Insurrection

The Bloody Events of May 1937 in Barcelona

Insurrection

The Bloody Events of May 1937 in Barcelona

Agustín Guillamón

Translated by Paul Sharkey

AK Press / Kate Sharpley Library

Insurrection: The Bloody Events of May 1937 in Barcelona

© 2020 Agustín Guillamón
Translation © 2020 Paul Sharkey
This edition © 2020 AK Press and The Kate Sharpley Library

ISBN: 9781849353601 | E-ISBN: 9781849353618
Library of Congress Control Number: 2018961635

AK Press
370 Ryan Ave. #100
Chico, CA 95973
www.akpress.org
akpress@akpress.org

AK Press
33 Tower St.
Edinburgh EH6 7BN
Scotland
www.akuk.com
akuk@akpress.org

Kate Sharpley Library
BM Hurricane
London WC1N, 3XX
UK
www.katesharpleylibrary.net

Please contact us to request the latest AK Press distribution catalog, which features
books, pamphlets, zines, and stylish apparel published and/or distributed by AK Press.
Alternatively, visit our websites for the complete catalog, latest news, and secure ordering.

Originally published by Editorial Descontrol in 2017, titled: *Insurrección: Las sangrientas
jornadas del 3 a 7 de mayo del 1937*

Cover design by Jared Davidson
Printed in the United States on acid-free paper

To César, taken from us by a lethal impact, because this book
is indebted to his generosity and shared enthusiasm

Revolutions like volcanoes have their days of flame and their years of smoke.
Victor Hugo, *Post-Scriptum de la vie*

What is known to none barely exists.
Apuleius, *Metamorphosis*

Historical memory is a theatre of the class struggle.
Fight For History: A Manifesto

The role of history will then be to show that laws deceive, that kings wear masks,
that power creates illusions, and that historians tell lies.
Michel Foucault, *Society Must Be Defended*

No more leaders and no more State
To leech upon our battles.
Raoul Vaneigem, *Life Goes By, Life Slips Away*

Contents

Introduction

In and of itself, the investigation, disclosure, and deepening of knowledge about the history of revolutions—rebutting the lies, misrepresentations, and slanders spewing from Sacred, Subsidized Bourgeois History and lifting the veil from the genuine history of class struggle, written from the viewpoint of the revolutionary proletariat—is a **Fight For History**.

Workers' striving to discover their own history is but one of the many battles being fought in the class war. It is not a matter of mere theory, nor is it abstract and banal, because it is part and parcel of class consciousness itself and can be classified as a **theorization of the world proletariat's historical experiences**. In Spain it must, necessarily, embrace, digest, and take ownership of the anarcho-syndicalist movements in the 1930s.

The mission of bourgeois History is to conjure up myths about nationalism, liberal democracy, and capitalist economics in order to persuade us they are timeless, immutable, and irreplaceable. A perpetual, complacent, uncritiqued present renders the past banal and is harmful to historical awareness. We are moving on from Sacred History to post-history. "Post-truth" is a neologism that describes a cognitive situation—commonplace these days—wherein the information source creates public opinion by subordinating facts and reality to emotions, prejudices, ideologies, propaganda, and beliefs. So post-truth can be a lie served up as a truth, but reaffirmed as a belief, ideology, promotional ad, or prejudice widely spread throughout society. If it has the appearance of truth and also flatters our vanity or satisfies our emotions, while reinforcing our prejudices or identity, it deserves to be true. A good advertising campaign can turn lie, deceit, and falsehood into a pleasant and handy post-truth. Post-history ceases to be what happens subsequent to the End of History (Fukuyama) and turns into the narrative that hacks of every hue and ideology fabricated for the publishing market, over and above the facts and historical reality that are these days deemed as secondary and dispensable, or exotic symbols for something we cannot quite put our finger on (Gallego).

1

The proletariat is drawn into the class struggle by its very nature as a waged and exploited class and does not need anybody to teach it anything; it fights because it needs to survive. Once the proletariat assumes the mantle of a conscious revolutionary class at odds with the party of Capital, it needs to digest the experiences of the class struggle, lean on historical gains (theoretical and practical alike), revolve issues not resolved in their time: it needs **to learn the lessons offered by history itself.** But this learning process can only be conducted through the practice of class struggle by the various affinity groups and sundry organizations of the proletariat.

Smoothing the way for this learning process is the point of each and every one of my books, the purpose throughout being to **let the protagonists of history speak** for themselves, respecting the reader's judgment, while at all times highlighting the fact if she is dealing with the author's opinion (indicated by italics) to which the reader need not subscribe.

The earliest books I published in 2007 and 2010 were *Barricades in Barcelona* and *Ready for Revolution: The CNT Defense Committees in Barcelona 1933–1938.*

Barricades explained how the ideology of antifascist unity was the ploy that allowed the higher committees to jettison all anarchist principles for the sole purpose of winning the war. My book on the defense committees in Barcelona brought to light how the Catalan CNT laid the groundwork for a clandestine revolutionary army. It deals with the origins of the CNT defense committees, the conversion of these into revolutionary committees in July 1936, their subsequent hibernation that December, how they overwhelmed the higher committees in May 1937, as well as how they were later dismantled and shut down once and for all. It is a local history zeroing in on the city of Barcelona and surrounding areas, and the justification for this is that that was the place where those committees were most fully developed and where they pushed the libertarian revolution the furthest.

Ready for Revolution, The Bread War, and *The Repression Targeting the CNT and Revolutionaries (1937–1938)* constitute the first, second, and fourth volumes of a quartet with the overall title "Hunger and Violence in Revolutionary Barcelona." They were published in 2011, 2014, and 2015, respectively. This present book, devoted to the bloody May 1937 events is, chronologically speaking, Volume Three of that quartet (although it was published in 2017).

Further volumes given over to significant aspects of the Spanish Civil War and Revolution in Catalonia were *The Friends of Durruti Group, History and Anthology of Texts,* and *The Stalinist Terror in Barcelona (1938),* both published in 2013.

Ready for Revolution offers an exhaustive explanation on the basis of previously unpublished, unknown, or unexploited documentation of how, in July 1936, the defense committees not only raised the frontline militias for Aragon but established barrio-based revolutionary committees throughout the city of Barcelona that spearheaded and defended one of the most profound social revolutions in history.

There was a **double TRANSFORMATION** of these defense cadres: into the **people's militias** that defined the Aragon front during the early days, launching collectivization of the lands in liberated Aragonese villages; and into **revolutionary committees** (RCs) that, in each barrio of Barcelona, and in many villages around Catalonia, enforced a "new revolutionary situation."

The "bread war" waged by Comorera against the barrio committees is the topic explored on the basis of exhaustive and often unpublished documentation in the quartet's second volume, *The Bread War: From December 1936 to May 1917*. The Bread War was designed for the sole purpose of wresting every vestige of power away from the defense committees, even though it meant the depletion of supplies in Barcelona and food shortages. Comorera was out to destroy the revolutionary war committees because he had identified them as potential organs of workers' power.

The barrio committees' supply warehouses controlled what, how, how much, and at what wholesale price, foods could be supplied to retail outlets, after the "revolutionary" needs of the barrio had been met—meaning its sick, its children, its unemployed, the people's dining halls, etc. Comorera called for an end of those revolutionary barrio-level committees and pushed for a free market. He was also aware that the one was implicit in the other and that, **unless the defense committees could be done away** with, the free market would be just a mirage.

Rational, far-sighted, and adequate provisioning of Barcelona and Catalonia would have meant caving in to the plans of the CNT's economy councillor, Joan Pau Fábregas, who battled unsuccessfully from October to December 1936 against opposition from all other political factions in Generalidad cabinet meetings for a monopoly on foreign trade. Meanwhile, on the Paris cereals market, ten or twelve major private wholesalers competed with one another, forcing up prices. But that foreign trade monopoly, which was not even a revolutionary proposition, but rather one appropriate for an emergency war-time situation, was a violation of the free market philosophy pushed by Comorera.

There was a thread linking bread queues in Barcelona and the irrational competition between wholesalers on the Paris cereal markets. A thread that would have snapped with the introduction of a foreign trade monopoly. Comorera's free market policy strengthened it. But in addition, the PSUC encouraged speculation by shopkeepers who imposed a virtual dictatorship over the pricing of all foodstuffs, lining their pockets by keeping workers hungry.

The fourth volume in my quartet *The Repression Targeting the CNT and Revolutionaries (1937–1938)* runs through the period from 8 May 1937 until 1

October 1937, that is, from the ending of the May Events to the storming of the Los Escolapios building by the PSUC and the bourgeois forces of order. From June 1937 onward, with the Control Patrols disbanded, there was a **reconquest** of various localities and comarcas by the Assault Guards and Civil Guard who deployed brutal repression against CNT personnel—especially against the erstwhile "patrollers" and the most prominent militants—to the extent where the CNT as an organization disappeared in many places.

This crackdown on anarcho-syndicalists was accompanied by a passive attitude in the higher committees, who chose to defend the prisoners on an individual, case-by-case basis rather than on a collective, political basis. The thousands of anarcho-syndicalist prisoners demanded greater commitment and solidarity from their higher committees, but all that was achieved was a safety valve response whereby the RCs of the CNT and FAI agreed to tolerate a clandestine press that mounted a campaign in support of the prisoners and exposed the brutality of the Stalinist repression.

Bit by bit, prisoners and revolutionary minorities distanced themselves from the collaborationist policy of the higher committees until a point was reached where a split seemed inevitable. That split was averted thanks to the Stalinists' SELECTIVE policy of cracking down and undermining the revolutionary opposition while absorbing the higher committees into the machinery of the state.

The Los Escolapios building was the headquarters of the Defense Committee of the Center, the Foodworkers Union, and other libertarian groups and committees. The storming of Los Escolapios on 20 September 1937 by the forces of order and the PSUC, using tanks, cannons, machine guns, and bombs, worked—not thanks to force of arms, but because of the order issued by the Regional Committee that it should be surrendered without a fight. It was a re-play, on a smaller scale, of the events of May 1937.

In the text, **bold face** is used to indicate dates, since the narrative is based on a chronological framework with each day making up a mini-chapter in the book. After each date, bold face is also used for the words that indicate the author and describe the type of document concerned: be it an article, a manifesto, a letter, a demonstration, a meeting of the higher committees, a meeting of the Generalidad cabinet, convening of some trade-union congress, and so on.

When it comes to the proceedings of a congress or of the Generalidad cabinet meeting or some gathering of militants, **bold face** is used to indicate the name of the rapporteur or councillor who is speaking. That way we can distinguish the various contributors and the reader is able at all times to have a clear grasp of who is speaking.

There is one last use of **bold face** that stands out plainly from the rest and that is to underline a particularly significant phrase or contention and these are usually followed by some explanation of why they carry such significance.

In this book, the task of the historian is quite simply to **let the protagonists of the story speak for themselves**, to give a platform to those who lived and suffered through these now historical events that, in their day, were establishing a present fraught with problems, wretchedness, illusions, struggles, and hopes.

The period of time covered by this book ranges from 3 to 7 May 1937. The aim, at all times and in every line, has been to allow the reader to form his own opinion about the events, speeches, and proceedings underway, and of the positions of the different protagonists and the street-fighting. **But documents never speak by themselves; they require interpreting, contextualization, and explanation.** If he is honest, the historian's task is not merely finding and selecting them, depending on how apt they may be, but also to render them understandable, or placing them in their chronological and ideological contexts. To which end we have resorted to footnotes; but also, when the narrator needs to intervene in order to complement the information within the document or offer his own (inevitable and necessary) slant on the facts, we have made use of italics, because this addition to the document or this author's interpretation, might be quibbled over and the reader need not buy into it.

Thus, italics are always used to show that the author is offering his own interpretation of the facts, in the hope of helping readers understand them, but also in the genuine hope of not confusing readers into believing that his is the only possible interpretation. Successful or not, the aim is absolutely to respect the reader's judgment; at all times, the reader is at liberty and empowered to hold on to his own opinion of the facts set out here.

Chapter 5 is the product of the need to offer the reader a summary of the May insurrection that enables him schematically but very clearly and precisely to follow the **revolutionary thread** running through the CNT. In Chapter 6, there is a series of bold or not so bold interpretations that seek to offer an historical perspective on the defense committees and a de-mystifying critique of the Friends of Durruti, the concrete aim being, not to deify or beatify that organization, because to do so would be squandering its legacy and its life and historical experiences that are too important to be thrown away with incense and eulogy.

The bulk of the **documentation used** here is previously entirely unpublished and it has been taken from archives all around the globe, ranging from Stanford University in California to New York's Tamiment Library, from the Russian Center for the Preservation of Contemporary History in Moscow, to the BAEL in Buenos Aires, not forgetting the BDIC in Nanterre, although the essential and richest archives have been those of the International Institute for Social History in Amsterdam, Salamanca's Center for the Documentation of Historical

Memory, the Tarradellas Archive in the Monastery of Poblet, Catalonia's Arxiu Nacional, the Fundación Anselmo Lorenzo in Madrid, and the Arxiu Enciclopèdic Popular in Barcelona.

Plainly this book is no mere anthology of documents bumped into at random, but rather a painstaking selection of telling documentary fragments that sometimes explain and sometimes contradict one another, but that are essential for any understanding of what was going on and what issues were burdening or concerning those men and women, whether they were leaders or at street level, helping the reader understand *the times* intensely, alerting him to the *climate* in which people were living, letting him *listen in* on the proceedings at meetings of the higher committees or at Generalidad cabinet meetings, so that he can *garner* an impression of the worries and fears of everyday life and be able to arrive *in the here and now* at a thorough knowledge of those events, now part of history.

Broadly speaking, the trading of information with other researchers dealing with the topics we have studied has been very gratifying and, without a single exception, it has taken place outside of academia, which is dominated by broomstick rigidity, neo-Stalinism, laziness, the whiff of incense, slave-driving, the most inane sectarianism, nationalism, and manipulation. The works of Bernecker, Ealham, and Godicheau command a mention and I would urge people to read them. And the same goes for the classics, such as Bolloten, Broué, Fraser, and Peirats.

I ought to express my **thanks**, for various reasons and out of heartfelt indebtedness, to the following: Manel Aisa from the AIP; Octavio Alberola and Agustín Comotto; Alessio from Naples; Lluis from Anònims in Granollers; K. Anderson and Svetlana Rosenthal from the CR in Moscow; Philippe Bourrinet; Paolo Casciola; Phil Casoar; Montserrat Catalán from the AMTM; Stuart Christie; Yves Coleman; Eulàlia Comas; Marc Dalmau from La Ciutat Invisible; Andy Durgan; David, Hector, Ibai, Pablo, and Sergi from Ediciones Descontrol; Luis Eemans and Jacques Lombard from the CERMTRI; Dino Erba and Mara Donato; Eulogio Fernández; Pablo Fierro from the *espacio radiofónico* Anábasis; Patrick Fornos from the Archivo Ascaso-Durruti in Montpellier; Carlos García Velasco; Antonio Gascón; Miquel Gómez; Daniel Guerrier; Miquel Izard, Stéphane Julien; Jean Michel Kay from Editions Spartacus; Marcelo López; Aurelio Martín and the staff at the FPI; Alex Martínez; César Martínez Lorenzo; Octavio Mondelo; Diego Murillo; Harald Piotrowski; José Ramón Palacios and the rest of the comrades at the FAL; Lourdes Prades and the staff from the Pabellón de la República; Leonardo Mulinas; Teo Navarro; Ramón Pino; Germinal Rebull; Michel Roger; Sergi Rosés; Jean Rosch from the CGT, Reus; Francisco Sala; Carles Sanz from the FELLA; Paul Sharkey; Quim Sirera; Kostas Tavlaridis-Gyparakis; the people who run the TSJC Archive; Rodrigo Vescovi and so many others whose names my poor memory have left at the dry cleaner's, only for them to torment me later over the unforgivable lapse.

My status as a member of the Ateneu Enciclopèdic Popular is something I regard as a duty and an honor and, given the increasing disrepute of the profession of manipulator-historian, I would rather be described as a history-worker or collector of old papers, if that could avert unwanted confusion. The process of researching and drafting this book has meant a long road filled with adventures, the constant welling-up of new questions, liaisons, and exchanges with third parties, interviews, bibliographical references, compilation of files, and the hours upon hours whiled joyously away surrounded by dossiers and archival documents, and pleasant, educational launches of previous books. How can I convey the joys and pleasure to be derived from the solving of a puzzle, the satisfaction achieved once all the pieces of the jigsaw finally fit?

The writing of the history of the events of May 1937 can no longer blithely omit the decisive parts played by Josep Rebull, Pablo Ruiz, Jaime Balius, Manuel Escorza, or Julián Merino, nor ignore the establishment of a secret CNT Revolutionary Committee. Although we must never under-estimate academia's bottomless ignorance and its ferocious short-sightedness.

Naturally, I bear the responsibility for all errata and shortcomings, which should be brought to my attention at Apartado de correos 22010—08080 Barcelona, so that I can amend and learn from them.

Agustín Guillamón
Barcelona, 19 February 2017

Table of Abbreviations and Organizations

AC: Acció Catalana (right-wing Catalanist Republican party)

AG: Anarchist Groups

BL: Bolshevik-Leninist (Trotskyist)

BOC: Bloc Obrer i Camperol (Worker-Peasant Bloc)

CADCI: Centro Autónomo de Dependientes del Comercio y de la Industria (Commercial and Industrial Staff Autonomous Center)

CAP: Comisión Asesora Política (Policy Advisory Commission)

CC: Central Committee

CAMC: Central Antifascist Militias Committee

CEIP: Comité Económico de la Industria del Pan (CNT-UGT): CNT-UGT Bread Industry Economic Committee

CNT: Confederación Nacional del Trabajo (National Labor Confederation)

CNT de Cataluña: CNT of Catalonia: (a sloppy expression often used as a synonym for the CRTC/ Regional Confederation of Labor of Catalonia)

CPV: Comité pro Víctimas (Victims' Aid Committee)

CRC: Regional Peasant Committee

CRTC: Regional Confederation of Labor of Catalonia

DAS: Deutsche Anarcho-syndikalisten (German Anarcho-Syndicalists in exile)

DOGC: Diari Oficial de la Generalitat de Catalunya (Generalidad of Catalonia Official Gazette)

ERC: Esquerra Republicana de Catalunya (Republican Left of Catalonia)

FACA: Federación Anarco-Comunista Argentina (Argentinean Anarcho-Communist Federation)

FAI: Federación Anarquista Ibérica (Iberian Anarchist Federation)

GBL: Grupo Bolchevique-Leninista (Bolshevik-Leninist Group)

GEPCI: Gremis i Entitats de Petits Comerciants e Industrials (Small Businessmen's and Industrialists' Guilds and Agencies)

GNR: Guardia Nacional Republicana (Republican National Guard: the new name bestowed upon the Civil Guard)

GPU (OGPU since 1923): The Soviet State Political Directorate. In 1934 it was subsumed into the NKVD

ICE: Izquierda Comunista de España (Communist Left of Spain: Trotskyist)

JCI: Juventud Comunista Ibérica (Iberian Communist Youth (aligned with the POUM)

JJLL: Juventudes Libertarias (Libertarian Youth)

JSU: Juventudes Socialista Unificadas (Unified Socialist Youth)

NC: National Committee

NKVD: Narodny Komissariat Vnutrennikh Del (People's Commissariat for Internal Affairs, the Russian secret police)

PO: Public Order

PC: Peninsular Committee (of the FAI)

PCE: Partido Comunista de España (Communist Party of Spain)

PE: Propaganda Exterior (Foreign Propaganda)

POUM: Partido Obrero de Unificación Marxista (Workers' Party for Marxist Unification, unorthodox Marxists). Party formed in September 1935 through the amalgamation of the Maurín-led BOC and the Nin-led ICE)

PSOE: Partido Socialista Obrero Español (Spanish Socialist Workers' Party)

PSUC: Partit Socialista Unificat de Catalunya (Unified Socialist Party of Catalonia). Catalan Stalinists.

RC: Regional Committee

SBLE: Sección Bolchevique-Leninista de España (Bolshevik-Leninist Section of Spain). Orthodox Trotskyists, led by Munis.

SIA: Solidaridad Internacional Antifascista (International Antifascist Solidarity)

SIM: Servicio de Investigación Militar (Military Investigation Agency). The Stalinist political police.

SURA: Sindicato Único del Ramo de Alimentación (CNT's Foodstuffs Union)

SURAB: Sindicato Único del Ramo de la Alimentación de Barcelona y Alrededores (CNT's Barcelona and District Foodstuffs Union)

UGT: Unión General de Trabajadores: Workers' General Union

UR: Unió de Rabassaires (Rabassaires Union)

Archives and Libraries Consulted

AEP: Archivo y Biblioteca del Ateneu Enciclopèdic Popular (Archive and Library of the Ateneu Enciclopèdic Popular, Barcelona)

AGMA: Archivo General Militar de Ávila (General Military Archive, Ávila)

AHCB: Archivo Histórico de la Ciudad de Barcelona (Barcelona City Historical Archive)

AHN: Archivo Histórico Nacional (National Historical Archive, Madrid)

AMCB: Arxiu Municipal Contemporani, Ajuntament de Barcelona (Contemporary Municipal Archive, Barcelona City Hall)

AMT3: Archivo Militar Territorial Tercero, Barcelona (Military Archive, no. 3 Region, Barcelona)

AMTM: Arxiu Monserrat Tarradellas e Macià. Monestir de Poblet (Tarradellas and Macià Archive, Monserrat, Poblet Monastery)

ANC: Arxiu Nacional de Catalunya, Sant Cugat del Vallès (National Archives of Catalonia, Sant Cugat del Vallès)

BA: Biblioteca Pública Arús, Barcelona (Arús Public Library, Barcelona)

BAEL: Biblioteca Archivo de Estudios Libertarios, Buenos Aires (Library-Archive of Libertarian Studies, Buenos Aires)

BAM: Biblioteca de la Abadía de Montserrat (Montserrat Abbey Library)

BDIC: Bibliothèque de Documentation Internationale Contemporaine, Nanterre (International Contemporary Documentation Library, Nanterre)

BN: Biblioteca Nacional, Madrid/ (National Library, Madrid)

CA: Ca l'Ardiaca, Hemeroteca Municipal de Barcelona (Ca l'Ardiaca, Barcelona City Newspaper Library)

CERMTRI: Centre d'Études et Recherches sur les Mouvements Trotskystes et Révolutionnaires Internationales, Paris (Center for the Study and Investigation of International Revolutionary Trostkyist Movements, Paris)

CR: Russian Center for the Study and Preservation of Documents of Contemporary History. Moscow

DEL: Archivo de la Delegación del Gobierno en Cataluña, Barcelona (Archive of the Government Delegation in Catalonia, Barcelona)

DIP: Archivo de la Diputación de Barcelona (Archive of the Diputación in Barcelona)

FAL: Fundación Anselmo Lorenzo, Madrid (Anselmo Lorenzo Foundation, Madrid)

FELLA: Fundació d'Estudis Llibertaris i Anarcosindicalistes (Libertarian and Anarcho-syndicalist Studies Foundation)

FPI: Fundación Pablo Iglesias, Alcalá de Henares/ (Pablo Iglesias Foundation. Alcalá de Henares)

HI: Hoover Institution, Stanford University, California

HL: Houghton Library, Harvard University, Cambridge (Mass.)

HMM: Hemeroteca Municipal de Madrid (Madrid Municipal Newspaper Library)

IISH: International Institute for Social History, Amsterdam.

PR: Biblioteca y Archivo del Pabellón de la Republica, Barcelona (Library-Archive of the Pavilion of the Republic. Barcelona)

SA: Centro Documental de la Memoria Histórica (de Salamanca) (Center for the Documentation of Historical Memory, Salamanca)

YL: Tamiment Library, New York.

TSJC: Archivo del Tribunal Superior Justicia de Cataluña, Barcelona (Archive of the Supreme Court of Justice, Catalonia, Barcelona)

1

The Background to May

Thursday, 4 March 1937

The Generalidad of Catalonia's *Diari Oficial* (Official Gazette, hereafter *DOGC*) made public seven Decrees and two Orders, under which the **Control Patrols were disbanded and a Unified Internal Security Corps set up**; the latter was based upon the amalgamation of the Assault Guard, which had already been under the orders of the Generalidad government, and the Republican National Guard (GNR)—formerly the Civil Guard—which had hitherto been answerable to the central government.[1] *These Public Order forces had not been disbanded back on 21 July 1936, nor had they been stripped of their weapons; they had merely been confined to barracks, armed, in the rearguard. They had not been dispatched to the front lines. In addition, the Civil Guard had been concentrated in Barcelona city and withdrawn from rural areas; its name was changed to Republican National Guard. Dionisio Eroles headed a so-called Workers' and Soldiers' Council that, despite its grand-sounding title, was nothing but a group that attempted to screen fascist personnel out from both police forces. The results of those efforts were very poor, not to say insignificant and practically zero. These forces represented a formidable weapon in the hands of the counterrevolution, which, by 4 March 1937, the government of the Generalidad wanted and was able to regain, in order to wrest back, once and for all, and fully, the power it had lost back in July 1936. The CNT unions caught on to this and the defense committees reacted immediately.*

The importance of the new corps lay in the fact that this brand new public order agency, serving the government only, was completely replacing the Control Patrols, which were the "revolutionary" police of the Central Antifascist Militias Committee (CAMC). No officer of the new Corps could be a member of a trade union or political party. At the same time, all of the town hall Security or Defense Departments

---

1   "Internal Security: Decrees of 1 March 1937 and Orders of 2 March 1937," *DOGC*, 4 March 1937.

were proclaimed abolished and arrangements were set in motion for pulling militia patrols and investigation or control committees off the frontier.

*This marked the conclusion of a lengthy process that **ended the duplication whereby both the CNT and Generalidad government managed Public Order in Catalonia**. However, the order disbanding the Control Patrols would not take effect until 5 June 1937, and even that was as a result of the defeat of the CNT following the May Events, the dismal finale to the disarmament of proletarians, prefacing a widespread crackdown on the anarchist workers' movement.*

★

The Olympia Theatre hosted the huge **closing rally of Catalonia's Regional Confederation of Labor's Regional Congress.**[2] Thousands of workers, unable to gain entry, milled around the adjacent streets "where powerful loudspeakers had been installed."

The rally was chaired by the CNT's regional secretary, **Valerio Mas**, who introduced the various speakers and announced the topic upon which each of them would speak.

Vicente Pérez (aka "Combina") talked about the unions' new structures; previously, they had been fighting agencies and now they were becoming Industrial Federations that would embrace the whole of the production process, from sourcing raw materials to their distribution to the public. Each Federation would see to its own transport requirements. Not that the idea of Industry-wide Federations was a new one; it had earlier been spelled out "at the last National Congress in Madrid." The Local Federation's existing twenty-six unions would be amalgamated into twelve Industrial Federations. "No more working for some bourgeois; now we will be working on behalf of the collectivity," and profits from one industry should pay off the debts of another. Differences between the two major trade-union centers had to be done away with.

Ramón Porté tackled agrarian issues that were entirely distinct from industrial issues and "the essence of the Revolution." Rural issues could not be resolved within the capitalist system. The land needed to be taken under social ownership, while at the same time there had to be respect for the small landholder, who otherwise might have felt dispossessed, thus creating a great malaise. "But we were in no position to parcel out the lands seized from the big landowners, because we were not about to conjure up new small landowners." They had created collectives instead. Over a two-month period, there had been pointless discussion

---

2   *Memoria del Congreso Extraordinario de la Confederación Regional del Trabajo de Cataluña* (Barcelona: Talleres Gráficos Juan, 1937), 397 ff.

with the UGT and with the *rabassaires*, but many of them knew nothing of land issues. "After 19 July, there could be no more grooms and no more day laborers, nor men subject to exploitation by other men." The international blockade would make complete social ownership of the land a necessity; otherwise, there would be the prospect of hunger.

The blindness of industrial workers precluded the granting of loans in sufficient time to ensure harvests better than the current ones. The industrial workers enjoyed advantages not extended to peasants. "We have lots of industrial workers who receive a wage and yet do no work"; if only such industrial workers would surrender a portion of their assets to the peasants, agricultural productivity would be boosted. There had to be an end of private ownership and they had to "beat fascism and ensure the triumph of the Revolution."

José Xena tackled the subject of the Councils of Economy. In the wake of the revolutionary insurrection, the workers had set up collectives, but they needed to familiarize themselves with the demands of domestic and foreign trade. Some collectives, wrestling with the war, were forgetting about the need to show solidarity with one another. Workers had to rid themselves of all parochial selfishness and get on with amalgamating at comarcal and regional levels.

And, for as long as money persisted, the Councils of Economy and their statistics were vital. The shared solidarity fund for which the countryside was crying out had to be set up. And international solidarity was the only means of breaking through international capitalism's blockade, by spreading the social war.

Just as lives were being offered up on the front so there was a vital need for production to be stepped up in the rearguard, without them giving up their weapons, these being the only guarantee against counterrevolution. The Councils of Economy needed to rise above trade-union differences and engage the workers with economic issues.

Helmut Rüdiger dealt with the international position. The fascists sought to dominate Spain, in the face of the indifference of the democratic powers. The fight currently was against international fascism.

In England and elsewhere, there was a deer-like fear of the Social Revolution and this had led them to the "Non-Intervention" policy that benefitted the fascist powers' massive intervention on Franco's behalf.

In actual fact, the democracies had opened the doors to fascism and their common enemy was the proletariat. "We here are fighting for the liberation of this country's workers, and at the same time we are fighting on behalf of the proletariat everywhere." World war was already upon us and it was being fought out on the soil of Spain.

José Viadiu addressed the CNT's stance on matters governmental, bridling at the fact that "we who hold positions of responsibility, entrusted to us by the people, should be the targets of systematic criticism." Such lack of respect for those who "hold positions of responsibility" was not to be tolerated.

Not that this absolved all who held such posts from displaying "the utmost responsibility." Bureaucracy needed mopping up and CNT members should know that their first duty should be to the Confederation.

Valerio Mas then offered a short summation of the Congress proceedings regarding the Industrial Federations, urging everyone to implement the resolutions passed. And Mas closed the rally "urging all to press on, for the Revolution."

*The Regional Congress had closed without any **emphatic and appropriate response to the decrees establishing the Unified Security Corps**, as published in the* DOGC *that very day.*

*The formation and structuring of the Federations of Industry at that Congress promoted and strengthened **the attempt to socialize Catalonia's economy**. Between March and May 1937, a new front was opened up for provocations and conflict, with gatherings of workers deciding in general meetings whether their industrial sector should be socialized, while their factories were being surrounded by police officers from the new Unified Security Corps. This new battlefield of **socialization versus collectivization**, already examined by others, was another factor that led to the armed confrontation during the May Events.[3]*

Friday, 5 March

There was a very serious incident this Friday "between four and eight o'clock in the evening," according to *Soli*.[4] "In one of several existing warehouses of war materials, which we will not identify for reasons of discretion, a number of individuals had arrived that day brandishing a document, at the bottom of which was stamped the signature of our comrade E. Vallejo, requiring that twelve of the most recently manufactured tanks be handed over to them."[5]

The person in charge of the transfer smelled something fishy and followed the tanks, which were "delivered to the Voroxilov [Voroshilov] barracks."[6]

Once Vallejo heard about this theft, he called the Control Patrols which surrounded said barracks, promptly meeting with the lieutenant-colonel in command and "insisting upon the swift return of the twelve stolen tanks." The

---

3   See the Bibliography below for Anna Monjo's outstanding works.

4   "Twelve Tanks Removed from Warehouse holding War Materials" in *Solidaridad Obrera* (7 March 1937), front page.

5   The actual location of the warehouse was the La Maquinista y Terrestre works which had been converted for use as a factory making armaments for the war effort.

6   This was a PSUC barracks ensconced in the former monastery in Sarriá.

lieutenant-colonel ignored Vallejo's demands, even though the latter told him that his signature had been forged.

Tarradellas and Vallejo made repeated overtures to the lieutenant-colonel, all to no avail. In the end Valdés (PSUC) the councillor of labor, stepped in, as did Almendros, the PSUC's military secretary and they got the lieutenant-colonel to acknowledge that he was in possession of the twelve stolen tanks.

When a disciplinary report was opened against him, the Lieutenant-colonel from the Voroshilov barracks "pointed out that he had simply been carrying out the orders handed down to him by the high command of the Karl Marx Division."

Soli's reporter commented: "What is beyond all doubt is that the stolen tanks were not taken for use in war operations," because distribution to the front lines was a matter handled by the Generalidad's Defense Department, and he went on to wonder: "If those tanks were not taken for transfer to the front, what was the purpose behind this 'brilliant' operation?"

The presumption was that it had been "a dictatorial dummy-run, against which everybody knows we will immediately rise up." *That is, the complaint was against preparations for a coup d'état that would oust the CNT and set up a* **strong** *government.*

The reporter closed with a beatific wish that antifascist unity might be preserved as the only thing capable of winning the war against fascism.

Saturday, 6 March

In *La Noche*, **Jaime Balius** printed an **article** entitled "Counterrevolutionary Attitudes. Positions of Neutrality Are Damaging" in which he listed the features of the new Security Corps set up by the Generalidad government, noting that it was a bourgeois force under the orders of the capitalist State and inimical to the most elementary rights of workers.

★

At 7:45 p.m., there was a meeting of **Control Patrol** delegates, attended by Tomás Fábregas, Asens, Coll, Nevado, Bonet, Gutiérrez, Sagristá, and Silvio Torrents.[7]

Tomás Fábregas, the Security Junta delegate, opened the proceedings by noting that he had called them together "because he felt it was his duty to brief them on the latest meeting of the now defunct Internal Security Junta and report to them on what had been agreed to there."

---

7   "Minutes of the meeting held on 6 March 1937" [AMTM-GC-33-22].

He stated that "with the demise of the Security Junta," those who had staffed it were out of a job and "all of the armed bodies making it up had been disbanded." As a result, "they would all carry on until the Unified Corps was up and running" and the councillor for the interior had asked that "all searches and arrests by the Patrols should cease."

José Asens took exception to Tomás Fábregas's final point, and said that the dissolution order, "for reasons of supposed prudence, is being applied only in regard to the Control Patrols."

After reminding, or chiding, Asens that he was indebted to him for his appointment as Chief of Services of the Control Patrols Department, **Tomás Fábregas** argued that, despite their complete autonomy, the Control Patrols were merely "an offshoot of the General Public Order Commission and, like every other armed body, should, as of now, cease operations."

Nevado stated that the decree disbanding all the armed bodies had to be accepted. But it was plain that the decisions of the councillor of the interior must have been shared with the rest of the Generalidad councillors, including the CNT councillors. He stated that he realized how disagreeable many people had felt the very existence of the Control Patrols had been, ever since their foundation; and he explained that they had managed to cling on to their identity thanks to a close relationship with the Security Junta. But his conclusion was that, despite this, the Patrols "ought not to cease operations until the Unified Corps starts to take over."

Tomás Fábregas asked those present if they agreed with Nevado, so that he could pass this on to the Council.

A fresh argument erupted and no concrete decision was arrived at.

Coll spoke at some length about some elaborate theory, according to which, once the Security Junta was wound up, the patrols would come under the remit of the councillor for internal security, who was also the person empowered to lead the new Unified Security Corps, the very essence of antifascist unity, over and above the particular interests of its component organizations.

Asens asked Coll to stick to the point and choose his words, adding that if the ERC's [Republican Left of Catalonia] preference was to abide by the dictates of the internal security councillor, he should withdraw "his representatives from the Control Patrols Department."

Coll turned on Asens, retorting that he was "mistaken in his views," in that the ERC was "ready to abide, not by this, but by arrangements emanating from the Generalidad government and, in obedience to them, will indeed pull out of the Control Patrols."

There followed a "lively discussion" between Coll and the CNT representatives, which Asens brought to an end by stating that, "above all else and with or without the cooperation of other antifascist parties and organizations, the

Patrols are going to carry on with their revolutionary work right to the end, that is, up until the Unified Internal Security Corps was formed."

Coll tried to make it clear to Asens that "the dispositions of the councillor [Aguadé] in no way reduce the authority of the Patrols since the latter now have the endorsement of the chief of staff of the General Public Order Commission, Dionisio Eroles."

Another argument erupted. In view of Asens's intention to leave the meeting, **Tomás Fábregas** asked for something concrete that he might forward to Internal Security.

The argument dragged on without coming to any resolution. Once Asens left, the meeting was wound up at 9:32 p.m.

Asens was against disbanding the Control Patrols and was prepared to carry on, even if every other antifascist organization pulled out. All he asked was that they carry on until replaced by the new Unified Security Corps, into which he naively imagined the patrollers would be incorporated.

Sunday, 7 March

This Sunday, declared "Madrid Day," came as the culmination of a week of rallies, parades, fundraisers, and gestures of solidarity "with the defenders of the capital of Spain, in the Monumental bullring."[8]

The Libertarian Youth handed out a manifesto in which they were critical of such parades, exhibitions, and band performances, which they described as "a continuous and odd partying in the rearguard."[9] The young libertarians were critical of the parasitical militiaman in the rearguard, of his dangerous messianism and how he was living "one continuous party, his conduct immoral and counterrevolutionary, as he finds excuses for turning out for every parade, celebration, etc."

They also insisted upon an end to the unutterable disgrace whereby there was hunger and privation in Madrid, while in Barcelona's fleshpots "one finds the most succulent foods and most 'aristocratic' aperitifs aplenty for the amusement and pleasure of the old and nouveaux riches and the shameless bureaucrats who make a mockery of the war-time economy."

They indicated that they were against and had nothing to do with the forthcoming exhibitionist celebrations scheduled for the 14th, in honor of the

---

8   T. Caballé, *Barcelona Roja. Dietario de la revolución* (Barcelona: Librería Argentina, 1939), 85.

9   RC of Libertarian Youth of Catalonia, "¡Mas acción y menos mascaradas!," manifesto (March 1937) [CA].

Unknown Soldier, and the ones due on the 21st, so-called Youth Day, in which they announced that they would not be taking part.

Their manifesto closed with their decision to bolster the Revolutionary Youth Front. They identified themselves as antifascist revolutionaries who espoused the slogan: "Fewer masked balls and more action!"

This manifesto from Catalonia's Libertarian Youth was damned up and down by Santillán at the next day's gathering of the Generalidad Council.

Monday, 8 March

La Noche carried one of those articles so typical of Balius's style, wherein, through an astute blend of news and opinion, he commented on the spectacle offered by **trains crammed with folk from Barcelona out looking for foodstuffs in country areas.** By means of a description of the people packed together inside the carriages, Balius was criticizing the new measures introduced by the Stalinist leader, Comorera, regarding supply arrangements.

The **Supplies Department**, headed by Comorera, announced that the production, warehousing, and distribution of **rice** all across Catalonia, was being taken over.[10]

A Plenum of the Local, Comarcal, and Inter-comarcal committees of the Anarchist Groups of Catalonia met, for the purpose of debating the decrees recently passed by the internal security councillor.[11]

The various provisions of the different decrees were read and discussed, some being approved, but the implementation of others was rejected and it was eventually determined that, on a transitional basis, while consultation was under way and how the decrees were to be implemented was being thrashed out, "the Municipal Defense Departments, the Control Patrols and other Corps must be respected just as they have been operating to date."

Which is to say that the Government could decree away but "for the time being," the CNT-FAI would not implement those decrees. This was an untenable situation of ongoing confrontation. In fact, the definitive winding-down of the Control Patrols

---

10   *DOGC*, 8 March 1937.

11   "Accords passed by the Plenum of Local, Comarcal and Inter-comarcal Committees of the Region's Anarchist Groups of Catalonia, Held on the 8th" [IISH-FAI-CP-17B1].

was not carried out until 5 June 1937, which is to say, three months later and then after a fresh Decree, but, above all, once the CNT-FAI had been defeated politically in the May Events.

★

At 6:30 p.m., the **Generalidad Council** assembled under the chairmanship of Tarradellas, with all the councillors in attendance, save for the justice councillor.[12]

Tarradellas reported on his trip up to the Cerdaña, a trip he had made with Santillán for company. They had held a meeting with all of the organizations represented in the government and were briefed on the situation in the co-marca. Together with Defense delegate Montserrat and by a detachment from the Death Battalion, they had travelled up to Alp castle, which was occupied by around eighty POUM militants, and where "purportedly as a sanatorium, they had ensconced themselves in a sort of a whorehouse where militia members and supposed nurses mingled. All of those militia members were being paid by the Generalidad and they had the comarca terrorized."

This foul slander of the POUMistas was made possible only by that party's expulsion from the government and it was part of the process of that party's marginalization and blackening, upon which was blamed all of the government of antifascist unity's difficulties. The aim was to defame it as a first step toward its expulsion from the comarca, since its presence there was undermining the counterrevolutionary forces of the PSUC, ERC, and Generalidad government.

Antonio Martín had been summoned to Puigcerdá to get him "to pull out all of the forces with which he had been blockading several villages, and he had complied." Tarradellas then pulled a lieutenant out of the area who, by dint of his conduct and character, had a tendency to make frictions worse, and ordered the release of all arrested persons.

Tarradellas reported on the "unfeasible innovations" making up the "program of those who govern Puigcerdá and the comarca" who "using the pretext of a general co-operative, have seized the whole town and shown no hesitation in using coercion in order to buy up all the produce at a low price and selling it off in Barcelona at a higher one," thereby creating an economic problem that was hard to resolve.

Antonio Martín, known as "the governor of the frontier" has set up an autonomous libertarian canton in the Cerdaña. He imposed reasonable pricing, but would not tolerate speculation, nor runaway price increases, which profiteered off

---

12   "Minutes of the 8 March 1937 meeting of the Generalidad Executive Council."

*the hunger felt by Barcelona workers. The Puigcerdá co-operative, **which had established a monopoly on the Cerdaña's trade**, prided itself on supplying milk and beef to Barcelona at fair and set prices, steering clear of profiteering and hoarding. The hatred the proprietors of Bellver felt for Antonio Martín and the libertarian canton in the Cerdaña derived from the "oppression and economic strangulation" inflicted upon them by the fact that Puigcerdá imposed the retail prices for beef and milk, at a time of rising prices due to the shortage of foodstuffs in Barcelona city. If we add to this the fact that the anarchists were also thwarting the traditional recourse to smuggling at a time when the latter, like the smuggling of priests and right-wingers across the border, represented a significant source of mouth-watering additional income, we can appreciate how the Bellver bourgeoisie might have hated the Puigcerdá revolutionaries. Tarradellas was echoing the Bellver bourgeoisie's interests. That anarchists should have had control of the border was unthinkable to the Generalidad government and the Valencia government alike. Antonio Martín was not "the Málaga gimp" as his enemies scornfully nick-named him, but "the Durruti of the Cerdaña."*

Tarradellas insisted that, in compliance with the new Public Order arrangements and the Decrees overhauling those agencies, all the forces currently in that comarca had to be pulled out. He suggested that Martí Feced be set up to sort the Cerdaña's economic issues, a suggestion that was agreed upon.

Santillán backed "everything the First Councillor has said." What had Santillán in common with Antonio Martín, other than that they were nominally members of the same organization?

Comorera asked for a suspension of the payment of wages to militia members not conforming with the government's orders.

The CNT's **Isgleas** alerted them to the fact that the central government's Finance Ministry had appointed a new commandant of carabineers, with whom they would have to reckon. He then requested that the UGT withdraw the armed groups that it had in Camprodón, Maçanet, and elsewhere.

Valdés stated that the UGT would do so just as soon as the Public Order Decrees came into force.

Tarradellas proposed that "*mossos de escuadra* be sent up to Bellver."

That was agreed to.

Comorera asked that an investigation be mounted into the man-handling his secretary had received at the border crossing in La Jonquera.

Aguadé said that what was required was a once-and-for-all settling of the borders issue. He accused *La Batalla* of not submitting its galleys to the censor and that it was persisting with "a campaign that seriously compromises military action." He moved that its publication be suspended for four days, supporting that request with a reading of several paragraphs. And added that he had already informed the press that steps would be taken against such infringements.

Isgleas indicated that he agreed, "because *La Batalla* is pig-headedly not abiding by the war censorship."

Herrera was of the view that some notification should be issued prior to the imposition of any sanction.

Tarradellas responded that it had already been asked to comply lots of times.

Herrera replied that "before action can be taken against the POUM, we would require that some sector [the PSUC-UGT] serving in the government refrain from systematically attacking it."

Tarradellas acknowledged that he agreed in part with Herrera, but that *La Batalla* needed sanctioning because it was a repeat offender and told lies that placed victory in jeopardy.

Valdés stated that the UGT had never raised any complaint about the campaign that the POUM had been running against the UGT and the PSUC. He added that he could not give a commitment not to attack the leaders of the POUM "because we believe and stand ready to demonstrate that they are engaged in counterrevolutionary work." He closed by endorsing Tarradellas's proposed sanction "without any thought of vindictiveness."

Tarradellas stated that he did not think that the POUM's leaders were counterrevolutionaries, but he did regard their behavior as "intolerable." He announced that he would again call Nin, but he asked, too, that the PSUC not provoke the POUM.

Sbert said that, plainly, the POUM comrades were not deliberately counterrevolutionaries, because, otherwise, he would be calling for more radical measures, but their stance played into the hands of the fascists, since, being Trotskyists, they have no interest in the war's being won under our leadership and they are afraid that the maximalist program will founder. Political debate would be possible if there was no war, but that war could not possibly be won with POUM tactics.

Doménech stressed that the suspension of *La Batalla* might backfire in the form of propaganda favorable to the POUM, since the CNT must be well aware "that it owed its strength to the persecution and suspension of its papers." He stated that he had no interest in discussing Communist Party policy.

Tarradellas reminded all that, for much less, the central government had suspended the FAI's *Nosotros* daily paper in Madrid and then he went on to bring up the editorial carried in *Solidaridad Obrera* that day, saying that he shared a lot of the thinking behind it.

He stated that there was no government campaign against the POUM and that, rather, it had been shown undue consideration, because when Nin was a councillor, *La Batalla* had set about attacking the decrees endorsed by its own representative on the Council.

Isgleas talked at some length to explain that *La Batalla* had persistently failed to honor all agreements and had ignored every warning. He was not of the opinion that the POUM was fascist, but *La Batalla* was carrying falsehoods and continually defying the orders of the Defense Department, and so had to be sanctioned.

Santillán said that he had suffered twenty years of censorship, even in relation to editorials that were of a doctrinal nature and on those grounds he had reason to reject it; but that, for some time past, every time he read the press, he had been convinced of the need to enforce censorship "especially relating to matters of the war."

He said that he **would not have allowed publication of the Libertarian Youth Manifesto** and many other outrageous statements.[13] He suggested that a fine be imposed and a warning issued to the editors that suspension would follow in the event of any repetition.

In the end, it was agreed that a five thousand peseta fine be imposed plus the cautions that Santillán had suggested.

Tarradellas informed them that the war industries would find themselves at a stand-still for want of foreign currency, unless they dipped into the existing million pesetas reserve.

Comorera indicated his agreement, asking that the commission provided for in the agreement with the central government be reactivated.

Santillán reported that Economy had placed thirty million at the disposal of the central government, but had not received any compensation in foreign currency.

It was agreed that Tarradellas be given authority to make use of the million pesetas in foreign currency.

Isgleas offered a briefing on his forthcoming trip down to Valencia to attend a meeting of the Higher War Council. He stated that Catalans "have the feeling that they are **unprotected against air and sea attack. The central government has abandoned us entirely.**"

Valdés set out his efforts to obtain arms for the Aragon front.

Santillán proposed a decree setting the norms by which the statutes of collectivized firms would be governed and this was passed.

Santillán and **Valdés** proposed a decree defining the powers of the Control Committees in un-collectivized firms and that was passed. After a number of decrees and exceptional loans had been passed, the proceedings concluded at 9:45.

Marginalization of the POUM as well as of the libertarian canton in the

---

13   See section dated 7 March 1937.

Cerdaña represented the first step, in which the CNT councillors acquiesced, toward their repression and definitive liquidation.

The charges leveled against the POUM, described here as a "counterrevolutionary party" according to **the possibilist and moderate program** of the ERC, UGT, PSUC, and even the Generalidad government, are surprising. Since the success of the workers' uprising of 19 July 1936, the government, the Stalinists, and the bourgeoisie had shamelessly been styling themselves as "revolutionaries."

The stance by Santillán, who was wholly compliant with Stalinist and government guidelines, or possibly worse, insofar as he stated that he would have censored a manifesto (authorized) by the Libertarian Youth, deserves to be described with appropriate rigor as perhaps signifying that he had fully **bought into** the responsibilities of the bourgeois Generalidad government. What with the Santillán of wayward declarations as a Generalidad councillor and Santillán, the libertarian columnist, the champion of anarchist purism, his schizophrenia is without parallel in the annals of political thought.

Even his Argentinean friends from the FACA who were very close to Santillán ideologically, were moved to deal very harshly with him. Jacobo Prince wrote a letter/briefing to his friends back in Buenos Aires, in which he stated: "There you have friend Diego, who, having been in positions of the greatest responsibility, in which all he succeeded in doing was to bring himself into disrepute in the movement's eyes, with his untimely and indeed catastrophic stances, now finds himself isolated, and, what is worse, pretending to be in opposition and speaking out against the very things he was doing just a few months back. A genuine case of lunacy."[14]

Finally, Isgleas's remarks about the people of Barcelona being defenseless against attacks from air and sea and **pinning the blame solely upon the central government,** raise a question mark over the responsibility of the Generalidad and all the antifascist organizations in terms of the patent reluctance and dereliction on their when it came to establishing **proper anti-air raid defenses;** effective, numerous anti-aircraft batteries and rapid anti-bomber fighter planes, ships forewarning of raids, etc.—such defenses were all but ineffectual or non-existent, while the people of Barcelona threw themselves into a magnificent **passive defense** program by building thousands of shelters for themselves. These passive defenses were the handiwork of the residents in each Barcelona street, investing their cash and their labor in the venture; whereas the active defenses, of which the government was in charge, allowed the fascist terror to dominate the skies over Barcelona, because it had not budgeted for more and better anti-aircraft batteries, nor for the purchase of fighters for the El Prat airfield, nor for the upkeep of a string of air raid early warning vessels. Then again, **bombs and hunger were the best ways of bringing the revolution to its knees.**

---

14   FACA correspondence, Letter 62, 28 October 1937 [BAEL].

Thursday, 11 March

La Noche carried an **article** devoted to commenting upon the figure of Durruti. **Balius** invoked the speech that Durruti had made over the airwaves just a few days prior to his death, a speech in which he deplored the fact that the war was not a "live" issue in the rearguard. As far as Durruti was concerned, the solution to this lay in waging the war properly, enlisting bourgeois into fortifications battalions and placing all workers on a war footing. According to Balius, Durruti's death was followed by a majestic funeral, but nobody had taken his thoughts to heart. Hence, the writer concluded, it could now be argued that the civil war was a war for independence rather than a **class war** as Durruti had advocated. Balius closed the article with the assertion that Durruti was more relevant than ever and that keeping faith with his memory meant standing by his ideas.

★

The **Generalidad Council** convened at 6:35 p.m., under the chairmanship of Companys, with a full attendance by the councillors, excepting the councillor for defense.[15]

Council was briefed on the appointment of the director-general of security and of the regional Public Order Commissioners, as well as the Internal Security decrees' coming into full effect.

After a long and heated debate about the posts to be filled, in which the Stalinists wanted to deny the CNT personnel the proportionality they were after, whereas the CNT personnel refused to discuss anything until the names of the actual appointees were made known, the proceedings went on and on, with no one giving an inch, until it was eventually determined that the issue should be postponed until the following day, so that they could get down to discussing the councillor for security's concrete proposals.

More trivial matters were then discussed and approved.

To the councillor for Agriculture, **Doménech** raised complaints that had come in from CNT farmworkers regarding the favored treatment received by the UR [Rabassaires Union] and ultimately asking for the establishment of a Higher Agricultural Council wherein all the peasant organizations might be represented. He also pressed for CNT participation in the Agricultural Trade Unions and Cooperatives.

Calvet denied any such sectarianism, or any UR intervention in the Agricultural Trade Unions and Cooperatives. He stated that seed and potatoes had been

---

15   "Minutes of the meeting of the Generalidad Executive Council on 11 March 1937."

distributed across the board. True, there had not been enough to go around, but the blame for that lay with the committees that had allocated for consumption a portion of what ought to have been their seed potatoes. Some had been forwarded to the front, although in inadequate amounts. He reported that, for the first time, potatoes "displaying Catalonia's coat of arms" had been exported to England, under the direct supervision of the Generalidad.

He explained that the membership cards of many Agricultural Unions and Cooperatives were from the UR because the UR had founded them and they had been in circulation long before his incorporation into the Agriculture Department.

Comorera took exception to the less than even-handed treatment doled out by the war censors, indicating *Treball* articles that had been censored, whereas he read out a *La Batalla* article that was insulting to the central government and that talked about a brand new *abrazo de Vergara*.

Vidiella said that the government resembled a beaten government, having no war and public order policy of its own and lacked the authority to enforce censorship: "The fact is that Franco is a bad general; the French ambassador has said as much; but he also said that **Franco commands and is obeyed, whereas hereabouts, the ambassador added, no one commands and no one obeys.**"

Valdés asked that *La Batalla* be hit with a four-day suspension.

Herrera was not opposed to this sanction, but asked whether the *La Batalla* article had or had not been submitted to the censor.

It was agreed that the sanction should be imposed, subject to the reservation articulated by Herrera.

The **chair** stated that if the article had been passed by the censor, the sanction would be rendered null and void, but the censor would be dismissed.

After a variety of accords and decrees relating to the Civil Register and other more trivial matters had been passed, the proceedings were wound up at 9:25 p.m.

Friday, 12 March

Balius had an article published in *La Noche*, entitled "Statements from Largo Caballero. The Counterrevolution Under Way." In it he criticized some recent statements made by the UGT leader, statements he characterized as counterrevolutionary since they brought to light the plan to revert to the situation as it was prior to 19 July by dismantling the collectivization and socialization of firms once the war had been won.

★

The **Generalidad Council** met at 6:30 p.m., under the chairmanship of Tar-radellas and with a full turn-out of councillors, except for the councillor for defense.[16]

Sbert reported on the Exhibition of Catalan Medieval Art in Paris. He noted that in diplomatic circles there was a reserved attitude toward relations between the French Republic and the Generalidad, even in the area of cultural relations.

He detailed the difficulties that had arisen over the flying of the Catalan flag at the *Jeu de Paume*. And announced that the opening on the 18th had been postponed in order to continue negotiations that might ensure "that the official representatives from the government of Catalonia would be greeted by a French government minister," and that matters would be suitably dignified.

Tarradellas reported on the serious situation on the Madrid front and ru-mors of a push by the rebels on the Aragon front. The central government had asked for all available war materials and manpower to be sent.

In the absence of the CNT's Isgleas, the defense councillor, who was away on a visit to the Aragon front, Tarradellas had ordered that preparations be made for an expeditionary force to deliver the available war materials.

Comorera asked "**that the Karl Marx Division be dispatched to the Madrid front.**"[17] Tarradellas's response was that no decision had been made regarding the sending of troops, because they had to wait for Isgleas's return.

Next up for discussion was Public Order.

Tarradellas then moved that the appointments to new posts be postponed, but that that they proceed with the immediate establishment of the Security Council, with an eye to organizing the Unified Security Corps.

Herrera asked how the existing incumbents would stand if the Security Council was launched and the Junta disbanded. The specific reference was to the Junta's secretary (Aurelio Fernández) "who would have to stand down, without further compensation."

Tarradellas insisted upon asking whether his proposal was being accepted "as he wanted to avoid the irresponsibility of getting into the nitty-gritty of an issue that might spark a crisis at a point where Madrid is under serious threat."

In a follow-up to Tarradellas's proposal, **Doménech** suggested that, until such time as a director-general had been appointed, Aurelio Fernandez or some other CNT member should take up the interim vice-chairmanship of the Secu-rity Council.

---

16   "Minutes of the Generalidad Executive Council meeting of 12 and 13 March 1937."

17   This implied an extraordinary weakening of the Aragon front. Isgleas was totally against this move, and it was behind his resignation as defense councillor. The crisis in the Gen-eralidad government was traceable to this proposal by Comorera that the Karl Marx Divi-sion be transferred to the Madrid front, and to the creation of the Unified Security Corps.

Aguadé urged that the director-general and public order commissioner be appointed forthwith.

Tarradellas stuck to his proposal. Aguadé announced that he would be travelling to Valencia to deal with the border police and passports issue. Tarradellas's proposal was carried and he stood in for Aguadé during the latter's absence from the Security Department.

Tarradellas informed all that *La Batalla* had not been presented to the censors and, that being the case, the article that had triggered its suspension, as agreed by the Council the previous day, had not been seen by the censor. It was agreed that the suspension was therefore ratified.

Santillán proposed a Decree on taking housing under municipal ownership and this was passed to the Inter-municipal Commission for consideration.

Doménech gave a briefing on the steps to be taken to stamp out abuses in vehicle traffic. He set out the assistance afforded to the CNT's taxis, reckoned at one hundred and twenty-five thousand pesetas a week. In order to avert any continuance of this financial assistance, it was agreed that they should be allotted ten thousand liters of gasoline per week and authorized to operate until 10:00 p.m.

After a range of decrees or draft decrees had been approved, it was agreed that the sitting should suspended until 11:00 a.m. the following day. This was at 8:35 p.m.

Saturday, 13 March

The **Generalidad Council** meeting resumed at 11:20 a.m. All councillors were present, except for Isgleas, who had yet to return from Aragon.

Tarradellas was critical of Isgleas's absence at a time when decisions of such import and urgency had to be made. Isgleas should act less like an inspector on the front lines and do more of his work in his office.

Santillán and others backed the criticisms made by Tarradellas.

Tarradellas reported on the air raid that he had witnessed that very morning on the outskirts of Barcelona, describing—as picturesque and regrettable—the sight of the enormous number of armed individuals who had been mobilized for it and who were helping to add to the panic. Then he stated that as a matter of urgency weapons not at the disposal of the government needed to be gathered up.

Herrera agreed with the gathering-up of weapons as something that should be carried out in conjunction with other government measures. He suggested that this four-point program be implemented:

1. Rifles to be gathered in within forty-eight hours.

2. Persons failing to surrender them would be drafted.
3. That draft should be in accordance with the published decrees.
4. The Armed Corps to be deployed for military operations.

Tarradellas, *who had caught on to the barely veiled challenge in point 4,* stated that he had no difficulty with implementation of the first three points, but the fourth was not needed "as the security forces are always at the disposal of the government."

And then Tarradellas briefed them that air-force officer Meana had failed to return the seven thousand pounds sterling in gold that had been entrusted to him for the purchase of a plane in France. It was agreed that legal proceedings should be initiated against the aviator.

At this point, in came **Isgleas,** defense councillor, to give a briefing on the meeting of the Higher War Council in Valencia, at which it had been announced that the situation on the Madrid front had been consolidated. He had found himself on the Aragon front at the same time as minister García Oliver, just as the Higher War Council was meeting down in Valencia and the [Generalidad] Council meeting was under way in Barcelona, and **had decided to stay in Aragon with García Oliver.** The latter had discussed with him the need to dispatch troops to the Madrid front and, afterward, he received a telegram asking for the Karl Marx Division. He was opposed to sending an entire division as he **thought it was dangerous to hand over an entire sector to rearguard forces.** He had haggled with General Martínez Cabrera, suggesting they send nine battalions, without their weapons, plus a company of Engineers, rather than the Karl Marx Division.

When the general had protested that those nine battalions were untried troops, Isgleas had retorted that these were troops tried and tested on the Aragon front and with the very same fighting qualities as the Karl Marx Division.

When Comorera pressed the point, Isgleas replied that the plan would have moved the Karl Marx Division to a post a hundred kilometers from the Guadalajara front and, from there, would have strung it out across a number of locations—meaning it would not operate together as one unit. It therefore offered no advantage over the nine battalions that he intended to send. They also discussed the imminent launching of a diversionary attack on the Aragon front.

Isgleas and **Comorera** then became entangled in a harsh continuation of the dispute about sending the Karl Marx Division to Madrid. **Herrera** sided with Isgleas and **Santillán** with Comorera. **Sbert** attempted to mediate, but was unable to persuade any of them.

Tarradellas was forced to agree that, just as there had to be obedience to the military command "it was also necessary that the defense councillor (Isgleas) at all times make whatever comments he deems necessary, so that he and the Generalidad Council could collaborate loyally with the central government and act responsibly."

In the end, the **Council** agreed that troops should be dispatched to the Guadalajara front and left to the disposition of the Central High Command, and that those troops should be the ones the High Command asked for. It also gave its approval to operations in Aragon being mounted in coordination with the Central High Command.

Comorera suggested that Defense and Internal Security handle the gathering-up of weapons jointly. **Herrera** pointed out that, if Defense agreed to it, there was no need for Internal Security to get involved. Defense Councillor **Isgleas** "expressed some reservations regarding the implementation of any such arrangement through his Department."

Tarradellas, possibly irked by Isgleas's reservations, said that he was ready to carry out the gathering-up of weapons from the Office of the Prime Minister, using resources furnished by Defense, or, if need be, using the Death Battalion that was under the direct orders of the Office of the Prime Minister. This was agreed.

Under the arrangements made with the Ministry of War, there was to be an immediate call-up of the classes of '34, '35, and '36, and no decision had as yet been taken regarding the classes of '32 and '33.

That there was a clash between Defense Councillor Isgleas and the rest of the cabinet was obvious. The main and most blatant reason for this was his opposition to the Karl Marx Division's being sent to the Guadalajara front. Pulling the Karl Marx Division out of the Aragon front would not merely weaken the latter, but would amount to that front being relegated once and for all to the status of a poorly armed, secondary front, with the CNT almost entirely responsible for it.

No doubt there were also personal issues, such as the public criticisms by Tarradellas of how Isgleas was performing in the Defense Department.

Maybe the ploy of burdening him with the gathering-up of weapons held in the rearguard broke the defense councillor's patience and tolerance. Tarradellas was signaling his annoyance with Isgleas when he impulsively offered to mount the operation from the Office of the Prime Minister, knowing full well that that sort of a gathering-up had failed on several previous occasions and that there was no practical prospect of success unless it was handled by a CNT council member, who might not run into quite the same resistance from armed CNT personnel: the ward defense committees, anarchist groups, and so on.

Santillán seems to have always backed Comorera, whereas Herrera was a loose cannon, making proposals so at odds with CNT interests, like the gathering-up of weapons held in the rearguard.

★

Item Six on the agenda of the **Plenum of Unions** related to continuing or disbanding the "Supplies Liaison Committee."[18] *That Liaison Committee was what was left of the old ward-based supplies committees.* Most of the unions lobbied for it to continue. The **Distribution-Workers Union** suggested that it amalgamate with the Foodworkers and Peasants [Unions] in order to get rid of Comorera, who had "blocked" the Liaison Committee. It declared that surrendering the Supplies Department to the PSUC had been a serious mistake.

Whereas the **Railways Union** noted that the Liaison Committee had failed and asked that it be shut down, the rest asked for it to be "re-evaluated," despite major sabotage by Comorera. The **Foodworkers Union** suggested that the peasant collectives funnel their produce through the Supplies Liaison Committee to ensure that it could compete with the official agencies.

This was the swan-song of the supplies committees in the wards of Barcelona; they were doomed, the life choked out of them by Comorera.

"In relation to a **visit made by First Councillor Josep Tarradellas**—who was standing in for the security councillor and accompanied by Security Junta Secretary-General Aurelio Fernández and Junta members Pons, Rebull, and Tomás Fábregas—to **the San Elías ex-convent**, the Control Patrols' remand prison, and having met with the entire Secretariat of the Patrols Department, made up of all the representatives who served on it, the First Councillor, with the assent of all present, ordered that all of those currently in detention within that building be transferred immediately to the Commissariat-General of Public Order."[19]

It was agreed, furthermore, "that the detainees would remain for no more than seventy-two hours in the relevant Sections" of the Control Patrols, so that the latter might carry out the requisite enquiries and that, once these were completed, "the prisoners would be brought before a Commission made up of one person from each of the three organizations, the ERC, the CNT, and the POUM,

---

18 "Plenum of Unions held on 13 March 1937. Second and last sitting" [SA-PSB-1401-16].

19 "Report to the Honorable First Councillor of the Generalidad of Catalonia, Josep Tarradellas, signed by the Security Junta Delegate [Tomás Fábregas Valls], the general secretary [González Batlle] and the ERC delegate in charge [Joan Coll] (Barcelona, 25 March 1937)." The letterhead reads: "Generalidad of Catalonia, Internal Security. Control Patrols." Written in Catalan, this document is on deposit in the Poblet Monastery [AMTM-GC-34-112].

who would operate as the Patrols Secretariat.[20] That Commission would then decide whether the detainees go free or are transferred immediately to the Commissariat 'along with the corresponding paperwork.'"

This was an attempt to usher in a new phase in the work of the Control Patrols, initiated by means of what would come to be known thereafter as the "San Elias Agreement." The phase of speedy application of "people's justice" had now ended and a "regularized" phase of collaboration with the Commissariat was beginning.

★

La Noche carried an **article above Balius's byline.** Entitled "Wage War We Must. Our Future Depends Upon It," it advocated a war economy and was critical of the Generalidad's economic policy.

★

Jacobo Prince, FACA delegate living in Barcelona, penned a **letter/briefing for his Argentinean comrades,** in which he tried to describe and analyze the existing complicated political situation as well as the tricky position of the anarchist leadership[21]: "It turns out that not only is the entire capitalist world, the democracies included, lined up against Spain, but that the Spanish anarchists face incomprehension and hostility from most anarchists elsewhere.[22] This is ridiculous and none too heart-warming for people here, who certainly have much graver things to worry about than thinking about what a few nitwits in Paris, New York, or Buenos Aires might say. They just shrug their shoulders, and are right to do so."

The Argentineans from the FACA, now members of "Nervio" and other likeminded anarchist groups, were the main champions of the higher committees' collaborationist line: "Political and military developments have forced the CNT into making a few real or perceived concessions and that of course has created unease and discontent within its own ranks." Criticisms of those concessions was, of course, doctrinaire and nit-witted and, if they came from abroad, were of no significance; but when they came from within, the form they took was not direct criticism but subterranean opposition "to Generalidad or central government accords to which our representatives have agreed." According to Prince, such lack of discipline on the part of the rank-and-file CNT personnel vis-à-vis the higher

---

20　The PSUC had pulled out of the Control Patrols in January 1937. The positions left vacant were then filled by the other organizations.

21　FACA correspondence, Letter 30, 13 March 1937 [BAEL].

22　The hostility sprang from the abandonment of basic anarcho-syndicalist principles.

committees was an encouragement to "the political enemies who are forever on the look-out and trying to reap maximum benefit from the circumstances."

Jacobo Prince listed as the higher committees' main problems: "on the one hand, shortage of personnel, the intrigues, speculation, and trickery of the politicians and, on the other, the indiscipline of the comrades as displayed in a range of publications akin to the ones over there, and also certain events that have sparked incidents in some villages."[23]

Prince was sounding the alarm about the emergence of a revolutionary opposition to the higher committees, one of which in terms of the foreign or international scene he was contemptuous, but that bothered him at the domestic level.

He warned that as far as most of the population of Barcelona was concerned, the war was far away and a secondary issue and visible only in a few very concrete facets of day-to-day life: "Even now, the only discernible signs that there is a war on are the queues outside the bakeries and tobacco stands and the fact that, at night, the lights are turned down by three quarters. Outside of that, the city looks normal." Such tranquility meant that people were not appreciative of the gravity of the situation, which in turn ensured that "nor is there any understanding of the concessions the CNT has had to make to the government and parties that, being a minority in Catalonia, have certain recourses that our people do not." Those concessions fed the discontent of a few comrades "who see certain gains whittled away, watch the expansion of government powers, quite apart from the innate defective comprehension of certain militants [who] are unhappy and lash out in an inappropriate manner."

According to Prince, what was called for was a discipline that was out of the ordinary, and he **deplored the fact "that the FAI is not a proper, organized party,** with the accouterments of cohesion and a uniform line."

Jacobo Prince made an excellent and closely argued case for the higher committees' collaborationism. His allusion to the FAI's turning into an organized party became fact at its July 1937 Peninsular Plenum, which embarked upon an overhaul of FAI structures, replacing affinity groups with a geography-based organization that would facilitate the training of cadres equipped to fill civil service positions. **The abandonment of principles necessarily had an impact on organizational formats.**

Sunday, 14 March

There was a meeting of **CNT area delegates from right across the Catalan region,**

---

23   The "shortage of personnel" was a reference to the dearth of militants equipped to fill positions of responsibility in the civil service or within the Organization.

attended by delegates drawn from the first, third, sixth, and seventh zones, plus a delegate from the Rail, Light, and Power Union, the RC's secretary and vice-secretary, and comrade Joan Pau Fábregas.[24]

Discussions covered the norms by which area delegates should abide; to properly perform their task, they would have to keep in close contact with the Local Federations and comarcal committees, the purpose being to sort out all the issues existing in that area.

In accordance with the resolutions passed by the last congress regarding the establishment of a Policy Advisory Council attached to the RC, Xena and Fábregas were commissioned to ferret out suitable comrades to act as advisors to the Generalidad Council Departments in the examination of whatever decrees were proposed, as well as framing suggestions to be put to CNT councillors serving on the Generalidad Council.

It was agreed that the area delegates moved to the RC would be paid their relocation expenses and that until "such time as the new Internal Security Council is set up, the defense councillorships at municipal level should not be disbanded." A notice regarding the matter would appear in *Soli*.

Several circulars issued by the NC were read, indicating to the RC that it was in agreement with across-the-board disarmament "of all civilian personnel" that was endorsed by the NC in its circular dated the 11th. It was determined that these circulars should be read out to the local and comarcal federations.

The proceedings were brought to a conclusion at 7:00 p.m.

★

Joan Pau Fábregas, who served as councillor for economy in the first Tarradellas government, delivered a **lecture** at the Coliseum cinema.[25]

He stated that the battlefront was inevitably dependent on the economic front for success. He described the Barcelona rearguard as "upbeat and trusting, witless and frivolous" and lacking in austerity or any sense of duty. The rearguard had to assume the same duties as the frontline militia members, who knew nothing of standard hours and did not succumb to tiredness.

He called for "a general mobilization of the rearguard."

24 "Plenum of the Regional Committee." Meeting with area delegates from around the region, held on 14 March 1937 [IISH-CNT-85C1]. For a biography of Joan Pau Fábregas, see Paolo Casciolo and Agustín Guillamón, eds., *Biografías del 36* (Barcelona: Descontrol, 2016), 56–77.

25 That lecture was published in pamphlet form as Juan P Fábregas, *Los factores económicos de la Revolución Española* (Barcelona: Oficinas de Propaganda de la CNT-FAI, 1937) [AEP].

And then he spelled out his "economic overhaul plan."

Industrial output had to be based on the formation of Enterprise Councils "on the basis of one representative per work-section, as determined by the corresponding union." Within each Enterprise Council "a Factory Committee should be set up," made up of three delegates: a bookkeeper, a technician, and a statistician; they would run the factory.

The most interesting part of the lecture was his admission that he had had two essential concerns during his time as councillor of economy. The first was the Collectivizations Decree: "a brand-new code governing Catalonia's brand-new socio-economic life"; it had been successfully passed in October 1936. The second was the "orchestration and the fixing of guidelines for our foreign trade, to end the chaos that had prevailed throughout the months of August and September." He had tried to put some meat on those bones through the "creation of the Foreign Trade Council," an effort that failed.

That **Foreign Trade Council**, consisting of a representative from the Finance Department, plus one from the Supplies Department, one from the Agriculture Department, and one from the Economy Department, under his chairmanship, was to have **"brought all of the initiatives together until an absolute 'monopoly' on foreign trade was arrived at."** The work of the Foreign Trade Council, coordinated with the producer and distributor unions, "was of inestimable importance."

It was to have cut unemployment, boosted the productive assets of the country, researched world markets, prevented the flight of capital, and centralized import-export operations, by optimizing the handling of foreign currency and acquiring "certain import goods" from a position of privilege "sometimes resorting to dumping and at other times to a regimen of temporary intake."

But that Foreign Trade Council had ended in a resounding failure: "The 'monopoly' on foreign trade, the imposition of which I asked for so often in vain, from my position as Generalidad councillor for economy" ran into steadfast opposition from the other political factions. *The substitution of Santillán for Fábregas in the Economy Department in mid-December 1936 spelled the end of any drive toward a monopoly on foreign trade.*

Joan P. Fábregas was sanguine about the S'Agaró financial decrees drafted by Tarradellas, although he insisted that, if they were to have any real impact, there was a need to sponsor a plan to reactivate economic activity. He did not criticize the political fallout from those decrees that left firms, whether collectivized or not, at the mercy of the Generalidad government. Likewise, he expressed support for the spread of industrial and peasant collectivization and called for antifascist unity as the only way of winning the war and "rescuing the essentials of our Revolution."

In fact, the incoming Generalidad government of 17 December, which replaced Joan Pau Fábregas by Santillán in the Economy Department, espoused the doctrine of the free market, through Comorera's influence. Implicit in this, as far as the PSUC was concerned, was making political clienteles of the GEPCI and the petite bourgeoisie and of all who were against the collectivizations and the revolutionary situation ushered in by the workers' uprising of 19 July.

The free market for which Comorera lobbied was diametrically opposed to the foreign trade monopoly. In practice, this made it possible for, at most, ten or twelve traders in the Paris cereals market making the wheat deals, driving up prices and encouraging profiteering, right from the outset.

This was the very point being made by Joan Pau Fábregas in rather technical, bombastic, and obscure language when he mentioned "dumping," the marshaling and centralization of currency management, or when he stated that a monopoly on foreign trade would place "in the hands of the public authorities ... the entire wealth of the country, the management of which would be handled through the National Bank, which would have to fund the extraordinary volume of commercial deals that would thereby be concentrated under a single direction."

In words less technical but plainer and more readily understandable, Joan Pau Fábregas was not saying in his lecture: **that the bread queues in Barcelona were the result of the failure to get that Foreign Trade Council up and running.**[26]

Joan Pau Fábregas's moderation and political compromise, completely in line with the higher committees and Generalidad government, were the inescapable consequence of the sort of deference one finds in any official where the bureaucratic machinery of his organization is concerned.

Tuesday, 16 March

The **Generalidad Council** assembled under the chairmanship of Tarradellas at 6:40 p.m., with councillors Doménech, Herrera, Valdés, Vidiella, and Sbert in attendance; the council dealt with the resolution of minor matters of no great import.[27]

Tarradellas briefed them on the incident that had befallen councillor Sbert on the border and on the sackings he had ordered, which had been resisted. He said that he was not about to tolerate such indiscipline, nor that such disobedience should go unpunished. He added that *La Batalla* had failed to abide by the sanction imposed upon it, as a result of which he stood ready to act with all due vigor as interim security councillor.

---

26 Compare this with the analysis made by a BL member, on 23 January 1937.

27 "Minutes of the 16 March 1937 sitting of the Generalidad Executive Council."

Sbert added additional details regarding the incident in La Jonquera, which boiled down to actions taken by a Control Patrol that, even after Sbert had been identified as a councillor, was so bold as to frisk him and record the foreign currency he was carrying. To prevent things from getting worse, Sbert had decided to turn back for Barcelona, and he highlighted "the government's lack of authority."

Sbert then briefed them that, the following day, the Exposition of Catalan Medieval Art was due to open in Paris and arrangements had been made for the French Education minister to attend and greet the councillor representing the Generalidad government. It was agreed that Sbert should attend the opening.

Proceedings were brought to a conclusion at 8:10 p.m.

Wednesday, 17 March

Tarradellas ordered that San Elías no longer be used as a prison: those arrested by the Control Patrols would from now on be going to the Public Order Commission.[28]

Thursday 18 March

The newspaper *La Noche* carried a notice reporting the formal launch of the Friends of Durruti the previous day. The unknown Félix Martínez, a long-time CNT member was listed as secretary of the Friends of Durruti, with Jaime Balius as vice-secretary. José Paniagua, Antonio Puig, Francisco Carreño, Pablo Ruiz, Antonio Romero, Serafín Sobías, and Eduardo Cerveró were listed as members of the leadership board.

Barcelona's Local Federation of [CNT] Unions sent a letter to the Regional Committee, dated 18 March 1937, wherein it reiterated its disapproval of the privileges awarded to workers in the War Industries: "We took exception to the War Industries' being allowed to make their own purchases of foodstuffs by setting up co-operatives and travelling out to the villages to make their purchases, which has meant that goods increase in price; in addition we have protested that the bulk of the populace had no such purchasing rights."[29]

---

28   Caballé, *Barcelona Roja*, 87; Govern de la Generalitat/Josep Tarradellas, *Crónica de la Guerra civil a Catalunya*, vol. 2 (Barcelona: DAU, 2009), 699.

29   "Letter from the Barcelona Local Federation of Sindicatos Únicos to the Regional Committee" (Barcelona, 18 March 1937) [IISH-CNT-43F].

Those privileges were based upon the need to maintain productivity in the War Industries, since their workers might otherwise have had to spend long hours waiting in queues. *Such prerogatives are a good illustration of the serious issues arising in the everyday lives of most workers.*

Friday, 19 March

The Libertarian Youth of La Barceloneta handed out a **leaflet** brilliantly setting out the contention that **food shortages were a ploy designed to harass the revolution and bring it to an end.**[30]

Aside from sounding the alarm and giving a nod to antifascist unity, it stated that "eight months into this war and we have yet to resolve the housing crisis or **the bread rationing** or control of **the cost of living,** or anything else." They remarked that the theorists of the New Economics had been duped "by a quiet conspiracy of warehouses and shopkeepers, those eternal worshippers at the altar of the god Agio."[31]

Workers and employees on starvation wages were being robbed in the rearguard by a petite bourgeoisie for whom the bourgeois and counterrevolutionary political parties were covering. A key aspect of this "cover" and of the parties' manipulative tendencies were "the demonstrations of women, those vile posters, those rabble-rousing rumors which led to the demand: Down with the Committees!" Those maneuvers and demonstrations had triumphed thanks to "the abdication of the trade-union forces, willing to sacrifice everything, so as not to disturb 'the antifascist order.'"

And what had they gained by their refusal to break ranks with antifascist unity? "**There is no more bread and no better bread to be had anywhere. No sign of a cap on the prices of basic necessities.** No advantage can be seen for the neighborhood with regard to rent payments, if they are now having to come up with impossible back payments."

There was recognition that the unions had lost and the politicians and petite bourgeoisie won "as they sell the most precious items to us at whatever prices they choose." And complaints about shopkeepers raking in "fabulous profits from the people's hunger." And moans about the dismal spectacle of combatants' families going hungry.

---

30 La Barceloneta Libertarian Youth, "The Hunger Ploy" [Around 19 March 1937. Fulls Volanders CA].

31 The 24 October 1936 Decree on Collectivizations and Workers' Control, drawn up by Joan P Fábregas, was regarded as the keystone of the "New Economics." December 5th and 6th saw the First New Economics Symposium, portrayed as the launch of a collectivized economy. *Agio* is a synonym for speculation, lucre, abuse, usury, fraud, and profiteering.

They described the differences between meals, which varied according to "each person's pocket," as shameful. "It is an outrage that we have chickens coming out of the drain-pipes and yet there are no potatoes. That we have lobster, but no dried cod. **That we have no bread, but we do have cakes.**"

They stressed the indecency involved in Barcelona's being able to live "high on the hog, as long as one has money." And denounced the sheer immorality whereby "Madrid goes without eating while Barcelona squanders."

They were scandalized by the thriving hordes of gilded prostitutes and the luxury restaurants, when workers lacked even basic necessities.

The conclusions they came to were admirable and profound: "The aim is to harass the Revolution and abort the very idea of Revolution. The gambit is clear. For once, let us spell it out. The aim is to wear the working classes down and bring them to heel through boredom and despair. From long experience, they know what relentless stomach pangs can achieve."

Consciously or otherwise, Kropotkin's thesis was that, for a revolution to succeed, it must be able to produce bread in abundance and avoid defeat at the hands of hunger.

That flyer closed with a call to the unions to stand up to the people's enemies and their intrigues, which were tolerated due to the demands of the war and out of support for the antifascist unity that was necessary if the war was to be winnable.

That hunger was a gambit on the part of the bourgeois and counterrevolutionary parties to defeat the revolution was a theoretical innovation that made sense of the Bread War that Comorera declared on the barrio committees from mid-December 1936 onwards. This thesis, formulated by Libertarian Youth from one Barcelona barrio who also articulated their radical criticism of the passivity of trade unions, was indicative of the conceptual and practical gulf that had already opened up between the real needs of the grassroots membership and the bureaucratic universe of the higher committees, subsumed into the machinery of state through the "antifascist unity" tactic.

Saturday, 20 March

Given the coming into force of the much-postponed municipal ration card, now scheduled for "this coming Monday, 22 March, the Bread Industry Economic Committee [CEIP] wishes to make it known to the general public that bread will be produced on a district-by-district basis," and press and radio notices would announce "the districts whose turn it would be to bake bread for sale on the following day."[32]

---

32   "District" meaning a municipal territory encompassing several barrios. These days, Barcelona is divided up into ten districts and sixty-three barrios. The Sants-Montjuich district,

The CEIP regretted the strict bread rationing in the city "but abnormal wartime circumstances ... require yet one more sacrifice of us," which should be accepted "without fuss or carping, so that Freedom may triumph." *But rhetoric fills no empty bellies.*

The notice closed with a sentence that reported yet another set-back for the ward committees in the Bread War: "any of the chits issued by the barrio and neighborhood commissions shall be null and void, with only those formally issued by Barcelona Corporation having any validity."[33]

★

The CNT's higher committees met in session at 10:15 p.m. under the chairmanship of Valerio Mas, the RC secretary: in attendance were representatives from these unions: Foodworkers, Metalworkers, Construction, Chemical Industries, Light & Power, Communications—and from Zone 1.[34]

Xena read out a list of the comrades chosen to serve as advisors to the RC, which Fábregas had drawn up. That list was approved, on condition that those named agreed.

Valerio Mas suggested that the entire range of RC activities be broken down into six secretariats, plus a general secretary.

A communiqué from the NC was read out; it warned that various villages had but a short span of time in which to argue the case for the loans they were seeking from the Ministry of Public Works as a means of reducing unemployment.

Next, Mas read out **two letters from Defense Councillor Francisco Isgleas,** one addressed to the RC and the other to the president of the Generalidad, in which he tendered his resignation from his post "due to dissatisfaction with the accords reached within [the Council]." It was resolved that the four CNT councillors should be summoned to a meeting with the RC the following Monday, at 9:30 a.m.

After a breakdown from **Domingo Canela** of the public order situation in Reus and the intolerable abuses of "three [CNT] individuals who had set themselves up as dictators and were bullying everybody," he drew attention to the activities of the Friends of Durruti "in that they shuttle around important cities and operate outside the supervision of the Organization."

---

for instance, takes in the barrios of Sants, Hostafrancs, Badal, El Poble Sec, La Font de la Guatlla, Marina, Prat Vermell, and so on. There is a measure of autonomy at both levels.

33 "The Sale of Bread in Barcelona," *La Vanguardia*, 20 March 1937, 3.

34 "Minutes of the Regional Committee meeting held on 20 March 1937" [IISH-CNT-85C1].

The RC's pool of advisors, distributed through a total of seven secretariats, was as follows:

Secretariat 1: Supplies – **Ausejo**; Trade – **Ausejo, Costelo**.

Secretariat 2: War – **Ascaso (Domingo) and Huix**; Navy – **Grünfeld**; Air Force – **Picas, Campos**; War Industries – **Martí, Vallejo**.

Secretariat 3: Public Order – **Aurelio Fernández, Dionisio Eroles, Asens**; Investigation – **Arias, Escorza, Riera, Porta [Portela?]**; Justice – **Batlle**.

Secretariat 4: Agriculture – **Ramón Porter**; Labor/Public Works – **Miralles, Barranco, Xena**; Industry – **Playans, Carbonell**; Mining – **Sala, LVC**.

Secretariat 5: Transport & Communications – **Combina, Castellote** – Light & Power – **Menassans**.

Secretariat 6: Finances – **Joan P.** Fábregas, **Gaston Leval**.

Secretariat 7: Public Education – **Ocaña, Puig Elías**; Health and Social Assistance, **FM, Ibáñez, Rosell**; Propaganda – **Carbó, Toryho**; Political Action – **Castellote, Xena, Doménech**.

The meeting concluded at 1:30 a.m. *The list included much of the elite of Catalan anarcho-syndicalism.*

Monday, 22 March

The Control Patrols' Section 7 drafted a **report** on events that had unfolded in a warehouse on the Calle Balmes that day.[35]

People from the Central (Borne) Market and others from the Defense Department (Supplies for the Front Section) turned up at the headquarters of the Control Patrols' no. 7 Section with a document "giving them the authority to collect a certain quantity of potatoes from the warehouse at 288 Calle Balmes, potatoes under the control of the Supplies Department.

The person in charge at the warehouse asserted that the document was not in order: it lacked the stamp of the appropriate department. Given the presence of a representative of the Supplies Department, he was handed the document in question to bring back to his department and have it completed properly.

At which point "two vanloads of Assault Guards" turned up and struck aggressive poses. The captain in command was called upon to "drop the attitude."

While they were waiting for the representative from Supplies to get back with the documents correctly validated, the aforementioned captain was overheard to say: "Since we knew in advance that a Patrols Section has set up

---

35   Control Patrols, "Internal Security," Generalidad of Catalonia (Barcelona, 22 March 1937) [AMTM].

shop here and knowing how they go about their business, we have taken our precautions."

When the representative from Supplies reappeared, he ordered the potatoes to be taken "under the protection of the Assault forces." The patrollers asked the members of the El Borne Committee if the presence of the Assault Guards was acceptable to them and were told that it was.

The presence of all these armed men caught the attention of passers-by, for which reason the patrollers telephoned the commissioner for public order who ordered that they all withdraw. The Assault Guard captain showed reluctance to withdraw until the Commissioner's order was repeated and then they decided to leave, the patrollers staying behind to be solely responsible "for what might happen."

Aside from the flamboyant attitudes on both sides throughout this tale, the climate of friction between the patrollers and the Guards was utterly unmistakable. What the report omitted to detail was what it was that "might happen"—a raid on the potato depot by women from the barrio.[36] In this episode, the patrollers looked like they were defending the people from the "same old" despised guards.

★

The Barcelona-based Argentinean **Jacobo Prince wrote a letter to his FACA comrades back in Buenos Aires.** He asked them to be wary about circulating the contents of the report "so as to forestall any loss of morale."[37]

He noted the existence of a "divorce between the nucleus of comrades holding down government and organizational leadership positions and the broad masses." This had led to a series of contradictions and anomalies.

He cited the example of what had happened in Public Order: "Our comrades sign up to a decree like the 'pubic order' decree, without first briefing the organization, and no sooner is the decree published, than, first in line to query it and not abide by it, are our own grassroots bodies."

Likewise, a decree coming from the Generalidad, with its CNT representatives, might offer a solution to a certain matter; but "a defense group from some ward or some village committee decides not to abide by it and the resolution falls into abeyance." It did not matter if the committee was right and the councillors wrong; the symptomatic departure from the norm, the disobedience was the point.

In this way, the grassroots militants had the same old suspicion of those in government that they had always had and the CNT councillors ducked out of

---

36   See below, for the account of the same incident as reported in *La Noche* of 23 March.

37   FACA correspondence, Letter 40, 22 March 1937 [BAEL].

attending assemblies when it came to explaining the decrees, adding further to the distrust between both sides. "Triggering a vicious cycle."

He could just imagine the sort of unpleasant and violent incident that might be triggered between some of the leaders and the membership, "if, say, Santillán were to show up at a plenum to give an explanation of certain positions, unpleasantness would doubtless ensue."

He reported on clashes between CNT personnel and UGT personnel in one Valencian village and on Maroto's having been arrested for criticizing the government.

He referred to the Generalidad government's having suspended *La Batalla*, the POUM mouthpiece for a matter of days, although he could not fathom the reasoning behind the CNT councilors' having voted in favor of such coercion. And he came up with this prophetic hypothesis: "I believe, however, that politically we should have stood by them [the POUM], for this is a party destined to be crushed ... before we are."

With regard to Public Order, he stated that the decree setting up the Unified Security Corps and breaking up the Control Patrols was still "in the air." As a result of that, he mentioned the interesting tidbit of news that "our defense groups and patrols are wary and not ready to disarm, not even for the sake of appearances." And he was unsure how the whole matter was going to be sorted out.

He criticized the organizational weakness of the FAI, made up of "whimsical" affinity groups, which there was talk of restructuring. He denounced the calling of plenums of old militants to discuss serious issues, thereby sidestepping the flood of new groups they had witnessed since 19 July. But what struck him as paradoxical was **the distrust those at the bottom had of those at the top, a distrust of all who were holding down government or organizational posts**. It required enormous amounts of "staying-power" to be able to handle any post.

He described the overall economic and political situation as highly complex, which made it hard to foresee whatever the future held.

The letter ended with a few slightly startling assertions for an anarchist: "**The absence of a strong party organization is more and more obvious.** With one, we would be invincible." He counseled against Argentinean FACA comrades' emigrating to Barcelona; it was pointless, unless they were to bring along their own Mausers and their own ammunition.

Prince's analysis of the mistrust the rank-and-file CNT membership felt toward their own leaders was very perceptive and spot-on. The "divorce" of which Prince was speaking in March 1937 was heightened with the ceasefire ordered by the higher committees during the May Events. The brutal Stalinist and government repression in the summer of 1937 pushed that divorce to unbearable levels, driving things in the direction of a split that nevertheless never came to a head.

Tuesday, 23 March

The **higher committees** met at noon; councillors, comarcal delegates, the director of *Soli,* and the responsible committees were in attendance.[38]

Valerio Mas mentioned that the RC was not happy with the resignation tendered, "in a personal capacity," by Isgleas from the post of defense councillor.

Isgleas then piped up to explain the reasons for his resignation, which were "all in all" his disgust at having to deal with folk as two-faced as those "who swarmed within the Generalidad," with the Catalanists and Stalinists' drive to "undermine" and bring him into disrepute "all for the good of the ideology they profess to stand for."

Santillán, Herrera, and **Doménech,** councillors of Economy, Health, and Public Services, respectively, indicated that they disagreed with the resignation because it created "the feeling that there was some falling-out between the CNT's councillors."

Xena reported on the deep-seated and widespread unhappiness in various comarcas around Catalonia regarding "the decisions relating to mobilization." He made no bones about his annoyance with "the unseemly propaganda being made about the same," which was heedless of the fact that, aside from those who were happy to go off to fight fascism, "those unmoved by any ideal go off to war painfully and not joyously." For that reason, in his view, the mobilization Decrees endorsed and signed by the CNT were disastrous. He regarded the unrelenting belittling of CNT activities and the constant sabotage of the collectivized economy as deplorable as they led to a reduction in the numbers of CNT adepts and sympathizers. **Manresa** expressed agreement with Xena. The **FAI's RC** stated "that the [anarchist] groups on the streets will create relentless pressure to ensure that everything is for the good of all."

The **Local Federation** urged Isgleas to spell out clearly the reasons behind his resignation, since it seemed as if he was hiding or disguising his real motives and "not telling the whole story."

Isgleas replied that "I have already told the whole story."

"In a moment of candor," **Santillán,** by now councillor for economy, explained "that in actual fact, Comorera has stuck his beak into countless areas under Economy's remit," leading them to understand that he had done the same

---

38   "Meeting of the responsible committees, councillors, comarcal delegates, and Toryho, held on 23 March 1937, at 12:00 noon" [IISH-CNT-85C1].

with the Defense Department run by Isgleas and that that was the essential reason behind his resignation.

The **Local FAI Federation** said that "the politicians are working against our Organization." It was their firm belief that the Public Order Corps would be impossible without widespread and majority participation by CNT members, because the old Assault and Civil Guard corps were not up to the job. *This was a piece of wishful thinking on the part of the higher committees*, which prompted them to demand that the command posts within the Corps also go to the CNT.

The FAI's delegate went on, prophetically: "Some day, triggered by an infinity of incongruous acts being performed by the socialists [PSUC], especially Comorera, there will be mayhem on the streets." And he cited the example of the recent discovery in one warehouse of "upwards of fifty thousand kilos of potatoes, nearly all of them rotten." When these were dumped in the street for the village women to sort through and avail themselves of, "along came a vanload of hunting dogs in Assault Guard collars," commanded by a young captain who, brandishing his pistol, threatened some CNT patrollers. The patrollers had threatened him with the same treatment until he desisted.

The conclusion that the FAI delegate drew from the incident with the potatoes was that, that same evening, the CNT councillors "contested and annulled the [Public Order] Decrees that they themselves had signed up to." If there was something awry in the Control Patrols, it had to be set straight: "but let Public Order slip from our grasp? Never."

Even though they still clung to certain illusions, they were starting to understand that this Unified Security Corps was going to be built on the amalgamation of the old, repressive, bourgeois police corps, for the precise purpose of smashing the CNT's armed hegemony in the rearguard.

Doménech asked whether Isgleas's resignation should be accompanied by that of the other three CNT councillors, or whether "both Isgleas and the others should stick it out for another fifteen days, which the Organization could use to bolster its position in the streets." He cautioned: "Over the airwaves, this very night, Companys would be sure to depict us as the bad guys, just to save his own skin."

Xena and Merino interrupted Doménech to say that "the Organization's rank and file will not allow this chump to bad-mouth, let alone poke us with a stick over the airwaves, because **such an insolent provocation will draw an immediate response in the shape of action on the streets.**"

As he was leaving the meeting, **Doménech** highlighted Companys's delicate position, as he was also being harried from Paris by Casanovas asking him to step down.

Xena reiterated the importance and possible fallout from a mishandling of the Public Order issue, concluding that the councillors "like it or not, should annul the Decrees signed."

In response to the allusions by Doménech (now no longer there) in opposition to meetings held at short notice in cinemas and other entertainment halls, in that he regarded these as negative propaganda counterproductive as far as the CNT was concerned, **Isgleas** said that he was not accepting the contention that the streets "are against us; the only people who are against us are the shopkeepers, the middle class, and the rich who, no matter how much propaganda we mount, will never be convinced by us, since they feel resentful and wounded [in] their private interests."

According to Isgleas, the CNT had on its side "the whole essence of humanity, kind, honest, decent people and workers," just as those who were working alongside the antifascist side out of fear were, for the most part, "one hundred percent fascists and they feed and sustain the communists and Catalanists."

Manresa referred to anti-libertarian demonstrations that they intended to break up emphatically, as they had done on a number of occasions already.

Portela brought up the usual arrests and murders of CNT personnel, insisting upon a swift purge of the security forces on the grounds that "otherwise, before the fortnight is out, we will be finding comrades dead on the streets." He cited the example of an item in *Soli* that very day, from which he gathered that they [the Stalinists and the Catalanists] "are in cahoots with all the world's fascists."

As far as **Comarcas** was concerned, the situation resembled a wall on the point of falling down.

The **Local Federation** asked that a commission should gather together all of the minutes written since the early days of the revolution, noting down all the accords, and if these had not been implemented, investigate why, because the Local [Federation] was sure that "had ALL the resolutions passed been implemented, we would assuredly be in a different position [a more favorable one]. *There was an unshakable belief in the infallibility of the accords reached by the Organization.* Then all the "true" militants ought to get together to see to it that every single thing that had been agreed upon was implemented, one step at a time. He closed his contribution with the assertion "that all the decrees that cannot be accepted should not be signed."

Xena, despite most of the councillors now having left, except for Isgleas, insisted that they should withdraw from the decrees they had signed.

Isgleas predicted that, at the Generalidad Council meeting that was about to start, the various political forces would try "to meddle more directly with the Higher War Council and the War Industries," because they had "a one-track mind when it comes to wresting fresh concessions from us." The Organization should see to it that the restructuring of Public Order "is carried out in a proportionate way and that goes for the posts too." He stated that he personally was fed up with governing and would rather devote himself to propaganda and educating the masses, which was what he reckoned was more sorely needed at that point.

It was agreed that "instead of being the accused, our representatives ought to be acting as ACCUSERS and getting to the root of the crisis; thereby coming up with a solution to our resolutions." The meeting concluded at 3:15 p.m.

Could Xena's and Merino's contributions to the proceedings, when they talked about **"such an insolent provocation drawing an immediate response in the shape of action on the streets"** *be considered a "call" to insurrection, or was it merely far-sightedness and the heralding of a "spontaneous" and unstoppable popular explosion? If the only thing holding back the outrage on the streets, the only brake on it, was the higher committees,* **would passivity on their part be enough to trigger the eruption?** *Was this the root of the May Events?*

The CNT's higher committees had decided that their councillors should turn away from the Public Order decrees to which they had signed on. That decision worsened and deepened the crisis within the Generalidad government, which was now the result not just of Isgleas's resignation "for personal reasons" but of **the CNT's frontal opposition to the Public Order decrees.** *Moreover, the CNT also wanted to put an end to constant anti-CNT sniping in the Generalidad Council because it was fed up with the usual government attacks. [The idea was that]* **the government would bring about a satisfactory resolution of the embedding of the CNT in government and in the Council.**

★

Under Companys's chairmanship and with a full turnout of its councillors, the **Generalidad Council** met at 6:25 p.m.[39]

Companys read out an impertinent telegram from the Republic's health minister, complaining about the lack of care shown in Catalonia toward people evacuated there from other areas. He then read out the response, addressed to the president of the Republic, refuting the insulting claims.

He went on to brief them on the incidents at the Port-Bou border crossing in connection with the entry of foodstuffs forwarded by the French Popular Front; they had held the authority of the government of Catalonia up to ridicule.

Companys and Vidiella reported on overtures made by the central government with an eye to a prisoner of war exchange through the good offices of the Red Cross.

---

39   "Minutes of the Generalidad Executive Council meeting of 23 March 1937."

At Companys's suggestion, there was agreement on exploring such prisoner exchanges with the central government, but the proposal was that the justice councillor would send Minister Giral a note alerting him to the fact that this was a matter that fell under the remit of the Generalidad and that, consequently he should be addressing himself to the president (and not to Vidiella) "refusing in advance any possibility of an exchange based on persons convicted by the People's Courts."

Companys passed on the news of the resignation of Isgleas, who had sent him a letter explaining that "he takes issue with the government's political orientation."

Companys explained that he had asked Isgleas to remain in office until "the Generalidad Council could decide whether or not there was a political issue to sort out," and asked him not to make his resignation public in the interim.

He stated that Isgleas had acceded to these conditions and he proposed to deal with this matter once the usual mailbag of orders and decrees had been gone through.

Aguadé reported on a meeting he had had with the interior minister who had raised no objection to the Public Order decrees, except where the borders were concerned, as he deemed that they fell within the exclusive remit of the central government. A makeshift solution had been worked out, whereby the central government and the Generalidad government would share their powers, but with the understanding that there was **an urgent need "to withdraw the control patrols from the borders,** especially the foreigners who have poked their noses in and given rise to complaints from the Embassies and who represent a standing danger that might lead to the complete sealing of the border, as has already been the case in Puigcerdá." The actions by the security councillor were endorsed.

A range of decrees and loans were approved. And the plan for a Housing Commission dropped once and for all. Approval was given to a one hundred million [peseta] loan to clear the bulk of the Supplies and War Departments' debts.

Isgleas and Vidiella suggested that they work out some formula whereby a number of those convicted by the People's Courts might be dispatched to the front. Sbert reported on his trip to Paris and that the Republican, Catalan, and Basque flags had all flown over the Exhibition.

Companys pointed out that there were several issues outstanding relating to the enforcement of the Public Order and Defense Decrees, as well as Isgleas's resignation "and since these, taken together, amount to a political problem, he asked the councillors for their opinions."

Tarradellas reported that the period of grace for appointment to posts and implementing the Public Order Decrees had expired. As had the time allowed for weapons collecting, without much success. The resignation of Isgleas "who represents an organization that can create a total crisis, if the entire [CNT] representation stood by the position of the defense councillor."

Tarradellas asked Councillor Isgleas to explain his resignation.

Companys read out the letter that Isgleas had sent him and then Isgleas expanded upon its contents, arguing that "the essential reason for his stepping down was disagreement with the government political outlook, because for some time, and even today, it has been tending, increasingly, to insert into Public Order affairs Corps and Forces that had been formed prior to 19 July and there is a danger that we may see resuscitation of persons and things that the people has rejected." He closed by saying that the government had boosted the role of organizations that represented nothing but bureaucracy, to the detriment of the revolutionary gains made in July.

Companys said that neither the government nor its various component organizations had wavered from the programs they supported. As to government policy, he said "that the revolution is made by means of Decrees and is directed by the representatives of the majority forces." **Anyone failing to comply with decrees was a counterrevolutionary.** It was pointless and bad faith to talk about the Security forces' being counterrevolutionary threats since they were under the orders of the government, which is the representative of the will of the people, and he added that it was those forces that had secured the victory on 19 July. *Companys's reasoning was as emphatic and democratic as it was false and reactionary.*

Comorera seconded Companys's words.

Valdés stated that all the decrees had been approved in council "by every single councillor" so it could scarcely be argued that enforcement of the decrees was the policy of one part; it was, rather, the government that had passed them.

Sbert said that public opinion was starting to question the government capabilities, that is, [the capabilities] of the organizations of which it was comprised, since they were the ones creating "difficulties for the direction of the war and the revolution."

People who were compliant were being mocked by the non-compliant who outnumbered them. The situation was beginning to look like the Middle Ages "and the watchword 'all power to the unions' bore too close a resemblance to corporatism and the guild organization that the French revolution had torpedoed," as it paid more heed to trade interests than to the public interest.

Ensuring compliance with the decrees was incumbent upon all councillors and all the organizations represented in the government. No one who did that could be accused of being a counterrevolutionary, nor was it conceivable that anybody thwarting the efforts of the government was any more revolutionary.

Isgleas stuck to his line of argument and stated that he felt alienated by this "tendency to place undue importance on a body of opinion that was nowhere to be found on 19 July and that is now making a stand with a counterrevolutionary impulse."

Tarradellas told Isgleas that his criticism of government policy could not justify the position of any organization, because it was incontrovertible that the government's decrees had long remained ineffectual, because no organization had managed to impose discipline of its members.

Tarradellas asked Isgleas if he was sticking to his resignation and the remainder of the CNT comrades whether they were standing by the defense councillor's stance.

Doménech replied that "councillor Isgleas's stance reflected opinion within the CNT, for it is the belief of our organization that just about any incident was being exploited for the purposes of politicking and that there was not enough revolution being carried out, with the war being the excuse." The CNT's thinking was that there was a retreat under way and that it was time, maybe not for a crisis, but for a change, because the CNT would not collaborate with the government if it sought a reversion to the old social organization.

Comorera said that the only option left was to declare that they were in crisis and to set about consultation, as there were programs in need of revision.

Vidiella could not understand the CNT's stance, as there was a new economy and Public Order was serving all the main organizations.

Companys said that it was not a question of debating whether the stance of Isgleas and the CNT had proper justification, because they had said already that it reflected "a mood within the organization," and, justified or not, its existence was a fact.

He acknowledged that the government had improved lots of things whenever it had been able to act and that in some departments brilliant work had been achieved. But it had to be conceded that Public Order "has thus far not been the government's doing."

He asked them to bear in mind that a time could come when the president might be unable to secure that agreement of all the existing organizations. "And since the president is stuck in this chair due to force of circumstances, it will be necessary for some solution to be adopted."

He asserted that he would never set a boundary to the revolution "insofar as it was the basis for a new society," but that henceforth he wanted to see "full responsibility and the whole of Public Order in my hands. And if that is not the case, I am redundant in my post."

He said that, now that a crisis had broken out, there would be no horsetrading with regard to Public Order and Defense. Everything else, he was willing to discuss. He did ask (with the aim of coming up with an internal solution) that the crisis not be made public for another eight days and that all the councillors remain in their positions.

Doménech reported on the air raids on a number of power stations and on them being left without defenses. **The president** drafted a telegram addressed to the prime minister, reiterating the need to protect the Catalan power stations.

The proceedings concluded at 9:35.

Wednesday, 24 March

In the **morning**, there was a meeting of the **libertarian higher committees**, with the RC, the Local Federation of [CNT] Unions, the Peninsular and Regional FAI Committees and the Local Federation of Anarchist Groups in attendance, plus Francisco Isgleas (the outgoing defense councillor).[40]

Isgleas reported that at the meeting of the Generalidad Council the previous evening, and because the other CNT councillors had resigned in solidarity with him, the government was now "in complete crisis." He explained that he had dissected the work of the current Council "pointing out its shortcomings in terms of Public Order, Economy, etc." He denounced "the counterrevolution in the making," the reason why "he could not carry on in his post." Companys, the Generalidad president, had indicated that he favored resolving the crisis "keeping the same coalition," but had stated that "he would make no concessions in respect of Public Order and Defense."

Xena set out his approach to Defense, his understanding being that all authority ought to be vested in the defense councillor, "especially where mobilization is concerned." As to Internal Security the Republican National Guard (formerly the Civil Guard) and the Assault Guard needed to be "dismantled" and amalgamated into a single, thoroughly purged corps. *This belief that the old forces of repressions could still be purged, was it witlessness, naivety, or pure rhetoric?*

Doménech suggested that the Defense and Internal Security Departments be amalgamated. Xena was opposed to this, insisting that it would be better if the Defense Department were to be passed on to the ERC, as long as Companys was president. He proposed that, in exchange, the current Supplies, Economy, and Public Services Departments be cut to two departments. Santillán pointed out that the Department of Foreign Trade was in the hands of the Valencia government.

Given that the RC was scheduled to be present at the Generalidad Palace,

---

40   "Minutes of the meeting held on 24 March 1937" [IISH-CNT-85C1]. The minutes mistakenly record "The meeting opened at five o'clock in the afternoon," contradicting the later reference to the meeting's having been adjourned and then resumed "at four o'clock in the afternoon."

proceedings were postponed until 4:00 p.m. The evening session resumed at 5:10, with the report that the meeting with Companys had been just going through the motions.

Xena completed the report, pointing out that Companys's main concerns were focused on Internal Security, War, and Economy. He stated that War ought to be run by experts and claimed the department should go to a military figure. The most serious issue facing Economy was the depreciation of the currency. He announced that the RC had "looked into the appropriateness of setting up an Advisory Council" to grapple with economic issues that, in his estimation, were "of most interest to us."

Toryho divulged that "there is spying going on at meetings of the Committees" because, he noted, "within a few hours of meetings, Antonov-Ovseenko knew the subject matter." Escorza pointed out that the Russian consul "has a complete dossier on our Organizations' meetings and accords."

Toryho complained about the Organization's lack of firm positions vis-à-vis collectivizations, propaganda, the war, etc., as a result of which everybody was confused and adrift; at Soli, he himself was merely spelling out his own "personal opinion," for want of clearcut guidelines.

Escorza sought to center the debate on the root causes of the crisis, because they had to know the reasons behind it if they were to come up with a solution. They also needed to look into "the positions we occupied at the beginning of the movement" so that these could be measured against the ones we came to occupy later. **In the absence of a "policy on power" and because "the word frightens us all,"** the issue was to find out "which positions we occupy and which it is in our interest to occupy."

Doménech warned of the danger of a "Vergara embrace" and of the preparations laid by the Valencia government for a prisoner exchanger. The **Libertarian Youth** reckoned that the higher committees needed to be bolstered "with comrades of sound reputation."

The **Local Federation** proposed that rather than asking anything of the government, it would be better to raise it with the people "so that they can bring pressure to bear on the government" from the streets.

Xena opened the discussion of which departments suited the CNT.

Escorza asserted that they were all related and inter-dependent. They had to "set the tone of government" and anybody "not complying with the accords reached previously" would be denounced in public. He noted that socialists and communists never used the press to brief their members about their own slogans; but the moment some CNT member uttered a word or some rallying cry, it was immediately rebutted by socialists and communists until it was drained of all value and effect. And as for the ERC, it had no trade-union support whatever;

all it had was Public Order, where "a series of arms-smuggling incidents have been unearthed."

The meeting carried on, in a pretty fruitless attempt to come up with firm yardsticks and clear-cut political positions to be put before public opinion, and with its "impassioned" debate on which ministerial posts to ask for and which to give away.

The proceedings were wound up at 8:04 p.m.

★

La Noche carried a lengthy **interview with Pablo Ruiz**, a member of the Friends of Durruti and spokesman for the Gelsa militiamen opposed to militarization of their columns. It offered an interesting short biography of Pablo Ruiz, from which we learn that he was a member of the Fígols revolutionary committee back on 8 January 1933, that during the July events he had fought in Las Rondas and on the Paralelo at the head of forty men, that he had played his part in the siege and ultimately the storming of the Atarazanas Barracks, shoulder to shoulder with Durruti and Ascaso, that he had set off for Aragon with the Durruti Column, where he had been fighting ever since in the Gelsa sector. After a paean to the virtues and advantages of the anarchist peasant collectivizations in Aragon, the interviewer asked him his opinion on militarization. His response was reasoned, cautious, and nuanced; but at the same time, it was rather coherent and radical, as if to underline the incompatibility between the anarchist outlook and the bourgeoisie and its republican state's management of the war: "We're not against a re-organization of the people's Army; remember, we were the first to call for a collective unified command ... overseen by delegates from the different columns, as a way of bringing some standardization to how they all operated. New structure? Bring it on, but as long as the people's Army does not end up dependent on the Generalidad, nor on the Central Government. Control must be vested in the Confederation."

In the interview, Pablo Ruiz alluded to the ongoing retreat from July's revolutionary gains and to the launch of the Friends of Durruti: "When we marched off to the front we left the victorious march of the Revolution—from the anarchist point of view—in the care of comrades. But political parties that had no feeling for the revolution, because they had to champion the interests of the bourgeoisie, and the UGT, which, compared with us, had only a tiny percentage in Catalonia, were given a say in its re-structuring ... by entering into a compact with them, we lost our hegemony in the Revolution, and have found ourselves obliged every day to reach compromises. Thereby, the Revolution has been disfigured, with the revolutionary gains made during the early days being whittled away. That led to the formation of the 'Friends of Durruti,' since this new organization has as its fundamental purpose the preservation, intact, of the postulates of the CNT-FAI."

Pablo Ruiz ended the interview by spelling out his own vision of how the revolution might be placed back on the right track: 1. The deployment of propaganda within the ranks of the CNT, without recourse to violence 2. Aim for trade-union (CNT) direction of the economy. 3. Exclude the political parties. 4. No compact or compromise with the forces harboring the counterrevolution, that is, with the PSUC and UGT: "let the direction of the economy and society be vested in the trade-union organization (the CNT), with the political parties playing no part in it, the idea being they don't deserve to be called remodelers (*renovadores*). All of this imposed, not by force, but by dint of propaganda within the CNT.… And I am against involvement of the political parties, my view is that would entail diminishing the revolution, which must flow one way or another, but never by giving ground to groups that not only have no feeling for revolution but are also in the minority."

Friday, 26 March

At 6:00 p.m., there was a meeting of former officials from the now disbanded Internal Security Junta, **members of the Secretariat of the Control Patrol Department**, and delegates from the Control Patrol sections.[41]

The meeting was chaired by Aurelio Fernández as secretary of the Security Junta. Tomás Fábregas, Joan Coll, Bonet, Gutiérrez, Sagristá, Nevado and Silvio Torrents were there representing the Patrols Secretariat. Present as delegates from the Patrols sections were Vicente Subirats Clos (ERC, Section 1), José Isalt Carreras (Section 2), Jaime Cornudella Olivé (Section 3), J. Casanovas, Guevara (standing in for Mario Gallud Maeda, CNT, Section 5) who arrived somewhat late, J. Sánchez (Section 6), Pedro R [Razzauti] Sulé (ERC, Section 7), Pere Olivé Martínez (Section 8), Vicente Vitalier Jáuregui (ERC, Section 9), Manuel (or Mariano) Pérez (Section 10), Antonio López Sánchez (CNT, Section 11), and Miguel González Batlle (from the secretariat). No one from San Elias was present (although Silvio Torrents was there, for the secretariat).

Aurelio Fernández explained that the subject matter of the meeting was "some executions carried out by certain Control Patrol personnel in defiance of the agreement reached on the 13th of this month with the Generalidad of Catalonia's First Councillor, José Tarradellas, at the San Elías center," which resulted in him receiving a protest note dated the day before.[42]

---

41   "Meeting of 26 March" [AMTM].

42   See above (under 13 and 25 March) for comment on that document, dated 25 March.

He asked that the letter in question be read out as an overture to "a friendly discussion, as is appropriate between comrades."

After Tomás Fábregas had read it, Joan Coll asked to speak in order to support the document and spell out his party's position on the incidents that had occurred.

Joan Coll (ERC) recalled "the formation of the Emergency Court" and its reorganization in early January. He himself served on that court as the representative of the ERC, as were Bonet for the CNT, Chueca for the UGT and Silvio Torrents for the POUM. He pointed out that one of the things that had prompted the ERC to insist on the formation of that court was **the expulsion from San Elías of Riera, who was sticking his nose in there even though he was not a member of the Patrols, nor of Investigations [Service].**[43] He recalled that the Emergency Court had carried on functioning after the UGT personnel left and on 13 March had come to an arrangement with Tarradellas. But he noted that "behind the back of that Court and heedless of the existence of any such arrangement, three detainees were murdered the previous day. The members of the Court protested against the killing "and did not in any way, shape or fashion, take responsibility for the act." **Bonet** (CNT) indicated that he wholeheartedly agreed with Coll.

Aurelio Fernández "having already set out the opinion of the comrades from the Investigating Commission or Emergency Court" yielded the floor to the delegate from the Control Patrols' Section 7.

Pedro R. Sulé regretted the fact that he did not have the reports on those executed to hand. He explained that, on the morning the incidents occurred, he asked, as was his custom, for the list of detainees "and was startled to find that in the one they handed him three of the detainees who had been on it the previous day were now no longer listed." When he queried this with the remand delegate, the latter's response was "that comrade Gutiérrez had turned up there with some other comrades the previous night, collecting them from the Section and executing them." When Sulé asked again on what authority this had been done, the answer was that "this was already known to the Secretariat."

Aurelio Fernández asked if the detainees' affidavits were always signed by the Section delegates, and Sulé stated that they were, insofar as his section was concerned "ever since the Investigating Commission was formed [in early January], adding that **in the early days only two executions had been carried out without approval**, and that at a time when his responsibility as a delegate was still ill-defined."

Gutiérrez explained his presence in section 7 away by saying that he had

---

43   He had been accepted at San Elías due to his having carried out similar repressive missions for the Patrols Emergency Court, under the Investigations Department of the now-defunct CAMC.

gone there looking for a member of the Municipal Band "who had mysteriously gone missing a few days earlier." He went on to say that he had searched for him throughout the night "arriving in Moncada in the morning, by which time the deed had already been done." He deplored the matter under discussion, but asked that they "**show indulgence regarding any mistakes that may still be being made by the Patrols** [Department], and blamed the whole delay in the convening of a meeting of Section delegates for the purpose of giving them a formal briefing on the San Elías arrangement."

He ended his statement by giving his opinion that the document that had been read out was the product of shoddy work by the ERC, in that it had been drafted without consultation with anyone else and raised questions over the responsibility of lots of patrol comrades.

Aurelio Fernández wanted him to clarify his involvement in the executions.

Gutiérrez's response was that everything he had said had been said as a denial of any such involvement.

Joan Coll described Gutiérrez's statement as "a product of the disorganization that has always prevailed within the Control Patrols Department," and he raised other past incidents, until he was cut short by **Aurelio** with a reminder that they were there to deal with one specific and current incident and not to discuss others "with which we are all too familiar."

Coll went on to claim that the previous day's incident had come about through "the Patrols' lack of guidelines" because there was no fathoming the moral aberration that presumed "to dispose of individuals and their fate, without anyone's knowing who was responsible."

His conclusion was that the letter would be sent out to every organization "as a protest over a deed with which we," those who had no hand in it, "could not show solidarity," and the disrepute of the Control Patrols was down to the prevailing indiscipline, and that it was high time to demand someone take responsibility for a deed "that might be repeated."

Nevado characterized Coll's remarks as "nasty, but fair." Rather mysteriously and menacingly, he spoke of the monitoring that he had ordered kept on the license plates of cars leaving Barcelona by the San Andrés highway and knew what he was talking about when it came to acts "ascribed by force of habit to the CNT." *Was this a veiled accusation that other organizations had been responsible for shootings in Moncada that were then chalked up to the CNT?*

Several section delegates spoke up to complain of "the slander campaign mounted against patrollers by certain parties."

Pérez, the Section 7 delegate, expressed the view that both the Section 7 patrollers and the persons who had drawn up the document that had just been read, had acted with undue "carelessness."

The Patrols were falling into disrepute because they were not now being allowed "to work like before." The ERC demanding to know who was in charge was part of a political maneuver. The most logical thing was to close the book on the matter by sending out a "watch your step" to those responsible for the appalling act.

Aurelio Fernández called upon them all to be more specific lest the discussion pointlessly broaden its focus. He said that they should not try to kid him, nor try to kid themselves: **"We have all played at Revolution and we are perfectly well aware of all the good and all the bad that has been done; but bear in mind that phase one is over and we are entering another, which should be one of collaboration rather than execution like the previous."**

He declared that it was plain that there was a campaign to bring the Patrols into disrepute and he had proof of that: but it was time to protest at these shootings "which are unauthorized by and known to none, when there is an arrangement already in place." He took issue with some of the section delegates and again reminded them that they were in "a brand-new phase," He closed by asking those present to decide upon the sanction to be imposed.

But when it came to the identification of which culprits to hit with the sanction, everybody dodged the issue or kept his head down. Several section delegates spoke up on behalf of López, the remand guard at Section 7 "at the time the detainees were removed" for execution, highlighting his merits, militancy and common sense. When **Gutiérrez** was asked for the name of those involved in the execution "he said he did not know the names" and then he himself asked for the writers of the accusatory letter to be sanctioned.

Since it seemed impossible to identify the guilty parties, **Aurelio Fernández** asked the comrades from his organization to raise the matter internally and for the CNT to decide upon whatever it reckoned was the most suitable punishment.

He recalled that **"under the San Elías arrangement, no section delegate, no one from the Secretariat, and absolutely no one from the Control Patrols Department, no matter who, may shoot or take action against any detainees,** [who] were to be handed over to Police Headquarters along with the appropriate affidavit."

He went on to issue a menacing caution, essentially directed at those who had not adopted **the change of behavior in the new phase**, citing some very odd arguments of a political sort: "Everybody needs to bear it in mind that those who, at a whim, carry out shootings or other undesirable acts, are simply playing into the hands of the fascist moles and those organizations out to see the CNT lose its representation in the government."

He ended with a call that the slandering of CNT personnel cease domestically as well as internationally, so that they were not defamed as "blood-thirsty executioners." He concluded that "a touch more common sense" and **adaptation to the new circumstances** would do the trick.

Coll piped up to place it on record that his party did not have, and never had, any interest in slandering anybody. He would leave the matter in the hands of the CNT to sort out. **Aurelio Fernández** assured him that it would impose a "fair and appropriate sanction." The meeting broke up at 9:45 p.m.

The statement from Gutiérrez was breath-taking. The absence of strict rules and the lack of rigor in the Patrols' handling of detainees were one of the major factors underlying the utter chaos that prevailed, leaving an opening for the personal whimsies of any unscrupulous individual. The power to carry out house searches, impose fines, or detain suspects and try them or to take sworn statements were too important to have been left to the whim of some brainless idiot. The power to execute detainees, arbitrarily or otherwise, could not be left to the whim of mere patrollers, outside of the purview even of their own section delegates. The facts really were very serious: but what Gutiérrez had had to say, when he referred to his belated search for a comrade in Moncada, also lifted the veil on a certain "tradition" and **common practices widespread throughout ALL the antifascist organizations,** *practices that were alive and well, and behind which Gutiérrez stubbornly and shrewdly was taking cover.*

The CNT had shown itself to be overly vulnerable and penetrable by criminal activities on the part of such dubious characters as Ruano (in the columns) and Gutiérrez (in the patrols). Sanctions were always internal and virtually secret, and at any rate were not widely publicized, so such criminality seemed to enjoy impunity (although Ruano was sentenced to death) and the sanctions never quite managed to repair the CNT's battered prestige.

As an organization within which these "uncontrollable" were actively and arbitrarily executing detainees without authority from any superiors—just as had been done "before" during the revolution's early days—the CNT was also answerable for such summary executions, even if only through negligence or organizational chaos, since it was not due to any policy decision on the part of the higher committees.

Aurelio Fernández summed up the situation perfectly when he explained to those in attendance that "We have all played at Revolution and we are perfectly well aware of all the good and all the bad that has been done; but bear in mind that phase one is over and we are entering another, which should be one of collaboration rather than execution like the previous."

The Gutiérrez case was regarded by all, including the ERC, as a failure to **adapt** *to this new collaborative phase. What mattered most, if any repetition of similar incidents was to be averted in the future, was not the punishment to be imposed but the threat hanging over the head of the patrollers.*

Good Friday, 26 March

A fresh crisis **formally** arises within the Generalidad government.[44]

Saturday, 27 March

In *La Noche*, Jaime **Balius** publishes an article "The Revolution Has its Requirements. All Power to the Unions."[45] Balius dissected the Generalidad government's crisis, which he interpreted as due to the heterogeneous nature of its component forces.

Balius highlighted the presence of other forces not included in the Generalidad government forces such as the trade unions, which could be constituted as the brand-new agencies the revolution needed. The industrial unions were an unprecedented and, as yet, untested force at loggerheads with the Generalidad government: "the duality of powers is self-evident."

Balius noted that "some Generalidad decrees have not been enforceable, because the unions, entirely within their rights, refused to abide by them, believing there was no question that their timing is ill-chosen, and, in addition, because they had not been consulted." The government crisis could not be resolved by rotten state agencies and bourgeois methods, but only by the workers acting through their unions. "The time has come for us to talk about '**all power to the working class**.'" And Balius concluded that "the revolution has its requirements. Let us not dither. **All power to the Unions**."

Toward the end of March
(or during the second fortnight of that month)

Barcelona's Confederal Defense Committee drew up a structural blueprint for the defense cadres and committees; *although it was undated, it seems to have been written in late March 1937.*[46]

The blueprint stressed **defensive preparations** at a point when, with the

---

44 Caballé, *Barcelona Roja*, 88; Govern de la Generalitat/Josep Tarradellas *Crónica*, vol. 2, 695. As to the relevance of the decision to transfer the Karl Marx Column from the Aragon front to the Madrid front in the eruption of a cabinet crisis and Tarradellas's withdrawal from the negotiations, see the report drafted by the latter: "The political crisis prior to the May Events. 23 days of mis-government in the Generalidad" [AMTM].

45 Jaime Balius, "The Revolution Has its Requirements. All Power to the Unions" *La Noche*, 27 March 1937, 3.

46 Barcelona Confederal Defense Committee, "A Structural Plan for Defense Committees" [IISH-FAI-CP-43-A6].

"all-round bankruptcy of the parties and systems, the only thing left standing is the Revolutionary Proletariat, with its program for work reorganization and economic and social equality."

Note was taken of **the ineffectuality and uselessness of the CNT personnel "representing us" in the Generalidad Council, as they were unable to do anything effective "in the face of the decrees looming and threatening to drown out any hint of revolution."**

They had enough personnel to confront any counterrevolutionary revolt, but it was acknowledged that their preparedness left something to be desired. The defense cadres were in need of intense and effective preparation. To which end, the Barcelona Defense Committee should be provided with everything it might need; capable personnel, suitable gear, and a study of the means and methods of struggle and of the tactics to be used.

There was a need for a pavilion to be established adjacent to the CNT's military training school, where trustworthy comrades might receive training.

The **ward defense committees** would make a painstaking study—surreptitious at all times—of all the locations occupied by the police, the parties, recreational centers.

Each individual comrade had to have his specific, well-defined mission, and it should not be forgotten that "if a prolonged struggle was to be sustained, efficient organization is indispensable."

These five aims were set out:

1. Investigation and instruction in fighting methods, ranging from weapons to electrical explosives.

2. Investigation into and preparation of arms-manufacturing workshops.

3. Training in the operation of motorized machinery, installation of communications, radio transmitters, wireless telephony, etc.

4. Procurement of enough appropriate equipment to arm all cadres.

5. **Organization of resources barrio by barrio, with a specific function assigned to each comrade,** "so that we can call upon complete fighting teams right from the outset."

Those cadres were to be organized and trained as follows:

A.   If they were to be effective, the **cadres were to be fifteen comrades strong**; seven riflemen, four dynamiters or bomb throwers, plus four auxiliaries serving the latter.

B.   Each machine gun was to be manned by a fifteen-man crew; nine for the transportation and upkeep of the gun; three providing cover as bomb throwers and three as "feeders" for the latter.

C.   "One comrade will be appointed to take charge of each of these teams and there will be comrades seconded to them as necessary, whether to handle communications, or other such services as may be required, such as food supplies, tending to the wounded, etc., etc."

D.   **For each ward, a sketch map is to be drawn up** on which would be marked, appropriately numbered and in different colored inks:

a.   Police posts, barracks and government buildings.

b.   Premises occupied by political parties and other organizations.

c.   Premises held by the Organization, unions, ateneos, ward committees, etc.

One would therefore simply have to state: Ward X, Letter X, and what needed doing, and no one not having access to the sketch map would be able to understand the message.

The report closed with two provisos addressed to the trade unions:

First: That the effectiveness of the defense committees would reflect the assistance and financial resources channeled into them.

Second: Only the people could defeat the counterrevolution. And today this was a life-or-death issue, just as it had been in the past, "and as pointed out at the start of this report **our collaborationist stance must not lead us to hope that we can make our revolution from the State. Quite the opposite.** We have to do all in our power to gradually recover our revolutionary identity."

*In the face of the government crisis, but above all, **in order to counter the undermining and threat to disband the Control Patrols** and in light of the hostility coming from the new Unified Security Corps set up as the amalgamation of the old bourgeois and anti-worker forces of repression, the Assault Guards and the Civil Guard, **there was a resurgence of the urgent need to overhaul, reinforce, and reinvigorate the defense committees** at barrio level.*

Between late November and early December 1936, the unions had placed the defense committees in sort of hibernation in the belief that they were unnecessary, given that there was an institutionalized "revolutionary power" in place in the shape of the Control Patrols within which the CNT enjoyed a sizable majority.

*In the second fortnight of March, or toward the end of that month, the Barcelona Defense Committee encouraged an overhaul of the barrio-level defense committees, deliberately gearing them up for a confrontation that looked imminent, while at the same time it drafted a very specific and detailed **defensive** plan of insurrection.*

Saturday, 3 April

It was announced that a brand-new provisional government had been agreed upon (it survived until 16 April). It was composed as follows:[47]

Josep Tarradellas (ERC), First Councillor and in charge of the Finance and Culture Departments.

Artemi Aguadé (ERC), Pubic Order Councillor.

José Calvet (UR), Agriculture and Supplies Councillor.

Francisco Isgleas (CNT), Defense Councillor.

Josep Juan Doménech (CNT), Councillor for Economy, Public Services, Health, and Social Assistance.

Joan Comorera (UGT), Councillor for Public Workers, Labor, and Justice.

This new lineup did not have the CNT's seal of approval, for which reason the CNT councillors did not, formally, take possession of their departments but merely worked within them, although without attending the meetings of the Generalidad Council.

Monday, 5 April

In the morning, **Companys** received a CNT delegation made up of Valerio Mas, Josep Juan Doménech, Joan P. Fábregas, and Manuel Escorza, which hammered home its view, "pointing out that there was no solution available other than to rectify the solution he had come up with for the crisis." **There was a "heated incident" between Joan P. Fábregas, Escorza, and Companys,** which merely worsened the relations existing between them all.[48]

★

---

47   Govern de la Generalitat/Josep Tarradellas *Crónica*, vol. 2, 714–15
48   Josep Tarradellas "The April 1937 Crisis," in ibid., 114–115.

Balius published an interesting article in which he delved into the meaning of the Generalidad government crisis.[49] As far as Balius could see, the Generalidad was a left-over from the past and not suited to the new revolutionary requirements: "The Generalidad government is a formula that belongs to the past, to a petit-bourgeois system entailing all manner of incongruences, fence-sitting, and hypocrisy."

Therefore, according to Balius, any solution to the Generalidad government's crisis would just be papering over the cracks. A change of names within the government would be utterly pointless. Balius issued **a call for the CNT to replace the Generalidad with workers' power and for the counterrevolutionary parties to be wiped out.** "Not that we are pessimists, but it is our honest belief that we have not been equal to the circumstances. The dilemma will brook no evasion. The future of the proletariat demands heroic decision-making. If there are some organizations out to strangle the Revolution, we must be ready to shoulder the responsibility for this historic moment, the very grandeur of which presupposes a range of measures and decisions that aren't out of tune with the present hour. On the side of the Revolution or on the sidewalk across the street. There is no middle ground."

★

At **7:20 p.m.**, there was a meeting of the **Control Patrols** Secretariat, attended by Tomás Fábregas, José Asens, Miguel González Batlle, Rafael Nevado, Juan Bonet, Joan Coll, Vicente Gutiérrez, Silvio Torrents, and Federico Sagristá, together **with all the delegates and sub-delegates from the various Control Patrol sections.**[50]

Nevado explained that the object of the meeting was to deal with the malaise and squabbles existing among the guards in the Montjuich fortress where some militia members and patrollers had come to blows due to inter-organizational animosities. Added to which there were the differential food rations and irregularities in how certain prisoners were being treated. The issue was whether the patrollers should carry on, or quit the fortress and leave it solely in the hands of militia members.

After a detailed report on the existing difficulties, delivered by Miguel Albert who was in charge at the Montjuich fortress, a heated discussion ensued. Asens promised that the food costs of patrollers would be defrayed by the Secretariat. After a number of arguments, it was agreed that the guard services provided by the Patrols would be handled by the Central Section.

This was the last surviving record of the Control Patrols Secretariat.

---

49   Jaime Balius, "An Historic Moment, A Categorical Dilemma," *La Noche*, 5 April 1937.
50   "Meeting of 5 April 1937" [AMTM].

Tuesday, 6 April

At **10:00 p.m.**, there was a meeting of the **Regional Committee** at the Casa CNT-FAI.[51] Comrade **Torres** from Perpignan was present and he set out the situation with the anarchist movement in France and its existing projects. He detailed the hurdles they were running into regarding the shipment of weapons and provisions to Catalonia, as well as the Stalinists' sabotage activity. And he announced that there was to be a huge rally held in Paris in support of the Spanish revolution.

Valerio Mas read out a letter "addressed to Companys regarding the current crisis," and the latter's response, which it planned to publish in *Soli* as the culmination of "a staggered attack in defense of the truth and as justification" of the CNT's stance.

Healthworkers Union recounted the recent incident in Olesa de Montserrat where, in a confrontation with the former Civil Guard, one of the latter had lost his life, leading subsequently to the arrest of eight CNT militants, their mistreatment and the ransacking of the village by the reinforcements sent in by the Civil Guard. Their orders had come down from Rodríguez Salas who could count on the cooperation of the PSUC. **Tarrasa, Esparaguerra, and Olesa called a general strike and the CNT had risen up in arms to insist that all of those detained be set free.**

At this point, into the meeting room came **Eroles**, stating that he had been involved in the matter right from the outset. Aguadé wanted to hold on to the prisoners. He himself had lobbied for the RC to register a vigorous objection, insisting upon the immediate release of all the detained persons.

Eroles analyzed the position as it presently stood, explaining that the willingness to step down expressed by Companys had made the Public Order issue even more serious, since the PSUC and UGT took advantage of every conflict in order to disrupt the situation, as had been seen, say, in the recent funeral of a guard.

Eroles put the defense committee (which was present at the meeting) **on notice** that such "undesirables" might, the following day, manage to get those attending the funeral of the guard killed in Olesa to create a disturbance.

Portela suggested that guards attending the funeral be banned from carrying weapons.

Construction [Union] submitted an extensive report on incidents in Valls arising out of strained relations between the Libertarian Youth, the FAI, and the CNT, pinning the blame on Prades, who had been invited to get out of Valls and make his way to Barcelona "to avoid any repetition of events."

---

51   "Regional Committee meeting held on 6 April 1937, at 10:00 p.m." [IISH-CNT-85C1].

After a long and fruitless delay for news of the release of the Olesa prisoners, the meeting was concluded in the morning hours of the 7th.

Wednesday, 7 April

The **funeral took place of Republican National Guard** (formerly Civil Guard) "Alfredo Aznar Gallego, murdered in Olesa de Montserrat on the 4th." It lasted three hours and a few incidents did occur.[52]

★

Jacobo Prince penned a **letter/report to his FACA comrades** back in Argentina, in which he remarked that the drawn-out crisis in the Generalidad government was far from settled.[53] By his reckoning, "this is a time of extraordinary gravity and anything could happen. There is even **talk of dictatorship**, of the Valencia government stepping in, and maybe of bloody clashes. Nothing can be ruled out."

He mentioned, merely to shoot them down, rumors blaming the freemasons for manipulating certain CNT councillors in order to trigger a government crisis, which had in any event benefited the PSUC.

He gave a painstaking account of how the crisis had developed, mentioning the tiniest details and underlining the lack of clear explanation coming from CNT personnel regarding the root causes behind its eruption. How the crisis had surfaced at two plenums that demanded all the important councils: War, Economy, Supplies, and Public Order. At the plenum, an extremist stance had been adopted. PSUC folk were screaming that the CNT was looking for too much and that it wanted to eliminate the *rabassaires* and the petite bourgeoisie, and they had successfully turned public opinion against CNT personnel. Following tough negotiations, they had come to an arrangement to share the portfolios equally between the CNT and the UGT, which had unexpectedly reported, while the Plenum was in session, that it was agreeing to a fait accompli. "This was on Thursday last, a week ago." But then the PSUC had insisted upon the signing of a commitment to accept and "faithfully comply with all Generalidad Decrees," which the CNT folk had refused to do. So the crisis was still unresolved. "On Saturday, Companys decided to appoint a cabinet on his own. He amalgamated some departments into one and nominated Isgleas to Defense and Doménech to Economy, Supplies, and Public Workers; the PSUC's Comorera has been nominated to Justice, Labor, and Social Assistance … but the whole procedure

---

52   Caballé, *Barcelona Roja*, 90.
53   FACA correspondence, Letter 32, 7 April 1937 [BAEL].

is unacceptable as the nominations have come, not from the organizations, but from the president."

At a plenum on that Sunday, bewilderment had ruled, but, thanks to Marianet's intervention, common sense had prevailed and they had decided to work out an accommodation. In Valencia, alarm bells were ringing due to the rumors carried in the newspaper *Nosotros* that "a CNT Defense Junta had been established in Catalonia." In the end, a commission had been appointed; it rejected the appointments made by Companys, but committed itself to ongoing negotiations.

"Wednesday the 7th saw a big CNT rally at which Cortés, Fábregas, and Doménech spoke, spelling out [divergent] points of view." It was publicly announced that the president's solution was not acceptable "and there was a reaffirmation of the revolutionary stance of the CNT, which was not prepared to give another inch beyond what it had already given." Doménech had gone furthest in his opposition to Companys when he had stated that "**One can govern alongside the CNT, or even without the CNT. But against the CNT? Never.**"

Prince remarked on how unstable the situation was, defining it as "the strangest sort of stop-gap solution" and very much at the mercy of extremists of every hue.

He concluded his letter by informing his Argentinean comrades that he had been appointed as "Propaganda Secretary of the Peninsular" [Committee], from which position he intended to defend "our Organization's fundamental stance, by way of consistency with the anarchist movement." It would be his task to champion the stance of the NC and combat the muddleheaded extremism that prevailed in Catalonia, which was "**inclined to 'extremism' and rupture.**" Newspapers such as *Ideas* he dismissed as extravagant, even though "it has stupendous things to say that are widely accepted."

Thursday, 8 April

At midday, Eusebio Rodríguez Salas, the commissioner-general of public order, issued a statement to the press that revealed the recent enormous tension of insisting "that no one controls the streets other than the security forces, or other organizations of the same ilk."[54]

He gave assurances that normality had been restored in Olesa de Montserrat "following breaches of the peace last Sunday."

Dionisio Eroles, PO Chief of Staff also issued a notice at noon the same day, in which he complained of repeated instances when nightwatchmen (*serenos*)

---

54   "Public Order," *Solidaridad Obrera*, 9 April 1937, 3.

had been disarmed and he threatened to pursue with the full rigor of the law any who might repeat the action.[55]

He explained that on Wednesday the 7th, at 5:00 p.m., he had received a telephone call informing him that a vanload of Assault Guards were en route to Olesa, having been dispatched there to stamp out any breaches of order that might be triggered following the announcement of a general strike, "called in response to the arrests that had been made on the previous day [the 6th] in connection with the death of a Republican National Guard."

Eroles briefed that he had dispatched agent Rafael Bardas to Olesa in the company of agents Balagué, Jofre, and Tudela "to work out a resolution of the dispute that had arisen."

Bardas spoke with the Assault Guard commander, who of course informed him that he was carrying out orders from above. Bardas assured Rodríguez Salas that if the latter would order the Assault Guards to pull out of Olesa, he had Bardas's word that normality would be restored in Olesa. Rodriguez Salas had insisted that Bardas supply him with a signed document recording that commitment. After that document was handed over to the officer commanding the Assault Guards, they withdrew and peace was restored to the town of Olesa.

Bardas got in touch with the CNT officials to get them to end the strike scheduled for the following day and it was called off by means of an announcement.

★

In *Ideas*, **Balius** published the article "In this grave hour. Let's make revolution," in which he delved into the reasons behind the protracted and insoluble crisis in the Generalidad government, which he ascribed to the strength of the revolutionary proletariat.

Balius held Companys up to ridicule, while also warning how dangerous he might be if he could muster enough forces of repression: "Over the course of the crisis, we have witnessed one move by the president who sits atop the body known as the Generalidad that has shocked us greatly. Lluís Companys has acted as if, in actual fact, we were back in the days prior to 19 July. The attitude of the big boss man of the 'Esquerra' has reminded us of the noxious paternalism of Macià and the presidential style of Pilsudski in Poland, De Valera in Ireland, and Masaryk in Czechoslovakia. At this moment, a presidentialist government is the starkest challenge to the times we are living in. It is intolerable that Power, which belongs solely to the working people, should come under attempted hijack by

---

55   Ibid.

an individual without the slightest support in the workplace. That is enough by itself to make us understand that, if only that same politician had a sizable contingent of armed forces at his disposal, he would again put the working class in the capitalist harness."

According to Balius, the only way of fending off the threat of counterrevolution was by boosting the revolution. "The blame for what is going on should not be laid at the door of the bourgeois politicians, because, in the final analysis, they champion [their own] position. Those to blame for the Revolution not having swept aside the working class's enemies are to be found in the workers' ranks [in] those whose lack of decisiveness in the earliest moments allowed counterrevolutionary forces to accumulate such strength that it will be a costly business to cut them down to size. Despite the difficulties littering our path, we have to surmount them by making revolution. The only way of countering the threat that is looming more clearly with each day that passes lies in the revolutionary effort that cannot be delayed a single minute more."

★

In *Soli*, a **short communiqué** was published, complaining of the rising cost of living and asserting: "We workers who live honestly on **our ten pesetas wages** are finding that our economic survival is becoming impossible."[56] It accused those charged with solving the subsistence problem of shying away from a solution, which consisted quite simply of coming down hard on "the legion of parasites, deadbeats, sharpsters, and speculators who, in broad daylight, sell all basic necessity items at highly inflated prices."

★

That night, in the Gran Price hall, there was a joint meeting held by the PSUC and the UGT "for the purpose of presenting to public opinion the Plan of Victory to secure our final triumph over fascism."[57]

Those who spoke included Rafael Vidiella, who chaired the meeting; Dolores Piera from the Women's Central Committee of the PSUC; Antonio Sesé, general secretary of the Catalan UGT; and Joan Comorera, PSUC general secretary.

The most highly anticipated speech was **Comorera**'s and it was greeted with a huge ovation as the band played "The Internationale."

---

56   "Soaring Subsistence Prices" in *Solidaridad Obrera*, 8 April 1937, 9.
57   "UGT and PSUC Rally to Present the Plan of Victory to the People," *Solidaridad Obrera*, 9 April 1937, 7.

The PSUC's councillor in the Generalidad opened by referring to the style of government over the previous eight and a half months as a "failure" and "a dead-end street." **"The Committees-and-uncontrollables system has failed; the system whereby the unions only abide by their own laws has failed and the tactic of paying for private armies mobilized on the streets of Barcelona has failed."**

He ran through the history of incidents that had arisen during the handling of the crisis in the Generalidad government, up to the current provisional government (formed on 3 April), the only common ground in which was "compliance with government accords." He described the crisis as out of the ordinary and detrimental to the struggle against fascism, declaring that the PSUC was not ready to go on collaborating with government that was not capable of imposing any authority.

He set out the **Plan of Victory.** He stated that the program of the UGT and PSUC was "clear and specific." **"First, win the war, and then make revolution."**

He then boiled the Plan down to two points: "Discipline plus responsibility, on the front and in the rearguard alike."

He closed with the statement that he was willing to govern alongside the CNT, "but not in the old manner, in advisory commissions that they later do not allow to govern." His conclusion was that the CNT was very powerful in Catalonia "and for that reason there will never be government in defiance of it, but, **if need be, they will govern in defiance of the gangs of uncontrollables,** since, in his view, there are men within the CNT who have and feel the working class's responsibilities at the present time."

As the meeting drew to an end, a military band played a range of anthems.

Comorera was drawing a clear distinction between two sectors within the CNT, distinguishing between collaborationists and revolutionaries, whom he chose to slander as uncontrollable. He knew that he had to be able to count on the connivance of the higher committees if he wanted to crush the revolutionary sectors.

Friday, 9 April

6:00 p.m. saw the convening of a **meeting at the Presidential Residence in the Generalidad,** attended by Pi Sunyer, Serra Húnter, Guinart, Galés, and Sauret, for the ERC; Mas, Doménech, Escorza, Joan P. Fábregas, Castellote, Alonso, Fernández, and Merino, for the CNT; Comorera, Sesé, Vidiella, Almendros, and Durán Rosell, for the UGT; Calvet and Josep Torrents, on behalf of the Rabassaires Union; and Tarradellas and Companys, on behalf of the Generalidad.[58]

---

58   Josep Tarradellas, "The April 1937 Crisis," 1139. Pi Sunyer was Mayor of Barcelona and Serra Húnter was Speaker of the Parliament of Catalonia.

Companys reiterated the old line about how they should squeeze him like a lemon. "just as I have been saying ever since 19 July." He called upon them all to come to an agreement, spelled out the seriousness of the situation on the Bilbao front, the push in Aragon, he "wouldn't dare ask that the CNT's representatives accept his decree" and take up their posts. Companys asked those assembled for their views. Nobody spoke. Companys again asked for everyone's opinion. Again there was silence.

Sauret asked that the document presented by the CNT be given a reading and discussed. **Serra Húnter** asked the CNT personnel why they had not taken up their posts, nor attended Generalidad Council meetings, even though they had been manning their departments. **The CNT representatives made no reply to his question.** Companys threatened to tender his resignation.

Valerio Mas (CNT) then spoke up to state that they had not taken possession of their posts because they had not been consulted and their ideology prohibited them from taking up a post without authorization from their organization. He declared that he was ready to work out a solution, "but while abiding by the CNT's accords at all times."

Companys set out the reasoning behind his decision and **Sesé** suggested that a working party be appointed, made up of two members from each organization, to thrash out a solution. **Escorza** asked for "a definitive government rather than one that was simply a caretaker," but agreed to Sesé's suggestion. After some toing and froing between the CNT and UGT personnel over who would chair the working party, it was agreed that it should be chaired by Companys. The working party would meet again in the same location on 11 and 13 April.

Saturday, 10 April

The CNT's Hilario Esteban, in a **detailed report to Dionisio Eroles on recent arms seizures**, announced that the ERC, PSUC, and Generalidad government were making ready for an imminent armed confrontation with the CNT.[59] The rapporteur's deduction was that

> the Esquerra de Catalunya and the UGT and the PSUC are as one in that Artemio Aguadé, Sesé, Rodríguez Salas, and who knows who else are getting together, and we are on the eve of events.
>
> I am certain that the provider of arms to the PSUC is the Esquerra Republicana whose arms are bought in France and imported with the stamp of the councillor for the interior.

---

59   "Informe 2a" [AHN Madrid, Causa General, 1791 (1)].

Rifles and cartridges have been delivered to the barracks in the Plaza de España and most of the members of said forces are a threat to the CNT, being loyal to the Esquerra Republicana and the PSUC. I cannot specify the quantities, but there will be no less than some 500 rifles and half a million rifle cartridges.

He detailed the preparations under way in some PSUC buildings: "[In] its central premises on the Paseo de Gracia, the PSUC has positioned a large timber board some seven centimeters thick, covering the lower part of the building and secured by metal rings to an inside wall, meaning that, when the time comes, it can be made to fall away from the façade, exposing sand-bagged openings and two machine guns."

The rapporteur recounted that "rifles have been collected from the [Unified] Socialist Party's members and the most trusted of these have been trained in the handling of small caliber submachine guns."

He concluded his report with the statement that "it is no secret that when UGT personnel express doubt as to what impact the preparation will have, they are told by their leaders that they have the Republic's government on their side, as well as CATALONIA'S LEGITIMATE AUTHORITIES."

*The concerted preparations by the PSUC, ERC, and Generalidad government for an imminent armed clash with the CNT was no secret from the CNT's higher committees. Besides, there were ongoing and unrelenting provocations. Such advance preparations by the PSUC, ERC, and Generalidad should not blind us to the fact that **the crucial gambit in the offensive by the reactionary PSUC-ERC-Generalidad axis against the CNT was being played out in terms of the constitution, reinforcement, and arming of the Unified Security Corps, which is to say, of the amalgamated Assault Guard and former Civil Guard corps.** The decision by the CNT unions to reorganize and rearm the dormant defense committees was due to the threat that a reconstruction of that repressive corps in the service of the bourgeoisie posed to the workers.*[60]

---

60   The May insurrection was the product of prior military planning and of provocation coming from the PSUC-ERC-Generalidad Government, as the existing documentary record shows and as most historians have explained. But it also formed part of the Stalinist strategy to create a strong state capable of winning the war against fascism. Disarming and weakening the CNT was, as far as the PSUC was concerned, a strategic necessity. The defensive resistance coming from the barrio committees in May 1937, when, for two days, they overwhelmed the CNT's higher committees, cannot be described as an anarchist insurrectionist initiative targeting the Generalidad. At all times, the preparations made for insurrection by CNT and POUM personnel were *defensive* in nature, designed to counter the offensive then coming from the counterrevolutionary PSUC-ERC-government coalition; the curtain-raiser for the latter would be the murder of Antonio Martín in Bellver. The attack

Sunday, 11 April

A **local plenum of anarchist groups** had been convened; it barely had time to meet, since it was interrupted to allow those there to attend the rally being held at the Monumental bullring. A working party was appointed to look into "the various proposals" and to consolidate these into one to be put to the upcoming plenum for its consideration. The working party agreed on four points. First, that there should be no movement from their stance regarding the current crisis, insisting that they get the bulk of the departments, "Public Order among them." Secondly, it was declared that there could be no reconciliation between anarchists and Comorera and Aguadé, "given the latter's dismissive and malicious performance." The third point agreed that the responsible committees should draw up "a revolutionary action plan in tune with current political events." Finally, it was agreed that, in the event that no solution could be found to the current crisis "the Organization will take the lead in events." That working party report, dated 12 April 1937, carried the signatures of **Modesto Ávila, Clemente, Pablo Ruiz**, and Pérez.[61]

At the **Monumental bull-ring**, rounding off the drive on behalf of the field hospitals, the CNT-FAI organized an important and very well attended demonstration, in which the speakers included Félix Martí Ibáñez, director-general of health, Joaquín Cortés on behalf of the RC, and Federica Montseny, the Republic's minister of health, *whose speech was booed and whistled at.*[62]

Also on that Sunday, representatives of different organizations met with Companys **at the Presidential Residence in the Generalidad** to carry on with talks aimed at thrashing out a solution to the government crisis. Herrera and Escorza represented the CNT, Pi Sunyer and Sauret represented the ERC, Sesé and Ferrer the UGT, and Calvert and Josep Torrents the Rabassaires Union.[63]

---

on the Telephone Exchange, which triggered the May Events, was a government initiative.

61   Attachment to "Second session of the Local Plenum of Barcelona Anarchist Groups … held in the meeting hall of the Casa CNT-FAI and attended by the confederal Defense groups and Libertarian Youth. Barcelona, 24 April 1937" [SA-PS Barcelona 1307-7]. Pablo Ruiz had been leader of the Gelsa militia members who quit the front lines, and he was a co-founder of the Friends of Durruti.

62   *La Vanguardia*, 13 April 1937.

63   "11 April. 1st meeting (Barcelona, 11 April 1937)" [AMTM].

There was talk of setting up Advisory Commissions for each councillor in his respective department; that proposal came from the CNT. **Sauret** took a dim view of that: "that would be like having another government inside each department." Herrera pointed out that, as the name suggested, "these Commissions would have a merely advisory role" and by way of comparison he cited bodies that were already in existence, such as the Security Junta at the Internal Security Department, the War Commission at the Defense Department, the Council of Economy at the Economy Department, or the Transport Council at the Public Services Department. **Calvet** confirmed that a sort of a Council had already been planned for the Agriculture Department. **Sesé**, **Sauret**, and **Ferrer** stated that such Commissions "are neither necessary nor appropriate." **Companys** wisely distinguished between one or more expert advisors freely selected by a councillor and, on the other hand, the imposition upon each councillor of an advisory commission "whose function would turn into one of social or political supervision." **Herrera** and **Escorza** defended advisory commissions on the grounds that they would offer "a guarantee to the organizations and might very well thereby avert many conflicts such as the ones we have seen in Supplies." The witty and provocative **Sesé** retorted that "Councillor Doménech may well not have been alone in the running of Supplies; maybe the entire Committee had a hand in it." The discussions carried on until it was decided to drop the matter, without any agreement's having been arrived at.

Ferrer (UGT) raised a different matter, the issue of the War Industries Commission, which the UGT thought should be constituted as a brand-new department, given its scale and importance. He moved that all the war industries be nationalized. **Herrera** argued that such nationalization was not appropriate for implementation in Catalonia alone and would in any case interfere with the coordination efforts already in existence at national level between the CNT and the UGT. **Ferrer** replied that that was the very reason why they need nationalize by arrangement with the Valencia government. **Sesé** sought the CNT councilors' views on nationalization of the war industries. **Herrera** answered that he was neither rejecting nor prejudging nationalization "as we shall see how it plays out." **Ferrer** wanted it placed on the record at any rate that the UGT aspired to nationalization of the war industries. Those assembled agreed to accept the concentration of armaments in the hands of the government, apropos of which "there are some decrees already." Militarization of transport was deferred pending agreement of the various organizations.

Next up for discussion was the issue of Supplies. **Companys** stated that "the fact that the government he formed [on 4 April] had allotted the Supplies Department and Agriculture Department to the Rabassaires Union representative should not be cited as a precedent." **Herrera** argued that Agriculture covered only a part of the requirements of Supplies, which was why he thought it more appropriate that a Department of Trade be set up, taking over the functions of Supplies and some of those of Economy, the object being to get to proper grips with "the collapse caused by the war." To Calvet's objections regarding the limits of that new Department of Trade, Herrera said that it was vital that they move toward a monopoly of foreign trade and strict monitoring of domestic trade; "otherwise it would be a disaster." Foreign trade had to be conducted by arrangement with the central government and town councils prevented from conducting it for themselves. **Pi Sunyer** stated that he had not yet made up his mind whether Supplies should be allowed to stand as a department or amalgamate with some other one, nor about the creation of a brand-new War Industries Department, but his experience as director of Trade had taught him that trade did need centralizing in some single agency acting in concert with the Valencia government. As to the town councils, he agreed that they should defer to the overall plan, but would have to be given a free hand in distribution, but never in buying and selling abroad. **Josep Torrents** expressed the view that exports should be handled by the agricultural unions. **Sesé** held that Supplies and Agriculture ought to remain wedded to each other, but never Supplies and Trade. **Herrera** belabored the need for a single agency to handle foreign trade. **Josep Torrents** raised the matter of disputes between peasants and the Supplies Department. **Herrera**'s answer to him was that it was not a matter of "riding roughshod over the contractual rights of the agricultural unions," but of monitoring trade through a single body.

The debate and haggling over the division of departments among the various organizations dragged on. **Companys** brought the proceedings to a conclusion, arranging for a further meeting to take place on the same day at 23:00 hours.

The **second meeting** assembled in the **Presidential Residence in the Generalidad** at 23:00 hours, with the same representatives as before; they continued to debate the (for them, impassioned) matter of how the councillorships or departments (as they interchangeably described the booty in contention) were to be divided up.[64]

The UGT representatives argued that the War Industries deserved a department of their own. **Pi Sunyer** argued that the issue was not so much the squabble over the different departments as the fact that "Public Order decrees were not being obeyed due to lack of authority"; there was some brouhaha about whether the UGT had more portfolios but the CNT's portfolios had more clout.

---

64   "11 April, 2nd meeting (Barcelona, 11 April 1937)" [AMTM].

Escorza stated that they should be seeking parity. **Ferrer** said that the problem lay in Defense and War Industries. For the sake of resolving the government crisis, **Pi Sunyer** stated that he was ready to hand over the Culture Department to the UGT, if that would help sort matters out. **Sesé** made some sardonic remark about Pi's acting as a mediator. **Companys** said that the government should be made up of them all. After a side argument between Herrera, Sauret, and Sesé regarding the portfolios that would suit each of them, no agreement was arrived at.

The debate then spilled over into an analysis of the causes behind the crisis. **Herrera** said that it was down to the spite directed at Isgleas within the Generalidad Council; **Sesé** said that the discontent within the various organizations had also had something to do with it and that the CNT had immediately tried to exploit the government crisis for its own purposes. **Companys** said that the causes of the crisis were more complex "but mainly he singled out the issue of the council's lack of authority" and he closed his remarks by asking those assembled there if they had any suggestions to make. **Escorza** answered that he was sticking to the ones made already. **Companys** agreed that they would reconvene the following Tuesday, the 13th, at 11:00 a.m., urging that the newspapers of the various organizations take care not to exacerbate the crisis and that they draw up "program agendas or commitments on which there is agreement."

Monday, 12 April

At the **Casa CNT-FAI**, the second sitting of the **local plenum of Barcelona anarchist groups** got under way, with the Defense Groups and Libertarian Youth groups in attendance.[65]

The panel for the discussion was made up of **Sánchez from the Los Mismos group** (chair), **Liberto Alfonso from the Acracia Confederal Defense Groups** (recording secretary) and **Vicente Micó** (as master of ceremonies).

Juan Santana Calero from the Devenir anarchist group spoke about the insubstantiality of the report drawn up at the previous session, because "it jettisons the principle underpinning organizations kindred to the anarchist movement."[66] Santana Calero reckoned that "the counterrevolution has gained significant ground, despite our having collaborated in government and, therefore, collaboration had proved counterproductive and ineffective." According to

---

65   "Second session of the Barcelona Local Plenum of Anarchist Groups..." [SA-PSA Barcelona 1307-7]

66   Juan Santana Calero had been active in the Libertarian Youth in Málaga. After May 1937, he joined the Friends of Durruti. Regarding the report he refers to, see above. The Resolution had been drafted on 11 April, although it was passed and dated the 12th.

whoever drafted the minutes of this second session, Santana Calero "asked the working party to explain to him what it means by collaboration and by anarchist principles." Santana Calero drew a comparison between the working party's stance on governmentalism and that of the POUM. Santana Calero sought to take to absurd lengths the gulf that existed between action and principles by making an exaggerated but telling comparison, stating that "the dilemma exists; either all the anarchist literature that has long informed our actions and conduct is put to the torch, or we all go off and 'carve out ourselves a niche' in governments."

Santana Calero succinctly spelled out where he stood: "No ministerial or departmental collaboration: accept collaboration only with regard to military oversight of the antifascist struggle that we are waging, and regarding Public Order, but let it be responsibly done, without our placing ourselves in laughable bourgeois-like positions, or engaging in mere politicking like the other petite bourgeois parties. He states that ministerial collaboration has been an abject failure."

Santana Calero's contribution ended by referencing the issues of the press and the prisoners, deeming "shameful" **the method of repression deployed against the confederal press critical** of the Organization's collaborationist policy, and "damning the action" of the higher committees in abandoning the prisoners.

Group 12, a defense group from the Gracia barrio in Barcelona, deplored the fact that the motions hardly ever reflected the mandate a delegate received, but his personal opinion instead. The Group 12 delegate claimed that "most of the delegates have spoken out against politics and in favor of the Revolution. We are anarchists and have enough strength to break out of the vicious circle that surrounds us." He rejected the working party motion because it resolved nothing. He talked of the events that had occurred in Cullera (Valencia) "upwards of a thousand Assault Guards, magnificently equipped with all manner of weaponry, mustered and stormed the Amalgamated Trades Union of the village. They looted and clubbed and did as they pleased with our comrades. This is fascism and our comrades in the councillorships and in the Valencia government acquiesce to it."

He repudiated the mechanical discipline of soldiery and called for "wholesale socialization of industry, trade, and agriculture," because "unless we do that, the war is not going to be won—we will lose it." He said that no revolutionary task could be carried out without some sort "of run-in with capitalism," whatever the guise in which it presents itself. He concluded that it "is better to take them all on and stay anarchists," because they would also "stand a better chance of success."

The **Galeotes por la Libertad** anarchist group indicated that it agreed with Santana Calero, and called upon all speakers to keep things short. **The Chair** asked to hear only from "those opposing the Motion and those who framed it." **Pérez**, a member of the working party, denied that "they could discern his private opinion in the motion." **Clemente, from the Armonía anarchist group**, reaffirmed its anti-political stance and moved "that a Revolutionary Committee be formed." He also stated: "Those who joined the government should have abolished the repressive Civil Guard and Assault Guard and have not done so, and they have failed by not having dared to."

The Libertarian Youth's Local Federation proposed that "lest we fail as an idea" ... "we set ourselves up as a revolutionary Convention" and then proceeded in a very mixed-up way to state that "what is needed is collaboration, but that we abide by our anarchist conduct at all times"

The **Eliseo Reclús anarchist group** sought to introduce some common sense to a session that seemed dominated by an extremism as witless as it was vague: "extreme positions were fine when we were wrapped up in the people. Now there is no one surrounding us and taking these sorts of decisions is dangerous." He closed by saying that the only thing to be asked of the higher committees was "greater accountability in everything."

The **Constancia anarchist group** reiterated its view, which it did not think had been reflected in the previous day's minutes, where "a request had been made that our representatives in the government pull out and that a *Central Committee* be appointed from among the ward committees."[67]

The importance of this proposal, coming from the Constancia anarchist group, is extraordinary because it tacked on to the withdrawal of anarcho-syndicalists from the Generalidad government the establishment of a Central Committee based on the ward committees. This CC of the barrio committees represented a brand new revolutionary authority, opposed to and an alternative to the Generalidad. The revolutionary events of May 1937 erupted twenty days later.

Caudet from the Constancia group talked about what had happened at the rally at the Monumental bullring on Sunday, 11 April 1937 (at which Federica Montseny had faced catcalls). At that rally, there had been **mass chanting of the slogan "Away with politics, away with the government"** and this, according to Caudet, "was the voice of the people reacting to the changes that have come over our organizations. It was an expression of opposition to the performance of those holding Public Order posts, because they are resorting to coercion and arrests, not only against rebels and questionable elements, but comrades as well."

Caudet also referred to the "agreement that payment would be cut off from those on sentry duty at the defense committees, due to shortage of funds"—which he described as "a ploy"—and to "incidents triggered by the efforts of some CNT collectives to raise the prices of basic necessities," efforts he saw as unpopular.

---

67   The emphasis appears in the original.

Abril from the Acracia Confederal Defense Groups stated that what was required was a change of direction, because federalism and anarchism "have vanished from our methods," adding that "the people primarily responsible for this are our ministers, who have undergone a complete transfiguration." He stated that the government was still "a tyranny against the people." And explained that in anarchist circles there was still a "bourgeois morality and practice" and, at the same time, **beggars were still "pleading for public charity."** He noted that "there are self-styled posts of responsibility with not an atom of morality to them." He brought up the incidents in Vinalesa, where "over 150 comrades, the only true anarchists, were ordered shot … [and] but for one captain with a modicum of humanity stepping in, that barbaric injustice would have been carried out."[68] He closed with a radical and pessimistic thought: "If this is organization and these are ideas, we demonstrate that they are worthless."

The Local **Libertarian Youth** Federation announced that it had to go, but before doing so it reported that outside its premises "the other night, comrades were being searched and stripped of their weapons by Civil and Assault Guards." It announced that they would put out a manifesto and would patrol the streets, inviting assistance from the various anarchist groups "in order to forestall such incidents."

Miguel, from the Convicción y Firmeza group, argued that there was no mistaking "the forward march of the bourgeoisie" and stated "that we have to act intelligently and in accordance with our principles."

Grünfeld, from the C group, spoke up against "our pulling out of politics" and argued that "if we take to the streets, we might well lose rather than increase the ground already won for anarchism." In his view, they had to get back into the trade unions in order to imbue these with an effective economic slant "to demonstrate the effectiveness of Libertarian Communism." He closed by rejecting violent and emotional solutions.

Alcalá, from the Bulgarian group, read out a motion regarding the CNT councillors serving in the Generalidad government: "Our councillors need to know that their mission in the Generalidad is to favor every working-class initiative that is geared toward social accomplishments, to stop the politicians from hampering the onward march of the social revolution, and to keep the CNT-FAI abreast of everything being done in the Generalidad, whether for or against the

---

68   The 8th of March 1937 saw violent, armed clashes erupt in Vinalesa (Valencia) between anarchists opposed to militarization and the Assault Guards who wanted to force them to return to the front; there were several deaths and wounded on both sides. Upwards of two hundred anarcho-syndicalists were detained, ninety-two of them militia members from the Iron Column. Eventually, on 21 March, the Iron Column agreed to be militarized and became the 843rd Brigade.

revolution and the war."

As far as Alcalá could see, the anarchists and anarcho-syndicalists' mission was the same as ever: briefing the people with the complete truth, protesting and exposing injustices, preventing the opening of a gulf between the people and the CNT-FAI, luring the workers away from the UGT and the bourgeoisie, and absolute unity between the CNT and the FAI, "steering clear of actions such as **the catcalling that targeted Federica Montseny at the Monumental,** catcalls only being advantageous against the reaction."

After a number of considerations, Alcalá suggested, as a resolution to the problem raised by Toryho as editor of *Solidaridad Obrera,* "the creation of a combative anarchist newspaper, should *Soli* refuse to publish notes sent in to it regarding matters going on behind the scenes.

Alcalá had struck a conciliatory note, as far from the swelling chorus of libertarian criticism as from the worst aberrations of the higher committees' bureaucracy. His essential purpose was to avert the growing chances of a split (which were plainly apparent at the 11 April rally at the Monumental) and, at all costs, to preserve the unity between the CNT and the FAI.

The **Humanidad anarchist group** contended that "19 July ushered in a counterrevolution and not a revolution. And that's where we still stand." It talked about the way the CNT's stance had evolved since July, and how anarchists had flooded back into the union in order to prevent the loss of their influence, getting the Local Federation of anarchist groups in Catalonia "to tinker with a few of the accords passed at the last CNT congress." And it deplored the excessive proliferation of plenums and accords with virtually no practical impact. It argued "the need for collaboration," insisting upon the highest standards of responsibility for post-holders.

Jiménez, from the A anarchist group,[69] came out against those who were critical of "ministerial collaboration." The Libertarian Youth's motion regarding setting up a Convention he described as "tyrannical and arbitrary." He stated that it wasn't "an option to break down the antifascist Front." He suggested that they "settle on a program" that would incorporate "most" of the libertarian "aspirations" and that could then be "put" to the Generalidad government "for its scrutiny." And he summed up by arguing "the need to carry on with collaboration, but on specific points, without our meddling in the inner workings of the other political representatives."

---

69   The A and C groups were offshoots of the Nervio group, led by Abad de Santillán and Pedro Herrera. Most of the Argentinean anarchists who showed up in Barcelona were active in these three groups. They were the hard core of the collaborationist camp and virtually all of them held important posts in the Generalidad government or within the Organization.

Die-hard defense of ministerial collaborationism and antifascist unity was firmly embedded inside the anarcho-syndicalist movement. The ideological rift within the CNT-FAI was plain and obvious to all. The issue was whether that rift would turn into an organizational split. Up to that point, the various anti-collaborationist strands had not gone beyond criticisms of the higher committees; they were unable to devise any alternative to the committees' possibilism and resignation in the face of the ongoing retreat from "July's revolutionary gains" and the constant trespass against principles. The higher committees supportive of collaborationism were running into growing internal and trade-union opposition, meaning that they barely controlled their own rank-and-file. Therein lay the root cause of the "social indiscipline" that annoyed Companys and the Generalidad government, and therein lay the source of the unrelenting attacks on the nebulous and mythical "uncontrollables." There was the hint of a solution even then in the approaching battle for control of Public Order.

The Devenir anarchist group deplored the fact that its proposal that "positions of leadership responsibility in respect to War and Public Order be abandoned" had not been debated; and the fact that "hints of Marxism" had cropped up in the odd contribution. It cited Malatesta as the authority validating its suggestions.

The **Zarathustra anarchist group** made common cause with the Devenir group.

Anarchist Group 27 stated that "the only people impugning the working party" were the Devenir and Constancia groups and it called for the motion to be more specific or to be re-drafted so that it might be discussed once more.[70]

On behalf of the Los Indomables anarchist group, Ordaz provocatively declared "that fear has crept into the CNT-FAI."[71] He insisted that CNT personnel "should be opposing everything by force of arms, but there is cowardice afoot." He identified with those impugning the motion. And said no to collaboration. "We have to take up arms for the revolution's sake. If we have all this time to bandy words around here, it is because we lack the gumption and courage to

---

70   At anarchist plenums, accords were traditionally adopted unanimously or on the basis of consensus.

71   Antonio Ordaz (1901–1950). CNT member and FAI propagandist. Deported to Bata (in Guinea) in 1931. Member of the CNT's Prisoners' Aid Committee. During the civil war, he was very active in repressive efforts in the rearguard. Some people described him as Aurelio Fernández's right-hand man. On 29 June 1937, he was placed in the Modelo prison in Barcelona and was tried along with Aurelio Fernández in relation to the scandal of the Marist brothers. While in prison, he figured in lots of incidents, serving on the antifascist prisoners' committee. In December 1937, he was moved to Manresa prison from where he managed to escape on 3 January 1938, along with seventeen other anarchists (prominent among them Justo Bueno Pérez) thanks to an effective escape network inside and outside the prison walls.

take to the streets."

The Chair stepped in here to clarify the meaning of a vote for or against the motion: "If the working party's motion is carried, collaboration will be embraced. If not, we must pull our representatives out of the government." So he asked that "a set, clear-cut determination be made."

Ordaz expanded upon and made the chair's clarification more specific: "In the face of transgressions to which our representatives have acquiesced, in the face of the ineptitude of all the politicians favoring national and international fascism, we have to come to some hard and fast and emphatic accord." And he moved that "at another gathering where there is a full house, a commission should be appointed so that, if there is any provocation, the commission can immediately take charge of the social response in Catalonia."

Group 12, from Gracia, offered a written proposal:

After full discussion, the Plenum, having given due consideration to the outcome of nine months of ministerial policy, and cognizant of the impossibility of the armed struggle against fascism on the front lines being won without the subordination of all private, economic, political, and social interests to the supreme objective of the war, and believing that only through comprehensive socialization of industry, trade, and agriculture can the crushing of fascism become feasible, and considering that any form of government is by its very essence reactionary and inimical to all social revolution, in addition, is agreed:

1.   That all the persons currently holding posts within antifascist government bodies should be withdrawn.

2.   That we aim for the construction of an antifascist Revolutionary Committee to coordinate the armed struggle against fascism.

3.   That industry, trade, and agriculture be taken under social ownership immediately.

4.   That we proceed with the introduction of the producer's card. Implement a general mobilization of all men capable of bearing arms and work tools, for deployment on the front lines and in the rearguard.

5.   And, lastly, that each and every one of us be made to feel the unyielding weight of revolutionary discipline, as a guarantee that the interests of the social revolution cannot, with impunity, be toyed with.

This text, in which there is a discernible echo of legal language, peppered with acknowledgments and considerations, carried all the weight of a manifesto, even though it was not one, and in any case was a brave and happy resolution from anarchist revolutionaries and, most of all, a revolutionary program and concrete plan of action designed to counter the antifascist collaborationism then prevailing within the libertarian ranks. Integral to this program was a call for comprehensive socialization of the economy, as opposed to the industrial and peasant collectivization that had proved to be a government tool for centralized, state control of the enterprises, collectives, and sectors expropriated back in July–September 1936.

The **Plenum** accepted the Group 12 motion unanimously. The view was that Ordaz's motion should be incorporated into the already approved Group 12 motion.

The chair concluded that, now that that motion had been passed, "**our representatives should pull out of the government of Catalonia.**" He then went on to ask the Plenum "whether that motion can be taken to apply also to the remainder of the nation" since "we have our representatives within the central government too."

That sparked a debate and "a minor incident" regarding which the writer of the minutes offers no detail. **Ordaz** from the Los Indomables group, stated "that whenever accords are being reached, there is always somebody trying to apply the brakes to them." He made it clear "that we are only here in Barcelona," which was to say, that the accord was valid only locally, but he went on to say that it might provide the spark that ignites a torch across Iberia," articulating the possibility, and his own wish, to see that accord applied to the entirety of republican Spain.

Estrada raised an organizational point, noting that it was not the FAI groups that had representatives within the government but the CNT's trade unions. **Pablo Ruiz** moved that "a Revolutionary Central Committee [be formed from] among all the defense committees."[72] **The Local Federation of Anarchist Groups**, which could see how the meeting was slipping out of its control, counterattacked, saying that it would not be held responsible if not issued with the "directives for how the accords were to be construed." The **Chair** tried to introduce a note of brotherliness by saying that what mattered now was forestalling any confrontation between the CNT and the FAI "so let that be an end of accords." **Caudet** suggested that a commission be appointed to that end.

Ordaz put his finger on what was worrying the Local Federation's representative and reproached him for it, saying that, after convening the plenum, "inviting

---

72   Pablo Ruiz, a militia member from the Durruti Column's Fourth (Gelsa) *Agrupación*, had been one of the founders of the Friends of Durruti Group in early March 1937.

the confederal defense committees and the Libertarian Youth to attend," now "that a vigorous accord had been reached on an item that this very same Local [Federation] had placed on the agenda, it was trying to wriggle out of its responsibility." Ordaz proudly underlined "that it is the anarchists who are passing this accord." Very tactlessly and even more politically incorrectly, he went on to add that "the CNT is a force that owes a debt to the direction that the anarchists have given it and not to what is most convenient for it." He ruled out appointment of the commission that Caudet had suggested. And in a contradictory flourish, like a bullfighter, he swiveled away from the accord that had been reached and that he himself had championed, and stipulated "that our comrades should not pull out of government. There is no need for that. What should be done is that they should have assistants seconded to them so that one day they can make themselves masters of the situation."

Ordaz was now misrepresenting the accord passed by the Plenum, ordering the abandonment of all government posts, and was embracing the option advocated by Escorza and Herrera, in favor of the establishment of expert panels in every department, so that CNT personnel could monitor them all.

Pérez, from the Armonía anarchist group, complained of the existence of a "pronounced interest in hobbling the confederal organization's steady progress" and warned that "no one should let himself be carried away by the guile or malice of certain comrades who have an abnormal understanding of the situation." He made it clear that "it is not that I want to characterize them as fascists, but they are dim-wits and have evil intentions." But this clarification struck everyone as being like an accusation, especially when he went on talking along these lines: "This is what we find at this Plenum." He closed his remarks urging "that before agreeing to any proposition, we should look into the political and social personality and background of whoever is making it, to keep ulterior motives from capturing the attention of Plenum members (*plenistas*)."

Given the gravity of these charges, the **platform party** asked Pérez to "point to the comrades to whom he is referring." **Pérez** once again made it clear "that he had not labeled anyone a trouble-maker," and also added that he would abide by the accords and "step down from his post."

Codina moved that "the accords reached be put into practice immediately, and that the comrades and the Committees take the appropriate positions in this instance." A comrade from **Gracia's Group 12** declared that, when 19 July 1936 happened and time for revolution rolled around, the CNT-FAI's anarchist leaders "took fright and lobbied again and again for collaboration. If, on that memorable day they had remembered that we are anti-statist, we would not now find ourselves in these circumstances."

The **Hispano-Suiza plant's anarchist group** proposed a written motion reporting on the arrest of three comrades from the Ortiz Column plus one female comrade, urging the anarchist groups present to lobby the Public Order Commission, once the Plenum was over, for their release. It also put the defense committees on notice that, from that night onwards, they should mount armed patrols "to prevent the Civil Guard and Assault Guard from disarming people."

Questioned as to the reason for the arrests of those comrades, the **Sants Defense Committee** stated that there had been "a fracas between the comrades and a number of personnel from the Assault Guard."[73] It was agreed that a commission made up of Ordaz, Santana Calero, and Griells be dispatched to seek a briefing at police headquarters. **The Plenum unanimously agreed that the defense committees be placed on armed alert,** as proposed by Hispano Suiza.

The **Local Federation**'s representative defended its actions in convening the Plenum, the intention having been "to marshal anarchism's might" and he regretted the fact that the first session had coincided with the rally at the Monumental. He stated again that the Federation "is still waiting to find out what it should do in light of the accords reached."

Papiol explained voting against the accord that had passed, arguing that similar resolutions had previously been passed in the Regional Committee and at other Plenums, but had never been put into effect. He contended that "there are comrades who are convinced that none of the accords reached here will ever be put into practice." He ascribed the passing of the resolution "to an extraordinary emotional state" and chided some whose outlook had altered since the previous session on 11 April. He stated that it would have been more practical and "maybe more revolutionary in the economic sense" to implement other aims, which "would take us much further than these present accords which will result in our being labeled crackpots." He predicted "that we will thereby be squandering a lot of energy in internecine, rearguard struggles," which would lead to libertarians being isolated. *This was actually a compendium of arguments in favor of anarchists deferring to the dictates of antifascist unity.*

The **Acracia group** stated that the accords should have been passed earlier and in different circumstances. After a range of digressions, it concluded that "our movement should hold fast to the sincerity of our anarchist principles."

Sosa from the Prácticos group was of the view that it was deplorable that the anarchist groups "should have convened this Plenum." He stated that "if some in their posts are not up to the task," they had merely to be replaced "but we should never pull our representatives out once and for all." He pointed out that the letter received from Maroto "is at odds with the report submitted by the

---

73   "Griells" may be a mistake on the part of the drafter of the minutes, who may have written that instead of Grünfeld.

CNT National Committee regarding his detention" and he demanded that that NC step down because of its "inaccurate and false report." In his view, by jailing Maroto, they were jailing "the entire CNT," since "he spoke for the real feelings of the Confederation." Sosa noted there was a growing "parting of the ways" between the CNT and the FAI, which he chalked up "to the performance of those holding the top posts," insisting that what they ought to be discussing was "a purge of post-holders" rather than a permanent once-and-for-all abolition of those posts.

Toryho, the managing editor of *Solidaridad Obrera*, denied that the Plenum represented "the local organization of anarchist groups." He denied that any of the accords arrived at had any "organizational validity." He declared that "the Barcelona FAI has not arrived at this accord, since the majority of those assembled there do not belong to the anarchist groups, but rather to the Confederal Defense Cadres, and the latter make up no accountable body, and any accords at which they might arrive are worthless."[74]

The **Barcelona Local Federation of Anarchist Groups** "stated clearly that they [the Local Federation] convened this Plenum with the agreement of the Local Committee of Defense Groups [Committees] and of the Libertarian Youth."[75]

Toryho belabored his point that "the anarchist groups are not represented at this Plenum" and that the confederal defense committees "are not entitled to set themselves up as a separate organization." He reiterated that this "is no gathering of anarchist groups" and thus "refuses to acknowledge the accords reached since they are worthless."[76]

The **Chair**, in order to refute Toryho, merely read out "the circular issued to all Groups," making it plain "that the Plenum was self-evidently convened by the Local Federation of Anarchist Groups."

The **Regional Committee of Anarchist Groups** repudiated episodes such as those evinced in the previous remarks, because they were unworthy of anarchists. It stated "that they cannot accept these accords" and expressed its intention of rescinding them in the forthcoming invitation to be sent out for a region-wide plenum.

---

74 Toryho's objection was based on the utter accountability of the defense committees to the CNT's Regional Committee, emphatically asserted ever since they had been launched—the object being to prevent any autonomous military decisions being made that were not under the organizational oversight of the trade unions. However, it was still a desperately bureaucratic quibble in face of the decision to which the meeting had come.

75 The Barcelona Local Federation of Anarchist Groups was saying in response to Toryho that it had convened the Plenum jointly with the Barcelona Defense Committee and that, as a result, the Plenum enjoyed full organizational validity.

76 The blunt opposition coming from Toryho contrasted with the radicalization of the meeting by the defense committees, that is, by revolutionary ward committees.

That announcement created mayhem. Once it was over, Ordaz gave a briefing on the outcome achieved by the commission that had been dispatched to Police Headquarters in relation to the arrests of a number of comrades. The three Ortiz Column comrades were to be brought to the Palace of Justice the next day and "may well be released immediately." The case of the female comrade was a lot more delicate and he withheld comment "due to the gravity of the matter."

The Dinamo anarchist group proposed "that a working group be appointed to delve into the details and make a definitive study of the contents of the motion that had been passed, together with the atmosphere at the Plenum," so that the accords reached by the gathering could be immediately implemented "after notice has been served to the respective Committees so that these may pass them on to their Groups." This suggestion was unanimously approved. Next up was the appointment of the five-man working party: Iglesias, Caudet from the Constancia group, the Cultura y Acción group, the Móvil group, and Mariano Ros from the Luz y Cultura group.[77]

The proceedings were wound up at 2:30 p.m. The minutes were signed by **Liberto Alfonso** from the Acracia Confederal Defense Groups in Barcelona and dated 12 *germinal* 1937. "Once the proceedings had been wound up, the **German anarcho-syndicalist DAS group** put forth the following motion: that a Peninsular Plenum of the Iberian Anarchist Federation be held with an eye to arriving at hard and fast proposals and the coordination of efforts. It proposed that the date be the First of May and the location, Valencia. The German DAS group's motion was passed and approval given "to the issuance of pertinent correspondence to ensure that this proposal goes ahead."[78]

This was a meeting that had escaped the control of the FAI bureaucracy. Several detractors of the accords that had been reached understood this when they referred to the "odd atmosphere" of the gathering or to "an abnormal appreciation of the situation." The Local Plenum of Anarchist Groups was nothing short of the authentic Barcelona FAI. And we say authentic, because it was the only place where the affinity groups were able to mingle and speak freely with one another without the dead hand of bureaucracy that was ensconced in organizational and/or government

---

77 The definitive draft of the Resolution was dated 24 April 1937.

78 The suggestion from the German anarcho-syndicalist DAS group that a peninsular plenum be convened at such short notice had two obvious purposes. First, to **preempt the accords arrived at from being revoked** at a regional plenum, which the bureaucrats would painstakingly arrange in such a way as to leave the revolutionaries high and dry. And, secondly, to make the **accords reached** in Barcelona regarding repudiation of collaborationism, withdrawal of all CNT personnel from the government, and the establishment of a Revolutionary Committee **applicable throughout the length and breadth of the Spanish state.**

posts, and somewhere where they also had, in theory at any rate, the power to determine the strategy of the anarchists from the Barcelona FAI.

The Barcelona defense committees—meaning the delegates from the ward-based revolutionary committees and the Libertarian Youth—had participated in this Plenum, and this naturally, radicalized the motions passed. This anarchist get-together took place in a revolutionary atmosphere in accordance with the desperate situation that existed on the streets—due to food shortages or speculative pricing of food that placed placing it beyond reach—and in line with the widespread protests against bureaucrats; on 11 April this had led to Federica Montseny's being booed in the Monumental bullring and to the raising of placards insisting that Maroto be set free, plus the chanting of slogans in favor of a withdrawal from government and calling for the release of anarchist prisoners.

And this Barcelona FAI, together with the defense sections of the revolutionary barrio committees and the Libertarian youth—heedless of the scandal and hysterical opposition coming from a few bureaucrats—had decided to end collaborationism. **To pull the anarchist councillors (ministers) out of the Generalidad government and to set up a Revolutionary Committee** *to direct the war against fascism.* **This was a crucial step in the direction of revolutionary insurrection, which erupted on 3 May.**

Moreover, this Plenum highlighted an ideological rift, not so much between the CNT and the FAI as between the revolutionaries (the defense committees, Julián Merino from the Local Federation of Anarchist Groups, Pablo Ruiz from the Friends of Durruti, and Santana Calero from the Libertarian Youth) and the collaborationists, which revealed an organizational split within the libertarian movement in Barcelona, seen in the growing opposition and unbridgeable gulf between the goals of the barrio committees and Libertarian Youth on the one hand and the higher committees on the other.

And within those higher committees a **tactical difference** *was established between the* **antifascist bureaucrats** *such as Toryho (and García Oliver and Montseny) who steadfastly backed loyal collaborationism with all antifascist organizations and with government, and the* **autonomous bureaucrats** *like Escorza, who pursued their own policy independently of the CNT, in the aim of accruing more power, sovereignty, and autonomy—and more clout—getting the Organization to show less deference to other antifascist organizations and to the Generalidad government.*

★

On the same premises, which is to say elsewhere in the Casa CNT-FAI and at roughly the same time the Local Federation of Anarchist Groups was meeting, at about 10:35 p.m. on 12 April and until 3:15 a.m. on the 13th, the **libertarian higher committees** were also meeting.[79]

We are talking here about simultaneous meetings of the CNT committees and of the anarchist groups. While in one room the anarchist groups, radicalized by the presence of the barrio committees and Libertarian Youth, were giving the seal of approval to the establishment of a Revolutionary Committee and insisting that the CNT councillors pull out of the government, in a different room, the CNT's higher committees were looking into and discussing which portfolios they should be asking Companys for.

Among the most outstanding matters was the report from secretary Valerio Mas on the current negotiations with Companys seeking to resolve the crisis, in which some of the CNT's suggestions had been agreed to, although there had been no agreement as to the distribution of ministerial positions. The other star issue at the meeting was the squabble between Herrera (the councillor for health) and the Healthworkers Union over insubordination on the part of ten nurses. After touching upon other lesser matters, the proceedings were concluded.

"Mingo" had had a number of articles published in *La Noche*; standing out because of their vehemence, they raised the alarm about the onward march of counterrevolution, eulogizing anarchism's revolutionary spirit (which he thought was incompatible with a governmental collaborationism that needed to stop) and attacking the UGT, the PSUC, Comorera, and Companys for their relentless defamatory remarks about the CNT. In addition he stressed the overriding need (as spelled out by Balius) to put an end to the Generalidad and to acknowledge the growing malaise among the people.[80] But the most interesting of all the articles was the one dealing with the municipalities, because his ideas

---

79 "Minutes of the Regional Committee meeting held on 12 April 1937, under the chairmanship of the comrade secretary and in the presence of the bookkeeper and delegates from the Printing Trades, the FAI regional [Committee], Agriculture, Fisheries and Food-workers, Distribution and Administration, Light and Power, Transport and Communications, health and Social Assistance, Manufacturing and Clothing, and Education and Liberal Professions [Unions]" [IISH-CNT-85C1].

80 Ponciano Alonso "Mingo," a tram-worker and author of several workerist novels, served as a councillor in the Barcelona Corporation and was a member of the Friends of Durruti. The articles signed by him and carried in *La Noche* were: "Our Task. The Revolution Has to Keep Moving Ahead" (2 April 1937), "We Have to Speak Clearly to the People" (8 April 1937), "The Revolution Demands Cleansing Efforts" (9 April 1937), "A Revolutionary Endeavor. Breathing Life Back into the Municipalities" (13 April 1937).

(only partially outlined) would, after May, be explored in full in the program devised by the Friends of Durruti in the columns of *El Amigo del Pueblo*. In this article, which appeared in the **13 April** edition of *La Noche*, Mingo declared: "The municipality is the real revolutionary government."[81]

According to Mingo, the Generalidad government had had no mission to perform since 19 July. The only politics left was political economy, and that was a matter for the unions. So, to Mingo's mind, the municipality, run by the workers and pursuing an economic policy directed by the unions, could and should have stepped into the shoes of the State by means of a municipal confederation.

Tuesday, 13 April

At 1:00 a.m. the working party appointed by the various organizations to devise some way out of the government crisis held its third sitting in **President Companys's Residence in the Generalidad**.[82] It was attended by the same lineup as the previous two meetings.

Sesé stated that the UGT was restating its position. **Ferrer** made it clear that the UGT could not surrender control of these two departments: War Industries or Defense. **Sauret** asked the UGT representatives if they were prepared to form a government on the same basis as the previous Council, as Herrera had suggested. After a protracted, tense, and complex negotiation between the UGT, the CNT, and the ERC regarding how the ministerial portfolios were to be allocated, especially the War Industries portfolio that they were now duplicating or amalgamating in order to keep all sides happy. They were promptly made into General Directorates and, as they were kept separate from the general oversight, both **Herrera** and **Escorza** rejected the setting up of any new War Industries councillorship and its separation from the planned Industry Department. No way out of the government crisis having been devised, **Companys** announced that, once the solemn commemorations of 14 April were out of the way, he would tender his resignation. It was agreed that they would meet for a fourth sitting (and for the second time that day) at 20:30 hours.

Under Companys's chairmanship, Herrera, Escorza, Pi Sunyer, Sauret, Sesé, Ferrer, and Calvet showed up for the working party's **fourth sitting** to continue with

---

81   Mingo, "A Revolutionary Endeavor," *La Noche*, 13 April 1937.
82   "13 April. 1st meeting (Barcelona, 13 April 1937)" [AMTM].

their deliberations from that morning and attempt to work out a resolution of the crisis.[83]

Companys asked those present if they could see any way out of the crisis. **Herrera** stated that the UGT had rejected the various formulas that had been put to it, so he could see no option other than the one articulated that morning, of "reverting to the lineup of the last Council, the one that [had been in place] when the crisis broke out." Ferrer was sure that the socialists' formula offered a way of settling the situation, without injury to the participation of the CNT, with the CNT taking part and a brand new War Industries Department being set up, run by the UGT. Herrera said that they would rather that the War Industries remain as they had been to date, under the oversight of the Prime Minister's Office (i.e. under the direction of Tarradellas).[84] **Escorza** added that the UGT had to understand that it was heavily committed to overhauling the current War Industries structures "due to the very fact that there was a crisis" in the government. **Companys** insisted that there should be no tampering with the arrangement whereby the War Industries fell under the remit of the prime minister's Office, and that they should be looking for a solution to the crisis on that basis. **Pi Sunyer** concluded that there were no differences in the programs of the two trade unions and that the digging in of heels was due solely to bickering over the portfolios to be divvied up. After some pointless oratory from Pi regarding the critical historical times Catalonia was going through, some grandiose Catalanist declamations, and some cloying appeals to antifascist unity, those present carried on with their hullabaloo until, with no prospect of a solution in sight, Companys decided to bring the proceedings to a close.

Wednesday, 14 April

Francisco Pellicer, an activist with the Foodworkers Union and with the Friends of Durruti, had an article published in *La Noche*, entitled: "The Present Moment."[85]

---

83   "13 April. 2nd meeting (Barcelona, 13 April 1937)" [AMTM].

84   What the CNT personnel and Companys were out to avoid was the CNT's Vallejo and Martín turning into subordinates of Comorera, thereby shattering the CNT's fruitful partnership with Tarradellas at War Industries. Vallejo and Martín had announced that they would be stepping down if made answerable to Comorera.

85   Francisco Pellicer was a prominent member of the CNT's Barcelona Foodworkers Union (SURAB). He ought not to be confused with the Pellicer brothers who were the Iron Column's delegates. The Foodworkers Union worked alongside the CNT's Supplies Committees that had, in July 1936, set up people's canteens and seen to it that Barcelona city was kept supplied. The SURAB became one of the mainstays of the Friends of Durruti. The article discussed here is Francisco Pellicer, "The Present Moment," *La Noche*, Wednesday, 14 April 1937.

A hawk-eyed scrutiny from atop the magnificent vantage point of more than eight months of struggle is called for and needed.

Are we satisfied with the gains made for the cause of the people's liberation? No.

No, because, no matter how we try to justify ourselves, we are no further down the road to our emancipation.

We could, and should, have made more progress and, by this stage, no political party and no would-be dictator would be daring to ask, insolently: And how many members does the CNT have in Catalonia?

We have been unduly gracious and unduly fainthearted in not having grabbed power in Catalonia and then brought it to bear on the boycott the Valencia government enforces against the CNT and the FAI in Catalonia and its shunning of Aragon—since talking about the Catalan region is tantamount to talking about the front in Aragon. Fainthearted, in that we were cowed by the threat of foreign intervention. **We could, and we should, have taken power** and I am more than convinced that the Revolution would have taken a different course, and the war too.[86] We now know that [the effect of] foreign intervention has been exactly equal to the fear that possessed us back in July.

In those days, no one could move through Catalonia without the CNT's say-so. Everything belonged to us, absolutely everything.

Companys said that it was up to us to give the orders and say what was to be done and that he stood ready to back our revolutionary endeavors politically in the face of Spain and the outside world. What remains, Señor Companys, of those plans of yours? Nothing.

The aim was to buy time so that the conservative political forces of bourgeois democracy and Moscow's brand of socialist centralism might be rebuilt. Once that happened, they would be the middle class and bureaucracy's best ally against the CNT and the FAI; our own indiscretions during months of antifascist collaboration did the rest, bringing us to the present grave pass....

In the Supplies area, we let all the money grubbers and speculators in the region suit themselves, instead of our taking over the food industry in its entirety in the main comarcas and cities of Catalonia, as a war measure, to prevent us from plunging into the chaos that currently characterizes this matter.

Today no one can feed himself on an average income in Catalonia. Yet the luxury hotels and restaurants are overflowing with food. This is an **affront to the people's hunger** and above all to the families of the militia members away

---

86   The belief that power should have been taken underpinned all subsequent theorization by the Friends of Durruti.

fighting. The luxury cafes, are awash with idlers forever ensconced around their tables instead of picking up a rifle or a mattock out in the fields.

Bureaucracy is the order of the day in all the government offices, where the most blatant confusion and ineptitude prevail. **Beggary and prostitution on the public thoroughfares.** A war industry in the making.

The countryside hates us because all we have worried about is living well in the cities, and especially in this putrid Barcelona, swamped with bourgeoisified oversight committees who drive cars everywhere, even on personal business.

Is this revolution? There was no need for all the calamity we went through prior to 19 July, no need for so many lives to be lost on that date and since, just for this. But enough of the lamentation and retrospective analysis, since what concerns us is today and tomorrow.

We should grab hold of Supplies, with consent or by force; we should do away with the hotels and cafes; the dance-halls and the prostitution. Introduce the family wage. Let the capital of each industry be owned by each respective union. Municipalize housing. The family wage must be applied to all. As a war measure, all large and small trading in foodstuffs must be taken over, so that we can restore order in the rearguard—and let anyone who disagrees with this scream as much as he likes, regardless of what membership card he carries. Add to the work hours and slash the wages of the hangers-on, so that everybody gets to eat. And anyone who feels ill at ease usefully employed in the city can just go and take the train; the countryside is crying out for manpower so that our peasant comrades do not need to work such long hours.

That is the work we need to be doing, in spite of all the hypocritical politicians out to crush the CNT and the FAI.

★

In the very same edition of *La Noche,* **Balius** published an article marking the anniversary of the proclamation of the Republic; in it, he underlined the petit-bourgeois character of the day and he attacked Catalanism, whether right-leaning or left-leaning, be it Maciá or Cambó, because they had both bartered away their nationalism when faced by the threat from the Catalan proletariat.[87]

These articles by Balius and other members of the Friends of Durruti, so widely varying in theme, generally offering a political opinion, but on occasion newsy,

---

87   Jaime Balius, "An Historic Date: 14 April," *La Noche,* Wednesday, 14 April 1937.

were without doubt the glue that held together a critical current of opposition to the CNT's collaborationist policy throughout the months of March and April 1937. Balius wasn't the only critical voice, but he was one of the most prominent ones and, of course, the most consistent, coherent, and radical. Balius's merit resides in his having secured the backing of a sizable group of militia members opposed to militarization of the militias. The banding together of these militia members, led by Pablo Ruiz, with other anarcho-syndicalist personnel opposed to the CNT's collaborationist policy, found in Balius's articles and criticisms the theoretical articulation of their political stances. Stances that would be crystallized in the program printed on the late April 1937 poster and that were to be explored in detail in El Amigo del Pueblo, *published in the wake of the May Events.*

So, although the Friends of Durruti was formally launched on 17 March 1937, its roots went back to the deep-seated malaise generated in militia members by the Generalidad decree militarizing the people's militias, which is to say, to around late October 1936, while Durruti was still alive. Besides, Balius had already made his name in 1935 as a journalist and anarchist ideologue and was well known for his interesting theoretical remarks about nationalism and his ferocious criticisms of the political performance of the Catalan bourgeoisie, his attacks on Maciá and Companys, his exposé of the Catalanist fascism embodied by Dencás and Badía, as well as his analysis, from a CNT viewpoint, of the events of October 1934 in Catalonia. Nor was there anything new about Jaime Balius and Pablo Ruiz working with each other, since they had already written a pamphlet together and had both been members of the same anarchist affinity group, "Renacer," a name it shared with the publishing house that, prior to July 1936, had published Balius's pamphlets.[88] *In addition to Jaime Balius and Pablo Ruiz, the membership of the Renacer group include Francisco Pellicer (a prominent leader of the Catalan CNT's Foodworkers Union) and Bruno Lladó (who served during the civil war as a councillor on Sabadell City Council and was comarcal delegate with the Generalidad's Economy Department).*[89]

---

88   The pamphlet (which we have not seen), jointly authored by Jaime Balius and Pablo Ruiz, was entitled "Fígols, 8 January, 8 December, and October" and was published (or maybe only its forthcoming publication was announced) by Editorial Renacer. The Balius pamphlets mentioned, though undated, came after October 1934 and prior to July 1936 and were as follows, in chronological order: Jaime Balius, *De Jaca a Octubre* (Barcelona: Editorial Renacer, undated); Jaime Balius, *Octubre Catalán* (Barcelona: Editorial Renacer, undated); Jaime Balius, *El nacionalismo y el proletariado* (Barcelona: Editorial Renacer, undated).

89   According to what Balius stated in a letter (in French) on 1 June 1978 to Paul Sharkey: "I was a member of the FAI's Renacer group along with comrades Pablo Ruiz, Francisco Pellicer, now deceased, and Bruno Lladó, likewise deceased." [Letter furnished by Paul Sharkey, whom we thank for the information.]

★

Also on that day, the Friends of Durruti issued a **manifesto** in which it opposed the bourgeoisie's celebration of the anniversary of the proclamation of the Republic, because it could only be a pretext for boosting bourgeois institutions and the counterrevolution.[90] Instead of commemorating the Republic, instead of the Generalidad and Lluís Companys, who were in the forefront of the bourgeois counterrevolution, the Friends of Durruti wanted to see celebration of 19 July and they encouraged the CNT and FAI to devise some revolutionary way out of the dead end street of the Generalidad government's crisis. That crisis actually began on 4 March with a decree disbanding the Control Patrols. As this had not been complied with by the CNT, the implication was that CNT personnel were pulling out of the Generalidad government.

The Manifesto cited a host of transgressions against revolutionaries, ranging from the most notorious incident with Maroto, which even drew an outraged objection from the meek and mild *Solidaridad Obrera*, through to lesser known examples like the incidents in Olesa de Montserrat.[91] The Manifesto laid out the program points that had been distilled since early March onward from the articles by Balius, Pellicer, Mingo, and others in *La Noche*. And these were distilled in the very first paragraph of the Manifesto:

> The capitalist state, which suffered a major setback in the unforgettable events in July, is still standing, thanks to the counterrevolutionary endeavors of the petite bourgeoisie.... The Generalidad crisis is a categorical demonstration that we need to shape a brand new world, dispensing entirely with state forms. The time has come for the legion of petite bourgeois, shopkeepers, and guards to be swept mercilessly aside. There can be no pussyfooting with counterrevolution.... This is a life-or-death moment for the working class.... Let us not dither. The CNT and the FAI, organizations that are the beating heart of the people, have to find a revolutionary way out of this dead end street.... We possess the institutions that are to replace the decrepit state. The Unions and Municipalities must take charge of economic and social life.

---

90   Friends of Durruti Group, "To the working people," Barcelona [14 April 1937].

91   Francisco Maroto was delegate of the militia column that bore his name. The column mounted a successful military campaign in Córdoba and Granada, though it failed to capture the latter due to lack of armaments. He had a run-in with the governor of Almería, Gabriel Morón, whom he criticized at a rally in February 1937. To the huge indignation of the libertarian movement, he was jailed, and it insisted upon his being released. On 1 May 1937, he was pardoned, but lost command of his column. At the end of the war he was arrested, tortured, and then shot by the Falangists in Alicante.

★

Because of the runaway inflation in subsistence prices, **groups of women demonstrated and protested throughout the 14th, and incidents were triggered in every marketplace in Barcelona.**

Thursday, 15 April

Whereas *Solidaridad Obrera* offered a brief commentary on the disturbances of the previous day, mistakenly comparing them with the usual, familiar women's demonstrations manipulated by the PSUC, the daily *La Vanguardia* carried an extensive and highly detailed report of the scuffles that had broken out.[92] The latter pointed out that these were different from previous women's demonstrations, when PSUC slogans had been prominently displayed, outlining the **telling differences: the spontaneity, the contagion or relocation from one market to the next in order to shut them down, the closing up of shops selling foodstuffs in the vicinity, the blocking of tram traffic, the complaints originally directed at "the comrades" from the Sants Revolutionary Committee in the Plaza de España, and the absence of the usual placards and slogans damning the committees.**

The disturbances led to a breach of public order when the demonstrators forcefully insisted that other women join them in the protest. A number of establishments and sales outlets had been closed down, although there were no reports of injury or serious incident.

The *La Vanguardia* reporter explained that "the incidents started in the La Torrassa, Sans, Hostafrancs, and Hospitalet markets, spreading like wildfire to other markets around the city as the morning wore on."

He also noted that "at seven o'clock in the morning, a gang of women turned up at the market in Sans protesting at the unjustified hike in food prices, especially eggs, and urging the vendors to close shop by way of a protest. The majority of them had locked the doors of their stalls and the rest followed suit until the market was completely depopulated, without further incident."

Once the Sans market had been shut down, a women's demonstration formed, shutting down all the shops in the adjacent streets that had foodstuffs for sale "and then storming onward to the Sans highway, where they carried on protesting in front of the grocery and vegetable stalls."

---

92   "Yesterday's Demonstration and the Same Old Politics," *Solidaridad Obrera*, Thursday 15 April 1937, front page; "Yesterday's Protests," *La Vanguardia*, Thursday 15 April 1937, front page.

Simultaneously, in Hostafrancs market, other gangs of women did the same as in Sans "also forcing the closure of sales outlets and the market gates."

With both markets now shut down, the women demonstrators took up positions on the Sans highway "stopping all the trams and urging all the women travelling on these to alight. Soon a sizable bunch of women had formed and **they made for the defense committee in the Plaza de España**, where they appointed a delegation to go inside for talks with the comrades from said Committee."

Those delegates "reported back to the demonstrators on their talks with the comrades" from the Sants Revolutionary Committee who "told them that they were not empowered to meddle in the dispute and that they had to address themselves to the appropriate authorities who were in a position to be able to settle it."

After that, the demonstration was dispersing, although several groups formed up and decided to head off down different streets, their aim being to carry on "getting various establishments to shut down." There was also some disorder in nearby Hospitalet: "The gates and food stalls there were also forced to close in the Collblanch market. In the Provenanza (formerly Santa Eulalia) market, the gates were shut for quite some time, in anticipation of possible incidents."

The disturbances and outcries were replicated pretty much everywhere: "At 1:30, there was a bona fide riot in the Boquería market, with the market gates being shut to avert incidents." That precaution of locking up was an example aped by shops in the vicinity. At 11:00, the market director called for assistance from the security forces.

"In Barceloneta market, other bunches of women, with one woman leading the way and brandishing a pistol, tried to force the market into closing," although all they managed was to get a few sales outlets to close, since the Control Patrols arrived to restore order.

"In the Libertad market [in Gracia] a number of women popped up, also objecting to the excessive pricing of basic necessities, and trade was interrupted for a while until the security forces showed up and restored order." Nearby shops, which had shut to avoid reprisals from the demonstrators, reopened for business.

Around 10:15, there were also demonstrators protesting at the San Antonio market, trying to smash up the tables of stalls and shut the place down, but "they were shown every consideration and given a full explanation by the [market] Management and the demonstrators withdrew in orderly fashion."

The protests that broke out in the market in El Clot failed "to close the doors of any establishment." In that market, an arrest was made, of a person "who was advising the women heading off to complain to **Comorera** to lift goods without paying for them."

In the rest of Barcelona's markets "a number of precautions were taken to prevent incident." But there was not the least sign of protest there "and sales there were proceeding absolutely normally."

Some of the groups that had tried to shut down the city markets headed for the Plaza de la República "brandishing placards that referenced the runaway rise in food prices. A commission of demonstrators called at the mayor's office to present him with the Barcelona women's objections to the rampant abuses."

The demonstrations were replicated that afternoon, "with the difference that now the demonstrators were barging into cafes and cinemas and trying to get the women in those places to follow them." At 6:00 p.m., "a demonstration comprising a hundred-odd women got as far as the Generalidad Palace, waving placards protesting at the inexcusable hike in food prices." A small commission of demonstrators got a hearing from **Martí Rouret** "who invited them to place their protest on record with the Supplies Department."

Later, "the demonstration made for the Vía Durruti and the commissioner-general of public order where again a commission was chosen to go up and meet with the chief of staff, comrade **Dionisio Eroles,** whom they lobbied for the release of the individual who had been arrested that morning in connection with the protest."[93]

The detailed narration of the disorder created in Barcelona's markets concluded by publishing a number of notes about the price of eggs, *bacalao* (dried cod), and bread.

The Mayor's office in Barcelona had it on record that the maximum retail price of eggs was: in Villafranca, 0.60 pesetas apiece; nationally, 0.55 pesetas apiece; in Holland, 0.35 pesetas apiece; in Belgium, 0.35 pesetas apiece; in Egypt, 0.25 pesetas apiece.

Barcelona Corporation's Supplies Department-Board reported that *bacalao* was for sale only as wet fish and specified these prices: de-boned top cut, 1.65 pesetas per 400 grams; as it comes, 1.50 pesetas per 400 grams; loin cut, 1.30 pesetas per 400 grams; tail cut, 1.20 pesetas per 400 grams.

The GEPCI released a lengthy self-justifying notice from the retailers' association that did not quote price per item but did attempt to explain the reasons behind the widespread hike in food prices.[94] It began by expressing its "enthusi-

---

93   That the female demonstrators were able to meet with "comrade" Dionisio Eroles (CNT) was another marked difference, indicative of the spontaneous, popular nature of that demonstration on the part of women who were closer to the CNT personnel than to the Stalinists and their anti-committee sloganizing.

94   The UGT-affiliated Gremis i Entitats de Petits Comerciants e Industrials, a PSUC-organized coalition, which brought together some 18,000 retailers, artisans, and small industrialists who shared a bourgeois and ferociously anti-labor outlook.

astic support for any drive designed to make basic necessities more affordable," after lamenting "the explosion of protests we are witnessing on a daily basis over the exorbitant pricing of food items."

Naturally the GEPCI was suggesting that the root cause for the price rises should be sought "in the centers of production or among the wholesale suppliers," and never in the grocery stores that the bulk of the population was holding to blame. The GEPCI condemned "any isolated instance of speculation that may have occurred or may be occurring among retail traders."

If there was any speculation going on among the retailers, these were isolated instances, according to the GEPCI. The blame lay with the wholesalers and they could produce invoices to prove that.

In the free market situation promoted and protected by Comorera from his position as Generalidad supplies councillor, added to which there was a chronic, ongoing shortage of food items, pricing was governed not by moral standards, nor by antifascist sloganizing, nor by solidarity of any sort, nor by coercive or repressive measures, but by the laws of supply and demand. That the constant and sharp rise in prices started with the wholesalers, as the retailers of the GEPCI were arguing, waving their invoices about, was an incentive for the retailers to get in on the speculation and line their pockets by exploiting the people's hunger. The disorderliness and demonstrations of 14 April 1937 were the result of such speculation and price gouging by food retailers. The hungry people had correctly identified those to blame and knew perfectly well who the culprit was and channeled their anger in the direction of the reviled Comorera, the PSUC general secretary. Not for nothing had the man arrested in the El Clot market been urging the women to make off with food items without paying for them and to go off and complain to Comorera.

★

La Batalla offered an account of the disturbances that complemented the one on offer in *La Vanguardia*.[95] Its focus was more on the incidents that had taken place in the **Pueblo Nuevo market**.

The report opened with an extensive restatement of the official price lists, wholesale and retail alike.

It noted the tedious queues that had formed just to buy potatoes, coal, soap, and olive oil, in the variety markets.

It explained how, in the incidents of "the day before yesterday" (13 April) at the El Clot market, women ready to kick up a stink if the price of bread went up, attacked other women who were paying 1.20 pesetas for a liter of milk, which

---

95   "Against Rising Subsistence Prices," *La Batalla*, 15 April 1937.

they regarded as a provocation. The paper carried a notice from the CNT's Dairy branch, warning that no one should be paying more than 0.90 pesetas per liter for milk.

In the Pueblo Nuevo market on the 14th, the protests turned more violent than elsewhere: "in light of the scandalous pricing of fish and eggs, a number of baskets were upturned and trampled underfoot." It was the same with the vegetables.

"My husband earns 7 pesetas—one weeping woman told us—and eggs are going for 0.60 each, cheaper cuts of fish for more than 3 pesetas a pound. How am I supposed to manage with two young children?"

Some two thousand women, coming from Pueblo Nuevo, mustered outside the Generalidad at 4:30 p.m. on 14 April "to protest at the high prices of basic necessities." After an hour and a half of waiting, a commission was allowed inside, only to be told that they should go and make their objections to the Supplies Department. The demonstration moved along the Calle del Call in the direction of the Ramblas and the Supplies Department, shutting down shops as they went. Cries of 'Death to Comorera' were frequently heard from the demonstrators."

The reporter complained of the presence of provocateurs from the PSUC who failed in their attempts to get the demonstrators to chant slogans targeting the committees and the Control Patrols.

★

Emblazoned across the back cover of the same edition of *La Batalla* was this: "What has triggered the runaway inflation in basic living costs? Three months of PSUC policy from the Supplies Department."

On the back page of the POUM's mouthpiece there was a political analysis of the protests: "The Supplies policy … has been a disaster. It began with Comorera's time in government, ordering a free market and providing an opening for unfettered price-gouging and an uncontrolled surge in product prices. And the problem is wider than just Barcelona."[96]

A link was made between the abolition of the comarcal supplies committees, as ordered by Comorera, and the dizzying rise in basic prices.

The writer wondered how it could be that olive oil was selling at 4 pesetas a liter and how Comorera could possibly want the price of a liter of milk to go to 1.20 pesetas.

---

96   "A Well-Deserved Protest That Should Not Be Turned into a Weapon in the Hands of Counterrevolutionaries," *La Batalla*, 15 April 1937, rear cover page.

The women's demonstrations and their protests at the price-gouging had triggered the **hunger riots** on the 14th.

The POUMists raised the alarm against the danger of such demonstrations being manipulated by supporters of the counterrevolution, as had already happened.

The free market that Comorera favored, plus the dissolution of the barrio and comarcal supplies committees, which had hitherto monitored food prices and the prices of basic necessities, had triggered a runaway escalation in prices and that, added to the shortage and unavailability of basic foodstuffs due to speculation, resulted in the hunger riots on 14 April 1937. And now the hungry were chanting "Death to Comorera."

★

Besides its excellent report on the disturbances occurring in Barcelona's markets, *La Vanguardia* the previous day had carried an **editorial** very tellingly and strikingly entitled "The dictatorship of the shopkeepers," in which it offered an outstanding analysis of the mood for riot existing among the Barcelona populace.[97]

The editorial was truly brilliant and got the reader worked up: "What we were afraid of, what would inevitably crop up, has cropped up. Yesterday, Barcelona witnessed our first stirrings of popular anxiety. Demonstrations by women roved the streets, venting their complaints about the high cost of living."

Following that concise and spot-on narration of the facts, their significance was calibrated by making it clear that "the people of Barcelona have never complained about the privations that circumstances have thrust upon them. The people are aware of the sacrifices required by the war and accept the inevitable with calm resignation. **When there was no bread, it ate no bread, but it never uttered a single word.**"

The writer of the editorial was, therefore, well aware that the previous mass demonstrations by the women bearing PSUC slogans were a very different kettle of fish from the popular protests that had erupted on 14 April.

"But what the people cannot brook patiently is the abuse, the deceit, the crime visited upon them when they are shown the counters of shops and market stalls groaning under displays of food, but food at unfeasible prices. And that is the truth, pure and simple."

In character, the demonstrations and protests mounted on 14 April were very different from the ones manipulated by the Stalinists and it was not so much a matter of identifying who was to blame as it was of coming up with solutions,

---

97   "Editorial: The Dictatorship of the Shopkeepers," *La Vanguardia*, Thursday 15 April 1937.

because they had turned into an intolerable blight, a **crime against the revolution**: "Where the blame lies for what is being done or left undone, we do not know, but we say in all sincerity: no one has done the revolution greater injury or damage."

The journalist skillfully dissected the arguments put by the retailers and lifted the lid on the intolerable inequality and sense of injustice on the streets: "These items, which go up by a peseta a day, for reasons known to none—the shopkeeper usually has a ready explanation for them, saying gruffly that he has to pay more for them at the source and he has to think about his livelihood; the shopkeeper has, as we can see, second sight: these items, which evaporate one day only to resurface three days later at double the price; these thousands of kilos of potatoes that one stumbles upon one day; these twenty-gram bread rolls; the disgrace, whereby, with the right money, one can eat as well in today's Barcelona as at any time in the past, all of this does more injury to the revolution than the Fifth Column, or the Sixth or the Seventh, if they exist."

His sympathy with the women demonstrating on the streets outside protesting the high cost of food prompted the editorial writer to explain the discontent and rebelliousness of the women, be they antifascist or neutral, vis-à-vis the misgovernment and maladministration that had introduced hunger into their homes: "We might have expected anything except our falling under a **money-grubbing shopkeepers' dictatorship**."

The editorial ended with a call for an immediate remedy to the soaring prices of basic goods, on the grounds that there was "no problem more serious." And he drew a delicate **distinction between what amounted to sacrifice and what amounted to abuse**. "We say it again: the people have a clear-cut sense of fairness and know perfectly well what sacrifice is and what abuse is. They stand ready to endure the former and have more than amply demonstrated this, but the latter they are not prepared to put up with."

The editorialist hoped that "the stink kicked up yesterday by the women in the streets of Barcelona" might have been effective enough to lead to devising solutions "for the good of the cause we all say we are defending, "although, being both pessimistic and scathing, he sardonically remarked "that it looks like some only defend it so that they can sell it out once the price has gone up."

Comorera's bread war was achieving its ultimate political and military purposes. The GEPCI had managed to displace the barrio-level supplies committees. That this meant rich pickings for shopkeepers, based on hungry bellies among the people, was a secondary issue about which the Stalinists did not much care, since it was also working to the advantage of their main clientele. **The slogan "More bread and fewer committees" was turning into the dismal reality of "Neither bread nor committees."**

★

In March 1937, a broad swath of POUM militants had raised a protest against the absence of internal debate and the further postponement of the party congress originally scheduled for December 1936, then delayed until February 1937, and now postponed again in March. Throughout March and April 1937, the weekly meetings of the political secretaries and organizing secretaries of the district committees, at the level at which the party's cells were organized, channeled the unhappiness of the rank-and-file membership. Which is how it came to pass that the **Barcelona POUM Local Committee** (or LC) became a staunch body in opposition to the POUM leadership, its Executive Committee (EC), and its Central Committee (CC)—and, in addition to pressing for the congress to be held, it launched a debate about political work on the front lines, which was running into opposition from commanders who were against the formation of cells in the ranks of militia members, and also about the party participating in a bourgeois government, as this implied disavowal of the strategy that the EC had hitherto been following.[98]

These protests, the fruits of a malaise widespread among the POUM rank-and-file, culminated on 13 April in the convening of a joint meeting of the Barcelona LC and the Central Committee (CC), at which **Josep Martí**, the secretary of the Barcelona LC, and **Josep Rebull** managed to secure endorsement and widely disseminated a **manifesto from the Barcelona LC** that was published in *La Batalla* of **15 April**.[99] Relating to the Generalidad crisis, it was critical of the POUM's participation in that bourgeois government and called for the formation of a Revolutionary Workers' Front to beef up the Workers' Councils as organs of power. It was also announced that the POUM's second congress would meet on 8 May, and ample consideration was made for the publication and dissemination, through internal bulletins, of the various cells' counterproposals to the EC's official theses.

The title of the manifesto by the POUM's Barcelona LC was: "For resolution of the crisis. Revolutionary Workers' Front" and it was carried by *La Batalla*.[100]

---

98 Correspondence between Negrete [Russell Blackwell] and Oehler, 1936–1937. (Extracts), Brandeis University, ALBA Archives [Photocopies. Extracts from letters written by Negrete, mostly addressed to Oehler and dated Barcelona, between 26 November 1936 and 4 November1937].

99 Josep Rebull was the leader of the so-called left of the POUM. See Agustín Guillamón "Josep Rebull de 1937 a 1939. La crítica interna a la política del CE del POUM sobre la Guerra de España," *Balance* nos. 19 and 20, May–October 2000. For a biography of Rebull, see Casciolo and Guillamón, *Biografías del 36* (Barcelona: Descontrol, 2016), 315–330.

100 *La Batalla*, 15 April 1937. The following day's edition of *La Batalla* rectified the mistake made on the 15th, when it had reported "United Revolutionary Front" instead of "Workers' Revolutionary Front." The error was telling.

The dragging out of the crisis for a fortnight highlights the contradictions of the current political situation.

Those contradictions consist of wanting to reconcile the power of a regime that was deemed obsolete on 19 July with the power of the Revolution; bourgeois interests presently embodied by the Generalidad government with the interests of a proletariat that lacks its own organs of power. Within the parameters of bourgeois institutions, only bourgeois solutions are possible. The Generalidad government and the Parliament of Catalonia are bourgeois institutions. No revolutionary situation has ever ended with a victorious revolution unless it has successfully created a Power at loggerheads with the former Power. Those organizations whose purpose is proletarian revolution—the POUM and the CNT-FAI—must immediately form the Revolutionary Workers' Front, ensuring that they recruit to their cause the masses torn between the bourgeois Republic and the socialist revolution.

The Revolutionary Workers' Front is going to have to make a start on the immediate creation of Councils of Workers, Combatants, and Peasants, and with the least possible delay, summon the Councils' congress, thereby restoring the dual power that is vital if power is to be won by the working class and a true Worker and Peasant Government installed.[101]

> For the creation of the Workers', Peasants', and Combatants' Councils!
> For a Worker and Peasant Government!
> BARCELONA LOCAL POUM COMMITTEE.

★

Soli carried an **article by Josep Tarradellas**, in which the Generalidad's First Councillor replied to the insults and mistakes published in *Treball* the previous day with regard to the War Industries.[102] *Treball* had demonstrated "an utter ignorance of the subject upon which it dares to speak.

Its advocacy of the political positions of the PSUC seemed to give it license to lie and to air "the most capricious comments with startling nonchalance."

He asked rhetorically whether it might not be better advised to keep its trap

---

101 See Josep Rebull's article: "For the Creation of the Workers', Peasants' and Combatants' Councils" (Clarification of Political Counter-theses)," in *Boletín Interior. Órgano de discusión para el II Congreso del Comité Local de Barcelona del POUM* no. 1, Barcelona, 23 April 1937.

102 Josep Tarradellas, "War Industries, a Political Pretext," *Solidaridad Obrera*, 15 April 1937, front page.

shut "rather than talking about matters it neither knows about, has any grasp of, nor understands."

He asked the PSUC not to make a football out of the War Industries, since the members of the Commission welcomed all criticism, but such criticisms should be voiced through the appropriate channels, which is to say, through "their representatives within the government and Generalidad." It was irresponsible to debate war-related matters in public and to mix them up with defense of party interests.

Tarradellas's article closed with a severe reprimand to the Stalinists whom he described as "curious *aficionados* of matters of war" and they were chastised for their disloyalty, manipulation, and partisanship and warned that "I do not believe that anyone acting thus is capable of carrying out any constructive plan, much less securing any victory."[103]

That Tarradellas should have published this letter upbraiding the PSUC in the anarcho-syndicalist newspaper Solidaridad Obrera *spoke volumes about the government crisis then current. Unlike Companys, Tarradellas was calling for an understanding between the Generalidad government and the CNT, because the 19 July uprising had made anarcho-syndicalist partnership in government a necessity. Tarradellas honestly believed that there could be no stable government without a CNT presence: whereas Companys was gambling on an alliance with the PSUC, the object being to belittle the CNT or oust it in order to form a "strong" government, capable of enforcing the decrees boycotted or defied by the CNT's "uncontrollables." For that reason, Companys had decided to drop Tarradellas from the negotiations for the formation of a new government.*

★

"**Companys held a wide-ranging meeting with Messrs Herrera and Escorza** from the CNT, without making any mention of this meeting."[104] This new meeting was a follow-up to the formal meetings they had had on 11 and 13 April in an attempt to resolve the government crisis, and it came right before the announcement of a new government lineup the following day, so it must have been some sort of a nod to the CNT, advance notification in the hopes, perhaps, of receiving its blessing. Be that as it may, **Manuel Escorza, at that point, looked like the CNT's strong man in Catalonia**, negotiating a way out of the government crisis directly with the Generalidad president.

---

103 Tarradellas was being sarcastic here about the Plan for Victory unveiled on 8 April by the PSUC.

104 Govern de la Generalitat/Josep Tarradellas, *Crónica*, vol. 2, 726.

★

A **report to Moscow** from a PSUC delegate in Paris, intercepted by the CNT intelligence agencies, disclosed the presence, in Paris, of two PSUC militants, one of them "someone of certain influence within the Catalan party; I refer to comrade Roldán Cortada, comrade Vidiella's secretary."[105] The mission that had brought the pair to Paris "was the purchase of arms, handguns," which the correspondent understood **was not a matter of buying arms for the Army, but for the PSUC:** "I attended to them, as the Party leaders had requested that I should and put them in touch with certain persons who might be of service to them."

Roldán had been heard to say "that we must take on the FAI and FAI members are armed." **The PSUC's delegate in Paris was of the view that disarming the FAI was a matter for the government, and the Party should play no part, since it could result in a disaster.**

After those two PSUC militants had returned to Barcelona, the delegate in Paris noted: "A large number of members of the Unified Socialist Party of Catalonia have paraded through Paris, and to anybody prepared to listen, they have all made the same argument as comrade Roldán Cortada, **that we need to take on the FAI."**

The correspondent provided details of the meeting in Paris between leading members of the PSUC, Comorera included, "and communist personnel from other countries and they came to an arrangement on a **plan of all-out attack on the FAI,"** all of which struck the delegate in Paris as extremely dangerous.

He forecast that "any day now Barcelona is going to be the theater for an unedifying spectacle that the [fascist] rebels will seize upon, and with more than good reason." His report closed with an apology for his having expressed his own opinion rather than confining himself to a bare-bones briefing.

Friday, 16 April

La Batalla carried an **article on the Control Patrols,** based on an interview with the CNT militant **Nevado,** "the CNT's delegate on the Patrols Secretariat."[106] He was preoccupied by "the risk that these street demonstrations might be exploited by the counterrevolution to degrade what are otherwise well-grounded protests at high food prices into a breach of public order."

---

105 "Reports on the May Events in Catalonia. Dossier no. 197. Sundry reports on those events, on which the Organization had advance information. Paris, 15 April 1936" [IISH-CNT-005-A15].

106 "The Effective Efforts of the Control Patrols," *La Batalla*, 16 April 1937.

Nevado expressed himself as greatly "interested in ensuring that there were no breaches of public order," but at the same time he appreciated "the righteousness that drives workers' spouses into protesting the high cost of living." He warned against those who were out to manipulate these women's demonstrations "for dark purposes," which might "result in clashes of no benefit at all to revolutionary order."

Questioned by the interviewer about the Patrols' intervention in the matter, Nevado replied: "We have been relentless in our pursuit of hoarders and people fleecing the consumers. Not long ago, a cache of soap was uncovered. Yesterday, Section 7 came across a rice hoarder who was selling it on to the public at the price of 2.80 pesetas a kilogram. That is self-evidently thievery, carried out under cover of shortages."

The reporter asked: "What was done with him?" **Nevado** replied: "He got his just deserts. We forced him to sell the rice at the current prices, with no surcharges of any sort."

Next the journalist described something he had been told by **Salvi Torrent**, "POUM delegate on the Patrols General Secretariat," regarding a grocery store in the Calle Valencia.[107] After reports were received about soda being sold at outlandish prices, the Control Patrols had imposed a five hundred peseta fine.

The reporter highlighted as crucial the work of the Control Patrols in price-monitoring and sanctioning speculators.

The focus then shifted to the recent incidents that had occurred in the markets on 15 April, which had been much less serious and intense than the ones on the 14th, thanks to the publication of price-lists for vegetables and fish, which appeased the women "who are the ones closest to the heart of the price-inflation tragedy."

Even so, in "Pueblo Seco, a women's demonstration roamed a number of streets, forcing establishments to close shop." In other markets, precautions had been taken "and the doors of lots of establishments remained half-open." The reporter's conclusion was that "broadly speaking, it has been a quiet day."

But it was also noted that there was a degree of "effervescence" in the bread queues, because rumor had it that the bread rolls selling at between 1.25 and 1.30 pesetas "were about to go up again." The women shouted loudly that "if the bread does go up, we won't put up with it, no matter what." There was a call for large salaries to be slashed. The reporter noted that, in light of the rumor of a rise in the price of bread, there was a threat floating in the air, "not so much a threat as a suppressed sob from the *compañeras* that were seeing their incomes under increasing pressure each day, while the bourgeois arrangement whereby profits

---

107   Otherwise known as Silvio Torrents.

were being funneled toward a minority behind the back of the working-class majority carried blithely on its way."

That the Control Patrols were running things contrary to the free market was proof enough to the bourgeois and anti-revolutionary forces, the ERC and the PSUC, of the need for them to be replaced immediately by the traditional forces of repression, the brand-new Unified Security Corps, essentially based on the Assault Guard and the former Civil Guard.

★

At 8:00 p.m., the Generalidad's press bureau issued this **roll-call of the new government**, the third lineup over which Tarradellas had presided (it lasted but a few days, until 4 May 1937):[108]

Josep Tarradellas Joan (ERC), First Councillor and Finance Councillor.

Antonio María Sbert Massanet (ERC), Cultural Councillor.

Artemi Aguadé Miró (ERC), Internal Security Councillor

José Calvet Mora (Rabassaires Union), Councillor for Agriculture

José Miret Musté (UGT), Supplies Councillor

Rafael Vidiella Franch (UGT), Councillor for Labor and Public Works

Joan Comorera Soler (UGT), Justice Councillor

Francisco Isgleas Piarnau (CNT), Defense Councillor

Andreu Capdevila Puig (CNT), Councillor for Economy

Josep Juan Doménech (CNT), Councillor for Public Services

Aurelio Fernández Sánchez (CNT), Health and Social Assistance Councillor

The new government was a revamped version of the second Tarradellas government (17 December 1936 to 3 April 1937). It looked as if the crisis had been sorted out **as Companys had wanted, with each organization holding on to the portfolios it had held prior to the onset of the government crisis in late March.** There had been only a few name changes, not many at all. Although the argumentative, reviled, and controversial Comorera was now out of Supplies and in charge of Justice. We should highlight the inclusion of Aurelio Fernández, the chief obstacle to the agreement to form a government, against Companys's personal objections. Demonized by the republicans and Stalinists, Aurelio was a strong personality. He stood ready to do battle with Aguadé within the Generalidad council over the red-hot topic of Public Order.

★

---

108   Govern de la Generalitat/Josep Tarradellas, *Crónica*, vol. 2, 730.

That day witnessed the **funeral of tram driver** José Gonzalvo, who had "passed away as a result of wounds sustained during one of the incidents on the 7th, during the burial of the National Guardsman murdered in Olesa. At union instigation, vehicular traffic through the city was suspended between nine o'clock and noon and lots and lots of businesses locked or closed over their doors in a gesture of mourning."[109]

Saturday, 17 April

The press covered the statements made the previous day by **Dionisio Eroles** who, asked by reporters about "complaints made by a range of citizens detrimentally affected by searches that had been carried out, in the course of which handguns under the control of trade union and political bodies had been unearthed," stated: "I am unaware of any dispositions instructing Public Order forces to carry out searches and impound firearms when the bearers are authorized by their respective unions or political parties that are part of the governing bloc. **Those in possession of such weapons have them for the sake of the personal safety of the militant, who is still mobilized, albeit in the rearguard."**[110]

After Eroles had denied that any order to impound weapons had issued from him, and ended the confusion existing in the Public Order field, he sought to remind all citizens, and most especially "the officers in charge of the Generalidad's Investigation and Watch Corps" of the arrangements arrived at in the Security Junta and published in the Generalidad Government *Official Gazette* on 25 October 1936, under which "authority to effect house searches will have to emanate from the commissioner-general of public order, from the commission's chief of staff or from whatever authorities to which they may delegate."[111] There was also the fact that it was mandatory for the authorization to feature the names of the officers charged with mounting the search.

*In actual fact, what Eroles was highlighting was that Rodríguez Salas had embarked upon systematic disarmament of CNT militants, in preparation for a planned confrontation that was plainly imminent. Eroles's allusion to the armed CNT militants being MOBILIZED, BUT MOBILIZED FOR SERVICE IN THE REARGUARD, is worth underlining as typical of the anarcho-syndicalist mindset at the time: **the war was being fought on the front, yes, but also in the rearguard.***

---

109 Caballé, *Barcelona Roja*, 92.

110 *La Vanguardia*, 17 April 1937, front page.

111 The Investigation and Watch Corps had escaped the screening to which the Assault Guards and Civil Guards had been subjected by the Workers' and Soldiers' Councils and, thanks to Gómez García, from August 1936 onward became a police force some four-hundred strong, implicitly loyal to the Generalidad government.

★

That very day, **Dionisio Eroles** sent out a note to all the union committees and presidents, informing them that he had authorized Riera to meet with them all, one by one, "in order to end the notorious disappearances of citizens and to stop certain things that do the Organization no favors," the aim being to standardize activities in the Public Order field.[112] "What was feasible during the early months of the upheaval is no longer possible.[113] We have entered a new phase, which will require us to act in a different format and manner."

★

La Batalla carried a novel and interesting article on the protests and demonstrations by the **female market traders.**

In light of the vegetable and fish price-lists posted on the 16th at the entrances to markets to inform the public and reassure the women who had recently been protesting the runaway rise in the cost of basic items, there had been many incidents in which female vendors had featured prominently.

"It must have been around 10 o'clock in the morning when, in the San Antonio market, the fruit and vegetable stalls started to close up. The female vendors split up into different groups, one of which headed for the Boquería market, another for the Generalidad, the aim being to force outlets to shut down and to mount a protest against the Central Markets Committee who, from what they say, are ones responsible for the escalation in the cost of living."

---

112   Eroles's note of 17 April 1937 [SA-PSB-1335]. Riera's input and his acceptance during interrogations at San Elías derived from the fact that he had previously served on the Patrols' Emergency Court, answerable to the Investigations Committee of the now-defunct Central Antifascist Militias Committee. At a Patrols meeting on 3 January 1937, reference was made to potential meddling by Riera and, at the 26 March 1937 meeting, it was reported that he had been shown the door at San Elías, as he was a member neither of the Patrols nor of Investigations. Now here was Dionisio Eroles entrusting him with a delicate and difficult mission that must have afforded Riera great authority and prestige within the ranks of the Organization.

113   Riera, on the part of the CNT-FAI, and José Gallardo Escudero, on the part of the PSUC, had served on the Court in San Elías that met two days a week to decide the fate of those arrested by the Control Patrols, at a time when these were answerable to the CAMC Investigations Department (July to October 1936). At the 27 November 1936 meeting, the Patrols' delegates decided to revamp that Court, which would now be made up of four members, one per organization: Coll, for the ERC, De Francisco (and later Silvio Torrents) for the POUM, Bonet for the CNT, and Chueca for the UGT. Chueca replaced Gallardo as a member of the Emergency Court, while Riera's influence started to slowly peter out.

The PSUC's social base, made up of shopkeepers and small businesspeople, was on the move once more.

One portion of the demonstrators headed for the Del Ninot market in the Calle Mallorca, forcing all the food, fruit, and vegetable stores they encountered along the way to shut up shop and calling upon the saleswomen to join their demonstration.

Once they reached the Del Ninot market, sales outlets were forced into shutting down "and in the course of the 'brouhaha,' the odd butchery was 'cleaned out' by the undesirable elements that got mixed up in the disturbances. The demonstrators mustered outside the market management office, where the manager spoke with the demonstrators "in an effort to discover precisely what the origin and purpose was behind this unexpected invasion by vendors from other markets."

The demonstrators' slogan was "No setting up stalls in the market." They were demanding that they should not be required to buy from the El Borne market, the central fruit and vegetable market controlled by a CNT Committee, because not only had they no desire to profiteer but they also did not want to fall into disrepute, and since they say that we should sell cheaply, let them set the example themselves, and then we won't be obliged to sell our fruit and vegetables at fantastic prices."

The reporter acknowledged that the retailers were largely justified in the complaints they were making and that shopkeepers and small traders did not bear sole responsibility for the price hikes, because the price list supplied by the El Borne Committee "**shows us that the price hikes originate in the countryside.**"

Interviewed by the reporter, a lot of the fish wives stated that they had bought no fish that day because "we are fed up with being told that we are money-grubbers, when we can just about earn a decent income." They showed him their invoices and the sale prices, and the reporter remarked "the price hikes are not down to just you."

The journalist reported that, having looked into the matter, he had established the sale price of fish at the source, noting that "one of the reasons for the price hikes is bloated administrative bureaucracy," that is, that middlemen had a lot to do with the cost of living and the runaway price inflation.

The reporter came to some very accurate conclusions regarding the rising costs of fish and he even hinted at political solutions to the problem. Even though the shopkeepers and retailers were "not without blemish," it had first of all to be conceded that what drove a businessperson was profit, but they should not be given all the blame. Likewise, he criticized the Central Markets Committees because publishing a list of source prices and setting the retail prices did not go far enough. They should have gone a lot further: "the consumer requires, if he is to be happy, that they tell him what is going on with the product prior to its going on sale in the Central Market, and what price they [the committees] pay for the stuff. When it comes to defending the Committees and rebutting the accusations made against them, there is nothing that speaks more eloquently than such an accounting."

The PSUC was accusing the supplies committees of forcing up produce at source, by means of levies and requisitioning. But no one, not the PSUC or the CNT committees, traced or disclosed the fabulous profits being raked in by middlemen whom no one was monitoring or denouncing, because they lurked behind a dense fog that prevented them from being clearly identified. And inside that fog lurked supplies officials, committee chiefs, politicians, public order officials, and a whole raft of dealing and corruption that didn't care about ideological opportunism and was simply out to get rich quick, abetted also by the defense of the free market that the PSUC was advocating.

The *La Batalla* writer concluded that what was required was "that the revolution be made moral." He said that speculating on the hardships of the populace, as was currently happening, was out of order. The problem of food supply cried out for an urgent solution, which could not be based on sacrifices by consumers only. But they had to forestall these women's demonstrations and the raids on markets. He noted that they were dangerous and might well degenerate into breaches of public order that might "be a boost to the counterrevolution."

It was articles along these lines and not just the sort that denounced the crimes of the Stalinists in Russia that earned the POUM the wrath of the PSUC.

In mid-April, a distinction needed to be drawn between two very different sorts of women's demonstrations, even if they shared the same root cause: the soaring prices of basic foodstuffs. Some women's demonstrations, the ones in January and February 1937, were controlled and directed by the PSUC, championing the interests of shopkeepers and retailers, carrying beautiful, elegantly finished placards with slogans attacking the committees and in support of strong government. These usually headed for the Generalidad to demand solutions. Other demonstrations, in mid-April, were mounted by working women and these were spontaneous, and displayed no placards nor handbills, spread through contagion and by moving market-to-market, for the purpose of shutting them down and closing down the nearby foodstalls, halting the tram service and directing their complaints to the quarters of the defense committees, without anti-committee sloganizing. The latter sort of demonstrations never looked to the Generalidad government for solutions.

The trader women's demonstration of 16 April displayed a mixture of features from the two earlier sorts of demonstrations. On the one hand, among the traders, we must differentiate between business owners, mostly affiliated to the GEPCI, and mere wage-earners affiliated to the UGT or CNT.

★

At a special session of the **Standing Municipal Committee** chaired by mayor Carles Pi Sunyer, it was agreed that a **notice concerning supplies** should be published in the press. It read:

> The Standing Municipal Committee, at its latest meeting, passed important accords regarding basic food prices. Given the proliferation of the abuses seen of late, it agreed to punish these with the utmost vigor, authorizing the councillor-manager to impose fines of up to twenty-five thousand pesetas, in the case of a first offense, and to close an outlet down in the event of a repeat offense, without prejudice to referral of the matter, as appropriate, to the People's Courts. However, being persuaded that while the direct motive behind protests is the retail pricing, since the latter is tied up with wholesale pricing, the City Council believes that the issue of supplies requires regulation in its totality; for which reason and in order to resolve the crisis in the Generalidad government, it agreed to endorse its being given the widest powers in the supplies sector, and, as a result, the responsibilities that it stands ready to embrace, naturally declaring its intention to act in close concert with the Supplies Department in order to resolve this matter that so rightly preoccupies the populace of Barcelona. The City Council asks once again for the co-operation of the citizenry and reminds them of the need for specific reporting of instances of abuse so that these may be sanctioned immediately. To this end, it has issued strict instructions to the inspectors and those charged with this task, so that they may act with all speed and without bureaucratic impediment. The City Council hopes that the citizenry will assist in the task upon which it is now embarked by reporting instances of abuses of which they may be aware to the Supplies Inspection Board to the City Hall Buildings or to the District Municipal Delegations, by way of facilitating and complementing the oversight and punitive functions carried out by the City Council.[114]

Barcelona City Council, then, thought of the city's supplies issues as a matter of reports, sanctions, and pricing "abuses." But it was self-evident that it was a political issue that, taken together with the existing Public Order squabbling, had triggered the Generalidad government crisis, which would ultimately lead to the armed clashes of early May.

---

114   *Gaseta Municipal de Barcelona*, 26 April 1937, 109–110.

At 1:25 p.m., the **Generalidad Council** met under the chairmanship of **Companys**, with a full turnout of all the councillors, except for the defense councillor.[115]

The chair greeted the former councillors and welcomed those joining the Council for the first time: Capdevila, Aurelio Fernández, and Calvet.

He said that the sole purpose of the meeting was to form a government that could get down to business on Monday. He explained that councillor Isgleas had apologized for his nonattendance, stating the he was "fatigued and in not very good health." The proceedings concluded at 1:50 p.m.

Sunday, 18 April

The **Friends of Durruti** called a **meeting**, which was meant to be a public presentation regarding its existence and program, **at the Poliorama Theatre**. This presentation of the group was reported in detail by Rosalio Negrete and Hugo Oehler in a report written and dated in Barcelona the same day.[116]

The meeting had been convened by means of handbills announcing the speakers as Francisco Pellicer (from the Food Workers Union) speaking on the issue of basic food supplies, Pablo Ruiz (delegate from the Gelsa *Agrupación* of the Durruti Column) speaking about the revolutionary army, Jaime Balius talking about the war and the revolution, and Francisco Carreño (a member of the Durruti Column's War Committee) on trade-union unity and political collaboration, plus Vicente Pérez "Combina," speaking on public order and the present situation.

As to how the meeting went, *La Noche* of the 19th carried this extensive notice:

> Yesterday morning, at the Poliorama Theatre, a meeting took place that was organized by the Friends of Durruti. There was a substantial attendance and comrade Romero, acting as chairman, said a few brief words regarding the import of the meeting before handing over the floor to Francisco Pellicer, who opened by sparing a thought to commemorate Durruti. Next, he dealt with the issue of basic food supplies and stated that **one cannot feed oneself on the wage currently being paid** ... next up was Pablo Ruiz, speaking on the subject of the revolutionary army.... Then Jaime Balius read out a few notes ... encapsulating what the initial fight against fascism was like on 19 July.... He stated that the Revolution had to be wedded to the war and that they both

---

115   "Generalidad Council Meeting of 17 April 1937."

116   This report was first published in *Fourth International* vol. 2, no. 12 (1937). See *Revolutionary History* vol. 1, no. 2 (1988): 34–35.

needed winning.... Last to speak was Francisco Carreño on the topic "trade-union unity and political collaboration" ... like the rest of the speakers, he was much applauded.

★

The press picked up on statements made by **Rodríguez Salas,** the commissioner-general for public order, who cynically expressed agreement with the note Eroles had published in the previous day's newspapers.[117] He then went on to blame the "disarmed" militants for brandishing handguns and rifles and noted that their loyalty was owed, not to the UGT or the CNT, but to the Generalidad government. He closed by insulting the armed militants walking around the streets as thieves.

He brought up the arrest of the three Civil Guards, detained by Section 5 of the Patrol Controls in the act of searching and disarming a number of citizens on the streets, while posing as agents of the Investigation and Watch Corps. In the end, they were handed over to Escobar, an officer of the ex-Civil Guard, now Republican National Guard. The weapons seized had been returned to their owners.

Rodríguez Salas's response to Eroles opened with lip service, which the rest of what he said not only contradicted but uncovered the real conflict between the two men—since Rodríguez Salas was encouraging the police to arrest anyone bearing unconcealed weapons out on the streets, even as he was slandering armed trade unionists as criminals. The involvement of these Civil Guards—disguised as Investigation agents—in such search-and-disarm tasks on the streets was indicative of a systematic plan to disarm CNT personnel in anticipation of, in a foretaste of, and in preparation for, an imminent confrontation that would eventually erupt two weeks down the line.

That very day, *Soli* carried a **note** alluding to the arrest of those Civil Guards "who were busily disarming workers who are armed because it is their duty to be."[118]

After agreeing that such an unacceptable "overstepping of their powers" (of what might have been seen back in the days of Arlegui and Martínez Anido) should be "ended," it stated that the workers who had defeated fascism on 19 July on the streets of Barcelona, were the very people most entitled to bear the arms "that are the guarantor of civic confidence."[119]

---

117 *La Vanguardia,* 18 April 1937, 4. A shorter piece appeared in *Solidaridad Obrera,* 18 April 1937, 10.

118 "There Can Be No Disarming of the Proletariat," *Solidaridad Obrera,* 18 April 1937, 6.

119 "The days of Arlegui and Martínez Anido" refers to when the CNT was being persecuted in Catalonia by joint employer–state terrorism.

Any legalities against the arming of workers or that insisted they produce their weapons permits were wrongheaded, because authority from any antifascist organization was permission enough.

The note ended with praise for workers who were on war footing: **"Today, a worker is a revolutionary. A revolutionary has to go around armed. His weapon underwrites the new order of things."**

That was a coherent train of thought, cognizant that there was a war on against fascists and reactionaries, both at the front and in the rear, but, front or rear, weapons constituted the sole guarantee on offer.

★

Jacobo Prince penned a letter/report to his Argentinean comrades, and in it he acknowledged receipt of the letters that had arrived and requested fresh addresses "so as to switch mailings around" and dodge the censors.[120]

He reported that the political crisis had been sorted out three weeks earlier by avoiding confrontation and reining in the demagogues and extremists. He described some of the motions endorsed at meetings of the anarchist groups as "catastrophic," *in all likelihood referring to the meeting of Anarchist Groups on 12 April, as cited above.*

The CNT was still extraordinarily full of life and "is standing up to the errors of its own people," whereas **the UGT had turned into a haven for the petite bourgeoisie.**

The situation was complicated because the masses were proving very diffident about the undue concessions made by the higher committees and, on the other hand, very receptive to the extremists.

He mentioned the "hate" existing "directed at the PSUC leaders" and the latter's attacks on the CNT-controlled war industries.

He complained about the influence and power of the PCE outside of Catalonia and within the police and censors' offices, the existence of *chekas* and maverick police, as well as some CNT comrades having gone missing. He foresaw an internal struggle within the UGT between wholesome elements and the Stalinists. "In any event, there is a brazen Russian mandate: **annihilate the CNT,** and all their agents are carrying this out, starting with physical elimination wherever possible."

PSUC people were not even waiting for the war to finish before finishing off the CNT and were using all means, "including exploiting matters of war." Things had happened that led him to believe that the PSUC folk were more interested in

---

120   FACA correspondence, Letter 33, 18 April 1937 [BAEL].

wiping out CNT personnel than fascists: "the tendency to corner us is apparent everywhere."

There was every indication that there was **no way out other than a outright showdown.**

However, "in the Centre [region] where the bolshies are taking over the UGT, lots of unhappy UGT workers are defecting to the CNT, which is growing, in the very zone where it is persecuted, whereas in Catalonia, where we bear the political responsibility of government," the CNT was stagnating.

Such bullying by the Stalinists and the drive to persecute CNT personnel was playing into the hands of

> irresponsible charlatans. Folk were coming out of their shells and there were repercussions. There is an association here by the name of the Friends of Durruti, Carreño being one of them, that reflects this trend.[121] These good folk operate like an opposition. The other day there was a big rally on behalf of the field hospitals and Federica went along to speak, and, by the way, she did ask the permission of the P[eninsulaur] C[ommittee], as we had her marked down for a different meeting.[122] **Well, those "friends" could find nothing better to do than to catcall at her and screech "What about 'our prisoners?'"** and other such nonsense. They hooted at the minister, a member of the cabinet and therefore, in their view, responsible for there being prisoners, when she did everything she could to get them out. The troublemakers were silenced by the audience, but none of them got the broken bones he deserved. **As for Federica, she was furious and told us that that would be her last time speaking in Barcelona,** until such time as some sanction was imposed on these people.

Prince explained that the settlement of the political crisis had not done away with the root causes of widespread discontent about unwarranted concessions made by the higher committees. That discontent was feeding all those "opposition" groups.

He gave his own opinion of the "impossible" Santillán, who explained everything away by throwing around random charges that people were "part of the old boy network (*enchufistas*) and spiteful."

He reported on a Libertarian Youth Regional Congress numbering 35,000 members, a congress that Prince himself had attended as representative of the

---

121   Rationalist schoolteacher Francisco Carreño, a prominent CNT member and public speaker in the 1930s. He served on the Durruti Column's War Committee and was a founder of the Friends of Durruti along with Jaime Balius and Pablo Ruiz.

122   Rally of Sunday, 11 April 1937.

P[eninsular] C[ommittee]. The congress had suggested the formation of a Revolutionary Youth Front, to which the POUM youth had already signed up. Accommodation with the PSUC youth had proved impossible, because of their reformist, democratic slogans.

He concluded his letter by pointing out, by way of a glimpse into day to day life, that the radio was at that moment broadcasting a football match, whereas just minutes earlier it had been raising the alarm about a possible air raid on the city.

Monday, 19 April

At 5:40 p.m., the **Generalidad Executive Committee** assembled in the Generalidad Palace under the chairmanship of Tarradellas, with all the councillors in attendance, except Justice.[123]

Tarradellas put forward a number of decrees approving special loans. He reported on the letter received from Giral, minister in the republican government, suggesting an exchange of prisoners, some of them convicted in the People's Courts. An argument erupted between Vidiella and Tarradellas over this, since the Generalidad government did not accept such handovers, whereas the republican government had begun to stake a claim to full powers in criminal matters. It was suggested (and approved) that the matter should be looked into along with the councillor for justice, Comorera, who was absent that day.

Asked by Tarradellas, **Doménech** stated that he was not conversant with the incidents that had occurred in Figueras castle.

Isgleas offered a briefing on the recent operations on the Aragon front and on the attack capabilities of the Karl Marx and Ascaso divisions. He appealed for the government to pay more attention to the Aragon front where an offensive could be mounted if additional war materials were supplied.

Miret asked if it was true that aircraft from Valencia were showing up late. **Isgleas** described the air force's performance as appalling.

Tarradellas raised the matter of the ineffectuality of passive air raid defenses. **Isgleas** pointed out that responsibility for that provision had been transferred to the Navy and Air Force Ministry. It was agreed that the defense councillor should expedite said transfer. **Vidiella** asked that those responsible for shortcomings in the passive antiaircraft defenses face sanction.[124]

Tarradellas's statements to Isgleas about the people of Barcelona being defenseless against air and sea attacks rehearsed arguments that had also been

---

123 "Minutes of the Generalidad Executive Council meeting of 19 April 1937."
124 The ineffectuality of the air raid defenses had been raised previously by the Generalidad Council on 8 March 1937.

outlined at a previous meeting of the Council. The solution to the problem did not lie in its being handed over to the central government. This was a blatant admission of incompetence by the Generalidad and an unconscionable and **criminal** dereliction of duty. **Besides, bombings and hunger were the best means of bringing the revolutionaries to heel.**

Capdevila, the CNT's councillor for economy, noted the central government's inroads into the powers of the Generalidad government.

Tarradellas moved that they pay no heed to orders not included in the agreement between the republican government and the Generalidad government.

Capdevila proposed seventeen decrees, endorsing the statutes of a range of Industrial Collectives and Groupings.

A number of decrees were signed up to in virtually every department.

Aurelio Fernández, councillor for health, asked **Artemi Aguadé,** councillor for the interior, to explain why twenty-one guards had been transferred from Lerida to Tarragona.

Aguadé explained the matter away. **Aurelio Fernández** persisted, asking for those guards to be returned to their previous posting, since it was the view of the CNT that their transfer was tantamount to an attack on the union. Aguadé stated that he could not accede to that request, because the transfer was proper, avoided confrontations and, besides, the rescinding of the order would be an undermining of his own authority.

Tarradellas intervened to underline the need to proceed with setting up the Security Council and establishment of the Unified Corps, with its personnel screened and its higher ranks and Commissioners appointed.

Aurelio Fernández warned of the need to prevent reprisals against former members of the Workers' and Soldiers' Councils.

Capdevila asked how things stood with the Housing Municipalization Decree. **Tarradellas** replied that they were awaiting a report from the Inter-Municipal Commission. The proceedings were wound up at 8:20 p.m.

The locking of horns between Aurelio Fernández and Artemi Aguadé within the Generalidad Council was an extension of their clashes earlier inside the Control Patrols secretariat and at meetings of the Security Junta. The Public Order issue that had triggered the government breakdown in March, was still unresolved.

At 10:00 p.m., the **Regional Committee** met at the Casa CNT-FAI.[125]

---

125   "Minutes of the Regional Committee meeting of 19 April, opened at ten o'clock at night, with full attendance of all its members" [IISH-CNT-85C1].

Valerio Mas, the secretary, briefed them on the excessive amount of paper that the Godó company had supplied to the daily *La Vanguardia*, on the campaign of slander targeting Maroto and the fact that the daily *Las Noticias* had referred to Maroto and the CNT as fascists.

It was agreed that "comrade Dionisios be told … to be extremely cautious about news items carried in the paper under his management."[126]

Mas read out "a communiqué from the Confederation of Co-Operatives in Catalonia, wherein the socialists sought to ensure that certain rights claimed by the Generalidad government were acknowledged and that its lead was followed." It was agreed that their response should be moderate, but that they should issue them with a reminder that "we already have accords that we have reached and cannot stray from them."

Domingo Ascaso reported on "the latest operations on the Huesca front and on the plummeting morale" in some battalions, to the extent that "**some four hundred comrades … have deserted** with a number of weapons and hand grenades and have come, willingly or not, down to Barcelona. The people in charge of the battalion having been unable to prevent this. And, to boot, there was the shameful fact that those deserters, as they fled the front, had had to be stripped of their weapons by some POUM battalions.

At this point an urgent telegram arrived "reporting the arrival of more deserters from the front." In view of the menace and urgency of the matter, serious decisions were made, implicit trust being placed in "the comrades from defense," who were urged "that, once we have clarity on these matters, the pair behind the first wave of desertion were to be shot and the other four hundred comrades (and we have a list of their home addresses, forwarded for this purpose) be placed under arrest that very night in their homes and taken to the Montjuich fortress," where the RC would determine which of them should be dispatched to the most dangerous fronts as a punishment and which were to be sent back to the front from which they had come.

The Commission charged with passing on these accords from the RC "to the defense comrades" was made up of Ascaso, Xena, and Berruezo.

Xena and Ascaso traded news about the arrest of "an adjutant of Reyes [a Stalinist] and those in charge of the airfield," who had been blamed for the loss of morale and the desertions from the front, since their planes had bombed a wooded area where CNT troops were located, whereas the enemy was on open ground. There was no question that air force, which as a rule did not support the troops, had bombed CNT personnel—which might account for "our comrades having deserted the Aragon front."

---

126   Antonio García Birlán, aka *Dionisios*, was managing editor of *La Vanguardia*.

After a serious and measured debate on loss of morale in the front lines, the discussion shifted to meetings to be held in concert with the UGT, to ensure that the 1st of May would be a working day, as long as "all that day's efforts were definitely toward the war effort."

Mas noted that the public had failed to turn out for most of the meetings arranged for the previous day, Sunday 18 April. Furthermore, he was critical of some of the things articulated by certain speakers and was passing a note on to the Propaganda Office. He specifically cited the speech given by "Tarrens from the Telephone Exchange," who had lashed out at Federica Montseny and the Generalidad government, overstated the losses in Santa Quiteria, and threatened to take revenge for the murders of CNT personnel in Seville, by killing thirty or forty fascists for every CNT fatality; Mas reckoned that, while the murders should be protested, no one had the authority to talk that way in the Confederation's name.

Severino Campos asked scathingly whether the remarks made by Toryho "in this morning's *Soli*" were also being "monitored by the Propaganda Section," a reference to the fact that, *at Mas's instigation, that Propaganda Section would be monitoring CNT speakers at meetings.* **Cortés**'s response was "No." **Mas** made a phone call to Toryho asking him "if his comments will be appearing in this morning's *Soli*," to which Toryho replied "No." A exchange on this matter then began between Campos, Clará, and Cortés.

A range of minor issues were hurriedly dealt with. **Berruezo** reported back on his meeting with Isgleas, who was already conversant with the business of the four hundred deserters and who was very happy about the accords reached by the RC, informing him "that he would issue orders to comrade Eroles that arrests were to be made this very night and the other pair to be summarily tried," once it had been determined what their responsibility was. He also informed him that at the same time "the aviators responsible for the recent failures were to be tried and severely punished" so that "our comrades will see that our justice is evenhanded and those who should fall, will."

Construction [Union] reported on the worrying inroads and expansion of the Friends of Durruti, "the fear being that a split might appear in our ranks." It proposed that the group be prohibited from using the CNT-FAI initials in its seal. The proceedings were wound up at 3:15 a.m.

*At these RC meetings, which usually turned into meetings broadened to include the CNT's higher committees or the broadly libertarian higher committees, all of the business and clashes of the day came up for discussion, with solutions and policy lines proposed regarding the most disparate matters, ranging from the military front to the divvying-up of councillorships, from the press to rallies. However, there was a glaring and almost utter **absence** of an issue very directly affecting the day-to-day* *existence of the working populace, one that had recently erupted into a violent hunger riot: the issue of Supplies, the extortionate price hikes, and the food shortages due to speculation. There was no mistaking the gulf between the problems dealt with by these higher committees and the real issues on the streets: air raids and hunger.*

Wednesday, 21 April

There were new riots involving women. One newspaper stated: "this morning the incidents in the markets were repeated. This time it was the turn of 'El Ninot' and El Clot. This time all it took was the presence of the security forces to break up the **women's demonstration** that had formed."[127] Another recounted: "again we had demonstrations by women, protesting the hike in food prices. A number of gangs of demonstrators forced some markets and shops to shut down."[128] It added that in the Calle Paris, one gang of demonstrators tried to bring a workshop to a standstill "so that they could join the demonstration" and the police were forced to intervene.

★

At 10:00 p.m., there was a meeting of the **higher committees**, with the RC, Local Federation of Unions, and the Libertarian Youth in attendance.[129]

Cortés specified the names of the speakers assigned to the rallies that were due to be held in concert with the UGT, to mark the First of May. Some thirty-three rallies had been scheduled and the speakers had been allotted the themes to be expanded upon. They were to abide strictly by these guidelines. He added the sneering comment "Anybody who doesn't like it should stay away."

The RC secretary, **Mas**, shared the news that the CNT's representatives in the Security Department were Aurelio, Eroles, Barrachina, and Portela, plus Castellote as security secretary.

Castellote delivered an oral report on the proceedings, reports, and accords arrived at by the Plenum of Regionals and Comarcals held recently in Valencia. With regard to Maroto, it was stated that he had fallen victim to "vile chicanery" and stood accused of having attended a meeting at which "it had been agreed that the Governor of Almería should be killed." As Maroto held the rank of lieutenant-colonel in his column, he had been "tried as a serviceman," but García

---

127 "Catalonia. Weekly Round-Up," *La Batalla*, 25 April 1937.

128 "High cost of living," *La Vanguardia*, 22 April 1937, 3.

129 "Minutes of the Regional Committee meeting held on 21 April at ten o'clock at night, in the presence of all its delegates, plus the Local Federation and the JJLL [Libertarian Youth] Committee" [IISH-CNT-85C1].

Oliver was going to move heaven and earth to see that he was "handed over to the civilian courts."

A detailed report was delivered on the horrific disaster in Málaga.

A letter was read out from Federica Montseny in which she threatened that she would not be speaking in public in Catalonia again "if she did not get satisfaction."[130] **Alfonso**, from the Local Federation, challenged the veiled accusations leveled at the Friends of Durruti as having been responsible for Federica Montseny's discomfort, declaring that "there was no way that anybody could be held to account when there was such a crowd of people."

Next up was the matter of the Industrial Unions and "the need for some sort of structure as a step in the direction of concentrating all our capital." The Local Federation reminded people of what a hindrance the "intervention law" promulgated by the Generalidad had been (because it left all the assets thus concentrated in Tarradellas's hands).

Aragon's contribution to the Plenum stood out as it denounced the activities of "state communists" out to seize power in the region, into which they had already sent "twenty three companies of carabineers—an armed, anti-revolutionary force par excellence—and, all the while, they will not let us have tanks, machine guns, or rifles," although these things were being sent to the luckier Guadalajara front.

The Catalan delegation tried to stand up to the prevailing anti-Catalanist sentiment, fostered by wrong-headed attitudes like Peiro's and by insults like the ones coming from councillor Isgleas who, on a visit to Valencia, never dropped in on the NC. It explained that Catalonia could not churn out more war material, for want of raw materials.

Attention then turned to the case of the Friends of Durruti, whose "propaganda should not be tolerated, given that Durruti is dead" and should not be "used as a recruiting sergeant by anybody." There was a suggestion that two agents be planted inside the group.

It was resolved that they should counteract the campaign to discredit the Confederation mounted by the "state communists," by promoting "a coordinated push against fascism in all its guises."

The Public Order situation was brought up for discussion again; things in Madrid were as disastrous as they were in Barcelona. It was reckoned that "to date" eighty-three CNT members had been murdered and a finger was pointed at Galarza as "the chief sponsor of this slaughter." His modus operandi consisted

---

130   Satisfaction for the boos, whistling, and cries for Maroto and other imprisoned antifascists to be set free that had interrupted her speech at the rally held on Sunday 11 April 1937 in the La Monumental bullring.

of dispatching "a company of security forces into the villages, where they murdered whomever they chose." Given that the situation was the same in the rest of Spain, they forecast a popular uprising that would "not leave a single guard behind to tell the story."

After some reports on other minor issues, Castellote concluded his report on the Valencia Plenum.

The Local Federation cut short the debate launched by the RC regarding the establishment of a confederal aid fund, with a further reminder that Tarradellas could do whatever he liked in that regard, since there was a decree empowering him to do so.

It was agreed that "once the notorious fifty-six decrees have been sorted out, the decree empowering Tarradellas to stick his nose" into collectivized ventures would have to be repealed.

The meeting ended at 3:30 a.m., and it was agreed to resume at 10:00 p.m.

Thursday, 22 April

At 6:35 p.m., the **Executive Council** met in the Generalidad Palace, presided over by Companys and with a full turnout of councillors, except for those from Justice and Economy.[131]

Companys remarked that "the republican government's policy of encroaching upon the powers of the Generalidad is becoming more pronounced by the day." He then alluded to the campaign to discredit Catalonia, which was no longer being depicted, as it had been initially, as the mainstay of the Republic. Catalans were now being portrayed as unscrupulous and it was clear to people abroad that the Generalidad was unable to resolve internal issues. All of which placed Catalan home rule "and, thus, the gains made by our revolution" in jeopardy.

He mentioned [Anthony] Eden's speech and dwelt on how the latter's words showed how poorly Catalonia was viewed in British government circles: **"Given a choice between Franco's government and Catalonia's, he preferred Euzkadi's."**[132] It was moved that examination of the decree establishing the Higher War Council be left for discussion at the next session.

Vachier's resignation as director-general of supplies and his replacement by Antonio Bertrán Suria were approved.

Tarradellas briefed them on the interruption of the monthly transfer of thirty million pesetas from the government of the Republic. He asked for

---

131   "Minutes of the Generalidad Executive Council meeting of 22 April 1937."

132   Anthony Eden was British Foreign Secretary between 1935 and 1938. *Euskadi* is the Basque name for the Basque region.

authorization to take the requisite steps, since the war would be a goner already, were it not for Catalonia's war production.

Isgleas reported that the airmen from Valencia who had failed to support the republican troops' advance in Aragon had been discharged, apparently because they had refused to fly. His request for arms to organize the divisions in Aragon had been postponed yet again, even though "our Aragon divisions are already organizing in conformity with central government orders." *Meaning that Aragon was still as poorly armed as ever, even though militarization and a unified command had been agreed to.* Later, he brought up the state of the artillery in Aragon, which, according to some expert reports, was practically defunct.

Aurelio Fernández suggested that a number of departments work together to look into an effective organization for tending to the refugees.

Tarradellas stated that assistance to refugees was costing Catalonia five million pesetas a week. **Companys** pointed out that such outlay should be defrayed by the central government, which was yet another reason to reactivate the economic relations between the two.

The supplies councillor, **Miret**, "raised the issue of meddling that stood in the way of a supplies policy and made it very hard to secure foreign currency from the government of the Republic." The **negotiated barter in goods** that had been worked out by the committees and town councils, which was ruining the Catalan economy, was spreading. He would not be held answerable for his department unless meddling by unions and local corporations was eradicated.

Aurelio Fernández declared that the Health and Social Assistance Department made its own provisions, as the Supplies Department had decided.

Miret brought up many examples of irregularities and abuses "in pricing, speculation, and fraud."

Isgleas indicated that he was all for unifying the Supplies service, but they would first have to endow it with the requisite efficiency, and, besides, the local committees could hardly be asked to cease operations as long as appropriate supply arrangements for them were not in place.

After a number of matters had been gone through, the proceedings were concluded at 9:05 p.m.

The complaints from the UGT supplies councillor, Miret, reflected the genuine chaos prevailing within that sector, which had quite plainly and simply reverted to barter at home, just as had happened in the summer of 1936, given that there was no foreign currency available for making purchases abroad. Supplies was in a free-for-all situation with committees and town councils in competition with one another, forcing prices up even higher.

★

At 10:00 p.m., there was a meeting of the **higher committees**, with the Defense and War Committees in attendance, plus **Arnau**, as the representative of the CNT's Catalan-language paper, *Catalunya*.[133]

Arnau laid out the paper's accounts and the losses it was generating and it was agreed that the *Soli* print-shop would lend a helping hand in its production and that a few improvements would be made to distribution arrangements lest the paper go extinct. It was also agreed that a referendum should be held among all the unions to determine who the managing editor and staffers should be, and this was to be held no later than 2 May. **Valerio Mas** offered to secure two vans from Public Services to help distribute the paper. Once this item had been dealt with, Arnau left the meeting.

Next, on to the situation within the Vivancos and Jover columns on the Aragon front.[134] **Jover** had awarded some furlough to a contingent of militias who had been hit hard during recent operations and whose morale was suffering badly after they had come under attack from their own air force. While on furlough in the town of Nunes, they had held some meetings at which they had agreed "to head off to Barcelona, like it or not" and not to return to the front "until fully equipped and endowed with tanks and planes." In light of that decision, the CNT commanders had put "the POUM comrades" on notice, getting them "to disarm the deserters."

A **debate erupted between Defense, War, and the RC**, and it was agreed that "tomorrow, the 23rd, *Soli* would issue an appeal along pretty much these lines: "Comrades from the Kropotkin Battalion currently in Barcelona are to report to the 'Spartacus' (Docks) barracks at 7:00 a.m. on Saturday, to move out immediately; with them will march the forty being held in Montjuich. Any others failing to present themselves to be arrested will also brought to the front."[135] The argument was that this step was necessary, lest the deserters' example spread to the entire front. Enlistment did not rule out an investigation that would sanction the guilty parties. The arrival of militia members from the Tierra y Libertad Column, with due permission, was also reported.

Half rabble-rousing and half in desperation, **Lara** stated that the higher committees should ask the same discipline of themselves as they required of the front lines, where "if we see a ship go by or a carriage laden with weapons," these had to be impounded and dispatched to the Aragon front.

---

133 "Regional Committee meeting held on 22 April, at ten o'clock at night, in the presence of all its members plus a delegation from the Defense and War Committee as well as comrade Arnau, representing *Catalunya*" [IISH-CNT-85C1].

134 Vivancos was the delegate from the Los Aguiluchos Column and Jover that of the Ascaso Column. The Los Aguiluchos Column eventually amalgamated with the Ascaso Column.

135 Being held in the Montjuich prison, we imagine, for desertion.

Juanel suggested the appointment of political Commissioners as a solution.

Jover stated that "we urgently need to appoint nine hundred Commissioners," and then gave an "apologia" for the political Commissioner, highlighting the merits he ought to have and his cultural efforts he would have to undertake "in order to knit together all the various ideologies" that might be found coexisting within the same Division.

After a far-fetched and nonsensical debate "about which flag should be the only one regarded as the Spanish flag and displayed at all gatherings, social or war-related alike," the meeting was brought to a close at 2:30 a.m.

Desertions from the Aragon front were a serious problem and added to the loss of morale due to inadequate weaponry, distrust of other units of differing political persuasions, a principled opposition to militarization, weariness with an interminable war that they had marched off to as "volunteers," and so on. It was a specifically CNT problem, because in other units, the slightest hint of indiscipline—and we are not talking here about desertion—was clamped down on immediately, without publicity, argument, or ethical torment, by having people shot.

The argument about the flag was as laughable and irrelevant as the people who raised it.

But still the higher committees were not addressing the serious supplies issue with which the city of Barcelona was beset.

Friday, 23 April

In the run-up to his party's congress, **Josep Rebull**, regarded as the leader of the **POUM Left**, published an internal bulletin in which he spelled out his **criticisms of Nin and the Executive Committee of the POUM, a party he considered adrift.**

> A party that does not speak plainly, that cannot tell black from white; that does not know what it wants and how to get it, is never going to be in a position to lead the working class to ultimate triumph. We think it might be of interest to quote a few extracts lifted at random from our central mouthpiece, *La Batalla*: "Dictatorship of the proletariat means authority wielded by the working class. In Catalonia we can state that dictatorship of the proletariat already exists." (From a report of a speech by Nin in *La Batalla*, 3 September 1936.)[136]
>
> Within a few weeks of saying that, the very same comrade Nin, representing our party, joined the Generalidad Council of Catalonia, which, according to *La Batalla* on 27 September, constituted the *government of the Revolution.*

---

136 This contention by Nin constituted a very serious flaw in his analysis, no matter what those who would make him a saint may say.

And we were still part of that Council when comrade Juan Andrade wrote the following in his "Political Diary Notes":

"The actual reason the old bureaucracy has survived is not technical but political. That means, or signifies, that the machinery of State has undergone no fundamental change and that the forms of bourgeois domination survive … The bourgeoisie machinery of State is still in operation, albeit bereft of the most vital necessary repairs." (*La Batalla*, 1 December 1936.)

Despite such statements, which in our view were never censured by the Executive Committee, whose members cannot have grasped the truth they encapsulated, the Party leadership regarded partnership in the Generalidad government as identical to the unity of action demanded by the fight against fascism. That stance was maintained until after the POUM was ousted from the government by the bourgeois political forces to which we had afforded *our loyal cooperation and our prestige*. (See *La Batalla* of 16 and 17 December 1935, editorials)....

The same confusion exists with regard to all the burning issues of our Revolution. Clarity is startlingly absent....[137]

And this is only a small sample of what we might say, which we will point out later to demonstrate the utter lack of political understanding and responsibility of our Party's leadership, something glaringly obvious to anyone reading our own press with care."

And in **another article** in the very same *Bulletin*, Rebull contended:

"The POUM's Second Congress is to meet in extraordinary circumstances.[138]

Although the revolution is in jeopardy, no advantageous exit is apparent. Plainly, the party of the revolution is not at hand.

The POUM could have been that party. But its political and organizational performance, mirroring the utter bewilderment among its leadership, has squandered the legacy that Maurín left us.[139]

---

137 Of the many confused notions of the POUM's EC, Rebull zeroed in primarily on the one he thought most important. The confusion about the body capable of becoming the agency of workers' power: council, committee, or trade union. In the very same *Boletín*, in an article entitled "For the Creation of Workers', Peasants', and Combatants' Councils," Rebull offered an outstanding definition of the terms "committee" and "council," as well as making a clear, precise, and emphatic comparison between both those bodies, while explaining why the unions could never be an agency of worker power.

138 The May Events and then the political persecution of the POUM from 16 June 1937 onward ensured that this congress was never held.

139 The severity of the attack on Nin, who, back then, **had not yet become a sacred icon immune from all criticism**, showed the intense unease that existed among many POUM

Can the POUM be saved? Can the POUM yet be the party of the revolution?[140] Many militants with a thorough knowledge of the POUM's situation, and who have witnessed the leadership's errors, are disheartened in this regard. They view the approach of the Second CONGRESS with a resignation unbefitting of revolutionaries.[141]

Well now, the Second CONGRESS can be, must be, the RECTIFICATION CONGRESS. This is a life or death issue for the Party and for the very Revolution. We are ready to fight all-out to see to it that this is so. We are against "Trotskyism"—which is in any case unknown within our Party—but we are similarly against those who are out, with no proof, to uncover "Trotskyists" within the POUM.

We are for a genuinely revolutionary Marxist party and it is our conviction that, if the membership reacts against the SECOND CONGRESS, the POUM will be the party of the revolution.

To this end, we need widespread and democratic debate. But the CC has not taken the same view. It has even gone so far as to trespass against the POUM's statutes, without even offering the party any explanation.

While this was happening, and before it happened, down in Valencia a deeply reformist faction has been allowed for months on end to control a weekly paper, through which it has been able to misrepresent our party's revolutionary essence in the eyes of the laboring masses of Levante.[142]

And already it has been announced that there will be no postponing of the SECOND CONGRESS.[143] To work, comrades! Let us harness every hour, ev-

---

militants, who were in mourning for Maurín.

140 The very posing of the question was itself an utterly devastating critique of the POUM EC's political strategy. Besides, this was the same question being asked by the tiny Trotskyist groups, although here it was coming from a prominent POUM member who was also making his criticisms from a BOC-ist (or Maurinist) perspective, levelling them at a leadership made up of ex-Trotskyists (or ex-Izquierda Comunista members), like Nin and Andrade.

141 Josep Rebull's criticisms of the POUM's EC, very well argued, devastating, and articulated with a certain radicalism to boot, could not tolerate any reconciliation with the existing POUM EC. However, it has to be admitted that they were made during the period of discussion in the run-up to a congress and, in that regard, were wholly respectful of party discipline.

142 Actually, it might rightly be stated that there was a range of POUMs coexisting within the POUM, ranging from the right-wing Valencia faction, whose positions were very close to Stalinism, through to Rebull's very critical attitude, to an EC led by Nin and Andrade.

143 Inevitably, there would, given the May Events. In the end, just as the Second Congress was about to be reconvened, the POUM was outlawed and all its members targeted for political persecution from 16 June 1937 onwards. The EC was rounded up by the Stalinists. Furthermore, Nin was kidnapped, tortured, and murdered by the GPU. He stopped being a militant susceptible to attack, and became a sacred, unassailable martyr.

ery minute, for the sake of the POUM's triumph. That triumph is not going to be secured unless the SECOND CONGRESS brings a complete rectification of political direction and unless there is a review of past conduct at the same time.

Let each cell make a stand. No militant is entitled to await the SECOND CONGRESS like a spectator. Let nobody say that we had the leadership that we deserved.

Saturday, 24 April

The finishing touches were put to the draft of the "**Motion presented to the Local Federation of Anarchist Groups, Confederal Defense Groups, and Libertarian Youth**," which, as had been agreed at the Plenum of Anarchist Groups held on 11 and 12 April, was to be issued to all the Barcelona anarchist groups, to the CNT defense committees, and to the Libertarian Youth.

The motion was even more radical and scathing than the initial motion by Group 12 from Gracia, and it reflected the revolutionary character that the barrio committees' defense sections had stamped on the proceedings of the plenary meeting of Barcelona anarchist groups.

In their foreword to the Motion, the drafters recalled how they had been appointed by the Plenum held on 11 and 12 April and they underlined how they were aware of the extraordinary nature of the time: "since we regard the historic times in which we are living as being of such transcendence that any deviation from them could cause serious upset to the revolution under way."

They also acknowledged the importance of "the bonds of principle that exist between the CNT and the FAI," denying that the anarchists' radicalism might alienate the syndicalists and cause a falling-out between the two organizations. There was no way that the FAI could wash its hands of its "revolutionary technique, since that would require it to espouse false positions." Their argument was that anarchists "as the vanguard of the Revolution, remain inviolable. It cannot be otherwise." The only thing that mattered was "driving forward the social revolution begun on 19 July."

The motion espoused the same stance as Group 12 had advocated, which had been passed unanimously, and the rejection of collaborationism as expressed by the Plenum.

Their conclusion was "the implementation of radical steps is an overriding necessity if we are to avoid our movement's slow deviation in the direction of the reformist camp; a justified fear, if we bear in mind the 'planting' within our movement of personnel of curious provenance."

With the foreword, with its narration of the political and social factors that had had an influence on the working party, now out of the way, "and in the belief that we speak for the feeling of the plenum," they set out the final Motion, which was blessed with great strength and beauty of expression, freely embodying the revolutionary wishes of Barcelona's anarchist militants, shorn of self-censorship and threats, and free from the higher committees' collaborationist horse-trading:

First

Comrades holding official posts should be disowned, the reasoning being that their performance has not been equal to the circumstances, nor has it matched the mandate they had been given.

Consequently, there should be a **reversion to the antistate revolutionary terrain in accordance with anarchism's theoretical and tactical principles.**

Second.

We are to proceed with the establishment of a Revolutionary Local Committee for the purpose of coordinating the armed struggle against fascism and the counterrevolution in all its manifestations.

Third.

For the sake of the proper progress of the revolution, the confederal Organization is going to have to implement the **socialization** of agriculture, industry, and trade with all due urgency; while at the same time introducing the producer's card and the family wage.

Fourth.

There shall be rigorous monitoring of the civilian population, so that no one may be excused from his obligation to lend his assistance to the great drive for liberation.

Fifth

The responsible committees shall take appropriate steps to ensure that all have a sense of **revolutionary discipline** as a guarantee that the social revolution's interests take priority over everything. **With classes abolished**, no one will be able to evade doing his duty for the benefit of the collectivity.

Barcelona, 24 April 1937.

This Motion, along with the poster distributed and put up on walls around the city of Barcelona by the Friends of Durruti in late April, constitute the two most forward-looking revolutionary texts from that point in time that culminated inevitably in the May insurrection.

Comparing it with the Group 12 draft, the Motion boasts the addition in its second item of a reference to the struggle's being not just against fascism but also against Stalinist counterrevolution.

The references in item three to the producer's card and to the family wage had been amply discussed within the libertarian movement and they addressed libertarian concerns about social justice. The producer's card was meant to exclude from the rationing system, and from the social benefits won back in July, any who were not proletarians or did not earn their living by working; it was a direct swipe at rentiers and bourgeois: the family wage was meant to favor and protect families with several underage children.

There was a determined push to bring the economy under socialized ownership, that being an idea that overrode and incorporated the notion of collectivization, which was considered to be a stage beneath socialization. It was also a counterattack against the creeping state control of the economy by the Generalidad government. In items four and five, the focus was on the need to resort to repressive measures against the Revolution's enemies. It was no accident that the May Events insurrection erupted nine days after this Motion was announced.

Sunday, 25 April

"At 7:00 a.m., as **Roldán Cortada**, personal advisor to Labor Councillor Vidiella (himself a leading light of the UGT) was out with some friends, spending the day outside Barcelona, a gang of five or six individuals stopped the car in which he was traveling, beside the bridge in Molins de Llobregat, and asked to see some papers. As Roldán Cortada climbed out of the vehicle, he was riddled with bullets and died on the spot."[144] The killing was attributed to a gang of CNT militants.

The press carried a **notice from the Supplies Department** urging town councils to "ensure an end of the difference currently existing between the prices set by the Supplies Department and wholesale prices."[145]

It was noted how frequently the complaints were coming in from the town commissions, who took exception to "the excessive price hikes in basic necessities"; these complaints were justified, but the department thought that it was up to the town councils to sort them out, because they were "the ones charged with overseeing the strict governance of the prices it set for the wholesalers, which in no way excuse the pricing hike." Then it made do with repeating the prices the department had set for sales to wholesalers, without any illusion that they might

---

144 Caballé, *Barcelona Roja*, 93.
145 "Rising Subsistence Costs in the Comarcas," *Solidaridad Obrera*, 25 April 1937, 8.

be adhered to, but simply in order to give "some idea of the huge difference there is between the department-set tariffs and the arbitrary pricing of sales to the public."

So, pricing was chaotic and entirely out of control. Neither the Supplies Department nor the town councils had the ability to actually impose prices. In the absence of the price control committees of the old supplies committees, which had been disbanded by Comorera, PRICES WERE SET BY THE SHOPKEEPERS' DICTATORSHIP. It was the foreseeable and inevitable consequence of the free market fundamentalism peddled by Comorera and the PSUC.

★

The **Construction, Woodworking, and Decorating Industrial Union** held a special assembly in the Victoria Theatre to boost socialization in its sector. The talk turned to the standard wage and there was a call for Maroto's release.[146]

Since 19 July 1936, the (CNT) Woodworkers Union had rationalized production by doing away with the smaller, economically unviable workshops, reorganized the productive arrangements in the sector by means of industrial concentration and rationalization, giving rise to so-called confederal workshops, in large, well-lighted and -ventilated hangars, outfitted with the requisite machinery and specializations. In addition, production was organized so that it would not be beholden to the outside world for raw materials. By late 1937, the sector would be employing eight thousand workers.

The Woodworkers Union was opposed to any sort of intrusion, funding, or interference by the State or other official institutions, bureaucracies, and inefficiencies. It was also opposed to the "trade-union capitalism" found in certain segments of the working class—meaning the introduction of inequality between the workers themselves, depending on the firm or sector to which they belonged—which flew in the face of the whole idea of socialization. "The easy thing, the logical thing for some people would have been to conjure up these collectivizations, which are nothing more than huge cooperatives within which only those industries with a life of their own will enjoy an enchanted life. But at the same time, they would leave the poor to their own resources, which is nothing short of creating two classes: the new rich and the eternally poor, an inequality that cannot be tolerated! We are all for the collectivization of all industries, but their funds should be pooled and shared out fairly. What we cannot accept is poor collectives and rich collectives."[147]

---

146   *La Vanguardia*, 28 April 1937, 2.

147   Carlos Semprún-Maura, *Revolución y contrarrevolución en Cataluña (1936–1937)* (Barcelona: Tusquets, 1977), 110.

Barcelona's Socialized Woodworkers [Union], even though it was one of the first to be set up and it operated consistently right up until Francoist troops entered the city, was never legally registered and at all times its stance was to shun any Generalidad role in revamping industrial activity, as already noted, as well as a critical line on the Collectivizations Decree.

★

Antonio Sesé, general secretary of the UGT in Catalonia, penned a letter to Companys in which he urged him to call a special and immediate meeting of the Generalidad Council because of the seriousness of the situation.[148] Sesé complained of the "military occupation of Puigcerdá and the entire northern part of Catalonia by FAI personnel, with leading personnel with government responsibilities playing an active part therein," preventing "freedom of circulation along the Barcelona to Puigcerdá highway." Sesé explained that the corps of carabineers was being ignored, allowing "the export of capital assets on the part of leading elements from the CNT," how UGT workers in the Barcelona metalworking plants were facing retaliation designed to "force them to join the CNT," how banditry was rampant in the Catalan countryside and how there had been calls for personal attacks to be mounted on Rodríguez Salas, Comorera, and "the craven murder carried out this very morning against the person of our comrade, Roldán Cortada." His conclusion was that appropriate action was required as a matter of urgency.

Sesé suggested that the defense councillor and interior security councillor should withdraw "the FAI forces and other irregular forces from the borders, disarming them," and he threatened that the UGT would pull its representatives out of the government, unless the Cerdaña was occupied immediately by Public Order troops as a first step, with the bullying of UGT workers and the banditry that was the scourge of the Catalan countryside tackled thereafter.

Antonio Sesé, the UGT's secretary in Catalonia, was insisting that the Generalidad government bring the FAI's rule in the Cerdaña to an immediate end.

Monday, 26 April

At 10:00 p.m., there was a meeting of the **CNT higher committees.**[149]

Aguilar reported on the smuggling operation mounted by comrades from

---

148 Antonio Sesé, "Honorable Sir (Barcelona, 25 April 1937)" [FPI-AH-43-24-00107].
149 "Meeting of the CNT Regional Committee held on 26 April 1937, at ten o'clock at night" [IISH-CNT-85C1].

the NC and involving gold, gems, and banknotes; it had been discovered on the border with people caught *in flagrante* and arrested. Those present at the meeting adopted the overall line that the comrades arrested should sacrifice themselves, thereby protecting "the honor of our beloved Organization." *This was not cynicism, but a grandiose cult of the Organization, for whose sake it was considered right that individuals should be sacrificed.*

Distribution [Union] added that the operation "might look criminal, when it was, at bottom, merely **one of many operations mounted in order to meet organizational needs.**" *Was this a euphemistic reference to purchases of arms or foodstuffs?*

It was agreed that the NC treasurer, Aguilar, and Batlle (its lawyer) should "sort this matter out as best they can." After a number of minor or procedural issues had been dealt with, the Workers' Control Committee from the Telephone Exchange described the problems created by the Esplugas town council, which wanted to impose a monthly levy of ten thousand pesetas upon them. The Telephone Exchange Committee argued that if every town was to follow suit, the Telephone service would have to "close its doors." He reminded everyone how the Committee was contributing a million pesetas a month, in hard cash, to the war effort, and was spending a further million a month on communication installed on the front lines. It was agreed that a delegation would pay the town council a visit to get it to reduce the excessive size of what appeared to be a municipal war levy.

There was a report on the constant incidents of provocation in Sadurní de Noya [Sant Sadurní d'Anoia] caused by the rivalry in the town between the long-standing CNT and a brand-new UGT, and a call went out for CNT militants to show more sensitivity.

A report was given on the "outrage yesterday targeting the person of Roldán Cortada" and a delegation was appointed to attend the funeral: it would be made up of Clará, Marcó, and Cortés.

It was also reported that the events in Castelldefels had been due to an attempted revolt by right-wing and monarchist elements who were formally socialists [PSUC members] but whose background was Catholic. Five people had been arrested. The task of monitoring the case brought against them in the courts was entrusted to Eroles.

Printing Trades [Union] requested that, before any meetings opened, a reading of the minutes from the preceding meeting be given, something that was never done. It launched into a lengthy history of mistakes detected in the minutes as drawn up by the RC's "perpetual" recording secretary and "amiably" criticized the manner in which they were being written, albeit that there was recognition that lately the minutes had not been "as imperative and facetious as before."

It censured the stance adopted by Merino, from the Local Federation of Anarchist Groups, at committee meetings and "what happened this morning with comrade Castellote." To avert such things, it moved "that the RC, meaning its members, refrain from being judgmental and involving itself in debates."

Liberal Professions [Union] lobbied on behalf of accords being at all times implemented "by CNT personnel," its view being that "if implemented by other comrades, the solutions arrived at might be distorted." *This union was carping about CNT accords being put into effect by FAI personnel.*

Valerio Mas felt that he was being criticized and enduring veiled reproaches. He explained that, given the gravity of certain events that cried out for swift resolution, he had relied upon the influence that the committees of the FAI or of the Libertarian Youth had in some places. Likewise, he had recently looked to Portela, Eroles, and Aurelio, on the basis that these were people well versed in public order issues. All of those present ratified their confidence in the RC secretary.

There was some discussion of the dispatch of excessive numbers of carabineers to Catalonia, urging the NC to step in to ensure that Galarza and Negrín were made aware of this concern.

Distribution [Union] launched into a very lengthy report explaining how Mas had commissioned it to answer questions from a Mexican journalist, and it passed one of the questions on to those present at the meeting: "whether the FAI and CNT do or do not have a program." This triggered "a very lively argument" that lasted "for more than an hour." Some, the majority, said yes; the rest said no. *The minutes offer no clear explanation of whether the Mexican journalist got his answer, nor what that program might have been. The front was shaky, the Stalinist threat was becoming more substantial by the day and, on the streets, hunger ruled. Meanwhile, the higher committees were caught up in byzantine, abstract arguments and debating whether or not they had a program.*

Light & Power [Union] reported that the central government had dismissed three hundred guards who had not made it through the selection procedure; but Aguadé was refusing to abide by that order.

Healthworkers [Union] reported that "seven of our comrades were on the verge of being shot by the Maciá-Companys Column," for wanting to leave it. A telephone call had been made to the officers to forestall any such outcome.

Proceedings were wound up at 3:30 a.m.

Tuesday, 27 April

Companys presided over the **burial of Roldán Cortada**. UGT members had arranged for shops to be shut throughout the city from one o'clock that afternoon. In Hospitalet de Llobregat, shots were fired when the police tried to arrest one of the alleged perpetrators of the Roldán Cortada murder "with bombs being hurled at the agents of the authorities!"[150]

Dionisio Eroles had the files on those being held in preventive detention at Police Headquarters and at the Remand Prison re-examined, and secured the release of a hundred detainees.[151]

★

Some days earlier, the Generalidad government had dispatched public order forces to **Bellver** and nearby villages, in anticipation of a probable confrontation with the anarchists of the Cerdaña.[152]

★

According to a French police report on the incidents in Bellver de Cerdaña on 27 April:

> On learning that a gun-battle had taken place in Bellver between the local residents, most of them members of the Esquerra Republicana of Catalonia, and men from the Puigcerdá FAI, and that there had been dead and wounded, notably MARTIN, Antonio, erstwhile head of the Puigcerdá government, I travelled to Llivia in order to gather all possible intelligence regarding the incidents that had occurred.[153]
>
> I ran into a member of the Committee in charge of providing victuals to Barcelona; he told me about Antonio's death and filled me in on how those tragic events had occurred.
>
> He stated to me that, there had been a number of incidents in Bellver due to the arrival in Puigcerdá of members of the Seo d'Urgell CNT who had just had an audience with the Puigcerdá committee regarding the arrival in the Spanish Cerdaña of a sizable contingent of carabineers.
>
> For a start, the **residents of Bellver had barred the way to the anarchists from La Seo** as they were arriving.[154] After a number of exchanges, they were allowed to proceed on their way to Puigcerdá, where meetings had been held

---

150   Caballé, *Barcelona Roja*, 94. See also the front page of *La Vanguardia* for 28 April 1937.

151   *La Vanguardia*, 28 April 1937, 2.

152   Joan Pons Garlandí, *Un republicà enmig faistes* (Barcelona: Edicions 62, 2008), 152.

153   Antonio Martín Escudero, murdered on 27 April 1937, outstanding leader of the libertarian La Cerdaña canton.

154   **Bold face** added by the author of this book to the original.

over the previous few days regarding the carabineers' arrival. In the course of one such conversation, what had happened in Bellver was brought up, and it was decided that several members of the Puigcerdá FAI would proceed, along with some from La Seo, to Bellver, to **parley** with the Committee in that village and forestall any repetition of such incidents. And this was done.

On reaching Bellver, their cars pulled up on the highway before coming to the bridge at the entrance to the village. Several spokesmen stepped forward, but **when they reached the half-way point on the bridge, they were greeted by a volley of rifle shots.** Nobody was hurt at that juncture and they made their way back to their cars. It was at that point that a heavy fusillade erupted, in the course of which two members of the La Seo Committee were killed and two people from Puigcerdá were seriously wounded.... They were taken to the hospital in Puigcerdá where MARTIN died during the night, at around 23:00 hours.[155]

The shooting continued until 20:00 hours, leading to several more wounded, whose conditions do not seem at present to give cause for concern. A number of them have been treated in Puigcerdá Hospital and most in their own homes.

The murder of Antonio Martin in Bellver, the result of an ambush, put the defense committees all over Catalonia on alert and they made ready to respond properly to the next provocation.[156] The higher committees were very much aware that the murder had been prepared by the Generalidad government, in league with the Stalinists (PSUC) and Catalan nationalists (Estat Catalá-ERC).

Wednesday, 28 April

In the morning, eight CNT militants from Hospitalet, who had happened to be arrested on the Barcelona highway at Molins, were placed in the cells at the Palace of Justice, arbitrarily accused of Roldán Cortada's murder.[157]

---

155   The driver, Joan Fortuny, a nineteen-year-old anarchist from La Seo de Urgel, was killed instantly.

156   The entire investigation into what happened in the Cerdaña represents the fruit of close collaboration between Agustín Guillamón and Antonio Gascón; together, they have published a number of joint studies on the subject. See the articles published in *Catalunya* and *Cuadernos Republicanos*, as well as the entry under Antonio Martín in Casciolo and Guillamón, *Biografías del 36*.

157   "Shedding light on What Happened in Molins de Llobregat," *Solidaridad Obrera*, 4 May 1937.

Thursday, 29 April

Following information supplied by the PSUC, several leading CNT militants from Molins, renowned for their part in the events of 19–20 July 1936 in the area, and four of whom were CNT members of the town council, were called upon to make statements at the Palace of Justice in Barcelona regarding their alleged part in the killing of Roldán Cortada.[158]

★

The Standing Municipal Committee discussed the proposal that the Municipal Supplies Commission "make meat rationing in Barcelona compulsory," as had previously been done with brown coal. Before starting to ration, it was necessary that the Generalidad's Supplies Department be contacted so as to achieve, for one thing, a reduction in meat prices and, for another, some adjustment of pricing to reality, in order to preempt "the complete absence of supplies."[159]

Rationing of foodstuffs became imperative when shortages in supply had become obvious, shortages that may well have been due to an actual absence or to their being swallowed up by the black market, when "legal" prices differed starkly from "actual" pricing. The fact that the authorities described the market prices as abusive and imposed sanctions did nothing to diminish the thriving black market, because that, always and everywhere, assumed that there was a disparity in both supplies and hunger among the populace, plus the wastefulness of those social strata capable of affording the "actual" prices.

★

Jacobo Prince wrote his Argentinean comrades a **letter** in which he recounted his continuous travel from place to place on a propaganda tour.[160]

He described the political situation as having "reached a supremely grave and complicated pass" in which the efforts of the comrades in charge "to avert something irreparable" appeared to "accord well with the seriousness [of the moment]."

It struck him as "obvious that political conspiracy is bearing fruit, but it is equally true that the absence of a disciplined movement leads to making mistakes and to provocations succeeding." **Officials wrestling with the situation felt that they were at risk of being swept aside by the masses:** "the enemy knows this

---

158   Ibid.
159   *Gaseta Municipal de Barcelona* (1937), 120.
160   FACA correspondence, Letter 35, 29 April 1937 [BAEL].

and plays upon it. When all is said and done, we can be sure that a lid will be kept on the situation, for now. Later, we shall see."

He reported the cancellation of all the rallies scheduled to be held on 1 May, concluding, very pragmatically, that "be that as it may, it needs to be proclaimed, loud and clear, that the blame for all this lies with the bolshies, first, because it is largely the truth and, secondly, because they will be saying the same about us all round the world."[161]

Late April

The French surrealist poet **Benjamin Péret**, the Fourth International's representative in Spain, having sought refuge in the Durruti Column following death threats from the Stalinists, wrote, shortly before his departure for Paris: "Throughout all this time, Barcelona workers have gone without bread and meat and so on, even as the luxury hotels and restaurants were brimming with food. But, exhausted from hours spent waiting in endless queues for a crust of bread or a little milk, the people are quietly beginning to grumble about the PSUC-protected small traders. Fifteen days ago, the women rebelled in Barcelona's markets, ransacking a number of ships. Taken aback, the Generalidad, has set up a commission of inquiry into speculation, but the cost of living continues to rise and basic necessities are more and more scarce."[162]

The Friends of Durruti set out their program in a **poster** with which they covered the walls of Barcelona toward the end of April 1937.[163] On those posters and BEFORE THE MAY EVENTS, they argued the need for the bourgeois Generalidad government to be REPLACED by a Revolutionary Junta; it read:

Friends of Durruti Group. To the working class.

1. A **Revolutionary Junta** to be set up, comprised of workers from city and country and by combatants.

---

161 The "bolshies" being the Stalinists.

162 Benjamin Péret, "Revolution and Counterrevolution in Spain," in *Oeuvres complètes*, vol. 7, 165–167. A footnote suggests that the unpublished article was written in the last week of April 1937. For a biographical note on Benjamin Péret, see Casciolo and Guillamón, *Biografías del 36*, 277–286.

163 There is a reproduction of the original in Agustín Guillamón, *Ready For Revolution: The CNT Defense Committees in Barcelona, 1933–38* (AK Press and KSL, Oakland, 2014), 93.

2. Family wage. Ration card. **The economy to be directed and distribution overseen by the trade unions.**

3. The counterrevolution to be liquidated.

4. A revolutionary army to be established.

5. Public order to be under the absolute control of the workers.

6. Steadfast opposition to any armistice.

7. Proletarian justice.

8. The exchanges of V.I.P.s to cease.

Attention, workers: our Group is opposed to the onward march of the counter-revolution. The Public Order decrees sponsored by Aiguadé are not to be implemented.[164] We demand the release of Maroto and other arrested comrades.

All power to the working class.
All economic power to the unions.
Instead of the Generalidad, the Revolutionary Junta.

That April 1937 poster anticipated and accounted for the leaflet circulated during the May Events and broached many of the topics and concerns dealt with by Balius in articles he had published in *Solidaridad Obrera*, *La Noche*, and *Ideas* (on revolutionary courts, prisoner exchanges, the need for the rearguard to live for the war, etc.). For the first time, we have broached here the need for a **Revolutionary Junta to supplant the bourgeois Generalidad government.**[165] That Revolutionary Junta was defined as a revolutionary government made up of workers, peasants, and militia members. *But the most significant thing was the articulation together of those last three slogans. The supplanting of the bourgeois Generalidad government by a Revolutionary Junta appears alongside the "All power to the working class" and "All economic power to the unions."*[166]

---

164 As noted in the Glossary below, Artemi Aguadé's surname is frequently spelled as Aiguadé, Aiguader, or Aguader.

165 How the Revolutionary Junta was characterized by the Friends of Durruti was subject to variation and it altered as the months went by. But no one was left in any doubt as to the importance of the slogans in that April 1937 poster. Not only did the establishment of a Revolutionary Junta signify the end of the bourgeois Generalidad government, but it also meant the establishment of an umbrella agency of the working class quite separate from antifascist organizations and state structures: "all power to the working class" and "all economic power to the unions." In 1939, Munis, in an interview he gave to *Lutte Ouvrière*, held that the terms "revolutionary junta" and "soviet" employed by the Group were synonymous.

166 Balius was very much alive to the importance of the watchwords set out in the April 1937 poster: "May 1937 is Spain's Kronstadt. It could only have arisen in Catalonia, given the

*The political program spelled out in that poster, right before the May Events, is without question the most forward-looking and far-sighted one from any of the existing proletarian groups and it makes the Friends of Durruti the **revolutionary vanguard of the Spanish proletariat** at that critical and crucial point in time, as was acknowledged by the POUM and by the Bolshevik-Leninist Section of Spain.[167]*

Saturday, 1 May

"**The talk in Barcelona** ... is of resolution of the Generalidad crisis, everyone wanting that government, reflecting the concord and unity of the great trade unions and antifascist parties, to be the government after the victory of the People's Army."[168]

The RC held a special meeting with the Commission dispatched to the Cerdaña. The Commission reported, first of all, upon the serious reasons that had impelled it to return to Barcelona "before peace was restored to that area."[169]

A certain **Villadiu** from Bellver had informed the Commission that "your comrade Martín was not murdered by us, as has been claimed." This Villadiu explained that "from various points along the highway, your people swooped on Bellver and, before they were across the river, they were shooting randomly at anything and everything; thereby squandering their ammunition—the empty cartridges were still visible on the ground, along with empty champagne and wine bottles."

He further explained: "Martín arrived by car—for who knows what purpose—and, as he got out of it, he was struck by one of the shots fired at him by the locals who were panicked about the anarchists coming to steal their land. Some came in from La Seo, others from Puigcerdá."[170]

---

might of the CNT. And just as the Kronstadt sailors and workers in Russia rose up to cries of 'All power to the soviets,' so the Friends of Durruti Group demanded 'All power to the Unions,' and we did so publicly in the many posters that were put up throughout Barcelona city and in the manifesto that we issued and that we managed to get printed in the heat of battle." Jaime Balius, "For the Sake of the Truth," *Le Combat syndicaliste*, 2 September 1971. See, also, Munis's remarks in *La Voz Leninista*, no. 2.

167 Juan Andrade, "CNT-POUM," in *La Batalla*, 1 May 1937.

168 *Mi revista* no. 14, 1 May 1937.

169 "Special Meeting of the Regional Committee of Catalonia together with the Commission that was dispatched to Puigcerdá, Bellver and La Seo de Urgel, held on 1 May 1937" [IISH-CNT-85C1].

170 The murder of Martín was followed up by excuses for it and demonization of the murdered man.

The delegates from the Commission went on with their report, recounting "their visit to Bellver village was, to say the least, dramatic, given the incidents that had taken place. At many points their very lives had been in danger, due to the edginess of the village's residents." The delegates recounted how, as they entered a particular home to speak to Villadiu, "they were able to see, reflected in some mirrors hanging there, that, while they were talking, a number of individuals outside were readying their weapons and showing signs of great excitement." When they stepped back outside, people shouted at them "calling us thieves" and accusing them of having commandeered the car they came in, tearing off the FAI banner and smashing the license plate.

During the discussion, an agreement was reached to return the detainees, withdraw "surplus forces" and appoint a commission, made up of all the parties in the village to sort out the remaining problems.

As they left, they had needed an escort "because some of them wanted to lynch us and the rest wanted to hold us there as hostages of war." The fear of vengeance being taken for those they had killed was so great that the villagers had threatened to flee en masse "if the security forces were pulled out of the village."

The Commission insisted that six *centurias* "armed with mortars and everything" had been pulled out of the front lines and that there were Guards four kilometers from Puigcerdá who had the place "almost entirely besieged."

The regional secretary (Valerio Mas) attempted to contact Yoldi by phone, but failed.

The Commission reported "that Bellver can call upon a thousand men," utterly blinded by their hatred of the CNT and an excessive selfishness regarding lands "that they say belong to them."

A certain Bru, from Bellver, had proposed that all those who armed themselves on 19 July be disarmed, or dispatched to the front lines; he had insisted upon the release of the seven Estat Catalá prisoners arrested in La Seo and "this individual, being very political, uses and abuses the word 'legality.'"

Rumors were circulating to the effect that the folk in surrounding villages wanted to wipe out the Guards sheltering in Bellver, as they were leaving that village. The access roads to Puigcerdá had been cut off. A lot of rumors relating to various armed actions in Alp and elsewhere, to Estat Catalá activity, and to Martín's murder were discussed.

Valerio Mas, speaking as regional secretary, explained that the Generalidad Council had touched on the matter that very day. The CNT members had suggested to the Council "that forces should leave those locations," but had run into opposition from the PSUC.

The PSUC's counterproposals to the CNT were as follows:

1. That the orders of the Generalidad be abided by in all the villages.

2. The dissolution of the Patrols and Committees.

3. That the five hundred rifles estimated to be held in Puigcerdá be surrendered.

4. That carabineers should not interfere in these internal squabbles.

Valerio Mas asked the commission-members to go back up to the Cerdaña and proposed these terms:

1. That "all surplus forces" be withdrawn.[171]

2. That CNT personnel on the border not be disarmed.

3. That a Commission "made up entirely of producers" be appointed to restore peace in the comarca.

The commission members showed a reluctance to return to the Cerdaña, for fear of reprisals, but in the end, they were talked into it.

The proceedings were brought to a close at 5:00 a.m.

★

On Saturday, the **First of May**, no demonstration took place in Barcelona. The Generalidad had declared it a work day, for the sake of war production, although the real motive was the fear of a clash between the different workers' organizations due to the increasing tension in a number of comarcas and locations around Catalonia. That same Saturday, the Generalidad Council met to examine the worrying Public Order situation in Catalonia. The Council approved of the effectiveness displayed by the internal security and defense councillors in recent weeks and passed a vote of confidence to resolve public order issues still pending.

★

---

171 Meaning all those other than the usual complement, i.e. those who had turned up days earlier to answer the call from the Bellver authorities, in anticipation of the supposed attack by anarchists from Puigcerdá, an attack that existed only in the form of frightened rumors among Bellver's smallholders.

According to the **Presidential Record for Saturday, 1 May 1937:**[172]

This year, marking the First of May in this country has stopped being the almost traditional popular commemoration it had become and is being turned instead into a tribute to the heroic frontline fighters.

In all government, political, and trade-union buildings, flags were flown from the balconies. Throughout the day, radio stations broadcast, in a range of languages, addresses intended for workers all around the world, reminding them of the tragic circumstances in which Catalonia and the Republic marked the First of May in 1937.

For their part, the CNT and UGT trade-union organizations released the following statement:

"On this, the First of May, the UGT Executive Commission and the CNT's National Committee jointly salute the Spanish working class and urge it to carry on strengthening its cordial relations so as to bring about the trade-union unity of the Spanish proletariat.

"For that reason, and for the sake of workers' unity, both sets of representatives declare that organizations set up outside of the trade unions' centrals we represent are to be considered divisive.

"Prompted by the staunchest revolutionary spirit, the signatories to this statement promise to work tirelessly, shirking no sacrifice, in pursuit of unification of the proletariat and to labor until we have completely achieved the noble, liberating purpose by which we are united.

"On behalf of the CNT National Committee: Mariano Vázquez, Galo Díez, Manuel Amil, Avelino C. Entrialgo, Pedro Sánchez, and José Espejo.

"On behalf of the UGT Executive Committee: José Díaz Alor, Pascual Tomás, Felipe Petrel, Mariano Muñoz, Ricardo Zabalza, and Carlos Hernández."

[...] The internal security councillor made a few statements to the reporters, telling them that the Public Order forces were under instructions to disarm and arrest all civilians who do not belong to the Generalidad's armed forces but who are walking around with rifles.

He added that he was satisfied with the state of public order and that there must be an end to the confusion in the rearguard.

The statement from the Ministry of War reported the surrender to the forces of the Republic of the rebels who had, since the outset of the army

---

172 Consulted at the AMTM.

revolt, been holed up in the Virgen de la Cabeza Sanctuary (in Jaén). Loyalist troops had taken 250 Civil Guards as prisoners and captured war materials galore. The news brought everyone great satisfaction.

Under the chairmanship of First Councillor Tarradellas, the government of Catalonia met in ordinary session.

The proceedings opened at 6:15 p.m. Expectations in the Generalidad Palace were running high as far as this meeting was concerned, since it was the continuation of the meeting held on Thursday 29 April, which the Council had agreed to postpone due to the irregularities in the public order situation.

The meeting lasted three hours. At 9:00 p.m., journalists questioned various councillors as they were leaving and they all stated that the Council had been merely a procedural affair. The Council's secretary, Councillor Sbert, did offer these comments about the meeting:

"The Council had decided to assess the overall public order situation, upon which the internal security councillor made a wide-ranging report.

"The government was pleased to see that considerable improvements had been made thanks to the measures taken at the last Council, these having been put into effect, generally speaking, effectively. **But the government has decided and is firmly resolved to bring normality to every corner of Catalonia, and to this end, it has held a vote of confidence in the internal security and defense councillors, so that, by common accord and each within the remit of his respective jurisdiction, they may proceed with the implementation of the necessary steps to resolve any outstanding issues.**

"Several decrees have been approved, a list of which will be issued as usual when it is finished."

The councillor for culture, once the aforementioned note had been issued, answered questions from the journalists, saying that the defense and internal security councillors had stayed behind with the first councillor to deal with the matter of pubic order.

In the president's under-secretariat, telegrams were still coming in protesting Roldán Cortada's murder. Such messages were pouring in from all antifascist organizations, without distinction.

Sunday, 2 May

The Friends of Durruti called another rally in the Goya Theater to introduce itself; the theater was packed to the rafters and filled with "delirious enthusiasm" among those attending. There was a screening of the documentary entitled "19 de Julio," reliving the headiest moments from the revolutionary events in July 1936. The speakers were Pablo Ruiz, Jaime Balius, Liberto Callejas, and Francisco Carreño.[173] During the meeting, a warning was issued that an attack by the reaction against the workers was imminent.

The FAI and CNT leadership committees did not pay too much heed to this new opposition that had sprung up within the libertarian movement, despite the scathing criticisms it was directing their way. In anarchist circles, the scintillating appearance on the scene of groupings that were meteoric in their rise, only to vanish into oblivion as quickly as they had arisen, was a frequent occurrence.

The program spelled out by the Friends of Durruti **PRIOR TO MAY 1937**, *was marked by the stress it placed on the economy being run by the unions, its criticisms of all the parties and their statist collaborationism, and a certain reversion to anarchist doctrinal purity.*

★

According to the **Presidential Record for Sunday 2 May 1937**: "The president of Catalonia received no visitors at the Generalidad Palace and remained working in his office. There was no political development worthy of mention. The social situation showed no signs of pacification, indeed very much the opposite. There was a discernible climate of nervousness that was to result in the serious events that occurred a few hours later. A number of precautions were put in place by the forces in charge of public order."

★

Jacobo Prince wrote a **letter/report** that he sent to his comrades in the FACA in Argentina, in which he passed on his "impressions in the wake of recent days that have us reeling from what might have happened."[174]

He reckoned that calm had been restored and that "yet again we have been spared the eruption of the volcano." He recounted what had happened; "the previous Sunday ... the UGT leader Roldán Cortada was killed by persons unknown." According to Prince, Cortada had been an obscure figure of no great importance and "there was nothing in his record to justify what happened, which we have to chalk up to a few dangerous *dechavatados* [halfwits]." The killing had "created a sensation" and the funeral had given rise to an impressive demonstration." The CNT repudiated the crime. On every side there was "a climate of

---

173 "The Friends of Durruti. Propaganda Rally at the Goya," *La Vanguardia*, 4 May 1937, 4.
174 FACA correspondence, Letter 36, 2 May 1937 [BAEL].

nervousness" and retaliation was expected, "since the PSUC elements were maliciously exploiting the deplorable deed."

Meanwhile, in the villages in the Cerdaña, there was another reason for conflict in the making: "carabineers, a special corps with customs duties that was answerable to the Finance Ministry, were massing in the border villages." Since July 1936, all the border passes had been in CNT-FAI hands. Puigcerdá in particular was a FAI fiefdom. There were rumors that there was fighting under way in Puigcerdá, but they turned out to be false. Conflict did eventually erupt in the neighboring village of Bellver, "with its reactionary tradition," when a CNT-FAI commission, under the command of Martin, showed up from Puigcerda. They were there to parley, but were shot at, and four of them were murdered—after which "all across Catalonia, the comrades went on to a war footing." The Guards were disarmed and facts were overstated; the expectation was that the incidents might spread, and who knew where it was going to end. **The worst thing about it is that the groups that were operating were under the control of the responsible Committees,** which gave rabble-rousers and irresponsible people a field day. In the end, the brakes were applied and common sense prevailed."

The PSUC and ERC back-pedaled, steering clear of provocative acts like body searches. Initially, Prince described the situation as "an attack of collective madness," but later delved somewhat deeper and explained: "

> at the root of it all is the fact that our people, at the grassroots, feel let down, that the gains of the revolution are slipping from their grasp, that we are sliding back into what there was before, and that elsewhere, where we are the minority, we are being persecuted in the old ways. And so they reacted violently and reckon that the best course is to take to the streets with whatever weapons they have, wrangling with the Guards and "all-comers." In a situation like that, the slightest incident might bring about a catastrophe. Faith in the [higher] committees had been lost and the tendency is to follow the lead of the local or "defense" groups. There are certainly grounds for the discontent. The [higher] committees fall well short of being equal to the circumstances.

Prince explained that on the one hand there was the attempt to make the revolution, but, on the other, the war imposed collaboration with other forces, with counterrevolutionary interests. "The old politicians maneuvered artfully" to stymie whatever does not suit them, while the comrades understand this and call for "a new 19 July" in order to recover their total mastery of the situation. In short, they think it a mistake to collaborate with other sectors and, though the term is not used, **"there is regret that the CNT's dictatorship had not been imposed across Catalonia,** something that was not, of course, an option."

Prince argued that Catalonia was not the whole of Spain and that Spain is part of Europe and that Europe included "Russia and planes, which Spain has too."

He summed up "that 'going for broke' was not and is not an option" and that collaboration was unavoidable, which included collaboration with bourgeois sectors. So, the option of "deftness and political strategy" was better than "drawing guns from holsters."

He stressed the absurdity and puerility of the belief that revolution through partnership with other proletarian sectors was feasible. And he also pointed out the impossibility of coming to any agreement with the UGT in Catalonia: "it is us or them, the saying goes."

Prince's conclusion was that, things being as they were, "there would be no other path toward actually making the revolution" than a CNT dictatorship, getting the jump on the Stalinist dictatorship. However, he declared that he was an advocate of compromise and negotiation, given that they had a truce: "For as long as the war continues on the front lines, we live in an armed peace."

Prince's detailed and specific report, to its credit, pointed out that the CNT's higher committees (Prince himself served on these and shared their tactics and ideology) were being swept aside by the defense committees in the wards of Barcelona and in a variety of locations around Catalonia.[175] And, prophetically, he forecast that any incident, no matter how small, might trigger a catastrophe, which is to say, a head-on clash between the defense committees and the Stalinists, the police, and the Generalidad government.

★

At 2:45 a.m., on **Monday, 3 May**, three truckloads of Assault Guards pulled up outside the Barcelona Telephone Exchange. They were under orders to seize the building and impose an auditor-manager appointed by the Generalidad. From the upper floors, the occupation was greeted by bursts of machinegun fire. Barely two hours later, the ward defense committees had erected barricades all over the city and implemented a revolutionary general strike. The barrios were in the hands of the defense committees. The only fighting was in a small area in the city center.

And so began the May Events in Barcelona.

---

175 As Joan Remi, a patroller from Sants, put it: "the rank and file was going to sweep the committees in charge aside, because [maybe] if they had paid no heed to the committees in charge, then there wouldn't have been any May Events." In Joan Casanovas Codina, "Joan Remi," Oral Source [AHCB 3-332-5D.102].

2

The Events of May 1937

Monday, 3 May

At around 2:45 p.m., three truckloads of heavily armed Assault Guards pulled up outside the Telephone Exchange on the Plaza de Cataluña. They were led by Eusebio Rodríguez Salas, activist with the PSUC (*a dyed-in-the-wool Stalinist*), the official in charge at the Public Order Commission. The Exchange building had been seized by the CNT back on 19 July 1936. *The supervision of telephone communications, the monitoring of the borders, and the Control Patrols were the sore points that, since January 1937, had been sparking a variety of incidents between the Generalidad republican government and the CNT masses. It was an inevitable contest between the republican state apparatus, which was staking its claim to absolute control of all of "its" jurisdictions, and the defense of the "gains" of 19 July on the part of CNT personnel. Rodríguez Salas was hell-bent on taking possession of the Telephone Exchange building.* CNT militants on the lower floors, caught off guard, allowed themselves to be disarmed; but dogged resistance was organized on the floors above, thanks to a machine gun set up in a strategic location.

*The news spread quickly. The defense committees, already in a state of alert, having been tipped off about a coup de main by the Stalinists and the Generalidad government, immediately threw up barricades throughout the city. There should be no talk of a spontaneous backlash from the Barcelona working class because the general strike, the armed clashes with police, and the barricades were all **the result of the initiative taken by the defense committees**, which swiftly received backing, thanks to the existence of widespread discontent, to the increasing economic issues in daily life—the soaring cost of living, the queues and rationing—as well as to the tension existing within the grassroots CNT activists between collaborationists and revolutionaries.*[1]

---

1   Gorkín states "In actual fact, the rising was entirely spontaneous. That spontaneity was very relative and needs to be explained. Since 19 July, a number of defense committees,

*The street-fighting was driven and conducted by the barrio defense committees (and only partly and at a secondary level by any segment of the Control Patrols). The fact that no direct orders for a mobilization or the erection of barricades across the city were issued by the CNT's higher committees, by those holding ministerial positions in Valencia, or by any other organization does not mean that these things happened spontaneously, but rather that they were the result of directives issuing from the defense committees. Moreover, not only did the higher committees at no time issue any such order to mobilize, but, from the very outset, they tried to rein in and contain the insurrection, but **they were pushed aside**.*

Soli was specific about the Public Order forces being made up of Assault Guards and Civil Guards (now rebranded as the Republican National Guard) who apparently failed to take the upper floors. It also noted that the deployment in the streets and on the rooftops adjacent to the Telephone Exchange was spectacular, "with armaments and military accouterments galore" catching the eyes "of thousands of people."[2]

Some rumors went around to the effect that the building was under attack from the FAI. Within a half hour of the launching of the raid on the Exchange, "Díaz from Defense, Asens from the Patrols General Secretariat, and Eroles showed up," for a "timely intervention," getting the CNT personnel in the Exchange to "set aside their righteous attitude." The personnel, "providing proof of common sense and level-headedness, acted on the advice of the aforementioned comrades."

The CNT's RC tried to work out the truth of what had happened; it met with Tarradellas and with (internal security councillor) Aguadé. Both professed ignorance of what had happened "and our [RC] comrades believed them." But, shortly after that, the officer in charge of the Public Order forces occupying the Telephone Exchange insisted that "he was following a seizure order bearing the signature of Internal Security Councillor Artemi Aiguadé [Aguadé] himself."

---

organized by grassroots personnel from the FAI and the CNT had been set up pretty much everywhere in Barcelona and around Catalonia. At times, these Committees led barely active lives, but it can be stated that on 3 May it was those committees that mobilized the working class. They were the rising's action squads. We know that none of the existing unions issued an order for a general strike." See Julián Gorkín, "Meeting of the POUM's International Sub-Secretariat (14 May 1937). Report by comrade GORKÍN on the 'May events'" [FPI-AC2-182-17]. The text is quoted at greater length in the Appendices, below.

2   "An Unfathomable Provocation," *Solidaridad Obrera*, 4 May 1937, 8 [*Soli* did not appear on 3 May 1937].

Soli stated that, following circulation of a notice from the RC "urging all workers to keep a level head" and asking that nobody should play into the hands of "maneuvers under way against the CNT," calm was swiftly restored in the city, *which was an absolute and blatant lie.*

Soli also said that the Public Order forces had been withdrawn to their barracks on orders from above and had left the Telephone Exchange, *which was an absolute and blatant lie.*

The paper picked up on the rumors and the questions everyone was asking as to "what the authorities' violent actions at the Telephone Exchange ... were all about."

Those *very interesting* questions were: "What was the [authorities'] purpose in this spectacular seizure? Was their action perhaps a foretaste of some previously prearranged plan? How far would they have gone had they not run into opposition in such activities?"

The *very disappointing* answers were these:

"We have no clue." After recalling that the Exchange had been in the hands of the CNT-UGT since 20 July, with representation from the Generalidad, and that any monitoring that the Internal Security Department had requested had been carried out, their conclusion was that "there is every reason to think that this is a provocation" by the security forces, "acting on Rodríguez Salas's personal orders," *starkly contradicting the claim made in the very same article that there was a seizure order bearing the signature of Internal Security Councillor Artemi Aguadé.*

Soli went on to narrate a number of "spin-offs from the incident"; throughout, it covered up or played down as being of no consequence that a barricade-filled city was the street-level result of a **revolutionary insurrectionist strike** promoted by the barrio defense committees. As far as *Soli* was concerned the only issue was "the attitude of the security forces, which, acting on guidance from above, was disarming the revolutionary workers. The latter ... refused to give up their weapons." *Now, why was* Soli *telling lies?*

★

According to the **Presidential Record for Monday, 3 May 1937:**

> At 9:00 a.m., the president of Catalonia set off by car from the Generalidad Palace, bound for Benicarló where he had a meeting with the leader of the Republic's government and minister of war, Señor Largo Caballero.
>
> Señor Companys made the trip in the company of the under-secretary to the president's office, Señor Rauret.

Señor Companys returned to Barcelona at 7:45 p.m. and made straight for his official office where he held talks with first councillor Señor Tarradellas.

At noon, in accordance with a government order, the commissioner-general of public order and officers acting on his orders arrived at the Telephone Company building located in the Plaza de Cataluña to install the government-appointed delegate in his post.[3]

The security forces accompanying the Commissioner came under gunfire from several places within the Exchange building.

At the end of the afternoon, and following talks between a delegate from the Home Affairs councillor and those showing reluctance to abide by the dispositions of the government, the latter vacated the Telephone Exchange building, which was taken over by the Public Order forces.[4]

This incident triggered a rash of regrettable incidents in several locations around the city. Numerous gangs of armed men roved the streets of Barcelona, especially the city barrios and adjacent areas. Barricades were erected in some locations. By around 5:30 p.m., workshops, offices, and stores were shutting down and the city had every appearance of being in the grip of a general strike.

On orders from the Internal Security Department, the following notice was broadcast early that night: "The internal security councillor is pleased to announce that the incidents that occurred in the Plaza de Cataluña over the ordered takeover at the Telephone Company have been resolved."[5]

The CNT-FAI organizations released the following **notice**:

The regional committees of the CNT and the FAI to all their affiliates in Catalonia:
Comrades: An incident occurred this afternoon outside the Telephone Exchange building. The regional committees stepped in immediately and made overtures to resolve the incident, which was sorted out on the basis that all

---

3   All of the historians and the eye-witnesses from the time set the time of the arrival of the Public Order forces at the Telephone Exchange at 2:45 p.m. The statement that there was "a government order" is a very significant claim on the part of whoever was maintaining the Presidential Record; it contradicts the speculation that the occupation of the Telephone Exchange was some whimsical or off-the-cuff act by the commissioner-general of public order, without the knowledge of his hierarchical superiors. See Manuel Cruells, *Mayo sangriento: Barcelona 1937* (Barcelona: Juventud, 1970), among others.

4   Not true. The security forces overran only the ground floor of the Telephone Exchange.

5   This notice, inserted in Spanish in the original document, was untrue.

forces mobilized as a result of the conflict were to withdraw while the competent agencies worked out a final resolution.

The responsible committees urge all bodies and affiliates to pay careful heed to this notice and abide solely and exclusively by the guidelines and accords emanating from the committees.

> On behalf of the CNT Regional Committee: The Secretary
> On behalf of the FAI Regional Committee. The Secretary.

★

As a result of the incidents that had taken place, and the nervousness generated on the streets, security measures appropriate to the circumstances were taken at the Generalidad Palace.

At 8:00 p.m., the Generalidad Palace hosted a special meeting of the Council. Given the city's grave situation in terms of public order, the meeting raised high expectations.

The gathering, chaired by Señor Companys, was attended by every councillor. Before the proceedings got under way, the councillors of Economy and Health and Social Assistance, Señores Doménech and Fernández,[6] held talks with Señor Tarradellas in the latter's office.

At 10:15, councillors Doménech, Capdevila, and Aurelio Fernández walked out of the meeting, telling reporters that, in actual fact, the Council sitting had yet to begin and that members of the government were to reassemble at midnight. The meeting ended at 3:45 a.m. No councillor was willing to make a statement. The president, Señor Companys, said: "Ready for the day ahead. We talked about the existing state of affairs, which I would describe as intolerable. In all likelihood, we shall meet up again tomorrow or the day after. You'll already be aware of what is happening. There are armed men on the streets. This state of affairs cannot be allowed. We have to sort things out. The government will have no option but to call upon its powers of coercion."

★

The economy councillor, Señor **Capdevila** (CNT) in his first meeting with the reporters handling news at the aforementioned government office made the following statements to them:

---

6   Both were from the CNT.

Over the past few days, I have been present at several meetings of the government Council of the Generalidad of Catalonia, to which I put some thirty decrees setting up a number of Industrial Groupings, in accordance with Article Two of the Collectivizations Decree. The plans corresponding to these decrees, like every other one relating to Industrial or Trade Groupings within the same sector, are drawn up by Catalonia's Council of Economy, and, since I am conversant with the way these bodies work in that I have spent upwards of a year serving on them, I want to stress that the business of setting up single ventures is handled by board member-councillors, with every assurance and safeguard for the overall interests of the economy, and, in that sense, and for the purpose of having a fully documented record, in each instance there is a period of public consultation, with which anyone with an interest in the planned concentration is welcome to engage.

He then raised the matter of his trip down to Valencia in an effort to thrash out some matters outstanding with the Republic's Industry and Trade ministers; these crystallized in the shape of the Order setting up the National Potassium Salts Export Council and the setting up of a Barcelona-based Regulatory Commission for Catalonia's Foreign Trade.

The National Potassium Salts Export Council is to be made up of equal numbers of State representatives from the Generalidad of Catalonia and from the workforces of each mine. This body will incontrovertibly enjoy full lawful agency when it comes to doing whatever is necessary for investment, hiring, exportation and sales, and payments for products derived from ores extracted from its mines in Cardona, Sallent, and Suria. The significance of this order from the Ministry of Industry resides in the implicit acknowledgement on the part of the State of our Collectivizations Decree. In fact, the aforesaid ministerial order, which acknowledges the same social arrangement currently in place, to wit, the collectivized arrangement with its basic organs—the Company Councils—the standing of which is explicitly recognized, and the pertinent management and administrative functions relative to mining operations is being ratified.

As to Catalonia's Foreign Trade Regulation Commission, it is to be made up of equal numbers of representatives from the republican government's Trade Ministry and from the Generalidad of Catalonia's Economy Department.[7]

★

---

7   "The Presidential Record for 3 May 1937" ends at this point [AMTM].

At 7:00 p.m., an hour ahead of the Generalidad Council's special meeting, the **Milicies Pirinenques** (Pyrenean Militias) also referred to as Companys's *margaritas* (daisies), showed up at the Palace "to offer their services to the president," assuming charge of the building's defenses and the personal protection of the members of the government.[8]

★

Shortly after learning of the serious incidents at the Telephone Exchange, the CNT Regional Committee called an **emergency meeting between the RC and the other higher committees.**[9]

Eroles reported that Asens had already been to the Exchange, "and that calm has all but been restored." He added that Asens would not budge from the premises as long as there was a single Guard remaining inside.

Trabal announced that traffic had ground to a standstill because the Guards were frisking and checking all drivers and passers-by.

The Local Federation of Unions sent its apologies for not attending.

Barrachina tried to read out a list of Guards who had been stood down, and the reports they had filed, with grave accusations leveled at Aguadé "as someone providing cover to professed fascists." But, given the gravity of the matters to be dealt with, he decided to postpone that plan.

Valerio Mas, regional secretary, said that what had happened was very straightforward: "Some government employees had gone to the Telephone Exchange to monitor communications and had run into dogged opposition from our people."

Torrents gave a lengthy list of the times "they have attempted to seize the Telephone Exchange and have not succeeded." The first time was an attempt made by a captain and thirty Guards who had given up in the face of the armed resistance they ran into. The second had come five days ago, when approximately eight individuals had barged in "carrying a concealed submachine gun." Once they were caught they were bundled outside. On this, the third occasion, they had seized upon the time when many were out to lunch and the raid had been led by an Assault Guard major plus Guards with a submachine gun.

---

8   They were called *margaritas* because of the edelweiss flower emblem they wore on their uniforms. According to Manuel Cruells, Antonio Gascón reckoned that the Pyrenean Militias were a very small and "green" force, and we are talking here about militia members captured by Antonio Martín at the La Molina chalet and then dispatched by train to Barcelona (*Mayo sangriento*, 59).

9   "Special Meeting held by the Regional Committee with the other Committees in charge, on 3 May 1937 in the city of Barcelona" [IISH-CNT-85C1].

Combina said that he and Eroles, who were having lunch themselves, were able to "see how the Guards pounced in their usual fashion ... with weapons loaded and ready."

The Local Federation of Anarchist Groups [Merino perhaps?] contended "we not lose sight of a detailed plan for the organizational formation of Defense Groups."

Valerio Mas used the comparison "we are where we were on 19 July."

Eroles corrected his earlier decision, asking now "that all forces be pulled out of the Telephone Exchange, including the six agents he had earlier thought might remain." **Combina** protested at Salas's actions. **Severino Campos** insisted that everybody had to be pulled out.

Escorza reckoned that the decision by Salas was a political faux pas, a mistake so huge that it might very well be exploited to our advantage.

The Local Federation told the RC that it should "spare a thought for all those who do nothing but abide by the orders coming from the Committees in charge."

Sousa asked that "every effort be made to ensure that the Generalidad reconsider things, because if it does not, our people are on the verge of taking to the streets."

Transport [Union] reported that three comrades had been arrested.

Doménech reckoned that "the [Generalidad] Council should proceed as normal and we will learn what happened over the airwaves."

It struck **Combina** that "there was something odd about the government's relying upon a commissioner [to] carry out its orders, rather than the councillor for the interior, as would be more appropriate."

Valerio Mas, speaking as regional secretary: "**read out the notice that is to be broadcast, urging calm and level heads.**"

Doménech reported that there was a **rumor afoot "that the CNT's RC intended to attack the Generalidad."**

The RC stated that "the Organization has fundamental accords in place" and that "we hold the formidable weapon of the unions."

Escorza argued that "we are investing this thing with a significance it does not have" and went on to declare that "this is run-of-the-mill stuff, carried out prematurely, without its having been at all thought through. Lame and counterproductive. Now we need to know whether or not we really do control our own masses."[10]

---

10   This comment makes nonsense of the hypothesis that the May insurrection was somehow directed or led by Escorza. Statements by various members of the RC point to the RC having been overwhelmed by the defense committees. The RC leaders are shown time and again to have been overruled by the ward committees and the pace of events. So Escorza's role was confined to his having tipped off the defense committees about an imminent coup de force on the part of Public Order forces. That warning was borne out

Torrens pointed out "that some comrades of ours have entered the Telephone Exchange and been very poorly received and poorly treated by some Central Government delegate sent down from Valencia; he is browbeating them badly."[11]

Valerio Mas summed the position up like this: "Given that there is a de facto normal process and that this could have been sorted out using diplomacy, a raid on the Telephone Exchange such as we have just been seeing can only be thought of as ill-timed."

Toryho turned up to read out the notice that was to be broadcast and after a few amendments it received approval. The meeting was wound up at 1:00 a.m.[12]

★

In Sarriá, the Civil Guard let itself be disarmed without a shot fired. In the Las Arenas bullring in the Plaza de España many anarchist militia members on leave were housed. Two factions had taken shape: the counterrevolutionary camp, which included the Assault Guards and Civil Guards (GNR), the Generalidad government, the PSUC-UGT, the ERC and Estat Català; and the revolutionary camp, made up of the CNT-FAI, the POUM, and the smaller organizations such as the Friends of Durruti and the SBLE. There were no taxis, no trams, no buses on the streets. The streets were deserted and the windows battened down tight. On the barricades, they were ready for whatever might come. There were no well-defined political objectives. Only two things were clear: 1. The police needed to vacate the Telephone Exchange and 2, Aguadé and Rodríguez Salas were going to have to step down.[13]

---

and exacerbated by the murder-ambush of Antonio Martín on 27 April in Bellver. The murder of Martín implied that the fragile arrangement that Escorza and Companys had arrived at on 15 April 1937—by accepting Aurelio Fernández on board, as a way of resolving the crisis festering within the government since March 1937—had broken down. Escorza provided the spark in a climate that was very heated as a result of Martín's murder: but after that, he had no way of controlling the flames. His tip-off was meant to alert the defense committees to the Stalinist and Generalidad coup de force. But he neither foresaw nor wanted to see the higher committees losing control of the defense committees and a revolutionary insurrection breaking out, because, if it failed, it might jeopardize the CNT's clout and autonomy. Escorza wanted a strong, independent CNT, not an insurrection that he thought was premature, badly prepared, and out of control.

11   That delegate was the author/anthologist of many of the documents or teletype messages relating to the May Events and that we reproduce below.

12   The minutes mistakenly record the time as "a.m.," something utterly impossible, given that the attack on the Telephone Exchange discussed at the meeting had occurred at 2:45 p.m.

13   Mario Signorino, *Il massacro di Barcellona* (Milan: Fratelli Fabbri Editori, 1973), 90–91.

★

Within just hours [of the attack on the Telephone Exchange], the whole of Barcelona was in arms.... From the days of the dictatorship and until the present, the CNT and FAI had had their defense committees. Those committee sprang immediately into action, their members took up arms. In order to prevent this incident from triggering worse collisions, the chief of police, Eroles, the general secretary of the Patrols, Asens, and comrade Díaz as the representative of the defense committee, made for the Telephone Exchange to get the raiders to pull out. The workers refused to work under threat from the police and it was foreseeable that there was not going to be any restoration of peace unless the latter left....

Meanwhile, blood had been spilled. Friction deteriorated into shooting; two people were gravely wounded. The nervous tension among the populace persisted. The workers were asking for assurances. They wanted no chance of any repetition of such things. Through the organizations, they called for the resignation of the public order director, Rodríguez Salas, and of Interior Councillor Artemi Aiguader. In the event that those resignations might not be forthcoming, the decision would be made to mount a general strike. They were not and work stopped the following morning....

The negotiations lasted through the night, up until 6:00 a.m. All to no avail. Overnight, workers had erected barricades in the outlying districts of the city.[14]

Tuesday, 4 May

The CNT's Regional Committee called another **special meeting of the higher committees** at the instigation of Julián Merino,[15] who proposed that the street-fighting be coordinated and spread and that the RC should assume the leadership of the insurrection.[16] **Valerio Mas** gave a rundown of the situation at the time, highlighting the dangers lurking within.

Merino, on behalf of the Local Federation of Anarchist Groups, stated that it

---

14   Agustín Souchy, *La verdad sobre los sucesos en la retaguardia leal. Los acontecimientos de Cataluña* (Buenos Aires: FACA, 1937).

15   According to what Severino Campos said in an article published in *Le Combat syndicaliste* of 23 December 1978. Although Severino Campos dated this meeting the evening of 5 May, there can be no doubt but that this special RC meeting took place on 4 May 1937.

16   "Special Meeting held on 4 May 1937 by the Regional Committee and the other committees in charge in Catalonia" [IISH-CNT-85C1].

looked to him like "we could not be in a better position."[17] The only mistake was that Eroles had abandoned the Police Headquarters.[18] The fact that they had now taken the Condal Theater and captured several Civil Guards "is an indication of our morale." He bluntly asserted: "**That the wards [*barriadas*] are entirely ours.** That the only ones who find themselves in delicate situation are the Distribution and Garmentmakers Unions. That inside the Exchange our comrades are on the upper floors and the ground floor is occupied by a company of Assault Guards. That there was no stomach in the Liberal Professions [Union] and Distribution [Union] for a surrender and that already there have been **fatalities and a number of wounded.**" He also added, although the draft of the minutes is a bit muddled here, that an Assault Guard captain had been taken prisoner and that some Guards had been wounded and shot.

The **defense committee** declared that "the comrades are engaged in the streetfighting and will not desist until these two clowns, who are to blame for the whole thing, are removed from their posts."[19]

Xena remarked that it was all too plain what the Generalidad wanted. "What they are after is a showdown between us and public opinion throughout Catalonia." He suggested that they should be blunt about "the reasons behind the events and why they have taken place." Moreover, he recalled that Tarradellas and other were already talking in terms of "the removal of those undesirables who answer to the names Aiguadé [Aguadé] and Sala [Rodríguez Salas] being up for discussion within the month." It was also telling that Comorera had for some time been trying to cozy up to Estat Catalá sectors.

Merino reported that ambulances were still coming under gunfire and would not come out to collect any of the wounded.

Barrachina proposed that they undermine "the Guards' determination" by drafting a note telling them how they had been deceived and that when the time came they would be thankful that they had remained impartial.

Xena reminded them of the ambiguity of the slogan "WEAPONS TO THE FRONT." He reported that all the comarcal committees had been briefed about the incidents. It was plain to see that there had been a systematic plan ranging

---

17   Merino, representing the Local Federation of Anarchist Groups, was one of the few RC members to afford full and unreserved backing to the insurrection in progress.

18   From the very outset of the occupation of the Telephone Exchange, Eroles and Asens attempted to mediate in the dispute, hoping to pacify things and prevent the CNT's appearing to promote the insurrection.

19   The defense committees had completely taken over in the streetfighting and were determinedly supporting the insurrection that was under way. The "clowns" reference is to the commissioner-general of public order, Eusebio Rodríguez Salas (PSUC) and Artemi Aguadé (ERC), the internal security councillor.

from the Catalanists in Bellver to the communists in Ripioll. One foreign correspondent had told Souchy in confidence a week prior that, come the First of May, the Telephone Exchange would be seized. All of these actions were being mediated by the Valencia government. He agreed that they should insist upon the resignations of the Commissioner and the internal security councillor: "A solution that, I think, will please everybody."[20]

Gerona stated there was no point holding joint rallies or antifascist unity rallies because "we are the fly and they are the spider." He pointed out that "we ought to go after the entire government" and that "if we calibrate our performance in government, there is no way that we are going to be able to operate with a completely free hand."

Nearly all of the union presidents in attendance supported continuing the fighting until they had secured the resignations of Aguadé and Salas.

The **Local Federation** gave notice that forces were on their way from Valencia and it was agreed that appropriate measures should be taken.

Healthworkers [Union] expressed its firm belief that they had been too easygoing "and that what counts now is that we knock these provocations on their head." He concluded that the only time government ever gave ground was when they were scared.

Castellote read out the final draft of the message to go out to the Guards.

The **Regional Committee and the Libertarian Youth** took it for granted that "battle lines have now been drawn" and that the point now was to work out how to grapple with them. A number of questions arose. "What position would foreign powers adopt? Should we take over the government? Would we know how to do so? Have we sufficient capability?" Their answer was that "if the CNT takes on the government we are going to finish up on our own. And the bottom line was that we can always argue that we are only defending ourselves after they attacked us."[21]

Aurelio Fernández said that, as he saw it, "This is going to end in chaos, due to weariness. They'll attempt it today and tomorrow as well; but after a few days' weariness forces everyone into surrender; if not lack of ammunition! The movement needs guidance: Does that suit the CNT or not?"

Santillán and Herrera, of Police Headquarters, gave assurances that "there'll be no more shooting from there," as if that meant that Aguadé and Salas were not directing the attack on the CNT personnel "from there." As it was their intention to make their way back to the Casa CNT-FAI "snipers were urged not to

---

20 For the May insurrection to have ended *just* with two resignations might well have suited the RC, but if fell far short of suiting those who had taken to the streets.

21 The lack of initiative and alternatives coming from the RC and the Libertarian Youth is surprising. Given such dithering, it was unthinkable that they could have coordinated the insurrection.

shoot and were told the color of the suits these two comrades were wearing, the better to avoid incident."

The proposals fell into two categories. A clear choice had to made regarding which was "the most feasible"

Sousa and Xena proposed that the CNT appoint the post-holders in the Internal Security Department, introducing a Director-General of Security.

The **Foodworkers Union** found it paradoxical that "we are about to parley with people who, only a few hours ago, or less, were calling us SUBVERSIVES AND UNCONTROLLABLES."

Sousa suggested that a CNT delegation demand over the radio that the Generalidad "stop the slander."

Castellote was afraid that anyone belonging to that possible delegation might wind up as a captive.

Xena said that "the crisis is actual fact."

A commission was appointed to go and talk to the Generalidad: **Santillán, Herrera, Alfonso,** and **Castellote** were appointed.

The proceedings were brought to an end at 12:00 noon.

The RC meeting of 4 May 1937 had been a special meeting called at Julián Merino's instigation.[22] The outcome of this gathering implied that:

1. **Merino was assuming leadership of the insurrection.**

2. **A (secret) revolutionary committee of the CRTC (Regional Confederation of Labor of Catalonia) had been established, made up of Merino, Ruano, and Manzana.**

3. **Two commissions were selected to coordinate and spread the fighting.**

A delegation headed by Santillán was appointed to hold talks in the Generalidad Palace with the rest of the antifascist factions.

Discussion of the situation provided an escape valve and a means of expression for the minority revolutionary sectors as well as a way for the RC bureaucrats to look for some way out of a revolutionary insurrection that was inconveniencing them and that they did not want. Very tellingly, Escorza failed to attend the meeting, because, to his mind., the insurrection was premature and its defeat might lead to the CNT's losing influence and political clout.

---

22   See the Bibliography in this volume for the article published in *Le Combat syndicaliste* of 23 December 1978. See also the documents in the Appendices.

The insurrection unleashed by the ward defense committees did not look to the RC for direction, nor for its revolutionary objectives; very much the opposite. It was offered the red herring of a speedy solution, essentially consisting of a demand for the dismissal or resignation of the pair responsible for the raid on the Telephone Exchange, by means either of the insurrectionist route (Merino) or through negotiations (Santillán). But Companys was not ready to assist the RC in coming up with a resolution and he doggedly opposed dismissing the men. **The CNT was playing with two different decks; the insurrectionist pack and the negotiation pack. Companys and Comorera were just playing the hand of provoking the CNT as a way of destroying it and thereby securing a strong government.**

In any case, as a result of that meeting, Merino and the Barcelona Defense Committee, protagonists of the insurrection in progress, managed to get two commissions set up to coordinate and drive the streetfighting; one in the Center and one in the Paralelo-Plaza de España area.[23] Moreover, at that meeting in the Casa CNT-FAI, the RC had managed to ensure that the chief object of the insurrection would be confined to a CNT delegation making its way to the Generalidad Palace to seek ... two dismissals, or rather, that those two dismissals would be obtained by means of insurrection.

As was common practice in CNT circles the two tactics proposed were not put to a vote; instead everyone was left free to espouse whatever tactics he had championed at the RC meeting. The proposal that a secret CNT revolutionary committee be formed and that two commissions be set up to spread the fighting was not mentioned in the minuted record, probably for safety and because those minutes were drafted and approved once the insurrection had already failed. How were they supposed to acknowledge in writing a proposal that placed the Organization and its own sponsors in such grave jeopardy?

According to *Soli*, throughout 4 May the working class faced down the provocation by the armed forces at the Telephone Exchange building.[24] The trams, which had been pulled out of circulation in the late afternoon on Monday, sat in their depots. Nor were the metro or the bus services running. Vehicular traffic through the streets was all but nonexistent. The widespread edginess and malaise ensured that "the vast bulk of the citizenry" refrained from "venturing out of their homes." And "in various locations around the city, barricades and parapets were thrown up."

---

23   Ibid.
24   "Grave Incidents in Barcelona Yesterday," *Solidaridad Obrera*, 5 May 1937, 1 and 5.

As the day wore on "a range of incidents occurred and there were clashes between the security forces and the people in arms," with many killed and wounded. The most intense clashes occurred in Armonía del Palomar (previously known as San Andrés), on the Paralelo, in the Plaza de Palacio, on the Via Layetana (around the Public Order Commission), and on the Diagonal (at the base of the Pi y Margall monument), although there were gun battles in a variety of locations.

There was intense gunfire coming from the Karl Marx barracks. The general strike had brought all of industry to a stop and it could be said that in the factories and workshops "work was at a complete standstill," except for the war industries. Commerce was also completely paralyzed.

From the Monday night on, there was great activity in progress in the barrios on the outskirts of the city in response to the raid on the Telephone Exchange. By the Tuesday morning, "the armed workers were rushing to throw up barricades at different strategic locations in the working-class wards." All the shops closed in the barrios as well as in the city center. The markets remained open for a couple of hours so that people could shop for food.

In the very early hours, some housewives tried to shop. There was no sound of gunfire and everything seemed to have calmed down. Soon, the first rifle shots rang out and people scurried for home. The battle had begun. There was fighting street to street. Rifle and machine-gun fire could be heard, as could the detonation of bombs. The fiercest fighting was in the Casco Viejo, in the winding barricade-blocked streets. At no time did the din of battle cease for more than three minutes. The city was deserted as the crackle of gunfire took over. Everyday Barcelona had evaporated. Most of the population, penned up at home, listened to the echo of a war that it felt was alien and odd. They did little more than endure it, just hoping that it might stop and normality be restored.[25]

★

"Toward five o'clock, there was a particularly violent and bloody incident on the Vía Durruti, not far from the CNT building. Two cars drove along the street from the direction of the port. They were trying to get through to the CNT Regional Committee.[26] Roughly three hundred meters away from it, they ran into a barri-

---

25 Signorino, *Il massacro di Barcellona*, 91.
26 The Regional Committee's headquarters were in the Casa CNT-FAI.

cade manned by men from the *mossos de escuadra* and PSUC members wearing red armbands. They halted the cars and told the occupants to get out and surrender their weapons. Even as they were complying with this "invitation" volleys of rifle fire struck them.... Since there was nothing to suggest that the police forces were about to cease hostilities and as ... the [police's] preparations were indicative of a plan to attack the Regional Committee's building, the defense committee decided at a meeting to bring in two armored cars to protect the premises and their occupants; they arrived that very night."[27]

★

Overnight an announcement was **broadcast from the Generalidad** that "at present the representatives of all the antifascist forces are gathered at the Generalidad to see if there is some way to halt the bloody strife that can only help fascism,"[28] and that not merely President Companys, but also Calvet, Vidiella, Alfonso, Hernández Zancajo, and García Oliver were about to speak over the airwaves. A watchword was launched that everybody was to obey blindly: **Ceasefire!**

Calvet, the UR president, spoke in Catalan, addressing his own people, pleading with them to stop the fratricidal strife that was staining the streets with blood.

Sbert, from the ERC, also speaking in Catalan, invoked antifascist unity, asking for a cessation to the fighting and that nobody exploit the lull to improve his own positions. The freedom of Catalonia was at stake. He issued a call for level heads and closed with four cheers for Catalonia, for Companys, for the Republic, and for Freedom.

Vidiella, speaking for the UGT, again in Catalan, explained that all the antifascist organizations were together under Companys chairmanship, to work out a solution. Also present at the meeting, he said, were Comorera and Miret, plus Muñoz and Hernández Zancajo, representing the UGT National Executive. It was vital that "all workers set aside their attitudes" and their arms and "that we have a ceasefire." Everyone should hold his ground without firing a single shot. A solution would be worked out that very night.

He reiterated the need for a ceasefire and close with five cheers, for proletarian unity, for antifascist unity, for the unity of all workers, for Catalonia, and for the Republic.

Alfonso, speaking, also in Catalan, for the Local CNT Federation, felt impelled to explain to the listeners that he was attending the gathering at the

27   Souchy, *La verdad.*
28   *Solidaridad Obrera*, 5 May 1937.

Generalidad, and was not under any sort of coercion. He called for an end to the fratricidal strife on the streets and for a ceasefire. He closed with the appeal: "No more shooting until we come up with a definitive resolution."

Juan García Oliver, minister of the Republic, spoke in Castilian, addressing all the workers in Catalonia, to explain to them that "all the representatives of the antifascist front [were gathered together] to see if we they could work out a solution to this big problem facing us all."

He recalled that the last time he had spoken over the airwaves of Generalidad radio had been "in the early days of the struggle when our forces were marching off to the front. Thinking that Zaragoza was about to be taken with ease.... I addressed the few workers left inside Zaragoza, telling them that our forces had set out from Catalonia to liberate them ... that they themselves had to help make the liberators' task easier; and I told them that the children, men, and women there should come out into the streets, that the comrades from Catalonia stood ready to come and free the Zaragoza comrades." And the few workers who had escaped the "huge fascist killing spree" came out into the streets "and almost every one of them was killed." *Was he boasting or criticizing his own speech?*

There was an oratorical flourish as he talked metaphorically about who was Cain and who was Abel in Catalonia. Then he talked about the half of Spain in the clutches of fascism. He tried another metaphor, which turned out to be a failure and unintelligible, about Mussolini and Hitler cracking the whip. He insisted that workers were "democrats" and knew where their duty lay and knew who the enemy was and knew that the enemy, at that point, was fascism.

He stated that he, who had never known fear, had felt scared as he crossed the streets of Barcelona, not on account of the gunshots, but because "he knew that all those who were doing the shooting were my brothers, my fellows; they all made up part of the antifascist federation; anarchists, communist, socialists, republicans."

He was scared because even though he might have been carrying a rifle or a bomb "I wouldn't have had any idea who to shoot at, because all of those who were shooting were my brothers, they could all kill me just as you may kill one another."

He harked back to his oration at Durruti's graveside, when he had said that the legacy left by Durruti "written in his blood through his life and his actions, was all about winning the war. And that, brothers, is what we have to do: win the war." That was the purpose behind the meeting under way at the Generalidad: ensuring that they were not "like Cain and Abel, slaughtering one another."

He asked, insisted upon, put the case for, and begged for "an end to the shooting." The only thing that mattered was antifascist unity. He asked that those recently killed not become the focus of a cult: "I want to state that the **Guards**

171

who have died this day are my brothers as far as I am concerned: I bow before them and kiss them. As far as I am concerned, the antifascists and anarchists who have perished are my brothers: I bow to them and kiss them. As far as I am concerned, the socialists who have perished are brothers. Yes, having said that, let me add: all who perished this day are my brothers: I bow to them and kiss them. They care casualties of the struggle against fascism and I kiss all of them without distinction. Salud! comrades, workers of Catalonia!"[29]

This was García Oliver's notorious "kiss" speech.[30] Many anarchists and CNT members who were listening to this speech were convinced that García Oliver had to be acting under threat and was a captive of the Stalinists. Some on the barricades or in the locals, overcome by fury and incredulity, shot up the radios broadcasting the speech.

Mariano Rodríguez Vázquez, the CNT's national secretary, insisted upon the danger that streetfighting in Barcelona posed to the Aragon front. Let it not be Franco that brings peace to the Barcelona rearguard. He asked that they place their trust with him in the talks under way at the Generalidad Palace as they looked for a solution and, in the meantime, that there be an end to the shooting.

Hernández Zancajo from the UGT National Executive, called for unity of the proletariat so that fascism could be vanquished, and he closed with two cheers, one for Catalonia and the other for the Republic.

According to the **Presidential Record for Tuesday, 4 May 1937:**[31]

Yesterday afternoon, after it looked as if calm had been restored following the incident that arose from the government's takeover at the Telephone Company, a number of deplorable incidents took place that brought the life of the city to a complete standstill.[32]

No public transport services of any sort were operating. There was a complete shutdown of shops, warehouses, workshops, and offices. No newspapers

---

29   Ibid.

30   For a fuller transcription of the "kiss" speech, see Juan García Oliver, *El eco de los pasos* (Paris: Ruedo Ibérico 1978), 425–427.

31   All quoted material from this point until footnote 38 is taken from "The Presidential Record for Tuesday 4 May 1937" [AMTM].

32   The correct time of the Telephone Exchange incident is given and here we have further confirmation that the Generalidad government had given the order for the raid to proceed.

were published.[33] The factories allocated to the production of war materials were the only ones working. The provisioning of the city operated almost normally and there was no interruption in water, gas, and power supplies.

Apart from ambulances and doctors' cars, the only motor vehicles circulating were those manned by the security forces, members of the committees, and other personnel from the trade-union organizations.

In different locations in Barcelona there were intense gun battles throughout the day between armed elements and the security forces, as well as between civilians. Barricades were thrown up at many points in the city.

The numbers of dead and wounded as a result of these things were high.

At 1:00 p.m., from the Generalidad Palace, where, right at the outset, the president of Catalonia had issued the requisite orders to quickly snuff out the conflict, the first official notice was broadcast warning all to be wary of certain orders that might be issued over the airwaves by certain groups or organizations.[34]

Another notice, broadcast shorty after that, stated the following: "At the behest of the Generalidad Council, the internal security councillor has deployed the forces under his command in order to stop the rebels. All Catalonia must rise up so that only the Generalidad's forces may move freely along the highways."

For their part, the CNT-FAI radio transmitters repeatedly broadcast notices informing their leading members in Alcañiz and Caspe that they should stay put. They added: "If we need anything, we shall call you. Keep calm."

At 12:10 p.m., a number of notices were broadcast by the **Rabassaires Union, the Unified Socialist Party (PSUC) and the UGT**, in which they immediately placed themselves at the disposal of the government of Catalonia.

At 1:20, notices were broadcast from the Republican Left of Catalonia (ERC) and from the Executive Committee of the Unified Socialist Youth (JSU), along the same lines as those just cited.

Later, a **notice was broadcast from the CNT**, asking everyone to lay down his arms and asserting that the target of the struggle was to be found on the Aragon front and not in the rearguard.

In light of the seriousness of events, the national bodies of the CNT and UGT, in accordance with the government of the Republic, dispatched representatives to travel to Barcelona by plane from Valencia at around noon.

---

33 Not quite. Publication and distribution were fraught with difficulties, but *La Vanguardia* did come out, although with a token edition. On the other hand, *La Batalla* and *Solidaridad Obrera* came out every day of the insurrection.

34 Thus far, the writer has been talking about the events of the Monday, 3 May. "At 1:00 p.m." refers to the Tuesday, 4 May, as does the rest of the text thereafter.

Those delegates were Muñoz and Hernández Zancajo from the UGT and Mariano R. Vázquez and Juan García Oliver, the justice minister, for the CNT.

Upon arrival in the city, they conferred with representatives from their respective organizations before making their way to the Generalidad Palace.

After this, there was a meeting, chaired by Señor Lluís Companys, of the following representatives of the antifascist parties and organizations: Antoni María Sbert attended on behalf of Esquerra Republicana; Comorera, Sesé, and Vidiella on behalf of the UGT; Hernández Zancajo on behalf of the UGT National Executive; Mariano R Vázquez on behalf of the CNT National Committee; Juan García Oliver, justice minister; Alfonso on behalf of the Barcelona Local Federation of [CNT] Unions;[35] and Calvet, representing the Rabassaires Union.

That night, at 8:45, from the Generalidad Palace the aforementioned representatives made **speeches over the airwaves in which they demanded again and again an end to the fighting** that was staining the streets of Barcelona with blood, and they called for everyone to lay down their weapons and abide by the ordinances of a government in which every antifascist sector was represented.[36]

The address made by the president of Catalonia, Señor **Lluís Companys** went as follows:

"People of Catalonia: You have listened to the representatives of the antifascist political sectors and trade-union organizations. Without going into the awful, bloody events that have occurred and that pose a threat to the antifascist cause, they have all highlighted the need to unite, the need to have an end to the violent struggle on our streets. Speech must be kept to a minimum, to the least possible minimum.

"Often it is in silence that men face the greatest sacrifice, which can only profit those who, having made the sacrifice, know how to match their moral thinking to their deeds. The fighting on the streets compromises many things. It has gone on too long and been too severe. We are living through difficult and glorious times that could be put in jeopardy by this conflict, one that I refuse to characterize and upon which I shall pass no comment, because I keep to myself all the bitterness and all the loyal, ongoing sense of having fulfilled my duty by trying to avert it. But the fighting must be ended, and there is but

---

35   Roberto Alfonso Vidal was head of the Barcelona Local Federation of CNT Unions. His name was put forward for the post of health councillor in the stillborn Generalidad government of 28 June 1937. In March 1938, he was vice-chair of the CNT-UGT Liaison Committee on the CNT's behalf.

36   These remarks were reproduced slightly earlier.

one thing to say, stripped of all commentary. One watchword: Ceasefire! It will be one of the aims of this meeting to highlight the seriousness of the moment and the responsibility we all bear. If this is done, we can all draw upon the very best within us. The greater the sacrifice made, the greater the glory, as long as no attempt is made to reap partisan benefits. How small-minded and petty that would be, measured alongside the grandeur of these moments!

"Our slogan and our cry must be: Down with fascism! We must live and win saying Down with fascism! I should not like to finish without calling to mind a message that makes my senses resonate: Catalonia! So beautiful! Of such soaring and profound possibilities! Catalonia, for the sake of the Republic in this struggle against fascism, Catalonia must invest all of her energies, all of her sacrifices and all of her selflessness.

"Brethren of the Catalan people: You have heard me speak so many times over the microphone in grave and peaceable times, and I know that I have stirred your souls; forgive me if I keep my comments to myself and if I am the one to send out the watchword: Ceasefire!

"For the sake of Catalonia, for the sake of the Republic, for the sake of antifascist brotherhood, for the sake of the task we shall carry out together tomorrow, let us in these solemn hours live up to our responsibilities. Long live freedom!"[37]

That address over, the meeting, begun at noon, resumed its efforts to devise a solution to the grave state of affairs.

The meeting concluded at 3:00 a.m. Reporters were issued with a statement reporting the solution devised, which amounted to a cessation of hostilities and progress toward the formation of a provisional government.

The new government was made up as follows:

Carles Martí Feced, from the Esquerra Republicana de Catalunya; Valerio Mas, secretary of the CNT Regional Committee; Antonio Sesé, general secretary of the UGT; and Joaquín Pou from the Rabassaires Union.

Martí Feced was put in charge of the Public Order portfolio.

The very grave events that had occurred in Barcelona generated great emotion throughout Catalonia, where they had some slight and very scattered repercussions.[38]

---

37 Companys's speech floated the ceasefire slogan without offering anything in return, hiding behind hollow Catalanist sentiments and saying nothing about the actual problems that had triggered the conflict, without acceding to even the least of the insurrection's demands and without conceding the resignations of the public order commissioner, as the CNT had been asking.

38 "The Presidential Record for Tuesday 4 May 1937" stops here [AMTM].

This comes from the **Copy of the notes taken by President Lluís Companys and the teletype exchanges between various political figures over the course of the street-fighting in Barcelona between 3 and 7 May 1937:**[39]

4 May 1937, which is to say the Tuesday when the revolt achieved substance.[40]

TALKS HELD VIA "HUGHES" BETWEEN THE HEALTH MINISTER AND MARIANO VÁZQUEZ AND THE MINISTERS OF JUSTICE AND THE INTERIOR REGARDING THE DISPATCH OF SECURITY FORCES TO CATALONIA.[41]

[**From Valencia**] Valencia here, Interior Affairs? Is that the minister of health?

[**From Barcelona**] Yes; speaking.

[**Federica**] Federica here with Mariano Vázquez. Listen, García, Mariano wants a word with you and then we'll speak to Galarza. We need you to fill us in on the situation there and the prevailing mood in the government; we'll give a briefing as well. Handing you over now to Mariano.

[**Mariano Rodríguez Vázquez**]: This morning at 8:00 a.m., the situation looked like it was nearing a resolution: there was considerable movement in the streets, lots of workers having gone back to work: the first few hours passed without a shot fired, but at noon the situation started to deteriorate due to the fact that the Security Forces were harassing the unions and preparing to attack. There was an escalation in nervousness as it became obvious that they were attempting to gain the upper hand. One crucial factor must have been the fact that Herrando has kept Rodríguez Salas on as head of the

---

39 All quoted material from this point until footnote 53 is taken from the entries for 4 May in "Copy of the notes made by president Lluís Companys of teletype conversations between different political figures during the street incidents in Barcelona from 3 to 7 May 1937" [HI]. The original is in Spanish. What we find here is a lot of colloquialisms and telegraphic language, with frequent syntactical errors. Francisco Aguirre, the managing editor of *El Día Gráfico*, who received the notes and teletype messages from Companys himself, was probably the one who drafted the finished text.

40 The original text mistakenly says 7 May (which was a Friday).

41 Federica Montseny (health minister) and Mariano R. Vázquez (CNT national secretary) were reporting from Barcelona and Juan García Oliver (justice minister) and Ángel Galarza (left-wing socialist interior minister) were speaking from Valencia.

Public Order Commission and the latter has carried on deploying the Security Forces and certainly guiding them in adopting the stance they have taken.[42] In many locations, there has been a systematic tearing up of CNT membership cards and piles of torn up CNT cards can be seen on the streets. **Five comrades belonging to Eroles's bodyguard have been dragged out of their homes and murdered.** The upshot of these things and others of the same ilk is that the comrades have made preparations to defend themselves. The climate has become more fraught since one thousand five hundred Guards reached Tortosa. Right now, there is no way of predicting what is going to happen. However, it is to be expected that in the absence of a swift about-face in the direction and attitude of the Security Forces, it will be impossible to prevent further spread of the fighting. Comrades' attitudes have been disciplined, with only a very few exceptions. I say again that the reason for the current fraught situation is the lack of tact and leadership in the performance of the Security Forces. There is no way to tell if a widespread crackdown on the Organization and its militants is in the offing. As a matter of great urgency, the minister needs to step in, make a change in the leadership at Public Order and give the Security Forces emphatic instructions that they are to give no provocation and must conduct themselves with all responsibility and impartiality. If the Security Forces on their way up from Valencia continue their advance, there will be no way of averting inflaming matters in the villages along the way that have, to date, not lifted a finger.

[**García Oliver**] The position in Levante and elsewhere is Spain is that there is absolute order, with the comrades and committees displaying the heightened sense of responsibility needed in these times. The interior minister has ordered Rodríguez Salas removed immediately and the minister is still ready to bring as fair a resolution as he can to the Catalonian problem. The Assault Guards en route to Barcelona simply have to get through to their destination, so that they can replace the Guards there who are overtired, edgy and worked up about the fighting because they have been influenced by the political and trade-union organizations fighting in the streets of Barcelona. It is imperative that you understand this and get the message across to the Committees and the comrades. Just as it is crucial that you get it across to all the comrades in the villages through which those Forces must pass if there is to be a genuinely impartial—utterly impartial—restoration of the peace. The government realizes that in the absence of fairness and impartiality on the part of the Security Forces, the conflict, far from being resolved, would

---

42   He means Arrando not Herrando, which is to say, Lieutenant-Colonel Alberto Arrando.

deteriorate, spreading to the whole of Catalonia and the rest of Spain, and the result would be the political and military failure of the government and of the fight on the battlefront against fascism. No one has a greater interest than the government itself in bringing the situation in Barcelona to a swift end, so the farthest thing from its mind is helping to feed such a serious situation by sending forces in with the deliberate intention of adding fuel to the fire. Sending forces to Barcelona is complementary to the takeover of Public Order Services because, without it, our interior minister and the government itself would fail because they would be obliged to rely upon worn-out, prejudiced forces, which is the situation now, when it appears as if the Barcelona Forces of Public Order are not carrying out instructions issued by the minister to the Public Order delegate—which is not to say that the interior ministers shouldn't consider the propriety of sending in those forces by some means other than overland, which is too long a journey and too fraught with obstacles, and which, in its wake, would only sow provocateurs interested in the continuation of the situation in Barcelona and in the failure of the government. With Public Order Services now taken over, I say again that you should quickly brief the comrades from the villages against placing obstacles in the way of these peacemaking forces; rather, have them extend every facility and welcome them warmly, because, otherwise, they are running a risk and the interior minister could not prevent those forces, should they be harried en route, from building up to a state of irritation that would inevitably work to everyone's disadvantage: meaning that we would only have succeeded in turning the problem of Catalonia into a national conflagration that will ultimately consume us all very rapidly. Above all, focus quickly on the province of Tarragona where the POUM and the separatists have great strength, so that they do not mingle with our comrades and provoke them into resisting the Public Order Forces by force of arms. That's it. Let me know if you want anything and I'll have a word later with the interior minister.

[**Marianet**] We are in complete agreement, in theory. Practicalities are something else and, even knowing the incontrovertible benefits of a changeover in Forces in Barcelona, we have to recognize that the problem here does not require Security Forces intervention. The way things stand is that if the Security Forces could simply be ordered to stay in their barracks for a few short hours, the situation could be restored entirely to normal. It is vital that we have a three to four hour breathing space during which there are no Security Forces harassing people or doing anything. That would provide enough time for confidence to be restored, for the barricades to come down, and for people to leave the buildings and places they are occupying.

[**Interior Minister Galarza**] On discovering at 7:30 p.m. that Commissioner Rodríguez Salas was still in post, I stated the following, which I copy from the teletype I have in front of me: "As of now, the Security Commission is still headed by a Police Commissioner, a member of the establishment, the man in whom you have the utmost confidence and representatives from the trade unions and parties have ceased involving themselves in Public Order." The Commander-in-Chief answered me: "Agree absolutely, and I will implement your orders immediately." I have made arrangements to place a call to him at 9:30 and I am sure that he will be reporting to me then that Rodríguez Salas is no longer at the Commissariat. I endorse what was said by García Oliver and, as for the period of grace you request for a resolution to be reached, I see no problem with doing the following. At 10:00 p.m. the forces will be issued with orders that they are not to fire a single shot, not to try to assault any building, and they will be confined on the streets to checkpoints, doing no searches or arrests for a period of three hours. You will undertake to tell people on the streets and in the Centers to withdraw to their homes during the interim and not fire a single shot. These are the orders I will be issuing to you. Plainly, you will appreciate that if they are not faithfully followed by both sides, nothing can be achieved. Hang on a minute, the Prime minister is calling me. García Oliver is here if you have anything to say to him.

[**Federica**] García, we can agree to what Galarza has said on the basis of its happening tomorrow between 6:00 and 9:00 a.m., to allow time for a huge peace demonstration to be prepared and organized, one for which the whole of Barcelona will turn out, led by interlinked flags and representatives from the organizations. We will put this to the UGT, in the belief that it will find it acceptable. However, I have to tell you right now that I reckon that what Galarza has just been saying to us is a very serious matter, given the blatant contradiction it represents. Around three hours ago I spoke with Herrando, enquiring yet again as to the replacement of Rodríguez Salas, who is still at Police Headquarters, lord and master of the Security Forces. Well, Herrando told me that he could no longer replace Rodríguez Salas because command was being transferred to the military authorities—and he said he had not done so earlier because all the bullying had kept him from asserting the principle of authority and excusing Rodríguez Salas who, he says, has done sterling work of late defending Police Headquarters from multiple attacks. As you can appreciate, I kept quiet about this, lest it inflame the comrades' minds even further; it is a very serious matter and flies entirely in the face of what has been said by Galarza, even supposing that Herrando has been acting in utter disregard of the orders he is receiving. Let Galarza read this when he gets back and let him respond to our suggestion, as well as to these details of the utmost significance.

[**García Oliver**] The interior minister should be back momentarily; but, holding the teletype in my hand, I can assure you that it is a fact that the order has gone out for Rodríguez Salas to be replaced, even though Herrando may have had his reasons for telling you that he never received it, since you spoke to him three hours ago, when the order was issued sometime between 8:00 and 8:15. Hang on a moment, here comes the interior minister and he can tell you himself.

[**Galarza**] Not only did I issue that emphatic order to Herrando at 8:00, but I handed him the order when I commissioned him to take possession of Police Headquarters; and today, when I spoke with him and fearing he might not have complied with my order, I put this specific query to him, which I copy from the teletype: "Has the commissioner-general been replaced yet and is there someone from the Police Corps now in his post?"

[**Dialogue between García Oliver and Federica**] The prime minister has sent for him again; now then —Get this, García. Galarza needs to answer regarding the extreme measure whereby Pozas has assumed complete command in Catalonia, because, if this is not right, as I imagine, I cannot fathom what Herrando's purpose in lying might be.

[**Oliver**] When Galarza gets back he'll answer your question in no uncertain terms. To my knowledge, it is not a fact that Pozas has assumed charge of the Public Order Services of a military nature and, so far, no government agreement has been arrived at.

[**Galarza**] Getting back to the business with Herrando. When I put that query to him, which just goes to show that the order had already gone out to him, he replied with something similar about Rodríguez Salas's defense of Police Headquarters; and I, knowing the value of that performance, said to him at that point that he should now be replaced. Herrando also told me that now that Pozas had taken over, the issue needed evaluating from the military angle and I gave him the response that I now copy: "I do not understand what you are at, talking about the presence and takeover by the General from the Fourth Division, necessitating that things be seen from the military point of view. —The General commanding the Fourth Division has, right at this moment, nothing to do with Public Order in Catalonia, although he might, if a state of war was to be declared, but not when the civilian authorities are in charge and they are the ones you represent. Is that clear, friend Federica? As to the three-hour interval, in the format in which I have described it to you, I see no problem with the period between 6:00 and 9:00 tomorrow morning. As for the demonstration, I would be all for that but for the presence of provocateur elements; I fear that such elements might exploit everybody's strained nerves and that the demonstration may finish up coming to grief. Perhaps the better option would be to agree on its being held and publicizing the fact in a joint notice issued by the two trade-union centers and, rather than tomorrow, holding it on the Sunday. Overnight I am going to order the Forces to act with the utmost caution. Give me until tomorrow after nine and I will have fresh and rested forces there, under the command of someone I trust implicitly.

[**Federica**] Right, Galarza. Now Mariano wants a word with you about the demonstration.

[**Marianet**][43] The truce may be our salvation but, just think, with the same people in charge of Public Order, I am not sure how much your orders will be obeyed. I am speaking from experience: about the host of contradictions there are at first glance between your position and people here. There will be others in command come tomorrow, but until that happens, they cannot get here, so have them flown up. But keep this a close secret so that there won't be anyone inclined to repeat it to Escobar.[44] Tell your people that, tonight, after 12:00, some of them should let themselves be seen heading for home, and if, as I hope, nothing and no one steps in to stop this, let all the rest follow suit and come morning we won't even need those three hours for the whole operation. This is very easy to put to the test. But it presupposes such a responsibility on me that I expect not just that you will help, but also that you will appreciate that this must be the last attempt on my part at this sort of a solution. Do not broadcast any arrangement of theirs over the radio, other than to your trusted men and on paper bearing your signature. Does that strike you as OK?

[**Federica**] An attempt is to be made to put this to the test overnight, although we can give no guarantees as it is hard moving around by night and

---

43 Nickname of Mariano.

44 Colonel Antonio Escobar of the Civil Guard received a gunshot wound on 6 May 1937, shortly after arriving in Barcelona to take up his post as recently appointed public order delegate.

giving instructions to people. That's it from me, Galarza. Mariano tells me that I should let you know that he is working on the basis of the six o'clock to nine o'clock interval, because that way we'll have time to get to work and it will be that much easier.

[**Galarza**] Give him my regards.

[**Federica**] Same to you. *Salud.*

Security Councillor Aguadé has long been asking for additional forces; those available to the Generalidad right at that moment were few in number. Only two thousand armed Security Guards, another six hundred without weapons, and a few National Guards. The unity-and-diplomacy policy should have been matched by an effort to boost the government's authority and by dealing with specific instances of so-called uncontrollable groups and coercion with regard to the government's directives.

His request was made not just through pressure from public opinion but also through the interior minister's own lobbying[45] and those by other Madrid authorities, plus comment in the foreign press about the borders, et cetera.

The complex[46] of the situation required additional forces, because, even with all the tact in the world, it was foreseeable that a clash could come. The Generalidad government was frittering away its resources on solving the situation and public opinion was breathing down its neck. The power of the government was being fortified more and more, but the majority of people in Catalonia were so annoyed that there was a danger that the government might lose the people's trust and that the climate of opinion and the very forces of public order in the government's service might suffer a loss of morale.

All conversations between the Generalidad authorities and its president and with the president of the Republic were being monitored at the Telephone Exchange.

The internal security councillor had the Exchange occupied and the response to that was an attack on the radio station and the eruption of a revolt. There was always coercion used whenever any attempt was made to resolve the passport issue or enforce the justice of the Courts against certain folk

---

45   Rather than "excitations" (*excitaciones*), maybe he intended to say "demands" (*exigencias*).
46   Perhaps he should have said "The complexity."

who were carrying out offenses (such as, say, the murders carried out with impunity in Manresa, Villanueva y Geltrú, et cetera).[47]

★

On the Tuesday, 4 May, there was a telephone conversation between Interior Minister Galarza and Councillor Aguadé.[48]

The minister enquired about how things stood and **Councillor Aguadé** stated: "Nerves are on edge, although clashes with the security forces have yet to begin, except for some minor friction. There's a general strike on. Please let me have your response regarding the issue I raised earlier." (Note: the reference here is to troops being dispatched).

Minister Galarza replied:

I have forces in Vinaroz who have come under air raids from the rebel air force this very morning. I have ordered forces to be mustered in Castellón, Murcia, Alicante, and Valencia should they be needed in the event of serious clashes arising in Catalonia. At the instigation of this government whichever of them may be needed would act on its instructions; but the *prime minister and I reckon that, since everything should be ready and waiting,* there is no advantage in intervention by forces that are not in Catalonia, whereas the ones that are there need not be fully deployed and may prove to be inadequate. In which case, since our solidarity with this government is absolute, the forces in barracks here would make their way in whatever numbers they might be needed and, in a short while, be in the positions indicated by the Generalidad government.

To which **Aguadé** replied: "Very good. Duly noted, and I'll be passing it on to the president."

★

Tuesday, 1:10 p.m.[49]

The **prime minister** enquires about the situation.

The **Generalidad president** answers: "Aguadé has just been telling me that it is not too bad, but it is still very serious. There are strong groups on the streets,

---

47   This text can also be found among the Tarradellas Papers at the ANC.
48   Emphasis in the original, where it mistakenly states 7 May.
49   Tuesday was 4 May 1937.

well equipped and sniping throughout the city. The Security Forces are too weak when it comes to swift action and are worn out. In short, the situation is not satisfactory. We are at a delicate juncture, with the tide turning rather in our favor. Aguadé had asked you for several things and received a telegram from Prieto endorsing his plans." (See the same day's conversation between the health minister, speaking from Barcelona, and the justice and interior ministers.)

The **prime minister** replies: "I've received your telegram regarding Sandino." (Note: the reference here is to a telegram that the Generalidad's president had forwarded to him to have Sandino ordered to place himself under the orders of the government of Catalonia.)[50]

The prime minister goes on: "Oliver and some CNT representatives have left for Barcelona in order to intervene and see if the conflict can be resolved. I think it is my duty to warn you that, having shared impressions with the ministers, we are all agreed that, unless the government's situation has improved by the start of this afternoon, in accordance with the Statute, we shall assume charge of Public Order. Let me know if you have any objection to that."

The **Generalidad's president** answers: "Let me answer your first point. The CNT has advised me that he is on his way although it did the same thing a while ago and he did not come. There are leadership elements who are doing their best but are being bypassed. Naturally, the Generalidad can listen but enter into no commitment, holding its ground against elements [that] have cunningly committed treason. As to Public Order, I think you should help beef up the resources of the internal security councillor as his responsibility in that field may get more difficult. The republican government can adopt whatever arrangements it may deem necessary."

6:00 p.m.

The Generalidad president informed the cabinet under-secretary that the rebels had brought artillery out onto the streets. He requested that Sandino be ordered to place himself at the disposal of the Generalidad government.[51]

Within moments, the **cabinet under-secretary** asked if comrades Muñoz and Zancajo had arrived to step in on behalf of the UGT.

The **under-secretary to the office of the president of the Generalidad's** reply was that Councillor Aguadé said that they had arrived, but they had yet to reach the Generalidad.

---

50   Sandino was in command of the air force and Companys wanted him to place himself at his disposal for air raids on CNT-FAI buildings and barracks.

51   Companys was still insisting that the air force make itself available to him for dropping bombs on the centers of the insurrection.

(At this point, García Oliver and Zancajo turned up and had a word with the under-secretary to the chair of the Council).

The **under-secretary** replied that the cabinet would remain in continual session and should be kept supplied with news.

Immediately, **García Oliver** presented himself at the telegram office and had a conversation with the Chair of the Council. In the course of it, he said that bringing troops in would aggravate things as they were all just about to meet to bring things to an end.[52]

Señor Zancajo, the UGT delegate, was of the same mind.

The Generalidad president immediately, and on the same tape as Oliver, spoke with the Council Chair who, in light of assurances from García Oliver and Zancajo's opinion—these having been sent in by the government and by the UGT—and of the fact that they were now all about to hold a meeting, stated that they could all wait for the transmission [dispatch?] of the forces "trusting once again in the loyalty of everyone." (The fact is that one thousand five hundred extra men would not have been able to reach Barcelona. More men were needed and they needed to be brought in by sea.)

One hour after that, again on 4 May, at 6:00 p.m., the **Generalidad president** reported the following to the cabinet: "We have been waiting to meet, but the socialist representatives have asked to exchange views with Zancajo and they are now meeting. Let me add to what I said earlier to the effect that I shall strive for conciliation, but it looks to me as if the CNT will be asking for conditions that allow it to emerge from the struggle stronger. *You are familiar with the methodology and characters involved. We must have everything sitting ready.*"

After that there were another two messages from **undersecretary to undersecretary.** One said: "That, making great efforts and in the overriding interests of the war against fascism, we have agreed, even though we were the injured party, to the 'ceasefire' formula and can announce that the representatives of all the organizations will be singing off the same hymn sheet."

In quick succession, there were further messages from **Vidiella** stating that the situation was, in spite of everything, very delicate and that troops should be sent as a matter of urgency.

The **president of the Generalidad** also sent off a message for troops to be brought in from Castellon to free the National Guard who were surrounded in their barracks in Tortosa.

---

52 This conversation can be consulted at FPI-AH-55-33. The prime minister told García Oliver that unless he had assurances, within fifteen minutes, that the streetfighting was at an end, the orders whereby the republican government was taking Public Order powers away from the Generalidad government would be made public.

At 10:00 p.m., the president of the Generalidad informed the Council: "At the outset of the meeting García Oliver broached a change of internal security councillor, asking that Public Order be under everyone's control and reiterated the usual points that have been so often discussed." He added: "Efforts will be made to secure a deal, though that is still a difficult task. Internal security councillor insists that reinforcements be dispatched because his forces are worn out."

The fighting on the streets persisted for the remainder of the night, and Internal Security, the President's Office, and Vidiella were in touch with Pascual Tomás to ask for troops to be dispatched swiftly.

At 12:30 a.m. on 5 May, the message came through that the state [Valencia] was taking over Public Order.[53]

★

Throughout the night the negotiations at the Generalidad Palace continued. The CNT and FAI had agreed to send out an order for an end to hostilities. As had all the antifascist organizations in the counterrevolutionary camp. But, that very night, the police and the Stalinists attacked the premises of the Leatherworkers Union (in the Calle Condal, at the intersection with the Pasaje de San José), "which was lightly defended." Gunshots and volleys of rifle fire continued all night long.[54]

Wednesday, 5 May

In the morning, since the minimal requests that Rodríguez Salas and Artemi Aguadé tender their resignations had not been met, there was a repetition of the previous day's scenes: "Housewives set out to do their food shopping, only to duck back indoors, while shopkeepers, who had opened their doors slightly, hastily locked them again. Momentarily bustling, the streets emptied once again and the people … were asked … in no uncertain terms to lock up again immediately and to retreat into their homes. Which they did without delay. And the fighting flared up again."[55]

---

53   The entries for 4 May in "Copy of the notes made by president Lluís Companys of tele-type conversations between different political figures during the street incidents in Barce-lona from 3 to 7 May 1937," end at this point [HI].

54   Souchy, *La verdad*.

55   Marcel Ollivier in *Barcelona, mayo 1937. Testimonios desde las barricadas*, eds. Carlos García, Harald Piotrowski, and Sergi Rosés (Barcelona: Alikornio, 2006), 130.

The **CNT Regional Committee** again convened an urgent meeting of the RC with the rest of the higher committees.[56]

Defense informed them that in Mollerusa "and one other village in Lérida," the Guards had attacked a number of unions.

Jover reported that, on the front, the CNT personnel had agreed not to come down to Barcelona. But a few *centurias* had proposed that they go down to Barcelona. Those at the meeting expressed their opposition.[57]

The demand on the front lines was that all the armed corps in the rearguard be disbanded. As to the matter of Supplies, anticipating what was about to befall them in that, after this, the government was not about to send them a thing, they warned the RC that it should "shoulder this burden" and it was reminded that there were a lot of people "to be supplied with clothing and food."

A number of more or less groundless rumors were reported and refuted as the meeting proceeded on its way.

A delegate reported that "our comrades in the Telephone Exchange have not eaten in two days and they have wounded."

Healthworkers [Union] responded that that was not an issue, because it could be sorted out by sending in an ambulance that would bring in food and munitions for those under siege and then ferry away the wounded. The same thing applied to those at the Distribution Union premises.

Isgleas described "the resolutions taken by the frontline comrades," which Jover had just brought up, as dismal. He reported that the Valencia government had taken charge of Defense and Public Order. He cautioned that this would make the situation of the comrades in the front lines worse if they decided to act upon their accords. He spelled out his own position, arguing that "we militants should be calling for a ceasefire." After which everything could be sorted out amiably. He raised the alarm by warning that they were not in control of the situation and that the "Casa [the Casa CNT-FAI, where they were meeting] is almost wholly under siege."

The **Defense Committee** declared that "we cannot hold out any longer, we are in eminent [imminent] danger unless we act swiftly. We cannot hold on to the wards any longer, they want to launch an all-out attack and nothing else. We have tried everything we could think of to bring the Generalidad around, but it

---

56 "Special meeting held [on 5 May 1937] by the Regional Committee for Catalonia and attended by virtually all the most responsible comrades from the Organization" [IISH-CNT-85C1].

57 Severino Campos mentions Jover as having arrived on foot to a summons to the RC meeting on 5 May. See Severino Campos's article in the Appendices, below.

has paid us no heed." It was agreed that a call be put through to Valerio Mas and the rest of the commission dispatched to the Generalidad Palace.

Xena reported that he had telephoned the Generalidad "briefing Herrera on the plan to mop up the Guards on the rooftops around this Casa, as their intention seemed to us to be to surround us," to which Herrera had replied that they should get on with it.

The **Local Federation** suggested "that a Defense Council be appointed" to look after the Casa CNT-FAI.

Trabal added that "if we do not have enough man-power, let's ask the barricades."

Light & Power [Union] asked "whether or not the wards should be provided with lighting, as something serious might very well befall the comrades engaged in that task." It was agreed that the city should have no lighting that night.

Barrachina insisted on the need to show the Guards that their officers had betrayed them, because, otherwise, the three thousand men making up their numbers were going to take on the CNT personnel. It was agreed that every facility should be extended to him.

Manzana warned of the danger of their being seized while all together and of a war rather a revolution being started. Every type of defensive measure had to be taken at the Casa CNT-FAI and a highly detailed plan drawn up. It was agreed that the existing Defense Committee at the Casa should be expanded, and Manzana and Xena were appointed to it and Isgleas and Jover undertook to serve on it for the duration of their time there. The Committee was accorded wide-ranging decision-making powers.

The meeting was brought to a close at 12:00 noon.

These minutes recount the "firefighting" role played by the higher committees and by the RC in particular. At no point did they take up a role leading and galvanizing the insurrection. At no point did they put revolutionary propositions forward. The very opposite: their role was one of containment and looking to the ward committees until they were no longer in a position to be able to rein them in. They also tried to seek a "political" way out of the insurrection, one confined solely to the insistence upon two resignations, which foundered on the curt refusal on the part of the Generalidad government. THE MAY INSURRECTION WAS SPEARHEADED BY THE BARRIO COMMITTEES WHICH SWAMPED THE CONTAINMENT EFFORTS OF THE RC AND THE REST OF THE HIGHER COMMITTEES.

At RC's 5 May 1937 meeting, two opposing stances had been advanced: the call for a ceasefire clearly articulated by Isgleas, and that of the defense committees, who wanted "to launch an all-out attack" immediately.

★

According to *Soli*, in the early hours of the morning "the streets of Barcelona were very crowded. Shops did not open and the only ones functioning were those engaged in trading in food items."[58] There was the odd, isolated shot fired now and then. Public transport was not in operation; "no trams, no buses, no taxis. The city appeared dismal."

As the morning wore on, the shooting escalated in certain wards, "having spread to the Plaza de Cataluña, the Calle de Claris, the [Vía] Layetana, the vicinity of the Generalidad, and the Avenida 14 de Abril, and the numbers of wounded were rising." "A number of tanks firing machine-gun bursts" drove down the Calle Consejo de Ciento.

Out in the barrios, the markets had opened for business and people were turning out in large numbers to buy food.

"There has been an outstanding trade in fish, as that item was in plentiful supply," whereas the meat counters were closed.

The official offices remained idle as a precaution against the intense gunfire. Nor did work resume at the Generalidad.

During the morning "the odd scattered gunfire could be heard" in the Plaza de España, but calm soon descended again. On the Paralelo, out by Vallhonrat, a number of hand bombs were thrown, claiming two lives and leaving several people wounded.

Several gangs of Stalinist provocateurs set about shooting down streets and arresting peaceable citizens and tearing up CNT membership cards. One such gang murdered Francisco Ferrer Guardia's grandson.

Pacos (snipers) cropped up, shooting from the rooftops in order to create "panic in barrios where there had been calm." Two of these *pacos* were detected at the junction of the Calle de Balmes and the Calle Mallorca.

Despite the shooting, by which they were occasionally struck, Red Cross ambulances carried on blithely with the business of picking up the wounded. The same could be said of the municipal ambulances and the ones from the War Department. Outstanding work was done by the emergency department and transfusion service at the Clinical Hospital where forty operations were performed.

At midday, Antonio Sesé, the UGT secretary, en route to the Generalidad to take up his appointment as councillor, was struck by gunfire that resulted in his death.[59] At 3:00 p.m., Vidiella, on behalf of the UGT, and Vázquez, speaking for the CNT, spoke over the Generalidad radio:

---

58   "General Information regarding Events," *Solidaridad Obrera*, 6 May 1937, 2.

59   Apparently, the vehicle in which he was travelling had ignored the call to halt coming from the CNT Public Entertainments Union barricade.

Vidiella said: "It is crucial that everybody lays down his weapons. Right now, all we are doing is playing into the hands of fascism. Our duty is to win the war."

Mariano Rodríguez Vázquez stated: "It is high time we had a ceasefire.... Everyone must abide by it and discipline must be enforced.... An hour from now, there should not be a single rifle, not a single armed man on the streets. We shouldn't be waiting for the others to do it. We should be doing it ourselves. We can argue later. If, once our performance comes up for discussion at meetings and you end up saying that we deserve to be shot, then go ahead and shoot us, but for the time being, abide by our instructions."

That afternoon, a notice was broadcast stating that the republican government "having greater resources" was taking charge of Public Order in Catalonia.

Barcelona's mayor ordered all city staff back to work, but the ferocious gunfire on the Vía Layetana endured and his order was carried out by very few "since movement through those places was impossible."

García Oliver had flown back to Valencia.

A note appeared, **disowning** the Friends of Durruti; it bore the signatures of the CNT's Regional Committee and the FAI's Regional Committee.

★

On the barricades, the Friends of Durruti were out distributing the notorious leaflet that made them famous; its text read as follows:

CNT-FAI, "Friends of Durruti" Group

WORKERS! A Revolutionary Junta. Shoot the culprits. Disarmament of all the armed Corps. Socialization of the economy. Disbandment of the political parties that have attacked the working class. Let us not surrender the streets. Revolution above all else. We hail our comrades from the POUM who fraternized with us on the streets.

LONG LIVE THE SOCIAL REVOLUTION!
DOWN WITH THE COUNTERREVOLUTION![60]

The leaflet was printed at gun-point on the night of 4–5 May in a print shop in the Barrio Chino.[61] The group's makeshift nature and lack of infrastructure

---

60   Original in the AEP and CA. Reprinted in *La Batalla* (6 May 1937).
61   Clara and Paul Thalmann in *Barcelona, mayo 1937*, eds. García, Piotrowski, and Rosés, 116.

were self-evident. The text was drafted after a meeting with the POUM Executive Committee, held at 7:00 p.m. on 4 May, by which time the Friends of Durruti and the POUM had already agreed on a policy of withdrawal, without giving up their weapons and with the proviso that guarantees against repression be established.

The leaflet endorsed by the POUM and reprinted in issue no. 235 (6 May 1937) of La Batalla *was not backed up by any plan of action and was merely a statement of intentions and an appeal to the spontaneity of the CNT masses to stick to their actions in response to the onward march of the counterrevolution. In actual fact, everything hinged on whatever decision the CNT leadership might arrive at. It was nonsensical and illogical to think that the CNT masses, despite their initial reluctance, or criticisms, would not fall into line behind the leaders of 19 July. Only if the CNT leadership was swept aside by some other revolutionary leadership could the masses have been induced (and even then, only with great difficulty) to abide by the slogans and plan of action of some new leadership. Could the Friends of Durruti shove the CNT leadership aside?*

The POUM never had any intention of unseating the CNT leadership nor did it have any pre-prepared plan of action. In practice, the POUM embraced a piggy-backing policy vis-à-vis the decisions of the CNT leadership. The POUM's Executive Committee turned down Josep Rebull's plan for seizing the Generalidad and the buildings still resisting in the city center, **arguing that this was not a military issue but a political one.**[62] *Fighting was confined to the city center.*

Also on 5 May there were talks between the Barcelona Local POUM Committee[63] and the Friends of Durruti, talks that the POUM described as negative because: "They [the Friends of Durruti] refuse to make direct approaches to CNT circles in order to unseat the leadership, but simply want to bring influence to bear on the movement without assuming any greater responsibility."[64]

---

62   Agustín Guillamón, "Josep Rebull de 1937 a 1939. La crítica interna a la política del CE del POUM sobre la Guerra de España," *Balance*, Cuadernos 19 and 20 (May–October 2000). See also Agustín Guillamón, *Espagne 1937. Josep Rebull, la voie révolutionnaire* (Paris: Spartacus, 2014), soon to be available in Spanish from Ediciones Descontrol.

63   Most likely with Josep Martí, secretary of the POUM's Local Committee, and with Josep Rebull, cell secretary.

64   Barcelona Local [POUM] Committee, "Report on the actions of the Local Committee during the May events, presented by the former to the Barcelona cells, for discussion." Type-written text [HI]. Partly reprinted in the Appendices, below.

★

In their leaflet, launched on 5 May, the Friends of Durruti proposed concerted POUM-CNT-FAI action. In the short term, they lobbied for the establishment of a Revolutionary Junta, **but at no time was this workable**. The suggested concerted POUM-CNT-FAI action was never anything more than a tribute to militants from different organizations who fought shoulder to shoulder on the barricades. *The leap from the wording of the leaflet to concrete agreement was never made. They did virtually nothing to brush aside the CNT leadership and wrest away control of the CNT masses that repeatedly turned a deaf ear to the calls for it to pack the street-ighting in.*

The Friends of Durruti were the most active combatants on the barricades and completely dominated the Plaza Maciá (today's **Plaza Real**)—where every approach was blocked off by barricades—and the full length of the **Calle Hospital**. In the intersection of **the Ramblas and the Calle Hospital**, under the gaze of a huge portrait of Durruti attached to the front of the building where the group had its headquarters, **they erected a barricade where they set up their operations center**. Their complete control of the Calle Hospital linked up with the CNT Defense Committee (the central HQ of the defense committees) in **Los Escolapios** on the Ronda San Pablo, and from there, with the **Brecha de San Pablo**, which had been overrun by about forty militia members from the Rojinegra column.[65] The latter were under the command of Friends of Durruti member (*durrutista*) Máximo Franco, who had "come down to Barcelona" on a "reconnaissance and fact-finding" mission, after both the Rojinegra Column and the (POUMist) Lenin Column had caved into pressures urging their respective units to return to the front.[66]

The POUM was in complete control of the **Plaza del Teatro** with some barricades protecting a wide perimeter around the base of the Local Committee (in the Principal Palace and the **Hotel Falcón**, which had been turned into a fortress).

---

65 In his reports to Moscow, "Pedro" (Erno Gerö) mentioned Los Escolapios as the directing center behind the May 1937 insurrection. See Agustín Guillamón *El terror eStalinista en Barcelona* (1938) (Barcelona: Aldarull/Descontrol, 2013).

66 In Gregorio Jover's absence (Jover had been in Barcelona since 5 May to attend meetings of the RC), García Vivancos was in command of the Ascaso Column and he confronted the Rojinegra column led by Máximo Franco and the Lenin Column under Rovira, forcing them to turn back to the front following orders received from the RC, orders he complied with after setting free CNT and POUM members being held captive by the Stalinists in Lérida. See García Vivancos, "The CNT's and FAI's Intervention in the POUM Trial," *Cultura Proletaria*, 4 February 1939; Ramón Liarte, *Entre la revolución y la Guerra* (Barcelona: Picazo, 1986), 241–242 and Antonio Téllez, *La red de evasión del grupo Ponzán* (Barcelona: Virus, 1996), 49–50.

The fiercest and most crucial clashes came during 4 and 5 May. The workers' barrios were in the hands of the CNT-FAI from the start. In the heart of Pueblo Nuevo, for instance, barricades were set up so that arrivals and departures in the city via the Mataró highway could be monitored, but things there were utterly calm, except in the area around the Karl Marx barracks held by the Stalinists, which shelled the nearby anarchist barracks on the Avenida Icaria and the Parque de la Ciudadela, the residence-cum-refuge of the president of the Republic, Azaña.

In those barrios where fighting became necessary, the balance quickly tilted in favor of the defense committees. In the case of **Sants**, the defense committee, ensconced in the Hotel Olimpic on the **Plaza de España**[67] stormed the nearby Assault Guard barracks (of six hundred men) before taking over the National Guard (formerly Civil Guard) **Casarramona** barracks (which these days houses the Caixa-Forum) in a preemptive attack of its eighty-man garrison.[68] The remainder of the garrison, some four hundred Guards, had ventured out under orders to seize the radio station on the Ramblas. As they approached **Los Escolapios** they were defeated and took to their heels. In **Pueblo Seco**, the defense committee used cannons to clear out the **América cinema** (Paralelo 121) where about sixty of those National Guard members had sought refuge as they retreated in the direction of their barracks.[69] **The bitterest fighting was in the city center, where it was often barricade versus barricade**, among barricades erected by the POUM, the CNT, the PSUC, the ERC, and the Generalidad, in defense of their respective locals.

The Plaza de Sant Jaume, where the Generalidad Palace and the City Council were located, was defended by barricades thrown up by the *mossos de escuadra*. POUM members had erected a barricade at the junction of the **Ramblas and the Calle Fiveller** (now the Calles Ferrán/Fernando), from where they were shooting toward the Generalidad barricade. PSUC personnel had erected a barricade at the **Calle Llibrería–Plaza del Ángel** (it was the Plaza Dostoievski back then) intersection directly facing the building that was home to the UGT Water, Gas, and Electricity Union on the Vía Layetana (then known as the Vía Durruti). Crossfire enabled them to dominate that stretch of the Via Durruti and it also commanded the doorway of number 2, Plaza del Ángel, where Camillo Berneri and

---

67 Now the main headquarters of the *Mossos d'esquadra*.

68 Juan Giménez Arenas, *De La Unión a Banat* (Madrid: Fundación Anselmo Lorenzo, 1996), 59. See also the oral evidence given by Joan Remi to Joan Casanovas, cited in the bibliography.

69 The cannons had been brought in by the defense committee from Sitges. In their haste, they omitted to secure them to the ground and at every shot the "kick" sent the little guns flying spectacularly into the air.

Francisco Barbieri were living; this pair was abducted and murdered by a UGT patrol. There were also skirmishes on the Vía Durruti itself, between the Public Order Commission and the Casa CNT-FAI, which was protected by tanks. In the Post Office building, every room and every floor was contested. On the Vía Durruti, in front of the Public Order Commission, an armored car was stopped by bomb blasts that forced the vehicle to a halt.[70]

In the Paseo de Gracia shots were traded among the PSUC's **Casal Carlos Marx** (formerly the Equestrian Circle), some furniture showrooms nearby which were under the control of the **Woodworkers Union**, and the base of the CNT's **Liberal Professions Union**, just across the street. In the **Calle Cinco de Oros**, there was shooting between the Assault Guards in the Palau Robert and a barricade erected across from the POUM headquarters in Gracia (in the Calle Córcega). One of the people attending that barricade was Albert Masó, a POUM militant.[71] In the same location, the German anarcho-syndicalists from the DAS group were occupying the former German consulate and had thrown up a barricade in front of it, running parallel with the POUM's (at the Diagonal–Jardinets de Gracia intersection), defended by a machine gun that had a clear line of fire right down the Paseo de Gracia. The PSUC-held La Pedrera was very close by.

On the Gran Vía between the Balmes and Paseo de Gracia intersections, Assault Guards allied with Estat Catalá personnel took over the **Oro del Rhin** café and erected a barricade on the Rambla de Cataluña, in front of the Estat Catalá headquarters. The defenders of that barricade faced CNT personnel from the nearby **Foodworkers Union**. The Control Patrol premises at Gran Vía 617, came under **sniper fire from the rear rooftops adjacent to the Hotel Colón**.[72] At the

---

70   We have two overlapping testimonials that differ on some significant details on this point. We have the evidence of **Conxa Pérez** who, in the February 2011 edition of the CGT paper *Catalunya*, states: "Those were days of great confusion. I was asked to make my way to the CNT Regional Committee's base in search of news of what was going on. A female comrade, one of the Carrasquers, said that she would go with me. In the end, an Italian lad with a car filled with scrap iron and wooden boards, which in the end proved useless, offered to take us there. We came under gunfire in the Vía Laietana, where the Commission was. They must have reckoned we were trying to mount an attack on them. The young driver was left badly wounded and they ferried me with my injured leg to the Clinic. When I was able, I escaped and made my way back with the comrades." The other testimony states: "An armored car passed by the front of the Public Order Commission several times, emitting a hail of gunfire at the guards on sentry duty at the entrance. The latter responded by tossing a grenade, forcing the car to a halt. A man and two girls climbed out, one of girls being about twenty. They were the ones who had been manning the machine gun." **Marcel Ollivier**, in *Barcelona, mayo 1937*, eds. García, Piotrowski, and Rosés, 131.

71   Correspondence between Agustín Guillamón and Albert Masó.

72   Domingo Ascaso was fatally wounded outside the Control Patrols' central base.

same time, the **Hotel Colón**, which shared an inner courtyard with the CNT's **Printing Trades Union**, which was getting ready to attack the hotel, was shooting at the **Telephone Exchange**.

Located between the Estat Catalá premises on the Rambla de Cataluña and the Hotel Colón, the **anarchist "Los de ayer y los de hoy" group** (at Gran Via, 610) and **Garmentmakers Union** had to fend off a constant siege.

On the upper part of the Ramblas, the headquarters of the POUM Executive Committee, under threat from a platoon of Assault Guards dug in at the **Café Moka**, had some protection from the **Poliorama** astronomical observatory across the street on the far side of the Ramblas, from where the entrance to the café Moka could be swept with gunfire.[73]

At the far end of the Puerta del Ángel, both the Healthworkers Union on the Plaza de Santa Ana and the Libertarian Youth headquarters on the Plaza Cucurulla, endured a worrying and prolonged siege and harassment, which they just managed to survive thanks to assistance from the Italian armored vehicles sent out from the Spartacus barracks.[74]

There was also fierce fighting in the **Parque de la Ciudadela**, around the **Parliament building, the residence of Azaña**, the Borne market, and the **Estación de Francia**, which was under CNT control but which troops from the nearby Interior Ministry building finally managed to capture on 5 May.[75] From the **Karl Marx barracks** (PSUC-controlled), the nearby **Spartacus, or Docks barracks** (on the Avenida Icaria), controlled by the CNT, was coming under hostile fire; barricades were set up a hundred meters from the latter's gates so that it would be better able to defend itself in the event of an attack.

Some troops on furlough from the Tierra y Libertad Column, as well as from the Durruti Column (who had been withdrawn from the Madrid front and were on their way back to the Aragon front) were inside the Spartacus barracks.[76] Their commanders, Sebas and Ricardo Sanz, were keen on keeping out of the streetfighting as best they could and abiding by the ceasefire orders issued by the RC. When the Spartacus barracks was shelled from the PSUC's nearby Karl Marx barracks, a mere six hundred meters away, the anarcho-syndicalists raised vigorous objections by phone on a number of occasions, always meeting

---

73   The British writer George Orwell was on guard duty at the Poliorama.

74   These days the Plaza de Santa Ana is no longer there; it used to be located at the end of the Puerta del Ángel, where it forked into two streets, the Calle Cucurulla and the Calle Arcs, opposite the Fuente de Santa Ana.

75   Azaña stayed in his official residence, paralyzed by his well-known physical cowardice.

76   They positioned six armored cars at the entrance to the Voroshilov barracks (in Sarriá) to prevent the Stalinist troops stationed there from venturing out. (Evidence of Marcel Ollivier, in *Barcelona, mayo 1937*, eds. García, Piotrowski, and Rosés, 129.)

with the same response: that the Karl Marx was unaware of any such shelling. Some two hundred Italian anarchists billeted at the barracks were the ones who responded—independently of the two Spanish column commanders—to the requests for assistance coming from the Casa CNT-FAI and a number of trade-union premises, bringing tanks out on to the streets to help whomever had requested their help, with weapons, food, medicine, or military muscle.[77] The figure of five thousand men inside the Spartacus barracks might seem a bit exaggerated, but, regardless, it was crucially important.[78] Those billeted at the Spartacus barracks may also have included around forty revolutionaries who had deserted from the Rojinegra and who were fighting on the barricades in the intersection of the Paralelo and Brecha de San Pablo, under the orders of Máximo Franco.[79]

Patrols from both sides were searching and disarming individuals and groups from other tendencies in the streets around the Ensanche.[80] There were lots of incidents, bursts of gunfire, and armed clashes erupting all over the place, but especially inside the triangle formed by the **Hotel Colón** (the PSUC's base), **the Generalidad Palace and the Public Order Commission** in the Vía Durruti. This counterrevolutionary bastion in the city center, made up of narrow, twisting lanes easily blocked by little barricades, though **still being contested**, might easily have fallen to a determined attack mounted by the Barcelona workers, as Josep Rebull insisted on proving to the POUM Executive Committee with a map of Barcelona in his hand. But the speeches broadcast by the ministers and other anarchist bigwigs had had a mighty demobilizing impact. Even though at the outset **there were those who shot at the radio when García Oliver had said there were kisses due to dead policemen** on the basis that they were brother antifascists, the message's demoralizing impact was soon evident on the barricades, with a slow but steady desertion by anarchist militants.[81] The Barcelona higher committees immediately fell into line behind their hierarchical superiors, the ministers from the Valencia government, hiding behind the cover of the "obvious" fact that the insurrection had been a "spontaneous" backlash against the provocation implicit in the taking over of the Telephone Exchange at the behest of the Generalidad.

At the Generalidad, the CNT hierarchs ("protected" by the artillery on

---

77   All the tanks or armored cars moving around Barcelona during the May Events were driven by those Italian anarchists from the Spartacus barracks.

78   Aldo Aguzzi, in *Barcelona, mayo 1937*, eds. García, Piotrowski, and Rosés, 157.

79   See above in the section dealing with 22 April.

80   Francisco Ferrer's grandson was murdered by a PSUC patrol at one such checkpoint, when he put up resistance to having his weapon taken from him.

81   Evidence of Albert Masó March (a POUM militant) in correspondence with the author: for a biography of Albert Masó (aka *Albert Vega*), see Casciolo and Guillamón, *Biografías del 36*, 224–236.

Montjuich trained on the Palace), the Stalinists, and the bourgeois Catalanists did the **only thing they could do: bring back the same government with a different lineup of names.**[82] The POUM leadership met with the CNT Regional Committee to … urge caution! On the barricades, a number of Committees for the Defense of the Revolution popped up but they failed to turn the formation of a Revolutionary Junta into a material fact.[83]

The most prominent theorist of the Friends of Durruti, Balius, crippled by progressive encephalitis along with spastic hemiplegia on his left side, which manifested itself in stiffness in his left leg and a twisting and tremor in his left arm, leaned on his crutches as he **read out a proclamation from the Ramblas Hospital barricade, sending out a call for** the European proletariat and especially its French representatives to demonstrate **revolutionary solidarity** with the Spanish proletariat's fight. It amounted to a formidable revolutionary snapshot of the moment, as beautiful as it was futile.

It was no easy undertaking to distribute the leaflet around the barricades and this had a lot to do with the mistrust in many militants and, indeed, physical repression. In fact, it cost a number of revolutionaries their lives (according to Jaime Fernández's oral testimony, he being one of those out distributing the leaflet on the barricades).[84]

On the afternoon of 5 May, the Bolshevik-Leninists Carlini and Quesada had an informal chat with Balius, arriving at no agreement or prospect beyond carrying on with the barricade fighting.[85] José Quesada stated:

> On the afternoon of the 5th, using our spare time, José María [Rodríguez] and I made our way to the hotel [Falcón] for a bite to eat, a cup of coffee and

---

82   According to Diego Abad de Santillán, *Por qué perdimos la guerra* (Barcelona: Plaza y Janés, 1977), 211.

83   Barcelona Local [POUM] Committee, "Report on the actions of the Local Committee."

84   For a biography of Jaime Fernández, see Casciolo and Guillamón, *Biografías del 36*, 82–97.

85   Apropos of the much vaunted but false claims of Trotskyist influence over the Friends of Durruti, Quesada claimed the following in the very same letter: "What influence did the GBL [Bolshevik-Leninist Group] have over the Friends of Durruti? None. In the true sense of the word, not even Carreño [could be said to have been influenced by] his friendship and dealings with Munis. On two occasions, all three of us [Carreño, Munis and Quesada] sat over a coffee, chatting about this and that; the first time was in the Café Brasil, which was, or is, on the Rambla, near where the Friends of Durruti had their premises; the second time was in the one at the far end of the Calle Goya, at the intersection with the Plaza de Cataluña [he must mean between the Plaza de Goya and the Plaza Universidad]. I was listening to the both of them, but took little part in the conversation." This letter from Quesada can be found in the Appendices, below. For a biography of Domenico Sedran (*Adolfo Carlini*), see Casciolo and Guillamón, *Biografías del 36*, 378–386. Regarding Quesada, see Agustín Guillamón, correspondence with José Quesada Suárez (1996).

a bit of rest. There we ran into Carlini and there was someone with him: he told us the name but I can no longer recall the name or the face. We chatted for a bit and reviewed the situation and agreed to go and see the Friends of Durruti and swap impressions about the overall situation; we all understood that since positions had been laid down by the leaderships of the CNT and the POUM, things were getting complicated, and the balance of forces in the fight was not going in our favor following the "treachery" of the traditional CNT-POUM organizations; but we had to carry on with the struggle to win the support of the people—"masses" not being part of the anarchists' vocabulary—in our fight. Again and again, Balius and Carlini reiterated that we either win the battle in which we were engaged, or July and the war would be goners. They were right, but not entirely right. It occurred to me that I should remind them of the much-repeated adage that the force of argument has always been just a snack for argument of force. Which led to Carlini's labeling me a pessimist. To which I replied: Pessimist or optimist, I've been behind my barricade these last three days and nights; I'm sticking there until the end, win or lose. The latter being the more likely.[86]

In the same letter, José Quesada penned these outstanding reflections, as well as a very significant note about Balius's anarchist mindset:

The meeting went on for a bit, but the underlying problems still hung in the air. Why? Because where we were in agreement—albeit that this was never said—was on staying united in the fight against all of the enemies of 19 July. About a centralized party or organization, not with the powers to order and command, but with a mandate and beholden to those in the grassroots, that is, with the people monitoring all authorities through their organizations. Whenever the word *authority* was invoked, when we talked about implementing the accords discussed and endorsed by the rank-and-file, the committees, or whoever, Balius's mood darkened. The interview or meeting ended without coming to grips with the real underlying issues or settling on a position vis-à-vis the insurrection, after the latter was condemned by the CNT-POUM.... As far as Balius and Carlini and the rest—though not all— were concerned, simply carrying on with the fight on the barricades was the right thing to do; and so we went our separate ways.

There was also a meeting between Jaime Balius and Josep Rebull, the

---

86   Letter from José Quesada to Agustín Guillamón (Tarbes, 16 October 1996), partly reprinted in the Appendices to this book.

secretary of the POUM's Cell 72, but, given the small numbers of both those organizations, it had no practical follow-up.[87] The Friends of Durruti turned down Josep Rebull's suggestion that they issue a joint Manifesto.

★

According to the **Presidential Record for Wednesday, 5 May 1937**[88]:

> As on the previous day, life in the city was completely paralyzed. No one reported for work. Nor were any newspapers published. Work in the war industries continued, however.
>
> In different locations around the city, there were bloody incidents, as a result of which many were killed and wounded.
>
> The speeches broadcast from microphones installed in the Generalidad Palace by the representatives of the UGT and CNT trade-union organizations and by the president of Catalonia himself, failed to restore calm in the city. Be that as it may, by that afternoon the situation was looking as grave as it had the day before.
>
> Throughout the day frequent messages were broadcast over the airwaves by a number of prominent antifascist personalities calling for a ceasefire and a return to work.
>
> At 3:00 p.m., it was the turn of CNT National Committee secretary, Señor **Mariano R. Vázquez**, and the UGT's representative, Señor **Rafael Vidiella**, who urged the rebels to lay down their arms and return to work.
>
> At 8:00 p.m., the Esquerra Republicana de Catalunya representative, Señor **Josep Tarradellas** and CNT representative **Pedro Herrera** both spoke to the same effect.
>
> Among the others who spoke were Señor **Jacinto Toryho**, managing editor of *Solidaridad Obrera*, and PSU members Messrs **Miquel Valdés**, **Víctor Colomer**, and **Pere Ardiaca**.
>
> The Generalidad government, provisionally constituted at 3:00 a.m., included Señor **Antonio Sesé** as the representative of the UGT, he being its secretary.

---

87   Author's correspondence and interview with Josep Rebull Cabré, See also Agustín Guillamón "Josep Rebull from 1937 to 1939: internal criticism of the policy of the POUM Executive Committee during the Spanish Revolution" in *Balance, Cuadernos de Historia*, nos. 919 and 20 (2000). A more extensive treatment can be found in *Espagne 1937. Josep Rebull, la voie révolutionnaire* (Spartacus). (Soon to be published in Spanish by Descontrol.)

88   All quoted material from this point until footnote 93 is taken from "The Presidential Record for Wednesday, 5 May 1937" [AMTM].

At noon, while making his way by car to take up his post as councillor, Señor **Antonio Sesé was gunned down and killed by pistol shots fired by persons unknown.** The two police officers escorting him also perished in the attack.

The dismal news, once known, produced deep emotion throughout the city.

On account of the death of Señor Antonio Sesé, Señor Rafael Vidiella was appointed to take up his place in the Generalidad government as representative of the UGT.

So the Generalidad government was constituted as follows:

President: Lluís Companys.

Councillors: Señores Carles Martí Feced (ERC), Rafael Vidiella (UGT), Joaquim Pou (URC), and Valerio Mas (CNT).

At noon the Republic's minister of justice and CNT representative Señor García Oliver left for Valencia.

During the afternoon a leaflet was in circulation in Barcelona signed by the Friends of Durruti Group. The aforesaid leaflet stated:

"A Revolutionary Junta. Shooting of the culprits. Disarmament of all the armed corps. Socialization of the economy. Disbandment of the political parties that have attacked the proletariat. Let us not surrender the streets. Revolution above all else. Long live the Social Revolution!"[89]

At 10:00 p.m., government radio stations broadcast a notice from the CNT-FAI in which it was stated that those organizations categorically disowned the manifesto signed by the Friends of Durruti Group and circulated in the city.

The aforementioned note closed by saying "Let everyone abide by the orders of the Generalidad government! Persons bearing arms, off the streets!

★

In the afternoon, the destroyers *Lepanto* and *Sánchez Barcaiztegui* arrived in Barcelona port.

The officers commanding the two destroyers, together with a commission of sailors, went to the Generalidad Palace where they greeted the president and placed themselves under his orders.

At 3:05 p.m., the following notice was broadcast:

---

89   In Spanish in the original. The reproduction is incomplete, in that there are two sentences missing: "We salute our comrades from the POUM who fraternized with us on the streets" and "Down with the counterrevolution!"

In light of the current circumstances, the government of the Republic has, on its own initiative, taken charge of Public Order in Catalonia. The Republic's government, which commands greater resources than the Generalidad will be able to meet the demands of the moment.

This is not the time for commentary. In light of the supreme interests of the war on fascism, the only option, and it should be recommended, is loyal and resolute collaboration with the Republic's government. Long live the Republic!

Alongside the Republic, the Generalidad's forces and personnel will not take long to re-establish the situation. We urge everyone to keep a level head. Yet again we urge that arms be set aside. We must have an end of this fratricidal strife. Enough of the disturbances on the streets.

Long live the Republic! Long live Catalonia!

★

Señor **Alberto Arrando,** lieutenant-colonel in the Security and Assault Guards, **was appointed as the republican government's delegate** in Catalonia in charge of Public Order services and acting chief of staff.

He took up office at 5:40 p.m.

He then went to greet the president of Catalonia, Señor Companys and the president of the Republic, Señor Azaña, telling them that he was ready to restore public order, one way or another.

The republican government's Public Order delegate, Señor Arrando, ordered that a notice be broadcast over the airwaves declaring that the Public Order forces belonged to the government and only the government, and they had no enemy save fascism.

The notice appealed to those who had been tricked into coming out into the streets to lay down their arms. Those who failed to do so—the notice added— were to be treated as fascists.

At 7:00 p.m., the new government of Catalonia assembled at the Generalidad Palace. Every one of its members attended.

At 10:15 p.m., the meeting concluded and the following notice was issued:

The new Generalidad Council, having met under the chairmanship of the president of Catalonia, Lluís Companys, and having been constituted on the basis of direct representation by the secretaries of the two trade-union centers, with representation from the Esquerra Republicana de Cataluña and from the Rabassaires Union, wishes to make one final effort to completely restore normality in Catalonia and avert continuation of the tragedy, written in blood and endured by the Catalan people, by sending out a peremptory call upon all those who are keeping up a fratricidal struggle that fills the whole of Catalonia with grief and compromises the overriding interests of the war against fascism.

The government, which is the ultimate and authentic representation of the entire antifascist front, calls upon all workers and upon the people of Catalonia to lay aside their arms, to forget these recent resentments and hatreds for the sake of the grandeur of the only struggle incumbent upon us all. Antifascists must stand by the governments of Catalonia and of the Republic, which the responsible organizations have supported through their representatives and to which they have entrusted the supreme leadership of the revolution and the fight against fascism.[90]

Long live Catalonia! Long live the Republic! Long live freedom!

★

Following this statement, the council agreed to meet in permanent session.

At midnight, health minister, Señora Federica Montseny, arrived at the Generalidad Palace in the company of Señor Mariano R. Vázquez, she had a meeting with the president of Catalonia.[91]

★

The Republic's Public Order delegate issued the following notice toward midnight:

The Republic's government in which all of the antifascist parties and organizations are represented, has assumed control of Public Order in Catalonia. From this moment forth, all officers are at the orders of the government and nobody—other than the blatantly malicious—can say that the forces are in the service of one party or one group. The forces belong to all, which is the very reason they belong to none. They are the forces of a lawful government

---

90   Even though it might have been part of the rhetoric of the historical period after 19 July 1936, it is still surprising to see it stated that the Generalidad and republican governments were the supreme leadership of the revolution. The hijacking of the notion of revolution was, of course, yet another battle in the counterrevolutionary struggle of republican governments against the working class.

91   The text actually has *Señor* and not *Señora*. Although, in CNT circles, there was a very familiar joke to the effect that "Federica was the CNT's best man," this was probably an oversight on the part of the reporter, or wholesale deference to the protocols in force, since hers was the first ever case of a female minister.

that is mindful only of winning a victory over fascism. The man who has assumed command this day regards no antifascist political or trade union organization as his enemy. He has no enemies other than the fascists, and he expects all of those who, carried away by passion or spurred into it by calculated provocation, have taken up arms, leading to these painful incidents, to lay them down forthwith. Those failing to do so are to be regarded effectively as enemy collaborators and will receive the treatment reserved for such.

It is high time that, on the streets, we sift the fascists from those who are not. Those who fail to do this must be doing it because they are in league with fascism. Which is why the entire people in whose name the government of the Republic acts, condemns them.

The PO [Public Order] Delegation must warn that uncontrollable elements have raided a warehouse holding GNR [Republican National Guard] uniforms.[92] In case these elements were intent on using those uniforms to some criminal end, which, in these times, would be tantamount to treason, all forces loyal to the Republic are being notified so that they may be forewarned against such eventuality.

★

Also around midnight, the UGT and CNT trade-union organizations released the following note:

The tragic occurrences that have happened in our city over the past forty-eight hours have prevented full attendance by Barcelona workers at their workplaces.

The conflict that triggered this anomalous situation that is injurious to the cause of the proletariat, has been satisfactorily resolved by the representatives of the antifascist parties and organizations assembled in the Generalidad Palace. Consequently, the CNT and UGT Local Federations have agreed to address all their members to order them to return to their usual employment right away. There must be a return to normality. Persisting in industrial idleness in these times of war against fascism is tantamount to collaborating with the common foe and to undermining our efforts.

---

92 *Republican National Guard* was the pious name bestowed upon the Civil Guard after 19 July 1936 in order to fend off popular rejection of that despised institution and forestall its abolition. In Catalonia, the Civil Guards were confined to barracks in the rearguard by the Generalidad government, rather than being dispatched into the front lines; May 1937 was a long-awaited opportunity to unleash these repressive forces on the revolutionary movement.

So, all UGT and CNT workers, without exception, are hereby ordered to report for work and we urge the workers from both unions to avoid any conduct that might provide a cause for disruptions and arguments at their production sites.[93]

★

Antonio Sesé's death inspired **these notes, written by Companys in his own handwriting and meant for Tarradellas:**

1. Generalidad president informs prime minister UGT secretary, comrade Sesé and escort murdered on way to take up office. Situation very grave. Urge dispatch of requested reinforcements, **aircraft,** and the rest. Asking quick response.
Over.
2. [*In Catalan*]
Friend Tarradellas: I think this note should be broadcast so that Defense can issue orders (Xena is there) and in case the Telephone Exchange cuts off outgoing calls and we are left with no other form of communications.
3. Friend Terra: Strikes me that the note I wrote for broadcast has to go out, come what may, and if another one is then needed, we can supply one.
Don't you agree?
In any event, give the go-ahead for its broadcast—if you think appropriate.[94]

★

According to the **Copy of the notes taken by President Lluís Companys:** "At 12:30 on the 5th [the night of 4–5 May] word came in stating that the state was taking charge of Public Order."

★

In the interim the situation had been contained, but by the Generalidad's own forces and the efforts of the leaders of the organizations and political parties. But the issue was still there with the same, grave internal implications. It was pointless thinking in terms of the five hundred men arriving via Tortosa, since

---

93   "The Presidential Record for Wednesday 5 May 1937" stops here [AMTM].
94   "Handwritten notes from Companys to Tarradellas, written in May 1937." Tarradellas Papers on the May Events of 1937 [ANC].

they could have been stopped from getting through to Barcelona by the simple expedient of blowing up some bridges. More had to come, and by sea.

★

By the time those forces got here, Colonel Torres was already in charge at Police Headquarters and Pozas in command of the Army of the East.

CNT Under-Secretary Molina is still at Defense and we have picked up a telephone message from the CNT regional [committee] to ex-Councillor Isgleas that he is to go to Defense and hand things over to Mas, the CNT's new councillor.

The president issued an official note to Molina stating that there is no new defense councillor and personally broadcast an announcement that he, the president, had earmarked that portfolio for himself, but, in light of the appointment of Pozas, he was handing over all the Generalidad's functions, in addition those conferred upon him by the State.[95]

Thursday, 6 May

According to *Soli*, the day began calmly, hinting that "the watchwords issued by the two sister unions had been heeded, as anticipated."[96] It was noted that "the streets seemed very busy" and that people were moving around optimistically and "with satisfaction reflected in their faces. Not a single shot was heard." The restoration of peace seemed to have been achieved. The Ramblas looked quiet. The Boquería market was very busy. There was "an abundance of meat and other foodstuffs."

However, a few bunches of *Stalinists* and Assault Guards were taking the papers of people passing by and ripping up CNT membership cards.

On the Vía Durruti, the scene of some very intense fighting on previous days, there was utter calm. The same could be said of the entire city.

But at 9:30 an exploding bomb was heard "and as if that was the signal," volleys of rifle fire followed in the Calle Pelayo and Plaza de Cataluña, shifting toward the left hand side of the Ensanche, where it persisted throughout the entire morning, spreading into Sants and other isolated pockets, albeit without the intensity and continuity of the preceding days.

---

95 The 5 May entry in "Copy of notes made by President Lluís Companys and teletype conversations between various political figures during the streetfighting in Barcelona from 3 to 7 May" [HI].

96 "General News from Yesterday," *Solidaridad Obrera* no. 1581, 7 May 1937, 1 and 2. A quite separate edition was issued on the same date, 7 May, numbered 1582 and displaying a masthead in red.

CNT personnel working on the metro, the trams, and buses reported for work, but were promptly told that damaged tracks needed repairs before the vehicles could be taken from the depots. The coaches that were brought out because the lines they used needed no repairs had to be returned to the depots because they came under gunfire. The metro was out of operation but "the Sarriá, Sabadell, and Tarrasa train services were operating during the day, until 7:30 p.m." The trains from Madrid, Zaragoza, and Alicante, as well as from the North, were operating normally.

At 9:50 a.m., the Generalidad broadcast a notice stating that the government was still in permanent session and that they had taken note "that the workers are preparing for a return to work." The government urged calm and said that people were to ignore false rumors and not let themselves be bullied. The notice was broadcast again at 10:45 a.m.

Later that morning "some volleys of gunfire rang out, followed by the explosions of ... small bombs, seemingly thrown in Sans." At 11:22 a.m., there was the sound of bombs and gunshots "followed by sniping." At 12:40, p.m., a further "burst of rifle fire" was heard. During the afternoon, rifle fire, gun battles, and sniping spread throughout the entire city, sometimes with intervals of an hour in between.

The Supplies Department broadcast a notice saying that it was working to ensure distribution of bread to all the bakeries that day.

The security forces had rounded up a hundred men in the vicinity of the Generalidad Palace. There had been a serious clash between the opposing sides in the Plaza Universidad, leaving a number of wounded and two dead. The La Batalla newspaper had its premises stormed and seized by the forces of public order.

A sizable group of women headed toward the wharves "where they attacked a number of trucks loaded with oranges, making off with all the produce." Barcelona City Council ordered every food trader and producer to reopen their establishments.

Given the revolt in a number of the wards close to the Modelo Prison, the decision was made to beef up the guard there in order to avert incident. Yet again the heroism of the Red Cross in tending to the victims of the revolt was plain to be seen. The bulk of the 160 detainees being held at the Public Order Commission were members of the Libertarian Youth, POUM, and CNT.

General Sebastián Pozas Pérez was appointed to stand in for General Aranguren as commander of the army's Fourth Division. Lots of false reports, rumors, and alarmist lies were flying around the city—for instance, that Aurelio Fernández, Marcos Alcón, Jacinto Toryho, and other prominent anarchist leaders had been killed—but the writer ascribed these to the fifth column and agents provocateurs.

The report on what was happening ended, not such much on an item of news as upon the wish that, with the supplies situation in the city easing, there was no need to "form queues nor to generate alarm."

★

In a goodwill gesture to help bring peace back to the city, **CNT militants vacated the Telephone Exchange building** where the conflict had originated; it was immediately overrun by police forces who gave UGT members guarantees that their jobs were safe and that telephone services should be restored.[97] When anarchist leaders objected, the response of the Generalidad was that "this was a fait accompli" and the CNT leaders chose not to publicize this fresh "betrayal" by the bourgeoisie, lest it inflame matters. *In common parlance, this was known as "firefighting," that is, dousing the flames and/or conflicts.* By then, the withdrawal of CNT personnel from their barricades was widespread. Exchanges of gunfire were rare.

When the news became known that a contingent of troops was en route from Valencia to pacify Barcelona, Balius suggested that a CNT column be raised to go out and meet it. Raised in Barcelona, that column would grow along the way and would be joined by quite a few militia members from the Aragon front: it might get as far as Valencia, and then storm the gates of Heaven! Commissions were set up to confer with the militants in the unions and on the streets, but there was no appetite for the proposal. *By that point it was utterly unrealistic.*

★

During the morning, there was a special meeting **of the RC** at the Casa CNT-FAI; the comrades holding down the top positions in the Organization were in attendance.[98]

Xena reported that talk of seven hundred guards "said to be in Tortosa" had been a false alarm.

He reported that a provisional government had been formed "charged solely with thrashing out a formula for calming minds that have been greatly convulsed of late." It was made up of the CNT, the UGT, the Rabassaires, and the ERC.

They needed to demonstrate that the CNT people had shown that they could defend themselves and were also up to displaying "the loftiest sense of responsibility" in order to ensure that calm was restored. This was the advice that had

---

97   According to the **Presidential Record** for 3 May, the Telephone Exchange had been **partly** occupied since 3 May. Now the talk is of a **complete takeover** of the building.

98   "Special meeting of the Regional Committee for Catalonia, in the presence of all the Organization's comrades holding the top responsibilities" [IISH-CNT-94D12] [The date of the meeting is not mentioned].

been issued to the Comarcas. They had to avoid the Valencia government's taking over Public Order.

Isgleas reported that he had had a telephone call from Herrera, telling him that "a number of mortars that had claimed victims" had been fired from the Casa CNT-FAI. Herrera had asked "if this could be stopped."

Xena reminded them that a defense committee for the Casa CNT-FAI had been set up and this should now be disbanded.

The vice-secretary stated that there had to be a ceasefire, but that they should remain vigilant "in case of what might happen."

The Regional of Groups piped up to say that they should not confuse the issue because "it was an issue of DEFENSE and not of ATTACK; if the other side did not implement a ceasefire, how can our comrades stop defending themselves?" It was up to the defense committee to decide.

Xena objected that they had to remain cognizant of "the matter of attacks on other Centers."

The Local Federation expressed the view that the defense committee could not "attack nor withdraw from any location, without the Organization's say-so." At this point, some loud explosions were heard, apparently mortar and cannon fire.

A lengthy debate was sparked by this change of mood and lots of suggestions for resolving matters as expeditiously as possible were advanced.

Costelo reported that there was "a certain leaflet signed by the Friends of Durruti [in circulation] that, due to its rather violent contents, strikes most comrades as unacceptable, and it is suggested that the comrades responsible for the drafting of it be disowned."[99]

Xena read out a note that he put to the Plenum for its approval, asking that neither the police nor any political premises be attacked or assaulted, lest this hinder the provisional government's peacemaking efforts.

The note was approved by majority vote.

Communications [Union] reported on the measures being taken to prevent forces from reaching Barcelona and for the defense of Casa CNT-FAI.

The meeting was brought to a close at 12:30 p.m.

★

Conversation between Pascual Tomás and Vidiella (morning):[100]

---

99   This leaflet had already been disowned over the airwaves on 5 May.
100   PRIME MINISTER'S OFFICE AND MINISTRY OF WAR. Telegraph office. Valencia, 6 May 1937 [FPI-AH-55-33].

[Tomás] Pascual Tomás here, requesting information, as the Executive is about to meet to deal with the Catalonian matter.[101]

[Vidiella] It looks like life is getting back to normal somewhat, but I cannot quite tell yet. Nerves are very strained. I suspect that this may be a plan aimed at making a better start. Those who unleashed this struggle [are out to] improve their positions and deliver the final blow. The Republic's government must be ready for them.

They are telling me now that a tank drove down the Paseo de Gracia: that can only be FAI personnel, the ones who have had all the armaments so far.[102] I am ill at ease because I cannot see things very clearly, however, we are doing all in our power to restore calm and tranquility, both the CNT Committee and the UGT, but I say again that I am ill at ease. I think there are elements with an interest in this not being stopped. Tell Caballero to have everything waiting and ready very soon because they may have something very serious up their sleeves for us. That's it. Let me have your answer.

[Tomás] Rest assured that every step has been taken to contend with [any] unpleasant contingency. I needn't tell you that you should keep a very level head so that you can control our defensive assets at all times. On behalf of the Executive, please convey our condolences to the Sesé family circle and let me have any news you have regarding the friends who stayed behind in Barcelona and whom I asked you yesterday to look out for.

[Vidiella] Those friends are with Foraste [?] and they are safe and I'll take care of issuing them a safe conduct pass from the government so that they may move around freely. Bear in mind that if the fighting flares up again, there is no way that we can avoid some terrifying eventuality today, given the resources available to the FAI, and if we don't receive the reinforcements today, it would be a catastrophe for one and all. Over and out.

[Tomás] I say again: keep a level head. We're keeping the government abreast of things. Keep calm. Call our friends and tell them not to budge from their

---

101 Pascual Tomás Taengua was a Spanish socialist activist born in 1898. In 1930, he was elected secretary of the UGT's National Metalworkers' Federation. In the February 1936 elections, he was elected a deputy. During the civil war, he belonged to the so-called *caballerista* faction and personally carried out a number of missions on Largo Caballero's behalf. In exile, he served as UGT general secretary from 1944 to 1968.

102 As mentioned earlier, all the tanks operating during the May Events came from the CNT's Spartacus (Espartaco) barracks and were driven by Italian anarchists.

hotel without my orders and that in Barcelona they are safe from whatever happens, for as long as need be. I'll call you again this afternoon, at around 5:00 p.m.

[Vidiella] I'll be here at five in the Telegraph Office and if you have nothing else to tell me, I'll pop out for a meeting with the Generalidad government. *Salud.*

[Tomás] Before you meet, call the comrades I left behind there and tell them we have just been speaking. Do not forget that message

[Vidiella] I won't. I'll deliver it to them right away.

Conversation between Pascual Tomás and Vidiella (at 5:00 p.m.)

[Tomás] Díaz Alor and Pascual Tomás here, asking for an update on the situation.

[Vidiella] We and the comrades [from the] CNT are making great efforts to restore normality. We are making headway, but it is hard going. There are strained nerves, which makes us fearful that the guns may talk again. There is no shortage of agents provocateurs everywhere exploiting the widespread psychosis, and I hesitate to offer any assurance that there will be no repetition of what we witnessed yesterday and the day before yesterday. There is some light gunfire that may be the prelude to widespread hostilities. Everybody reckons he is about to come under attack from his adversary, which shows that nobody wants to attack, but the very same edginess is straining the atmosphere. We have to be very cautious because, if things erupt, the consequences will be worse than on previous occasions.

[Tomás] I revert to what I told you this morning. To wit: that the vital steps be taken to ensure that the lawfulness of the Republic endures. You must step up your efforts to avert fresh clashes, so that you can operate with greater peace of mind, that being the only way of coming up with a solution. Let me know what government has been formed and what you have heard from the friends we left behind there.

[Vidiella] A government under the chairmanship of Companys and including the Catalonia Regional Secretary of the CNT, myself on behalf of the UGT, Martí Rouret for the Esquerra, and a Rabassaire, Joaquín Pou. It is a provisional government until another can be put together once all the antifascist organizations have agreed, if calm is restored. A moment ago, the president broadcast a memo according to which, since the erstwhile Defense Department persists in issuing orders, when the only person empowered to do so in regard to war-related matters is General Pozas, the appointee of the government of the Republic, the Defense Department has therefore been abolished. Your friends are still at the Hotel Nouvel and, thankful for the guidance you asked me to pass on to them, they will not venture out of the hotel but await your instructions.

Federica Montseny had a conversation over the telephone with Galarza, telling him that dispatching troops is adding to misgivings among the CNT masses and she fears that something catastrophic might be triggered as a result. Galarza calmed her by saying that they are going to relieve them [something unintelligible here] and are not under orders to take action against anybody, nor to mount reprisals. I say again that there is a climate [of confrontation] looming between us and the other side, which we are striving to banish, but whether we will succeed in this, I do not know.

[**Tomás**] Much obliged. We shall continue to monitor events as they develop minute by minute and will call again tomorrow morning. Let us leave it there, unless there is something else you want. *Salud.*

★

According to the Presidential Record for Thursday, 6 May 1937:[103]

Despite the notice released to the public jointly by the UGT-CNT trade-union organizations ordering their members to return to work, work has not resumed and life in the city was at an absolute standstill.

For all that, there were lots of people on the streets. Virtually all of the newspapers resumed publication, which was a powerful factor in creating the impression of normality. Catalonian Railways and the metro were operating as normal.

From the early morning hours onward, Generalidad transmitters were repeatedly circulating the following official notice:

"The government wants all citizens to know that they can come out onto the streets, safe in the knowledge that they will not be bothered. Let everyone

---

103 All quoted material from here until footnote 109 is taken from "The Presidential Record for Thursday 6 May 1937" [AMTM].

get back to work and move around so that the life of the city can get back to normal. Let no one be interfered with. Have confidence, citizens! Do not succumb to nervousness nor to false rumors. Go to your job. Above and beyond nervousness and false rumors, a level head on everyone's part will help restore the peace between the antifascist elements."

★

At around **10:00 a.m.**, this additional notice was broadcast:

"The Generalidad government, which is in permanent session, has seen for itself that workers are getting ready for a return to work. It is only natural that there is still some nervousness to overcome, but it is vital that no one let themselves be swayed by anyone with an interest in sustaining the agitation.

"The government calls upon everyone to display the same serene approach and to pay no heed to anyone, no matter whom, that, by phone or using any other medium, says things designed to breach order, since it must be borne in mind that there are fascist elements with an interest in keeping the fighting going.

"Keep a level head and let no one pay any attention to bullying.

"Long live antifascist unity!

"Long live Catalonia! Long live the Republic!"

★

Despite these notices, the serious incidents that had occurred over the previous two days in the city were repeated in a number of locations around Barcelona and, because of them, many people became victims, one being **Domingo Ascaso**, a leading light of the CNT.

★

At **11:30 a.m.**, the following notification from the **Internal Security Department** was broadcast over the government radio station:

"By agreement of the organizations that make them up, the Control Patrols have agreed to line up behind the lawful government of the Generalidad and have placed themselves at the disposal of the central government's delegate, Lieutenant-Colonel Arrando, to act in accordance with his guidelines and to ensure the triumph of the antifascist cause."

★

That afternoon, the cruiser *Jaime I* reached the port of Barcelona.

Barcelona City Council released a notice ordering all grocery stores to open for business so that city dwellers might make whatever food purchases they needed.

Throughout the day, the Generalidad government was in permanent session. From the early morning hours onward, a variety of notices from the government and from the general secretaries of the UGT and CNT urging a return to work were broadcast.

At 11:00 a.m., The minister of health in the republican government, Señora **Federica Montseny**, a member of the CNT's National Committee, arrived at the Generalidad Palace for talks with the president, Señor Companys. There was a repeat of that meeting during the afternoon.

★

Toward noon, Señora Federica Montseny, on behalf of the CNT, and Señor Rafael Vidiella, on behalf of the UGT delivered radio addresses along the same [peace-making] lines as earlier ones.

At 1:30 p.m., Generals Sebastián Pozas and Aranguren arrived at the Generalidad with their adjutants and held a meeting with the Catalonian government.[104]

Both upon entering and upon exiting from the Generalidad Palace, the two generals were applauded and cheered by a large crowd standing in the Plaza de la República.[105]

When en route to the Public Order Commission to take up his Public Order duties, the Republican National Guard colonel, Señor Escobar, was attacked by persons unknown who fired a number of shots at him.[106]

Colonel Escobar was left seriously wounded.

The Supplies Department broadcast an announcement to the citizenry that it was actively working to ensure a supply of flour to all the city's bakeries.

---

104 General Aranguren was commander in Barcelona of the Civil Guard, now rebranded as the Republican National Guard, which is to say he was in charge of troops of questionable loyalty to the Republic who had not been dispatched to frontline duties and whose name had been changed as a means of averting their disbandment.

105 Today's Plaza de Sant Jaume, where the Generalidad Palace and Corporation are located.

106 Republican National Guard: that is, Civil Guard.

That **afternoon**, the **president of Catalonia**, in the flesh, read out this notice:

"Lest there be any confusion, the president makes it known that, not having been appointed defense councillor in the new Council, a post that I had wanted to set aside for myself, and by virtue of the appointment by the [Republic's] government of General Pozas, who commands the Fourth Division, all of the functions of the Defense Department are vested in the general, along with all the authority and full range of military representation of the government of the Republic and of the Catalan government.

"Calm and unity of authentic antifascists!

"Long live freedom! Long live Catalonia and long live the Republic!"

The following notice, bearing the UGT and CNT trade unions' stamp of approval, was broadcast:

"This morning the unions have broadcast a notice urging all comrades capable of doing so to rise above this historic date and let no one dare raise the prospect of a split.

"Above and beyond anything else, the unity of the proletariat must be maintained. Respect one another, do not threaten one another. Long live the unity of the proletariat!"

At 6:00 p.m., the incoming internal security councillor, Señor Martí Feced, took up his post.

The security forces serving in the department greeted him with cries of: "Long live the Republic!"

The remit of the department was handed over to Señor Martí Feced by ex-Councillor Señor Artemi Aiguader.[107] The transfer was witnessed by Gen-

---

107 Internal security councillor in the Tarradellas government, 28 September 1936 to 5 May 1937. The winding-up of the CAMC had not ended the division of powers within the police forces. Artemi Aiguadé had control of the Assault Guards, the Republican National Guard (formerly Civil Guard), and the militias of the moderate parties. Artemi Aiguadé chaired the Internal Security Junta, whereas the CNT's Aurelio Fernández was its general secretary. From early March 1937 onwards, the contest for sole control of the Public Order forces and border forces, to disarm the Control Patrols and the rearguard generally, led to a government crisis in the Generalidad. This festered on until it erupted into the

eral Pozas, divisional commander and councillor for defense, plus the security force delegate Lieutenant-Colonel Arrando.

Señor Antoni Soler was appointed director-general of the local civil service and took up office.

★

At **6:00 p.m.**, the government radio stations broadcast the following note:

"The Council remains in session in order to oversee the restoration of normality and assure the prestige and good name of Catalonia and the Republic. The government has made the requisite appointments in the departments and is keeping in touch with the organizations, and it urges that people remain calm so that those defying the authorities may be isolated

"Keep level heads to avert a reopening of hostilities."

★

The general secretary of the [CNT] National Committee issued the following document:[108]

"We have recently seen a number of discordant, painful events move, through factionalism, into the dangerous terrain of fratricidal struggle.

"When the reason behind the disagreement, which has saddened the whole of loyalist Spain, reached our ears, we thought we were entitled to step in directly and actively to ensure an end to the hostilities and bring everyday life back to normal. Bent on achieving this purpose, we have exerted all our influence, continually dispatching delegations where events were happening. Meanwhile other representatives visited the government in search of a satisfactory solution that might encourage common sense, mindful of the enormous responsibility incumbent upon our actions in this the supreme juncture in the life of our people.

"As of today—we find ourselves compelled to say—we have issued no public statement, confident that quiet, well-attuned efforts would be the best means of reaching what our desire, and the people's interest, required; we

---

clashes of May 1937. Companys ordered his internal security councillor to take over the Telephone Exchange, even though the latter was to take the blame in the event of failure. Hence Companys's reluctance to dismiss him, as the CNT's councillors were insisting, as a step toward calming things down and restoring normality.

108 This was, Mariano R. Vázquez.

have abided strictly and cautiously by that silence, broken only to give an appropriate and brief answer to those determined to impose antifascist unity and bolster the government by means of a public scandal as well as unfair and disloyal allegations.

"As soon as we learned the implications of what was happening, we ordered the whole of our organization to keep a level head and steer clear of propaganda of the deed that might have fatal consequences for us all; we ensured that the same recommendation went out to all the frontline combatants.

"From that hour to this, we have engaged in countless efforts designed to ensure that calm is restored in our rearguard, efforts that those with bad intentions ignore and are incapable of duplicating.

"We finished up, warned one and all that, as soon as the opportunity afforded itself, we would speak out loudly and clearly so that the whole of Spain might know where to look for the provocateurs and where to look for those who want unity of action to be our victory flag. Meanwhile, we stick to the path that we have outlined—a path that isn't one of intemperate screaming—so that our people may regain the confidence that allows it to crush fascism once and for all."

Toward morning, the following message was broadcast:

"The responsible committees of the UGT and the CNT hereby reiterate the order, issued yesterday to all workers, to get them to return to work without delay.

"Once again, we direct ourselves to the membership of both union centers, urging them to heed no orders beyond those emanating from the Committees of the responsible organizations.

"We know that there are disruptive elements determined to impede a return to civic normality. We shall deal as harshly with them as the case requires and as circumstances recommend. No one has any authority to stand in the way of the workers returning to their usual employment. Anyone who does so is to be regarded as an agent provocateur in the service of fascism, and punished as such.

"We again urge the workers to set aside hostile attitudes and give a wide berth to anything that might cause discord in the centers of production. UGT and CNT membership cards are sacred. Anyone trespassing against them is trampling on the dignity of the working class. The Control Committees in every firm have an inescapable duty to see that these guidelines are implemented and all workers assured of respect in the workplace.

"Comrades: those victims of the nonsensical strife who have been hospitalized need to be tended to. Do not delay a single second more your return to normal productivity. Only thus, by working, will we be able to attend properly to their needs.

"So, to work, comrades!

"The Local Federation of UGT Unions. The Local Federation of CNT Sindicatos Únicos."

★

The tragic events rolled out in our city over the past forty-eight hours have prevented the totality of the workforce of Barcelona from reporting for work.

The conflict that triggered this anomalous situation, which is detrimental to the proletariat's cause, has been satisfactorily resolved by the representatives of the antifascist parties and organizations assembled in the Generalidad Palace. So the Local Federations of the CNT and the UGT have agreed to address all their members, to order them to return to their normal tasks. We have to get back to normality. Lingering industrial idleness in these times of war against fascism is tantamount to collaborating with our common enemy and to weakening ourselves.

Thus, all UGT and CNT workers, without exception, are hereby ordered back to work and we urge the workers from both unions to avoid any behavior in the centers of production that might give rise to disruptions.[109]

★

According to the **Copy of the notes taken by President Lluís Companys:**

On the 6th, the **Generalidad president** sent out a teletype stating: "that Federica Montseny has been here since yesterday and has asked that she be able to communicate by teletype with the prime minister in her capacity as minister, and she has been duly authorized so to do."

The president also issued another teletype, stating that: "Unless we have disarmament and a mopping up of the frontiers, there will be a repetition of the situation, because the same problem will obtain."

So here we are. It remains the same unless we have disarmament, not just on the streets, but also through a takeover of the arms depots. (Which has not been done).

109　"The Presidential Record for Thursday 6 May 1937" ends here [AMTM].

The new Public Order authorities dabble in politics. Giving talks, talking, coming up with formulas, making compromises, etc. **General Pozas** tries to organize Defense on the basis of commissions from all of the parties. **Colonel Torres** comes to an arrangement with the Control Patrols and rings the president and reads to him a note that opens: "The Control Patrols have come to an arrangement with the Generalidad and with Colonel Torres, the Republic's Supreme Head of Public Order." The colonel states that he means to have this notice broadcast over the airwaves. The **Generalidad's president** warns him that he must not in any way involve the Generalidad, which has reached no such agreement and will have no truck with the Control Patrols. Later **Colonel Torres** calls to say that instead of "have come to an arrangement with the Generalidad," the text reads "together with the Generalidad." The **president** warns him that he has not authorized nor given his consent to any mention's being made at all to the Generalidad apropos of the Control Patrols.[110] Later, the text is released without a word said to the president, as if it were a spontaneous declaration from the Control Patrols. The Public Order delegates are forever issuing statements and political comment.

Colonel Torres sets up a censorship office for the newspapers and an officer from the newly arrived forces, Don José María Díaz de Ceballos, formally tells the president to end the censorship introduced by the Generalidad-created Press. The same dispatch states that censorship applies to "news and political commentary."

The **president** phones the colonel who apologizes for the formality. The president agrees with Public Order enforcing censorship using whatever methods and scale as might be thought necessary, but wants it understood that the rules for "association, press, entertainments" do not fall under its remit, although the Generalidad government will afford it every facility it might wish for the moment, and if there is anything that needs to be discussed regarding such facilitation, it should be left until another time.

The president is insistent, however, that since the forces had arrived and since the State had reserved Public Order for itself in order to deploy its forces for that purpose and since the Generalidad had not been afforded sufficient troops, the State should act as assigned and without delay in respect to borders, disarmament, etc., since its political and general powers were not susceptible to seizure, nor was there any reason for it to hold on to Public Order.[111]

---

110 As a soldier, Colonel Torres was trying to arrange a peace between the two warring sides. As a politician, Companys was never going to recognize the Control Patrols as an equal with whom he could negotiate anything.

111 The entries for 6 May in the "Copy of the notes made by President Lluís Companys and teletype conversations between various political figures during the street-fighting in

At 22:15 hours, Vidiella and Llopis conversed by means of teletype:[112]

Vidiella: Vidiella here.

Llopis: Llopis here, sending you his greetings and wanting to know how the Generalidad government was formed and the current status of the situation in Barcelona.

Vidiella: A provisional government has been formed under the chairmanship of the Generalidad president; I am part of it, on the UGT's behalf; Valerio Mas, secretary [of the Regional CNT Committee; Martí Feced on behalf of the Esquerra and somebody called Joaquín Pou, representing the Rabassaires. This government will be expanded as soon as normality has been restored. Today there was some shooting, but quite a reduction in the fighting on the streets. Then again, minds are more agitated because everybody is expecting the other guy to attack him. So much so that I am almost inclined to believe that the fratricidal struggle will erupt again and will this time be a lot more vicious than yesterday and the day before. The FAI, which has thus far held virtually all the power in matters of the war and the war industries, has access to plenty of war materials, cannons, machine guns, hand grenades, rifles, etc. But the morale [of the] security forces and [of] our people is very high and will be able to fend off aggression with vigor. Be that as it may, the government of the Republic needs to monitor the situation, due to the formidable resources that the FAI possesses and to the natural weariness of our fighters.

I am in permanent contact with the Generalidad [and] with the CNT Regional Committee and we are making superhuman efforts to avert such a catastrophe [and] we might just pull it off, because as [I have already] said, there is a general psychosis with everybody thinking that the adversary is out to exterminate him. That is the real situation right now, although things might take a turn for the worse this morning or tonight."

Llopis: Thanks very much for your news, which I shall pass on to the prime minister. Rest assured that the Republic's government has taken the requisite steps and arranged matters to bring the situation in Barcelona to a swift

---

Barcelona between 3 and 7 May" [HI].

112 All quoted material from here until footnote 125 is taken from the Tarradellas Papers on the Events of May 1937 [ANC].

conclusion. Tell me, in this provisional government, have any departments and portfolios been allocated and how were they distributed?

Vidiella: I'm looking after Justice, Labor, Public Works, and Supplies. The Rabassaire is handling Agriculture. The CNT guy is looking after Public Services, Health and Social Assistance, and Economy. The Esquerra does not have any department since it had been in charge of Internal Security, which, now under the remit of the Republic, is represented by its security chief, Lieutenant-Colonel Herrando. The Generalidad has also lost its Defense Department since the republican government has entrusted that, by decree, to General Pozas, commander of the Fourth Division. The Generalidad president himself [has] broadcast a notice, in light of the fact that the old Defense Department was still issuing orders, saying that "this matter was under the exclusive remit of the republican government through the good offices of General Pozas."

Llopis: Do you know if General Pozas has had any difficulty at the Defense Department since that notice was given by the Generalidad president?

Vidiella: So far, none, to my knowledge, although we can take it for granted that his holding that councillorship will not have gone down well with the faction that used to hold it.[113] Pozas and Herrando get along well together and this seems to be lifting the morale of the security forces and the city dwellers. However, I say again that they are working with little in the way of visible resources. Do not overlook that point.

Llopis: I ask that question of you because, according to our surveillance associate, at seven o'clock this evening, it seems Radio Asociació de Catalunya has made it known that there is a new appointee, a new defense councillor, in the shape of Martí Feced. They added that he took up office in the presence of General Pozas, Tarradellas, and Aguader. Since we thought that odd, we assumed that it was a mistake on the part of whoever had been listening to the radio, so we were keen on the having any confirmation or correction you might have to offer."

Vidiella: I can deny it categorically. It must have been a rebel station as Radio Asociació and Radio Barcelona are under Generalidad government control and nothing gets said there without its say-so.

---

113   The CNT.

Llopis: Right, thanks a lot. Nothing else?

Vidiella: *Salud*, till next time.

Llopis: *Salud*.

★

The night of Thursday-to-Friday was decisive. The CNT and the FAI had not yet fully exerted themselves and remained on alert. There was no desire to break antifascist unity once and for all, much less come to an armed showdown. The anarchist higher committees were leaning in the direction of negotiations, but the situation was very fraught with dangers, and they were not even being offered the two resignations they had called for. There was also fighting in Tortosa and Tarragona. The troops from Valencia were closing in on Barcelona. The Casa CNT-FAI found itself under siege again. Anything might happen.[114]

Friday, 7 May

At 12:15 a.m., Uribe, the PCE minister of agriculture had a teletype conversation with a Stalinist source [Comorera, perhaps?] in Barcelona.

Source: Señor Uribe, greetings to you.

Uribe: Same to you.

Source: I was calling to brief you on the situation. Barcelona is bristling with barricades and despite the efforts of some CNT leaders, the anarchist gangs are not withdrawing from their fighting posts, nor have they desisted from their intentions to press ahead. I regard the calming reports that Federica Montseny and others have passed on to Largo Caballero and Galarza as extremely dangerous, and designed to have a counter-order issued regarding the troops now heading to Barcelona. Those forces have to get here, for one thing because ours are worn out by now and also because, with them, Pozas and Herrando will be able to sort out the underlying problem: which is to say, **disarm the FAI and break up the defense committees and the POUM, the real leaders of the subversion.** You should contact Galarza and warn him that Supreme Police Chief Lieutenant Herrando is a bit lame and on the brink of

---

114   See the texts by Aguzzi, Bonomini, Ollivier, and Souchy, cited in the Bibliography below.

making a tremendous mistake: absorbing the Control Patrols into the Assault Guards. You know that the Control Patrols are the scariest weapon in the FAI armory and have earned themselves a name for greed and cruelty. They are deeply despised by public opinion and by the Assault Guards themselves. You know, too, that some three months ago, we pulled our own patrollers out, lest we get any more compromised and be held answerable for that agency.[115] Consequently, their absorption or an acknowledgment of them on the part of Lieutenant Colonel Herrando would be a blow to the morale of the only force we have with any real morale, and to public opinion, which now expects to see the resolution of the situation that has prevented us from operating effectively. I reiterate this because it is very important that Galarza tackle Herrando this very day and warn him against this ploy by the rebels and forbid it in the clearest and most categorical terms.

Uribe: Right. Troops have set off by sea so that they will not run into any hurdles en route, so they tell me. I will immediately pass on what you have just been telling me to Galarza, and I too think it is a serious error to amalgamate the Control Patrols into the Assault Guards, and I will do all in my power to stop it from happening. Besides those matters, do you have any other news regarding the party and the masses at this point.?

Source: Thank you for the information and for your help. The [PSUC] party is working splendidly. Our militants have fought and are fighting with great courage.[116] I have to inform you that comrade Sesé was murdered on the Public Entertainments Union premises. The UGT General Secretariat had appointed Del Barrio as his replacement. Tell Galarza that there is an urgent need for machine guns and machinegun ammunition.

Uribe: See if you can get me the approximate number of the gangs [that] have rebelled and gauge the people's frame of mind and who seems to be the leader of the subversives.

Source: The revolt is by all the groups from the FAI and the POUM, the latter having acted as an out-and-out provocateur. The "punch" [coup] was planned meticulously, since, within a few hours of the order going out, Barcelona was covered with barricades. The people's mood could not be better and it would be [a bad thing] for us all if, due to some mistaken viewpoint

---

115   The PSUC had ceased its involvement in the Control Patrols back in late January 1937.
116   Plainly, the source was a PSUC member.

or whatever, the underlying problem I mentioned to you before was not swiftly resolved.

The leaders of the unrest are: the Barcelona unions, the defense committees that have the Control Patrols under their control, and the POUM, which has influence within the Libertarian Youth.[117] The defense councillorship has also had a hand in the crackdown on the unrest.

With regard to the last point, I have to tell you that, even now, messages are going out from Defense by Morse telegraph and Hughes to the front lines and to a variety [of locations] in Catalonia, giving orders contrary to the Republic and [line missing].[118] Communications should be issued [marked] urgently for the Chief in central Barcelona, ordering that Defense be denied communications facilities, which should be handed over to the Fourth Division until General Pozas himself gives the word on taking possession of the Defense Department. The staff of that agency should heed no one other than Pozas and, should they feel compelled to use lines of communication, the authorities should be extended the resources they may have within their reach.

Uribe: Any idea what Isgleas is doing and where he is?

Source: Isgleas has been very cowardly and is hiding out in the Regional Committee [of the] CNT. The real work is being done by the undersecretary, name of Molina.

Uribe: What's your opinion of this undersecretary Molina?

Source: At the moment, Molina is no longer undersecretary because our government's Defense Department has been done away with, but, even so, he spends all day working there. I reckon he is one of the greatest dangers.

Uribe: How have the [central] government's moves gone down there, and how about the takeover of public order? What is the position in the towns around the region as well as Barcelona?

Source: The measures have gone down well, but once this is over and the political situation gets back to normal, it will be necessary for public order [to be returned] to Catalonia. I have just been told that Galarza has granted the FAI a truce, which will end [at] nine today and I say again that this policy

---

117   Both these assertions are erroneous.
118   Hughes is a brand of teletype.

is utterly wrongheaded and that you should use your influence to ensure that there is no repetition.

All in all, there has been no breach of normality in the towns. There was some fighting in Tortosa, Tarragona, and Lérida, with the outcome favoring us. There has been a lot of unrest on the front but, thanks [to the] collaboration [of] Reyes, we reckon we will be able [to overcome] any situation.

Uribe: If you have anything new to tell me tomorrow, you can call me between one and two. My best wishes to the comrades, and I hope this disgraceful situation can be brought to an end as soon as possible.

Source: It would be better if you were to ring me at five [in the] afternoon, here at the Generalidad. *Salud.*

Uribe: Can't call at five. I have a cabinet meeting. I'll call you at two.

Source: Fine. *Salud.* Until tomorrow.

★

At 1:25 a.m., **Vidiella** sent off a **teletype** briefing on the plan drawn up by Jose del Barrio for ending the troubles in Barcelona by bombing Barcelona:

7 May 1937. **1:25 a.m.**

Alcubierre: Alcubierre here.[119]

Vidiella: Comrade Vidiella here.[120] Comrade **del Barrio's** Order goes like this:[121] "Situation Barcelona very grave. Should strive to have air force ready

---

119 Miquel Alcubierre had worked at the Lámparas Z firm alongside José del Barrio. He was a leading member of the UGT.

120 Rafael Vidiella, a typesetter, had been a prominent member of the CNT up until 1932, when he became a Barcelona Corporation official and joined the UGT and the PSOE. In July 1936, he was appointed liaison secretary of the PSUC and head of the CAMC's Investigations Committee. In December 1936, he took over from Nin as justice councillor. In the crisis government of 5 May 1937, he had just been made councillor for labor, public works, and justice.

121 José del Barrio was the PSUC's military secretary at the time. Since the events of July 1936, he had raised and led a military column on the Aragon front, made up of members of the recently launched Unified Socialist Party of Catalonia (PSUC). During the 1930s, he had been employed at the Lámparas Z plant and had been active in the CNT

to bomb, when we give the word, Los Escolapios, the Monumental bullring, the Campo Sagrado tram depot, the San Andrés, Pueblo Nuevo, and Pedralbes barracks, plus the Hotel el Reloj at no. 1, Plaza de España.[122] It is absolutely imperative that the air force strikes this morning (it is already seven o'clock). We shall brief by radio whether its presence is needed and where; we will state whether such-and-such a site is suitable and that should be enough to get the message understood. In addition, we need planes to drop us ammunition, which should be dropped at the Casal Carlos Marx in the Paseo de Gracia. We absolutely must have rifle ammunition. And some of those standard caliber ammunition clips for Colt automatic rifles. Have to report that the Army's Third Mountain Battalion is in Sabadell but unarmed, having gone there for rest. It is a great and absolutely reliable battalion, an it's asking if it can step in. It could be armed by air drop as the airfield is ours and so is Sabadell. If there is no better solution, we must send in our weapons so that the battalion, plus any forces that can be scraped together, may march on Barcelona as soon as possible. Insist upon this being done as a matter of urgency. Insist. Apart from that, spirits are good and we are certain of victory despite the great hurdles. Fraternal greetings. Del Barrio."

Vidiella: Vidiella here. Tell me how things stand on the front and if you have observed any movement by Francoist troops.

[**Del Barrio**]: Fine. Anarchist and POUM troops mobilized this morning with artillery, armored trucks, and machine guns; digging in in Binéfar, they had talks with an emissary from Lieutenant-Colonel Reyes, from what I have been told. At six this afternoon they returned to the front. However, I am not in a position to guarantee that they all did. This afternoon we intercepted a telephone conversation, Albero Barracks, Ascaso Division talking with Barbastro, which stated: "Landing a blow impossible. Valencia government has outplayed us by sending two-hundred truckloads of GN and we have to conform as it also has control of communication." I think that message provided

Metalworkers Union, from which he had been expelled after standing as a PCE candidate in the 1933 elections.

122   All of the buildings listed were barracks or buildings held by the CNT. The Pedralbes barracks had been dubbed the "Bakunin" barracks; members of the Durruti Column just back from the Madrid front and awaiting return to the Aragon front were in the Docks barracks in Pueblo Nuevo; Los Escolapios was the base of the Defense Committee of the Center which played a crucial part in the May insurrection (and which was only brought to heel after it had been attacked and pounded with artillery by public order troops and the PSUC in September 1937).

to me by Del Barrio should be passed on. There was also a Hughes message to Lieutenant-Colonel Reyes from Lérida airfield, the latter feeling very optimistic and, seemingly, he has doubts as to the veracity of our messages, believing that they are motivated by our nervousness, while he would be better placed to inform you of the forces that have relocated to Binéfar. For my part, I have already sent rifle munitions to the airfield. I intend to do likewise with the other gear and, if Lieutenant-Colonel cannot arm the Mountain Battalion in Sabadell, I will forward the rifles, by disarming a battalion of those serving on the front. It all depends on the Lieutenant-Colonel's fleetness of foot and I mean to contact him immediately, but should prefer if you would do so first. Troops' morale good, our anti-anarchist companies just waiting for their chance to show that they are Marxists. Greetings.

[**Vidiella**]: Message received. I shall let Comorera know about the Reyes thing and, if I deem it appropriate, I will be in touch with Lérida.

★

At 2:55 a.m., Interior Minister Ángel Galarza and Health Minister Federica Montseny conversed by means of teletype.

Galarza: Interior minister here.

Montseny: Health minister here. Greetings. I have some good news for you. Not a shot has been heard here for a fair number of hours now. The truce has been accepted and will be implemented if you can ensure that the forces sent up from Valencia do not enter Barcelona before daybreak and in batches so as not to draw attention. That would be great. We could all take it that the matter was settled. I don't know how far from Barcelona they are and we have ensured that the appropriate orders have gone out for them not to be harried, given, as García Oliver stated, that they were peace-making troops designed to resolve a situation. If you could just hold them back for a few hours, in, say, Villafranca, that would go down well. Over.

Galarza: You know that I always keep my word and those troops will not enter Barcelona until after nine o'clock. As long as the comrades whom you are so zealously leading can show that they have kept theirs. Moreover, I can tell you that their entry will be with enough of an interval between one batch and the next that they do not draw attention, and it would be very interesting if the reception from everybody were to be warm, since their mission is to pacify minds. Take Tortosa, where, as I told you, there had been a very tricky situation since Wednesday on account of personnel there having laid siege to the 150 guards in the post there at the time, through trickery, disarming them, and leaving a number wounded. By the time the forces coming up from Valencia arrived, there was already a battle raging between the UGT and the CNT. The troops came under fire on the bridges but so conducted themselves that, with very few shots fired and with no losses on either side, they entered Tortosa. The people who were on the bridges came out and I have it that, despite the constant sniping between the two union groupings, both sides bade the troops heartily welcome, because they saw that their mission was to bring peace.

Montseny: We shall strive, and are striving all day, along the lines you indicate, gradually persuading more and more people that we need to give a warm welcome to the troops you sent, who will stand as guarantors that minds are not going to be poisoned, nor inflamed by the inevitable political posturing that has brought Catalonia to this tragedy. In the morning, a new back-to-work order by the CNT and UGT will be made public and our belief is that if [nobody prevents the trams from coming out, the metro from running, and life from getting back to normal], everyone will turn up for work. Mariano is still enamored of his notion of a demonstration, though I have the same reservations as you. I reckon that in the end it will be pushed back until Saturday or Sunday. Provided that you show tact and we do likewise, it will be sorted out.

Galarza: I won't try to hide it from you that pressures have been brought to bear on me, including reminders about which party I belong to and even flattery, like the sort used by the witches who told the classical character "Thou shalt be king";[123] but my duty is to demonstrate that in this position there is not, nor can there be, any obsession other than keeping the peace between all the antifascists in the rearguard.

Montseny: Mariano sends you his greetings. He cannot speak to you because he is right now swapping impressions with Herrando. Without wearying you further, he sends you his best and urges you to carry on displaying your usual proverbial intelligence and tact…

Galarza: My best to Federica and Mariano, and rest assured that I shall not deviate from my line of conduct. *Salud.*

---

123 Namely, Macbeth.

Telephone conversation, Vázquez—Valerio Mas. At 1:45 p.m.[124]

That they have no idea where Isgleas is and that (Vázquez) should get in touch with the chief of public order in order to establish his whereabouts. That Xena had gone off to get some sleep.

That the Prisoners' Aid Commission will not be open for business until 3:00 p.m. That Santillán is nowhere to be found.

They have not made any joint intervention with the POUM.

That the Estat Català guys are gullible types.

That they must see to it that the death is pinned on Estate Catalá and the POUM.[125]

According to the Presidential Record for Friday, 7 May 1937:

Normality has returned completely to the city of Barcelona.

Things have been absolutely calm since the early hours of this morning. Scarcely an isolated gunshot has been heard in the city that, for three days, lived through violent events that claimed a huge number of victims and that crushed the spirits of citizens whose attention has been solely focused on developments in the war the Republic's soldiers are waging against fascism on a number of battlefronts.

At 5:05 a.m., a CNT representative spoke on that organization's microphones and urged workers to answer the vital need for a return to work. He stated that an agreement had been reached and that not another shot should be fired.

All workers, without distinction, returned to work. The public services and city transport service are operating. The newspapers were published. The grocery stores, factories, and workshops have opened. In the port, the business of loading and unloading was proceeding as normal. The city at last reverted to its normal rhythm. Bunches of passersby roamed the city streets that had been the scene of recent cruel events. The streets hit hardest by the fighting were the Petritxol and Boquería streets, the former Calle del Bisbe, Cardenal Casaña, Durán i Bas streets, and the streets surrounding the Casa CNT-FAI building on the Vía Durruti.

---

124   Translated from the Catalan.
125   Quoted material from Tarradellas Papers on the Events of May 1937 ends here.

Throughout the day the police set about arresting those walking around armed without the proper permit for the use of a weapon.

The tragic cost of the three days of cruel strife that bloodied the streets of Barcelona can be estimated at around four hundred dead and upwards of a thousand wounded.

Since the afternoon of Monday, 3 May, when stirrings of the serious incidents that later erupted were first observed, requisite precautions have been taken at the Generalidad Palace to thwart a potential attack on the part of the rebels.

The Mossos de Escuadra took up positions inside and outside the Palace.[126] A section from the Pyrenean Militias also manned the Palace from Monday onwards.[127]

On several occasions and from different locations on the streets leading to the Plaza de la República, the rebels attempted to attack the personnel charged with the defense of the Generalidad. At no time did they succeed in breaching the lines of defense set up around the Palace and the adjacent streets, and, as a result of the gun battles that erupted, the rebels sustained many losses.

The forces defending the Generalidad Palace made a hundred arrests over the three days that the incidents lasted.

Despite the intense gunfire continually directed from the Generalidad at the troublemakers, the Mossos d'Esquadra sustained only four casualties. One, Francisco Ferrer Prat, was killed. Lieutenant-Colonel Félix Gavari, Sergeant Josep Sabater Vigatá, and Mosso Emili Vilalta Santamaría, were all wounded.

In the early hours of the morning, Major Emili Menéndez López took charge as commissioner-general of public order.

The full normalization of city life was, of course, mirrored at the Generalidad Palace. Business resumed at the primary government center and most of the offices ran completely normally.

In accordance with the agreement worked out, the members of Catalonia's provisional government carried on holding meetings and conversing pretty much throughout. The meetings were always chaired by the president, Señor Companys. At noon, when the reporters showed up at the President's Office, Señor Companys ordered that they be informed that he had no news to offer them.

---

126 The Generalidad's police.

127 Catalanist militias, the embryo of an army of Catalan nationalists with their sights set on independence for Catalonia; instead of manning positions on the Aragon front, it just so happened that they were in Barcelona city.

The communist deputy Señora Margarita Nelken visited the Generalidad Palace to meet the president of Catalonia.

A friendly communiqué from Euzkadi's Delegation in Catalonia was received in the office of the president's undersecretary; in it, the government of the Basque Country reaffirmed its support for the Generalidad president and once again expressed its affection to the Catalan people.

Journalists reporting from the Generalidad Palace showered the councillor, Señor Vidiella, with questions, asking for a breakdown of the situation.

Señor Vidiella stated that the fighting was over and that normal life had not been disrupted in the slightest throughout Catalonia as a whole. Except for Tortosa—Señor Vidiella added—where a few isolated incidents had been recorded.

In the early afternoon, the internal security Councillor, Señor Marti Feced, declared to reporters that they could take it that normality had been completely restored to the city and that virtually every civic activity was functioning.

Ex-councillors Comorera, Calvet, and Miret said the same.

That afternoon, infantry Lieutenant-Colonel Emilio Torres Iglesias, the government's appointee as Barcelona's supreme Chief of Police, and Vigilance Corps agent José María Díaz de Ceballos, appointed commissioner-general at the Supreme Police Headquarters in Barcelona, flew into Barcelona from Valencia.

They both took up their posts immediately upon arrival in Barcelona and presented their compliments to the Generalidad president.

Toward evening, eighty truckloads of Assault Guards, amounting to a total of five thousand men, plus two motorized companies, arrived in Barcelona from Valencia.

The caravan's progress through the city streets provoked great enthusiasm.

On stepping down from his post as commissioner-general for public order, Señor Rodríguez Salas released the following statement:[128]

"As I step down from my position at the General Public Order Commission, I wish publicly to hail all who, on account of the posts they have filled and of the relations they have had with me, have assisted me in my duties.

"I have to register my gratitude to all of the Watch and Security personnel

---

128   The standing-down of Rodríguez Salas had been demanded repeatedly by the CNT as a step toward re-establishing normality in the city. Companys's dogged refusal to accede to this helped exacerbate events. Friction between CNT personnel and the public order commissioner had taken a tremendously serious turn some weeks prior to the May Events when, at a meeting of the Security Junta, Aurelio Fernández had put a pistol to Rodríguez Salas's head.

who have at all times afforded me their unconditional aid, above all during the grave times from which we have just emerged.

"I leave the Commission the same as when I entered it, the only difference being the result of actions upon which public opinion will pass judgment. That opinion and nothing more concerns me, since I cling to the moral satisfaction of having done all that I could to accomplish what was asked of me. At the Commission-General, I have merely been a loyal servant of a government that includes all organizations and on whose orders I have acted, regardless of whether or not it agreed with my political outlook, carrying out the instructions issued to me.[129]

"Today, as I step down as Commissioner, I revert to being what I always have been: an ardent militant of the Unified Socialist Party of Catalonia, to which I owe everything."[130]

★

The CNT released the following statement:

The tragic incidents in Barcelona have ended and, so that everyone may know what to abide by, the CNT Regional Committee and the Local Federation of Sindicatos Únicos express their unanimous determination to cooperate with the utmost efficacy and loyalty in the re-establishment of public order in Catalonia and end the partisan activity that led to the situation that triggered the tragedy.

Therefore, we reiterate our support for the Generalidad government and for the Public Order delegate sent in by the central government, Lieutenant-Colonel Torres, whose outstanding diligence in the performance of such a delicate mission in Catalonia we have seen for ourselves.

Unity and trust. Loyalty and equality of rights and duties for all antifascist groups in every regard.

That is the watchword of the moment and we all must be unanimous in abiding by it.

—The CNT Regional Committee
and Local Federation of Sindicatos Unicos."[131]

---

129 The Presidential Record makes it crystal clear that the order to take over the Telephone Exchange was issued by Companys. It was not in any way a personal initiative on the part of Rodríguez Salas.

130 Proclaiming his status as a Stalinist activist? An odd way of displaying his neutrality as commissioner.

131 "The Presidential Record for Friday 7 May 1937" ends here.

★

On Friday, 7 May 1937, *Solidaridad Obrera* published two editions. In *Soli* no. 1581 the headline read "The CNT and UGT reiterate back-to-work order" In *Soli* no. 1582, in a red, banner headline, we read the more confident and assured "The Fighting Is Over." *Things had progressed from orders to accomplished facts.*

★

According to a **copy of the notes made by President Lluís Companys:**

7 May 1937, 5:00 p.m.

Generalidad president here. The undersecretary wants to speak to Sr. Llopis's undersecretary.

Sr. Llopis's Undersecretary speaking.

Sr. Rouret's under-secretary here. Greetings from my president. Transmit the following to them. By means of our telephone monitoring, we have eavesdropped on a phone conversation according to which Mariano R. Vázquez from the CNT, and the undersecretary for Heath in the republican government, told Valerio Mas from that organization's Regional Committee the following: "We must see to it that the death is pinned on Estate Catalá and the POUM."[132] We would point out that the allegation as regards Estat Catalá is a slander, a stunt by the CNT to bring the focus back on separatism, because the tiny Estat Catalá group fought bravely on the side of the forces of Public Order against the rebels. The bit about the POUM, on the other hand, they are the leading agents provocateurs.[133] Read today's *La Batalla*, which is a disgrace, and they had to have it printed on a different press because its own has been seized by the Assault Guards. This morning that newspaper was being sold on the streets by POUM people in helmets and bearing rifles. The contents are a violent incitement to carry on with the fighting. I have only just found out that delegates from the POUM are at the Interior Ministry talking with the Public Order delegate,

---

132   The CNT leaders were even then suggesting two scapegoats.

133   Companys cleared Estat Catalá of all blame and singled out the POUM as the sole scapegoat.

Lieutenant-Colonel Arrando. I don't know what instructions the government has issued to its Public Order delegates, nor what the needs or intentions are regarding circulation generally, but I have to issue a warning about clarity for the future; we shall come to an arrangement with the Public Order delegate and General Pozas so that the Generalidad government can publish policy arrangements reflecting the capabilities of the Public Order forces and authorities. There has been no shooting today but the barricades still stand and the rebels are striving to consolidate and improve their positions. They are making no bones about the fact that at the first opportunity, they will launch a nationwide uprising—remember, all the warehouses holding war materials have been overrun, as has the Artillery Depot, and huge amounts of gear and ammunition are being stashed in locations around Barcelona. Their plan is to irritate and regain ground, while more responsible figures closer to the government politically bully and beaver away so that they are allowed to consolidate or hold onto positions. If total disarmament is not feasible—and the swift mopping up of the borders likewise—I have no doubt that, for all the talk, we will soon be confronted not just with the same state of affairs but one extended to other places around Spain, chiefly the Levante region.[134] Over.

[**Llopis**]: Many thanks, my dear Rouret, for the greetings you have sent on behalf of your Honorable President and for your own as well as for the interesting news you have sent me. Neither you nor I can be surprised by the tactic of pinning the deaths on somebody else or playing down responsibilities. The information available here is more than sufficient to decide how much to believe this one or that one. However, speaking for myself, I would venture to ask you to obtain a copy of *La Batalla* for me and that, as soon as you can, provide me with an objective assessment of the motives or pretexts that have set off the situation we are grappling with as well as the stances adopted by the political and trade union organizations. As you will appreciate, all of this will have to be raised again when everyone's representatives meet, and the prime minister has to have the fullest information, including whatever information you can furnish beyond the intelligence he officially receives. You should forward it all as securely and as swiftly as possible; the best way is probably by air. Tell the president that HE, the president of the Republic, has been in Valencia since this morning.

---

134   Complete disarmament of the rearguard and control of the borders were the goals Companys had set himself, to be achieved at all costs.

[**Rouret**]: I'll do as you say and, although you will appreciate that we have a lot of work to do relative to your request, the president asked me to pass on his most respectful regards to the president of the Republic.

[**Llopis**]: I'd be grateful if you could let me know Colonel Escobar's current status and if there is any truth in what the press says about loads of weapons' having been found in the Telephone Exchange building.

[**Rouret**]: My current impression is that Colonel Escobar is in a pretty satisfactory condition, although his injury is quite serious. Arms were found in the Telephone Exchange but not in any huge amounts. Many thanks. *Salud*.[135]

★

On the morning of 7 May, Barcelona looked like a different city. The workers left the barricades. Sometimes they dismantled them totally or in part. They withdrew to their homes but held on to their weapons, to the great regret and annoyance of the Generalidad government. The counterrevolutionary barricades were left standing, untouched and armed. Patrols of Assault Guards were disarming isolated workers and tearing up their union cards.

Unarmed, some young anarchists proceeded from Calle Portaferrissa and Calle Cucurulla (where the Libertarian Youth had premises) to the Plaza del Pi where the Assault Guards were, to suggest that both sides dismantle its barricades. A few hours passed before the Assault Guards agreed to this peacemaking gesture. The city center looked like a military encampment: there were barricades and trenches protecting the buildings or sealing off streets; the windows and balconies were covered by sandbags, furniture or mattresses; with rifle barrels poking out from behind them, from makeshift openings. But the people were delighted after three days of enforced confinement due to the unrelenting gunfire. They poured out on to the streets to shop, to gawk and gossip, and to take in the sun, forming "queues to pass through the barricades. The children were playing at revolution. In the cafes and bars, there was chit-chat."[136]

At around midday, a few incidents in the Boquería and Calle de San Pedro area were triggered by Assault Guards, but the overall feeling was that calm had returned for good.

---

135   The entries under 7 May in "Copy of the notes made by President Lluís Companys and conversations by teletype between various political figures during the streetfighting in Barcelona from 3 to 7 May 1937" end here [HI]. See also the Tarradellas Papers at the ANC.

136   Souchy, *La verdad*.

As darkness fell some gunshots were heard in the Puerta del Ángel and near the Arco del Triunfo, and the car in which Federica Montseny was travelling was shot at, one of her companions being wounded.

In accordance with the agreements, the captives on each side were to have been set free immediately. The CNT complied with this, starting with the six hundred Civil Guards detained in Sants, but the Catalan nationalists and the Stalinists showed greater reluctance and greater hesitancy. It was noted that even after some days, many libertarians were still prisoners.

★

From 7:00 p.m. onward, the troops from Valencia paraded along the Diagonal and the Paseo de Gracia. *Only a few barricades would be left to stand, the PSUC wanting to hold on to them to mark its territory and show others who the winners had been. The same old bourgeois order as ever prevailed once more in Barcelona.*

Albert Masó witnessed the desertion of the barricades and the parade by the troops:

> As time went by, the CNT leaders—Montseny, García Oliver, Vázquez, and so on—kept repeating over the radio their calls for an end to the strike, for a ceasefire, for the barricades to be abandoned, for us all to go home, plus their promises that they were going to sort everything out peaceably since "we are all brothers", and, since nobody was offering any credible and acceptable way out, the CNT comrades were losing heart and they abandoned our barricades and took off with the machine gun and we were left there on our own; yes, we POUMists were the last ones to quit the barricades. In our Gracia section, we paid the price for that; one comrade dead and two wounded ... the rising was primarily defensive.... So, as night fell on the 7th, I was able to see from behind a half-dismantled barricade the caravan of tens of truckloads of Assault Guards up from Valencia singing *The Internationale* to "restore order" in our city.[137]

As night fell that same day, the Libertarian Youth secretary, **Alfredo Martínez**, making his way back to his parents' home after having played a very active part in the negotiations for a ceasefire, **went missing**.[138]

---

137 Letter of Albert Masó to Agustín Guillamón, 14 July 1996.
138 Ramón Liarte (*Entre la revolución y la Guerra*, 250–252) quotes the evidence of Ramiro Rueda, Libertarian Youth secretary, arrested by Rodríguez Salas who, when he came to interrogate him, said of him and Merino "you have been the cornerstones of the anarchist resistance. And you're going to pay dearly for it. You're going to suffer the same fate as

The political speeches from the various leaders and virtually all of the contemporary newspapers noted, without any rigor, that the "round" figure for the victims of the May events was around five hundred dead and a thousand wounded. The 8 May edition of *Solidaridad Obrera* gave this breakdown: at the Clinical Hospital, 193 dead; General Hospital, 11 dead; Military Hospital, 5 dead; Red Cross, 8 dead; at La Alianza, 1 dead; making a total of 218 dead. If we add to this figure the twelve corpses of the libertarians murdered at the Karl Marx barracks then taken out to Cerdanyola by ambulance, the total figure adds up to more or less 230, which comes close to the 235 dead that the experts mention for 3 to 11 May 1937.[139]

★

Important Note: The sequence of what happened from 8 May 1937 onward is spelled out in the fourth volume of the tetralogy *Hambre y violencia en la Barcelona revolucionaria*, entitled *La represión contra la CNT y los revolucionarios. De mayo a septiembre de 1937* (Barcelona: Ediciones Descontrol, 2016). That tetralogy is organized as follows:

Hambre y violencia en la Barcelona revolucionaria

1. *La revolución de los comités. De julio a diciembre de 1936.*[140]

2. *La guerra del pan. De diciembre de 1936 a mayo de 1937.*

3. *Insurrección. Las sangrientas jornadas del 3 al 7 de mayo de 1937.*[141]

4. *La represión contra la CNT y los revolucionarios. De mayo a septiembre de 1937.*

---

your running mate Alfredo Martínez." Shortly after that, on discovering that the driver who had brought Rueda had managed to escape, he changed his attitude, stopped threatening him, and had him held on remand in prison to await trial.

139　The most recent rigorous studies into the tally of victims during the May Events (3–11 May 1937) speak of some 235 killed and do not dare offer a rough guess for the wounded. See the works of Aguilera, Solé, and Villarroya, cited in the Bibliography below. Aguilera also insists that the number of fatalities on the revolutionary side was double that among the counterrevolutionaries.

140　Published in English as *Ready for Revolution: The CNT Defense Committees in Barcelona, 1933–1938* (Oakland: AK Press and KSL, 2014).

141　The current volume.

3

The Epilogue to May

*The barrio and comarcal defense committees were in open and irrepressible revolt against their higher committees, and meetings were barely able to disguise this fact, much less come up with an appropriate response to their complaints and concerns. In actual fact, **a rift had opened up between the rank-and-file membership at ward and comarcal levels and the leadership**. If this did not crystallize into a formal organizational split it was due to the bureaucratic sway that the officers of the higher committees wielded in an authoritarian way over militants and members incapable of standing up to their own leaders and walking away from their organizations.*

*This lay at the root of the hatred that the higher committees felt toward the Friends of Durruti. **There was a chance that the rank-and-file membership in the barrios of Barcelona and out in the comarcas**, who had spearheaded the fighting on the barricades and whom they were intent on disarming and over whose head the threat of repression was looming and to whom they had already dealt brutal blows, **might find the group an ideological and organizational alternative** to the CNT-FAI, given the ineffectuality, uselessness, and indifference of the higher committees.*

Mariano Rodríguez Vázquez dated the CNT National Committee's report (on what had happened during the first week of May 1937) 13 May 1937.[1]

---

1   We know of three versions of that report, with notable differences between them:
     "Report on What Happened in Catalonia. To the FAI Peninsular Committee, in *[FAI] Reports of the May 1937 Rising and the Latest Crisis in the Government of the Republic* [AHN. Causa General. Bundle 792 (1), 15-23]. This was the original version.
     "Memorandum: The May 1937 Events in Barcelona. Document no. 17: Report Presented by the CNT's National Committee on What Happened in Catalonia" [BAEL]. This is a variation on the draft above.
     "The CNT and the Barcelona Events: We Cannot Keep Silent While Others Slander

The NC's report referred only to the work done by the NC during the May Events. However, it offered some very interesting detail that lifted the lid on the **nature of the provocation by the Stalinists, the ERC, and Estat Català and their intent to wipe out the libertarian movement in Catalonia.**

A mere reading of the report, without any additional comment, discloses the criminal intent and conspiratorial preparatory activities of that anti-CNT, counterrevolutionary bloc. But we stress again that the report centered only on the intervention made by the NC.

On Monday, 3 May, the NC had its first reports of "something serious going on in Barcelona," but decided not to step in because the situation in Catalonia had been out of kilter for some days already. "The political adversary was acting in a provocative manner," with the aim of "getting the confederal Organization to revert to streetfighting." The NC noted "that at numerous meetings and plenums things had been brought up in an inopportune way." That is, **provocation by the adversary and bad timing at meetings.**

On **Tuesday 4 May**, the anarchist ministers "were summoned by the prime minister" so that he could brief them on the very serious situation unfolding in Barcelona, and asked for their help. Largo Caballero confided to them that the Internal Security Council of Catalonia (actually the Generalidad government) has asked the interior minister for "the urgent dispatch of 1,500 Guards, crucial if the [insurrectionist] upheaval was to be snuffed out." The Largo Caballero government refused to send in that force "to act at the behest of someone who might well have had something to do with the conflict that has arisen." Rather than send in the troops, it stood ready to proceed with a "takeover of Public Order Services." It requested that the "CNT and UGT National Committees travel up to Barcelona immediately" to smooth over the conflict and look for solutions.

The CNT's NC decided to send in Juan García Oliver and Mariano Rodríguez Vázquez for the purpose of securing a ceasefire. For its part, the UGT sent Hernández Zancajo and Muñoz. "The trip was made by plane."

Us. Valencia, June 1937" [AEP]. This is a re-evaluation by the NC of the May Events. It is the text that Peirats reprints in *La CNT en la revolución española*, vol. 2 (Paris: Ruedo Ibérico, 1971), 162–165. He underlines the parts stricken out by the censor, in which there is an exposé of those who hatched a plot on behalf of the ERC and PSUC against the CNT, culminating in the May Events. Specifically, the finger is pointed at Comorera, Aiguadé, Dencás, Casanovas, Ventura y Gassol, Lluhí Vallesca, and the police officers Sancho Xicot, Polo, and Castañer. It was the publication of the findings of the devastating reports drafted by Dionisio Eroles and Manuel Escorza who, from as early as January 1937 onward, had detected and denounced preparations for a coup de force against the CNT. See above for Hilario Esteban's 10 April 1937 report to Escorza. *Such preparations are, in terms of the historiography, undeniable, unless sectarianism blinds the historian-manipulator to their duty.*

Together, the CNT and UGT representatives visited the RC. The latter was ready "to wrap the situation up just as soon Aiguadé and Rodríguez Sala step down," those two being held directly to blame for the conflict. There had been constant provocations, and the seizure of the Telephone Exchange "over the heads of the CNT-UGT Control Committee" was the last straw for the CNT's patience.

There was a meeting of all factions at the Generalidad Palace. Prior to the meeting, the CNT raised the matter of the "desirability of us representatives of the organizations making an address over the radio to launch the proposition of a ceasefire." They paused for the radio broadcast. They reconvened and, after a wide-ranging debate, the CNT's NC suggested "that a caretaker Council be formed, made up of four representatives," chaired by Companys, but with no one serving on it who had been part of the previous Council lineup and, on that basis, the longed-for resignations of Aguadé and Rodríguez Salas were obtained. The caretaker remit would last for about ten to fifteen days. This proposal was acceptable after broad discussion.

The fly in the ointment was whether this provisional government should be formed straight away, as the CNT's NC believed, or the following day, as the PSUC and ERC advocated "arguing that there would first have to be a total ceasefire on the streets." At 2:00 a.m. (**Wednesday, 5 May**) the determination was made that there should be further radio addresses ordering a complete ceasefire.

In the morning, Companys announced the formation of the new government.

In Valencia, the central government was meeting in permanent session to deal with the Catalan problem and discussing the order for the takeover of public order in Catalonia. For four hours, Federica Montseny stood up to the communists and republicans who were arguing in favor of the takeover. When news that the situation was improving arrived from Barcelona at 2:00 a.m., the meeting broke up.

But in Barcelona the situation was rapidly deteriorating and at around noon the news broke that the central government was taking over "public order and defense and appointing Arrando and Pozas to take charge at Security and War."

The takeover was gleefully welcomed by communists and republicans.[2] "Some French and some British warships had anchored" in the port of Barcelona. The CNT's NC carried on trying to arrive at a ceasefire. Then came news that muddied the waters. "Sesé, the new Generalidad councillor and national secretary of the UGT, had been killed en route to the Generalidad. And the word was that he had been murdered from the Public Entertainments Union premises.... Furthermore, the new Public Order delegate, Escobar, had faced

---

2   The NC of the CNT was opposed to the takeover on the grounds that it thought that the central government would come down hard on CNT personnel, as proved to be the case.

an attempt on his life while he was en route to take up office. From Valencia, Lieutenant-Colonel Arrando was chosen to replace him."

On Wednesday, 5 May, at night, the CNT NC decided to make a radio broadcast jointly with the UGT's Vidiella and a fresh appeal was issued "spelling it out that the CNT was ready to disown anyone still armed and on the streets an hour from now."

The CNT and UGT Local Federations jointly "drafted the back-to-work order." The CNT and UGT press directors agreed "that on Thursday they would come out with a message of concord."

On Thursday, 6 May, "day broke with relative calm on the streets." Work began on repairs to the tram tracks. But, as the morning wore on, the repair vehicles had "to withdraw after coming under gunfire." The Metro cancelled its services "because at some station entrances communist police officers and Estat Català were laying siege to travellers." People were being frisked on the streets and "CNT cards were being torn up." The CNT workers and some CNT premises "were under siege." Their adversaries were using the truce to consolidate their positions. Which was why "by midday, the fighting had deteriorated and the strife was spreading again." *At no point does the NC acknowledge that the failure of its call for an end to the* **strike** *was also down to the revolutionaries' refusal to obey the orders coming from the higher committees.*

That afternoon, the situation was graver than ever. "The comrades were ready to take to the streets straight out. Up until that point not everyone who could have been mobilized had been mobilized." The Organization was feeling "cornered." The Casa CNT-FAI was under siege, the Healthworkers Union was under constant attack. All CNT personnel were waiting for the full mobilization order "before throwing themselves into the decisive battle." There were reports of the arrival in Tortosa of "1,500 Guards sent up from Valencia." There was even talk of not letting Pozas take up the post to which the central government had appointed him.

In its report, the NC reckoned that if the CNT were to make up its mind to finally join battle, victory was a very tricky prospect. But it also raised this issue: "What would we do with victory?" The response it came up with was that it would be a disaster, an outright catastrophe: "the front lines would collapse," the ships at anchor in the port would step in "to impose the armistice for which so many yearn" and "with the war lost, the revolution would be lost and every revolutionary gain with it." *Deference to the ideology of antifascist unity was absolute, and complicity with the government-driven counterrevolution could not have been more blatant and the question that should have been posed was not "What would we do with victory?," but "What had become of libertarian principles and what would we do with counterrevolution?"*

The NC had determined to turn a blind eye to the provocations, confine the insurrection to Catalonia, and stop it from spreading to other regions or to the front lines, and, above all else, to prevent Franco's victory.

The NC rejected the abuse hurled at it by the rank-and-file membership and the charges that "it was not representative of the Organization." They soon managed to ensure that General Pozas was welcomed to the Defense Department. But above all, they had managed "to remain on the defensive rather than going on the offensive, as had been decided."[3] Next up, the NC volunteered its services to the central government "to see if there was some way of ending the fighting."

The NC contacted the Interior Ministry by means of a functioning teletype machine in the Generalidad Palace.[4] It proposed a three-hour truce during which the security forces should not intervene under any circumstance, because that was the only way to allow armed individuals to pull back from the barricades "and wherever else they were occupying."

"Galarza went along with our suggestion." It was agreed that from 6:00 a.m. to 9:00 a.m. on **Friday, 7 May,** "the security forces would not bother anybody." It was also decided that Rodríguez Salas should step down and that the Guards on their way up from Valencia should be allowed through. The NC ordered CNT members to start dismantling their barricades at 6:00 a.m. The CNT and UGT Local Federations again ordered a return to work. The Control Patrols, "**which had kept out of events,**" set out to patrol the streets at 6:00 a.m., on orders from the new Public Order delegate, Arrando.

The NC had come to a direct arrangement with the central government (Galarza), circumventing the Generalidad government: "the representatives from every antifascist faction, from Companys through to Comorera, pouted," as this was a very bad blow to their "calculations."

Over the morning of Friday 7 May CNT members left their barricades. Their adversaries exploited every possible opportunity to rattle their cages. On occasion the CNT personnel had a hard time refraining from retaliating against such provocations. That was how the existing, serious problem in Barcelona was sorted out.

---

3   Which is to say that they had successfully thwarted the attempt by Julián Merino and the CNT's Revolutionary Committee to go on the offensive. That attempt had the backing of the POUM on the streets. The Friends of Durruti and the SBLE also distributed flyers setting concrete goals for the insurrection underway. The failure of the efforts by Merino and the Revolutionary Committee to take the offensive—and the resolve evident in the flyers to endow the insurrection with some goals—highlighted **the absence of an offensive and the insurrection's lack of goals.**

4   All the phone lines were being monitored by the defense committees.

The report closed with a series of considerations, some correct and others less so, typifying the mindset of centralistic functionaries.

1.   What happened was no isolated incident nor was it spontaneous, but was part of a very elaborate program of provocations.

2.   That program had been spearheaded by the PSUC, Estat Catalá, and the ERC.

3.   They wanted the central government to take over at Public Order and to wipe out the CNT and the anarchists.

4.   With the anarchists crushed, the Generalidad government, the PSUC, and the [Catalan] nationalists would, facing no opposition, impose "bourgeois hegemony and separatist politics."

The first two points were self-evident and have been accepted by most historians as such. The latter two points, on the other hand, were a bit interrelated and fanciful. The report closed with a series of pretty exotic denunciations that would be hard to authenticate and that were indicative merely of the NC's powerlessness and lack of realism. The abyss that had opened up beneath the feet of the NC led to disaster, and Mariano Rodríguez Vázquez would not be the man to undo it.

The CNT NC's complicity with the counterrevolution and bourgeois order was as blatant as it was obscene. The NC had drunk deeply from the ideology of antifascist unity. Its abdication of anarchist principles was absolute. A reading of the NC's report on the May Events in Barcelona is not deserving of any further comment or characterization beyond a critical scrutiny.

It is worth pointing out that the NC was very conscious that it had successfully stemmed the offensive mounted by the Catalan CNT's Revolutionary Committee, led by Julián Merino and aided and abetted on the streets by the Friends of Durruti, the SBLE, and the POUM.

★

Jacobo Prince wrote his FACA comrades in Argentina a **letter/report** in which, after bemoaning the fact that a number of his previous letters and bulletins had gone astray, he delved deeply into the causes of and the bloodstained events that had occurred recently, during the first week in May.[5]

---

5   FACA correspondence, Letter 4, 16 May 1937 [BAEL].

As to the background:

It was plain that for some time a plot had been hatching against us.... The recent breakdown in the Generalidad...thoughtlessly caused by our comrades... and the manner in which that was resolved did not hold out the prospect of any normality, and in particular I had the impression that something serious was in the offing. The Esquerra's Aguadé had been left in charge at Public Order, and the guy's main feature is his hatred of the FAI. Our people were unhappy and there was an air of menace in the air. Even so, nobody on our side was prepared for anything serious.... And days went by like that and then along came the murder of Roldán Cortada, a matter yet to be clarified" [that was] explicitly condemned [by the Organization]. Some days after that (and cashing in on the atmosphere) Rodríguez Salas, commissioner-general of PO, mounted spectacular raids on the villages, making provocative arrests. There were violent incidents. At the same time, the carabineers, whose lawful assignment is to guard the borders, tried to enter Puigcerdá, which was under the complete control of our comrades, and there were clashes—with the carabineers being stripped of their weapons. Some comrades from here [Barcelona] stepped in and peace was restored. There was a further conflict in Bellver, near Puigcerdá. **Comrade Martín from there [Puigcerdá], someone highly regarded in the movement, whom the bourgeois and the PSUC folk utterly despised, made his way to that location. They laid an ambush for him and murdered him** along with his companions.[6] Nerves snapped and there were scattered clashes everywhere, without further consequence.

There were lots of isolated confrontations. On the streets of Barcelona, both sides were frisking passersby, disarming them and tearing up their membership cards "and there was a feeling that a provocation was in the offing. **There were talks between commissions from our committees and those from the PSUC and the Esquerra** with an eye to avoiding these things. But none of it amounted to anything more than fine words to which no one lived up.... There would be grounds for a range of bitter reflections upon the **tremendous harm done to us by the lack of ongoing discipline and the existence of irresponsible, rabble-rousing elements."**

As to the start of the insurrection, he recounted the attempt by an Assault Guard detachment to seize control of the Telephone Exchange; after the initial

---

6   This sentence is correct. See the various articles and studies of the Bellver incidents by Antonio Gascón and Agustín Guillamón, in the journals *Catalunya* (published by the CGT) and in *Cuadernos Republicanos*.

surprise, this was fought off by the CNT personnel who worked there and the Guards had been pinned down in the lower floors. "The news promptly spread like wildfire and within a short time groups armed with rifles appeared on the streets...the fireworks began on the Monday night." The CNT personnel took to the streets as a precaution, suspicious people were disarmed and positions were taken up. The following day, the situation deteriorated and it became clear that, on the part of the Stalinists, the ground had been prepared in advance, in contrast with the spontaneous reaction from the CNT people who were "without a plan, without a methodology, and without any concrete objective."

In his letter, Prince explained how he would not chronicle the events, this having already been done in pamphlet form and in the bulletin he was sending them, but would confine himself to offering his own impressions.

There was intense fighting all day on the **Tuesday**. It was apparent then that **the folk from the PSUC, the Esquerra, and Estat Catalá were prepared, with their buildings in the center fronted by parapets and barricades;** they were shooting at anything that moved. No doubt their own people had some sort of a password for identifying themselves.... By the end of the day the impression was that a wave of madness had swamped the streets.[7] I did not miss a single day at my post at *Soli*, capitalizing on the fact that it was in an area dominated by our guys and relatively peaceful. So I was in a position to find out all the details. The impression was of chaos and disaster. **Whereas our people had the upper hand across much of the city, the Casa CNT-FAI, being located in the center, found itself all but blockaded. At times, there was no way of approaching without running the risk of being slaughtered. That was sheer oversight. No precautionary measures had been taken** and they had seized the nearby buildings and were firing machine guns, sweeping the streets. Luckily, there were some *carritos* available that could defy the hail.[8] Every union premises, our own and theirs, was a fortress. Barricades went up everywhere. Several Civil Guard barracks were overrun, some of them surrendering without a shot fired. A number of Guards sought shelter in a moviehouse and they were bombarded until they gave themselves up and were shown every consideration.[9] In short, after 24 hours it was apparent that

---

7   Such "collective madness" was the favorite explanation of the higher committees who portrayed themselves as the only one in "their right minds" at that point. It was their way of describing the fact that the higher committees had been overwhelmed by the barrio defense committees.

8   An amusing way of referring to tanks.

9   The cinema was the *America* on the Paralelo. The cannons were of small caliber and had been brought in by the Sitges defense committee. Due to haste, they were not secured to

the whole business had been more intense than on 19 July. [On] the afternoon of the Tuesday, a commission made up of Santillán, Herrera, Souza, and Vázquez, from the NC, and some others besides, visited the Generalidad in an effort to end the mess. Two delegates from the UGT Executive also came and they conducted themselves very well. García Oliver came too, and later, after he had left, Federica showed up; her conduct throughout these events has been very proper. I need not go into the detail of the negotiations. To make a long story short, the point was this: our comrades, especially the ones who had come up from Valencia, caught onto the game and tried to thwart it at all costs. The game was this: the movement [insurrection] having been sparked, to push it to the limits and force the Valencia government to step in violently, ensuring that our forces would fight it out with the government forces until they were defeated or exhausted and, if need be, to trigger a landing by foreign troops, to which end Companys had sought help from the British and French navies, several vessels from which were at anchor in the port. That way they could successfully "liquidate" us under cover of the slander that we had placed the resistance to fascism in jeopardy.

As to the political backdrop to the May Events, the Argentinean Jacobo Prince pointed to the agreement between all political forces, with the exception of the CNT, that the revolution should be wound up: "The obstacle to that plan was the CNT, plus the Largo [Caballero] tendency." The Stalinist campaign to discredit Largo and CNT personnel was under way and the Aragon front was being blockaded. Companys had thrown in his lot with the Stalinist plotters.

Regarding the ceasefire order, Prince recounted how, despite the Tuesday night agreement that hostilities were to be suspended without any positions being abandoned as yet, there was an upsurge in clashes on the Wednesday, creating the impression that no one was in control of his rank-and-file on the barricades and that chaos and lack of leadership prevailed.

However, "the barrios had not sprung into action but were awaiting orders.[10] That had cost some lives as the other side had gone all out to provoke things, but it was a great boon, as things would have been an utter catastrophe but for this restraint."

According to Prince, "order was beginning to emerge from the chaos. A military leadership was set up under two former column commanders" who managed to seize the reins. "The people from the Committees put their heads

---

the ground and would leap a meter into the air with every shell that was fired.

10   Which is to say that by Wednesday the higher committees were successfully bringing the ward defense committees under control, holding them back and stymying them.

together: Was there a chance that they might wind up as masters of the situation if the entire membership was to be mobilized?" and, for another thing, "Could they sustain this?"

The first query was answered in the affirmative, "setting aside the ferocious fighting," but the second query drew a negative response because it would be hard to hold up for more than a week, given the "foreign forces, the blockade, the hunger pangs and all the rest." Patently, there had been no forward planning or preparedness since even the Casa CNT-FAI had been in imminent danger of being attacked.

Regarding Thursday night, Prince made a tragic assessment of the final cost of the bloody fighting in May: that **Thursday**, tram workers had been shot at while preparing to restore normal tram services. The Valencia government had sent in several thousand Guards, at the request of the Generalidad. "There were foreign vessels in the port. Provocations were continuing on the streets. People were impatient and furious. The Casa Central [Casa CNT-FAI] was under siege." As it happened, the most serious-minded comrades at the standing plenum of higher committees could see no way out other than perishing "in the ruins. The implication of which was to go for broke"—until, in the end, Vázquez came up with the opposite viewpoint: "letting the troops inside, applying the brakes to everything, sorting it all out, steering clear of catastrophe." Federica argued the same case forcefully. The "equanimity" of the troops from Valencia was known and trusted. Reason returned to the plenum and on the Thursday night there was "a revolution in many minds. The meaning of strategy and political sense was revealed." They had been to the brink of disaster and it took a lot of courage "to tell the comrades: **halt your fire even if they fire at you, even if they kill your comrade.**" Even though the bulk of the membership was persuaded "there were a few maverick and maladjusted types like these guys from the Friends of Durruti (Carreño being one of them) who put out a provocative flyer and were disowned."[11]

In his letter, Prince also disclosed a number of very interesting details that he described as "diplomatic." "We found out that Aguadé had issued **orders to the air force to bomb** our redoubts, orders that were not carried out because they needed to come from the minister."[12] He accused the Stalinists of having shot at and wounded the first PO head sent up from Valencia, just to put off Rodríguez Salas having to step down. The CNT press sang the praises of Largo and Galarza as a counter to the Stalinists' propaganda and provocations.

---

11   Leaflet or flyer. Remember that the Argentinean FACA subscribed to the viewpoint of the higher committees.
12   In actual fact, the orders for the bombing had come from Companys.

General Pozas, who took over at Defense, asked all the CNT personnel there, and especially Molina "Juanel" to stay on in their posts. Juanel had prevented the CNT columns from coming down to Barcelona and stopped the militia members in their barracks in Barcelona from taking to the streets. "He was congratulated by the government and by the High Command." Prince remarked that he had averted the collapse of the Aragon front.

Prince devoted a section of his letter to denouncing the **crackdown in the villages** during the May Events. He claimed that the five hundred Guards arrested were immediately released, whereas there were still CNT personnel being held "with no guarantee that they will be getting out." In the CNT-controlled villages, there had been no incidents, except for a few killings in the initial clashes. But wherever the Stalinists had emerged as the victors, aided and abetted by the security forces, "there were brutal, fascist-style reprisals taken. Prisoners murdered, torture, etc. This Catalan bourgeoisie carries a ferocious hatred for us, a hatred skillfully exploited by the bolshies, their allies. As they have already shown. The most murderous of all are the Estat Catalá guys, who murdered twelve lads from the [Libertarian] Youth who had been taken prisoner:[13] before they finished them off, they savagely tortured them." Prince warned of the chances of a Catalan bourgeoisie-sponsored "St Bartholomew's Night against *faístas*."

Prince closed that portion of his letter with *one of those all-embracing thoughts from the higher committees when they congratulated themselves on their inexcusable and depressing breach of principles*: "We will have accomplished a great historical task **EVEN THOUGH IN PRACTICE WE HAVE HAD TO CONTRADICT EVERY DOGMA OF ANARCHISM.**[14] We need to have the courage to state that, although, for didactic reasons, it's not appropriate those precise terms. But honesty above all else."

He then went on to describe the **murders of Berneri and Barbieri** by the *cheka*. He accused Antonov of having ordered the murders: "Berneri's specialty of attacking the bolshies had not gone unnoticed." His conclusion was that "the truth is that Berneri was murdered under cover of the fighting on the barricades when there was no control over anything." He also remarked upon and regretted the murder of the Argentinean comrade Tuffró in Tarragonas.

Prince called to mind a meeting of militants prior to the May Events at which **Federica Montseny** had delivered "a brilliant and daring accounting"

---

13 Prince's information was incorrect. As is plain from the TSJC (Catalonian Supreme Court of justice) file on the twelve murder victims whose corpses were found dumped in Bellaterra, they had been arrested, tortured, and then murdered in the PSUC's Karl Marx barracks.

14 The capitalization is by Prince. But the bold face has been added by the author of this book.

expounding on her government "and how she, as purist as anyone, realized that for the revolution's own good, every weapon had to be deployed and that included the weapons of politics; that they needed to employ shrewdness and trickery like all politicians do and enter into alliances with whomever we need to, et cetera."

The object of that meeting had been to "set up a sort of an Executive Committee covering the three organizations, the CNT-FAI-JJLL, and to stop with these endless plenums and assemblies." It would be for that Executive to lay down guidelines to be followed.

Prominent among the propaganda guidelines in the immediate term were the heaping of praise upon and exalting of the personality of Largo Caballero and the CNT-UGT alliance. *Fragua Social, Castilla Libre. Soli* immediately ran with this slogan, to which many anarcho-syndicalists took extraordinary exception. Prince closed his letter by invoking the uncertain prospects ahead, the only sure thing being the determination of the Stalinists and the bourgeoisie to "have done with the Revolution by finishing us." Even though he did not know which was the correct response in the present circumstances, Prince ruled out "voicing criticisms of a classical purist sort, which, unfortunately, still happens, and we can anticipate it spreading, so we have to mount out-and-out opposition." Prince could not imagine anything "more irksome and imbecilic than this purity business."[15]

★

On 21 May 1937, there was a **Plenum of the Barcelona Local Federation of Sindicatos Únicos,** at which the bloodstained events of the first week in May came up for discussion.[16]

The **Garmentworkers Union** described the performance of the NC as "far from capable," complained of the "unseemly propaganda mounted in favor of Largo Caballero," and concluded by asking for the resignations of the NC.

Printing Trades [Union] agreed with the description of the propaganda in favor of Largo Caballero as "misguided" but did not propose any motion of censure because, in its view that, in the situation currently facing them, there was no need for any further aggravation of the Organization's problems.

Transport [Union] requested that the NC step down.

Foodworkers [Union], on the other hand, endorsed the report from the NC's delegate, which it thought a proper account of what had happened.

---

15   This is nothing new; it was a classic excuse. In every split or debate, those who trespass against principles accuse their adversaries of being purists and/or dogmatists.

16   "Minutes of the Plenum of Unions held on 21 May 1937" [FAL-R109-409/414].

Steel- and Metalworkers [Union] advocated coming to a broad agreement with the wholesome part of the UGT. It stated "that we have dabbled in politics and we have lost, which suggests our militants should withdraw from all things political" and re-engage with trade-union activity.

Public Entertainments [Union] insisted that the NC should be stripped of all executive authority and pull out of politics, and it asked the NC to quickly step down and for militants to get back to trade-union activity.

Building and Woodworkers [Union] reckoned that the experiments in collaboration alongside political parties had not borne fruit and moved that "all official governmental bodies be abandoned" and that they return to the unions.

The Local Federation of Anarchist Groups approved of the performance of the NC and suggested that the CNT, FAI, and JJLL coordinate their tasks "by means of joint committees" that might facilitate "agile and homogeneous" action. They should be working "on behalf of the revolutionary worker alliance." At the same time relying upon all measures likely to help win the war, and that included governmental measures, they had to defend revolutionary gains and abide by "a policy of watchful opposition vis-à-vis the bourgeois democratic government." *That is, a carrot-and-stick policy; supporting the government in winning the war against fascism, while at the same time defending the gains of the revolution from that same government. Neither fish nor fowl. Fighting simultaneously on behalf of the revolution and of the war.*

The Anarchist Groups [GGAA] closed their contribution by urging comrades to remain in their posts and to thrash out a new organizational format for the FAI.

The JJLL made a declaration of apolitical faith, calling for a return "to anarchist principles" and for a recruitment campaign. They took exception to the anarchist press's campaign in favor of the socialist Largo Caballero's government.

Healthworkers [Union] accepted the NC report in its entirety.

Chemical Industries [Union] was rather hesitant about accepting the NC report and protested at the pro-Largo Caballero campaign.

Liberal Professions [Union] came out in favor of the NC report.

Distribution [Union] expressed unhappiness with the NC and asked that *Solidaridad Obrera* be censured for its pro-Largo Caballero campaign.

According to **Manufacturing** [Union], the blame lay, not with *Soli*, but with the committees who had suggested just such a press campaign.

By a majority, the Plenum passed a vote ratifying its confidence in the NC.

Discussions then turned to the stance to be adopted by the CNT "vis-à-vis the new [socialist] government" headed by Negrín. Some unions (Transport, Woodworkers, Printing Trades, Steel and Metalworking, Entertainments, plus the JJLL Federation) came down in favor of CNT personnel's withdrawing from posts; against collaborationism in any guise, and even in favor of encouraging a split within the UGT, but a lot of dissenting voices were heard, like those from the Garmentworkers, Chemical Industries, Distribution, Healthworkers, and Liberal Professions, in favor of collaborationism "on matters relating to the war" and of agreeing to "a minimum program with the UGT."

The union-by-union voting arrangement ensured that those who were favorably disposed toward political collaborationism had the majority.

The plenum carried on debating the political and social orientation of the libertarian movement, the collectivizations, cooperativism, and the need to set up a Prisoners' Aid Committee (which passed by unanimous vote): "sheer necessity demands it."

Transport asked "that the disarming of our comrades and unions be prevented."

This Plenum had ratified its confidence in the NC, had endorsed ongoing political collaboration, this time with the new Negrín-led government, forcefully argued in favor of the prospects of CNT-UGT unity, and set up the crucial Prisoners' Aid Committee against the backdrop of an exasperated government and Stalinist crackdown.

The political (though not military) defeat of the May insurrection was borne out at this Plenum, along with a second and even more terrifying political setback: Ratifying their confidence in an NC that had led to the defeat of the May insurrection? Pressing ahead with collaborationism? Unity with the Stalinized UGT? Relaunching the Prisoners' Aid Committee "in the middle of a period of revolution"? What did it all mean?

The keynote of this Plenum was the abdication of revolution and adapting to the ascendancy of the counterrevolution. Anarchist principles lay in ruins by then; all that was left standing was the ideology of antifascist unity.

In the wake of this Plenum, the Confederal Defense Committees submitted a resolution addressed to the Barcelona Local Federation of [CNT] Unions, putting their finger on "a matter crucial to the welfare of our organization and ideas."[17]

The **Defense Committees** introduced themselves like this: "It is an open secret that the Confederal Defense Agency has played and is playing a highly praiseworthy [brilliant] role in the Revolution, sacrificing everything for the sake of our Organization, something...that has been overlooked, and the proof of that

---

17   "Resolution put forth by the Confederal Defense Committees to the Barcelona Local Federation of Unions" [FAL-R-109/415].

is that the Trade Union organization passes accords but, in practice, does not abide by them."

Once again, they called upon the unions to acknowledge their agency and autonomy "as afforded us by the Revolution" because that was the only way of "reinforcing the unity of our bloc" and, going forward, avoiding "the entire series of organizational differences we have blundered into."

So they summed up the "fundamental issue" in these three points:

1. They ought to be consulted in all decisions affecting them.

2. They should control all the Organization's arms.

3. In the event that the agency of the defense committees was not acknowledged, the matter of their funding had to be resolved.

Given that they were organizationally dependent upon the unions, the defense committees, those potential agencies of power, were still having to beg for their own autonomy and status, for some acknowledgment of the outstanding role they had played in the recent insurrection, for a monopoly over the weaponry within the Organization, and for adequate funding. They would soon find themselves having to fight for their very survival and to withstand repression coming from the government and counterrevolution, enforced with the complicity of the higher committees.

4

The Insurrection in Summary: Clarifying the Revolutionary Thread of the CNT

At the 12 April 1937 gathering of the Local Federation of Anarchist Groups, radicalized by the invitation that had been issued to the Libertarian Youth and the delegates from the defense committees, there was insistence that all CNT personnel withdraw from any municipal or governmental office and that an insurrectionist committee be set up. **Julián Merino, Pablo Ruiz, and Juan Santana Calero** had played outstanding roles in that radicalization.

In mid-April 1937, Manuel Escorza del Val directly negotiated a way out of the Generalidad government crisis with Companys; that crisis had erupted in early March 1937 over the decrees setting up the Unified Security Corps and abolishing the Control Patrols. Companys kept Tarradellas at arm's length from those negotiations because, to Companys's mind, Tarradellas was unduly soft on the CNT. Companys sought a rapprochement with the PSUC within the Generalidad government and was out to sideline or even exclude the CNT once and for all. He had it in mind to establish a strong Generalidad government by doing so.

After some tough negotiations that included some violent arguments and threats, they came up with a flabby agreement that provided for a government that Aurelio Fernández would join as a Generalidad Council member.

The murder of Antonio Martín in Bellver de Cerdaña on 27 April shattered the fragile temporary compromise agreed to during the talks of 9–11 April and the personal accommodation reached between Companys and Escorza on 15 April.

Manuel Escorza tipped off the defense committees that he had intelligence regarding a foreseeable and imminent coup or violent operation by the Generalidad's Public Order forces, one that would be aided and abetted by the PSUC and the ERC.[1] Events in Bellver on 27 April plus the murder of Antonio Martín were the overture to the coup de force being hatched in Barcelona.[2] **Escorza lit the spark that triggered the insurrection by placing the defense committees in a state of alert**. The constant frictions, the disarming of one side by the other, and the repeated brushes between the Control Patrols and the Assault Guards certainly heralded the imminent and definitive confrontation.

The higher committees (**Dionisio Eroles and José Asens**) stepped in right at the outset of the takeover of the Telephone Exchange, their purpose being to avert the eruption of the insurrection, and, once the insurrection was under way, to capture control of it and bring it to an end; but they had been swept aside by the defense committees and very soon found themselves utterly overwhelmed.

The 4 May 1937 meeting of the RC was called at the instigation of Julián Merino who spoke as the (military) sponsor of the insurrection in progress, asking the RC to lead it and succeeding in having a (secret) revolutionary committee of the Catalan CNT appointed, plus two commissions: one for the Center and one for the Paralelo-Plaza de España sector.[3] Lucio Ruano played a very active role in breaking the cordon around the Casa CNT-FAI building, by hurling bombs at the forces surrounding the building, as well have by having control of the artillery in Montjuich, the guns of which were trained on the Generalidad Palace after that.

The Paralelo-Plaza de España commission led the fighting on that street and in the Plaza de España, attacking the Casarramona Civil Guard and Assault Guard barracks in the Plaza de España, capturing some six hundred (Assault and Civil) Guards who were held on the premises of the Hotel at no. 1 and in the España Industrial building.[4]

The Center commission operated alongside the Friends of Durruti (**Pablo Ruiz** and **Jaime Balius**), taking over the whole of the Calle Hospital from the Ramblas end, where the Friends of Durruti headquarters were, as far as the Los Escolapios building, where the Defense Committee of the Center (and Pueblo

---

1 César Martínez Lorenzo, *Le movement anarchiste en Espagne. Pouvoir et révolution sociale* (Les Éditions Libertaires, 2006), 347.

2 For a biography of Antonio Martín, see Casciolo and Guillamón, *Biografías del 36*, 202–223.

3 "Special meeting held on 4 May 1937 by the Regional Committee and other committees in charge in Catalonia" [IISH-CNT-85C1]. Escorza did not attend this meeting, because he regarded the insurrection as premature and worried that its failure might lead to a loss of strength and influence for the CNT. For the revolutionary committee, see Severino Campos, "Ideas and Men. Objections to the Foreword of a Book," *Le Combat syndicaliste*, 23 December 1978, 6.

4 For details of the attack on the Casarramona, see the writings of Joan Casanova, as cited in the Bibliography, below.

Seco) and lots of anarchist groups were based. On the far side of the Ramblas, they took over the bottom end of the Calle Fiveller (Calle Ferrán these days) and the Plaza Maciá (now known as the Plaza Real) and, forging past Los Escolapios, they met up with Máximo Franco on the Brecha de San Pablo; with around forty militia members (revolutionaries who had deserted from the Rojinegra column), Máximo Franco had thrown up barricades on that portion of the Paralelo.

The RC appointed a delegation to parley at the Generalidad Palace. Santillán was one of the delegates, and he had ordered the Montjuich gunners (Lucio Ruano) to shell the building should they not receive his half-hourly updates.

The main anarcho-syndicalist spokespersons, ministers Juan García Oliver and Federica Montseny, travelled up from Valencia to broadcast their peacemaking addresses over the radio. They were the "firefighters" who doused the flames.

Xena, Jover, and Manzana orchestrated the military defense of the Casa CNT-FAI building. The seizure of the Casal del Metge, facing the Casa CNT-FAI, on the far side of the Vía Durruti by foreign militia members drawn from a variety of nationalities (primarily Italian and French) was part of their defensive strategy and was dictated by the need to break the siege.

The abandonment of the barricades on 7 May consolidated the political defeat: the threat of repression necessitated the covering of tracks, the concealment of responsibilities, and the assumption of a lower profile. And this impacted on the drafting of the minutes of CNT meetings.

Now eighty years after the events, the role played by each of the protagonists seems plain.

1.   Julián Merino, Pablo Ruiz, and Juan Santana Calero served on the revolutionary committee that was set up on 12 April 1937 to confront what was a foreseeable counterrevolutionary coup de force.

2.   On 15 April, Escorza and Companys personally reached agreement on a new Generalidad government lineup, with Aurelio Fernandez joining it. The 27 April murder of Antonio Martin in Bellver inflamed the situation already in place throughout Catalonia. By revealing and passing on intelligence regarding an imminent coup de force by the Stalinists and the Generalidad, Manuel Escorza placed the defense committees on a war footing.

3.   On 3 May, efforts by Eroles and Asens to urge restraint and pacify minds following the storming of the Telephone Exchange building proved spectacularly unsuccessful: the defense committees had swept aside the higher committees, declared a revolutionary general strike, taken control of all the working-class barrios, and erected barricades in the city center

and at the main access routes leading to and from the city. Streetfighting erupted between the barricades different factions, barricades that had gone up in the triangle at the heart of the city, traced by:

a.   The Generalidad Palace.

b.   The Public Order Commissariat and the Casa CNT-FAI, both of them on the Vía Layetana.

c.   The area around the Plaza de Cataluña and the Paseo de Gracia, where the main antifascist organizations—the ERC, Estat Catalá, and the PSUC—had their headquarters, between the Hotel Colón, the Casal Carlos Marx and La Pedrera.

4.   On the morning of 4 May, **Julián Merino** requested that a special meeting of the CNT's RC be summoned for the purpose of broadening and coordinating the insurrection that had erupted the previous day, and asked the RC to assume command of it.

5.   Escorza reckoned that in the **absence of proper coordination and clear-cut goals,** the uprising was a ramshackle affair doomed to failure and that this would suggest a severe defeat that would undermine the CNT.

6.   A CNT revolutionary committee was established (Merino, Ruano, and Manzanas) and two commissions were appointed to coordinate and **widen** the fighting: the Center commission and the Plaza de España commission. At the same time, a delegation from the RC was chosen; headed by Santillán, it would negotiate with the Generalidad: the RC was adopting a **two-pronged approach.**

7.   On the afternoon of 4 May, **radio broadcasts** by the various antifascist leaders, including the anarcho-syndicalist ones, **aborted the offensive unleashed by the CNT's Revolutionary Committee and the two commissions, preventing it from fully unfolding and from showing sufficient daring.**[5]

---

5   This offensive, driven by the CNT's (secret) Revolutionary Committee, was **aborted** in the late afternoon/evening of the 4th by the radio addresses in favor of a ceasefire, addresses delivered by García Oliver and others. I recommend a close reading, from that perspective, of the texts by Bonomini (151–152) and Aguzzi (160), both listed in the Bibliography.

8.   On 5 May, the Friends of Durruti distributed a flyer on the barricades, trying to endow the revolutionary upheaval with hard and fast revolutionary **goals**, which it had hitherto lacked:[6] replacement of the Generalidad by a Revolutionary Junta, the culprits behind the provocation (Rodríguez Salas and Artemi Aguadé) to be shot, socialization of the economy, fraternization with POUM militants, etc. The distribution of this flyer breathed fresh life into the fighting on the barricades.

9.   By 7 May, it was plain to see that the insurrection had failed. The troops sent up from Valencia, around five thousand Assault Guards, paraded along the Diagonal. Over the ensuing days, the higher committees strove to cover up everything that had happened, bowdlerizing minutes that were in the process of being drafted and, ultimately, doing all in their power to ward off the anticipated Stalinist and government crackdown on the Organization and the most prominent players.

10.   The POUM and the Friends of Durruti were chosen as the **scapegoats.** As far as the higher committees were concerned, this was **a two-pronged gambit** intended to help them wriggle out of their own responsibilities and deflect this onto the POUM, their old, minority rival, which was now defenseless, and, especially, onto the Friends of Durruti who looked like a dangerous opposition and internal revolutionary alternative to the CNT's collaborationist leadership.

★

Book Four in the quartet *Hambre y violencia en la Barcelona revolucionaria,* entitled *The Repression Targeting the CNT and the Revolutionaries* offers full details and documentation to show:

1.   The higher committees' collaboration with the Generalidad and central governments in the crackdown on all revolutionaries, including CNT personnel.

---

6   The SBLE had issued its own flyer the night before. The May insurrection **lacked effective coordination and clear objectives.** Merino did his best to deal with those shortcomings at the RC meeting on 4 May by trying to get the RC to handle that coordination, in military terms at any rate. So did the Friends of Durruti who, in their flyer on 5 May, tried to equip the insurrection with some very clear-cut and concrete minimum objectives. To which efforts the flyer launched by the SBLE on 4 May has to be added.

2. The prosecutorial onslaught and the Stalinists' chekist drive against the revolutionaries and those officers of the higher committees who had held office in the Courts Office or in Public Order.

3. Manuel Escorza's input to the meeting of the higher committees on 19 May 1937.[7]

4. Merino's "I accuse" at the gathering of militants on 20 May 1937.

5. The establishment of the CAP and Liaison Committee as dikes designed to ensure that the CNT's higher committees were not overruled again. The offensive against the Friends of Durruti and the defense committees, designed to thwart the emergence of a revolutionary internal opposition.

6. Julian Merino's unrelenting revolutionary lobbying from within the Transport Union over the summer of 1937 in favor of the calling of a revolutionary general strike in opposition to the rampant Stalinist and government repression.

7. The attempt by the Friends of Durruti through their newspaper *El Amigo del Pueblo* to devise a theory based on the firsthand experiences the revolutionaries had been through.

8. The final crushing on 20 September 1937 of the unions, defense committees, and anarchist groups holding out in the Los Escolapios building, in a miniature replay of the May Events.

9. The attempt by Rafael Vidiella to oust the viscerally anti-CNT Comorera from the leadership of the party and to effect a rapprochement with the CNT's higher committees in order to avoid the PSUC's being isolated.

---

7   During the May Events crisis—and in the search for a clear-cut, determined stance that might allow them successfully to grapple with the struggle that was approaching, organizationally and politically—Manuel Escorza stated that "our ballast let us down, not our engine." They needed coolly and calmly to learn "from this knock." He highlighted the importance of the CNT having control of "that economic assets." He suggested "a unitary, uniform, specific body" that would also have room for the POUM and which would parade the tremendous fighting strength of the revolutionaries. It would be "articulated organizationally," regardless of "whether our action is dressed up in a red frockcoat or a black one."

10.　The evaporation of the CNT as an organization from many comarcas and locations around Catalonia, because of the summer 1937 crackdown, with thousands of anarchists and CNT personnel now behind bars.

5

From the Defense Cadres to the Friends of Durruti's Analysis of the Organs of Power. Plus Some Untimely Considerations

A. THE CNT DEFENSE COMMITTEES

The Republic had been proclaimed on 14 April 1931. On 25 April, eleven days later, at a Plenum of its Locals and Comarcals, the CNT adopted two organizational measures that were going to prove tremendously successful later: the formation of **barrio unions** in Barcelona city and the launching of **defense committees**.

During the 1920s and 1930s, the CNT was rather more than just a trade union in the classical sense, an organization championing its members rights in the workplace. The CNT was part and parcel of a **network** of solidarity and action that encompassed every facet of the life of the workers, whether social or cultural, family-centered, recreational, political, or trade union related. That network was made up of the barrio unions, the *ateneos*, the rationalist schools, cooperatives, the economic defense committee (which resisted evictions), affinity groups, defense groups (coordinated at barrio level, rising to district and then citywide levels), making up, in everyday practice a sturdy and effective autonomous society based on solidarity, with a set of values different from capitalist values.

Unless we grasp the importance of this solidarity-and-action-based libertarian network, as outlined in the paragraph above, we will never be able to appreciate the strength and radicalism of the libertarian movement in Barcelona and Catalonia, as well as the consequences that flowed from it:

1. Utter repudiation of the way of life foisted upon them by capital, exploring, in theory and above all in practice, new paths in terms of social and personal relations, in culture, economics, etc.

2.　　Theoretical and practical rejection of the State in the post-revolutionary society of the future; holding out against the spread of statism within the reformist socialist parties and Stalinist counterrevolutionaries, as well as against the CNT's own higher authorities and their gamble on collaborationism.

3.　　The practice of new social relationships and experiments in new societies, dispensing with money, wages, private ownership, social hierarchy, and the commodification of everyday life. Expropriations, collectivizations, and socialization of the economy were practical trials and experiments by a profoundly revolutionary subversive movement that set its sights on making a tangible reality of the communist utopia.

4.　　The fight was not on behalf of some abstract ideology, but rather through a practical collective experience that was changing society and reality.

5.　　The barrio-level revolutionary committees were the actual social movement that, in its everyday practice, replaced all the functions of the state. By their very existence, these embodied the social revolution in progress.

In 1923, with support from Aurelio Fernández and Ricardo Sanz, Juan García Oliver had boosted the practical organization of what had come to be known as "revolutionary gymnastics." Those were the days of *pistolerismo*. The CNT had to defend the lives of its militants from physical liquidation at the hands of the alliance between the terrorism of the employers and the state, which were funding the so-called Sindicato Libre and affording carte blanche to killings by the police and Civil Guard through the practice of the so-called *ley de fugas,* which amounted to murdering prisoners and detainees at the point of transfer or release, on the pretext that they had tried to escape.

In 1931, the setting up of the defense committees amounted to a relaunch of the action groups from the years of *pistolerismo* (1917–1923), although now they were not geared solely toward protection of strikers and campaign demonstrations. The defense committees offered a crucial guarantee that of basic rights of assembly, expression, association, press, demonstration, unionization, or strike, not as yet recognized by a constituent Republic that had yet to approve a constitution, but that also had not yet disbanded the Somatén (the odious, right-wing minutemen, specializing in strikebreaking and persecuting trade unionists) in Barcelona.

On 1 May 1931 at a May Day rally, huge red-and-black banners, the identifying mark of the CNT, made their first appearance. It was agreed that a schedule of demands should be drawn up that would be carried on a march to the Generalidad Palace. When the demonstrators reached the Plaza de San Jaime, they were greeted by gunfire. The shooting, to which the defense committees replied, went on for three quarters of an hour, until Juan García Oliver was allowed to hand the demands over to the authorities and to step out on to the Generalidad balcony to dissolve the demonstration.

The defense committees were not presenting themselves as a "terrorist" or military group disconnected from the working class and the people, but rather as just another vital accouterment of the class struggle, alongside the union, the *ateneo*, the rationalist school, or the cooperative. The defense committees stood guard over the workers' rights as there were no rights beyond what could be extracted by means of streetfighting, no rights beyond whatever rights they could defend by exercising them.

But the insurrectionist tactic of "revolutionary gymnastics," amounting to quickly arming oneself for the occasion, spontaneously proclaiming libertarian communism in some tiny village or entire comarca, and waiting for the remainder of the country to join in the insurrection exposed its limitations and, above all, its drawbacks and disadvantages. The insurrections of January 1932 and January and December 1933 had led to the disarming of the defense committees, which had come in for very severe repression—that had dispatched most of their members to prison—so that the "revolutionary gymnastics" tactic had merely led to the dismantling of the defense committees. A different approach and a change of tactics were called for.

At a time when the Asturian uprising was still in progress, the National Committee of the Defense Committees (NCDC) noted in a resolution dated 11 October 1934 that the insurrectionist tactic, popularly known as "revolutionary gymnastics," had failed, and it blamed the failure on the CNT's lack of preparedness when it came to participating at a nationwide level in the October 1934 insurrection. The time had come to move beyond those tactics because they had demonstrated the nonsensicality and dangerousness of a localized, ill-timed insurrection without proper groundwork laid in advance, in that it left libertarians open to state repression without ever spreading to the populace nationwide, nor attracting support from other organizations—all of which was required if the state's military and repressive machinery was to be successfully grappled with. In October 1934 when the conditions were in place for a revolutionary proletarian, statewide insurrection, the anarcho-syndicalists were utterly spent and disorganized, unarmed with thousands of their militants behind bars.

The determination to work on reinforcing the defense committees by overcoming their flaws, correcting their mistakes, and, above all, harnessing the state's repression as a spur to carrying on with the struggle was the motivation for the NCDC resolution in October 1934. The old tactics were jettisoned in favor of serious, methodical revolutionary groundwork: "There is no revolution without preparedness; and the more intense and intelligent the latter, the better the former will fare when its day comes. We have to have an end of the makeshift, hothead-inspired approach as the only feasible option in times of difficulty. That mistake—of trusting the creative instincts of the masses—has cost us very dearly. The indispensable battlefield resources required to fight a state that has experience, mighty assets, and superior offensive-defensive resources on its side cannot be conjured up as if by spontaneous generation."

In the view of the NCDC "the great importance that the defense committees have for the CNT and for the libertarian revolution must be reflected in unrelenting scrutiny of their structures so that these can be transcended [improved upon] and afforded whatever financial and liaison resources, moral and technical, that renders them more effective when it comes to bringing about the desired end soon and directly."

The defense committees' clandestine military apparatus should at all times be obedient to the orders and requirements of the CNT: "the defense committees are to be an organizational offshoot of the CNT." The Resolution based the defense committees on "volunteer militants," just like participation in the specific organizations, i.e. the FAI and the Libertarian Youth. But it should never be forgotten that the defense committees were a clandestine military arm of the CNT, funded by its unions, which "will set the percentage of the dues payments to be dispensed to them [the defense committees] monthly through the CNT committees in a given locality or comarca."

The October 1934 Resolution from the NCDC argued that the basic defense group or cadre had to be small so that it might more easily operate in a clandestine way and be flexible, as well as fully know the character, expertise, and skills of each militant. It had to be comprised of a secretary, whose essential task was to liaise with other groups in the same barrio and to form new groups. A second militant would take on the task of identifying and noting down the names, addresses, ideologies, personal data, habits, and dangerousness of enemies existing within the group's assigned bailiwick. "Dangerousness" meant the profession or ideology of the person identified as an enemy: "servicemen, policemen, priests, civil servants, bourgeois and Marxist politicians, gunmen, fascists, etc." A third militant had to make a study of buildings and premises inimical to the labor movement, recording their vulnerabilities and importance. It was a matter of drawing up plans and building up a database of persons, things, and weapons to be found in "barracks, police stations, jails, churches and monasteries, political and employers' premises, strongholds, etc." A fourth militant from the group was to check out strategic and tactical locations such as "bridges, underground passages, sewers, basements, buildings with rooftops or escape doors leading to other streets or some yard offering an escape route or refuge." The reckoning was that a fifth member of the group would concentrate on the public services: "lighting, water, garages, tram depots, metro, transport routes, and their vulnerability to sabotage or seizure." A sixth militant was in charge of locating and looking into how to mount attacks on places where weapons, cash, and supplies for the revolution might be obtained; "armories, fortified private homes, banks, lending houses, warehouses holding clothing, foodstuffs, etc."

It was thought that a six-person team was the ideal size for a defense group or cadre, albeit that, on occasion, extra members might be added to cover tasks "of prime importance." The Resolution added that when it came to cadres, it was quality rather than quantity that mattered and that the militants should be "reserved, able-bodied types."

So, after October 1934, the defense groups were characterized by their small numbers: six militants, each handling a very specific assignment. The group's secretary was the liaison with other groups from the same barrio. These were intelligence-gathering and combat teams who were to play "the part of righteous revolutionary vanguard," who "will be an inspiration to the people," that is, come the moment of insurrection, they would have the ability to mobilize a larger number of secondary groups. And the latter, in turn, the entire populace.

The defense group was the basic building block of the CNT's clandestine military structure. A ward defense committee was set up in every barrio to coordinate all these defense cadres and it would be issued monthly with a report from each of the group secretaries. The barrio secretary/delegate compiled a summary that was passed on to the district committee and the latter in turn passed it on to the local defense committee "and the latter to the Regional and on to the National."

This organizational blueprint, suited to the larger cities, was simplified for the villages where the different groups were coordinated directly through the local committee. The Resolution even went into detail as to how and where "to set up defense groups or cadres, drawing upon personnel from the unions and distributing them through the wards of the industrial cities, assigning them to an operations area drawn on a map of the city and from which they shall take care not to stray without express notice."

The detail and precision with which these defense committees were formed is well known. The Resolution urged that the groups be made up of men drawn from the same union or trade sector, "not that this means that they should keep in contact with or be beholden to their union, since they are at the exclusive disposal of the defense committees and, in order to fulfill the purposes these have set themselves," but because this "approach has the merit of turning these militants, banded together within the defense committees, into guardians of principles within the union and overseers of its internal and public performance."

The NCDC Resolution also delved into the organization of the regional and national defense committees, marshaling workers from specific sectors such as railwaymen, coach drivers, telephone and telegraph operators, mailmen, etc., all who, by virtue of their trade or organization, operated throughout the country, highlighting the importance of communications in a revolutionary insurrection. There was a special section given over to the tasks of infiltration, propaganda, and recruitment of sympathizers in the barracks. After considering the need to discuss and continually improve the defense committee's insurrectional tactics and planning at local, regional, and national levels, and formalizing the working relationship with the FAI, the Resolution closed with an appeal to CNT members to give some thought to the importance of consolidating, extending, and perfecting a clandestine CNT military apparatus "to face up to the military and police might of the state and of the fascist or Marxist militias."

For the most part, the defense cadres were trade union cadres. From 19–20 July 1936 on, these trade union cadres were marshaled into *centurias* in the people's militias that promptly set off to fight fascism on Aragonese soil. So, within the various confederal columns, there was talk of "the metalworkers' centuria" or "the woodworkers' centuria" or the "construction workers' centuria," made up of militants drawn from the same union.

The defense committees had two essential functions:

1. Procurement, upkeep, and storage of arms and training in the handling of weapons. The defense committees' authority was rooted in their being an armed organization. Their power was the power of the workers in arms.

2. Quartermaster duties, in the broadest sense of the term, from the supply of victuals and people's kitchens through the establishment and upkeep of hospitals, schools, *ateneos*, or even, during the first few days of the people's victory, recruitment of militia members and supplying the columns heading off to the front.

During the 1930s the unemployed were marshaled into defense cadres on a rotation basis, the purpose being to show them solidarity by affording them an income, preventing them from becoming strikebreakers and training as many militants as possible in the handling of weapons. For those very same reasons, and to preempt their "professionalization," care was taken to ensure that the remuneration never became permanent. Throughout the time of the Republic, it was armed pickets and trade union defense groups that protected demonstrations and strikes or promoted local insurrections.

The NCDC Resolution of October 1934 implied a brand new organization and guidelines for the defense cadres that, without saying so, understood the criticisms of "revolutionary gymnastics" voiced by Alexander Shapiro and the CNT's internal critics (as spelled out in the "Manifesto of the Thirty").

The Local Revolutionary Preparedness Committee

In Catalonia, the practical implementation of the new defense committee structure was the subject of a motion proposed by the anarchist groups Indomables, Nervio, Nosotros, Tierra Libre, and Germen at the January 1935 Plenum of the Federation of Barcelona Anarchist Groups. The motion set out the establishment in Barcelona of a Local Revolutionary Preparedness Committee.

The preamble to the motion characterized the times as "a period holding out immense revolutionary prospects primarily on account of the manifest inability of capitalism and the state to devise equitable solutions to pressing economic, social, and moral problems." It was noted that, since the end of the Great War, politics had failed internationally: "Upwards of fifteen years of unrelenting effort on the part of the leaders of economic life and as many trials of multiple forms of state, without forgetting the so-called dictatorship of the proletariat, have not come up with as much as a glimmer of equilibrium bearable by the broad masses, but have accentuated the widespread malaise and brought us to the brink of physiological ruin and to the verge of a fresh slaughterhouse of warmaking." Faced with an historical vista that was really depressing—fascism on the rise in Italy, Nazism in Germany, Stalinism in the Soviet Union, economic depression with mass and ongoing unemployment in the United States and Europe—the motion contrasted the hopes of the world proletariat: "In the universal bankruptcy of ideas, parties, and systems, the only thing left standing is the revolutionary proletariat with its program for reorganization of working conditions, the economic and social reality, and solidarity." The optimistic drafters of this motion saw the labor movement in Spain as being strong enough and capable enough "to do definitive battle against the aging edifice of capitalist morality, economics, and politics."

In the definition that the authors of the motion offered of revolution there was a profound criticism of the childish tactics of revolutionary gymnastics and improvisation jettisoned back in October 1934. "The social revolution cannot be construed as a stroke of daring like Jacobinism's coups d'état, but will be the consequence and outcome of unleashing an inevitable civil war, the duration of which it is impossible to anticipate." Not only was this a startlingly clearsighted forecast of the civil war that would follow eighteen months later, and of its immense cruelty, but there was an insistence that preparations had to be made for it immediately by endowing the defense cadres with a brand new structure: "While in modern times the coup d'etat demands great technical and insurrectionist preparedness, with resources and personnel trained to perfection for the intended purpose, a civil war is going to demand all the more a fighting machine that cannot be cobbled together in the heat of mere enthusiasm, but must be structured and articulated with the greatest amount of foresight and personnel possible."

It was known that there were plenty of men available, but it was noted also that they lacked the organization "for a sustained struggle against the enemy forces." So their training needed accelerating. "The present structure of Local Revolutionary Preparedness Committee that we propose is the answer to that." That committee would be made up of four members: two would be appointed by the Local CNT Federation and the other two by the Local Federation of Anarchist Groups. Those four would also organize an auxiliary commission. The chief task of this Local Revolutionary Preparedness Committee was "to look into the means and methods of struggle, the tactics to be employed, and the articulation of the insurrectionist organizational forces." A clear distinction was drawn between the old shock cadres from prior to October 1934 and the brand new defense cadres: "Just as the defense committees have hitherto been primarily organized shock groups, they must, henceforth, be bodies capable of investigating the realities of the modern struggle."

Revolutionary preparedness for a protracted civil war brought fresh challenges, unthinkable in the context of the old, shock group approach; "Given that we cannot, in advance, stockpile the weaponry necessary for a sustained struggle, the Preparedness Committee must look into ways of converting the industries in certain strategically important areas ... into industries supplying the fighting gear for the revolution."

The CNT's regional committees were to be the bodies coordinating these Local Revolutionary Preparedness Committees. The latter could meet up for special Plenums for trading initiatives, intelligence, and experiences. At the national level, it was anticipated that there might be meetings of regional delegates.

The Preparedness Committee was at no time to take the revolutionary initiative "that will at all times have to come from the confederal and specific organizations, they being the ones that must choose the opportune moment and assume leadership of the movement." The funding was a matter for the CNT unions and the anarchist groups, though there was to be "no preset mandatory general contribution [levied]." As to the "training of fighting cadres, the insurrectionist groups in the cities are to be based on the wards, with nuclei of unlimited size, but the affinity groups wanting to stay connected shall also make up part of the insurrectionist cadres, but will fall under the remit of the Preparedness Committee."

Both the NCDC resolution in October 1934 and the motion from the Barcelona anarchist groups in January 1935 insisted upon new structures for the defense cadres, revising the old idea that they were merely shock groups and converting them, instead, into defense cadres with strict, revolutionary preparedness duties, grappling with issues of intelligence, armaments, tactics, and research in anticipation of a protracted civil war. They had moved on from the shock groups they had been prior to 1934 and become intelligence gathering and combat cadres

July 1936: The Revolutionary Committees and the Militias

On 19 and 20 July 1936, even as the fighting on the streets of Barcelona was at its height and the military rebels were facing defeat, the defense committee members began to refer to themselves and to become known to others as "the militia members." Without any transition, the defense cadres turned into the people's militias. The defense cadres' basic structure had provided for a broadening and expansion through the incorporation of secondary cadres. It was just a matter of making room in them for the thousands of worker volunteers who were joining the fight against fascism, now that it had spread into Aragonese territory. The confederal militias became the vanguard of all the armed units that set out to find and fight the fascist foe. They were the armed organization of the revolutionary proletariat. Their example was mimicked by other workers' organizations and even organizations of bourgeois extraction. In the absence of a single proletarian army, as many militias surfaced as there were parties and organizations in existence.

The defense cadres underwent a double transformation: into the people's militias that in those early days defined the Aragon front, introducing collectivization of the land in the liberated Aragonese villages; and into the Revolutionary Committees that imposed a "new revolutionary order" in every Barcelona barrio and every village in Catalonia. Their shared origins in the defense cadres ensured that the confederal militias and the Revolutionary Committees were always very united and interconnected.

In the wake of the victory over the fascist and military revolt in Catalonia, the defense committees in each barrio (or village) set themselves up as revolutionary ward (or local) committees, adopting a huge variety of titles. These *barrio* revolutionary committees in Barcelona city were made up virtually exclusively of CNT members. By contrast, the *local* revolutionary committees were usually made up by making room for all the local workers' and antifascist organizations, imitating the make-up of the Central Antifascist Militias Committee (CAMC).

These revolutionary committees performed these functions in each ward or locality, especially during the nine weeks following 19 July 1936:

1. They commandeered buildings to set up the Committee headquarters, a supplies depot, an *ateneo,* or a rationalist school. They commandeered and maintained hospitals and newspapers.

2. They carried out armed searches of private homes in search of foodstuffs, money, and valuables to commandeer.

3. They carried out armed searches of private homes, hoping to arrest "*pacos*" (snipers), bushwhackers, priests, right-wingers, and fifth columnists. (Remember that the "gunplay" by snipers in Barcelona city went on for a week.)

4. In each barrio, they set up recruitment stations for the militias, which they armed, funded, kept supplied, and paid (up until the end of August) out of their own resources, with each ward keeping up, until after May 1937, an intense and unbroken relationship with its very own militia members on the front lines and welcoming them home when on leave.

5. In addition to arms held at the defense committee premises, there were also some buildings or warehouses in which the ward's Supplies Committee set up shop, being kept victualed by the requisitioning of food carried out in rural areas by means of confiscation at gunpoint, through barter, or purchases made using vouchers.

6. In each barrio or locality they imposed and collected a revolutionary levy.

The Supplies Committee would set up a people's kitchen; initially, meals were free, but as the months passed and as food items became scarcer and dearer, it had to introduce a voucher system subsidized by the barrio's or locality's revolutionary committee. At the defense committee's headquarters there was always a cabinet for the storage of weapons and, sometimes, a little jail in which arrested persons might temporarily be held.

The revolutionary committees did important and widely varying administrative work ranging from issuing vouchers, food stamps, safe conduct papers, passes, establishing cooperatives, officiating at weddings, and supplying and maintaining the hospitals through to confiscation of food items, furniture, and entire buildings, funding rationalist schools and the *ateneos* run by the Libertarian Youth, and making payments to militia members or their families, etc.

The coordination of the ward revolutionary committees was handled at regional committee meetings, attended by the secretaries from each of the ward defense committees. In addition, there was a standing Confederal Defense Committee, based in the Casa CNT-FAI.

For matters relating to the seizure of significant sums of money and items of value, or all things having to do with arrests, intelligence, and investigations that, by their very significance, were beyond the jurisdiction of the ward revolutionary committee, they looked to the CNT-FAI Investigation Service, run by Manuel Escorza from the Casa CNT-FAI.

So in the city of Barcelona, the ward defense committees were answerable to the following higher committees:

1.   In respect to the recruitment of militia members (in July and August 1936) and the victualing of the people's militias (up until mid-September 1936), they answered to the CAMC.

2.   In respect to the supply of foodstuffs and basic necessities, to the Central Supplies Committee.

3.   In respect to organizing and the resolution of issues, to the CNT Regional Committee, which issued them their orders and guidelines by which to abide. This had to do with the well-known dependency of the defense cadres upon the unions and the denial to them of their autonomy as awarded in the 1934 Resolution.

4.   Experiences were coordinated and shared through a Barcelona Defense Committee, which was simply the organizational level that came after the district committees. This Committee was a tokenistic presence.

5.   In respect to intelligence-gathering, investigation, pursuit of fifth columnists, and other armed "policing" tasks, they were answerable to the CNT-FAI Investigation Service.

Organized on a geographical basis in areas clearly marked off from other groups and made up of six members, each with very precise intelligence-gathering, espionage, and investigative missions, the defense cadres were the

CNT's basic clandestine armed wing. Come the insurrection, these initial cadres were swollen by secondary teams of trade-union militants, FAI affinity groups, *ateneo* members, and so on. After 19 July, intelligence-gathering tasks and the business of spying on the enemy and investigating the strength and leadership of the class enemy were coordinated by the CNT-FAI's Investigation and Intelligence Service, while other matters were coordinated through meetings between the secretary-delegates from each barrio committee and the Regional Committee at the Casa CNT-FAI.

Against Militarization

The real upshot of the CAMC and its nine-week lifespan was the transition from locally-based revolutionary committees wielding all the power on the streets and in the factories to these being wound down for the sole purpose of fully restoring the Generalidad's power. The decrees signed on 24 October 1936, regarding the collectivizations and the militias' being militarized from 1 November onward, completed the disastrous stewardship of the CAMC, which is to say the shift from worker militias made up of revolutionary volunteers to a bourgeois army along classical lines, subject to the monarchist military code and led by the Generalidad: and a shift from expropriation and workers' control over factories to a centralized economy under the control and direction of the Generalidad.

The decree militarizing the people's militias generated enormous discontent among the Durruti Column's anarchist militia members on the Aragon front. After protracted and heated arguments, in March 1937 eight hundred volunteer militia members based in the Gelsa sector decided to quit the front and return to the rearguard. Arrangements were made for the militia members opposed to militarization to be relieved over the space of a fortnight. They quit the front, taking their weapons with them.

Once back in Barcelona, alongside other anarchists (who were all for pressing on with and entrenching the July revolution, and who were against the CNT's collaboration in government), the militia members from Gelsa (Zaragoza) decided to launch an anarchist organization separate from the FAI, CNT, or Libertarian Youth; it mission would be to channel the anarchist movement along a revolutionary path. So this new grouping (*Agrupación*) was formally launched in March 1937, after a long period of gestation of several months, stretching back to October 1936. Its leadership board was the one that decided upon the name the Friends of Durruti Group, a title that was in part an invocation of their shared background as former militia members with the Durruti Column and, as Balius made clear, that was not a reference to the thinking of Durruti, but rather to the popular mythology surrounding him.

This revolutionary opposition to militarization of the people's militias was also echoed, to a greater or lesser degree, within all the confederal columns. In terms of its impact outside of Catalonia, there was the Maroto affair: Maroto was sentenced to death for his refusal to militarize the column he led—the sentence was never carried out but it was enough to keep him in jail. Another prominent example was the Iron Column, which decided on a number of occasions to "go down to Valencia" to give the revolution a boost and confront counterrevolutionary elements in the rearguard.

Between 5 and 8 February 1937, there was a gathering of the confederal columns to deal with the militarization issue. Threats that the supply of arms, food, and manpower would be withheld columns that did not agree to be militarized, adding to the conviction that the militia members would be absorbed into other already militarized units, had their effect. To many it seemed better to embrace militarization and adapt it to their own column in a flexible way. In the end, the ideology of antifascist unity—and of CNT-FAI partnership in the business of governing to defend the republican state—won out over the resistance to militarization, which was eventually accepted, even by the recalcitrant Iron Column.

There is an extraordinary document that allows us to follow the **process that induced a significant majority of the Durruti Column's 4th *Agrupación* in Gelsa to instinctively repudiate militarization and ultimately to quit the front lines, taking their weapons with them back to Barcelona.**[1]

After lengthy discussions and talks on the part of the members of the CNT-FAI Regional Committees, as far as Catalonia goes, the militarization that had initially been agreed on behalf of both organizations was accepted by our columns.

However, and even though the frontline comrades were offered, apropos of the business of militarization, all manner of reasons why the confederal and specific organizations had consented to it, there were some comrades from the Durruti Column in the Gelsa sector, who categorically refused to accept what the organization had agreed to, even though the other confederal columns had.[2] These comrades gave as their grounds for not agreeing to militarization the fact that anarchist ideas and militarization could not be reconciled. Another of their reasons for not agreeing to it was that, to their mind, military hierarchies could not be countenanced in a revolutionary movement

1 FAI, "Report submitted by this Anarchist Groups of Catalonia Liaison Committee to the region's comrades" (undated, no place of publication indicated, no publisher identified).
2 This was the Durruti Column's Fourth *Agrupación* in the Gelsa sector, led by Pablo Ruiz.

and in columns that had marched off voluntarily to the field of battle, since they implicitly castrated the revolutionary spirit of the respective columns, while reverting to the old structures of the Spanish army against which they were fighting at the time. In spite of all these considerations, which we appreciate are of great import and which are indicative of a purist view of our ideas, our understanding and that of the organization generally was that this was not the appropriate time for entering into a debate about our beliefs, but called, rather, for pressing ahead with militarization since that was the only way of combatting fascism. Having taken stock of the situation in which we find ourselves, this Liaison Committee was one of the first to lobby for acceptance of militarization, in that our understanding was that anarchism in Catalonia, upon which most of the world was keeping an eye, had an ineluctable duty to do all in its power to win the war, since, if it did not, anarchism would vanish entirely from Spain due to the triumph of fascism, and from the rest of the world, due to our ineptitude, in that we would have shown ourselves incapable of prioritizing the imperative demands of the war we are fighting over our view of our own ideas.[3]

Our arguments failed to get the necessity of militarization across to our comrades from the Durruti Column's 4th *Agrupación*, in Gelsa. After a number of face-to-face meetings and trips to the front lines and into the rearguard on both our parts, we could not come to any agreement in principle. The comrades from the fourth *Agrupación* in Gelsa never missed a single Plenum, showing up at them in order to spell out the grounds that had prompted them to adopt the stance they had.[4] At every plenum they could, they set out their reasoning, but at none of them were they able to make any progress with the delegates in opposing that plan.[5] On several occasions, they were

---

3   We are dealing here with brutal enforcement of the collaborationist, circumstantialist arguments of anarchism's reformist element. But if ideas are of no use in dealing with reality, what purpose do they serve? Where did the setting aside of principles lead, other than to the abjuring of one's own program, one's own tactics, one's own identity, and to being dragged along by the ideology of the Catalanist bourgeoisie or crushed by the Stalinists? Could fascism not have been fought with a revolutionary army rooted in a thoroughgoing social revolution in the rearguard, could Morocco not have been declared independent and international solidarity of the European working class promoted?

4   The most significant Plenum was the one held in Valencia on 15 February 1937. The minutes of the plenum were published as a pamphlet by the Friends of Durruti as *Minutes of the Plenum of Confederal and Anarchist Columns, held in Valencia on 5 February 1937"* [SA].

5   As we can monitor through the minutes cited above, faced with bureaucratic obstacles to them having their say, the antimilitarists were blackmailed that, unless they agreed to militarization, they would receive neither arms nor pay. The only option they had was to embrace militarization or leave the front "and let fascism win." In spite of all this blackmail, the Gelsa *Agrupación* stuck by its antimilitarist stance of "Militia members, yes; soldiers, never."

cautioned that they should drop their opposition and abide by the organization's accords. Such hints, coming from the CNT-FAI regional committees, went entirely unheeded. Not only did they refuse to be militarized, but they also ignored the insistence of both Committees that they lay down their arms and quit the front.

After several weeks had elapsed and given that there was no way of papering over the difference of opinion there was within the Durruti Column, a commission chaired by comrade Manzana came to talk to those Committees and at a joint sitting of both he spelled out the delicate situation through which the Column was passing, since tensions between the two sides were such that it was feared they might degenerate into a bloody clash.[6] At that meeting, it was resolved that the Gelsa comrades be invited yet again to bring the situation to a final resolution in whichever fashion they thought most appropriate.

When those comrades took up the invitation issued by the organization's Committees, and after much consideration, they agreed that within a fortnight of the date of the meeting, they would quit the front, handing off their weapons to the comrades arriving as their replacements.[7]

At the time of writing of this report, most of the comrades from the Gelsa *Agrupación* have quit the front, in spite of the entire outlook and accords of the specific and confederal organizations. Some of the comrades from it, realizing the times we are in and the historical import of quitting the front, opted to remain, in defiance of the views of most of the *Agrupación*.[8]

Toward the end of February, nearly all of the militia members from the Durruti Column's Fourth Agrupación *in Gelsa made up their minds to quit the front because they rejected militarization.[9] The pressures and threats to which they were subjected were unbearable and were on the brink of triggering an armed clash within the Durruti Column. In the end, they left the front lines, taking their weapons with them. These militia members were behind the launch in Barcelona of the Friends of Durruti.*

---

6   The fear was that argument about the acceptance or nonacceptance of militarization might erupt into an armed confrontation within the Durruti Column itself.

7   The departure from the front probably occurred in late February 1937, and those who quit the front returned to Barcelona with their weapons.

8   Some eight hundred men, which is to say, virtually the entire Gelsa *Agrupación*. An *Agrupación* was the equivalent of a Battalion. See "Letter from Balius to Bolloten (Cuernavaca, 24 June 1946)," in Agustín Guillamón, *Los Amigos de Durruti Historia e antología de textos* (Barcelona: Descontrol, 2013), 153.

9   See Balius's letters to Bolloten, dated 10 and 24 June 1946, in ibid., 149–157.

The Defense Committees in May 1937

At around 2:45 p.m. on Monday 3 May 1937, Rodríguez Salas, a member of the UGT, dyed-in-the-wool Stalinist, and the officer in charge at the Public Order Commissariat, tried to seize possession of the Telephone Exchange. The CNT militants there put up tough resistance thanks to a strategically positioned machine gun. The news spread swiftly. Barricades were promptly erected all around the city. There should be no talk of a spontaneous backlash from the Barcelona working class because the general strike, the armed clashes with the police forces, and the barricades were products of the initiative taken by the CNT-FAI Investigation Service and the defense committees and were swiftly supported thanks to tremendous, widespread discontent, the increasing economic straits caused by the soaring cost of living, the queues and rationing, as well as the tensions at the CNT's grassroots between collaborationists and revolutionaries.

The streetfighting was driven and conducted by the barrio defense committees (and only partly and at secondary level by any part of the Control Patrols). That no order had come down from the CNT's higher committees serving as ministers in the Valencia government, or from any other organization, for a mobilization and erection of barricades throughout the entire city, does not mean that the latter were entirely spontaneous—just that they were the results of watchwords issuing from the defense committees.

In April 1937, Pedro Herrera, "councillor" (minister) of health in the second Tarradellas government, and Manuel Escorza were the CNT leaders who tried to thrash out with Lluís Companys (the Generalidad president) a way out of the government crisis that had erupted at the start of March 1937 following the resignation of the defense minister, the CNT's Francisco Isgleas. Companys had decided to drop Tarradellas's tactics—Tarradellas could not conceive of a Generalidad government that was not a government of antifascist unity, in which the CNT would not be a partner—to switch instead to the line advocated by PSUC secretary Joan Comorera, namely that force be used to impose a "string" government that would no longer put up with a CNT that had proved incapable of reining in its own militants, the so-called "uncontrollables." Companys was determined to break with the policy of entering into arrangements with the CNT, a policy that was proving more and more difficult, and he thought that the time had come (thanks to backing from the PSUC and the Soviets) to use force to impose the authority and decisions of the Generalidad government, which however, as the facts demonstrated, was still not quite powerful enough to dispense with making deals with the CNT.

The breakdown in the talks between Companys and Escorza and Herrera, after they failed to come up with any political solution after two months of talks, was averted at the eleventh hour by a personal agreement between Companys and Escorza on 15 April; they agreed upon a new cabinet lineup for 16 April; Aurelio Fernández would be joining it on behalf of the CNT.

The ambush and murder of the Cerdaña's anarchist leader, Antonio Martín, on the bridge into Bellver on 27 April shattered that fragile agreement and led directly to the armed clashes in Barcelona in May 1937, when Companys, without alerting Tarradellas (let alone Escorza and Herrera, of course) ordered Artemi Aguadé, the interior "councillor," to seize the Telephone Exchange. The order was carried out by Rodríguez Salas.

Seizure of the Telephone Exchange was a brutal answer to the CNT's demands and a slap in the face of the April negotiations that Manuel Escorza and Pedro Herrera, representing the CNT, had held directly with Companys and from which the latter had deliberately excluded Tarradellas. Escorza had reason enough and resources enough to respond to Companys's provocation from the CNT-FAI Investigation Service and he tipped off the defense committees about an imminent coup de force by the Stalinists and the Generalidad government and aimed at the CNT.

Escorza lit the spark that started the fire. But the man who led and coordinated the defense committees' insurrection and who suggested that it be broadened, and that the RC should take the lead, was Julián Merino.

On the barricades, the Friends of Durruti were the most active fighters and completely controlled the Plaza Maciá (today the Plaza Real)—where they had all access routes blocked off—and the entire length of the Calle Hospital. At the Ramblas-Calle Hospital intersection, under an enormous portrait of Durruti draped across the façade of the building where the group had its base, they threw up a barricade where they set up their operations center. Their unchallenged control of the Calle Hospital linked them to the headquarters of the Confederal Defense Committee (the central HQ of the defense committees) in Los Escolapios on the Ronda San Pablo, and, from there, to the Brecha de San Pablo, which had been taken over by forty-odd militia members from the Rojinegra Column who, under the Durruti Column's Máximo Franco, had "gone down to Barcelona" on a "reconnaissance and fact-finding" mission, after both the Rojinegra and the (POUMist) Lenin Columns, the latter under the command of Rovira, had caved in to pressures brought to bear, at the instigation of Abad de Santillán and Molina (the CNT personnel who gave the orders at the Generalidad's Defense Department in Isgleas's absence) that their respective units return to the front lines.[10]

---

10   There is a chance that Máximo Franco alone came down to the city and that the forty militia members were deserters from the Rojinegra, already in Barcelona. See the chronology under 22 April above.

Bewildered by their leaders' call—the same leaders of 19 July!—for them to leave their barricades, the CNT masses had eventually chosen to withdraw from the fight, even though they had initially defied the CNT leadership's calls for concord for the sake of antifascist unity.

How were the Defense Committees dissolved?

In Barcelona, the barrio defense committees had emerged on 19–20 July 1936 and they lasted up until 7 June 1937 at least, at which point the reconstituted public order forces of the Generalidad dissolved and took over the various Control Patrols headquarters and a few defense committees premises besides, like the one in the Les Corts barrio. Despite the decree that required all armed groups to vanish, the bulk of them held out until September 1937 when they were systematically broken up and their premises attacked, one at a time. The last to be overrun and the most important and strongest was the headquarters of the Defense Committee of the Center in the Los Escolapios de San Antonio building, which was stormed on 20 September 1937 by Public Order troops who deployed a whole arsenal of machine guns, tanks, and hand grenades. However, those resisting inside Los Escolapios were overwhelmed, not by gunfire, but by eviction orders emanating from the Regional Committee, acting on advice received from the Policy Advisory Commission (CAP) headed by García Oliver.

After that, the defense committees clung on under the designation of CNT Coordination and Intelligence Sections, engaged solely in clandestine investigation and intelligence-gathering tasks like before 19 July—but now (1938) against an unmistakably counterrevolutionary backdrop.

However, they were still strong enough and pugnacious enough to publish a clandestine mouthpiece entitled *Alerta!*, of which seven issues appeared between October and December 1937. Number 1 appeared on 23 October 1937. A consistent thread running through this paper was **solidarity with "revolutionary prisoners,"** calls for their release and exposés of the management and abuses in the Modelo Prison; a **critique of collaborationism** and of the politicization of the FAI; denunciation of the disastrous war policies of the Negrín-Prieto government and of the **Stalinist ascendancy** within the army and the state. It sent out fraternal greetings to the Libertarian Youth and the Friends of Durruti. One indelible feature of the publication was the constant calls to "make the revolution" and for the high committees to give up all their posts: "Revolution cannot be made FROM THE STATE, but only AGAINST THE STATE." The late edition, dated 4 December 1937, denounced the Stalinist *chekas* and the brutal persecution of CNT personnel in the Cerdaña.

By 1938, the defense committees, like all revolutionaries, were either under-ground, behind bars, or operating in the utmost secrecy. It was not Franco's dictator-ship that finished off the Revolution it was Negrín's Republic.

B. A CRITICAL AND DE-MYTHOLOGIZING CRITIQUE OF THE FRIENDS OF DURRUTI

The Friends of Durruti was a very significant anarchist *agrupación* (it issued around five thousand membership cards and several hundred of them took a hand in the fighting in May) that was set up as a revolutionary opposition to the CNT-FAI's collaborationism.[11] It was more like a branch of the libertarian movement, like the Mujeres Libres, than a mere affinity group (affinity groups usually had between twelve and thirty members). It was not at all influenced by the Trotskyists, nor by the POUM. Naturally they were conversant with the economic writings of the leading 1930s anarcho-syndicalist theorists like Pierre Besnard and Christian Cornelissen and they relished the writings of Malatesta and Mella. Their ideology and watchwords were quintessentially confederal: at no point could it be argued that they displayed a Marxist ideology. In any event, they showed great interest in the example of Marat during the French revolution and maybe we should speak of a mighty attraction to the grassroots movement of the Paris sections, the *sans-culottes* and the *enragés,* the revolutionary govern-ment of Robespierre and Saint-Just, and great interest in reading Kropotkin's *The Great French Revolution.*

Their purpose was nothing short of grappling with the contradictions within the CNT, injecting some ideological coherence into it, wresting it away from the sway of personalities and committees of officials, and bringing it back to its class-struggle roots. Their *raison d'être* was to criticize and oppose the CNT's policy of forever making concessions and, of course, of COLLABORATION be-tween anarcho-syndicalists and the national or Generalidad governments. They were against abandoning revolutionary goals or the basic ideological principles that characterized anarchism, something that the CNT-FAI leaders had made great play of, all in the name of antifascist unity and the need to adapt to circum-stances. In the absence of revolutionary theory, there is no revolution. If princi-ples serve no purpose other than to be cast aside at the first obstacle reality places in our path, it might be better to concede that there are no such things as princi-ples. Spanish anarcho-syndicalism's top leaders thought of themselves as skilled negotiators and were manipulated like puppets. They conceded everything and

---

11   See Balius's correspondence with Bolloten, available in Agustín Guillamón, *Los Amigos de Durruti,* 146–162.

got nothing in return. They were opportunists unable to seize their opportunity. The insurrection on 19 July 1936 had not been able to call upon any revolutionary party with the ability to take power and make revolution. The CNT had never asked what it would do once the rebel military had been defeated. The July victory had left anarcho-syndicalist leaders at a loss and bewildered. They had been overtaken by the revolutionary élan of the masses, who had organized themselves into myriad revolutionary committees. And since they were clueless as to what to do, they agreed to Companys's suggestion that they and the other parties should form an Antifascist Front government. And they posed the phony dilemma of *anarchist dictatorship versus antifascist unity and partnership with the state*, in order to win the war. They had no inkling of what to do with power, when failing to take it meant leaving it in the custody of the bourgeoisie. Not only did they not marshal and centralize the power of the committees, but they felt a measure of distrust toward a form of organizing that sidestepped the unions and that had not been anticipated by anarcho-syndicalist ideology. The Spanish revolution was the tomb of state anarchism as a revolutionary theory for the proletariat. Which is where the Friends of Durruti came in and where their *raison d'être* was.

The prime purpose of the group was to criticize the CNT leadership and to end the policy of CNT partnership in government. Not only did they mean to hang onto the "gains" made in July but they wanted to see the revolutionary process continued and deepened. But their resources and their organization were still very much limited. These were barricade fighters, not good organizers, and they were even worst theorists, although they had some good journalists among them. In May, they staked everything on the spontaneity of the masses. They failed to counter the official CNT propaganda. They neither used nor organized the militants who were serving in the Control Patrols. They issued no orders to Máximo Franco, a Friends of Durruti member and delegate from the CNT's Rojinegra Division, who had wanted to "go down to Barcelona" on 4 May with his division, although it eventually turned back toward the front lines (as did the POUM column led by Rovira) due to overtures made by Molina and García Vivancos.

The high points of their activity were the poster distributed toward the end of April 1937, in which they proposed that the Generalidad be overthrown and replaced by a Revolutionary Junta; their control of a number of barricades on the Ramblas during the May Events; the reading given to an appeal addressed to all the workers in Europe to show solidarity with the Spanish revolution;[12] the

---

12   According to the claims made by Pablo Ruiz in "Posthumous Praise for Jaime Balius," *Le Combat syndicaliste-Solidaridad Obrera*, 9 January 1981.

distribution on the barricades of the notorious flyer on 5 May; and the summing up of the events in their manifesto of 8 May. But they were never able to put their slogans into practice. They suggested that a column be raised to head off the troops on their way up from Valencia, but that idea was quickly dropped when they found little response to the suggestion.

After the May Events, they started publishing *El Amigo del Pueblo*, even though they had been disowned by the CNT and the FAI. In June 1937, even though they were not outlawed like the POUM was, they experienced the political persecution that hit other CNT militants. Their mouthpiece, *El Amigo del Pueblo*, was published clandestinely from issue 2 (26 May) onwards and its editor-in-chief, Jaime Balius, was jailed time and time again. Other Friends of Durruti (or *durrutistas*) lost their posts or influence, like Bruno Lladó, a member of Sabadell council. Most of the members of the group found themselves targeted for expulsion from the CNT, on the recommendation of the FAI.[13] In spite of it all, they carried on with the clandestine printing of the aforementioned newspaper and in January 1938 their pamphlet *Hacia una nueva revolución* (Toward a Fresh Revolution) was published; by that time the counterrevolution was finally and crushingly victorious and the war already lost by the republicans.

Their most outstanding tactical proposals could be condensed into the following slogans: union direction of the economy, a federation of municipalities, a militia-based army, defense of a revolutionary program, replacement of the Generalidad by a revolutionary Junta, and concerted CNT-FAI-POUM action.

If we had to summarize in brief the historical and political import of the Friends of Durruti we would say that they were a failed attempt emanating from the bosom of the libertarian movement itself to form a revolutionary vanguard that would end the CNT-FAI's collaborationism and champion and entrench the revolutionary "gains" of July 1936.

They failed in the attempt because they showed that they were incapable, not so much of implementing their slogans, but even of effectively propagating their ideas and offering practical guidelines as to how they might be fought for. Perhaps the terror-stricken bourgeois and the disguised priest saw them as a bunch of savage brutes, but their membership numbered journalists like Balius, "Mingo," and Liberto Callejas, militia column commanders such as Pablo Ruiz, Francisco Carreño, and Máximo Franco, councillors such as Bruno

---

13   See the articles in which the FAI proposed that the Friends of Durruti face expulsion, in *Boletín de Información y orientación orgánica del Comité peninsular de la Federación Anarquista Ibérica*: "Disavowal of the Friends of Durruti entity" in issue no. 1, 20 May 1937; "Public Sanction on members of the 'Friends of Durruti' Group" in no. 3, 6 June 1937.

Lladó, leading trade unionists like Francisco Pellicer, Libertarian Youth leader Juan Santana Calero, leading anarchist militants, and public speakers such as Vicente Pérez "Combina'; and that is not in any way to downplay the existence, courage, and much-needed men of action such as Progreso Ródenas. For their remote origins, we must reach back to the libertarians who shared the revolutionary experience of the uprising in the Alto Llobregat back in January 1932 and to the Renacer affinity group between 1934 and 1936. Their more recent origins can be traced to the opposition to militarization of the militias (particularly in the Durruti Column's Gelsa sector) and, their championship of revolutionary gains, and criticisms of CNT collaborationism as articulated in articles carried by *Solidaridad Obrera* (July to early October 1936), *Ideas,* and *La Noche* (January to May 1937)—which came especially from Balius's pen. Their arsenal was the flyer, the poster, the newspaper, and the barricade: but they never advocated a split or a breakaway as a weapon, or the denunciation of the counterrevolutionary role of the CNT, or at least, during the May Events, or a confrontation with CNT leaders in an effort to counter the CNT-FAI's defeatist dictums.

Nevertheless, the historical importance of the Friends of Durruti cannot be denied. And it resides precisely in their having been an internal opposition to the libertarian movement's collaborationist outlook. The political import of their emergence was grasped immediately by Nin who devoted an article to them that was full of praise and hope, because they had opened up the possibility of the CNT masses' espousing a revolutionary approach, opposing the CNT's policy of compromise and collaboration.[14] Hence the interest that both the POUM and the Trotskyists showed in bringing their influence to bear on the Friends of Durruti: something at which they never succeeded.

The group's main theoretical contributions to anarchist thought can be summed up thus:

1. The need for a clear and precise **revolutionary program**, defended at the point of a rifle. All economic power to be exercised by the unions.

2. **Revolutions are either totalitarian or they fail.** "Totalitarian" meaning embracing every facet of life: political, social, economic, and cultural.

---

14   Andrés Nin, "The Time Has Come to Act in the Face of the Counterrevolutionary Danger," *La Batalla*, 4 March 1937.

And it also indicates the requisite violent crushing of bourgeois counter-revolution and the need for a revolutionary leadership.

3. Replacement of the Generalidad government by a Revolutionary Junta, understood as a **unitary revolutionary agency of the working class, opposed to class collaboration, outside of state structures, and with no place either for the bourgeoisie or for the Stalinists.**

★

Traditional anarchist apoliticism meant that the CNT lacked a theory of revolution. In the absence of theory, there is no revolution and not taking power meant leaving it in the care of the capitalist state. **As far as the Friends of Durruti could see, the CAMC was an agency of class collaboration** and it had served merely to shore up and strengthen the bourgeois state that it neither would nor could destroy. Hence the need stressed by the Friends of Durruti, to form a Revolutionary Junta capable of coordinating, centralizing, and fortifying the power of the many workers' committees, be they local committees, defense committees, factory committees, militia committees, and so on, which had been the only ones holding power between 19 July and 26 September 1936. Authority atomized into a plethora of committees that "usurped" all power locally, but that, by not federating with one another, being centralized and fortified by one another, were steered, undermined, and transformed by the CAMC into Popular Front town councils, unionized factory managements, and battalions in the army of the Republic. Without total destruction of the capitalist state, the revolutionary events of July 1936 could not have led on to a new workers' power structure. The degeneration and ultimate failure of the revolutionary process was inescapable. However, the clash between the reformist state anarchism of the CNT-FAI and the revolutionary anarchism of the Friends of Durruti was not precise and emphatic enough to trigger **a split that might have shed light on the gulf between their positions.**

Although the political thinking articulated by the Friends of Durruti was an attempt to comprehend the reality of the war and the Spanish revolution from the viewpoint of anarcho-syndicalist ideology, one of the main grounds on which it was rejected by the CNT membership was its authoritarian, "Marxist," or "bolshevistic" flavor. The Friends of Durruti found themselves in a dead-end street. They could not countenance the collaborationism of the leadership cadre of the CNT and the onward creep of the counterrevolution; but if they theorized about the experiences of the Spanish revolution, that is, the need for a Revolutionary Junta to overthrow the bourgeois republican Generalidad government of Catalonia and use force to repress the agents of counterrevolution, then they were written off as Marxists and authoritarians and thus forfeited any chance of making recruits from among the CNT grassroots.[15] One wonders whether the Friends of Durruti's dead-end street was anything more than a reflection of the theoretical inadequacy of the state anarchism that thrived and was ascendant in the higher committees, when it came to grappling with the problems raised by the war and the revolution.

Our conclusion, therefore, has to be that the Friends of Durruti simply could not circumvent the limitations imposed upon it by the ideology of antifascist unity; indeed, quite the opposite; it was the starkest expression of the contradictions existing within anarchism's revolutionary aspiration; **they aspired to revolution, but they were operating within the confines of capitalist logic.** The Friends of Durruti posed the problem of the revolution in its totality, but were unable to come up with an answer that was **viable** within the historical conditions of the Spanish revolution. Especially if we bear it in mind that their starting point was implicit loyalty to the CNT and their ultimate purpose to restore the credibility of that trade-union organization. **Patriotic commitment to those initials was an insuperable taboo.** The limitations of anarcho-syndicalism were not going to be overcome from the inside of libertarian ideology per se, because that would have necessitated a split that they were unwilling and unable to contemplate.

May 1937 had been hatched in July 1936. The group had realized that revolutions are either totalitarian or they are defeated: this was greatly to their credit. The great lesson to be drawn from the 1936 Spanish revolution was that the task of destroying the state is necessary, urgent, and cannot be postponed; that the state must be replaced by the coordination and strengthening of new working-class organs of power, which in 1936 existed in the shape of the committees—local, barrio, defense, and workers' control committees; in the revolutionary committees. That is, in the shape of what the Friends of Durruti dubbed the **Revolutionary Junta, the group's essential theoretical contribution to revolutionary theory.**

---

15   The tag "authoritarians," an insult when used among libertarians, was simply a by-product of CNT propaganda, since one of the group's most significant learning experiences was that it asserted the authoritarian, totalitarian nature of any revolution. This contention by the Friends of Durruti was reiterated on several occasions. Its first use was in an article by Balius on 6 December 1936, entitled "Durruti's Legacy" and he had it coming from Durruti's own lips in a harangue delivered on the Madrid front on 5 November 1936. The last time he used it was in the 1978 introduction he wrote for the English-language version of the pamphlet *Toward a Fresh Revolution* in which he states: "In our 1938 pamphlet, we affirmed that all revolutions are totalitarian."

C. UNTIMELY CONSIDERATIONS

Eighty years on, the lessons of the defeat of the revolution in 1937 Barcelona affords us an understanding of the fact that a revolution must not just be simultaneously economic and political, but **total** as well. That is, it must be **anti-economic and anti-political** and thereby preempt any possibility of a restoration of the power of capital. Anti-economic, because it is not confined to collectivization or to socialization, nor does it lapse into an obsession with productivity, but rather **does away with waged labor and surplus value.** Anti-political because it is organized through workers' councils that **tear down all state structures and do away with all borders,** which is what makes the revolution necessarily international in scale.

6

Conclusions

1

May 1937 represented the defeat of the most advanced revolutionary proletariat, a defeat **needed and sought after by the Stalinist counterrevolution** and republican **reformists,** so that they might defuse the threat the defense committees posed to bourgeois institutions, unleash a **selective** repression, lock the higher committees into the machinery of state, and annihilate the revolutionaries.

2

In the 1930s, antifascism was fascism's greatest success. The sacred union of all antifascists for the purpose of defeating fascism and defending democracy implied that the workers' movement would turn away from its own principles, a proletarian revolutionary program, its revolutionary gains, everything—which is to say, that notorious catchphrase incorrectly attributed to Durruti: "We renounce everything ... except victory"—and defer to the program and interests of the democratic bourgeoisie. It was this program of antifascist unity, out-and-out loyal collaboration with all antifascist forces, that led the CNT-FAI swiftly and unwittingly into a partnership with government for the sole purpose of winning the war against fascism. It was this embracing of the antifascist program (which is to say, of defending capitalist democracy) that explains why and how yesterday's revolutionary leaders had, within a few months, turned into ministers, firefighters, bureaucrats, and counterrevolutionaries. It was the CNT that produced the ministers and those ministers betrayed nothing and no one; they merely and loyally did their duty as best they could.

3

The May 1937 insurrection was the fruit of the defense committees' resistance to the looming and foreseeable military coup de force of the counterrevolutionary

PSUC-ERC-Generalidad government bloc, and the provocation implicit in the order to storm the Telephone Exchange, as is demonstrated by the documentary record and as virtually all of the rigorous historiography explains.[1] It was also a part of the Stalinist strategy designed to achieve a **strong state** capable of winning the war on fascism. Disarming and weakening the CNT was a strategic necessity as far as the PSUC was concerned, and the murder of Antonio Martín in Bellver had been the curtain raiser. It is obvious that the raid on the Telephone Exchange, which triggered the May Events, was the Catalan government's idea: the CNT personnel inside resisted the attack (they had not started it).

Or perhaps the Stalinists and post-historians would now like to argue that the CNT personnel working inside the Telephone Exchange and attacked by the Guards, were the provocateurs who started the May Events by putting up resistance?!

Talk of May '37 as being a harebrained, whimsical, spontaneous, and needless insurrection by anarchists, as some nationalists and neo-Stalinists would have us believe, is a historical untruth and a sectarian interpretation that also arbitrarily leaves out the POUM's intervention.

4

The detailed report on January–April 1937 that Manuel Escorza's Investigation Service had drawn up in conjunction with Eroles's agency and entitled "The Sancho-Casanovas-Lluhí-Gassol Affair, from the Paris Embassy and the Toulouse Consulate" left no room for doubt as to the painstakingly prepared plot against the CNT-FAI, in which Catalan nationalists and the PSUC worked hand in glove, with the explicit approval of the *mossos de escuadra* and the Generalidad government.[2] Those preparations culminated in the days of bloodshed in Barcelona from 3 to 7 May 1937.

5

Julián Merino's leadership at the morning meeting of the higher committees on

---

1   See Hilario Esteban's report to Eroles (10 April 1937); the report from Moscow disclosed by Escorza's Information Service; the letter from Sesé to Companys; the murder of Antonio Martín in Bellver (25 April); Prince's 29 April 1937 letter to the FACA. And above all, because this was blatantly the PSUC's political strategy, as ordinary people were able to see for themselves on a daily basis.

2   This was a collection of personal dossiers, tracking the movements of individuals, trips to Paris, lists of addresses, and family, financial, and interpersonal reports covering the January to April 1937 period. It is a stunning and incontrovertible piece of documented research into the plot that was being hatched against the CNT.

4 May 1937, the formation of a secret revolutionary committee of the CRTC (Regional Confederation of Labor of Catalonia), and of two combat teams to extend the streetfighting constituted, no question about it, an attempt to go on the offensive. It failed because of the ceasefire appeals broadcast that very afternoon (4 May) by García Oliver and Federica Montseny. The swift collapse of that intended offensive merely underlines the predominantly defensive nature of the May 1937 workers' insurrection.

6

On the afternoon of 4 May, the CNT's revolutionary committee laid the groundwork for a final offensive by the defense committees and marshaled its forces for an attack on the city center, which was still being contested. In the end, that attack was not carried out due to the broadcast ceasefire call ordered by the CNT's higher committees.[3] At the 8 and 19 May meetings of the higher committees this revolutionary committee is charitably designated as a "war committee."[4]

7

The insurrection of 3 to 7 May was essentially a Barcelona affair, although there is no denying that there were significant antecedents throughout Catalonia and in the País Valenciano, as well as (sometimes startlingly similar) reverberations in many Catalan towns: Tarragona, Reus, Tortosa, Amposta, Lleida, Gerona, Cadaqués, Manlleu, Vic, Bisaura de Ter, Montesquiu, La Farga de las Lloses, Villafranca del Penedés, Sitges, etc., which would merit detailed study beyond the limited scope of this book.

8

The Friends of Durruti had no hesitation in stating in its 8 May manifesto that the battle had been won in military terms by the workers and that, this being the case, they should have finished once and for all with a Generalidad that meant nothing. The group accused the CNT's leaders and higher committees, who had brought a victorious workers' insurrection to a halt, of "treachery":

---

3   There is plenty of testimony to this: see in the Bibliography: Aguzzi, 169; Bonomini, 152; Casanovas: *Joan Remi*, 135–136; the NC's report on the May Events, etc.

4   See the meetings of the higher committees on 18 and 19 May 1937 in Agustín Guillamón, *La represión contra la CNT y los revolucionarios. Hambre y violencia en la Barcelona revolucionaria. De mayo a septiembre de 1937* (Barcelona: Descontrol, 2015).

The Generalidad represents nothing. Its continuation is a bolster to the counterrevolution. We workers have won the battle. It is inconceivable that the CNT's committees should have acted with such timidity as to venture to order a "ceasefire" and even imposed a return to work when we were on the very brink of total victory. The provenance of the attack was ignored, no heed was paid to the true meaning of the current fighting. Such conduct has to be described as treason against the revolution and nobody should commit or foster it in the name of anything. And we do not have the words to describe the poisonous work done by *Solidaridad Obrera* and the CNT's most prominent militants.

The mention of "treason" cropped up again when remarks were made about the CNT Regional Committee's disavowal of the Friends of Durruti as well as in relation to the transfer of the Security and Defense jurisdictions (not those wielded by the Generalidad but those controlled by the CNT) to the central government in Valencia: "This is treason on a huge scale. The working class's two essential guarantees, Security and Defense, are being served up on a plate to our enemies." The 8 May manifesto closed with a brief self-criticism regarding some tactical shortcomings during the May Events and with an optimistic look forward to the future, which the impending wave of repression launched against the group on 28 May would expose as vain and lacking in substance. **May 1937 did not end in failure, but it was a severe political setback for the proletariat.**[5]

For all the mythology surrounding the May Events of 1937, the fact is that it was a very chaotic and confused situation characterized by an appetite for negotiation on the part of all sides involved in the conflict. May 1937 was at no time an offensive, determined workers' insurrection; it was merely defensive and lacking in precise goals, even though it was part and parcel of the tussle under way between socialization and collectivization, and remained in defense of the "gains" made in July 1936. What detonated the conflict was the raid on the Telephone Exchange by the Generalidad's security forces. And that act, the real provocation, fitted in with the Companys government's rationale of slowly reacquiring all the powers that the "anomalous" situation of the 19 July 1936 worker insurrection had, for a time, wrested from it. The recent counterrevolutionary successes in the Cerdaña, with the murder of Antonio Martín, opened the way for a final push in Barcelona and throughout Catalonia. Plainly, Companys felt that he had the backing of Comorera (PSUC) and Ovseenko (the Soviet consul), with whom he had been working very closely and effectively since December

---

5   The Group's local in the Ramblas was attacked and an order from the higher committees for their expulsion was published in *Solidaridad Obrera*.

1936, when the POUM had been ousted from the Generalidad government. Stalinist policy overlapped with Companys's aims: weakening and nullifying the revolutionary forces—that is, the POUM and the CNT—was one aim of the Soviets, achievable only if the bourgeois Generalidad government was strengthened. The lingering crisis in the Generalidad opened with the CNT's rejection of any transfer to the Madrid front of the (PSUC's) Karl Marx Division. Added to that initial friction there was the direct opposition to the **decree of 4 March 1937** regarding the disbandment of the Control Patrols and disarming of the rearguard, while simultaneously establishing the Unified Security Corps (combined Civil Guards and Assault Guards). The widening gulf with the CNT was inevitably resolved through violence in the raid on the Telephone Exchange (following a number of armed clashes in La Fatarella, Olesa, Bellver, Cortada's funeral, etc.) and the bloodshed in Barcelona that May.

The stupid blindness, the unbreakable belief in antifascist unity, the large measure of collaboration with the republican government on the part of the main anarcho-syndicalist leaders (ranging from Peiró to Federica Montseny, from Santillán to García Oliver, from Marianet to Valerio Mas) were not irrelevant, nor were they any secret to the Catalan government and soviet agents. The latter could count on their idiotic sanctimony, as was amply demonstrated during the May Events. But Companys and the soviets had not reckoned on the possibility that the CNT's higher committees might be sidelined and swept aside by "the uncontrollables" and by the barrio defense committees. Companys was driven to despair by the Valencia government's refusal to have (air force commander) Díaz Sandino act on his orders and **bomb the CNT's barracks and other buildings.** Companys ended up with a Generalidad stripped of all its Defense and Public Order powers, which had never been that broad anyway.

As to the activities of the Friends of Durruti during the May Events, we need not indulge in any misleading mythmaking about their involvement on the barricades and their leaflet, since the Friends of Durruti did not have their sights set on replacing the CNT leadership and confined themselves to directing harsh criticism at the leadership and its policy of "treason" against the revolution. Maybe there was nothing else they could do, given their small numbers and flimsy influence on the CNT masses. **They avoided a split and expulsion at all costs.**

The part they played in the streetfighting, their control of several barricades on the Ramblas, especially outside their own clubhouse, and their part in the fighting in Sants, La Torrassa, and Sallent deserve mention. Naturally, their attempt to offer direction and some minimal political demands in the flyer they handed out on 5 May needs to be highlighted. Distributing that flyer was no easy undertaking and it cost the lives of a number of the group's members, although its distribution also attracted the sympathy and assistance of many

CNT militants. Among the actions to be highlighted during the May Events, we should not forget the call that Balius sent out from the barricade located at the intersection of the Ramblas and the Calle Hospital, calling upon all European workers to show active solidarity with the Spanish revolution. On hearing the news that an Assault Guard column had been raised and was on its way up from Valencia to snuff out the rebellion, the response of the Friends of Durruti was to try to raise an anarchist column to head it off. But that never went any further than the proposal, as it was not taken up by the CNT membership who were beginning to dismantle their barricades. Meanwhile, Ricardo Sanz, the delegate for the Durruti Column militia members newly returned from the Madrid front and awaiting reassignment to the Aragon front, sat idly in the Docks barracks on the Avenida Icaria.[6]

Finally, and from a political viewpoint, we need to highlight the agreement reached with the POUM to issue an appeal to the workers **to insist, before they dismantled their barricades, upon guarantees that there would be no repression to follow**; and, above all, to point out that the best guarantee of that was for them to hold on to their weapons, which ought never to be surrendered. Even if a beaten workers' insurrection refuses to jettison its weapons, it can scarcely expect repressive forces to refrain from cracking down on the insurgents, as indeed happened from 10–16 June onwards.

But the fact of the matter is that, once the fighting was over, the May barricades were a bother to everybody; the troops newly arrived from Valencia tore up CNT membership cards and forced peaceable passersby to dismantle the barricades, while the CNT's Regional Committee called for the barricades to be taken away as a token of normality. A few days later and the only barricades still standing were the ones the PSUC chose to keep as a sign and token of their victory.

From the theoretical point of view, the Friends of Durruti played a much more prominent role after the May Events, when they began publishing their mouthpiece on 19 May; it borrowed its name from the paper (*L'Ami du people*)

---

6   Ricardo Sanz, *El sindicalismo y la política. Los "solidarios" y "nosotros"* (Toulouse: Self-published, 1966), 306. The Docks (renamed the Spartacus) barracks was attacked by the Stalinists from the nearby Karl Marx barracks, but Ricardo Sanz's troops confined themselves to passively fending off the attack, without taking to the streets. Inside those same barracks, militia members from the Tierra y Libertad column who had been involved in the streetfighting, complied on the night of 5 May with orders from the CNT's RC that all attacks should be called off. The only ones to venture outside to fight on, on the defensive barricade erected in the Avenida Icaria, were a bunch of Italians, who had fetched four tanks to defend the Casa CNT-FAI on 4 May and, on 5 May, six armored cars to defend the Gran Vía to defend the Control Patrols' base and the Foodworkers Union local.

that Marat had published during the French revolution—*El Amigo del Pueblo* (The People's Friend).

9

July 1936 was an offensive insurrection against the military-fascist mutiny; the May Events of 1937 were a defensive insurrection against the coup de force planned by the Stalinists, the nationalists, and the Generalidad.[7] Comparison of the two insurrections leaves no doubt as to their chief characteristics: **July 1936 was offensive and May 1937 was defensive.**

The crucial difference between the July 1936 and May 1937 insurrections is that, in July, the revolutionaries were unarmed, but had a precise political purpose: defeating the army revolt and fascism. Whereas, in May 1937, despite being better armed than in July, they were openly stripped of their weapons; **they lacked effective coordination and clear cut, precise goals.**[8] The defense committees launched a defensive insurrection targeting the Stalinists and the bourgeois Generalidad government **in spite of** their own organizations and **without** their own leaders, but proved incapable of seeing the fight through to a finish **without** their organizations and **in defiance of** their leaders. In May 1937, as in July 1936, there was no revolutionary organization with enough clout and prestige to defend anarchist principles: destroying the state and imposing a social alternative to capitalism and state structures.

The proletariat had not managed to mold such an organization during the 1930s. Nor were the POUM or the CNT-FAI the necessary revolutionary vanguard (nor could they be); quite the opposite. They were the greatest impediment to its emergence. The incompetence of the anarcho-syndicalist leadership and the absence of any revolutionary theory meant that the only thing on the horizon was antifascist unity and the republican bourgeoisie's democratic program. **The proletariat's methodology and goals had vanished from the scene.** Not only had the CAMC failed to beef up the revolutionary committees but it collaborated with the Generalidad government in undermining and doing away with them.

---

7   Most of the historiography and the protagonists who manned the barricades are agreed in pointing out the defensive character of the May insurrection. See, for instance, Hugo Oehler, "Barricadas en Barcelona: la primera revuelta del proletariado contra el Frente Popular capitalista: relato de un testigo. Barcelona, 15 de mayo de 1937," in *Barcelona, mayo 1937: Testimonios desde las barricadas*, eds. García, Piotrowski, and Rosés (Barcelona: Alikornio, 2006), 55; See also Albert Weisbord in ibid., 89–90.

8   Hence, Julián Merino's failed attempt to get the RC to take over the coordination, in military terms at least. Hence, the belated and failed efforts of tiny organizations with hardly any influence, like the Friends of Durruti and the SBLE, to endow the insurrection with clear and precise **goals.**

The barricades that went up in July 1936 were still up months afterwards; the ones that went up in May 1937 vanished immediately, except for a few that the PSUC chose to leave as testimony to its power and its victory.

Viewed in this light, May 1937, even though it was without doubt the result of the growing discontent—with soaring prices, food shortages, the contention within firms over socialization of the economy and workers' control, the Generalidad's escalating efforts to disarm the rearguard and assume control of Public Order, etc., etc.—was primarily the **essential defeat of the proletariat, a defeat that the counterrevolution needed in order to exorcize, once and for all, any revolutionary threat to bourgeois republican institutions.**

By 1938, the revolutionaries were under the soil, in jail, or in hiding. The antifascists in prison numbered in the thousands. Hunger, air raids, and Stalinist repression were lords and masters in Barcelona. The militias and work had been militarized. Bourgeois order now prevailed throughout Spain, in the Francoist camp and in the republican camp alike. The revolution was not crushed by Franco in January 1939; Negrín's Republic had done that many months before that.

10

In July 1936, there was a revolutionary situation that sustained the working class's hegemony and its threat to the republican bourgeoisie for ten months. There was no COORDINATION or CENTRALIZATION OF (workers') POWER, because that power was fragmented around hundreds of committees— local, factory, attached to different workers' organizations and the various party militias, control patrols, etc. What there was, was POWER ATOMIZED.

May 1937 did not come out of the blue but was the result of the resistance to the dissolution of the Control Patrols, the militarization of the militias, and, above all, to the fact that, in the struggle to entrench and monitor the process of socializing the Catalan economy in the face of the erosion of the "gains of July," workers' resistance happened in an isolated way within each individual firm. Because the Generalidad's "normalization" process, as it sought to enforce the S'Agaró decrees approved by Tarradellas back in January 1937, implied the end of "revolutionary gains" and the Generalidad government's being left in absolute control of the Catalan economy.

The lessons to be drawn from this are, obviously, the need to destroy the capitalist state utterly and to disband its repressive agencies, as well as to implement the proletariat's program of social revolution, which the anarchists organized within the Friends of Durruti believed meant setting up a Revolutionary Junta made up of all the organizations that had done their bit in the revolutionary street-fighting in July 1936, while steering clear of collaboration with bourgeois organizations or with the state. May 1937 was the consequence of mistakes made in July 1936.

In Spain, there was no revolutionary organization or vanguard, but there was thoroughgoing and powerful REVOLUTIONARY ACTIVITY by the working class that thwarted the fascist would-be coup and that overwhelmed all the workers' organizations in existence in July 1936, and that, come May 1937, took on the Stalinists and the reconstruction of the machinery of state in Barcelona, although, in the end, it failed because it neglected to confront its own trade union and political organizations (CNT and POUM) when they came to the defense of the bourgeois state and the program of the counterrevolution. The fact that the revolutionary movement that existed in Spain between July 1936 and May 1937 went up in smoke and was lured away from its class goals toward antifascist aims does not alter the fact that a revolutionary situation existed. No proletarian revolution so far has succeeded, and the failure of the Commune, or the existence of Stalinism, do not disprove the revolutionary character of the Commune or of October 1917.

Plainly, without the proletariat's seizing power,[9] the Spanish collectivization process was doomed to failure, and all of the collectives would have been tainted and denatured by that failure to take power; but it is equally plain that, for all its limitations, the expropriation of the bourgeoisie was the result of the proletarian revolutionary upheaval in July. The essential lesson of the "Spanish Revolution" (or, to be more precise, of the revolutionary situation existing in Barcelona and nearly all of Catalonia and parts of Aragon and the País Valenciano) is that there is an ineluctable need for a vanguard to champion the proletariat's revolutionary program, the first two steps in which are the utter destruction of the capitalist state and the installation of a **Revolutionary Junta**, like the Friends of Durruti said. That Revolutionary Junta would be a novel body, beyond politics and parties, and organized on the basis of workers' councils, and it would have to come to grips with the inevitable violence from the counterrevolution by destroying state structures, the way that some churches have been destroyed: with only the bell tower and the floor remaining.

But to make the leap of arguing, as *Bilan* did, that in the absence of a party there is no revolution and no revolutionary situation, fails to understand that **the revolution is made, not by the party and not by the vanguard, but by the proletariat,** even though a proletarian revolution will inevitably fail unless there is an organization capable of defending the proletariat's revolutionary program (as the barrio committees, the Friends of Durruti, or the Bolshevik-Leninist Section of Spain [SBLE] tried unsuccessfully to do).

---

9   Or, better, without the destruction of the power of the bourgeoisie and its state.

The analysis offered by those who purport to "be the party"—be they *Bilan* or the Stalinists—and who missed the revolutionary situation that was playing out under their very noses—remains tragicomic.

Bilan's analysis is very valuable when it comes to exposing the weaknesses and errors in the Spanish revolutionary process, but it is dire and irksome when that analysis is taken to the absurd lengths of **denying the revolutionary, proletarian character of the historical process through which the Spanish working class lived between July 1936 and May 1937**. In short: it is a fact that **without a party** or revolutionary vanguard, a proletarian revolution will fail; and we have the Spanish example and *Bilan*'s splendid analysis there to prove it. But **it is not the case that there can be no proletarian revolutionary situation unless there is a (Leninist) party to lead the revolution**. And this is the claim that led *Bilan* to the mistaken analysis of the situation created in Catalonia on 19 July 1936, as well as to its failure to understand the events that spurred the proletariat into a second revolutionary insurrection in May 1937.

11

The Stalinist camp, including both the PSUC and the PCE, was the party of the counterrevolution. It welcomed the hapless petite bourgeoisie into its ranks, rejected the launching or possibility of any revolutionary "adventure" and concentrated all its efforts on the building of a **strong state** capable of winning the war on fascism. Its antifascist unity program was the program of the counterrevolutionary petite bourgeoisie.

The characteristic features of the **Stalinist counterrevolution** were these:

Relentless, omnipresent, and omnipotent police terror.

An essential misrepresentation of its own nature and of the nature of its enemies, especially the revolutionaries.

Exploitation of the workers by means of a state capitalism led by a Party-State, embodied through a program of municipalization and nationalization measures tending toward progressive militarization in the workplace and in everyday life.

The Negrín-Stalin government turned the initial inter-class collaborationism within the CAMC and the ideology of antifascist unity into a **national unity** and law-and-order government; it turned the reformist powerlessness in the face of revolution, which characterized socialists, Catalanists, and the anarcho-syndicalist bureaucracy, into a rounded counterrevolutionary program that stamped out every vestige of worker democracy and turned bourgeois democracy into the police dictatorship of the GPU and the SIM.

The Stalinists have never been a reformist faction within the workers' movement. Collaboration with Stalinists has never been feasible, only a struggle with no quarter asked nor given. Always and everywhere, Stalinism headed and steered the counterrevolutionary forces, drawing its strength from the idea of national unity, the practice of a law-and-order policy, its battle to establish a strong government, to plant militants from the Stalinist party in the machinery of state, and, above all, its ability to hide its reactionary nature from the workers' movement.

12

Stalinist, democratic, and nationalist historiography is trying to make fashionable a partisan interpretation of May 1937, one that amounts to lamenting **the crisis and fratricidal breakdown in antifascist ranks**. It is trying to impose the post-truth that May implied a **terrific loss to antifascist unity**, and that this opened the doors to Franco's victory. However, there is no fathoming the May Events of 1937 unless one appreciates that Barcelona's revolutionary workers **were not fighting for a bourgeois republic, nor for a democratic state**. The barrio revolutionary committees, which had grown out of the defense committees' victory over a mutinous army and a fascist coup attempt, were **fighting for social revolution and for a new world, IN A CLASS WAR**. They fought to bring about the destruction of the state by replacing it in every one of its functions, expropriating factories and properties from the bourgeoisie, raising an army of volunteer militia members, taking charge of the political, social, and economic management of a city with more than a million inhabitants. And this is something that nationalist, social democratic, fascist, reformist, leftist, rightist, or Stalinist historiography can neither stomach nor contemplate.

That simple premise—that **the barrio committees were fighting on behalf of revolution**—leads on to these **three inescapable conclusions**:

1. In July 1936, the essential issue was not the **taking of power** (by a minority of anarchist leaders) but rather the committees' coordination, boosting, and deepening of the **destruction of the state**.

The revolutionary committees (and some of the local committees) neither made nor did they stop making the revolution: they **were** the social revolution.

The revolutionary committees' destruction of the state was a very concrete and real task, through which those committees took over all the functions performed by the state prior to July 1936 **and this is the great lesson to be learnt from the revolution of 1936: the vital necessity of destroying the state.**

2. During the civil war, the political project of **state anarchism, constituted as just another antifascist party** that used methods involving class collaboration and partnership in government, failed spectacularly on every count; but the social movement that was **revolutionary anarchism, organized through revolutionary committees**—barrio-based, locally-based, defense, etc.—represented the embryonic forms of a worker power that reached into management of the economy, revolutionary popular ventures involving proletarian autonomy, which to this day highlight and herald a future that is radically different from capitalist barbarism, fascist horror, or Stalinist enslavement.

And even though that revolutionary anarchism eventually succumbed to the coordinated and conspiratorial repression by the state, the bourgeoisie, the Stalinists, and the higher committees, it bequeathed to us the example, the thoughts, and the fight put up by minorities such as the Friends of Durruti, the Libertarian Youth of Catalonia and certain anarchist groups affiliated to the Barcelona Local Federation, and on that basis we can theorize today about their experiences, learn from their mistakes, and lay claim to their struggle and their history.

3. In May 1937, the revolutionaries and the defense committees **swept aside** the CNT's higher committees. And after May those higher committees implemented the requisite organizational measures needed if they were to avoid being overwhelmed again: to wit, the CAP and the Liaison Committee, as we shall see in Volume 4 of the quartet *Hunger and Violence in Revolutionary Barcelona*, entitled *The Crackdown on the CNT and the Revolutionaries.*

13
TO SUM UP:

The **4 March 1937** Generalidad decrees created a Unified Security Corps (made up of the Assault Guard and the Civil Guard) and (immediately thereafter) disbanded the Control Patrols. Those decrees spurred the CNT members of the Generalidad Council into resigning and triggered a serious government crisis.

On **15 April**, after difficult, lengthy negotiations, Companys and Escorza personally agreed upon a way out of the crisis and the formation of a new government (with the CNT's Aurelio Fernández joining the Generalidad as a *conseller* [councillor]).

The **27 April 1937** murder of Antonio Martín in Bellver signaled the breakdown of the laboriously worked out agreement. Escorza placed the defense committees on the alert by disclosing intelligence regarding an imminent coup de force by the counterrevolutionary bloc.

The provocation given on **3 May 1937** when Eusebio Rodríguez Salas raided the Telephone Exchange, mobilized the defense committees, which, within two hours, called a revolutionary strike, took over all the working-class barrios, and erected barricades in the city center and at strategic points. The CNT higher committee (Eroles and Asens) tried to rein in the defense committees, but were swept aside.

On the **morning of 4 May**, Barcelona's revolutionary workers, armed on their barricades and ready for anything, were not defeated, not by the PSUC, nor by the ERC, nor by the public order forces of the Generalidad. **They were annihilated over the radio.** The revolutionary attempt to come up with coordination and a precise direction for the insurrection under way, failed. **When the whole of Barcelona was one huge barricade, the workers in arms were beaten and humiliated by radio broadcasts made by the CNT's higher committees, most especially by the "kissing" speech of Juan García Oliver.**

On **5 May**, the Friends of Durruti launched a flyer that was an attempt to endow the insurrection with specific aims: replacement of the Generalidad by a Revolutionary Junta, the execution of those behind the provocation (Rodríguez Salas and Artemi Aguadé), socialization of the economy, fraternization with the militants of the POUM, etc. That flyer was promptly disowned by the higher committees, but it had the merit of resuscitating the fighting on the barricades.

5 and 6 May were the dates on which the streetfighting was at its height. CNT talk of a truce or of abandoning the barricades, as the radio and the press had urged, was exploited by the counterrevolutionary bloc in order to consolidate its own positions; this in turn spurred the revolutionaries into renewing the fighting and returning to their barricades.

By **7 May**, it was plain that the insurrection had failed. The troops sent up from Valencia marched along the Diagonal and occupied the whole of the city. Those troops began to dismantle the barricades. Over the days that followed, the higher committees tried to cover up everything that had happened, tried to bowdlerize the minutes that were in the process of being drafted and, ultimately, to do whatever they could to avoid the predictable Stalinist and government crackdown on the Organization and on the leading protagonists.

If we had to sum May 1937 up in a single sentence, we would have to explain that the revolutionary workers, armed on their barricades and ready for hell or high water, were beaten by ceasefire appeals broadcast over the airwaves: **Barcelona was an insurrection beaten by radio.**

14

IN CONCLUSION:

For the first time in history we had the case of an insurrection launched and sustained against the wishes of leaders [of the Organization] to which the vast majority of the insurgents belonged. But although an insurrection can be improvised, a victory cannot (Escorza); especially not when all the antifascist workers' organizations—from the UGT to the CNT's own higher committees—turned on the revolutionary proletariat.

The higher committees came to play a double game, allowing the formation of a CNT Revolutionary Committee while simultaneously forming a delegation to negotiate at the Generalidad Palace. But the insurrectionist card was very quickly discarded in favor of the trump card of ceasefire, which assured the bureaucrats of their future.

The UGT and the CNT, the ERC and the Generalidad government, the Stalinists and the higher committees, all of these together, turned the glittering military victory that was within reach of the insurrection (Merino, Rebull) into a ghastly political defeat. All of them together, each in their different ways, played their parts effectively. The Stalinists and republicans directly on the barricades of the counterrevolution. The anarcho-syndicalists and the POUMists amid the ambiguity of "I would, but I can't" and "I am, but not anymore"—the former urging an end to the fighting and the evacuation of the barricades and the latter through their daring practice of **riding the coattails** of the former.

Only two tiny organizations, the Friends of Durruti and the SBLE tried to avert defeat and invest the insurrection with precise goals. Barcelona's revolutionary proletariat, essentially an anarchist proletariat, fought for the revolution, even against their own organizations and their own leaders, in a battle that had already been lost back in July 1936, the moment the machinery of state had been allowed to stand.

But there are some lost battles that need fighting, for the sake of generations to come, and that serve no purpose other than to make it clear who is who, exposing which side of the barricade each stands on and marking where the class lines are, which is path should be taken and which mistakes need to be avoided.

Appendices

APPENDIX A
The Karl Marx Barracks Massacre

The judicial investigation into the twelve corpses of anarchist militants dumped at a bend in the Cerdañola-to-Bellaterra road on 10 May.[1]

On 10 May 1937, Judge Josep Vidal Llecha was chosen to draft an indictment following the discovery of twelve corpses in the town precincts of Cerdanyola, as well as in relation to the disappearance of the town's mayor and his abandonment of his post.

The aforementioned judge went to the place where the twelve bodies had been piled up, in order to retrieve the corpses and proceed with whatever measures he felt appropriate.

At 15:40 hours, the examining magistrate, accompanied by three investigation agents from the Special Brigade, set off by car, collecting the pathologist in Sabadell so that he might assist in any enquiries made. They reached the scene at 17:00.

A Special Court was set up in Cerdanyola cemetery "inside which twelve corpses were found, laid out, supine, upon the ground, their faces very dirty and in the early stages of decomposition and, to all appearances, showing the outward signs of violence." *Meaning that they had been tortured before being murdered.*

The judge ordered that the corpses be identified, since every one of them was without identification papers or cards. Juan Minguilla Fernández, a Barcelona resident, identified the corpse of JUAN CALDUCH NOVELLA, aged twenty, a native of Arenys de Mar, the son of Enrique and Francisca, a bachelor resident in the San Andrés barrio of Barcelona at 31 Calle Batreina, lower.

Barcelona residents Pascual Coello Coumat and Amadeo Gómez Pahisa also came forward to identify five of the cadavers: stating that these were FRANCISCO VIVIANA MARTÍNEZ, a twenty-seven-year-old native of Valencia,

---

1   (In Catalan) "Overview of the discovery of twelve cadavers on the Bellaterra road. Special Court, 1937" [TSJC].

married to Montserrat Uch Moré and the son of Francisco and Agustina; he left two children, Josefa and Francisco: CÉSAR FERNÁNDEZ PACHECO, twenty-five-year-old bachelor, the son of José and Victoria , a native of Barcelona; JUAN ANTONIO ROMERO MARTÍNEZ, twenty-four, bachelor, native of Águilas and the son of Lázaro and María; LUÍS CARRERAS ORQUÍN, nineteen-years-old, unmarried native of Barcelona and son of Victoriano and Joaquina; and JOSÉ VILLENA ALBEROLA; we have at present no further details regarding them, home addresses included.

Judge Vidal Llecha ordered that the twelve corpses be collected and taken to the court morgue. The six unidentified cadavers were put on display to the public in accordance with the law, even as notices were being posted in well-frequented public places, requesting assistance from anyone who might assist with details toward their identification.

The unidentified bodies were numbered from 7 to 12, their chief physical features being described and scraps of their clothing being attached, as well as full figure photographs.

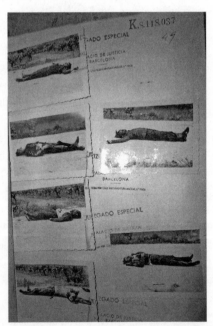

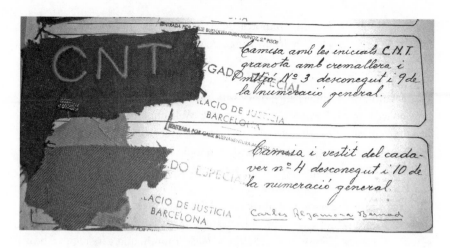

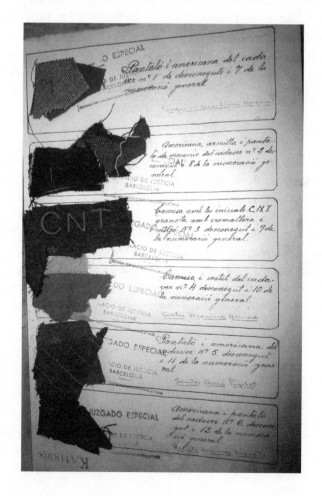

Cadaver no. 7: Person Unknown no. 1: Twenty-year-old male, 1.72 meters tall, chestnut eyes, black hair, no fringe, regular nose, eyebrows, and lips. Was wearing a light brown woolen, small check jacket. Brown sports shirt. Leather belt. White cotton undershirt, and brown trousers matching the sports shirt. White cotton brief underpants. Black shoes and black cotton socks.

Cadaver no. 8: Person Unknown no. 2: Well-built male, 1.68 meters tall, greying hair, prominent forehead; sparse hair of eyebrows, moustache, ear-lobes and beard; chestnut colored eyes, aged around 55 to 60. Wearing a black woolen jacket with brown stripes, a white cotton shirt, black-laced sandals, and a large checkered kerchief wrapped around the torso.

Cadaver no. 9: Person Unknown no. 3: Well-built male, 1.60 meters in height, looks to be about eighteen years old, chestnut hair, slightly prominent forehead, single, very thick eyebrow. Chestnut eyes. Nose, mouth, and ears regular, beard sparse. Wearing a tartan windbreaker, blue shirt, white cotton undershirt, black woolen belt. Blue denim trousers. White cotton briefs, zip-fronted trousers, lilac silk socks, brown shoes.

Cadaver no. 10: Person Unknown no. 4: Male, height 1.80 meters. Dark hair, hair combed back, reasonably thick beard, mouth, and nose regular. Wearing a brownish-grey jacket, black trousers with spigot pattern. Khaki shirt, white undershirt, white silk underpants, light brown striped socks.

Cadaver no. 11: Person Unknown no. 5: Male, 1.85 meters. About twenty-five years old, chestnut hair, hair combed back, eyebrows average, light brown eyes, aquiline nose, regular mouth, black eyes. Wearing tartan-patterned, brown, zip-up windbreaker. Brown woolen jersey. Blue-striped brown sports shirt, blue striped trousers, white underpants, brown socks, blue suspenders, and dark brown leather belt.

Cadaver no. 12: Person Unknown no. 6: Male, 1.55 meters, around twenty-six years of age, redhead, hair combed back, eyebrows normal, light chestnut-colored eyes, flattened nose, bushy beard, and normal ears. Wearing a dark blue striped windbreaker and white cotton shirt. Black trousers with thin white stripe. Brown and white underpants. Black cotton socks. Brown, rubber-heeled shoes.

★

Also on 10 May, Tomás Truyols Altayó presented himself before the examining court in Cerdanyola, to state that at 8:45 a.m. the previous day (9 May 1937), his brother José had called him on the telephone to let him know that the *masover* (farm manager) at Can Fatjó del Xiprès had told him that twelve dead bodies had been found on the Bellaterra road, asking him what he needed to do as the person handling the funeral arrangements and telling him that the matter had already been reported to the councillor for health. That later, around 9:30, somebody (he knows not who) advised him that they could go and pick up the corpses, which he did in the company of his brother and his father. A car with a photographer on board arrived to collect them. That they came upon twelve dead bodies on the Bellaterra road, five hundred meters from the intersection with the Sant Cugat road, beside a ditch. There were about fifty people there, onlookers. That they could not identify the cadavers. The photographer immediately started taking photographs and samples of clothing to help identify the corpses. That later they loaded them into the car for removal to the cemetery.

★

On the same day, in Cerdanyola, a statement was taken from Emili Giner Pertelas, a twenty-eight-year-old resident of the San Andrés barrio in Barcelona.

Under questioning, he stated that he was the brother-in-law of JUAN ANTONIO ROMERO MARTÍNEZ, aged twenty-four, one of the cadavers identified, from no. 32 Calle Llenguadoc, lower second, a native of Águilas and son of Lázaro and María. That he had no knowledge of what had occurred. That the family's wishes were that the cadaver be surrendered to him for burial in Barcelona.

★

That same day, in Sabadell, a statement was taken from Francisco Gómez Giménez, aged thirty, a resident of the San Andrés barrio in Barcelona. He declared that, on behalf of the family of FRANCISCO VIVIANA MARTÍNEZ, he was claiming his corpse for burial in Barcelona. That he lived with the deceased's family at 14 Calle de Mir in San Andrés.

★

On the dame date, in Cerdanyola, Antoni Carreras Orquín, the brother of the deceased LUIS CARRERAS ORQUÍN, aged nineteen, living in the family home at 115 Calle Ignacio Iglesias, lower, in the San Andrés barrio, presented himself. That his supposition was that his brother had been arrested in connection with the recent bloody events, from what he had been told by Antoni Torres, a friend of his brother's, who had been with him at the time of arrest and who is at present in the Military Hospital, wounded. He asked for his brother's corpse to be brought back to Barcelona.

On the same day and in the same location, Jaime Villena Alberola, residing at 14, Calle Estevanes, *principal primera*, in the La Sagrera barrio of Barcelona and brother of the deceased JOSÉ VILLENA ALBEROLA, made a statement that he lived in the family home. He asked that his brother's body be brought back to Barcelona.

Josep Badía Conell identified the body of his brother-in-law, the deceased CÉSAR FERNÁNDEZ PACHECO, twenty-five-year-old son of Josep and Victoria, a native of Barcelona who lived with the deponent at 32 Calle Montpellier, lower. "That he knows nothing of what occurred. That all he knows is that since last Tuesday, we have heard nothing from him since he left the house. That he supports the request that his brother-in-law's body be removed to Barcelona."

Luís del Valle Mandileuna reported to the Cerdanyola bench on 10 May 1937. He stated that in the Barcelona district of Armonía del Palomar (known prior to the revolution as the San Andrés district) the talk was that the corpses of several of his comrades from that barrio had been found on the Cerdanyola to Bellaterra road. And in fact, when he got sight of the cadavers, he recognized the bodies of Joan Calduch Novella, Francisco Viviana Martínez, César Fernández Pacheco, Joan Antoni Romero Martínez, Lluís Carreras Orquín, and Josep Villena Alberola. That, except for Carreras, these had left the barrio on Tuesday 4 May in a, eight-cylinder vehicle driven by Calduch, Madrid license plate number 52846. Dark crimson in color, although he could not be certain that the last figure was a 6. That it must have been around six o'clock in the evening when they set off for the CNT Regional Committee, since when nothing more had been heard from them, nor was it known what had become of the car, but apparently it had been spotted, riddled, in the courtyard of the Karl Marx barracks, but that this had yet to be confirmed. Likewise, there had been no clarification regarding his death. That, as for Lluís Carreras, he had left the district that same Tuesday around noon, by car, in the company of one Antoni Torres, presently in the Military Hospital, and another fellow by the name of Boreadas and a third person, of whom nothing was known, making off in the direction of the barricades in the vicinity of the Karl Marx barracks, where, according to Boreadas [or something of that sort] they were called upon to "Halt!," immediately after which several gunshots were heard, leaving Valle [the deponent] wounded. Boreadas and the other comrade got away but Lluís Carreras was left there, expecting to be arrested. Since when there had been no more news.

That the call to "Halt!" had come from some individuals wearing steel helmets adorned with a red star and, during the shooting, it seemed that some members of the National Guard were shooting from behind.

★

On **11 May**, Defense Councillor Mariano Tejero Regales turned up at the court, stating that he was delivering photos of the twelve deceased, plus twelve clothing samples that had been cut from the clothing of the corpses. He also handed over a length of gilded metal chain discovered on the ground beside the aforementioned deceased persons.

★

The judge ordered that these photos be added to the file and that, for identification purposes, a record be made of which clothing belonged to which person and that the piece of metal found be retained by the commissioner for oaths.

★

The clothing samples, attached and stitched to a sheet of paper, specified the number of the cadaver from which it had been taken. There was an eyecatching scrap from a blue shirt with the letters CNT embroidered on it in red, belonging to Cadaver no. 9, Person Unknown no. 3.

★

On 11 May the doctors who had carried out the autopsies on the twelve corpses reported to the judge, offering their anatomical findings.

From the analyses carried out, an approximate calculation of the age of each corpse had been arrived at. They had all died violent deaths, and exhibited bullet wounds in different parts of the body: thorax, stomach, legs, etc., which would fit with death by gunshots. They all displayed indications of a coup de grace in the head, mostly in the temples, but in some cases in the forehead or in the mouth. The time of death was three days previously. Some of the corpses displayed visible bruising and indications that they had been beaten, manhandled, or tortured prior to being shot.

The court authorized Tomás Anguera Constanti, delegate from the Barcelona Health Services, and acting for the relatives, to remove the corpses of Juan Calduch Novella, Francisco Viviana Martínez, César Fernández Pacheco, Juan Antonio Romero Martínez, Lluís Carreras Orquín, and Josep Villena Alberola to Barcelona for burial in the **San Andrés cemetery**.

The court sought and received medical consent for the removal of the corpses and the removal arrangements, and was assured that they posed no threat to public health.

On 11 May 1937, Josep Ribatallada Casamiquela presented himself at Cerdanyola court, to state that on Sunday the 9th, at around ten o'clock, the defense councillor for Cerdanyola had told him that he should go with him to take photographs of the corpses that had been found on the road. He immediately boarded the car and went with him to the scene, which is to say, to the Bellaterra road, some 250 meters from the road to San Cugat (known at the time as Pins del Vallés), and climbing down into the culvert on the left, found twelve corpses stacked up, many of them with **facial disfigurement. The deponent took photographs of all the cadavers.**

He stated that there were lots of people, strangers to him, who were looking at the deceased.

That same day, the special judge, escorted by Marià Tejero, Cerdanyola defense councillor, driver Joan Tatxer Pol, witness Josep Mas Puigbó and the investigation officer from the Special Intelligence Bureau of the Barcelona High Court, travelled out to the place where, according to what Triguero, Tatxer, and Mas had said, "after swearing to be truthful," the corpses were discovered.

On the edge of a vineyard on the left hand side of the unasphalted road that leads from the Cerdanyola to Pins del Vallés road to Bellaterra, 168 paces from the intersection and adjoining a track four paces in width that led into that vineyard, which is located some three *palmos* below the level of the road itself; the various witnesses pointing out that that was where the corpses had been stacked up, in a clearing two paces wide, between the road and the edge of shrubbery, on the left hand corner of the road.

For the sake of greater clarity and precision, a small sketch is to be added to the file.

There are no buildings in that location, which is close to a dip in the terrain.

Doubtless on account of the numbers who had been there watching the removal of the corpses, the soil at the crime scene looked rather churned up and as a result had nothing of interest to offer the investigation. Witnesses pointed out that just in front of the trail from the vineyard there were signs of vehicle tire tracks.

At the entrance to the vineyard were found a wrapper from a pack of "Smoke Clouds-High Grade Virginia Cigarettes," a printed paper from the Instituto Libre de Pins … two scraps of an identical paper and a piece of paper that had been torn into shreds but upon which one could make out some numbers and letters written in pencil … The visual inspection was brought to a conclusion and the signatures collected from all the witnesses. There being nothing else to be seen, the inspection ended. The materials noted were filed.

★

Twenty-year-old Josep García Ladevesa, unmarried, a construction worker and native of Lorca (Murcia) and resident of Pins del Vallés, living at 12 Calle de Las Marchas, stated that last Saturday, between eight and nine o'clock, p.m., as he was leaving the barbershop on the Rubi road, he watched a pale white ambulance pass down the road, with two or three men seated on the driver's side. The ambulance was travelling at great speed, without slowing down to make the turn on to the Cerdanyola road.

Asked by the judge if he noticed the make and license plate of that ambulance, his response was that it looked like a Hispano-Suiza to him. Asked by the judge if it carried any insignia and if so, what shape and sort, he stated that out in front, beside the fender, it displayed a white flag bearing a red cross in the center and that there was also a painted circle on the side and rear with a red cross against a white background. Having nothing further to contribute, he was cautioned by the judge that he was duty-bound to report any changes of address and then he read and he and the judge signed his deposition.

★

Solidaridad Obrera of 12 May 1937 carried an article entitled: "The Crimes of the Uncontrollables," condensed in the subheading as follows: "In the town precincts of Sardañola-Ripollet, a mystery ambulance dumped the barbarously butchered corpses of 12 Libertarian Youth militants."

In capital letters, the article stressed: "WE CANNOT STAY QUIET ABOUT FRESH ACTS OF BARBARISM." The writer spelled out the contradiction between the frequency of "a series of criminal acts committed with the utmost 'impunity' and the fear that exposure of them may strain the atmosphere, with our urge to expose such outrages in order to see if for once they cease being construed as an intent to breach the peace of the rearguard."

The writer from the main anarchist mouthpiece complained of the pressures and calumnies hovering over his trade "and, graver still, the twisted, criminal activity of some people who, shielded by a certain antifascist sector,[2] operate without restraint of any kind, inflicting the most barbaric tortures[3] upon the unfortunates who fall into their clutches, as if their cruelty were guided by some atavistic nostalgia for sadistic oriental torments."[4]

Wisely but courageously, the unnamed writer stated that "in the face of this proven and repeated practice," keeping mum for the sake of peace and civic serenity, was being dropped in favor of systematic denunciation of "whatever outrages may occur."

And he stated that, starting today, and with "nothing in mind save the wish to see downtrodden justice restored," he was going to denounce the "unpunished murder" that had taken place the previous Saturday and claimed the lives of twelve libertarians.

He explained how, that Saturday, 8 May, the residents of Cerdanyola had seen an ambulance pass by "and judging by the direction it was moving in, it seemed to have come from Barcelona," stopping at a crossroads before setting off again for a destination unknown. That ambulance had drawn people's attention and they had approached the spot where it had stopped "whereupon, suitably dumbfounded, they were able to gaze upon twelve corpses" dumped there, beyond any shadow of a doubt, by that ambulance.

From lengthy examination of the twelve bodies, it was plain that **not only had they died by violence, but also after horrific torture, judging by the mutilation, bruising, and terrible blows on display."[5]**

The pathologists determined that the corpses were those of young men who had died two days earlier. "At the same time, they stated that before they were finished off they were barbarously tortured, as proven by the fact that the bodies

---

2   The Stalinists from the PSUC-UGT.

3   Which is to say, torture was used, and then they were murdered.

4   Stalinists were sometimes referred to as "the Asiatics," due to the USSR's stretching from Europe into Asia.

5   Bold face added by the author of this book.

displayed bruising and blotching all over the belly, which looked swollen and misshapen." One of the cadavers showed signs of having been hung up the feet. One of the heads looked as if it had been "smashed in by the butt of a rifle."

In the course of the identification of the corpses, it turned out that every one of them had belonged to the Libertarian Youth in San Andrés.[6] "On account of the huge facial damage," only four of them had been recognizable: César Fernandez, José Villena, Juan Antonio, and Luís Carreras. All of them from the San Andrés Libertarian Youth.

From enquiries made by the reporter, it transpired that on 4 May "and at the time of the troubles in Barcelona on that date," a bunch of libertarian youths from San Andrés set off for the premises of the RC, via the Paseo Pujades, until, as they reached the Parque de la Ciudadela near the Karl Marx barracks, a large group of armed men called upon them to halt; they put up no resistance and were arrested and taken to the Karl Marx barracks.[7] After which, nothing.

The following day (5 May) at the same spot, another libertarian group was shot at and several left wounded, their lives being saved thanks to the commitment of the comrades from the Red Cross who rescued them from the vicious gunfire coming in their direction. "There was no way of averting the capture of one of the members of the group under attack, comrade Luís Carreras, who has now been identified as one of the corpses found."

The writer closed with the evidence that showed that the twelve cadavers had been done to death at the Karl Marx barracks and subsequently removed to Bellaterra. "This latest incident is striking proof to us that the perpetrators of both incidents were, undeniably, the same criminals who, under cover of the peace symbol of an ambulance, ship their victims, after torturing them barbarously, to out of the way places that lend themselves to the required impunity for their vile crimes."

In reporting on the (11 May) funerals of "the young innocent victims of cruelty and political savagery," the writer was defying the orders and watchwords issued by the higher committees to the effect that there was to be no fanning of libertarians' discontent and indignation at the Stalinists' brutality, since displays of mourning and newspaper reports of such had been banned.

The *Soli* writer stated: "Upon seeing the mutilated remains of the poor lads, the large crowds who filed past the corpses expressed outraged condemnation of

---

6   This "every one of them" refers only to the four cadavers identified up to that point. Later, other cadavers were identified which did not belong to Libertarian Youth members. One of the two unidentified corpses looked to be around fifty-five years old.

7   The so-called Karl Marx barracks stretched over two former barracks, the Jaime I barracks and the Intendencia (Quartermaster) barracks close to the Parque de la Ciudadela; both have now been absorbed by the Pompeu Fabra University campus.

the barbarism committed."[8] He noted that the "CNT's RC, the Artillery Depot, and Defense Committee, etc." had been in attendance.

The article closed with expression of the forlorn hope that the killers might be brought to book and sentenced, as well as an even lamer wish that there might be no repetition of such things.

★

On 22 May 1937, police officer Jerónimo Jiménez Villalba declared before the judge that on Sunday, 9 May, acting on orders received from the commissioner-general in Barcelona, he went to the town of Cerdanyola to look into the appearance of twelve corpses within its precincts. On arrival, he found that the corpses had already been removed to the cemetery. Carrying out a visual inspection of the scene where the cadavers had been found, he found nothing to indicate that they had been killed there, finding only a small bloodstain, a scrap of rope and remnant of a pack of tobacco, both of them stained with blood, plus a button that he supposed may have belonged to one of the victims. Enquiries having been made into how they had been brought to the scene where the cadavers had been discovered, some residents of the village of Pins del Vallés (San Cugat) indicated to him that an ambulance heading in the direction of Cerdanyola had passed through that village at around half past eight. Efforts made to trace the ambulance in question had been fruitless. He had had a word with Señor Samblancat's driver,[9] Francisco Bascada, who told him that during the bloody incidents in May he had been with a group in the Parque de la Ciudadela, a group that had included Antonio Torres, Luís Carrera, some others and himself (Francisco Bascada), when they were surrounded by Republican National Guards and Socialist Party members.[10] He had made a run for it, taking cover with [illegible here] in a stairwell. That Antonio Torres was brought down wounded and was now in the Military Hospital and he supposed that Carreras had been arrested there. That these were the only enquiries the deponent had made in respect of the incidents of concern to this indictment. This statement was read and cosigned with the judge.

★

---

8   Not all twelve corpses, just the two belonging to the young libertarians from the La Armonía barrio (Sant Andreu del Palomar).

9   Samblancat was the legal counsel to CNT members.

10   The Unified Socialist Party of Catalonia, that is, the Stalinists of the PSUC.

On **26 May 1937**, Vicens Priñonosa Palomares, residing at 23, Calle Amelia in Barcelona, appeared before the special magistrate, to state that, on account of his being employed in the Pharmacy branch of the Generalidad's Department of Health, he was acquainted with a fellow employee from the same branch, named Santos Carré Puplet, who had not reported for work since 7 May, for which reason his comrades looked into where he might be. Having learnt from the newspapers of the discovery of twelve corpses on the Bellaterra road, he was presenting himself before the court to find out if his work colleague could be identified among the photographs of the twelve cadavers. When the photographs were shown, he recognized the photo of the cadaver of Person Unknown no. 5 (no. 11 overall) beyond the shadow of a doubt and identified said cadaver as that of Santos Carré Puplet, married father of four, who lived with his family at no. 2, *segundo piso*, in the Pasaje Serrahima.[11] That he was not aware of the name of his friend's wife, or other personal details of the deceased. He just remembered that he had been transferred to the Health Department on the instructions of the Defense Committee of the Center and so was a member of the CNT, but as to who could have murdered his comrade, he had no clue, as he was not aware of his friendships as he was a lad that was not one to stick his nose into things, let alone social offences and simply got on with doing his work. That he recognized the clothing samples from page thirty-four of the file as indeed matching the dead man he had just identified.

On 26 May Carme Cosials Onfins appeared before the special magistrate to declare that she was the mother of Agustí Lasheras Cosials, who was employed on the MZA railways and who had, on 4 May 1937, as normal, set off for work at the Estación de Francia, and, to ensure that the trains were kept running, they had given him a rifle so that he could stand guard over a section of the track, the section running from the station to the San Carlos bridge.[12] That, while guarding said track, the aforementioned Lasheras had headed toward the Parque to see what was going on there, at which point he was approached by two individuals who grabbed his rifle from him, disarming him and telling him that if he wanted it back he should accompany them to the Karl Marx barracks, since when her son had disappeared and had not been seen since.

11   The Trotskyists and SBLE militants Carlini and Kielso were arrested on those premises where they had been lodging since the end of May 1937. See the biographies of both in Casciolo and Guillamón, *Biografías del 36.*

12   The San Carlos bridge ran in a straight line from the Parque de la Ciudadela to the seafront area occupied by the Sailing Club, overlooking the railway tracks.

The deponent was making these statements on the basis of what she had been told by her son's comrades who were a short distance from Lasheras when the incidents related occurred. His mother was unable to provide the names of those comrades, but the people at the Estación de Francia had to know.

That having learnt through the newspapers that some corpses had been found on the Cerdanyola road, she was appearing before the court for the purpose of identifying, if need be, one of the corpses. Having been shown the photo from page 46 of the file, the one marked as Person Unknown no. 8 (no. 12 overall) and the clothing samples attached to page thirty-four, she recognized the photograph as that of her son Agustí Lasheras Cosials, a twenty-five-year-old unmarried man, employee of the MZA railroad company, shunting section, born in Estación de Sant Vicenç de Calders, baptized in the town of Vendrell, son of the deponent and her husband Agustí Lasheras and likewise she identified the clothing sample as belonging to her son.

That she did not know who his killers may have been, nor the reasons behind his murder. That she believed her son belonged to the CNT. That his father was unable to approach the court due to mental illness. That, having been briefed on Article 109 of the Law of Criminal Prosecution, and having read and agreed with her statement, she cosigned it with the judge.

That same day María Cabanellas Planen, doctor's assistant by profession, a divorcee living on the first floor at no. 15, Calle Tapias in Barcelona, appeared before the judge. She stated that for the past three years she had been in a relationship with Carles Alzamora Bernat who was a lieutenant-militian with the Durruti Column and that she was a doctor's assistant with the medical section of the same column. That they had both returned to Barcelona on a ten day furlough and that, at the suggestion of some comrades, she had been lending a hand at the Defense Committee of the Center, located on the Ronda Sant Antoni, her intention being to remain in Barcelona permanently.

That on the Monday, 3 May her partner had told her to put lunch off for a moment as he had some business with some comrades from the Defense Committee of the Center, but would be along shortly. That she waited for him until just before four o'clock in the afternoon, but her partner had not appeared and she had not set eyes on him since. Later, she found out from the CNT member Muñoz, a member of the aforesaid Defense Committee of the Center, that her partner had spent 3 and 4 May manning a barricade at the Estación de Francia; she had no idea why her partner might have been killed, any more than she had any notion of who his assailants might have been.

That the clothing samples recorded on page thirty-four as having belonged to Person Unknown no. 1, the cadaver she identified beyond the shadow of a doubt as the cadaver of her partner, were not what he had been wearing; his were the ones indicated as having belonged to the unidentified Cadaver no. 4. That her twenty-four-year-old partner was a native of Cuba, the son of Carles and Bernard and was unmarried. The whereabouts of his mother had not been known for many years and his father was dead.

★

In a letter bearing the letterhead of the Karl Marx Barracks and dated 17 May 1937, it was stated, in response to the court's enquiry of 5 May, that one Antonio Torres Marín had not attended at the barracks and nor had anyone else.

★

The judge drafted a report dated 29 May 1937 in which he went over the evidence compiled to date: letter from the Karl Marx barracks, the appearances by the relatives of the deceased Calduch, Viviana, Fernández, and Carreras. He wrote to the judge in Sabadell urging him to get the Cerdanyola Local People's Committee to issue a fresh death certificate for Francisco Viviana, amending the initial misidentification of the cadavers of Agustí Lasheras and Carles Alzamora in light of the statements made by María Cabanellas and Melchor Martínez. It was agreed that driver Francesc Bescada and the wife of Santos Carré Puplet should be called before the court. An order was also sent out for an appearance by the person in charge at the Estación de Francia so that he might say which employees were with Agustí Lasheras Cosials on 4 May when he was arrested by persons unknown in the Parque de Ciudadela, who, it seems, disarmed him, taking away the weapon he was carrying while guarding the railway track. A further reminder was issued to the police, as a response was still awaited. The report was signed by magistrate Josep Vidal Llecha.

★

Twenty-one-year-old driver Francisco Bescada Navarro came in on 2 June 1937 to make a statement, declaring that on the Wednesday of the week the incidents occurred, if memory served, he left the San Andrés barrio bound for the Regional [Committee] in search of news from a brother of his fiancée. With him in the car were several neighbors, Antonio Torres and Lluis Calduch, who, as far as he could remember, were armed. On arrival in Pueblo Nuevo, they were warned by some locals not to proceed any further by car due to the risks involved in doing so.

That they left the car there and carried on, on foot. His two friends were ahead of him. Walking with them, there were also two other young, unarmed fellows, heading in the same direction. At around eleven o'clock, as they came to the Parque de la Ciudadella, they came across a number of individuals wearing military headgear and, from a barricade, these beckoned them to come closer, but, being afraid that their CNT union card might be ripped up, they dithered there quietly for a few moments, at Carreras's instigation. That the two unknown comrades from Pueblo Nuevo whom he mentioned earlier then said: "Civil Guard," after which he heard several gunshots behind him, so, not even bothering to check who was doing the shooting, he tried to escape from the area, ducking into a stairwell along with the two strangers and they had stayed there until the shooting was over and they were able to move on. That he had not seen if Carreras or Torres had managed to get away or been wounded or arrested, because he had lost sight of them as soon as he had ducked for cover. That some days after that, it was learnt that Carreras's corpse had been discovered in Cerdanyola. That he had no further information to offer.

Police officer Jerónimo Jiménez Villalba submitted a report addressed to the Public Order delegate regarding clarification of what had happened in Cerdañola following the discovery of twelve corpses in the vicinity of that town. The corpses had been discovered at around 20:30 hours on 8 May 1937 by a resident who later could not be traced. The twelve corpses had been roughly stacked up beside the left-hand ditch on the side of the Bellaterra road, around fifty meters from the Cerdanyola-to-Pins del Vallés (now San Cugat) road.

All that was found at the location was a small bloodstain, from which the deduction was that they had been killed somewhere other than the location where they were found.

Wednesday, 21 July 1937

The Olympia Theater hosted a CNT rally that drew a large attendance, on a par with the largest CNT mass gatherings ever.[13]

The rally was a replacement for the demonstration that had been planned to mark the first anniversary of the July insurrection, which had, in the end, been banned by the Generalidad government.

---

13   CNT-AIT, *El mitín del Teatro Olympia en Barcelona (21 de julio 1937)* (Barcelona: Talleres Gráficos Bosch, 1937).

Hours in advance of the opening of the rally, the place was packed to the rafters. There was no way of reckoning how many were in attendance from every one of the barrios and from the *comarcas* too. The crowd was waving placards, portraits, and flags. The rally's organization commissions marshaled the crowd along the full extent of the Ronda de San Pablo, the Calle Aldana and the Paralelo. The numbers admitted were reduced by the presence of a band from the Entertainments Union that played revolutionary CNT-FAI anthems.

At 6:00 p.m. precisely, **Joaquín Cortés**, who was chairing the rally, spoke to the audience to tell them that the band would be playing *The Internationale*, "in honor of the workers from the UGT," this drawing "great applause once the band had finished."

Reference was made to the banning of the demonstration to mark the first anniversary of the crushing of the fascists in Barcelona; not so much a protest as claiming the current rally as a CNT show of strength.

Liarte spoke on behalf of the Libertarian Youth, touching upon a number of subjects, among which one sentence stuck out slightly: "The morality of ideas, authentic revolutionary morality must be our victory over all political repression."

Isgleas spoke in Catalan. He repudiated the criticisms leveled at how he had been performing at the Defense Department since the Valencia government's takeover of that department (councillorship). He made a connection between the band's playing of *The Internationale* and the need for CNT-UGT unity "if we want to win this war." He talked about the active and passive aspects of antifascist unity, saying that anybody opposing it was a hindrance to be cast aside.

As Isgleas finished his address, Cortés called upon the band to play the anthem *Hijos del Pueblo* in memory of those who had perished on 19 July and in honor of **imprisoned revolutionaries and antifascists**. The crowd, "on its feet and fists held high," joined in with the band and the whole thing finished with a "deafening ovation," until **Federica Montseny** got up to speak on behalf of the RC.

"A year has gone by since 19 July. A year of struggle. A year of war. A year of Revolution," and it was tremendously painful that, one year on, "the people are still having to shout What about the prisoners! The prisoners! We need to address this matter per se and let us state how deplorable it is that, with the battle against fascism raging, there are antifascists imprisoned in Spain's jails."

Deploying her brilliant gift of gab, on she went, turning the subject of antifascist prisoners this way and that and the incontrovertible fact that a year had elapsed since 19 July. And then she brought in a third matter: away with dictatorships and above all, away with dictatorships like the Bolshevik dictatorship in Russia.

Federica's sparkling speech closed with a reference to thankfulness for the aid from Russia and Mexico, but a reminder that only the Spanish people could win the fight against fascism.

She rejected certain methods imported from abroad, which merely served "to have the membership of a entire party accused of spying, being put in prison and a trial being cooked up against them in the shadows."[14] And, as if by accident, she let it drop that "**they have just told us that the corpses of Nin and another two comrades have been found, in Madrid.**"

The audience was greatly shocked at this.

She remarked that the news had yet to be confirmed, "but until such time as the Government denies it and tells us where Nin is, we have to take it as true."

She complained that no one could, with impunity "grab a bunch of people, level unproven charges against them, hold them in a private dwelling adapted to the purpose and then take them out under cover of night and murder them."

Nin might be accused of being a fascist agent; but that accusation needed to be proved and, if correct, he needed shooting; but they could not countenance murder in the shadows.

She closed her speech by praising the Spanish people's struggle for its freedom and with the slogan: "Neither Rome, nor Berlin, nor Moscow."

This was greeted by great applause.

Returning to the thread of her speech, she cautioned "beware of politicians" only to proceed to *make the wisecrack* "I've only just remembered that I'm an ex-minister myself," provoking laughter from the audience. She went on to say that "he that screams loudest is not the one with the most right on his side" and was able to speak up, albeit that she might be put on trial for doing so "everybody in Spain is going to be put on trial," a remark that drew further laughter.

She went on to say that there would be too much required to put her on trial, given her immunity.

Federica was feeling comfortable, loved, and in fine fettle and told the audience as much: "I'm enjoying speaking here today, comrades … because I haven't spoken in Barcelona for a long time.[15] Here I am, back in touch with the genuinely revolutionary Barcelona that the CNT is never going to lose, no matter how much it is slandered about queues and dead bodies being dug up around the villages.

---

14   The imported methods referred to the Soviet Union's, and the accused party was the POUM.

15   This was the first occasion on which she had spoken publicly in Barcelona since the time she had been whistled at and heckled by the Friends of Durruti and others at the 11 April 1937 rally in the La Monumental bullring, when they demanded that Maroto and the many other jailed antifascists be set free.

Again, loud clapping erupted at this denunciation of Judge Quintana's "clandestine graveyards" trial.

She launched into a historical review of the three categories in the typology of revolutions: the English one, with the beheading of Charles I and so many others, although it never occurred to his successor to "dig up the dead," although it had, to Comorera.[16] The French revolution witnessed this faction and the other dispatching one another to the guillotine, up until Napoleon came along and then he in turn was overthrown as a tyrant, and it had not occurred to the restored monarchy to "put on trial the revolution that had sent so many heads rolling." Nothing of the sort had occurred to anybody "because **a revolution is a hurricane, the blind force of the body of society, which is let loose, fertilizing the soil like a river that has burst its banks. Such is the Revolution and such are all revolutions.**"

She regretted that she was no longer health minister "as I would make the finest quarters in the Instituto Pere Matas in Reus ready for many of you here."[17]

Further laughter.

She went on to say that "all these gents devoted to vampire-like chores ... are afflicted with a neurosis that cries out for swift treatment," concluding that she could not fathom any such boycott of the antifascist unity that was so sorely needed if the war was to be won.

She pressed the point and asked: "**Persuading Catalonia that the men of the CNT are murderers and that the fascists executed on 19 July died at the hands of the CNT alone ... what is the purpose behind it all?**"

Her answer was that there could be only two expected outcomes: either the preceding vampire neurosis or the collapsing of the CNT's morale and its withdrawal from the fight. With the second a much more serious matter than the first.

She laid into the problem of antifascists in prison, most of them there, not on account of the May incidents, since the blame for those was being pinned on the POUM, "because it was in the minority and because there are some people who bait only the weak and never the strong."

This contention on the part of Federica Montseny deserves to be explored because the fact was that the PSUC, the Generalidad, and the Valencia government could not brazenly confront the Catalan proletariat, most of which belonged to the CNT and was irreplaceable as the driver behind the output from war industries, which were vital if the war on fascism was to be prosecuted. The tactic to be adopted was to make an example of the POUM by means of exemplary repression, to draw

---

16   This was a reference to the so-called "clandestine graveyards" inquiries opened in response to complaints made regarding murders, robberies, or disappearances that had occurred during the revolutionary upheaval all across Catalonia in July 1936.

17   This was an insane asylum.

*the CNT leadership into the orbit of the authorities and to be **discriminating in the crackdown** on the rebellious sectors within anarcho-syndicalism, in order to prevent the **emergence from within the CNT of a revolutionary opposition; this was a concern shared by the higher committees and their antifascist allies, ranging from the PSUC to the ERC and including soviet agents and the Generalidad and Valencia governments.**

Federica went on to say that the vast majority of antifascists behind bars were there because of anonymous allegations about deaths that had occurred during the revolutionary events in July.

All it took was for somebody to write an anonymous letter to the president of the High Court, complaining about the death of some priest that had been killed on 19 July in such-and-such a village and off they went to search out the priest's corpse and open up an indictment: "And we have numbers of CNT-FAI militants in prison already."

And when brought against CNT personnel such allegations moved full speed ahead, whereas when the accused were PSUC members, like the ones who had murdered thirty-six CNT members in Tarragona, they did not. "In Sardanyola, twelve horrifically mutilated [Libertarian] Youth corpses were found in the cemetery, with eyes gouged out and tongues cut out. Brought there by am ambulance that dumped them in the cemetery. I insisted that an indictment be drawn up.[18] This has not been done."[19]

*Federica Montseny was complaining here about the courts' harassment of CNT personnel who were monstrously being prosecuted for the revolutionary incidents back in July,[20] on the grounds that **she did not regard the killing of priests, servicemen, pistoleros, or right-wingers just for being such as an offence or crime.**[21] And this was a view shared by the vast majority of anarcho-syndicalists. In*

---

18   "Investigation into the discovery of twelve cadavers on the Bellaterra road, Special Court, 1937" [TSJC].

19   An investigation had been opened but it was set aside, like all the inquiries opened into the "clandestine graveyards." The bodies found on the Bellaterra road had been dumped there from a van that had originated in the Karl Marx barracks. All of the bodies bore obvious signs of torture. They had all been detained in the Karl Marx barracks and there was no record of their having been released. It was plain that the PSUC had been involved since all inquiries showed that the killers must, of necessity, have been free to operate inside the Karl Marx barracks.

20   See Agustín Guillamón, *La represión contra la CNT y los revolucionarios. Hambre y violencia en la Barcelona revolucionaria. De mayo a septiembre de 1937* (Barcelona: Descontrol, 2015) for how, on 8 September 1937, Vidiella had also argued along these lines.

21   They were not guilty on the basis that, individually, they might have been implicated in the cruel, criminal fascist coup attempt, which was sometimes hard to prove, but because they were part of rebel institutions or certain social strata that had sponsored or been complicit in the fascist army revolt.

September, by which time such harassment had been extended to include UGT members, Vidiella came up with a line of argument similar to Montseny's. The republicans' bourgeois courts were criminalizing the July '36 revolutionaries.

She invoked the dictum, wrongly ascribed to Durruti, "We renounce everything except victory," and stated that she could not retreat from destroying the fascist enemy.

She reiterated that "those of unsound mind cannot make us lose this war," by alluding to trials over "clandestine cemeteries," because they were shattering antifascist unity.

She said, "We have to organize production and ensure basic subsistence needs in the rearguard," but *failed to come up with a single concrete measure.*

She denied that antifascism was a program: "any more than the Popular Front is in competition with our Antifascist Front."

There was no program but socialism, regardless of whether it was described as libertarian, federalist, or state socialism.

They had to resist all temptation, which cropped up in any revolutionary process, to impose a dictatorship: "Had we so wanted, we were the absolute masters of the situation in Barcelona and Catalonia and **we could have imposed an anarchist dictatorship.**"

But she was abjuring any such dictatorship, for the sake of antifascist unity. "What we will never countenance is anybody becoming dictator at our expense." *Applause.*

The sole solution was a libertarian regime "that trumps bourgeois democracy"; socialism and federalism: "Which is why we cannot talk of anarchist or of communist socialism. We are talking about federalist socialism."

She closed her address with a paean to antifascist unity. A unity that had to overcome every obstacle: "They want to dig up the dead? Dig them up! They want to mount trials to put our comrades in prison? Then fight to get them out, even should it be with the weapons that we have thus far not used because we are overly scrupulous." Be that as it may, "the war has to be won and the Revolution has to be made" by the working class, by maintaining antifascist unity and CNT-UGT unity.

"Don't forget that in Spain **there are two UGTs.** There's the UGT of the small businesspeople, shopkeepers, proprietors, and industrialists, the UGT of the small shopkeepers formerly members of the Lliga and who are now in the UGT because they have to unionize in one center or the other…. So much for the UGT in Catalonia. The Madrid UGT is another matter [conscious and wholesome]." The CNT needed to enter into a pact with that revolutionary UGT.

This was a leftist, populist speech from Federica Montseny, out at all costs to buy the applause and warmth of those attending the rally. Hovering over Federica's head was the memory of the catcalls and whistling that greeted her at the meeting in the Monumental, with its displays of placards and shouts in support of the prisoners. She did not want the same thing happening to her at the Olympia rally.

It was a brilliant if incoherent speech. How could they make the revolution and maintain antifascist unity when the two were utterly incompatible and contradictory? How could they take up arms to free the prisoners and simultaneously sue for re-admission to government? These contradictions grew out of the rabid populism spewed out at the rally and only the most naive expected there to be any followup to them.

The Catalan UGT was a Stalinist, counterrevolutionary organization, as Montseny herself conceded, one with which there could be no compact and no unity of any sort. The bit about there being two UGTs might have been true in Madrid, but in Barcelona? No. It was absolutely suicidal in Barcelona to suggest a tactic of CNT-UGT unity because it implied handing oneself over, bound hand and foot, to the anti-worker repression coming from the PSUC Stalinists. And Federica, who had roundly denounced the Stalinist character of the Catalan UGT, was **confusedly lobbying for Spanish UGT-CNT unity,** *at a rally being held in Barcelona,* **without issuing a clear warning that such a pact was not feasible in Catalonia.**

Joaquín Cortés summed up the rally, describing Federica Montseny's speech as "magnificent." *She was elated at having taken the sting out of the Monumental rally.*

He highlighted the fact that the speakers had touched upon two issues: "the war problem and the problem of the rearguard." The rearguard was the main thing if they were to keep up the war effort. And the rearguard was demoralized, because at the end of a year of struggling and after the incidents in May, it could see the PSUC dismantling peasant collectives by lawful means or, acting outside the law, through violence.

He complained to the workers of the UGT that CNT-FAI militants were being systematically persecuted and jailed and that this was crushing the morale in the rearguard and consequently "the way is being cleared for fascism to succeed."

Cortés noted that ever since the CNT had left the government, it had been subject to persecution, its collectives were being dismantled and the groundwork was being laid for a PSUC dictatorship to the great amazement of its ERC allies. *Loud applause.*

The ERC would soon have to join in with the protests coming from the CNT and POUM "over the persecution being mounted against their militants and organizations."

He pronounced that "in actual fact, there is no government in Catalonia today." Applause. It had previously been said "that government was impossible because **uncontrollables** were venturing out into the countryside and the comarcas and attacking private property, as well as **cleansing** the fertile soil of heroic, revolutionary Catalonia **of fascists.** I say that the **controllables, handled and led by Comorera,** are venturing out into the comarcas to loot everything "and they are **implacable in their pursuit of CNT and FAI comrades.**"

There could be no lawful government countenancing persecution of "the revolutionaries of 19 July 1936, due to denunciations from fascists in the rearguard, nor the jailing and, **very often, vanishing** of revolutionary workers with **nobody knowing whether they are in some party or government jail.**"

A government that dismantled the industrial and peasant collectivizations could not be countenanced. Without an antifascist morale, the war was unwinnable. The PSUC, through **slander and terrifying persecution,** was destroying labor and antifascist unity.

After yet another idealist hymn to unity and trade union management of the economy, Cortés proposed "a heartfelt commitment in memory of those who fell on 19 July on the streets of Barcelona and those who perished on the fields of battle over this awful year … and that we spare a thought … for antifascists and revolutionaries, for the POUM and CNT personnel or those who have no party and who are **suffering in prison for the crime of having risked their lives during the heroic, blood-stained hours of 19 July.**"

After the usual ritual outcries and a prolonged ovation, the CNT band brought the meeting to a conclusion by playing *Los Hijos del Pueblo* as thousands of voices chorused the lyrics.

On **3 December 1937,** as agreed by the Government Branch of the Barcelona District High Court, the order went out for the Special Court to stop its work on further indictments regarding clandestine cemeteries and for Judge Bertrán de Quintana to wind up those already in progress as quickly as he could. As the files, including the ones relating to the twelve Cerdanyola corpses, were being closed, a trial was held without further delay and all of those tried were acquitted by the People's Court and so the Cerdanyola indictment was finally dismissed.

Ten of the twelve cadavers had been successfully identified (their ages are given in brackets).

Juan Calduch Novella (20).

Francisco Viviana Martínez (27), married father of two.

César Fernández Pacheco (25).

Juan Antonio Romero Martínez (24).

Luís Carreras Orquín (19), militia sergeant. Student at the School of War.

José Villena Alberola (33).

Calduch, Romero, Villena, Fernández, and Viviana were all from the Libertarian Youth from the Armonía (formerly, Sant Andreu del Palomar) barrio and were buried in the barrio's graveyard, along with Carreras.

Santos Carré Poblet (30). Married father of four. Skinner, domiciled in Poble Sec. CNT member.

Agustín Lasheras Cosials (25), CNT railway worker arrested in the vicinity of the Estación de Francia while making a safety inspecting of the tracks.

Joaquín Martínez Ungría (18). Shop assistant.

Carlos Alzamora Bernard (27). Linotype operator. Cuban, militia lieutenant from the Durruti Column, in Barcelona on leave.

Antonio Torres had witnessed by first hand the arrest at the Karl Marx barracks of Luís Carreras Orquín, a pupil at the School of War. **The presence of Carreras's body in the pile of twelve corpses in Bellaterra was the thread connecting those detained at the Karl Marx barracks to the cadavers ferried out to Bellaterra by ambulance.**

Joan Calduch was the driver of the car carrying Francisco Viviana, César Fernández, Joan Antoni Romero, and Josep Villena, which, at 6:00 p.m. on 4 May, drove toward the CNT Regional Committee premises until stopped in the vicinity of the Parque de la Ciudadela. They were all members of the Sant Andreu Libertarian Youth.

★

The twelve cadavers dumped in a pile on the Cerdanyola-Bellaterra road from an ambulance belonged to people who had been arrested in the vicinity of the Karl Marx barracks during the May Events. The corpses showed signs of having undergone barbaric torture and having then been shot or finished off at gunpoint (around 8 May), as perhaps the only way of concealing the savagery to which they had been subjected.

Ten of the twelve murder victims had been successfully identified. Of the two not identified, the one registered as Person Unknown no. 2, was around fifty-five years old and, beyond that, nothing more is known about him; of the other, Person Unknown no. 3, we know that he was aged about 18 and was wearing a blue shirt with the letters CNT stitched into it in red. Eleven of the twelve cadavers belonged to members of the Libertarian Youth. That was their crime: being libertarians. Their murderers were the Stalinists from the Karl Marx barracks.

APPENDIX B
Correspondence between Agustín Guillamón and José Quesada Suárez (1996): The Trotskyists in May 1937

1. Letter from José Quesada[22]

Tarbes
October 1996
Guillamón
Barcelona

Dear Friend,

These lines are a belated response to yours of 10 September. As ever, I am very late in replying. Many thanks to you and your friend for the greetings from Romualdo Fuentes....

Now to Carlini. But first let me answer the question posed:[23] Together with Dositeo Iglesias, we arrived—I am going by memory here—on 20 to 22 February [1937]. Our mission was to brief the POUM EC on the military situation in Madrid and on what resources the Madrid Local Committee could call upon, in terms of personnel and supplies....

Iglesias and I did not go back to Madrid: we stayed on in Barcelona, hoping to be posted to the front or to some other task. With Madrid's agreement, the EC decided to transfer those party members not serving in units, plus its wounded members, to Barcelona so that, if there were enough numbers, a company might be raised for posting to the Aragon front, or to be added to the POUM forces already fighting in that region. Among those who arrived in Barcelona there were lots from Llerena, which is to say, from Munis's old stomping ground; knowing me from Azuaga and Madrid, they put me in touch with him. Along with Munis, his *paisanos* and myself, the tiny GBL was formed in Barcelona.[24] Whether there was some foreigner with him, I cannot say. None showed up at our meetings. As for Jaime Fernández Rodríguez, I never saw him in Barcelona. Maybe he had

---

22 A few amendments have been made to the original through the insertion or removal of commas, removal of certain abbreviations and other trivial matters, for no purpose other than to make for easier reading.

23 To wit: When did you relocate to Barcelona?

24 This was a cell, then, composed exclusively of Spaniards and POUM militants, unbeknownst to the rest of the SBLE membership.

stayed behind in Madrid with other militants to ensure that the organization retained its foothold in the capital.[25]

Once Julio Cid and G. Baldris arrived in Barcelona with a large contingent of militia members, people well used to a scrap, the Lenin Battalion was formed; with Cid as Commissar and G. Baldris as Commander. We were posted to the Huesca front; and took up position in the El Carrascal trenches, near the cemetery, held by the other side. We spent only four days on that front; then we were transferred to the Belchite sector. After waiting in that sector for four or five days, we were not moved into the trenches; next, we were dispatched to the Tardienta–Santa Quiteria hermitage sector.

We come now to Carlini: I never met or spoke to Carlini any more than twice: on the day Munis introduced him to me—early March—and in the afternoon we went for a talk with Balius at the premises they had on the Ramblas, almost facing the POUM local. Starting on the afternoon of 3 May—as the light was fading—four CNT youngsters and three from the POUM—José Maria Rodríguez, Pedro de Cristina, and yours truly—built a barricade on the Calle Hospital—you'll know where that leads to. We stood guard over it, facing the PSUC guys, day and night, until seven o'clock in the morning, when, giving the whole thing up as a waste of time, each group (the four and the three) went off in search of information from its organization.

On the afternoon of the 5th, José María and I went to the POUM local, which was pretty much opposite the Hotel Falcón and near the spot where Ascaso perished. The POUM Local Committee was based in the hotel: there, I would sometimes bump into Quique, Antonio Rodríguez's brother. He, Antonio Guerrero, Teodoro Sanz, Roberto Montero, and I were in the same concentration camp in Argelès-sur-mer for two months....

In the hotel, the Committee occupied the upstairs rooms and downstairs there was a cafeteria that was still serving—to militia members and non-militia members—coffee, refreshing drinks, and sandwiches.

On the afternoon of the 5th, having some spare time, José María [Rodríguez] and I went to the Hotel [Falcón] for a bite to eat, a coffee, and a bit of a rest. There, we ran into Carlini and there was somebody else with him; he told us his name, but I cannot call it to mind nor see the face now. We chatted for a bit and reviewed the situation and agreed to go and see the Friends of Durruti to swap impressions regarding the overall situation; all of us appreciated that things were complicated, what with the positions laid down by the CNT and POUM leaderships, and that the correlation of forces in the fighting was not in our favor, following the "treachery" by the traditional organizations, the CNT-POUM;

---

25   He was imprisoned in the Modelo prison in Barcelona.

but that the fight had to be pursued so that we might win the support of the people—"masses" is not a word used in the anarchist vocabulary—for our fight. Balius and Carlini were saying time and again that we either won the battle that was under way or July and the war were lost. They were right, but not entirely right. It occurred to me to quote them the oft-cited adage about the force of argument being just an "entrée" for the argument of force. Which made Carlini tagging me as a pessimist. To which I replied: Pessimist, optimist, I've been behind a barricade for the past three days, and I'll stay there until this is all over, win or lose. The latter being the more likely.

Win or lose, to this day I have stood by my own, the working class. Our meeting lasted a while longer, but the essential issues were left hanging in the air. Why? Because what we were agreed about—although this was not said—was clinging on to unity in the fight against all enemies of 19 July. On a centralized party or organization, not one with powers to order and command, but one with a mandate and answerable to those at the bottom, which is to say, with all authority being monitored by the people through its organizations. Once the word Authority was mentioned, authority to enforce accords debated and approved by the rank-and-file, committees and such, Balius's mood darkened. The interview or meeting ended without coming to grips with the real, underlying issues or settling upon any stance vis-à-vis the insurrection, after the latter had been condemned by the CNT-FAI. I am still asking myself: what was the point of sending the best of the Barcelona working class (or from other places where there was still fighting going on) to their deaths? As far as Balius and Carlini and others— but not everybody—were concerned, the right thing to do was just to carry on fighting on the barricades: and that was how we parted.

What sway did the GBL [Bolshevik-Leninist Group] have over the Friends of Durruti? None. In the true sense of the word, not even Carreño [could be said to have been swayed by his friendship and dealings with Munis]. On two occasions, the three of us [Carreño, Munis, and Quesada] sat over coffee, chatting about this and that; the first time was at the Café Brasil, which was, or is, on the Rambla, near where the Friends of Durruti had their local; and the second occasion was in the one at the far end of the Calle Goya, where it meets the Plaza de Cataluña [he must mean between the Plaza de Goya and the Plaza Universidad]. I was listening to the pair of them, but contributed little to the conversation.

Carreño was listing, starting with the Asturian working class's insurrection back in February 1934, the failure of every uprising attempted in our country by the FAI-CNT. Which is why, he said, the National Confederation of Labor [CNT] had to begin a serious analysis of all those failures and rethink action, or the act of insurrection, and the seizure of political power. Anybody else who claims they had some sway is mistaking wishful thinking for reality.

What has not been said and written about the May Events? And that includes by the people who claim to have lived through it. That they lived through it, I do not doubt; but the ones who write about it have nothing to do with the reality of the events they describe. Later, I will mention one of the heavyweights....

Signed: José Quesada Suárez.

2. The Trotskyists in May 1937

If it is possible to speak of a foundational meeting in the forming of a tiny group launched over a lengthy process, then we can say that Munis set up the pro-Fourth International SBLE—Bolshevik-Leninist Section of Spain—in Barcelona in November 1936. But the tiny number of members, almost all of them foreigners, with scarcely any command of the language and even less of a social base, plus the fact that most of them had enlisted in various frontline units and the fact that they were split into two rival groups, the discredit into which the Fourth International had fallen as a result of Rous's disastrous mission and the POUM's refusal to let them organize as a fraction, all of these things prevented the Trotskyist organization from consolidating itself. The 12 December 1936 report from the GBL (Bolshevik-Leninist Group) in Barcelona is very revealing in this regard.[26] One could speak of a second foundation or relaunch of the SBLE from April 1937 onward, with the publication of the very first edition of *La Voz Leninista* and the establishment of an Executive Committee made up of Munis, who took on the post of secretary, the Dane Aage Kielso, plus the Italian Adolfo Carlini.

So, from November 1936 onwards, there were two competing Trotskyist groups in Spain; these later came to be known by the titles of their respective press organs; the official, Munis-led group that published *La Voz Leninista*, and the Molinier-ist group led by Fosco, publishing *Le Soviet*. The official organization took on the name of SBLE—Bolshevik-Leninist Section of Spain—while the Fosco group became the "Le Soviet" Bolshevik-Leninist Group.

An attempt in January 1937 to reunify the two groups foundered when the SBLE refused to discuss "the personal case of Fosco," which in reality amounted to a refusal to discuss the existing political differences of opinion.[27] And so, the splitting of the Spanish Trotskyist movement into two factions would defy resolution until 1943.

---

26   See Agustín Guillamón, ed., *Documentación histórica del trosquismo español (1936–1939). De la Guerra civil a la ruptura con la Cuarta Internacional* (Madrid: Ediciones de la Torre, 1996), Doc. 1.12.

27   See ibid., Document 1.39.

As the months passed, the numbers of Spanish militants joining the ranks of the official group grew. In any case, the Bolshevik-Leninists [BL] were always a small nucleus outside of the POUM, but above all, there was a BL fraction (de facto, if not de jure) within the POUM ranks.

Leading militants from the SBLE were Esteban Bilbao, Jaime Fernández Rodríguez, Julio Cid Gaitán, José Quesada Suárez, Miguel Olmeda, Antonio Guerrero, the German Hans David Freund (aka Moulin), the French surrealist poet Benjamin Péret, the Italians Adolfo Carlini and Lionello Guido, the Pole Casanova (real name Myeczyslaw Bortenstein), the Australian May Low, and the Cuban surrealist poet Juan Brea, among others.

The Trotskyists from the "Le Soviet" GBL made up a motley crew that, in spite of the initial rejection and clash between Fosco and Molinier in Barcelona in August 1936, was drawn toward the political stances of the dissidents Raymond Molinier and Pierre Frank (who, in France, following the breakdown of the fragile unity achieved on 1 June 1936 by the launch of the POI [Internationalist Workers Party], reverted from 23 October onwards to publication of the *La Commune* newspaper as the mouthpiece of the PCInt (International Communist Party]). The "Le Soviet" GBL was outnumbered by the official group and was made up of Fosco (who also employed the literary aliases of *Emiliano Vigo* and *Rolano*), his partner Virginia Gervasini (aka Sonia), the Italian Cristofano Salvini (aka Tosca), and the Frenchmen Henri Aïache and Georges Chéron (aka Romeo Julio and Remy), plus Chéron's partner, Louise. They managed to recruit the Spanish militant Antonio Rodríguez Arroyo (aka Rodas). Between January 1937 and January 1938, they managed to publish fifteen issues of a French-language bulletin, eight to ten copies of which were typed up by Sonia; entitled *Le Soviet*, it gave the group its name.

The organization founded by Munis published two editions of a *Boletín* in January and February 1937 and, from April onward, that *Boletín* took the title *La Voz Leninista*. Unable to join the POUM and form a Trotskyist fraction there, the SBLE did its best to influence the POUM and radical anarchist sectors from without. An attempt was made to steer segments of the radical left unhappy with those organizations in the direction of revolutionary positions. The CNT and POUM were chided for their partnership with the government of the republican bourgeoisie, while there was also lobbying on behalf of the formation of a Revolutionary Workers' Front that might seize power, make the revolution, and win the war.

Munis and Benjamin Péret (who had seen action in the POUM militias and later served in an anarchist unit) left for Paris in mid-April. Péret did not return to Spain. Munis spent a few weeks in Paris, and there wrote a report on the SBLE's situation for Trotsky, and the May Events caught him off guard there.[28]

---

28   Ibid., Document 1.50.

So the First of May flyer was probably the work of Freund (Moulin) who was leading the SBLE, along with Sedran (Carlini) during a pivotal moment in the Spanish revolution. Moulin, who had regular dealings with the Friends of Durruti Group had been working to reunite the two existing Trotskyist groups. In any case, too much has been made of the contacts between Balius and Moulin and some authors, like Pavel and Clara Thalmann, have automatically, and displaying more imagination than evidence, transformed this into Moulin's having irresistibly influenced Balius's thinking.[29] It takes only a cursory reading of the issues of El Amigo del Pueblo to register that Balius and the Friends of Durruti were not only not Marxists but were not in any way influenced by Marxism. In late July, Moulin had arranged a rendezvous with another militant by the name of "Martín" near Fosco's home and had laid the groundwork, along with Sonia, for a meeting with Fosco "most likely to come to some arrangement."[30] A few days after that, on 2 August, Moulin was detained and later murdered by the Stalinists who thereby deprived the SBLE of one of its most valuable leaders.

Munis arrived in Barcelona in mid-May, most likely in the company of the delegate from the International Secretariat (SI), Erwin Wolf, known by the pseudonym Nicolle Braun. Erwin Wolf drafted a detailed report dated 6 July 1937, which is a superb X-ray of the SBLE's political problems and membership in the wake of the May Events and the beginnings of the Stalinist repression targeting revolutionary organizations.[31] It is known that Wolf was arrested twice in succession in late July and then he vanished for good, joining the long list of Stalinism's victims.

Given its larger numbers and superior social and political foothold, the SBLE was able to engage in more wide-ranging and thoroughgoing work than anything the "Le Soviet" GBL could accomplish, and it successfully distributed copies of its newspaper and flyer in the thousands, even producing news bulletins in French and German. Its dealings with various critical factions within anarchism and the POUM offered it a real prospect of broadening its political influence and conjuring up factions likely to collaborate with a Revolutionary Front. The activities of the "Le Soviet" GBL were at all times tightly constrained by its inability to equip itself with a newspaper deserving of the description. The use of French, due to its poor command of written Spanish, was a very significant impediment to its propaganda and recruitment efforts and this proved an insurmountable obstacle as far as the group was concerned.[32]

---

29   See García, Piotrowski, and Rosés, eds., *Barcelona, mayo de 1937. Testimonios desde las barricadas* (Barcelona: Alikornio, 2006), 109–112.

30   Testimony of Virginia Gervasini (*Sonia*) given to Paolo Casciolo (Varese, 8 March 1993).

31   See Guillamón, ed., *Documentación histórica del trosquismo español*, Document 1.57.

32   Although *Le Soviet* no. 14 (1 December 1937) carried a reproduction in French with the

In May 1937, there was a workers' insurrection in Barcelona, spearheaded by the defense committees. In response to alarming reports of the police storming the Telephone Exchange building, run by the CNT and UGT unions, the Control Patrols and barrio defense committees threw up barricades and CNT workers quickly gained the upper hand in the city, except for the city center. In the contested city center, there was a camp on each side of the barricade; on one side, the republican security forces, the Generalidad with its Pyrenean Militias, the Catalan anti-CNT nationalists from Estat Català, and the (Stalinist) PSUC; on the other side of the barricade stood the CNT, the FAI, the POUM, but above all, the workers in arms.

The Friends of Durruti and the Trotskyists from the SBLE were alone in issuing leaflets advocating continuance of the fighting and opposing the ceasefire. These were the only organizations that tried to steer the workers' spontaneous uprising in a revolutionary direction. Most of those workers being CNT personnel, the vast majority of them opposed the defeatist calls for peace coming from their own leaders, but in the end, they caved due to the absence of any revolutionary alternative coming from the CNT.

The Friends of Durruti and the Bolshevik-Leninists were both virtually organizationless, with tiny memberships and virtually no sway over the working class.[33] We can assert that their activity was almost entirely restricted to publication of their newspapers and the flyers circulated in May 1937.

Nor can we speak of collaboration between the two organizations; they merely found themselves on the street at the same time in May, issuing similar appeals addressed to the workers.[34] During the May Events, Adolfo Carlini and José Quesada spoke with Jaime Balius and other Friends of Durruti leaders in an attempt to give a boost to the revolutionary insurrection.[35]

As to the setting up of a left fraction inside the POUM favorable to the arguments for revolution, despite repeated invitations issued through *La Voz Leninista*, there were no contacts or practical collaboration between them worth talking about.[36] Only Josep Rebull, the administrator of *La Batalla*, a member

---

comment (in French): "We offer a translation of this flyer which was distributed in Spanish." See Guillamón, ed., *Documentación histórica del trosquismo español*, Document 1.72.

33 It is interesting to try and gauge the membership sizes of the minority revolutionary organizations in May 1937. The Friends of Durruti had between four thousand and five thousand members, the Trotskyists from the SBLE around thirty, the Trotskyists from the "Le Soviet" GBL about eight, and Cell 72 of the POUM around a dozen.

34 See ibid., Document 1.53.

35 According to José Quesada's evidence. See also the correspondence with Guillamón and Leon Trotsky's book *La revolución española (1930–1940)*, vol. 2, (Barcelona: Fontanella, 1977), 123–124 [Anthology of texts with an introduction by Pierre Broué].

36 From Guillamón's interview with Munis in Barcelona on 16 November 1984:

of the POUM Central Committee, and himself the author of some countertheses drafted for the POUM's Second Congress, countertheses highly critical of POUM collaboration with the Generalidad government, had submitted to his party's Executive Committee a plan of the city detailing and advocating a military seizure of power during the May events.[37] That plan had been rejected by Nin, Andrade, and Gorkín on the basis that they saw the issue as *not a military one but a political one.* Contacts between Josep Rebull and Jaime Balius had no practical outcome.[38]

So, May 1937 failed to find or produce any revolutionary leadership or coordination capable of turning the insurrection into a revolution. In May 1937, all of the mass workers' organizations, one after another, turned down the chance they were offered to become a revolutionary vanguard.

On 4 May 1937, the SBLE issued a flyer on the barricades.[39] The following day, the Friends of Durruti did likewise. These were the only two organizations to try to endow the insurrection under way with clearcut revolutionary objectives. The activities of the "Le Soviet" GBL were confined, it seems, to a token presence by Fosco and Georges Chéron ("Remy") on the POUM barricade outside the Hotel Falcón.

Q: Was there collaboration between the Bolshevik-Leninist Section and groups from the revolutionary left such as the Friends of Durruti or Rebull who had been critical of the POUM's Executive Committee and Nin?

G. Munis: I have no recollection of any such thing. I can't recall the details any more, but of course I knew nobody from the "Friends of Durruti," any more than I knew Rebull, or any of those people prior to May.

Q: And after the May Events?

G. Munis: I did try later to contact Rebull [in France] to see if there was any possibility of our doing something together, but that fell through. During the war [Second World War] Rebull worked with Franc-Tireur. He was in the Resistance and our stance was that the Resistance was one of the sides in an imperialist war in which revolutionaries ought not to get involved.

37 See the "Counter-theses of Cell 72 of the POUM Local Committee," drafted by Josep Rebull, in *Boletín interior no. 1. Órgano de discusión para el II Congreso del Comité local de Barcelona del POUM,* Barcelona, 23 April 1937, and *Boletín Interior no. 2. Órgano ...* Barcelona, 29 May 1937.

38 Guillamón questionnaire to Josep Rebull, 16-12-1985:

Q: Did Cell 72 try to make contact with other groups with the intention of creating a revolutionary front with, say, the Friends of Durruti, Libertarian Youth, Balius, Munis, or other POUM factions?

Josep Rebull: Our only contacts with the Friends of Durruti came during the May Events, but the numerical insignificance of that group, and its lack of ties to the rank-and-file, and C72's modest representativeness did little to favor a practical agreement on, say, our agreeing to issue a manifesto to the struggling workers. I do not recall having spoken to Munis until I was in exile, in Paris, when our conversations got nowhere.

39 Probably drafted by Moulin.

Munis claimed that the bourgeois state had evaporated in Spain back in July 1936. The committees government were the only real authority in existence. However, there being no revolutionary party around capable of unifying and beefing up those committees at the national level, the democratic counterrevolution, ideologically embodied by Stalinists and organizationally by the Popular Front, encroached, step by step, upon the revolutionary gains made in July. It took until early October 1936 and the entry of the CNT and POUM into the Generalidad government and the order disbanding the local workers' committees, to conjure up a dual power situation pitting the republican government against the new organs of workers' power: the committees. The counterrevolution, which had the wind behind it by then, made ground until, by May 1937, it was able to strike a definitive blow against the revolution's nerve center: the Barcelona working class.

The Stalinist repression that followed the downfall of the Largo Caballero government ensured that the POUM was outlawed and put on trial, as were the Friends of Durruti and the Bolshevik-Leninist Section. The murders of the anarchists Camillo Berneri, Francesco Barbieri, and so many other less well-known individuals were followed by the murder and disappearance of the POUMists Andrés Nin and Kurt Landau, to name but two, as well as of Munis's comrades Hans David Freud and Erwin Wolf.

An SBLE flyer of 4 May 1937 (reproduced in *La Lutte Ouvrière*, no. 48, 10 June 1937) read as follows:

LONG LIVE THE REVOLUTIONARY OFFENSIVE

No compromise. Disarm the reactionary GNR and Assault Guards. This is a crucial time. Next time, it will be too late. General strike across every industry not working on behalf of the war effort, until the reactionary government resigns. Only Proletarian Power can guarantee military victory.

Armament of the working class.

Long live CNT-FAI-POUM Unity of Action.

Long live the Revolutionary Front of the Proletariat.

Revolutionary Defense Committees in the workshops, factories, on the barricades, etc.

Bolshevik-Leninist Section of Spain (for the IV International)

APPENDIX C
The Murder and Burial of Camillo Berneri and Francesco Barbieri in Barcelona, May 1937

[Top image] Barricade erected in May 1937 in the Plaza Dostoievski (Plaza del Ángel these days) at the end of the Calle Llibretería. This photo shows the view of the barricade visible from the doorway where Berneri lived, looking to the right toward the Generalidad Palace. It was facing the premises of the UGT's Water, Light, and Power Union. This barricade had been put up by PSUC militants as protection against any move to attack the Generalidad from the Vía Layetana side.

[Bottom image] The same barricade, seen from the Calle Llibretería side. In the background, underneath the flag, there is a poster reading "UGT Water, Light, and Power Union" on a building that is on the Vía Durruti (now Layetana). On the left, between the two columns, the doorway where Berneri lived, right on the Plaza Dostoievski Ángel (Plaza del Ángel), at no. 2.

The photograph clearly shows that the doorway to the building where Berneri was living was wide open to crossfire exchanged between the PSUC barricade and the balconies of the UGT union premises.

It is also plain from the photograph that the doorway to where Berneri was living was surrounded by a barricade running from the Vía Durruti (today's Vía Layetana) into the middle of the Plaza del Ángel. No one could have entered or left through that doorway without the permission of those manning the barricade. Machine guns had been set up on the roof of the building, trained on the Vía Durruti and the Casa CNT-FAI located some two hundred meters distant.

Thus, the location was totally monitored by the PSUC-UGT: the barricade in the Calle Llibrería, the barricade in the Plaza, and the UGT union local. It was a basic security precaution for the Stalinists to investigate and search the apartments in the building in which Berneri was living, which was at the heart of the Stalinists' defensive arrangements.

Berneri and Barbieri were in the worst possible place, at the worst possible moment.

The Italian anarchists living in the building were identified during a first visit (on Tuesday, 4 May at 10:00 a.m.); their weapons (three rifles) were confiscated from them on a second visit (Tuesday 4, May at 3:00 p.m.) and they were ordered not to leave the building. On the third occasion, their visitors returned (Wednesday, 5 May at 6:00 p.m.) with "orders from above" to arrest Berneri and Barbieri.

On the night of 5–6 May, Berneri's corpse turned up very close to the Generalidad Palace, barely fifty meters from the Plaza de Angel. Barbieri's corpse was found on the Ramblas.

No one but the Stalinists could have arrested them, no one but the Stalinists could have murdered them and the word from above that they were to be executed could only have come from a few; the Soviet consul Antonov Ovseenko, or the man who led the PSUC from the shadows, Gerö (aka Pedro).

The Murder[40]

At 10:00 a.m. on the morning of Tuesday 4 May, two individuals wearing red armbands presented themselves at apartment 1, 2 Plaza del Ángel. They were received by comrades Berneri and Barbieri, whom they told not to shoot as they were friends and there was nothing to fear.[41] Our comrades replied that,

---

40   "Report on the Murder of Comrades Camillo Berneri and Francesco Barbieri" [IISH-CNT-005F-9]. Fragment of the report lifted from Virgilio Gozzoli's article in *Guerra di Classe*, 19 May 1937.

41   For the life of Berneri, see Francisco Madrid Santos, *Camillo Berneri, un anarchico italiano (1897–1937): Rivoluzione e controrivoluzione in Europa (1917–1937)* (Pistoia: Archivio

as antifascists who had come to Spain to defend the revolution, they had no reason to be shooting at antifascist workers.

The two individuals then left and were seen from the window to enter the premises opposite belonging to the UGT union. At around 3:00 p.m. the same day, five or six individuals wearing the same red armbands as the ones who called that morning, plus steel helmets and shotguns, called on the apartment again, stating that they had authority to effect a search. Seeing that the search was thorough, comrade Tantini handed three rifles over to them, stating that they had been left there for safekeeping by three militia members who had turned up on leave from the Huesca front. After collecting the rifles, the UGT personnel and policemen left, just two of the latter staying behind to complete the search. Papers found in comrade Fantosi's room and a few books and maps from comrade Mastrodicasa's room were taken away. As for comrade Berneri's room, given the volume of the material there, they made off with only a portion of it, stating that they would be back with a car.[42] As they left, they warned our comrades not to venture outside and to keep away from the windows, unless they wanted to get themselves shot. The searchers, upon being questioned, replied that they had had reports of armed Italian anarchists in the apartment.

On the afternoon of the Wednesday, around 6:00 p.m., a dozen persons showed up, among them some UGT militia members in red armbands, armed police officers, and someone in plain clothes, stating that they were there to arrest Berneri and Barbieri. The latter asked why he was being arrested, and the response was that they were counterrevolutionaries. Whereupon Barbieri replied that in his twenty years as an anarchist militant, this was the first time he had had that insult thrown at him. The policeman replied that he was a counterrevolutionary precisely because he was an anarchist. Incensed, Barbieri asked for the name of the one who insulted him so that he could reserve his right, when the time came, to hold him accountable, whereupon the policeman showed him his lapel on which he was wearing a metal badge bearing the number 1109 (which was jotted down by Barbieri's partner who happened to be there at the time.)

Comrade Tantini objected that, whereas the arms had been left in her care and they were letting her go free, they had no right to arrest Berneri and Barbieri, on whom they had found nothing. That *compañera*, as well as Barbieri's

---

Famiglia Berneri, 1985). For a life of Barbieri, see Antonio Orlando and Angelo Pagliaro, *Chicco il professore* (Milan/Ragusa: Zero in Condotta/La Fiaccola, 2013).

42   For an anthology of Berneri's writings, see Camillo Berneri, *Pietrogrado 1917, Barcelona 1937*, eds. Pier Carlo Masino and Alberto Sorti (Ragusa: La Fiaccola, 1990). Contains an Appendix on the Berneri affair.

partner asked to be allowed to accompany the detainees, only to be told by the police that, if need be, they would be back to arrest them. At around 9:30 on the Thursday morning, two individuals in red armbands showed up at the apartment door to tell the two *compañeras* that the two detainees had been released the previous day at noon, after which they left.

According to the registers of the Clinical Hospital, Barcelona, Barbieri and Berneri were brought in, dead, on the Wednesday-to-Thursday night, having been collected by the Red Cross from the Rambla, in the case of the former, and from the Plaza de la Universidad in the case of the latter [this is a mistake: he was found in the Plaza de la República or de Sant Jaume, across from the Generalidad Palace.]

The Autopsy on Camillo Berneri[43]

The autopsy carried out on the cadaver of our comrade Berneri demonstrates the ease with which the killers acted in order to accomplish their feat. Let us see how.

The body displays a firearm wound with an entry hole behind the right axillar line, exiting via the right breast at the level of the seventh rib. The bullet moving in a right-to-left direction. FORWARDS FROM BEHIND AND FROM ABOVE DOWNWARDS.

Similarly, there is a further firearm injury in the right temporo-occipital region, TRAVELLING IN A DOWNWARDS DIRECTION FROM ABOVE AND FORWARDS FROM BEHIND.

Going by the location of the edges of the wounds, they were produced at close range measured at a distance of no less than 0.75 meters. The injuries were caused when the assailant was behind or on the side of the victim, as far as the abdominal injury is concerned and from a position looking downwards as far as the head injury goes.

[Meaning that the first bullet put into him penetrated his chest from the right shoulder-blade to the right nipple and then, once he had fallen to the ground, a coup de grâce was fired into his right breast, with the bullet exiting through the nape of the neck.]

Such was the death of comrade Berneri, along with Barbieri. The very same methods have been used today, just as similar methods were deployed in mid-April to disappear Mark Rein, son of the Menshevik Abramovich,

---

43   *Solidaridad Obrera*, 11 May 1937, 2.

editor-in-chief of the newspaper *Democratic Kraten*. The Police then conducted enquiries to locate the missing man. And met with no success. Exactly the same as will happen in this instance when they embark upon showy enquiries into these comrades' deaths.

The Funerals of Berneri and Barbieri

Tuesday, 11 May 1937

The Regional Committees of the CNT, the FAI, and the Libertarian Youth distributed a joint manifesto, weighing up the May Events.[44] It had been a provocation, centering upon the storming of the Telephone Exchange by Rodríguez Salas and Artemi Aguadé "unbeknownst to the Generalidad Council." So the blame was being pinned on those two individuals and the Generalidad government was being absolved.[45] The reply to that provocation had been "spontaneous"; they did not exploit that point any further.

The May Events boiled down to "three awful days of fratricidal strife in Barcelona. Three days of a systematic and terrifying manhunt."

A link was drawn between the murders of twelve CNT militants in San Andrés "brought to the cemetery in Sardañola in an ambulance," the five members of Eroles's bodyguard, the fifteen militants murdered in the Tarragona area and the finding of the body of the Italian Berneri, only to finish by lamenting "all the victims on both sides."

It highlighted the danger of foreign intervention, what with the presence in the port of Barcelona "of six French and English vessels" during the "Wednesday and Thursday of last week."

The CNT and the FAI "were spurred into revolt by a monstrous maneuver involving many, diverse sectors and men whom we shall name, with the appropriate proof, when the time comes."

The only lesson drawn was denunciation of provocateurs and provocations yet to come, about which the security forces and UGT were warned, with an appeal to worker unity "in the face of the common foe, within and without, the enemy of the vanguard and rearguard alike."

That same day witnessed the discreet burials of Domingo Ascaso that morning

---

44   CNT-FAI-FIJL-AIT, "The regional organizations in Catalonia attached to the CNT, FAI, and FIJL, To Public Opinion," manifesto/flyer [AEP-C606].

45   There is more than enough documentary proof to show that the order to seize the Telephone Exchange building came from the Generalidad President, although it had not been run past the Council, on which the CNT was represented.

and Camillo Berneri that afternoon. The Public Order authorities, abetted by the CNT higher committees' calls for concord, had banned the funeral processions lest passions become inflamed. In defiance of that ban, the corpses of the Italian anarchist activists Camillo Berneri and Francesco Barbieri, Adriano Ferrari, Lorenzo De Peretti, and Marco Pietro were escorted from the Clinical Hospital by a procession of several thousand comrades and friends, walking behind the black flag of the German DAS group.[46]

The editors of *Guerra di Classe* pointed to the presence, right from the outset, of Barbieri's *compañera* and the fact that Berneri's daughter joined the cortege in the street, having arrived by car from the border at Port-Bou. "There was no oration," and no more homage than the dipping of the black flag over the five coffins that were laid to rest the following day in the different graves assigned to them, graves owned by the CNT's Italian section.[47]

On 30 December 1940, the remains of Marco Pietro and Francesco Barbieri were removed to the mass grave in the cemetery in Sants.[48] On 7 November 1941, the same was done with the remains of Adriano Ferrari and Lorenzo De Peretti.[49] Finally, Camillo Berneri's remains were removed to the mass grave in the cemetery on 16 November 1951.

---

46 A letter to the author from Barcelona Cemeteries (9 October 2013) clarified that Marco Pietro's name had been erroneously recorded in *Guerra di Classe* as "Pietro Macon"; See Nelles, Piotrowski, Linse, and Garcia, *Antifascistas alemanes en Barcelona (1933–1939)* (Barcelona: Sintra, 2010), 353, n. 12. And *Guerra di Classe*, 25 May 1937.

47 *Guerra di Classe*, 25 May 1937, front page.

48 According to Aldo Aguzzi in *Barcelona, mayo 1937* (Barcelona: Alikornio, 2006), 159, "On the morning of the Wednesday [5 May] a further risky sortie was attempted. Six armored cars set off from the Spartacus barracks. It took them three hours, fighting every inch of the way, to get through to the Control Patrols headquarters in the Calle Cortes [Gran Via]. The Italians who took part in the defense of that building included, among others, Cafiero, Marcon [Marco Pietro], Zamboni, etc. and they fought heroically. The second named perished and the last of those named was seriously wounded." According to Severino Campos's evidence, Domingo Ascaso also perished in the attempt to step outside the besieged Control Patrols' headquarters.

49 According to Aldo Aguzzi (ibid., 158), "[Ferrari and De Peretti], on reaching the Plaza del Ángel were stopped by PSUC personnel and shot."

APPENDIX D
The POUM Local Committee's Report on May 1937

{"Report on the Actions of the Local Committee during the May Events, presented by it to the Barcelona cells for discussion" [AHN. Causa General. Bundle 792(1)]. Translated from the Catalan. Bold face added by the Spanish translator.}

Report on the actions of the Local Committee during the May Events, offered for discussion by the Barcelona cells[50]

Triggered by the attempt to storm the Telephone Exchange, the handiwork of a bunch of reformist provocateurs commanded by Rodríguez, the incidents of which we are all aware ensued and showed that the working class was not ready to allow the gains made at the cost of such sacrifice on 10 July to be snatched from it with impunity....

The tension in the proletariat throughout the week prior to the events had been escalating so that all that was missing was a spark to send everything sky high. A simple rehearsal of the happenings, by way of proof of this: the UGT activist Roldán [Cortada] had lost his life and his corpse was used as an excuse to organize a demonstration that showed every possible sign of counterrevolutionary and provocative intent toward the rest of the organizations. Backed indirectly by Estat Catalá, the security forces attacked the hamlets of the Cerdaña; they arrested and murdered worker militants and, with weaponry aplenty, made their preparation for an attack on the town of Puigcerdá. An expeditionary force of carabineers seized the strategic villages around Figueres and from there marched on the city, thwarted in their efforts thanks to the measures that workers throughout the entire comarca put in place to prevent this. We could go on quoting other instances of blatant provocation, all of them geared to the same purpose: liquidating the revolutionary positions still retained by the workers and paving the way for abolition of their class organizations.

All of this brought about a rarefication of the political atmosphere in our city (Barcelona), the outcome of which was not hard to foresee. The spark eventually came on 3 May. At the head of his gang, Rodríguez made his historic intrusion into the Telephone Exchange building and the workers, already weary of

---

50   Josep Rebull was on the POUM Local Committee, but was not its secretary. How much influence he had over the committee and how involved he was in the drafting of the report, we do not know.

provocations and provocateurs, greeted it with gunfire.[51] The news immediately spread throughout the city. Workers poured out of the factories, workshops, and construction sites. Groups of armed workers set about securing the most strategic streets. Barricades proliferated. The proletariat was stirring and on a war footing; it declared a general strike and was taking up arms.

That mobilization took place **spontaneously**.[52] The CNT's leadership was utterly **outflanked**.[53] The Confederation's committees moved heaven and earth to ensure that the Telephone Exchange incident would remain localized to the Generalidad government and even on the Monday afternoon they were telling their membership that the conflict was on the verge of being sorted out.[54] But by then the working class had run out of patience and, heedless of the [CNT] leadership, it took to the streets ready to risk everything rather than tolerate any further loss of ground.

That being how things stood, what stance should our Party [the POUM] adopt? What stance should the [POUM] Local Committee espouse?

Given that our party operates on the basis of revolutionary Marxism, the only viable option was to support and engage with the uprising. That being the view of the Local Committee, that very day, the 3rd, it requested a joint meeting with the Executive Committee for the purpose of studying the situation and putting our points of view along the lines mentioned. At that meeting, there was agreement between the two committees and the reckoning was that the party's mission was to engage actively with the movement, our members being ordered to take up arms and act in concert with the CNT's defense committees. On the morning of Tuesday the 4th, there was a further meeting of the Local and Executive committees. At that meeting, after a fresh look at the situation, the decision was made, at the suggestion of the Local Committee, to issue the **directive to proceed with the creation of Committees for Defense of the Revolution and for a Central Defense Committee**.[55] Our reckoning was that if we could endow the workers with the essential organs of struggle, then the greater the likelihood of that struggle's losing its spontaneity and turning into a

---

51 He was not leading any "gang"; he was leading three truckloads of Assault Guards.

52 Gorkín was clear in explaining that this was a "spontaneity" driven by the CNT's defense committees.

53 This notion is key to the May insurrection: the CNT's higher committees were **shoved aside** by the defense committees.

54 "The Confederation's committees" refers to the CNT's higher committees, the Local Committee, and the Regional Committee.

55 The POUM published a flyer entitled "The committees for defense of the revolution" [AHN Causa General] dated 10 or 11 May 1937, clear evidence of the POUM intention of hijacking the CNT defense committees organization: "they emerged as the anarchist comrades' military organization."

coordinated activity with hard and fast aims, whereby the working class might score a great victory.

And those **organs of struggle, which might later on turn into organs of power,** had to be the Committees for Defense of the Revolution. On the 4th, we sent orders out to all our district and ward committees to proceed immediately to the establishment of those defense committees:

"Set up Committees in every ward, go and put it to the CNT and, if they are in agreement, launch a Committee for Defense of the Revolution in each barrio."

"All the Committees should appoint a delegate to attend a meeting that very night to set up the Central Committee for Defense of the Revolution."

Those were the orders we issued to our comrades on 4 May.

The following day, the 5th, the fighting persisted, more intensely than ever. However, nobody quite knew where it would lead. There was a **meeting with the Friends of Durruti**; it was negative. They had no desire to lobby the CNT rank and file directly in order to oust the [CNT] leadership; they merely sought to influence the movement, without assuming any other responsibility. We were summoned by the Local Libertarian Youth Federation to a meeting with all the CNT and FAI local bodies, a meeting that did not proceed due to the poor turn-out by those invited to it.

We used the opportunity to have **talks with the CNT's Revolutionary Committee.**[56] They told us that they could not set up any joint committee with us, but that we could establish contact with them and they informed us that the National and Regional Committees were parleying with the Generalidad.

The *manguera* (as they called García Oliver) would shortly be deployed.[57] The stance of that [CNT Revolutionary] Committee was absolutely nonsensical. If the higher committees of the CNT ordered a withdrawal, they were going to remain on the streets, but they would leave it up to the combatants to do as they saw fit. The impression the delegation from the Local Committee came away with was also negative.[58]

From then on and given that the movement might end in utter defeat for the proletariat, both the Local Committee and the Executive Committee reckoned

---

56 Compare this with Severino Campos's testimony in *Le Combat syndicaliste* and with that from Matías Suñer Vidal, according to César M Lorenzo. This was a Revolutionary Committee propelled by Julián Merino. Therefore, this document corroborates and ratifies the existence of the CNT's secret Revolutionary Committee.

57 *Manguera* meaning fire hose.

58 This is a simplistic analysis but one that suited the POUM Local Committee very well. If the Friends of Durruti and the Revolutionary Committee left them with a "negative impression," then they had no allies to look to and it was fine for them to fall back in order to salvage their party cadres.

that we had to choose an opportune moment to begin a strategic withdrawal.... There was no way that we could be the first to step back, but neither could we be the last. We had to rescue the party from a potential defeat.

After that audience with the [CNT's] Revolutionary Committee, our two committees got together again and after assessing all the factors we have just spelled out, we came to the conclusion that, if we wanted to avert the movement degenerating into a putsch, we needed to publish a note urging a return to work. In that note, carried by *La Batalla* on the 6th, it was stated that all the workers should lay down their arms and go back to their workplaces, while remaining on standby. Nevertheless, the order issued to our comrades over the telephone was that if the CNT comrades, in spite of all the warnings from their leaders, were to remain on the streets, that they were not to abandon their barricades.

Thursday the 6th opened with the workers starting to withdraw. In some barrios, lots of barricades were abandoned. This persisted until noon, when, since the security forces were treating the workers' withdrawal as if it were an act of cowardice and seizing their chance to better their positions, the fighters caught on to the chicanery and returned to their battle stations and the fighting persisted throughout the remainder of the day.

As night fell, the [CNT] Committee of the Center barrio asked to speak with a commission from the [POUM] party. At that meeting, the anarchist comrades asked us how we saw the movement's being brought to a conclusion. We put forth the view that the party had adopted at the afternoon meeting, to wit, that we had to **order a withdrawal**, contingent upon the security forces being taken off the streets and that the working class should hold on to its weapons.

The comrades from the [Defense] Committee of the Center [and of Pueblo Seco] appeared to be in agreement with our view and, the following day, the 7th, *La Batalla* issued the withdrawal order, making it contingent upon the two stipulations mentioned. The order [to pull back from the barricades] that we reissued [a second time] to our [POUM] comrades ensured that they stayed on the barricades as long as the CNT comrades carried on manning them, but that they should keep in close touch with the latter so that they could begin to pull back together.[59] This wait-and-see stance was advisable because, in some wards, the barricades had been captured and abandoned several times over, depending on the judgment of the comrades manning them.

The pull back began in earnest on the Saturday. Positions were being abandoned throughout the day. Elsewhere, they were not abandoned until the

---

59   The POUM's coattailing of the CNT is patently obvious here. The POUM's priority seems to have been nothing short of a childish competition to avoiding being accused of having been the first to quit the barricades.

Sunday. The pull-back proceeded in a perfectly orderly fashion. The working class had not been beaten but was making an orderly withdrawal and was holding onto its arms.[60]

It immediately occurred to the Local Committee that it needed to rescue the party from potential repression and it ordered all districts to prepare the [POUM] party to go underground.[61] It was absolutely vital that you adopt organization on the basis of cells in such work and put intense effort into it.

Such, in broad outline, was the Local Committee's stance and activity during the May events....

Our position was that sloganizing about proceeding to seize power was not a possibility. Taking into account the balance of forces, and that we had no direct input into the direction of the movement, the party could not risk releasing such instructions without, at the very least, there being organs in existence that might replace the bourgeois authorities.[62] By our reckoning, it would not have been hard to overrun the Generalidad Palace, but then what? How could we have stayed in power? On what foundations might we have built it?...

So, drawing the lessons to be learnt from this movement, the party in Barcelona must focus its activity upon creating the conditions favorable to ousting from power the bourgeoisie, and the reformists who are a lot more dangerous than the bourgeoisie itself.[63] That can only be achieved through a coming together of the revolutionary organizations, which are going to have to form the WORKERS' REVOLUTIONARY FRONT in order to prevent the reaction from gaining new ground. The mission of the Workers' Revolutionary Front will be to create the grassroots organs upon which the working class in power will have to rely. Those organs can only be the Committees for Defense of the Revolution....

Comrades: For the Revolution to triumph, get to work selling these watchwords: WORKERS' REVOLUTIONARY FRONT—COMMITTEES FOR DEFENSE OF THE REVOLUTION.

---

60   This was not so much a military defeat as a political one.

61   In any event, the POUM made no serious preparations to operate from clandestinity. Josep Rebull was alone in urging the party to take such steps. Whether this sentence was drafted due to his input, we cannot say.

62   The whole line of argument in this document is erratic and inappropriate for a revolutionary organization. Power had not been seized because there were no organs of power on standby to take it on. But, without taking power, how were the Committees for Defense of the Revolution supposed to turn into organs of worker power? Besides, if they came away with a "negative impression" of the Friends of Durruti and the CNT's Revolutionary Committee, with whom were they going to form this Workers' Revolutionary Front? And at no point is there any mention made of the Revolutionary Junta that the Friends of Durruti had been suggesting since late April 1937.

63   In the jargon of the day, the notion "reformist" referred to the PSUC Stalinists.

APPENDIX E
Companys Ordered Aerial Bombing of Barcelona

Report submitted by the Political Commissar of the Airborne Forces in
Barcelona to their political Delegation at the Defense Ministry of the
government of the Republic in Valencia regarding recent incidents in
Barcelona at the beginning of this May. Barcelona, 24 May 1937.[64]

The political commissar of the airborne forces in Barcelona drew up a report
on the May Events, which he submitted to the Republic's Defense Ministry.

As "precursor events," he cited what had happened in "La Fatarella, Bellver
and Hospitalet, plus the excavations carried out to uncover certain cadavers,"
culminating "in the disgraceful attack on the Telephone Exchange, the seizure
of which was made at a time when worker unrest was at crisis point."[65] He described that raid as "a provocation launched in order to detonate that unrest in
order to satisfy purely selfish interests." *That is, it was a provocation by the PSUC.*

In support of his contention, he quoted the 9 April edition of *La Vanguardia.*

He harked back to the start of the May Events and the seizure of the Telephone Exchange: "On the 3rd and with the lack of government accountability
we cited in the paragraphs above, three truckloads of Assault Guard troops under the command of then Public Order Commissioner-General Rodríguez Salas
pulled up outside the building housing that facility at half past three in the afternoon, and without further ado or dialogue with those in charge of that facility,
forced their way inside, training their rifles on all those present on the ground
floor of the building, calling upon them to surrender.[66] Once the occupants of
the upper floors caught on to what was happening and witnessed the violent
attitude of the Guards who were disarming those who normally had custody
of the building, uttering insulting cries targeting a certain labor organization,[67]
they called upon them" to withdraw, as "they were not about to surrender" without some trade union or government resolution "of the matter, the response to

---

64   "Report on the incidents which occurred in Barcelona at the beginning of this May, submitted by the Political Commissar of the Barcelona Air Forces to the Political Delegation
of same at the Defense Ministry of the government of the Republic in Valencia. Barcelona, 24 Mat 1937" [IISH-CNT-002-A11].

65   The "cadavers" were a reference to the so-called "clandestine graveyards" trial which was
looking into deaths that had occurred during the July 1936 insurrection and the subsequent establishment of local committees as the new revolutionary authorities. This was a
trial targeting the revolutionaries of 19 July 1936.

66   A lot of testimony said the time was 2:45 p.m.

67   The CNT.

which was an intense volley of gunfire that in turn drew a response from those under attack, all of this in the presence of Commissioner Rodríguez Salas."

"The Operations Chief of Public Services in Zone One, Dionisio Eroles" immediately arrived on the scene, "mediating between the two sides and asking them to stop the violence until the unions, in concert with the government, could clear the matter up."

The incidents at the Exchange and the most nonsensical rumors and inaccuracies raced through the city, complicating "the position in an extraordinary way" and triggering lots of clashes, "the upshot being the armed response from the workers who, in the face of the fait accompli of the war declared on them on the streets, found themselves obliged to take up defensive positions, clashing, inevitably, with the attacking forces." However, as soon as the unions and the government "laid down the guidelines to be followed, such as the ceasefire orders, the strictly defensive stance, the return to work, the destruction of the barricades, etcetera, the workers abided by them, even though this might, and did, imply losses in their ranks due to the persistent attacks they were still enduring."

In an entirely contrasting stance, the security forces and PSUC militants and, to a lesser extent, those from the ERC and Estat Catalá "kept up the shooting throughout, in spite of the accords agreed by the Generalidad and other political and trade union representatives. The barricades erected by them were left to stand and still do, in defiance of the arrangements."[68]

The writer of the report pointed to the brutality and alacrity of the Stalinist repression, listing raids on locals, the seizure of "prisoners of war," the murders of many CNT members, such as those "of the antifascists Berneri and Barbieri," the armed checkpoints on the streets, the tearing up of CNT membership cards, and other excesses.

The Stalinists had acted like "out-and-out uncontrollables," heedless of the orders jointly issued by the Generalidad government and all the organizations. "If would be unfair not to place it on record that a goodly part of the Republican National Guard and Assault Guards kept absolutely cool heads and refrained from getting involved in the fighting, which they saw as having nothing to do with their remit, by virtue of its very derivation."[69]

As for the Air Forces in Barcelona "they deserve fulsome praise and respect" for their professionalism. The commanders of the Aviation Corps had a clear

---

68 That the PSUC's barricades were still standing two weeks after the end of the May Events was a provocation and above all, a signal as to who the political winners had been.

69 We think the reference here must be to the crackdown coming right after 8 May, because, during the May Events they had played a prominent role. In any event, the attempt is to justify the Air Force's own neutrality by citing the alleged neutrality of the Assault Guards and former Civil Guard.

vision of the incidents,

> as is shown by the fact that the commander of the Air Base, ordered by the councillor for internal security, over the telephone, to **bring out his planes to bomb that part of the city known as the Ronda de San Pedro**, lived up fully to the responsibility incumbent in his post and replied that **he took his orders only from the government of the Republic**, to which he was answerable for his command, which decision was wholly endorsed when it was put to the officer commanding no. 3 Air Region, Colonel Sandino, who ordered that it be borne in mind that they could only obey orders from their commanders and from the lawful government of the Republic.[70]

Once the Republic's government took charge of Public Order, it immediately appointed Colonel Escobar, but, he being injured, his place was taken by Arrando.[71]

This report clearly indicated that the May Events had been planned as a provocation by the PSUC and how the workers' insurrection **swamped** the hopeless craving displayed by the CNT's higher committees for dialogue, agreement, and restraint FROM THE VERY OUTSET.

The most striking part of this report from the Aviation Corps is that it confirms something documented and remarked upon before: **Companys and the Generalidad government had repeatedly insisted that the Air Force bomb the main CNT buildings in Barcelona.** Such insistence shows that the Generalidad and the PSUC were prepared to go to any lengths, ABSOLUTELY ANY LENGTHS, **just to destroy the revolutionaries** within the CNT ranks. They did not pull it off during the bloodletting in May 1937, but they persisted in the attempt during the subsequent selective crackdown over the summer of 1937, until they were fully successful.

---

70   The Ronda de San Pedro refers to the Los Escolapios building, the headquarters of the Defense Committee of the Center, and Poble Sec barrio which had played a leading part in the May Events. Sandino had worked in close association with CNT personnel in the insurrection of 19 July 1936. He had served as defense councillor of the Generalidad government up until 17 December 1936.

71   Escobar was a Civil Guard officer and Arrando an officer in the Assault Guards. Both had taken part in the streetfighting of 19 and 20 July 1936 against the rebel military.

APPENDIX F
Meeting of the POUM's International
Secretariat (14 May 1937)

Comrade Gorkín's Report on the May Events[72]

We have to confess that the scale of the uprising that started on 3 May (1937) came as a surprise to everybody, but our Party, which for months had been relentlessly denouncing the intrigues of the counterrevolution, had foreseen the Stalinists' provocation in league with the reformists.

The rising came about in an atmosphere of *persecution directed at revolutionaries* (at the POUM for months previously and against rank-and-file CNT and FAI personnel) and of *reactionary politicking by the Generalidad government* that, over the preceding months, had ceaselessly been attacking the revolution's gains. The masses who, week after week, had been witnessing this phase of counterrevolution, made it plain on that date that they would not tolerate any further movement down that road.

It has to be understood that, in Catalonia on 19 July, the masses had defeated fascism and right away had taken over the economic reins of the country, control of transportation and the means of communication, living in the dream that they had established worker power. They did not appreciate that if they did not hold political power, all of their gains might some day be wrested from them.

The very next day [after the May Events ended] the Stalinist and republican press tried to sell the story that the uprising had been provoked by the POUM through its direction of the "uncontrollables." In actual fact, the rising was entirely spontaneous. That spontaneity was very relative and needs to be explained. Since 19 July, a number of *defense committees*, organized by grassroots personnel from the FAI and the CNT had been set up pretty much everywhere in Barcelona and around Catalonia. At times, these Committees led barely active lives, but it can be stated that on 3 May it was those committees that mobilized the working class. They were the uprising's action squads.[73] We know that none of the exist-

---

72   (In French) "Meeting of the POUM's International Sub-Secretariat (14 May 1937). Report by comrade GORKÍN on the 'May events.'" [FPI-AC2-182-17]. All emphases are Gorkín's.

73   In an article dated 19 May 1937 and published in French in the first issue of the review *Juillet*, this was how the POUM's political secretary, Andrés Nin put it: "The May Events in Barcelona led to the revival of certain bodies that, over recent months, had played a certain role within the Catalan capital and in a number of important locations: the defense committees. Mainly, these are agencies of a technical-military variety, formed by the

ing unions issued an order for a general strike. But, having realized what sort of fight the Committees had begun to commit to, the workers failed to report for work. Given the lack of other options, that the uprising should have begun in this way should come as no surprise, for it is the traditional practice of workers in Barcelona to trigger a general strike by taking over strategic positions in the city (tram and bus depots, power stations) to bring the city to a standstill.

Right from the start of the upheaval, the POUM realized that it was going to take a chaotic turn due to the absence of precise goals for the action of the masses and that this movement could not lead to the conquest of power. But, given that, in its earlier struggles against reformism and Stalinism, the POUM had continually alerted the laboring masses to stand up to the counterrevolution, and given all its traditions, the POUM had to side with the masses in their struggle. Besides, the POUM's militants were already involved in the fight and would have refused to back down. But the POUM's role had to be to place itself at the head of the masses and commit to the struggle in order to try to give it a direction.[74] And that is what it did.

From day one, the POUM strove to ally itself with the CNT Regional Committee with an eye to steering the movement in partnership with the RC.[75] On the afternoon of 3 May there was a meeting with the CNT's RC. The POUM leaders highlighted the significance of the Telephone Exchange incident, rehearsing what had led to it and who was responsible for it. The Esquerra [ERC] and the PSUC were behind the takeover of the Telephone Exchange. Had that move been successful, they would have pressed on down that road. That operation was part of an entire reactionary plan. But the counterrevolutionaries had not been expecting the proletariat to respond on such a scale.

But we now know, concretely [and in some detail] that that plan of attack had been agreed in Paris at a meeting of 17 communist partners. At present, a mediation plan is being hatched between Paris, London, and Moscow. In parallel with the work that has been done in the fascist camp (the disbandment of the Falange Española, with all power being vested again in Franco's hands). The plan is to annihilate the revolutionary vanguard in our camp.

In Valencia, there is resistance to that mediation plan, coming from the CNT, the socialist rank-and-file and from Largo Caballero himself. Every attempt thus far to set up a government without the CNT and without Caballero has failed....

CNT's unions. In actual fact, it was the latter which led the struggle and which, in every barrio, provided the attraction and organizational center for revolutionary workers."

74 The POUM was a heterodox Leninist party, persecuted by Stalinists, but **Leninist** for all that; that is, it was a Marxist party leading the "unconscious" masses who "needed leadership."

75 Other organizations criticized this as "coattailing."

The day after the uprising, the CNT sought to justify itself. It explained: we are revolutionaries. We cannot permit the crushing of the masses. But even before the rising started, 6 French and English destroyers were steaming toward Barcelona. We were facing a plan for foreign intervention against the Spanish revolution. The CNT was extraordinarily afraid of criticism from the POUM.

The POUM could envision itself being outlawed. But that will not be the case.[76] The Communists are clamoring for our elimination. They understand that power is still in the streets. That, had we so wanted, we could have seized it, for a time at any rate. Hence their fury.

The Stalinists have not been entirely successful in their plans. And proof came on the morning of the 6th [of May 1937] when, after the order for a return to work had gone out (the POUM was obliged to abide by it, since the word had already gone out from the CNT), the masses pulled back from their battle stations [but], on noting that the ERC and PSUC were out to reap political benefits from this, they went back on the attack. That was the day when the struggle was at its most violent. Cannons were even used. On that day, the Friends of Durruti met with the POUM. The Libertarian Youth insisted that the POUM should attend a meeting with the FAI [Local Committee].

The issue had been starkly posed that day: if a Central Revolutionary Committee could be successfully formed, then maybe the following day the issue of the revolutionary organizations' jointly taking power might have been on the agenda.

However, that afternoon, the CNT's Vázquez, who enjoyed a measure of popularity, had intervened over the radio calling for an end to the fighting. It was plain to see that there was movement toward ending the turmoil. A pullback was imposed.

Today, though, it is clear that, by winning over the CNT's rank-and-file, the POUM can become the Center of the Revolution.[77]

There was a betrayal on the part of the CNT. But, tactically, we must be cautious about making that criticism, lest we are left isolated.[78] Had the heads of the CNT come under frontal attack, the CNT's grassroots would have come

---

76　On 16 June 1937, the POUM was outlawed, its EC arrested and its members persecuted. Andrés Nin was abducted, tortured, and eventually murdered around 24 June. The EC was put on trial for treason.

77　And how might this happen? The sentence reads like a forlorn aspiration. Regarding his mention of "today," Gorkín's report is undated, but must date from late May or early June 1937.

78　Now this is straightforward "coattailing" tactics. In any case, revolutionaries are duty-bound not to shy away from denouncing such betrayal, if this analysis is of any relevance at all.

unanimously to their defense. The POUM will explain that it is not after hegemony in terms of revolutionary power, but instead is out to wield it in partnership with the other revolutionary organizations: Committees for Defense of the Revolution, Workers' Revolutionary Front. These Committees for Defense of the Revolution must be formed, now, in every barrio, factory and locality. They can be turned from defensive organs into organs of power. By our reckoning, it would be sectarian to believe that such organs of power have to be created prior to the taking of power. Those organs can be set up immediately after it....

The POUM's congress has been scheduled for 19 July.

The International Conference is to meet on 19 July.[79]

---

79   The POUM was outlawed on 16 June, so neither that POUM congress nor the International Conference ever went ahead.

APPENDIX G
The May Events at La Batalla (Notes by Molins i Fábrega)

{"The May Events at *La Batalla*" (Notes by Molins) [FPI-AC2-182-17]. Translation from the Catalan original.}

On the day the May Events erupted, I received word from the EC saying that we were to go for talks with the CNT Committee and FAI at sunset.[80]

Nin, Andrade, Gorkín, and I think Bonet as well, turned up at *La Batalla* at around eight or nine o'clock that evening and off we went together to hold the talks. I don't remember who was there for the CNT but I do know that we met up at the Fomento de Trabajo on the Vía Layetana.[81]

We put our views regarding the incidents to the CNT leaders and proposed a political solution to them. We told them that, as we saw it, if the movements stayed an armed insurrection, it would finish up being overwhelmed by the government forces, but that, as long as the workers stayed on the streets and on the offensive, we needed to come up with some sort of a solution for them, one that would be to the advantage of the Revolution.

The CNT guys replied that it would all be over that same night since they had ordered the workers to withdraw from the barricades and return to work....

After the exchange, I headed back to *La Batalla*. It was pretty calm that night and until noon the following day. That morning—day two of the events—*La Batalla* found itself completely hemmed in. Facing us, separated by a street not more than six meters wide—the Calle Banys Nous—was the police station—the one that had been set up at the beginning of the civil war on the former premises of the Institut Catalá de Sant Isidre. The police had taken over the entire Calle de Banys Nous. On the Calle de la Paja side, some Estat Catalá forces were barracked, and, further down, in the Plaza Nova, were the *mossos d'esquadra*. In the Calle del Pino…there was an Estat Catalá local. On the other side of the Calle de Banys Nous—on the Boqueria and Calle de Call side—there were policemen and Estat Catalá members. Around midmorning, we began negotiations with the police station—at their request—and came to a sort of a nonaggression pact. In return, they offered us "coupons" that we could use to buy food from an imported goods store right there on the Calle de Banys Nous. Speaking for

---

80 3 May 1937.
81 Ever since 21 July 1936 the building had been known as the Casa CNT-FAI. The Casa CNT-FAI comprised two adjoining buildings, the former Fomento de Trabajo and the Casa Cambó.

ourselves, coming to an accommodation was not hard. Virtually the entire guard on *La Batalla* had been done away with some time ago and all that remained was two militia members with rifles. That was all the weapons we had, nor did we have any munitions beyond three or four pistols with one or two clips. There was no one on the premises save for five or six of the newspaper staff and two or three members of the editorial team. As a precaution, we put up a barricade on the first landing of the staircase to make it look as if we had access to more weapons. Which is what the Estat Catalá people and policemen must have believed when they refrained from attacking us and offered a non-aggression pact.

At mid-morning the same day, Nin rang me on the telephone from the Executive Committee's place, to tell me to go there to attend meetings. I tried, but it was impossible. The government [Generalidad] forces that were occupying the far end of the Calle de Banys Nous near the Boquería and Calle de Call recognized me and said that I was free to get out that way, if I wished, but warned me that they would not accept the responsibility if I was to be killed by "your guys, shooting from the other side of the street." To be sure, that was a danger, but I was more afraid of their shooting me in the back once I made a move to cross to the other side.

That night—around eleven o'clock—a pretty forceful attack was made on the police station in the Plaza del Pino. We made ready to attack the station from the rear, provided that our guys could make enough ground and enter from the front, although there was little we could do with the weapons we had. After a little while, the attack died down and nothing happened. Later I found out that the attack had not been an attack at all but a brush between some patrols of ours and a scouting patrol from the station. As those who played a part in the Events—and as is the tradition in streetfighting in Barcelona—a truce was arranged on the morning of the following day, during which one could move around the streets relatively freely, if one was lucky enough not to be recognized by enemy patrols. I used this time to slip away from *La Batalla* and went off to meet with the EC in the Plaza del Teatro. I was able to get through by showing the government patrols my Generalidad official's card. As for the guys on the other side, luckily, they recognized me and nothing happened.

La Batalla was unable to appear for some days, due to the Executive Committee's being under siege, so it was ordered that an alternative edition be produced at the Nuñez printworks on the Calle San Ramón, on a flat-bed press. The editorial staff met up there under Gorkín's leadership....

For those few days, the *La Batalla* printed in the Calle de San Ramón became the organ of the insurgent workers. *La Batalla* was being read on the barricades and in the working-class barrios and they were burning *Solidaridad Obrera*, which was toeing the line of the unconditional peace policy peddled by the CNT leaders: García Oliver, Vázquez, et cetera, who were speaking over the airwaves with the Generalidad government's acquiescence.

Especially in Sants, Hostafrancs, and Gracia, the POUM comrades in the working-class areas came to an arrangement with the CNT and FAI workers, setting up joint Committees—called, if memory serves, Defense of the Revolution Committees, in accordance with a watchword given by the EC in *La Batalla*....

Was there a day when there was almost complete peace, [during] a truce arranged prior to the arrival of the troops from Valencia? My inclination is to believe that there was, although I cannot recall the details. Nin and I were delegated by the Executive Committee to approach the Interior Department to come to some accommodation with Major Herrando, the commanding officer who wore a wig and who is now in Mexico, an employee of the Property Bank.[82]

As we arrived we were insulted by a number of functionaries and civilians, among whom I remember Josep Picó—the gimp with the missing arm—who told me aggressively that we ought to make our way to Montjuich to be shot. Major Herrando was punctilious in his dealings with us.[83] We agreed to a prisoner swap, with no one allowed to retain any captives, the handing over of premises to the local committees and an entitlement to bear arms. This was all that we were able to get at a time when things were already falling apart. We never even tried to come to an accommodation with the CNT because it had made its own arrangements throughout the fighting and without asking for anything in return, and given its commitment through the mouths of its leaders. We pointed out to the major that the PSUC people would not abide by the agreement unless compliance was forced upon them. The major said that he would enforce the agreement against everybody, but what we had anticipated came to pass....

[T]he EC delegated me to parley with the councillor for the interior, the object being to avert a clash with the government forces. I found Señor Artemi Aguadé in his private quarters at the Interior Department and our conversation was short and to the point. [Whereas] I was trying to get him to appreciate our right to defend ourselves against the PSUC's foul attacks, his answer to me was curt and concrete: "*Look, it's going to take a day of bloodletting in Barcelona to*

---

82   This refers to Alberto Arrando Garrido, not Herrando. In July 1936, when he was a major, he headed the Security and Assault Forces in Barcelona. He remained loyal to the republican authorities and made a decisive contribution to the routing of the rebel military in the Catalan capital. By the time of the May Events he was a lieutenant-colonel. Arrando was appointed public order delegate for Barcelona, replacing Colonel Antonio Escobar, who had been wounded. In February 1938, he was put in charge of the Aragon front. He suffered from complete alopecia which gave him an odd appearance as he lost his eyebrows and was totally bald. He wore a wig and drew on some eyebrows so that his face was capable of some sort of expression. At the end of the war he left for exile in Mexico.

83   Again, this is Arrando. See previous note.

finish once and for all with certain things and certain people. I don't care whether today is the day...."

My response was that we had forces at our disposal too and were also prepared to do battle. *"Well then,"* he said *"it's up to you. We can start whenever you like."* To which I said that we had a greater sense of responsibility than he did and that we were not about to play into his hands.

He was able to understand me, as he must have known that we were aware of a plan he had worked out months before with Estat Català and later with the PSUC people, to provoke a civil war, their intention being to finish off the CNT and the POUM.

That plan had fallen into our hands because they had sent it in 1936 to a friend in New York who had sent it on to Nin. At the time, we had not been able to do anything, but they had embarked on making their preparations since we had left the government. We had alerted the CNT to all this on several occasions and had furnished it with the evidence and let it in on the chicanery; which included pulling whole battalions out of frontline communist divisions, back into the rearguard and **turning them immediately into carabineers.**

Those were the forces that initiated the overtures to the May Events, in the shape of the Events in Figueres and Puigcerdá. But the CNT was never willing to listen. They reckoned they were too strong and were not unduly bothered by scruples when they thought about the Stalinists mounting a *pogrom* against POUMists.

APPENDIX H
Josep Rebull article on the May Events

This article by Josep Rebull on the May Events of 1937 is extraordinary. Extraordinary in terms of Josep Rebull's own personality and his critical stance on the POUM leadership. And an extraordinary analysis of the May Events of 1937 in Barcelona, from a revolutionary vantage point. And we say "extraordinary" because:

a.   It registered the **worrying absence** of a revolutionary party from the Spanish revolution.

b.   It represented a rigorous and radical **critique** of the POUM coming from a prominent POUM militant, coming **from inside the party, a part of the runup to the congress debate.**

c.   It asserted that the CNT bureaucracy had showed its counter-revolutionary character in May 1937.

d.   Its conclusion was that **May had been a serious defeat for the proletariat,** that any future insurrection had to grapple with the destruction of the bourgeois state, the counterrevolutionary forces (PSUC and ERC) and at the same time take on the reformist bureaucracies (CNT and UGT).[84] Josep Rebull was the **only** POUMist **to warn of the overriding need to go underground in the wake of the May events** in order to make provision against the predictable repression that was inevitably unleashed on the POUM from 16 July 1937 onwards.

In Rebull's eyes, May 1937 was the predictable onslaught of the counterrevolution (embodied in the PSUC and ERC), a direct consequence of the failure to destroy the bourgeois state and take power back in July 1936. The speed of the encroachments of the counterrevolutionary forces had been made possible thanks to the CNT-FAI's collaboration with bourgeois institutions and the absence of a revolutionary party. In May 1937, the proletariat spontaneously bridled at the seizure of the Telephone Exchange, erecting barricades all over Barcelona. But leadership, coordination, and political goals were missing from the battle they launched. The CNT bureaucracy could only come up with one

---

84   The POUM leaders, by contrast, came to refer to it as a victory for the workers.

firm decision: **unconditional withdrawal**, which Rebull had no hesitation in describing as a BETRAYAL of the workers' movement and a CAPITULATION without parallel to the bourgeoisie. Rebull also noted that the POUM leadership had lagged behind events throughout and that **the Friends of Durruti alone deserved kudos for having called for a fight AGAINST the Generalidad.**

Rebull described the May insurrection as an unmitigated defeat for the proletariat, even though the seizure of power might have been feasible had the fight been pursued with determination by a revolutionary party, of which there was none…because the POUM not only did not fit the bill but could not ever have done so with the political strategy followed by the existing leadership of that party.

"The May Events"[85]

[Endorsed by Cell 72, District V][86]

(After publication of the political Counterthesis of Cell 72, District V, Barcelona, the May events were triggered. Cell 72 offers this addendum, now part and parcel of its Counterthesis).

Background

The second power having faded away as an organized entity, which is to say, the organs generated in July in opposition to the bourgeois government now gone, the counterrevolution, represented these days by the petit-bourgeois and reformist parties, have successively attacked—initially warily and later aggressively—the proletariat's revolutionary positions, mainly in Catalonia, it being the region where the revolution had had the greatest momentum behind it.

The potential of the working class was partly stymied by such attacks; on the one hand by the counterrevolutionary dictatorship of the leaders of the

---

85   There are two versions of Josep Rebull's text. The first was published in the *Boletín del Comité Local del POUM* and was dated 19 May 1937. The second appeared in the *Boletín de discusión editado por el Comité de Defensa del Congreso [de POUM]* Paris, 1 July 1939. Where something has been added, this is shown inside square brackets like these […]. The most relevant amendments have been pointed out in the footnotes. What few contributions have been made by the compiler of this book appear inside curly brackets like these {…}.

86   *Boletín Interior. Órgano de discusión para el II congreso del Comité Local de Barcelona del Partido Obrero de Unificación Marxista*, no. 2, Barcelona, 29 May 1937.

UGT in Catalonia and, on the other, through the CNT's partnership with the bourgeois governments in Valencia and Barcelona.

That handicap notwithstanding, the proletariat—parting company from its reformist leaders who were collaborating with the bourgeoisie—had been coming around to the view that only its vigorous action on the streets could head off the advance of the counterrevolution.[87] The armed clashes that occurred in several locations in Catalonia over the month of April were the overture to the May Events in Barcelona.

In broad terms, the fight was posed (and still is) between revolution and counterrevolution, in the following circumstances, as far as Catalonia goes:

The CNT-FAI and POUM revolutionary sectors could call upon the bulk of the proletariat in arms, but, ever since last July, they lacked hard and fast goals and effective tactics. As a result, the revolution lost the initiative.

The PSUC-Esquerra counterrevolutionary sectors, while lacking such a broad base—and having had virtually none back in July—have, right from the outset, been going after well-defined goals and employing appropriate tactics. Whereas the CNT—the decisive force in terms of numbers—has been getting tangled up in the labyrinth of bourgeois institutions, while at the same time talking about nobility and loyalty in dealings, its adversaries and partners have been painstakingly making their preparations and pursuing a whole, phased plan of provocation and defamation, phase one of which was the elimination of the POUM. Prior to these attacks—which initially were mounted in disguised fashion and later, after their cover was blown, in brazen fashion—both the POUM and the CNT leadership were off balance, so they have allowed the counterrevolution to seize the initiative.

These were the circumstances in which the May Events came about.

The Struggle

The fighting begun on [Monday] 3 May was provoked, piecemeal, by the reactionary PSUC-Esquerra forces when they tried to take over the Telephone Exchange in Barcelona. The most revolutionary portion of the proletariat replied to the provocation by taking possession of the streets and digging in. The strike spread like a trail of gunpowder and covered absolutely everywhere.

Even though it was headless to begin with, the movement cannot in any way be described as a "putsch." It can be stated that virtually all the arms in the

---

87   In the 1939 text, the English word "handicap" was replaced by the Spanish word "*desventaja*" (disadvantage).

workers' possession were present on the barricades. During its first two days, the movement was greeted sympathetically by the broader working class—the scale, speed, and unanimous support for the strike being proof of this—and it left the middle class in a condition of expectant neutrality, terror being one factor in this, of course. The workers mustered all their fighting spirit and enthusiasm, until they realized that there was no proper coordination and ultimate goal behind the upheaval, at which point hesitancy and demoralization set in among a range of fighters. Only in terms of such psychological factors can we understand why, in defiance of their leaders' orders, the workers themselves stopped just a few meters short of the Generalidad Palace itself.

On the side of the government there was only a part of the forces of Public Order, the Stalinists, Estat Català, the Esquerra—with these latter forces showing little stomach for the fight. Some Public Order companies declared themselves neutral; they refused to fight the workers, and others let themselves be disarmed. The Control Patrols were, the overwhelming majority of them, on the proletariat's side.

There was no central leadership or coordination on the part of the revolutionary organizations. However, the city was so much under the control of the proletariat that, from Tuesday on, liaison between the different working-class strongholds was perfectly achievable. Only the odd one was cut off; but a concerted onslaught on the government strongholds was all that it would have taken to ensure that, at no great effort, the city was brought completely under the power of the workers.[88]

As a rule, the fighting was marked by expectancy on both sides. The government forces because they did not have the manpower to seize the initiative. The worker forces because they lacked leadership and goals.

Outside the city, but liable to join in the fighting at any point, there were the frontline forces who were ready to swoop on the city—forces in the revolutionary camp who had already made a start by blocking the path of the Karl Marx Division—and those forces the Valencia government had dispatched, and it was none too certain that these would make it through. From Wednesday on, a number of French and English ships were moored off Barcelona, probably ready to step in.

For four and a half days—from the Monday through to the Friday—the proletarian forces were masters of the streets. The CNT bodies reckoned the movement lasted one day—the Tuesday. The POUM bodies thought that it

---

88   {Note no. 1 by Rebull, which was removed from the version published in 1939}: Cell 72 has a plan of Barcelona showing the barricades and positions of both sides during the fighting. It makes for very interesting reading. It is accessible to all comrades.

lasted three days. Which is to say, each of them regarded its respective order to pull back as the end to the upheaval. But in actual fact, the workers pulled back AFTER those orders went out, for want of any leadership to point them toward a progressive way out and, above all, in light of the betrayal by the CNT leadership; some in the form of actual radio broadcasts; others through their collaboration with Companys, as the latter himself put it: "The government had little in the way of defensive resources and not because it had not anticipated this, but because it could do little to remedy it. In spite of which, it unhesitatingly contained the subversives, using only those forces and assisted by the people's enthusiasm and the *talks opened with different trade union delegates* in the Generalidad and, with the aid of some delegates from Valencia, bringing about a return to normality." (*Hoja Oficial*, 17 May).

Such, in broad outline, were the May Events.

The CNT's Leaders

The proletariat went into that movement in a spontaneous, instinctive fashion, without any solid leadership, and with no concrete goal to be resolutely pursued. By failing to explain clearly to the working class what the incidents in April meant, the CNT-FAI leadership had left the incipient movement headless.

At the outset, not all of the CNT leaders were against the upheaval. The Barcelona local committees not only backed it but tried to coordinate it in military terms. But there was no way of doing that without first having goals of a political type to be achieved. The dithering and hesitancy of those committees translated in practice into a series of ambiguous and wrongheaded instructions, halfway between what the rank-and-file wanted and the higher committees' capitulation.

The latter—the National and Regional Committees—had but one staunch decision to offer: a pullback. That withdrawal, ordered without conditions, without securing control of Public Order, without the reassurance of Security battalions, without any de facto workers' front agencies and without a satisfactory explanation given to the working class, lumping all the fighting personnel—the revolutionary and the counterrevolutionary alike—together in the same basket, stands as one of the greatest capitulations to the bourgeoisie and an act of betrayal of the workers' movement.

It will not be long before the leaders and the led will be paying a heavy price, unless the Workers' Revolutionary Front becomes a reality.[89]

---

89 {The distinction that Josep Rebull is making here between the Barcelona local committees and the national and regional higher committees is an interesting one.}

The POUM Leadership

In keeping with its policy line since 19 July, the POUM leadership lagged behind developments. As these happened, our leaders would subscribe to them, even though they had no hand, act, or part in calling for the movement, nor in how it was subsequently channeled. The—belated and hard to disseminate—call for defense committees without a word said about how such Committees were in confrontation with bourgeois governments, cannot be deemed as such channeling.

From a practical viewpoint, all the credit for the activity belongs to the lower committees and party grassroots. The leadership published not a single manifesto, not one leaflet during the early days, to offer the proletariat-in-arms any guidance.

When—like those who were fighting on the barricades—our comrades in the leadership realized that the movement was not actually in pursuit of any ultimate object, the pullback order went out.[90] After events had run their course, without any decision to lead it from the outset and in face of the capitulation of the CNT leaders, the withdrawal order was plainly designed to prevent carnage.

Despite this lack of guidance from our leaders, the reaction is depicting them as the leaders, the driving force behind the upheaval. This does them a quite undeserved honor, even if they reject it and insist that it is a calumny.[91]

The Popular Front

As far as all who believed in the Popular Front as the working class's salvation are concerned, this uprising has been highly instructive. An upheaval provoked by the component parts of the PF itself and their deployment to bolster the bourgeoisie's machinery of repression, stand as the most emphatic proof that the PF is a counterrevolutionary front that, by thwarting the

---

90 ["As the workers fighting on the streets lacked concrete goals and a responsible leadership, the POUM could not help but order and coordinate a strategic withdrawal" (CC resolution regarding the May Events, Point 3).] {This note did not appear in the 1937 version.}

91 ["On the part of certain domestic and foreign newspapers, the most extraordinary efforts have been made—and they were needed—to depict us as 'agents provocateurs' of the incidents that occurred last week in Barcelona. Had we issued the order to launch the rising on the 3rd, there would be no reason for us to disguise the fact. We have always stood by what we say and what we do. What our party did—and we have stated this several times and reiterate it today simply—was join in. The workers were on the streets and our party needed to be alongside the workers." (*La Batalla* editorial, 11 May 1937.)] {Note not included in the 1937 version.}

crushing of capitalism—the root cause of fascism—paves the way for the latter, while on the other hand coming down hard on any attempt to carry the revolution forwards.

The CNT, apolitical prior to 19 July, fell—as it stepped into the political arena—into the Popular Front's trap and that unfortunate experience is going to cost fresh rivers of proletarian blood.

As to the POUM's political standpoint prior to 19 July, this brutal parting of the ways from the PF represents a political triumph, in that it had foreseen and issued forewarnings about it.

As for Stalinism, for the first time it has been unmasked openly as the enemy of the proletarian revolution, having stood on the far side of the barricades, fighting against the revolutionary workers and on behalf of the PF bourgeoisie, of which Stalinism is the creator and chief protector.

[In the] future, the working class can no longer entertain any doubts as to the role set aside for the PF in each country.

The Danger of Intervention

The fear in certain quarters, during the May upheaval, of the danger of armed intervention on the part of England and France is indicative of a lack of understanding of the role played by those powers to date.

Anglo-French intervention against the Spanish proletarian revolution has been underway for the past several months, in a more or less covert manner. Such intervention consists of the sway that those imperialisms wield, through Stalinism, over the Valencia and Barcelona governments; it consists of the recent struggle—again with Stalinism the vessel—inside the Valencia government, a struggle that ended with Largo Caballero and the CNT being eliminated and, lastly, it consists of the "Non-Intervention" agreements that are only enforced when there is a chance of their favoring the Spanish proletariat. Overt intervention by sending in warships and occupation troops would merely be a change in the form of the intervention. Overt or covert, that intervention will have to be beaten or it will be beating us.

Just like any other workers' revolution, ours not only needs and will have the need to eliminate our home-grown exploiters, but will also, ineluctably, be required to fight to defeat all attempts at intervention by international capitalism. There can be no victorious revolution unless that aspect of the war is tackled and overcome. Trying to sidestep it is tantamount to giving up on victory, as the imperialist will never voluntarily give up on meddling in our revolution.

Fair international policy on the part of Spanish revolutionaries can rouse and win over to our side the proletariat in those countries that are out to mobilize it against the Spanish proletariat and may even turn it against its own governments. That was the example set by the 1917 Russian revolution.

Discussing the Uprising

The uprising having come about spontaneously, there are two main positions that might be adopted regarding its progress [we are disregarding any inhibition of it]:

a) Looking at it as a protest revolt, in which case a brief term should quickly have been placed on it and appropriate steps taken to avoid pointless sacrifices. In July 1917, the Bolshevik leaders strove to stem the proletariat's premature rising in the city and this did their prestige no harm at all, as they were able to justify the decision made.

b) Looking at the rising as vital for the conquest of power, in which case the POUM, as the only revolutionary Marxist party, ought to have placed itself resolutely, firmly, and unshakably at the head of the rising so as to coordinate and direct it. Of course, to do that, it was not enough just to hope to accidentally find itself crowned as the High Command of the revolution, but rather it needed act swiftly, broaden the battlefront, extending it to the whole of Catalonia, bluntly proclaiming that the rising was directed at the reformist government and making it clear, right from the outset, that the defense committees and their Central Committee should be formed without delay and establishing these, come what may, as organs of power IN OPPOSITION TO THE GENERALIDAD GOVERNMENT and unhesitatingly attacking strategic positions, capitalizing upon the bewilderment and panic by which our adversaries were beset.

But if the Party leadership's obvious fear of confronting the CNT leaders right from the outset—later was too late—is an instance of an inhibition that cost the party dear, which is to say running counter to the initial measures adopted once the rising had erupted and counter to the POUM's political independence, the potential excuse, that the party was in no position to assume the mantle of leadership, is no loss counter to its interests, since the POUM is only going to be able to assume the role of a real Bolshevik party by assuming such leadership rather than "modestly" declining to offer determined guidance to the working class's movements. Being on the side of the struggling workers is not enough for the party to style itself "revolutionary"; it needs to act as their vanguard.

But for its dithering, but for its waiting yet again to find out what the *treintista* personnel in the CNT leadership thought, the POUM, even in the event of defeat, persecution, and being placed outside the law, would have emerged from the fray enormously strengthened.

The only group that did try to play a vanguard role was the Friends of Durruti Group, which, without espousing entirely Marxist slogans, did and does have the incontestable merit of having proclaimed that they were fighting—and urging others to fight—AGAINST THE GENERALIDAD GOVERNMENT.

The short-term outcomes of this workers' insurrection add up to a defeat for the working class and a fresh victory for the pseudo-democratic bourgeoisie.[92] But a more effective and more practical performance by our party's leadership might have scored at least a partial victory for the workers. At worst, a Central Defense Committee might have been built on the basis of representatives from the barricades. But that would have taken, first, a meeting of delegates from every POUM barricade and the odd CNT-FAI barricade, in order to appoint a Provisional Central Committee. By means of a little manifesto, that Provisional Committee might then have summoned a second meeting, sending invitations out to delegations from groups not represented at the first meeting, and a central defense body formed. In the event of its advocating for a pullback also, it would have been possible to sustain the Central Defense Committee as an embryonic agency of dual power, which is to say, as a Provisional Workers' Revolutionary Front Committee that, being democratized through the creation of defense committees in the workplaces and barracks, might have been able to carry on the struggle against bourgeois governments more advantageously than at present.[93]

But we cannot exclude the possibility of an infinitely more beneficial variation. With the Central Defense Committee up and running along the lines indicated, it might well have proved possible to seize political power. Demoralized and surrounded in the city center, the bourgeois forces might have been defeated in a swift, organized offensive.

Naturally, such proletarian power in Barcelona would have had repercussions across Catalonia and many other places in Spain. All the forces of domestic and international capitalism would have rallied to destroy it. Its destruction, would have been inevitable, of course, unless it was immediately bolstered by the following means: a) the POUM's prompt decision to act as

92   {Note added by Rebull in 1939} [In ordering a withdrawal, the POUM leadership took the contrary interpretation, that victory belonged to the workers. A bloody repression came as the epilogue to that "workers' victory."]

93   {Note included in the first text published in 1937} [Over the afternoon of the Tuesday, this coordination was worked on in the L{ocal} C{ommittee}, but the leadership lacked the enthusiasm to see it through.]

a revolutionary Marxist vanguard, capable of steering and leading the new power in concert with the other sectors active within the insurrection; b) the organization of this new power upon the basis of appropriately centralized workers', peasants', and combatants' councils; c) the spread of the revolution to the whole of Spain by means of a lightning offensive in Aragon; d) solidarity from workers in other countries. In the absence of these conditions, the Catalan working class could not have retained power for long.

By way of conclusion to this section, let us say that the hypotheses formulated here are designed to bring data to the broader debate that the May Events are fated to inspire in revolutionary quarters for a long time to come.

CONCLUSIONS

The working class remains on the defensive in circumstances that are worse than before the May insurrection. It could have launched its offensive in May, had betrayal and capitulation not brought about a partial defeat, though not [yet] a final defeat of the present Revolution. The workers are better armed than before the May events and, if they avoid being dragged into a premature conflict due to provocation, they may yet find themselves once more in a position to go on the offensive after a few months.

The failure to take power back in July led to a second insurrection in May. The defeat suffered then makes a further armed struggle for which we must prepare ourselves inevitable. Until such time as the bourgeois state is overthrown, and our revolutionary struggle should be directed against it, the proletariat's armed insurrection remains a prospect for the future.

The May uprising has demonstrated the true role of the anarcho-syndicalist leaders. Like all reformists at all times, they have been—knowingly or otherwise—the enemy class's instruments within the ranks of the workers. The revolution in our country is only going to be able to succeed by means of simultaneous struggle against the bourgeoisie and against the reformist leaders of every hue, including the CNT-FAI.

We have seen that in our revolution there is no genuine Marxist vanguard party in existence and that this essential instrument of final victory remains to be forged. The party of revolution cannot have a leadership that dithers and is forever waiting for things to happen; it needs to be a leadership firmly convinced that it must precede the working class and guide push it, and win with it.[94] It cannot make its stand only on the basis of *faits accomplis*, but

---

94   {Josep Rebull notes that the POUM is not a revolutionary party and will never manage to become one by sticking to the political strategy of its present EC.}

must have a revolutionary political line underpinning its actions and pre-empting opportunistic adaptations and capitulations.[95] Its action cannot be based on empiricism and improvisation, but must make advantageous use of modern technology and organization. It cannot allow even the slightest carelessness at the top because these resonate painfully and are magnified at grassroots levels, planting the seeds of indiscipline, lack of selflessness, and, among the weakest, a loss of belief in the triumph of proletarian revolution.

We have seen yet another proof of the inescapable need for a Workers' Rev-olutionary Front, which can only be founded upon a thoroughgoing struggle against the bourgeoisie and its state, at the same time as a fight against fas-cism in the front lines. Unless the leaderships of the revolutionary workers' organizations embrace such foundations[96]—and this is certainly at odds with their performance since July—the pressure from below is going to have to create them.

None of the lessons learnt can be of any use unless the proletariat, and above all the revolutionary Marxist Party, commits to intense practical agita-tional and organizational effort. The final struggle against the threats and re-strictions of clandestinity itself calls for unrelenting activity, unless we want to be crushed beyond all recovery. The view that the Party is not going to be forced underground can only be construed as testing the waters for a fresh adaptation and a further renunciation of the revolutionary struggle in these quite possibly crucial moments.[97]

Cell 72, District V

---

95   {A direct criticism of the POUM's EC.}

96   {Note added by Rebull in 1939} [Foundations that make up part of the political Counter-thesis we mentioned at the outset.]

97   {Note added by Rebull in 1939} [Indeed, the leadership failed to take the requisite steps regarding illegal work and clandestine organization. Unfortunately, those very same lead-ers were, as we have seen, the first victims of such lack of foresight.] {This is the only instance of a POUM leader issuing a warning about the imminence of a crackdown on revolutionaries and, thus, of the pressing need to make ready to go underground, which came to pass from 16 June onwards, with the outlawing of the POUM, the arrest of its leaders, the kidnapping and murder of Nin, and the persecution of its membership.}

APPENDIX I
Testimony of Severino Campos and Matías Suñer Vidal[98]

Julián Merino's Leadership of the May Insurrection and the Formation of the CNT Revolutionary Committee

A) Severino Campos's Testimony:

[T]he undersigned [Severino Campos] was secretary of the Catalan [Regional] Federation of Anarchist groups. I had to engage widely with this conflict in performance of the duties I had taken on.

On the 3rd, when the incidents occurred and in light of the way things were shaping up, telephone calls starting coming to us from the various wards around Barcelona; they agreed "as to what was going on and what we had to do."[99] In the [FAI Regional] Committee secretariat, there were Serapio Pérez, Gabaldá, Eusebio Magriñá, and myself. We monitored how things were going and issued warnings to the effect that precautions needed to be taken. In light of these circumstances, we chose to involve comrade [Valerio] Mas, at that point secretary of the CNT's Catalan Regional. After consultation, we agreed on a joint meeting, attended by personnel holding no posts in any of the three libertarian branches.

Having analyzed the situation, we could see that it was serious. Which is why, as a temporary and first step, a Commission was set up to collate information; it was made up of José Xena, Lunazzi, and myself. We were in permanent communication with the wards around Barcelona, and at the same time kept the various committees from our libertarian homestead up to date.[100] The violence was on the increase and by the 4th, the situation was a lot more complicated. By late that night and without prior notice, Gregorio Jover showed up on our premises, fresh from the front, accompanied by five of his trusted confidants. We held a meeting with what comrades we managed to alert; the comrades who had come from the front asked us to inform them about what was going on, which we did in as

---

98 Severino Campos, "Ideas and Men. Objections to the Foreword to a Book," *Le Combat syndicaliste*, 23 December 1978, 6; César M Lorenzo, *Le movement anarchiste en Espagne. Pouvoir et révolution sociale.* (Saint-Georges-d'Oléron: Les Éditions Libertaires, 2006), 347. Translated from the French.

99 This fits with Sara Berenguer's testimony with regard to the importance of telephone links between the various barrio defense committees when it came to mobilizing. See Berenguer, *Entre el sol y la tormenta* (Calella: Seuba Ediciones, 1988), 88.

100 He meant the Casa CNT-FAI.

much detail as was required.[101] They proposed to return in strength to sort out the communists and, after weighing that suggestion, we came to the conclusion that it was neither necessary nor wise to go to those lengths.

On the 5th, Barcelona was in a frightful state. We found out that libertarians were being arrested on the streets and in their own homes; that many of them, taken to La Pedrera, were being murdered under a prior arrangement [... and] that whenever he set foot outside the door to the Control Patrols offices, a burst of machinegun fire from the communists in the Hotel Colón had killed Domingo Ascaso.

By afternoon that same day and as night was falling, Julián Merino, the then secretary of the Local Federation of [Anarchist] Groups summoned a general meeting.[102] It drew a wide attendance. Among those attending was Aurelio Fernández, with the Ruano brothers in tow. Everybody was beside himself. The overwhelming feeling was that it was time "for an all-out attack, come what might." As a result of all this, the decision was made to form two commissions, one to operate in the Center, the other on the Paralelo, near the Plaza de España.

The commission that had to get to the Paralelo had its work cut out just getting out the door of the Casa CNT-FAI. From one corner of the Bank facing us and from on top of that building, we were under machinegun fire.[103] In light of this, the elder of the Ruanos asked whether we were in a hurry to get out of where we were and when we stated that we were, he asked to be provided with some hand bombs. With masterly expertise (which he also deployed against fellow libertarians in the front lines, among others),[104] he forced a passage using the bombs and got the commission through to where it needed to go.

In any event, there had never been so much debate within the CNT and FAI about whether we needed to take power.

B) Page 347 of César Martínez Lorenzo's book:

These defense committees had been tipped off by Manuel Escorza who, thanks

---

101   That RC meeting, attended by Gregorio Jover, was held on 5 May, not 4 May.

102   It was actually on the morning of the day before (4 May).

103   Banco de España back then. Later it became the headquarters of the Caixa de Catalunya.

104   This is a reference to Ruano's criminal conduct on the Aragon front. See Agustín Guillamón, *La Guerra del pan: Hambre y violencia en la Barcelona revolucionaria. de diciembre de 1936 a mayo de 1937* (Barcelona: Descontrol, 2014), entries for 18 December 1936 and 27 January 1937. For a biography of Lucio Ruano, see Antoine Gimenez and Les Giménologues *Les Fils de la Nuit* (Montreuil: L'Insomniaque, 2006), 493–503 and passim. Published in English as *The Sons of Night: Antoine Gimenez's Memories of the War in Spain* (Chico, CA: AK Press, 2019).

to his network of informants, knew that a counterrevolutionary coup de force was imminent....

Matías Suñer Vidal (body mechanic and welder, born in Nonaspe in 1915, and a militia member with the Control Patrols): "I was a fanatical *faísta*, and even though I had no contact with the Friends of Durruti, I wanted to finish off the communists. I followed the guidelines from the secret Revolutionary Committee—made up of Julián Merino, Lucio Ruano, and Sergeant Manzana—who were directing the military operations against the PSUC.

C) Conclusions

Matías Suñer Vidal's evidence about the existence of a secret CNT revolutionary committee in May 1937, a committee made up of Julián Merino, Luco Ruano, and Sergeant Manzana is conformed and nuanced by Severino Campos's testimony, which affords us an understanding of the part played by each of them: Merino as the insurrection's leader, Ruano as the action man adept in streetfighting, and Manzana as the strategist behind the military defense of the Casa CNT-FAI.[105]

Severino Campos, therefore, refines Suñer's evidence by drawing a clear distinction between the different tasks performed by each member of the committee.

Comparison between the two testimonies from Severino Campos and Matías Suñer Vidal and the minutes of the special meeting of the RC on 4 May 1937, allows us to reach the conclusions that, at that meeting:[106]

1. Merino assumed leadership of the insurrection.

2. A (secret) CRTC revolutionary committee was set up.

3. Two commissions were set up to coordinate and spread the fighting.

---

105   For a similar assessment, see Danny Evans, *Revolution and the State: Anarchism in the Spanish Civil War, 1936–1939* (Chico, CA: AK Press, 2020).
106   Not forgetting the POUM Local Committee's report, reprinted in these appendices.

APPENDIX J
Biography of Julián Merino

Julián Merino Martínez was born on **21 January 1897** in Palacios de la Sierra (Burgos). From 1 November 1919 onwards, he was affiliated to the Marcilla (Navarra) branch of the Sindicato Único of Sugar and Alcohol Workers, to which he paid his dues until April 1920, at which point he switched to paying his dues in Calatorao (Zaragoza). There, within a month, he was signing things as president of the Peasants and Amalgamated Trades Sindicato Único. He stopped paying his dues that October, having been arrested in the station in Marcilla. At the time of arrest, he had on him two trade union membership cards, one from Marcilla and the other from Calatorao, plus some letters and flyers, an address book containing trade union addresses and notes on books sold, dues received, collections made for prisoners, outlay, travel costs, receptions prepared, and the musings of an activist.

For a few months he lived in Zaragoza, working as a sugarworker and was active in the anarcho-syndicalist movement. On **12 May 1921**, armed with a pistol, he was arrested in the Plaza del Mercado in Zaragoza together with Segundo Martínez Fernández, while they were collecting dues for the Sindicato Único.

Having moved away to Catalonia, he was arrested again on **29 August 1922** in the course of a raid on the CNT's Railwaymen's Center in Barcelona, which had been shut down by the authorities. During the Second Republic, he was active in the Maritime Section of the Barcelona CNT's Transport Union and was appointed its secretary.

On **10 March 1932**, from inside the Modelo prison in Barcelona, he signed a manifesto against Ángel Pestaña and *treintista* tactics, as did his comrades Ángel Continente Saura, Jaume Giné, Jaume Riera Arbós, Antonio Rodríguez, Luzbel Ruiz, Fernando Tiscar, José Vernet, and so on.

In **November 1933** he was tried by the Fourth Section of the Barcelona High Court as the author of an article, published by *Solidaridad Obrera* in late May 1932, under the pseudonym "José Bonet," that included an incitement to sedition. The case was eventually dropped.

Julián Merino was the FAI's delegate for the defense committees. Along with the Nosotros group, and Alcodori's group, he had a hand in laying the groundwork for an attempt on the life of Josep Dencás that, in the end, was thwarted.

On **10 January 1934**, he was arrested during a large raid on the La Tranquilidad bar, as the police suspected that a union meeting was under way there. The many people arrested were nearly all CNT members and most of them were tramworkers or employees of the Bus Company, many of whom had been dismissed because of the recent strike.

On **31 August 1935**, he was arrested in the port of Barcelona in connection with his trade union propaganda and organizational activities. In November the same year, he stood trial for unlawful association and incitement to sedition, but once again the charge was dropped.

On **16 July 1936**, two days ahead of the fascist revolt, he led the raid on the ships anchored in the port of Barcelona to seize the weaponry on board.

During the streetfighting on **19 and 20 July 1936**, he had a hand in the operations of the Maritime Section of the Transport Union, alongside Patricio Navarro and Manuel Lecha "*el artillero*," known also as Maeztu.

In July 1936, after the insurrection of the Barcelona workers against the rebellious military and the fascists succeeded, the CNT dockworkers settled old scores with the UGT dockworkers who had prevented them for months from working in the port.

At the **6 October 1936** Special Plenum of the unions of Aragon, attended also by representatives from the columns operating on that front, militia members Julián Merino, Francisco Carreño, and Pablo Ruiz were very active participants in the Bujaraloz Plenum, which promoted the formation of the Regional Defense Council of Aragon.

On **24 October 1936**, at a meeting of the higher committees, Santillán complained of a report furnished to him by Julián Merino from the Marine Transport Union, telling him that, given the chances of Valencia and Catalonia "wanting to declare themselves independent," the central government was commandeering all vessels and moving them to safe loyalist ports.

At an RC meeting on **30 October 1936**, Merino, who had returned from the front lines asking for war materials, explained that his unit was in a bit of a pickle in that it might be surrounded unless it had access to appropriate equipment: several machine guns and three hundred rifles. If his unit was encircled, Barbastro was in jeopardy. The Barcelona Defense Committee offered him three machine guns "until such time as the three hundred rifles could be retrieved from the barracks of those attack dogs that wear Assault Guard or Civil Guard collars." Which is to say that the defense committee was prepared to dip into its own arsenal, as long as its enemy in the rearguard was proportionately weakened. Santillán, with Eroles's assistance, would see to it that he got hold of those rifles "so that the defense committee can honor its pledge."

On **12 February 1937**, the higher committees met—the RCs of the CNT and FAI, the Local Federation of [CNT] Unions and the Libertarian Youth—with Manzana attending on behalf of the Durruti Column. Manzana reported on developments in Gelsa, a sector of the Aragon front where the militia members "will not countenance militarization in any form [and] manifestos to other sectors, explaining [why they do not accept] militarization and the dangers implicit within it." Some eight hundred militia members, led by Pablo Ruiz, had threatened to quit the front, taking their weapons with them, if forced to do so. During the proceedings, some people (such as Federica Montseny) even suggested that they should open fire on the men in Gelsa to force them into accepting militarization. **Merino** heatedly rejected the use of violence "to force some comrades into abiding by something that, to their way of thinking, is an affront to their sensibilities." He rejected the sort of methods that belonged to the monarchist *ancien régime* and complained about the Gelsa comrades' being depicted as criminals, or indeed, "traitors to the Revolution." **Merino** argued that they were conscious anarchist comrades and he imagined that they were intelligent enough not to cling "to the suicidal and fratricidal notion of seeking confrontation with the Manzana Column." Virtually everyone else there turned on Merino "with all manner of abuse," saying that he "was a crackpot who did not know what he was talking about, but was only a windbag and an ignoramus, who was talking about things he knew nothing about."

The minutes of that meeting are explicit enough to make it obvious that their embrace of the ideology of antifascist unity, together with the shelving of their anarchist principles, had prompted most of the members of the higher committees to take reactionary stances, bringing them into conflict with those who still supported ethical and political principles that boiled down to a rejection of militarization of the columns. Most members of the higher committees were coming out with the same repressive response that might have come from any bourgeois government.

On Tuesday **23 March 1937**, the higher committees assembled in the presence of councillors, comarcal delegates, the managing editor of *Solidaridad Obrera*, and the accountable committees.[107] Isgleas spelled out the reasons behind his resignation as defense councillor; the transfer of the PSUC's Karl Marx Column to the Madrid front and the decree setting up the Unified Security Corps. Doménech asked if Isgleas's resignation ought not to be matched by those of the three other CNT councillors and warned "Tonight, over the airwaves, Companys would strive to depict us as the bad boys, to take the heat off himself." Xena and Merino interrupted Doménech, to state that "the Organization's rank-and-file will not allow this puppet to speak ill, nor dole out any beating over the airwaves, because there would be action on the streets in response to any such insolent provocation."

---

107   "Meeting of the responsible committees, councillors, comarcal delegates, and Toryho, held on 23 March 1937, at 12:00 noon" [IISH-CNT-85C1].

From **9 to 11 April 1937**, Merino was present at the talks held in the Presidential Residence in the Generalidad, attended by Barcelona's mayor Carles Pi Sunyer; the speaker of the Parliament Jaume Serra Húnter; Guinart, Galés, and Sauret from the ERC; Valerio Mas, Josep Joan Doménech, Manuel Escorza, Joan Pau Fábregas, Castellote, Alonso, Aurelio Fernández, and Merino himself on behalf of the CNT; Joan Comorera, Antonio Sesé, Rafael Vidiella, Joaquín Almendros, and Frances Durán Rosell on behalf of the UGT; Josep Calvet and Josep Torrents from the Unió de Rabassaires; and Josep Tarradellas and Lluís Companys representing the Generalidad. The aim was to resolve the Generalidad government crisis. In the end, a commitment was given that Aurelio Fernández would be appointed a *conseller*.

At the **12 April 1937** meeting of the Local Federation of Anarchist Groups, which was radicalized by the invitation issued to the Libertarian Youth and the defense committees, there was insistence that all CNT personnel withdraw from any municipal or government post and that the economy be socialized. An insurrectionist committee was set up. A prominent part had been played in this radicalization by **Julián Merino, Pablo Ruiz**, and **Santana Calero**. Pablo Ruiz was one of the founders of the Friends of Durruti, Santana Calero joined the group after the May Events. Even though, for obvious reasons, there is no document in existence identifying the lineup of the insurrectionist committee, that **Julián Merino, Pablo Ruiz**, and **Juan Santana Calero** belonged to it, which they had all championed so enthusiastically, is a likely and very reasonable assumption.

At the meeting of the higher committees on **26 April 1937**, Printing Trades [Union] censured the extremist stance adopted by Merino and the Local Federation of Anarchist Groups at committee gatherings.

The murder of Antonio Martín in Bellver on **27 April 1937** shattered the delicate balance agreed to in the group discussions between the delegations headed by Companys and Escorza during 9 to 11 April and, above all, at the personal meeting between them both on 15 April. Manuel Escorza tipped off the defense committees that he had intelligence regarding a predictable and imminent counterrevolutionary coup de force by the Generalidad and that it would have the backing of the PSUC and the ERC. By placing the barrio committees on a war footing, Manuel Escorza was not only **tacitly giving the go-ahead** from the higher committees but was **lighting the spark** that ignited the insurrection.

On **3 May 1937**, the Assault Guards' attempt to seize the Telephone Exchange at 2:45 p.m. triggered a response in the form of a revolutionary insurrection by the defense committees that, having been prepared and alerted beforehand, coordinated with one another by telephone to come up with their response within two hours; they dominated the working class barrios, threw up barricades in the city center, and called a insurrectionary general strike. **Dionisio Eroles and**

José Asens strove from the outset to curtail the spread of the insurrection and to mediate in order to pacify and ultimately "channel" it. But they failed. The higher committees had been **overwhelmed** by the defense committees.

The special meeting of the RC on **4 May 1937** was called at the instigation of **Julián Merino** who spoke as the **promoter of the insurrection** underway, inviting the RC to assume leadership of it.[108] Two combat teams were formed: one for the city center and another for the Paralelo-Plaza de España, to spread and coordinate the streetfighting. Lucio Ruano played a very active part in breaking through the armed cordon around the Casa CNT-FAI building, allowing the two commissions to leave under cover of handheld bombs tossed at the forces surrounding the building.[109] Later, Lucio Ruano seized control of the cannons on Montjuich, training them on the Palace of the Generalidad, where Abad de Santillán was. Santillán had instructed the Montjuich gunners to open up on the Generalidad Palace if they didn't receive a telephone call from him at half-hourly intervals.

Xena, Jover, and Manzana organized the military defenses of the Casa CNT-FAI, which faced a bit of a tactical dilemma, being completely surrounded by hostile forces. The seizure of the Casal del Metge by foreign anarchist militants, mainly French and Italian, was crucial in breaking through the cordon.

The higher committees (Eroles and Asens) had stepped in right at the start of the insurrection, with the intention of seizing the reins and bringing it to an end, but they had been overwhelmed by the ward defense committees and soon found themselves isolated and bereft of any influence.

The main anarcho-syndicalist leaders and public speakers, Juan García Oliver and Federica Montseny, came up from Valencia to broadcast pacifying speeches over the radio. They were the firefighters who doused the flames.

At the **8 May 1937** meeting of committees at the Casa CNT-FAI, **Merino**, on behalf of the Local Federation of Anarchist Groups, made an evaluation of the May insurrection and gave assurances "that the comrades out in the wards have taken a very DIM VIEW of the Guards and others having been set free." At all times, Merino seemed to be the spokesman for the barrio committees at meetings of the higher committees. As secretary of the Barcelona Local Federation of Anarchist Groups, he had a regular and very fluid relationship with the defense committees in the wards around Barcelona, as befitted his function as the **FAI representative on the Barcelona defense committees**.

---

108 Testimony of Severino Campos. RC meeting of 4 May.

109 Testimony of Matías Suñer Vidal in César M Lorenzo "Libertarian Socialism's Spanish Roots" (in French, unpublished). Correspondence and debate between the author and César M. Lorenzo on this score.

In his memoirs, Juan García Oliver intuitively "accuses" the leadership of the Marine Transport Union—made up of Julián Merino, Patricio Navarro, and "Maeztu"—and most especially Merino, of having been responsible for **starting** the May Events.

At the **19 May 1937** get-together of the higher committees, Merino asked to speak "just to say that he prefers to have his say at the meeting of militants tomorrow, because he wants lots of comrades to have the chance to hear him, as he has an **I Accuse** message to deliver," in which he probably offered his analysis of what led to the defeat of the May 1937 insurrection, pointing the finger at the Organization's own "firefighters."[110]

On Sunday **6 June 1937**, at a special meeting of the higher committees called by the Regional Committee for the purpose of dealing with the issue of the disbanding of the Control Patrols, Merino alluded to the rumors that anybody not handing in his weapon would be prosecuted for thievery, in light of the incidents that had occurred in the Calle del Cardenal Casañas and at the Chicago bar. Asens's response to this was that it was deplorable that anyone should try to heap the blame on him personally. Asens pointed out that it was not only a matter of the Patrols being wound up; there was also "the matter of their weapons and the buildings occupied by the comrades."

Merino persuasively told Asens that there was a need for him, personally, to banish all existing doubts, especially as to whether "you would hand over the names and addresses of those who might refuse to hand in their weapons."

The Regional Committee met on **21 June 1937** together with other higher committees, at the Casa CNT-FAI. Merino reported that "even as he was talking with the delegate for Public Order, at that very moment, an arrest warrant was issued against comrade Gonzalo de Reparaz."[111] The lawyer Barriobero, who was on hand, was unable to get the delegate "to show some respect for our comrade's age" and a house arrest order was imposed, the argument being that "he had to abide by the orders he had received."

Eroles read out a fragment from a talk by Federica Montseny, disclosing the reactionary and Catholic nature of several of the decrees drawn up by Irujo, who "went so far as to propose that Catholics might celebrate Mass." He also read out the report from the commission "that had gone to see the Public Order delegate."

Merino accused Gómez Sáez of having failed to honor the promises made to the CNT and of having released "55 proven fascists and 5 from the Partido

---

110 See the meetings of the higher committees on 18 and 19 May 1937 in Agustín Guillamón, *La represión contra la CNT* (Barcelona: Descontrol, 2015).

111 "Meeting of the Regional Committee for Catalonia, held on 21 Padial [June] 1937. The other responsible Committees were present" [IISH-CNT–39 A]. Gonzalo de Reparaz (1860–1939) was on the editorial staff of *Soli*.

Popular."[112] Gómez Sáez stated that it made no difference to him as "he was unaware of what party they belonged to." Threatened with a hunger strike by the CNT prisoners, he had replied with his usual indifference: "Let them refuse food and if somebody dies, we'll bury him." He had undertaken to release those held in preventive detention (*presos gubernativos*), though he mentioned his fear that there might be "blackguards" among those set free; Merino's response to that was that "there are no blackguards in the CNT."

Gómez denied that there had been any trespasses committed against the CNT and stated that he was not looking for any confrontation with CNT personnel. When Merino replied that if that was the case, then what was happening was that his subordinates were being disobedient to him, Gómez retorted that they were obedient to him in everything. **Laborda** concluded that Gómez was being misled by his subordinates.

A Regional Plenum of the Anarchist Groups of Catalonia was held from **1 to 4 July 1937**.[113] Merino was present as representative of **Cultura y Acción**.[114] He went over at some length "a number of mistakes within the organization," numbering among the gravest of these the mistake of militarization that had been precipitately embraced "without the frontline comrades being consulted." Another serious error was disarmament, something suggested "by a comrade from the Nervio group, albeit on condition that the weaponry of the government institutions should be dispatched to the front."[115] He complained of inactivity on the part of the committees and concluded that the comrades on the RC had not been equal to circumstances. During the afternoon proceedings, Merino insisted that for some time now the FAI's groups had been drifting away from the CNT unions, which accounts for the regional secretary's present dithering stance. He had his doubts about the effectiveness of their present plenum and it seemed to him as if there was a deliberate concern to ensure "that the FAI not arrive at a fixed position on issues of importance. We have taken the wrong path. No one has been willing to set things right and so the enemy has had things his way."

He remarked that the mistakes made were not merely countless but that, as Severino Campos had stated, anarchism was under the sway of "hidden powers" and nobody was preoccupied with setting these mistakes straight. Like others before him, he announced "that the FAI was once the vanguard of the CNT, but,

---

112   Paulino Gómez Sáez took over from Echevarría Novoa early in June 1937 as public order delegate, at the same time as Torres was replaced by Burillo as Chief of Police.

113   FAI Catalonian Regional Federation of Anarchist Groups, "Minutes of the Regional Plenum of Groups held on 1, 2, and 3 July 1937" [IISH-FAI-CP-17B1].

114   J. Merino was a member of that group and had been delegated by it to attend this Plenum on its behalf.

115   The Assault Guards and Civil Guards.

ever since 19 July, it has been lagging behind the Confederation." Nobody was putting a stop to that. There were comrades who had slipped down a path that was not anarchist. The movement had a duty to point out what was happening, but it had not done so. "The RC tells us it couldn't," something that was unacceptable unless it could be shown that there had been no breach of principles.

He recalled how, in Gelsa, vis-à-vis militarization, "there were 800 comrades who rejected it on the basis that the appointment of officers would end the free initiative of the individual."[116] The Organization had resorted to the use of violence against those "conscientious objectors." As a result, "today we have an army with a penal discipline the same as before 19 July. The Organization forced acceptance of militarization and still there were no weapons."[117]

He charged the government with wanting and working toward the destruction of the CNT and the FAI. Catalan anarcho-syndicalism was being denied arms, hard currency, and gold. After General Pozas was sent in, in the wake of the May Events, the arms had arrived: "the comrades were duty-bound to appreciate that Companys, Largo Caballero, and Azaña could not stop being bourgeois."[118]

He went on to add that "in May we were too easy on Aiguader [Aguadé]," to the extent that they had permitted a "moral victory for gentlemen hell bent on sinking our organization." Economic gains had not been consolidated by their ministers in the Valencia government.

He moved, first, that **all who held government posts should step down from them** and return to the unions, and, secondly, that the **FAI strike back against persecution** "forgetting for one moment that the fascists are in Aragon."[119]

The chairman reminded them that the proceedings would go into recess at 7:00 p.m., to attend the unveiling of a plaque in Durruti's honor. Severino Campos was appointed to represent Catalonia's anarchist groups at that ceremony.

Los Mismos expressed the view that the course that anarchism had been on since 19 July had proved a failure. It endorsed "Cultura y Acción's brilliant

---

116   Many of those militia members [led by Pablo Ruiz] who quit the Gelsa front, taking their weapons with them, later took part in the Friends of Durruti Group. But consideration should be given to the fact that incidents and departures from the front were features of many other CNT columns and not exclusive to Gelsa.

117   This reference is to the fact that the rationale for embracing militarization had been the promise that arms would be forthcoming for militarized columns, a promise that was not honored.

118   The weapons were not just to ensure success on the Aragon front, as the Cultura y Acción group argued, but primarily in order for reprisals to be taken against revolutionary personnel.

119   The first was the same resolution that had been passed at the 12 April 1937 gathering of Anarchist Groups, at which Julián Merino, Pablo Ruiz, and Juan Santana Calero had been very active participants.

exposition." It recalled how "the communists murder our comrades on the front and also force them to tear up their membership card." It pronounced that it was high time that things were set straight "since the CNT was obliged to back off in the recent crisis for the sake of its dignity." They had proven incapable of appropriately advising those holding government office and had been shunned by Catalan public opinion. If the RC knew about the communist conspiracy, it should have exposed it and acted in a timely fashion. The collectivizations were being trampled upon and imprisonment and murders countenanced. They had to oppose "folk being disappeared that way."

The discussions had polarized around whether the RC or the groups were to be held to blame for the FAI's loss of standing, dereliction of principles, and the serious mistakes made. Those who held that the RC was to blame showed support for the CNT-FAI withdrawing immediately from official office; those who blamed the groups for their lack of activity and made excuses for the RC proved to be supporters of sticking with CNT collaborationism in the institutions, especially in order to prevent CNT personnel's being swept aside by repression.

There was an out-and-out, irreconcilable ideological gulf emerging between collaborationists and anti-collaborationists. **The contributions made by Julián Merino and by the Cultura y Acción group were telling and they radicalized the debate.**

The Plenum closed by appointing a working party made up of the groups Cultura y Acción (**Merino**), Nervio (Lunazzi), Hispania (Tapia), the Gerona group (Pedro Serra), Amor y Verdad (Viladomiu), Irreductibles (Peirats), and Asturias (F. Alberola), to draw up a consensual resolution on whether the trajectory that the FAI had been on since 19 July needed to be ratified or amended.

On the morning of **10 August 1937**, there was a special meeting of the CNT higher committees, summoned by the RC.[120] The meeting opened with an exhortation from regional secretary Doménech directed to the Transport Union "to desist in its plans to stand up to the Police when the latter tries to search the Union for all available weaponry": for the rest of the unions either to endorse the Transport Union's stance or for Transport to be left to its own devices and isolated by the rest of the unions "and thus find itself outside of the Organization." It was not so much an option as a threat from the regional secretary.

The **secretary of the Transport Union's Junta** (in all likelihood, Merino) responded by saying that it was not the Transport Union that was being provocative

---

120 "Special meeting held on 10 August 1937 by the Regional Committee for Catalonia; in the presence of the following delegates: Printing Trades, Foodworkers, Chemical Products, Transport, Secretary Mas, Light and Power, Eroles, Isgleas, García Oliver, Metalworkers, and the Junta of the Transport Union" [IISH-CNT-39-A2].

but rather "our enemies." And, half in reproach and half in reflection, he went on to say: "we are leaving our gains in tatters. We have lost nearly all of the centers of production we captured in the heat of the revolution. We have surrendered two garages to the police and they have undertaken to pay the staff there; which they have not done and are not doing." He then launched into an endless litany of trespasses and excesses, to finish up declaring that, weary of all this, the CNT's militants had, by a majority, made up their minds to defend themselves while they were still able to do so. The Junta had simply confined itself to implementing those accords. In a long speech, Doménech argued that what needed implementation was long-term "appropriate and dogged activity" rather than some actual, short term, localized confrontation.

Xena complained that, just the day before, the Transport Union "was on standby to stop, by force of arms, the Guards from entering to effect a search and that **the groups and the wards were already in the know about that stance and were also standing by to show solidarity with such ambitious action.**[121] Rather than laying preparations for such defiance, they ought first to have briefed the Liaison Committee about it, as it has the oversight of all such movements, should any be needed."

Xena, then, was complaining that the Liaison Committee, established after the May Events to monitor and prevent any such actions—on the part of the anarchist groups and barrio defense committees in solidarity with the unions—from overruling and overwhelming the higher committees, had not worked. This was a case of a genuine workers' insurrection, triggered by the Transport Union's refusal to submit to a degrading police search. Doménech's threat that they might find themselves out on a limb was merely a bureaucrat's ploy. The fighting solidarity of the barrio defense committees and anarchist groups in Barcelona was immediate and unconditional; and there was every likelihood that the remainder of the CNT unions would follow suit. The Liaison Committee stood exposed as a dike that was not fit for its purpose, that would not stop the higher committees from being overwhelmed again, as they had been in May.

García Oliver delivered a long speech full of intimidation and menaces: "we should always gauge the impact of our words and actions"; people were being shot on the front lines for a lot less. He indirectly described the Transport Union as a traitor: "whoever is behind this unrest is a TRAITOR, and if there are ten people behind it, they are TEN TRAITORS." He threatened that "if we take to the streets and lose, our losing would be THE GREATEST SELLOUT EVER." And he answered his detractors at the meeting: "Those of you who depict us as reformists, note that we are no less revolutionaries than any of you. If things are

---

121   "Groups and wards" refers to the anarchist groups and barrio defense committees.

as comrade Xena has described them, there would definitely be a call for People's Courts TO PUNISH THE HOTHEADS."

He then referred to "what happened with comrade Aurelio Fernández," which struck him as a bit of a mystery. **Merino** asked what was behind the persecution of comrade Aurelio who went to make his statement in the morning and was arrested the same afternoon. García Oliver's reply was that it looked as if "our enemies" were out to break the CNT-UGT pact and he could not see any solution other than the establishment of a Revolutionary Court "to crack down HARD and KNOCK HEADS TOGETHER." In light of the turn the meeting was taking, **Transport** insisted that Xena "produce the evidence for what he said." **Merino**, greatly irked by García Oliver's innuendoes, which were not entered into the minutes, insisted that he clear up a few dubious points, as it seemed he had been involved in the persecution of Aurelio Fernández when, very much to the contrary, "what you want is for nobody to be arrested." The uproar spread and a bitter argument erupted "the final impression being" that the Transport Union did not seem disposed to drop its attitude. Doménech and other CNT leaders were confident that they could talk them round "at the meeting of Juntas scheduled for this afternoon." The proceedings were wound up at 3:15 p.m.

The bureaucratic style was stunning. The higher committees had resources galore with which to control the CNT membership. And it was all done to please and assist the police, so as to allow them to carry out needless, humiliating searches, based on no logic other than bourgeois authority. Instead, Merino and the Transport Union were pushing an insurrectionary revolt.

On **11 September 1937**, all of the unions excepting the Metalworkers Union, attended the **Barcelona Plenum of Unions** that was held over **11 and 12 September 1937**.[122] The platform party having been appointed, the chair asked if there was any need to read out the report submitted by the National Committee (NC), "since the unions are already familiar with it."

Transport had issues with the manner in which the report was passed, that is, vote first and then the debate, as there had been an overwhelming majority in its favor, and argued that they would have to wait for a congress "so that we can discuss how to bring a swift end to the outrages perpetrated against the CNT." It also complained that the report did not tackle "how to stand up to the repression" and it asked if the Local Federation might expand upon the figures given in the NC report. There was then a debate about the political and social line to be adopted.

Transport (Merino?) took the line that forgetfulness regarding "our goal, which is to say, Libertarian Communism, has entailed the loss of much ground,

---

122 "Minutes of the Barcelona Plenum of Unions held on 11 and 12 September 1937" [IISH-CNT38/B3].

to the benefit of the Communist Party, and he indicated that, prior to 19 July, the CNT-FAI had been the only force in Catalonia and, thanks to our readiness to compromise, the Communist Party has gained what it hadn't previously had." He spoke extensively about the period before entering the Generalidad government, and he was dubious about the benefits of collaborationism, which the other delegations were glorifying. He agreed with Construction that the republican parties were itching to end the Communist Party's hegemony. But he disagreed with Construction regarding the respect for the petite bourgeoisie, something heard before at previous plenums, because he believed that petite bourgeoisie ought to get the same treatment as the great bourgeoisie. "So Transport reckons that collaboration should be off the table," because, as one comrade had stated earlier, the CNT was apolitical and "must always act in accordance with our ideals, which is to say, Libertarian Communism."

As to dealings with the UGT, his view was that, in Catalonia, they had to be wary because "there can be no relationship with the Communist Party," since it does nothing but attack us. Same goes for the Socialist Party. As to the republican parties, bourgeois every one of them, they only deserved a hearing "when they come looking for us."

The **Foodworkers Union** took issue with the Transport Union. It stated that the revolution had been a big mistake. The first thing CNT members had to do was to realize that they had to stand firm to win the war. It asked: "Should we collaborate?" and answered in the positive "because that way there will be an increased likelihood of our holding onto our gains." It summed up its stance in a short slogan "Collaborate in a measured and dignified way." Finally, it reckoned, somewhat contradictorily and paradoxically, that "it should be the workers defending the collectives, and not the CNT."

Most of the delegations there seemed to have agreed on the same points: governmental collaboration, with minimal conditions or with a program of protection for social gains, and this as the only means of avoiding the establishment of dictatorial rule, which looked inevitable if the CNT-FAI were to withdraw from political life. Some unions still insisted that social gains be retained, that the prisoners be freed, and even that the CNT receive proportionate representation in government. Whereas a few unions called for united action with the UGT and even for a trade-union-based government of unity, others, more realistic, reckoned that any involvement with the Stalinist UGT was out. Still other unions were prepared to give up on everything, for the sake of antifascist unity and victory over fascism. The unions (with Transport being a notable exception) had therefore given up on the slightest revolutionary aspiration, could not see beyond governmental collaborationism, and were even afraid that a tyrannical regime might be established. By then, the defeat of the revolutionaries was complete and all but final, despite the resistance put up by diehards like the people from the Transport Union.

So between 1937 and 1938, Merino served as secretary of the Barcelona Local Federation of Anarchist Groups and, in July 1937, he attended the Catalan FAI's plenum as the delegate of the Cultura y Acción group.

On 2 April 1938, he took part in the plenum of anarchist groups, union delegates, and members and committees of the CNT-FAI and Iberian Libertarian Youth Federation (FIJL) that was held in Barcelona. As the representative of the CNT-FAI, he joined the Executive Committee of the Spanish Libertarian Movement (MLE) and, the very next day, signed the resolutions of the plenum's working party on behalf of the Barcelona Local Federation of Anarchist Groups.

On 19 January 1939, the FAI appointed him general secretary of the Commission raising volunteer battalions; it had its recruitment office at 11 Calle Pi Margall.

With the fall of Catalonia and the Francoist army occupation, he was obliged to cross the border into France. His name appeared in a list of 279 dangerous anarchists kept under special surveillance by the French police. On 30 May 1940, he reached the Dominican Republic on board the *Cuba*. In the end, he went into final exile in Venezuela where he died in April 1977.

★

Note on Julián Merino

What follows is simply a question, an inkling and an open line of historical investigation, rather that a documented fact: *Was Julián Merino the author of a number of anonymous articles or articles signed with the nom de plume of* Fulmen, *in* El Amigo del Pueblo, *musings upon the reasons for the failure of the revolution in May 1937?*

In Chapter 2 of this book, devoted to the background to May 1937, the close relationship existing between Julián Merino, Pablo Ruiz, and Juan Santana Calero (all of them protagonists of the revolutionary committee set up between 12 and 14 April 1937, as agreed by the Local [Barcelona] Plenum of Anarchist Groups, broadened to include the Libertarian Youth and the defense committees) has been delved into. It is also blatantly obvious that in the streetfighting in May 1937 there was an alliance between the City Center Commission (formed on 4 May 1937 to extend the insurgents' fight), the committee at Los Escolapios, and the Friends of Durruti.

So, the possibility that Merino may have contributed copy to *El Amigo del Pueblo* (the mouthpiece of the Friends of Durruti) is not some far-fetched or startling **hypothesis,** but, rather, the logical consequence of a close ideological, activist, and revolutionary kinship. Whether Merino was ever officially a member of the Friends of Durruti is a formal issue that may well never have been raised, perhaps in order to avoid organizational frictions.

Plainly, the answer to all these questions, assuming that one exists, is still lurking in the archives; we must ferret it out! However, if we are to find answers, we must first frame the appropriate and pertinent questions. Hence this note.

GLOSSARY

A GROUP: Made up of: **Jacinto Toryho**, Jacobo Prince, Abelardo Iglesias Saavedra, Federico Sabaté, Miguel Tardaguila, Palmiro Aranda, Francisco López, Juan Osó, José Jiménez Sánchez, etc.

AGUADÉ, Artemi (The surname is often written as Aiguadé, Aiguader, or Aguader): One of three ERC representatives on the CAMC, along with Jaume Miravitlles and Joan Pons. Following the dissolution of the CAMC, he was appointed councillor for internal security in the first Tarradellas government, chairing the Internal Security Junta, the body charged with managing Public Order and, consequently, with running of the **Control Patrols**. In fact, the establishment of the Security Junta, as a result of the dissolution of the CAMC, institutionalized a duplication of powers in the Public Order arena, between Artemi Aguadé of the ERC on the one side and, on the other, the CNT's Aurelio Fernández, who held the position of Control Patrols Secretary. Frictions between Aguadé and Aurelio were constant and increasing. In May 1937, Aguadé ordered Rodríguez Salas to seize the Telephone Exchange. He had the backing of **Comorera** and Vidiella from the **PSUC**, out to oust the anarchists from the government. The CNT called repeatedly for Aguadé's and Rodríguez Salas's resignations, but Companys's dogged refusal dragged out the streetfighting unnecessarily. The upshot was that the **Generalidad government** was stripped of all its Public Order responsibilities. In 1939, he left for exile in France, living in Paris until the German Occupation. In 1941 he secured passage to Mexico.

ALCÓN, Marcos: Anarchist, active in the Glassworkers Union. He took part in the CAMC, taking over from Durruti when the latter marched off to the front, and was in charge of War Transport. In 1937, the defense committees asked him to take over the general secretaryship of the CNT. He went into exile in Mexico where he was closely associated with Katia Landau and became a leading member of the group publishing *Tierra y Libertad*.

ANTIFASCIST UNITY: The absence of any organization, vanguard, or platform capable of championing the historic program of the proletariat was crucial, as it enabled and encouraged all the workers' organizations to embrace the bourgeois program of antifascist unity (the sacred union between the working class and the republican, democratic bourgeoisie), with the sole purpose of winning the war on fascism. The revolutionary vanguards that did crop up, like the Friends of Durruti, the left of the POUM (Rebull), a few anarchist groups from the Barcelona Local Federation, the Libertarian Youth of Catalonia, or the SBLE (Munis), did so belatedly and badly, and were crushed in the first moments of their attempt to offer a revolutionary alternative capable of breaking away from the bourgeois "fascism or antifascism" option.

ASCASO, Francisco (1901–1936): The Aragon-born, youngest son of a family with an anarchist heritage. Baker and waiter by trade. From a very early age, he was active in the Aragonese action groups. In December 1920, he was jailed for an attack, mounted along with his brother Domingo, that claimed the life of the *El Heraldo de Aragón* journalist who had denounced the soldiers who mutinied in the El Carmen barracks that January. He served two years in prison, emerging with his health broken by the mistreatment he received. In 1922, he moved to Barcelona, joining the Los Solidarios anarchist group alongside **Durruti, García Oliver, Aurelio Fernández, Gregorio Jover, Ricardo Sanz**, etc. He was involved in many armed operations and *attentats*. In June 1923, he was arrested and jailed, but managed to escape that December. During the Primo de Rivera dictatorship, he was in exile in Paris. In December 1924, he, along with Durruti, went on a "tour" of Latin America, a tour characterized by numerous bank holdups, in several countries, to raise funds to secure the freedom of anarchists in prison in Spain. By May 1926, he was back in Paris, where he was arrested in July, along with Jover and Durruti, for laying the groundwork for a planned attempt on the life of Alfonso XIII, and he spent a year in prison. Extradition to Argentina and Spain was averted thanks to an intense popular campaign to secure his release. He lived "under the radar" in a number of countries. At the start of 1929, he secured a permit to live in Brussels.

He returned to Barcelona right after the proclamation of the Republic on 14 April 1931. And joined the **Nosotros group** (the new name the Los Solidarios had to assume when they discovered that there was another group using their old name) with Durruti and García Oliver, among others. A member of Barcelona's Textile Union, he was a regular writer for *Solidaridad Obrera*.

Deported to the Canary Islands and to Guinea in February 1932 as punishment for his part in the January 1932 uprising in the Upper Llobregat, he was released in September 1932 and served on the Revolutionary Committee driving the 8 January 1933 uprising in Barcelona. In April 1933, he was arrested with Durruti and both were jailed in the Puerto de Santa María prison until their release in October.

He worked as waiter and played a part in the pro-abstention campaign vis-à-vis the November 1933 elections. He threw his weight behind the December 1933 uprising. At the beginning of 1934, he was appointed CNT general secretary and backed the general strike in Zaragoza.

He was against the Asturian CNT's signing of any Workers' Alliance pact with the UGT. On 6 October 1934, he called off the general strike that was supposed to have supported the Generalidad government in its quarrel with the central government and, for that reason, was ousted from his post as general secretary. He spoke at the Zaragoza Congress (May 1936) as the representative of the Barcelona Textile Union. A member of the Confederal Defense Committee, he was one of the leaders of the workers' uprising against the military mutiny on 19 July 1936, playing a prominent part in the streetfighting, displaying excessive daring and boldness. He perished on 20 July when shot while attacking the Atarazanas barracks.

ASENS, José (?–1985): In July 1936, he was secretary of the Barcelona Local Federation of CNT Unions, a member of the CNT's Regional Committee, and of the Confederal Defense Committee. He was—with **Durruti** and **García Oliver**—one of the CNT's representatives on the CAMC, as well as Head of Operations for the **Control Patrols**. He made numerous trips abroad to buy arms. He defied the Republic's bourgeois courts, which wanted to discipline him for his activities with the Patrols,and, in August 1937, left for exile in France, for which he was "barred" from holding any post within the Organization, although in April 1938 he was appointed the CNT representative on the Libertarian Movement's executive council. When the civil war ended, he was fully rehabilitated within the CNT and had a hand in reestablishing it in France. Asens died in 1985.

BALIUS, Jaime (1904–1980): Balius was afflicted with a degenerative illness that left him disabled and palsied in one arm. In his younger days he was a Catalan nationalist, taking part in the El Garraf attack on Alfonso XIII. For a few months he belonged to the **BOC**. In 1933, he joined the anarchist movement while in prison. On 21 July 1936, he produced a flyer that was a supplement to *Solidaridad Obrera*. Along with **Pablo Ruiz** and **Francisco Carreño**, he launched the **Friends of Durruti**. In May 1937, from atop a barricade, he read out a manifesto calling for active solidarity from French workers.

In 1939, an exile in France, he founded, along with Ridel, Prudhommeaux, and a number of French anarchists, the French-Spanish chapter of the Friends of Durruti, and in the review *Révision* and in a triple edition of *L'Espagne nouvelle* (nos. 67–69, July–September 1939), they published an unconventional analysis and some rigorous reflections upon the reasons for the defeat of the Spanish revolution.

After the Nazi invasion of France he spent many years in exile in Mexico. For a few months, he stayed at **Munis**'s house and, for two years after that, at the Sanatorio Español, when his illness took a turn for the worse and he found himself utterly penniless. He corresponded with the California-based historian, Burnett Bolloten, who afforded him some moral and financial assistance. In the 1960s, he managed to move back to France. From 1964 onward he contributed to *Le Combat syndicaliste*. He died in Hyères at the Bon-Séjour rest home for Spanish republicans in exile. See *Los Amigos de Durruti. Historia y antología de textos* (Barcelona: Descontrol, 2013).

BARCELONA LOCAL FEDERATION OF ANARCHIST GROUPS: The authentic FAI in Barcelona city, or, if one prefers, the only forum where Barcelona anarchist groups could air their differences with, and criticisms of, collaborationism.

BARRIOBERO, Eduardo (1880–1939): Republican lawyer, politician, federalist, and freemason. Based in Madrid. He was looked upon as the architect of the assassination of Dato, who lost his life while prime minister of the Spanish government. He was exiled twice under the Primo de Rivera dictatorship. He was elected to the Constituent Cortes under the Republic and was at the forefront in criticizing the government in the wake of the **Casas Viejas** incident. He acted as legal counsel to CNT personnel. On 21 July 1936, he moved to Barcelona to take over from Ángel Samblancat as head of the Courts Office, the functions of which he strengthened and broadened. In that task, he had help from Antonio Devesa from the CNT's Prisoners' Aid Committee and from José Batlle, who liaised with the defense committee from the Center ward.

From June 1937 on, he defended many CNT members charged in relation with the May Events. In October 1937, he himself was jailed over alleged irregularities at the Courts Office. The republican authorities failed to release him when Barcelona fell to the fascists and he was shot by the Francoists.

BERNERI, Camilo (1897–1937): Active in the Socialist Youth in his younger days. A veteran of the Great War, lecturer in humanities at Florence University, and a member of the UAI (Italian Anarchist Union). Following the fascist takeover, he was exiled from Italy, arriving in Spain in July 1936 and, together with Carlo Rosselli, he organized the very first column of Italian volunteers to fight in Aragon. His impaired hearing prevented him from staying on the front lines. In Barcelona, he published the *Guerra di Classe* newspaper. He was scathingly critical of collaborationism and his open letter to **Federica Montseny** earned him great notoriety and was widely distributed. He helped make radio broadcasts over CNT-FAI Radio. During the May Events of 1937, he was murdered by the Stalinists along with Francisco Barbieri. See his biography in *Entusiastas olvidados* (16–21). For his death and burial, see the appendices of this book.

BLOC OBER I CAMPEROL (BOC): A breakaway from the PCE in 1931. It was led by **Maurín**. In 1935, it amalgamated with the ICE (Communist Left of Spain) to form the POUM.

BOC: (See Bloc Ober i Camperol)

BREAD WAR:

    a.   The **PSUC's councillor** for supplies, **Comorera**, clashed with the **ward supplies committees** and this also affected the Barcelona Cooperatives Union.

    b.   **War erupted between three different flour and bread distribution (and rationing) networks:** one run by the barrio committees, one run by the cooperatives, and Comorera's nonexistent one, which he ordered Barcelona City Corporation to conjure up out of nothing. It lasted from 20 December 1936 until the May Events of 1937. Comorera imposed a **free market policy** very different from the **monopoly on foreign trade** previously advocated by Fábregas.

    c.   PSUC-manipulated **women's demonstrations**, displaying placards with counterrevolutionary slogans such as "More bread and fewer committees."

CAMC: (See Central Antifascist Militias Committee)

CAMPOS, Severino (1905–2006): Born in Montserrat (País Valenciano) on 26 August 1905. At a very early age, he went off to Barcelona, joining the CNT in 1918. He was known by the nickname "Little Jacobin." In the 1920s, he was part of the editorial team at *El Productor*. Under the Primo de Rivera dictatorship, he was in exile in France and Belgium, where he played an active part in a range of anarchist groups and tried his hand at a wide variety of trades. In March 1931, he returned to Spain and by November that year was on the RC of the CRTC, stepping in for Mira. He worked as a miner in a number of places and was very actively involved in the January 1932 uprising. Arrested in March 1933, he was held on the prison ship *Arnús*. During the 1930s, he worked in various rationalist schools, particularly the La Torrassa rationalist school run by the Ocaña family, of which his partner, Igualdad Ocaña, was a member.

In November 1936, at RC meetings, he clashed with Santillán over the latter's ineptitude when it came to arming and supplying the militias and over Santillán's forbearance in the face of plotting among the officers of the republican army, dubbing the Pyrenean Militias "fascists." On 19 February 1937, Campos complained about pressures coming from García Oliver and others trying to silence the criticisms targeting governmentalism that came from *Acracia* and *Ideas*. Campos pointed out that, as he saw it, the CNT was following "a mistaken path," and he added that, when the agreement had been made to appoint ministers to the republican government, it was on the condition that things would be quickly resolved and that, if this was not the case, the ministries would be given up immediately; but "time has slipped by, nothing has been done, and still our comrade ministers are in the same posts."

As of 1 **April 1937**, he was appointed a member of the FAI's RC, holding the post of secretary. In May 1937, he insisted that the police withdraw entirely from the Telephone Exchange building. After May, he expressed dissatisfaction with the CNT press campaign lauding Largo Caballero.

On **9 June 1937**, he spoke up during a meeting of the RC and clashed harshly with José Xena over whether the **Committee of Committees** that had been running the libertarian movement since July 1936 was viable or not. The clash between Campos, who argued that it had already disbanded itself, and Xena, who argued that it was still around and still viable, was due to the fact it was an exceptional, centralist, elitist, and authoritarian body, better suited to some Leninist party than to a trade-union organization like the CNT, or a libertarian one like the FAI. In Campos's view, the exceptional circumstances that had justified it were long gone. Xena took the line that the Committee of Committees still had its uses.[1] The argument came at a very critical point for the higher committees, when they were being belittled and bad-mouthed by the rank-and-file membership over their counterrevolutionary performance during the May Events. Hence the virulence of the sniping between Campos and Xena over the relevance or dissolution of the Committee of Committees, even though it had been brought up at a number of meetings since 24 May. Here, Campos, defending a certain loyalty to principles; whereas Xena was championing the ascendancy of the higher committees and their leadership role vis-à-vis the rank-and-file membership.

Be that as it may, a few days later, at an RC meeting, the decision was made to set up the Policy Advisory Commission (CAP), which was a sort of a revamped version of the July 1936 Committee of Committees, but this time specializing in ensuring that the higher committees were not overwhelmed as they had been in May 1937.

When the war ended, Campos left for exile in Mexico where he was active in the Mexican Anarchist Federation (FAM). After Franco's death, he returned to Hospitalet

---

1   In a letter to Bolloten dated 27 October 1950 [HI], Severino Campos gave this definition of the Committee of Committees: "The Committee (or, rather, the two Regional Committees, FAI and CNT) for Catalonia had agreed during the early days of the Uprising [July 1936] to meet daily, early each morning, together with the personnel they had scattered through the various political and administrative positions, with the aim of swapping impressions and outlining lines of policy."

and rejoined his old union. In 1979, he was made director of *Solidaridad Obrera* and from 1982 to 1983 he was on the staff of that paper. In July 1984, he was a delegate to the Regional Plenum of the CNT of Catalonia, held in Badalona and took part in numerous conferences and meetings. In 1993, he returned to Mexico and donated his newspaper collection to the FAL (Anselmo Lorenzo Foundation). Over his lifetime he contributed to numerous libertarian movement publications.

He died on 25 March 2006 in Mexico, of a respiratory disease. He was buried in a coffin swathed in the red-and-black flag.

CARBÓ, Eusebio (1883–1958): Anarcho-syndicalist journalist. At the CNT's 1919 congress, he defended the Russian revolution and the entry of the CNT into the Third International. He travelled widely throughout Europe between 1917 and 1920, with lengthy stays in Italy, where he met Malatesta, Fabbri, and Borghi, and he accompanied the latter to lots of trade union rallies. From 1930 on, he was on the editorial staff of *Solidaridad Obrera*. He launched the weekly *Más Lejos*. During the civil war he held a number of posts in the Generalidad's Propaganda Commission and in the **Council of Economy**. He was the CNT drafter of the **Collectivizations Decree** promulgated by **Joan Pau Fábregas**. He died in exile in Mexico.

CARLINI, Adolfo: Pseudonym employed in Spain by the Italian Trotskyist Domenico Sedran. See Casciola and Guillamón, *Biografías del 36*, 378–386 and the letter from José Quesada in Appendix B of this book.

CARREÑO, Francisco: Rationalist schoolteacher, outstanding militant, and public speaker in the 1930s. A member of the Durruti Column's War Committee and founder of the Friends of Durruti along with **Jaime Balius** and **Pablo Ruiz**. Great friend of Munis. In May 1937, he met with **Adolfo Carlini** and **José Quesada** at the Hotel Falcón.

CENTRAL ANTIFASCIST MILITIAS COMMITTEE (CAMC): A short-lived government agency serving as an umbrella for all revolutionary, reformist, and counterrevolutionary antifascist organizations, parties, and labor unions, along with antifascist bourgeois. It was created in Barcelona on 21 July 1936 as the bitter fruit of the victorious insurrection against the army and of the CNT's refusal to take power. It was a **class collaboration** agency that survived for just nine weeks. Many historians talk mistakenly of the CAMC's having be an organ of dual power.

CENTRAL SUPPLIES COMMITTEE: The **Central Supplies Committee** emerged as a crucial auxiliary to the CAMC. It was chaired by **Doménech** and found a "natural" extension in the form of the Supplies Department of the first **Tarradellas**

government, with Doménech still at the helm. Its foundation and strength grew out of the coordination and cooperation with the barrio committees in Barcelona city and with the local committees across Catalonia.

CNT: *See Confederación Nacional del Trabajo.*

COLLECTIVIZATION AND WORKERS' CONTROL DECREE: The CNT's Joan Pau Fábregas, councillor for economy, issued the **Collectivizations and Workers' Control Decree** on 24 October 1936. This decree was the result of CNT negotiations with other antifascist forces and with the Generalidad government. It applied the brakes to and marked the beginning of the regulation of the spontaneous process of expropriations that the workers had embarked upon in the wake of the success of the July 1936 insurrection. With Fábregas's departure from the government formed on 17 December 1936, the practical implementation of this decree was shaped and manipulated by **Josep Tarradellas** through fifty-eight financial and tax decrees issued in January 1937. The Collectivizations Decree was thus turned into a Generalidad tool for effectively controlling all firms and planning the Catalan economy. The workers' revolution, won on the streets, was being lost in the offices, as weapons were "outgunned" by finances.

COMORERA, Joan (1895–1958): Represented the USC (Socialist Union of Catalonia) in the Catalan Parliament. Served as councillor for agriculture and economy in the government formed by Companys in 1934. Served as secretary of the PSUC from that party's foundation on 24 July 1936. During the civil war, he headed several Generalidad departments, one after another. In concert with the Hungarian Gerö (aka "Pedro"), he **led the PSUC** with a very personal, authoritarian style. In 1949, he was expelled from the PSUC, accused of Titoism. In 1951, he slipped back into Catalonia. Arrested in 1954, he was tried and imprisoned. In prison, he was shunned and boycotted by his Stalinist comrades. He died in 1958 in Burgos prison.

COMPANYS, Lluís (1882–1940): Successor to **Maciá** and president of the Generalidad (in 1931, Maciá had been the first president of the republican Generalidad) having previously served as mayor of Barcelona, civil governor, and minister of the Republic's Navy. A one-time friend of Salvador Seguí and, as a lawyer, closely associated with anarcho-syndicalists.

In July 1936, he managed to preserve the existence of the Generalidad government through his oft-repeated "lemon" speech. In November 1936, CNT personnel exposed a planned coup against Companys on the part of pro-independence militants from **Estat Catalá**, the basis being that the separatists regarded him as not much of a Catalanist and as unduly inclined to ally himself with the CNT. During the week of bloodshed in May 1937, on learning of Sesé's death, he **repeatedly ordered air raids on the main buildings occupied by the CNT in Barcelona, in accordance with a plan drawn up by José del Barrio**. While in exile in France, he was arrested by the Gestapo and extradited to Spain. In October 1940, he was shot in a ditch in Montjuich fortress. Regarded as a martyr and as the founding father of his homeland.

COMMUNIST LEFT OF SPAIN (ICE): Part of the International Trotskyist Opposition. In 1932, it broke away from the PCE and began to distance itself from Trotskyist discipline. **Nin** and Andrade were flirting with **Maurín**'s BOC, whereas Fersen, Estaban Bilbao, and **Munis** opposed the establishment of the POUM, looking upon it as a centrist, counterrevolutionary party.

CONTROL PATROLS: The Control Patrols were formed between 21 July and mid-August 1936 as a "revolutionary" police answerable to the CAMC. Only about half of the patrollers were card-carrying CNT or FAI members; the other half were drawn from other organizations making up the CAMC: the **POUM, the ERC, and the PSUC**, essentially. Only four out of the eleven section delegates belonged to the CNT, in the working-class barrios of Pueblo Nuevo, Sants, San Andrés (or Armonía), and El Clot; another four belonged to the ERC, three to the PSUC, and none to the POUM. The Control Patrols were answerable to the CAMC's Investigation Committee, headed by **Aurelio Fernández** (FAI) and Salvador González (PSUC). The delegates in direct charge of the Control Patrols were **José Asens** (FAI) and Tomás Fábregas (Acció Catalana). The patrollers ten-pesetas-a-day wages came from the Generalidad. Even though arrests were made in all of the sections, their central prison was in the San Elías former convent of the Poor Clare nuns. After the dissolution of the CAMC on 1 October 1936, the Patrols found themselves answerable to the Security Junta, which CNT personnel argued was autonomous, whereas the PSUC, ERC, and Generalidad government regarded it as answerable to Security Councillor **Artemi Aguadé**.

CONFEDERACIÓN NACIONAL DEL TRABAJO (CNT): Anarcho-syndicalist trade union founded in 1910, in which, by July 1936, four-fifths of the Catalan proletariat were active. In Barcelona city, it enjoyed an absolute majority.

COUNCIL OF ECONOMY: The revolutionary situation that was obtained in Barcelona following the success of the 19–20 July 1936 insurrection, was quickly built upon three brand-new agencies: the **CAMC, the Central Supplies Committee**, and the **Council of Economy**.

There were others as well, such as the CENU and the War Industries Commission, but the three named above were the most important ones, and they embodied the new "revolutionary order." The **CAMC**, undoubtedly the most decisive of the trio, given its early refusal to step up and make itself a revolutionary government replacing the Generalidad government, ended up specializing in matters military and public order related. The **Central Supplies Committee** emerged as an indispensable auxiliary to the CAMC. It was chaired by Doménech, and evolved "naturally" into the Supplies Department of the first Tarradellas government, the latter being also headed by **Doménech**. It was rooted in and drew its strength from coordination and cooperation with the barrio committees in Barcelona city and with Catalan local committees.

The third essential agency was the **Council of Economy**, charged with regulating and coordinating collectivizations and the Catalan planned economy. Two members of the Council would end up as the first anarchist ministers in history to join a government, Antonio García Birlán and **Joan Pau Fábregas**.

CRTC: *See Regional Confederation of Labor of Catalonia.*

DECREE ABOLISHING THE LOCAL COMMITTEES: The decree of **9 October 1936**, complemented by the one published on 12 October, declared that **all the local committees** that had sprung up on 19 July were being **abolished** and replaced by brand new town councils. Despite resistance from many local committees regarding their abolition and several months of delay in the establishment of the new town councils, this was a fatal blow from which there would be no recovery. The resistance from the CNT rank and file, who ignored the orders coming down from the higher committees or emanating from the Generalidad government, posed a threat to antifascist unity.

DECREE ORDERING MILITARIZATION OF THE MILITIAS: 24 October 1936 saw the promulgation of the decree militarizing the militias, a decree that would come into force on 1 November. It implied a shift away from the volunteer militias of revolutionary workers to a bourgeois army along traditional lines, subject to monarchist code of military justice and under the direction of the Generalidad.

DISTINGUISHING BETWEEN CONFEDERATION, SPECIFIC, AND ORGANIZATION:

    Confederation: refers to the confederation of unions, or CNT.

    Specific: refers to the FAI, which is to say, the anarchists' own, separate or specific organization.

    Organization: In the 1930s, given the *trabazón* (working relationship) between the unions and the specific branch, this word was used to refer to the CNT-and-FAI umbrella organization and in general parlance replaced the term "Confederation," which had been in use prior to the foundation of the FAI.

DOMÉNECH, Josep J. (1900–1979): Trade unionist and cooperativist. Secretary of the CRTC in 1934 and in 1937. Headed up the Central Supplies Committee and later served as Generalidad councillor for supplies. In December 1936, he was councillor for Public Services, at loggerheads with **Comorera** and the latter's "bread war" against the barrio committees. In April 1937, he served for a few days as councillor for economy. Exiled in France, he returned to Barcelona in 1975.

DURRUTI, Buenaventura (León 1896–Madrid 1936): Mechanic. From a very young age he was involved in social disputes through the labor movement. His pugnacious involvement in the August 1917 general strike led to his being expelled from the UGT. A few weeks after that, he left for exile in France in order to evade military service. In October 1922, he—along with **Francisco Ascaso, García Oliver, Aurelio Fernández, Ricardo Sanz**, and others—launched the Los Solidarios anarchist group. Early in 1923, he was arrested in Madrid and released again in June. On 1 September, he took part in the holdup at the Banco de España branch in Gijón and after the proclamation of the Primo de Rivera dictatorship on 23 September of the same year, he decided to leave the country. In January 1924, Ascaso and Durruti settled in Paris. In November 1925, they were involved in the Vera de Bidasoa plot that planned for Spain to be invaded by small guerrilla teams. In December 1924, after it failed, Durruti and Ascaso took off to the Americas where they combined working at a variety of trades with robberies to raise funds to secure the release of prisoners, launch rationalist schools, and other schemes. Their jaunt took them to New York, Mexico, Cuba, Chile, Argentina, and Uruguay. By May 1926, they were back in Paris. In July 1926, Durruti, Ascaso, and Jover were arrested on charges that they were plotting an attempt on the life of Alfonso XIII, who was on a visit to Paris on 14 July 1926. An intense and massive popular campaign was launched to ensure that these Spanish anarchists were not extradited to Argentina or back to Spain. They regained their freedom in July 1927. After a period living below the radar and repeated expulsions along the French–Belgian border, Durruti was granted the legal right to reside in Brussels at the beginning of 1929. With the proclamation of the Republic on 14 April 1931, Durruti returned to Barcelona, living in the working class Pueblo Nuevo barrio. He set up the **Nosotros group** along with Garcia Oliver, Francisco Ascaso, Ricardo Sanz, and others.

In February 1932, he was deported to the Canary Islands and then to Guinea as punishment for his part in the January 1932 uprising in the Upper Llobregat. He was released in September 1932. He served on the Revolutionary Committee behind the 8 January 1933 uprising in Barcelona. He was arrested in April 1933, along with Francisco Ascaso, and they both served time in the Puerto de Santa Maria prison, being released that October.

He worked as a mechanic and was involved in the campaign calling for abstention in the November 1933 elections. He backed the December 1933 uprising, as a result of which he was arrested and jailed in Burgos up until amnestied in October 1934. In June 1934, he took part in the CNT's National Plenum, which rejected the Workers' Alliance that the Asturias CNT had entered into with the UGT. He was arrested in connection with the events of 6 October 1934 in Catalonia, even though he had had no hand, action, or part in them. He was left locked up in Barcelona's Modelo prison until April 1935. For the remainder of that year he was variously, briefly, but repeatedly jailed.

By July 1936, he was on the Confederal Defense Committee that defeated the army. On 20 July 1936, he was part of the delegation that held talks with **Companys** and that took the provisional decision to set up the CAMC. He was appointed delegate of the Column that set off for Zaragoza on 24 July. He was against militarization of the militias and collaboration within government. A section of the Durruti Column was transferred to Madrid, which was in danger of falling into Francoist hands at the time. On 19 November 1936, he sustained a gunshot wound on the Madrid front, dying the next day. His funeral in Barcelona on Sunday, 23 November 1936 drew an impressively massive turnout. Within a year of his death, Stalinist propaganda was falsely crediting him with the slogan that its propaganda machine made famous: "We renounce everything, except victory."

ERC: *See Esquerra Republicana de Catalunya.*

EROLES, Dionisio (1900–1940): CNT militant active in the action groups in the Barcelona barrio of Sants. Sentenced to a twenty-year prison term for an attack mounted during the years of *pistolerismo*, he spent the entirety of the Primo de Rivera dictatorship behind bars. He took part in the January 1932 and January 1933 uprisings. During the civil war, he held the position of Secretary of the Workers' and Soldiers' Council (a body put in charge of purging the army, Civil Guard, and police) and, by October 1936, he was Chief of Staff of the Internal Security Junta, ferociously competing and clashing with the General Security Commission and the security councillor, both dominated by the Stalinists and the ERC. After May 1937, he served for a few months as caretaker secretary of the CRTC. He was murdered in 1940 in exile. See his biography in *Entusiastas olvidados* (93–111).

ESCORZA, Manuel (1912–1968): Stricken by polio that left him partially and permanently paralyzed. Because of atrophy in his legs, he wore enormously built-up shoes and that, together with his crutches, gave him a woeful appearance. He was highly intelligent, very tenacious, and highly cultured. He was active in the Libertarian Youth and eventually served on the Peninsular Committee of the FAI. At a CNT-FAI gathering on 20 July 1936, he argued in favor of a third way, rather than **Garcia Oliver**'s "going for broke" or the collaborationist line argued by **Montseny**

and **Santillán**; his idea was to use the Generalidad government as a tool in the socialization of the economy; the CNT could then cast it aside once they no longer needed it. He was the man at the top of the **CNT-FAI Investigation Service**, which carried out all sorts of repressive activities after July 1936, as well as handling espionage, counterespionage, and intelligence-gathering tasks. Some arrested persons were interrogated in the attic of the Casa Cambó by Manuel Escorza in person. He was feared and hated by his own and by outsiders because of his powers of repression and the reports he drew up for court proceedings. In the summer of 1936, he was involved in conversations between the CAMC and Moroccan independence campaigners with an eye to demobilizing the Moroccan volunteers serving in the Francoist camp by granting Moroccan independence. In October 1936, he signed the CNT-UGT-PSUC-FAI unity agreement along with **Eroles** and **Herrera**. In April 1937, he and Pedro Herrera negotiated directly with **Companys** a way out of the Generalidad government's crisis. In late April, he tipped off the defense committees that a counterrevolutionary coup de force was imminent. But he was of the opinion that the May insurrection was premature, badly prepared, and lacking in clearcut purposes and effective leadership. His fear was that the foreseeable crackdown coming after the insurrection would weaken the Organization. Ensconced in his attic at the Casa CNT-FAI, he was beyond the reach of the Republic's (and Stalinist chekas') prosecutorial crackdown, unleashed in Barcelona over the summer of 1937. He left for exile in Chile, thanks to Masonic connivance and solidarity between the Chilean consul in Toulouse and his brother-in-law Minué, a fellow-Mason. He led a very austere existence. He was a stringent and terrifying theatre critic. He died in Valparaíso.

ESQUERRA REPUBLICANA DE CATALUNYA (ERC): Republican Left of Catalonia, a republican, Catalanist, petit-bourgeois party with a measure of workerist leanings; it was led by **Maciá and Companys** and scored a huge election success in April 1931. It was the party that provided the Generalidad with two presidents— Maciá, who died on Christmas 1933 and Companys, who took over from him.

ESTAT CATALÀ: Catalan fascists. This was a nationalist, pro-independence, right-wing, radical political party that emerged in July 1936 from the amalgamation of several small Catalanist organizations. It was not part of the CAMC. It was undermined by many personality-driven rivalries. Its first secretary, Josep Dencás, fled to fascist Italy when he felt he was under threat. His successor, Torres Picart was arrested in November 1936 over his part in an abortive attempt at a coup d'état against Companys that also planned to physically eliminate CNT leaders like **Aurelio Fernández** and **Dionsio Eroles** and to end "the anarchist influence" within the Generalidad government. The replacement general secretary, Cornudella, stepped up the party's visceral opposition to the CNT, a rapprochement with the **PSUC**, and support for the **Generalidad government**. In May 1937, it was involved in the streetfighting, harrying CNT personnel, and defending its own headquarters at the intersection of the Gran Vía and the Rambla de Catalunya.

FÁBREGAS, Joan Pau (1894–1966): CNT member and economist. During the eighty days (26 September to 16 December 1936) he served as councillor for economy, he attempted to plan and accomplish three objectives, only one of which he managed to implement, albeit only on paper: legalizing the seizure of factories, firms, and workshops under the **Collectivizations and Workers' Control Decree**. This took effect in January 1937. **Tarradellas** was the person responsible for their practical implementation, and his orders and arrangements proved to be wholly contrary to the spirit and the letter of the Decree promulgated by Fábregas.

His other two objectives never got off the drawing-board. Those were his plan for civilian mobilization of the labor force in the rearguard, something the workers deeply grasped and desired; and the plan for a Foreign Trade Board that sought to impose a **Monopoly on Foreign Trade**, the aim being to halt the rising prices of food, arms, and raw materials from abroad.

Fábregas was dropped from the government at the same time as Nin, on 17 December 1936, and his removal was unopposed. The historiography usually just highlights the significance of the ouster of **Nin**, but says nothing about Fábregas's removal, which had greater economic, political, and social implications. Fábregas had made himself too many enemies, both inside the government (**Companys** and **Comorera**) and within the CNT itself (**Santillán** and the **Nervio group**). See Casciola and Guillamón, *Biografías del 36*, 56–77.

FAI: Iberian Anarchist Federation.

FAISTAS: Militants of the FAI, obviously. But the term was also used in a sneering way to designate those who championed the technique of insurrections, regardless of objective circumstances, in the belief that sheer example would spread through the people like a contagion, thanks to the daring displayed by the revolutionary action groups. The **treintistas**, or reformists, took exception to FAI meddling in the unions and advocated a gradualist trade union activity, with stringent groundwork laid for insurrections that had to be mass events that were mounted when the objective circumstances were in place whereby they might spread nationwide and to the whole of society.

FASCISM OR DEMOCRACY?: Whether in its fascist form or in its democratic form, the **capitalist state has to be destroyed**. The proletariat cannot come to an accommodation with the republican (or democratic) bourgeoisie in order to defeat the fascist bourgeoisie, because, implicit in any such accommodation is, *ipso facto*, the defeat of the revolutionary alternative and a renunciation of the **proletariat's revolutionary program** (and its attendant methods of struggle) as a prelude to adoption of the antifascist unity program alongside the democratic bourgeoisie, for the sake of winning the war on fascism.

FERNÁNDEZ SÁNCHEZ, Aurelio (1897–1974): Born in Oviedo in 1897, mechanic by trade. Resident in Barcelona from 1922. Member of the Los Solidarios group. Mounted an attempt on the life of **Martínez Anido**. On 1 September 1923, he was involved in the holdup at the Banco de España's Gijón branch, the proceeds from which were to be used to buy weapons. He was in exile in Paris during the Primo de Rivera dictatorship. In July 1926, he had a hand in the plan to assassinate Alfonso XIII in Paris. That October, he crossed into Belgium. Shortly after that, he was arrested in Madrid, in possession of bombs and weaponry. Held in Cartagena prison up until the Republic was proclaimed in April 1931. He then joined the **Nosotros group**. He was involved in laying the groundwork for several revolutionary uprisings, such as the one in January 1933. Served on the Regional Defense Committee of Catalonia. He was a FAI representative on the CAMC, handling the Investigation and Watch Department. Organizer of the **Control Patrols**. From October 1936, he served as general secretary to the Internal Security Junta of Catalonia and was constantly running into problems with the Stalinists and with Councillor **Artemi Aguadé**. In April 1937, he was appointed health councillor in the Generalidad government. By 28 August 1937, he was being held in the Modelo prison. Subjected to several trials by summary process; the first was for an attempt on the life of the president of the High Court, Andreu Abelló, and he was acquitted. Before he could be released, he had to face another trial by summary process for murder and fraud in the case of the Marists. Thanks to **García Oliver**'s intervention, he was freed on 6 January 1938. By April 1938, he was on the Executive Committee of the Libertarian Movement, as the FAI's representative. Was exiled in France and Mexico.

FOUS: *See Workers' Trade Union Unity Federation.*

FRIENDS OF DURRUTI GROUP: The Friends of Durruti Group (*Agrupación*) was a substantial anarchist grouping with around five thousand members. It was founded in March 1937. They were opposed to militarization and highly critical of the CNT's entry into the republican government and Generalidad. On 2 March 1937, *La Noche* newspaper carried an insert setting out the aims, features, and membership conditions of the Friends of Durruti, which was formally established on 17 March 1937. Its chief promoter, **Jaime Balius**, became its vice-secretary. **Pablo Ruiz** and **Francisco Carreño** were on the steering committee.

On Sunday 11 April, there was heckling and whistling during Federica Montseny's speech at the rally in the Monumental bullring. The Friends of Durruti carried a placard insisting that **Maroto** and other imprisoned antifascists be set free. The Friends of Durruti were accused at meetings of the CNT's RC of shunning the minister.

On Sunday 8 April 1937, the Friends of Durruti held a rally at the Poliorama theatre, chaired by Romero, with contributions from Francisco Pellicer, Pablo Ruiz, Jaime Balius, Francisco Carreño, and Vicente Pérez "Combina."

In late April, a poster from the group was stuck up on trees and walls all over Barcelona city, making known its program: "All power to the working class. All economic power to the unions. A Revolutionary Junta instead of the Generalidad."

GARCÍA OLIVER, Juan (Reus 1901—Guadalajara, Mexico, 1980): Outstanding anarcho-syndicalist militant, waiter by trade. He started out in the social struggles in his native comarca and in 1922 helped set up the **Los Solidarios group** along with **Durruti, Ascaso, Jover, Sanz, Aurelio Fernández**, etc. and took part in lots of robberies and attacks, prominent among them the murder of the fascistic Cardinal Soldevila. He was jailed in Burgos. In 1924, he left for exile in Paris, negotiating with Maciá's supporters for an invasion to be mounted that would end the dictatorship, and, with Italian "exiles," for the assassination of Mussolini. He joined with **Durruti, Ascaso**, and Jover, back from their "tour" of the Americas, to prepare an attempt on the life of Alfonso XIII, and managed to escape to Brussels without being arrested. He took part in the attempted invasion of Catalonia by Maciá's Catalan nationalists. He was then arrested and convicted and was only released from prison when the Republic was proclaimed in April 1931.

He took part in the January 1933 uprising. Arrested and tortured, he was released from prison shortly before the November 1933 elections. He joined the **Nosotros group** and, in May 1936, attended the Zaragoza Congress. On 19 and 20 July 1936, he played a crucial part in the street-fighting, as an organizer and strategist with the Nosotros group, which had set itself up as the Confederal Defense Committee. At CAMC meetings he played a leadership role, taking on the post of secretary of war. In November 1936, he agreed to become justice minister in the Largo Caballero government. In May 1937, he was one of the anarchist leaders at the forefront of the call for a ceasefire.

In the summer of 1937, he served on the CAP (Policy Advisory Commission) that advised and directed the RC of the Catalan CNT. In September 1937, he lobbied to get the CNT insurgents in the Los Escolapios building to surrender to the Stalinists and the police. In 1938, he strove to get an Executive Committee of the Libertarian Movement formed. After a short stay in Sweden, he finally left for exile in Guadalajara (Mexico) where he died in 1980. He wrote a highly controversial set of memoirs *El eco de los pasos*, published by Ruedo Ibérico.

GELSA: In October 1936, the decree militarizing the people's militias generated great discontent among the Durruti Column's anarchist militia members on the Aragon front. After lengthy and heated discussions, in March 1937, eight hundred volunteer militia members from the Durruti Column's Fourth *Agrupación*, based in the Gelsa sector, made up their minds to quit the front and rejoin the rearguard. Once back in Barcelona, many of them joined the **Friends of Durruti.** Pablo Ruiz played a prominent part in this process of "revolutionary defeatism" on the part of the militia members from Gelsa.

GENERAL UNION OF WORKERS (UGT): A socialist trade union, in the minority in July 1936. It experienced enormous growth due to an influx of petite bourgeois and anti-CNT shopkeepers, thanks to the Stalinist counterrevolutionary policy that turned the UGT into a transmission belt obedient to the orders coming from the PSUC.

GENERALIDAD GOVERNMENT: Catalonia's bourgeois home rule government, all but swept away entirely by the workers' insurrection against the army and the fascists in July 1936. The dissolution of the CAMC on 1 October 1936 eased its re-establishment. The collapse of the central state made it easier for the Generalidad home rule government in Catalonia to take on certain defense, public order, and border control functions that were not provided for in the Statute of Autonomy. These functions were lost beyond recovery in the wake of the May Events in 1937, when they were reclaimed by the central government.

HERRERA, Pedro: Railway worker. Active in the **Nervio group.** Friend of **Santillán** and **Toryho.** On behalf of the FAI, he signed up to the UGT-CNT-PSUC-FAI unity agreement in October 1936. He served as the Generalidad of Catalonia's health and social assistance councillor from 16 December 1936 until 3 April 1937. In mid-April 1937, he and Escorza held direct negotiations with Companys to thrash out a way out of the Generalidad government crisis.

HIGHER COMMITTEES: Antifascist ideology, plus CNT participation in various municipal posts, Generalidad councillorships, and even ministries of the central government conjured up a bureaucracy of higher committees, with interests different from and contrary to the revolutionary committees emerging in the Barcelona barrios. Whereas the higher committees made everything else subordinate to victory in the war on fascism, the barrio committees still clung to the program of a workers' revolution.

The process whereby these CNT-FAI higher committees were **institutionalized** turned them into lackeys of the state, making **the barrio revolutionary committees** their worst enemies, as was stated by the RC at a get-together of the libertarian higher committees held on 25 November 1936. The naïve and simplistic thesis that separates the anarcho-syndicalist leaders into traitors or heroes, as if the bulk of the membership was amorphous or apathetic, is no explanation at all. **The clash between the higher committees and the ward revolutionary committees was yet another chapter in the class struggle** and came within a hair of triggering a **split**. This was ultimately resolved by a **selective** Stalinist crackdown that annihilated the revolutionaries and integrated the higher committees into the machinery of the state.

The **institutionalization of the CNT** had significant and inescapable implications for the organizational and ideological nature of the CNT.

The leadership and power functions performed by the higher committees, which included a very tiny minority actually capable of exercising them, generated a series of interests, approaches and aims different from those of the active CNT membership. Hence, on the one hand, the unresponsiveness and widespread disenchantment to be found among the membership and grassroots militants, who were having to contend with hunger and repression, and receiving absolutely no help from the higher committees. Hence also, the emergence of a revolutionary opposition, essentially embodied by the Friends of Durruti, the Libertarian Youth of Catalonia, some anarchist groups from the Barcelona Local Federation of Anarchist Groups, especially after May 1937. But that opposition had already surfaced much earlier, during the summer of 1936, in the barrio committees and defense committees in the wards of Barcelona.

ICE: *See Communist Left of Spain.*

LARGO CABALLERO, Francisco (Madrid 1869–PARIS 1946): PSOE and UGT leader. He collaborated with the institutions of the Primo de Rivera dictatorship. Served as minister of labor (1931–1933). Jailed in the wake of the events of October 1934, he took a radical turn, becoming the leader of the left wing of the PSOE. He advocated a revolutionary workers' front policy. He was dubbed "the Spanish Lenin." He was prime minister from 5 September 1936 until 17 May 1937, when he tendered his resignation following pressure from the Stalinists to outlaw the POUM. He was marginalized in the PSOE and UGT. In 1939 he took refuge in France. He was deported to a concentration camp in Germany.

MAROTO, Francisco (1906–1940): Delegate from the militia column that bore his name. His column mounted a successful military campaign in Córdoba and Granada, the latter of which it failed to capture for want of arms. He clashed with the governor of Almería, Gabriel Morón, whom he criticized at a rally in February 1937. He was jailed, to the great indignation of the libertarian movement, which insisted that he be set free. On 1 May 1937 he was pardoned, but lost command of his column. At the end of the war, he was arrested, tortured, and shot by the Falangists in Alicante.

MARTÍNEZ ANIDO, Severiano (1862–1938): Military governor of Barcelona in 1920–1922 and head of the repression targeting workers' organizations, especially the CNT. His activities were characterized by brutality and recourse to terrorist methods. He set up the *Sindicatos Libres*, funded by the employers, with the aim of murdering CNT trade unionists. Under the Primo de Rivera dictatorship he served as home affairs minister and was public order minister in Franco's first cabinet.

He was one of thirty-five high-ranking Francoist commanders indicted before the Audiencia Nacional in the indictment brought by Judge Baltasar Garzón, on charges of unlawful detention and crimes against humanity during the Spanish Civil War and the early years of the Franco dictatorship.

MAS, Valerio (1894–1973): Acting secretary of the CRTC from 20 November 1936 to 2 March 1937. He was then secretary elect from 2 March to 5 May 1937, at which point he was made a Generalidad councillor in the provisional government appointed at the height of the fighting during the May 1937 week of bloodletting in Barcelona.

MAURÍN, Joaquín (1896–1973): Founder of the BOC. Undisputed leader of the newly established POUM, the product of the amalgamation of the BOC and the ICE. The outbreak of the civil war caught him inside Francoist territory and his comrades had given him up for dead, but he was held in Francoist prisons until October 1946. Disenchanted with politics, he left for exile and abandoned political activism.

MERA, Cipriano (MADRID 1895–PARIS 1973): CNT bricklayer. Mera's column became the 14th Division, of which he was appointed commander. That division played a crucial part in the defense of Madrid in November 1936, and in the March 1937 battle of Guadalajara, where Italian troops were beaten. He commanded the IV Corps of the Army of the Center. In 1938, by then a lieutenant-colonel, he set up his headquarters in Alcohete (Guadalajara), near the Villa de Horche and, from there, protected the entire eastern sector of Madrid. He backed Colonel Segismundo Casado's coup d'état on 5 March 1939. He was imprisoned until 1942. Eventually left for exile in France where he returned to bricklaying.

MERINO, Julián (1897–1977): *See his biography in the appendices.*

MOLA, General (1887–1937): Emilio Mola was the general responsible, from the February 1936 elections that were won by the Popular Front, for the painstaking preparations for the 17 July 1936 coup. The so-called "Mola Plan" provided for the extermination of the enemy in the rearguard, this being regarded as the only appropriate military strategy for an army confronted by a huge popular majority hostile to it.

MONTSENY, Federica (1905–1994): Daughter of anarchist intellectuals, she was very young when she began writing for *La Revista Blanca*, which was run by her parents "Federico Urales" and "Soledad Gustavo." She wrote a number of "proletarian" novels. Her articles drew their inspiration from apoliticism and ideological purism. In 1936, she served on the PC of the FAI. She was health minister in the Largo Caballero government from November 1936 until May 1937. During the May Events, she played a very prominent role in dousing the streetfighting in Barcelona. In exile, she reverted to her anarchist purism and apoliticism. Together with her partner, Germinal Esgleas, she dominated the CNT apparatus in exile, being permanently ensconced in paid posts and helping to keep it hidebound and ineffective.

MUNIS, Grandizo (1912–1989): Manuel Fernández Grandizo y Martínez, known by his pseudonym "G. Munis." Leader of the SBLE. See his biography in Casciola and Guillamón, *Biografías del 36*, 241–261.

NEGRÍN LÓPEZ, Juan (Las Palmas 1889–Paris 1956): Specializing in physiology, he was an eminent scientist who had trained in Germany. Professor in Madrid. Minister of finance in the Largo Caballero government. Responsible for shipping the Bank of Spain's gold reserves to Moscow. On 17 May 1937, he took over from Largo Caballero as prime minister. He organized the "government of Victory," dropping the UGT and the CNT from the lineup and securing the support of the Stalinists. In August 1937, he dissolved the Council of Aragon. On 31 October 1937, he ordered the government to relocate to Barcelona. In April 1938, he set up a "government of national unity," bringing back the CNT and the UGT. The bloody battle of the Ebro (July–August 1938), plus severe rationing based on lentils, jokingly referred to as "Dr. Negrín's pills," marked his time in government. In September 1938, he tried to negotiate an end to the war on the basis of a thirteen-point program. That October he decided that the International Brigades should pull out of Spain. With the fall of Catalonia to the fascists, he crossed the border only to return to the Center-South Zone and to insist on resistance to the bitter end. Casado's coup d'état on 4 March 1939 forced him to flee to France. In 1945, he stepped down from his position as prime minister of the Government of the Republic.

NERVIO GROUP: Made up of **Santillán, Pedro Herrera,** Jacobo Maguid, Germinal de Sousa, Adolfo Verde, Ildefonso González, José Mari, Juan Rúa, Vicente Tarín, Horacio Baraco, Simón Radowitzky, etc. The group was led by Santillán and was made up almost entirely of Argentineans. Together with the Group A and others, it formed an anti-Nosotros front.

NIN, Andrés (1892–1937): Started off as a trade unionist in the CNT, serving as its general secretary in 1921. He was an official of the Profintern up until he was expelled from Russia in 1929 for his Trotskyist leanings. In 1930, by which time he was back in Barcelona, he helped organize the Spanish Trotskyist Opposition, which adopted the name **Communist Left of Spain** (ICE) in March 1932. In 1934, he broke once and for all with Trotsky, after a long process of flirtation with **Maurín**. He called for amalgamation with the BOC, leading to the foundation of the **POUM** in September 1935. Maurín's disappearance right at the start of the civil war left him a political secretary of the new party. In August 1936, he served on the **Council of Economy**. From 26 September to 16 December 1936, he held the position of Generalidad justice councillor, undoing the work done by **Barriobero** and ordering the dissolution of the Courts Offices. On 30 September, he accompanied **Tarradellas** and **Comorera** on a trip to Lérida to get the Lérida People's Committee to back down. Together with the CNT's **Joan Pau Fábregas**, he was dropped from the Generalidad government formed on 17 December 1936. In January 1937, with repression targeting the POUM raging at full tilt in Madrid, he wrote a letter insisting that his party take part in the talks about an amalgamation of the PSOE and the PCE. In May 1937, he tried to douse the streetfighting and avoid isolating the POUM by imposing a "coattail-riding" policy of deference to the CNT's **higher committees**. He turned down Josep Rebull's suggestion that the Generalidad be attacked, on the grounds that this "was not a military matter but a political one."

On 16 June 1937, the POUM was outlawed and its Central Committee arrested. Nin was removed to Alcalá de Henares where he was abducted by agents of the Soviet police, tortured, and murdered.

NON-INTERVENTION COMMITTEE: The Non-Intervention Committee, known also as the **London Committee**, was an organization set up in 1936 at the instigation of France, its purpose being to monitor the degree of compliance with the Non-Intervention Pact, an attempt to avert foreign meddling in the Spanish Civil War and preventing the internationalization of the conflict at a time when the tensions between the democracies and the dictatorships were at their highest point. Germany and Italy signed up to the Non-Intervention Pact on 8 August 1936. In the end, as many as twenty-seven European nations, including the Soviet Union, joined the Pact. Whereas the United Kingdom and France refrained from meddling in the conflict, Germany and Italy systematically and decisively backed the Francoist side, while the Soviet Union sent intermittent aid to republican Spain. The Committee was a huge farce that worked to the detriment of the lawful, democratic government of the Republic, by placing it on the same level as a bunch of military would-be coup-makers. While the republican government was prevented from buying arms, the Axis supplied Franco with all the arms and manpower he wished, right from the outset. The Committee was the product of the French and British governments' fear of a successful revolution in Spain.

NOSOTROS GROUP: This was the new name assumed during the 1930s by the former Los Solidarios group. It was made up of **Buenaventura Durruti, Francisco Ascaso, Juan García Oliver, Antonio Ortiz, Aurelio Fernández, Ricardo Sanz,** etc. There were around twenty active militants at the forefront of the group; they were supported by numerous auxiliaries who would prepare and assist the various actions to be mounted, bringing the total number up to around eighty. On 19 July 1936, the Nosotros group set itself up as the Confederal Defense Committee, leading the workers' insurrection and the street-fighting against the army. Subsequently, several of them (Durruti, Ortiz) became column delegates, held a range of military posts (Jover, Sanz) or police posts (Aurelio Fernández), and even held ministerial office (García Oliver).

ORTIZ, Antonio (1907–1996): A member of the CNT Woodworkers Union, he had a hand in the preparation of the January 1933 uprising, for which he was imprisoned. In 1931, he joined the **Nosotros anarchist group**, alongside **Durruti, Ascaso, García Oliver,** and others. And played a prominent part in the 19–20 July 1936 insurrection. On the afternoon of 24 July 1936, he set off by train for the Aragon front, as delegate for the Ortiz or South Ebro Column.

On 14 September 1937, as a result of his opposition to the Stalinist general Enrique Líster's dissolution of the Aragon collectives and the dissolution of the Council of Aragon, he was removed as commander of the 25th Division and was left for several months on end with no military posting. Eventually, in July 1938, he left for exile in France with Joaquín Ascaso (former president of the Council of Aragon) and several colleagues. He accused the top echelons of the CNT-FAI of having issued orders that he and Joaquín Ascaso were to be murdered. He was interned in the Le Vernet concentration camp. Having enlisted with a shock battalion of the French army, he saw action in a number of countries in Africa and Europe. And was decorated several times over. His most brilliant operation was the liberation of Belfort (France). Ortiz's battalion continued the push into German territory, taking the cities of Karlsruhe and Pforzheim, where he was wounded. In 1948, he featured in a planned attack on Franco and the attempted bombing of his yacht, the *Azor*, from a light plane. Wanted in France in connection with this, he left for exile in several Latin American countries. He died in the La Verneda home for the elderly in Barcelona. See José Manuel Márquez and Juan José Gallardo, *Ortiz. General sin dios ni amo* (Barcelona: Hacer, 1999).

PEIRÓ, Joan (Barcelona 1887–Valencia 1942): Outstanding anarcho-syndicalist leader and glassworker. In 1918, he spoke up at the Sants Congress (named after the Sants barrio of Barcelona) and took part in the discussion around the topic of **direct action**. At the congress held in the La Comedia theatre in Madrid, he championed Industrial Federations. He was jailed for his trade union activities from June 1920 until the end of 1921, from January to September 1925, in May 1927, and again in August–September 1927. He served as general secretary of the CNT in 1922 and again in 1928–1929. In 1931, he signed the *Manifesto of the Thirty* (Treinta) and was industry minister in the republican government (1936–1937). While exiled in France, he was picked up by the Gestapo and extradited to Spain. The Falangists invited him to work for them as a union organizer, but his refusal led to his being shot.

PENINSULAR AND REGIONAL FAI COMMITTEES: The PC was the coordinating and leadership agency of the FAI, peninsula-wide (Spain plus Portugal), and the RC its equivalent as far as Catalonia was concerned.

PESTAÑA NÚÑEZ, Ángel (1886–1937): Prominent union leader and veteran CNT member. Watchmaker by trade. Managing editor of *Solidaridad Obrera* in 1917. The CNT's 1919 congress decided to affiliate on a provisional basis to the Third International and dispatched him to Russia to look into how the soviets were organized. Pestaña drew up a report condemning the Soviet regime, triggering the CNT's withdrawal from the Communist International. In 1922, he, **Seguí, Peiró**, and Viadiu signed a restatement of the CNT's apoliticism. In August of that year, he was targeted by gunmen from the *Sindicato Libre*. During the Primo de Rivera dictatorship, he was behind bars from 1924 until 1926. In August 1931, he signed on to the *Manifesto of the Thirty*. In March 1933, he was expelled from the CNT. In April 1934, he launched his Syndicalist Party. When the civil war started he moved to Madrid. Deteriorating health (never the same since that attempt on his life in 1922) forced him to retire to the little village of Begues (Barcelona) where he died.

PORTELA: This was the pseudonym of CNT activist Vicente Gil. He was in charge of border control and of issuing of passports, first for the CAMC (July to October 1936) and later for the Security Junta (October 1936 to March 1937).

POUM: *See Workers' Party for Marxist Unification.*

PRIMO DE RIVERA DICTATORSHIP: During the reign of Alfonso XIII, General Primo de Rivera mounted a coup d'état on 13 September 1923, awarding himself dictatorial powers. He thereby ended *pistolerismo* in Barcelona and covered up the King's involvement in the rout of the Spanish army at Annual (the Spanish war in

Morocco). He persecuted the CNT and cozied up to the UGT. He implemented a policy of great public works and a measure of statist dirigisme. He set up a single party, called the **Patriotic Union**. He was father of the Falange's founder, José Antonio Primo de Rivera. The 1929 economic crisis eroded his social base. On 28 January 1930, he stepped down from office and was replaced by the "*dictablanda*" (soft dictatorship) of General Berenguer. Municipal elections on 14 April 1931 brought about the end of monarchist rule and led to the proclamation of the Republic.

PRODUCER'S CARD: In April 1937, a "workerist" measure, **revolutionary in nature,** was attempted. It aimed to introduce a producer's card, offering rationing entitlements to ensure that no one could survive just because they had money. The point was to flush the rentiers and the bourgeois out from the hiding places in which they were lurking and to get them to enlist in the army or play an active part in military defense efforts. It never came to pass. Not to be confused with the "work card" the Stalinists imposed in 1938 as part of the process of militarization of the working class and work relations.

PSOE: *See Spanish Workers' Socialist Party.*

PSUC: *See Unified Socialist Party of Catalonia.*

RABASSAIRE: Tenant farmer whose lease was tied to the lifespan of his vine roots. The Unió de Rabassaires (Rabassaires Union) was a Catalanist peasant party, close to the ERC.

REBULL, Josep (1906–1999): Josep Rebull Cabré was born in Tivissa (Tarragona) in 1906. He got involved in social struggles following the precedent set by his older brother, the famous POUM militant Daniel Rebull (aka "David Rey"). His first arrest came when he was just eleven years old, and that was in his brother's house in Barcelona, in connection with the 1917 general strike. He studied industrial engineering during the Primo de Rivera dictatorship (in 1927). In 1929, he joined the Catalan-Balearic Communist Federation (FCCB). In November 1932, he stood in the elections to the Catalan parliament. In 1933, he was one of the founders of the Bloc Obrer i Camperol (Worker-Peasant Bloc) in Tarrasa. From October 1934 on, he was paid for editorial work on behalf of the BOC and achieved excellent results thanks to imaginative and efficient distribution of the party's press. He was involved in the founding of the POUM in Las Planas (September 1935). This new party was the result of the amalgamation of the BOC with the ICE. In February 1936, he stood for election on the POUM ticket in Tarragona. During the revolutionary upheaval of 19 and 20 July 1936, he was involved in the streetfighting in Barcelona, in the Plaza de Cataluña and surrounding areas, as part of a group of around a hundred militants that included Carmel Rosa (aka "Roc'), Rovira, Algemir, Vidal, etc.

After the presses of *El Correo Catalán* were commandeered, he reorganized the POUM press and the publications of the Editorial Marxista (Marxist Publishing House) and carried on with his administrative efforts for both. In March 1937, a broad section of POUM militants voiced objections to the lack of internal debate and the further postponement of the party congress, which had previously been postponed in December 1936, February 1937, and now again in March. During March and April 1937, weekly meetings of the political and organizing secretaries from the district committees, at which party cells were organized, channeled the discontent of the grassroots membership. Which is how it came to pass that the POUM's Barcelona Local Committee (LC) turned into a staunch body opposing the POUM leadership, which is to say, opposing the Executive Committee (EC) and the Central Committee (CC). On 13 April 1937, such protest activity, the result of widespread malaise among the POUM's grassroots members, culminated in the convening of a joint meeting between the Barcelona LC and the Central Committee, at which Josep Martí (secretary of the Barcelona LC) and Josep Rebull secured the endorsement and widespread distribution of a Barcelona LC manifesto that was then published in the 15 April edition of *La Batalla*; it related to the crisis in the Generalidad, was critical of the POUM's participation in that bourgeois government, and called for the formation of a Revolutionary Workers' Front to boost Workers' Councils as agencies of power. It was also announced that the POUM's second congress was being convened for 8 May and that there would be ample opportunity to publish and distribute the various cells' countertheses to the Executive Committee's official theses. On 16 April, Nin attended a meeting of the Barcelona LC at which he managed to thwart publication of a pamphlet that did not toe the party's official line.

Josep Rebull was secretary of the POUM's Cell 72 in Barcelona. The countertheses endorsed by Cell 72 (some twelve militants), which were printed in the *Boletín de discusión del II Congreso del POUM*, published by the Barcelona Local Committee, emanated from him and all they did was collate, explore, and theorize the controversies and demands coming from the POUM's grassroots in opposition to the EC's political strategy. The reason why those countertheses were signed by Cell 72 rather than by Josep Rebull had to do with the requirements of the regulations relating to the Second Congress.

During the May Events, Josep Rebull was held for two days as a hostage by a Stalinist platoon. There were three highlights to his part in the May Events, but at no time did he ever call upon his CNT comrades to seize power; he confined himself to putting the matter to his own party's EC. Those three highlights were:

a.   A meeting between Cell 72 and the Friends of Durruti (on the night of 4 May), involving Josep Rebull and Jaime Balius; at which it was decided that no initiative would be taken, given the minority status of both organizations and on the basis that this would depend on what action the CNT took.

b.   A meeting with the EC of the POUM—Nin, Andrade, and Gorkín—where, with a map of Barcelona in hand, Rebull explained that military victory was a certainty if the POUM would just make up its mind to attack the government buildings in the city center. The response to this was that the situation was a **political matter and not a military one**; seizing power meant a breakdown of antifascist unity and would hasten a swift victory for Franco's armies.

c.   He made the presses of the POUM available to the Friends of Durruti (8 May) so that they, having been disowned by the CNT by that point, might launch a manifesto taking stock of the recent May incidents.

Josep Rebull was **the only POUMist alert to the overriding and immediate need to go underground** in order to prepare for the repression that could be anticipated. With the chances of holding a party congress now gone, the so-called left of the Barcelona POUM was down to just one militant by early 1938: Josep Rebull. During the year he spent living below the radar in Barcelona city, he lived in, alternately, Manuel Maurín's apartment in the Calle Padua or a rented room in the Calle Llibretería. He was still active in publishing and distributing the POUM's clandestine press (up until April 1938), as well as in bringing solidarity and aid to prisoners, repeatedly paying visits to Justice Minister Irujo to get him to have POUM militants removed from the Communist chekas (from which they might vanish without trace) to republican prisons. He enlisted in the army under the alias of Pau Mitjá, in late 1938. After the fall of Barcelona, he and his partner Teresa, made the trek on foot to cross the border via Coll d'Ares and on to Prats de Molló and Perpignan. For some months he worked, as many far-left exiles of every nationality did, at the Croque-Fruit jam factory that was run by Trotskyists. Josep Rebull secured phony identity papers in the name of Robert Verdeaux. During a stay in Marseilles, he struck up a friendship with the writer Jean Malaquais, his neighbor in Air-Bel. In the summer of 1941, he joined the French Resistance in the Var department, until he was arrested by the Gestapo, only to be freed eventually in 1944. In 1947, he moved again, to Paris. During his lengthy exile in France, he survived as the administrator of a small publishing house and as a journalist for *Franc-Tireur*, later renamed *Paris Jour*. For a full biography, see Casciola and Guillamón, *Biografías del 36*, 315–330. See also the appendices of this book for his article on the May Events of 1937. There is also a book analyzing his political thinking: *Espagne 1937. Josep Rebull, la voie révolutionnaire* (Paris: Spartacus, 2014), released in Spanish in 2017 by Ediciones Descontrol.

REGIONAL AND LOCAL CNT COMMITTEES: Respectively, the coordination and leadership body of the CNT covering the whole of Catalonia (the RC), or at local level.

REVOLUTIONARY BARRIO COMMITTEES IN THE CITY OF BARCELONA: In Barcelona city, the **revolutionary** *barrio* **committees** and various local committees around Catalonia were the working class' **potential organs of power.** They campaigned for **socialization** of the economy and opposed militarization of the militias and collaboration with the government and antifascist political parties. They were armed and were the **clandestine army of revolution.** Their main shortcoming was their inability to organize and coordinate themselves outside of the machinery of the CNT. The higher committees drowned out, politically and organizationally, the revolutionary committees, which became their worst enemies and the greatest obstacle to their longed-for and necessary absorption into the bourgeois state's apparatus, the ultimate aim of the process of their institutionalization. Comorera declared war on them, prioritizing their defeat over the hunger pangs of Barcelona residents.

REGIONAL CONFEDERATION OF LABOR OF CATALONIA (CRTC): Commonly, but incorrectly, referred to as the CNT of Catalonia.

REVOLUTIONARY PROGRAM OF THE PROLETARIAT: The revolutionary program of the proletariat entails internationalization of the revolution, socialization of the economy, the laying of sound foundations for the abolition of value and waged labor around the world, proletarian leadership of the war and the workers' militias, society reorganized along councilist and assembly-based organizational lines, and the repression by the proletariat of bourgeois and petite bourgeois strata of society as a means of crushing the inevitable armed backlash from the counterrevolution. The main theoretical advance made by the Friends of Durruti was to assert the totalitarian character of the proletarian revolution. Totalitarian, yes, all-embracing, reaching into every realm: social, economic, political, cultural, and into every single country, overriding all national borders; and authoritarian too, in that it faced military opposition from the class enemy, which is to say, the petite bourgeoisie pampered by the PSUC.

RUIZ, Pablo: A militia member from the Durruti Column's Fourth *Agrupación* based in **Gelsa**, he led the eight-hundred militia members who quit the Aragon front and returned, armed, to Barcelona, to fight on for the revolution. At the beginning of March 1937, he was one of the founders of the Friends of Durruti.

SANTANA CALERO, Juan: Had been active in the Libertarian Youth in Malaga. He joined the Friends of Durruti after May 1937.

SANTILLÁN, Diego Abad de (1897–1983): This was the outlandish pseudonym adopted by the anarchist writer and leader Sinesio Baudilio García Fernández. In 1905, his family, made up of workers and impoverished peasants from the mountains of Leon, emigrated to Argentina. Santillán returned to Spain in 1913. He completed his baccalaureate and started studying at university. Shuttling between Spain and Argentina, he came into contact with the anarchist movement in both countries. He was a regular contributor to *La Protesta*, the mouthpiece of the Argentine FORA. In 1922, he travelled to Germany to study medicine and took part in the IWA congress in Berlin in 1925 and in the one held in Amsterdam in 1926. In 1933, he settled in Spain, on the run from the Argentinean police. In 1934, he joined the Barcelona editorial team of *Solidaridad Obrera* (organ of the Catalan CNT), ran *Tierra y Libertad* (the FAI mouthpiece), and was the driving force behind *Tiempos Nuevos*. He set up the **Nervio group**, which built an anti-Nosotros front and played host to all Argentine anarchists arriving in Barcelona, assigning them significant positions of leadership during the war.

Although he did not distinguish himself in the streetfighting, he served as a member of the CAMC's War Department headed by García Oliver. In the summer and autumn of 1936, he amassed countless positions of responsibility, all of them equally ineptly performed. Between December 1936 and April 1937, he was councillor of economy in the Generalidad government, replacing **Joan Pau Fábregas** (Fábregas had promulgated the Collectivizations Decree), and was always ready with a defense of the government's viewpoint against the CNT. In May 1937, he joined those calling for a ceasefire, only to regret it within days.

In September 1937, he published a book saying the war was a lost cause. He had no problems reconciling the contradiction between drafting theoretical articles that were immaculately purist, and collaborationist political activity in favor of CNT partnership in the business of government. In the summer of 1938, he launched the prestigious theoretical review *Timón*, returned to his activities as a translator, and resurrected Ediciones Tierra y Libertad. He left for exile in Argentina.

SANZ, Ricardo (1898–1986): Textile worker from the Pueblo Nuevo barrio of Barcelona. Syndicalist and anarchist. In 1922, he joined the **Los Solidarios group** with **Durruti, Ascaso, García Oliver**, and others. In Pueblo Nuevo, he set up an arms depot and bomb-making workshop. In 1925, he was taken into preventive detention.

In 1926, he was again arrested and held for twenty-six months. From 1928 to 1930, he was inactive. In 1931, he turned to training the CNT defense cadres. He served on the Revolutionary Committee behind the January 1933 uprising and was involved in the streetfighting on 19–20 July 1936. During the summer of 1936, he worked on supplying the columns serving on the Aragon front. After Durruti died, he was appointed to succeed him as the column delegate (which had become, following militarization, the 26th Division). He went into exile in France. See Casciola and Guillamón, *Biografías del 36*, 369–375.

SBLE: *See Spanish Bolshevik-Leninist Section.*

SEISDEDOS GROUP: Made up of **Manuel Escorza del Val**, Liberato Minué, Abelino Estrada, José Irizalde, Manuel Gallego, etc. Many of them were assets of the CNT-FAI Investigation Service run by Manuel Escorza.

SESÉ: Antonio Sesé Artaso started out as a trade unionist with the CNT. He then was active in the Catalan-Balearic Communist Federation and became a cofounder of the **BOC**. In 1932, he joined the Partit Comunista de Catalunya and moved on to the **PSUC** in July 1936. He took over from José del Barrio (who had been appointed as delegate of the Karl Marx Column) as **secretary of the UGT in Catalonia**. In the spring of 1937, he was at the forefront of confrontations with the CNT. In April 1937, he wrote Companys a letter insisting that the frontier areas be swept clean of anarchists. During the May Events of 1937, he was appointed councillor-without-portfolio and was murdered (5 May 1937) by gunfire in the Calle Caspe, outside the premises of the CNT's Public Entertainments Union, while en route to take up office at the Generalidad Palace.

SINDICATO ÚNICO: The Sants Congress of the Regional Confederation of Labor of Catalonia met in the Barcelona district of that name from 28 June to 1 July 1918. Its major achievements were **direct action** and the *sindicato único* or *sindicato de ramo*. In addition, it was agreed that women needed unionizing and that the exploitation of minors had to end. It was agreed that no overtime was to be worked while there were workers without jobs. It was resolved that those trades that had already secured the eight-hour working day would help the ones who had yet to do so. And that their sights should be set on a standard wage.

The chief advance was the organization of the CNT into *sindicatos únicos*. It was a matter of ending the old guild organization that remained in a number of trades, with their differing interests within the same factory or firm. The various autonomous trades societies were disbanded and the object was to have all who worked in the same branch of industry organized in a single, united organization. In, say, a textile plant, the various trades distinctions—spinner, weaver, boilermaker, machinist, etc.—would be done away with and these would all amalgamate into a single textile workers' union, bringing great organizational strength to workers in their dealing with the employer, who, in the event of a strike, could not rely any longer on the distinctions between the several trades within his firm. It was the same for the unions of woodworkers, health-workers, construction workers, bank workers, etc. The old trades unions were done away with and replaced by single unions covering each branch of industry.

The *sindicato único* implied a higher degree of unity vis-à-vis the employers and it was a boon to strategies such as the general strike and to direct action. The lobbying on behalf of the *sindicato único* was led by Salvador Seguí and Emilio Mira who stated that: "Workers have to display unity in the face of a close-knit, organized employer class."

SINDICATOS DE OFICIOS VARIOS: Amalgamated trades unions. The *sindicatos únicos* covered each branch of industry. Thus, in Barcelona, there was a woodworkers *sindicato único*, one for construction workers, one for textile workers, one for hospitality workers, one for healthworkers', and so on. But in a small town, where the numbers for the establishment of several *sindicatos únicos* were just not there, up popped the *sindicato único de oficios varios*, embracing all workers in that small town, regardless of what trade they plied. In Barcelona, there was also a *Sindicato Único de Oficios Varios*, covering those workers who could not affiliate to any of the branch unions already in existence, perhaps because there was none to suit them, because they lacked the numbers, or because they were in the process of being established. This was the case with intellectuals, artists, and so on.

THE SOCIALIST UNION OF CATALONIA (USC): Founded in 1923. Joan Comorera was made its general secretary in 1932. It was one of four small parties that amalgamated on 24 July 1936 into the PSUC.

SOCIALIZATION VERSUS COLLECTIVIZATION: By the spring of 1937, there was growing tension between worker-advocated socialization and Generalidad-managed and -manipulated collectivization. On the one hand, the Generalidad government, supported socially by petit-bourgeois sectors—civil servants, technicians, ex-entrepreneurs, the liberal professions, and even some ideologically Stalinist or right-wing workers (very often marshaled by the UGT) embarked upon an offensive to expand its control over firms, basing itself on the Collectivizations Decree and enforcement of a battery of decrees approved by Tarradellas in S'Agaró in January 1937. In parallel with this, a radical sector of the CNT's membership attempted to SOCIALIZE production, which implied a boosting of the powers of the Industrial Unions within firms. In the view of that radical sector of the CNT,

SOCIALIZATION meant that the Catalan economy would be run by the (CNT) unions and there would be a break with the dynamic of trade union capitalism, with a fair distribution of assets that would end to the scandalous differences between rich collectivized industries and the poorer ones, and between the latter and the unemployed. In turn, this approach to a Catalan **socialized economy** required the creation of appropriate bodies within the CNT, which is to say, the replacement of *sindicatos únicos* (fine for running a strike but not for running firms) by Industrial Unions (better equipped to run the various sectors of the economy) and this was done in the first few months of 1937. SOCIALIZATION of the Catalan economy implied that the CNT would be in charge of the running the economy (and the war), and that, in turn, required doing away with the Generalidad government.

So, the Generalidad's counterrevolutionary offensive, designed to beef up its control by reaching into every firm, clashed head-on with the radical segment of the CNT's plans for socialization.

During the spring of 1937, there was a firm-by-firm battle whereby meetings that had to give their approval to socialization came under pressure and were manipulated in a wide range of ways, from the most ruinous politicking intrigues through to the deployment of police. In this firm-by-firm tussle, which the CNT's higher committees never wanted centralized, because that would have meant breaking the antifascist unity pact, there emerged an ever plainer and more "painful" rift in the union membership, between the pro-collaboration sector and the radical segment of the CNT. In that attempt to bring the Catalan economy under social ownership, the radical CNT membership attempted to challenge the pro-collaboration militants for the support of the bulk of the union members. But in almost every case the radical elements were in the minority in factory meetings, given the huge influx of opportunists who had joined up after 19 July and the dispersion that the revolution had caused in the revolutionaries' ranks, what with their having enlisted in the militias or been hoisted into positions of responsibility.

Examples of the contest between socialization and Generalidad-manipulated collectivization are the following pamphlets:

Barcelona CNT-IWA Metalworking Industrial Union: *Colectivización? Nacionalización? No: Socialización* (Barcelona: Imp. Primero de mayo, 1937)

Memoria del Primer Congreso Regional de Sindicatos de la Industria de la Edificación, Madera y Decoración (Barcelona: Gráficas Inicial, 1937)

The protagonists wrote: *Balances para la historia. Las colectivizaciones y la autogestión obrera durante la Guerra civil española* (No indication of publisher, place or date of publication)

SPANISH BOLSHEVIK-LENINIST SECTION (SBLE): An orthodox Trotskyist group in which **Munis**, Domenico Sedran (aka "Adolfo Carlini'), Hans David Freund (aka "Moulin'), Erwin Wolf, and Jaime Fernández were active. During the May Events, it launched a flyer. For biographies of all of the above, see *Biografías del 36*.

SPANISH WORKERS' SOCIALIST PARTY (PSOE): In Catalonia, the PSOE's Catalan federation evaporated completely after it amalgamated with three other parties to form the **PSUC**. In the Madrid and Valencia governments, the PSOE held the premiership of the central government from 5 September 1936 until the end of the war, first in the person of **Largo Caballero** and later in the person of **Negrín** (from 19 May 1937 on), though the latter was heavily influenced by the PCE.

STATE CAPITALISM AND TRADE-UNION CAPITALISM: Stalinism was a counterrevolutionary option, championing **state capitalism** and advocating a Stalinist party dictatorship over the proletariat. The **state anarchism of the libertarian higher committees** was also a counterrevolutionary option, in that it championed a **trade-union capitalism** and called for a strengthening of the state, for antifascist unity, and for a single aim: winning the war on fascism, abjuring the revolution.

TARRADELLAS, Josep (1899–1988): Catalanist bourgeois politician. He was the former private secretary to **Macià** and was married to his daughter. In 1931, he was elected a deputy and, in December, joined the Generalidad government, holding the portfolios for Interior and Health. Stood trial in relation to the events of October 1934. When the civil war erupted he placed himself at the disposal of **Companys**, the Generalidad president, at a time when the ERC had largely abandoned public office. In July–September 1936, he served as Public Services councillor. He was prime minister (or, in Catalan, *primer conseller*) of the Generalidad Council from September 1936 until May 1937, subsequently taking up the Department of Finance. In April 1937, Companys kept him at arm's length from negotiations meant to thrash out a solution to the Generalidad government crisis. In 1954, while in exile in France, he was elected Generalidad president, a position in which he was confirmed in 1977, and he was one of the mainstays of the so-called Transition. Tarradellas stepped down from that office in 1980.

TORYHO, Jacinto: Anarchist journalist. In 1932, he was on the editorial staff of *Solidaridad Obrera* and *Tierra y Libertad*. In 1933, he joined the **anarchist A group**. In the wake of the events of July 1936, he set up a CNT-FAI Press and Propaganda Section. In November 1936, he took over from Liberto Callejas as managing editor of *Solidaridad Obrera*, purging the editorial team of veteran anarchist staffers and replacing them with bourgeois professionals and collaborationist ideologues. He was the very prototype of the bureaucrat ensconced in his post. His ineptitude and bullying manner, the unhappiness of the unions and the irritation of his readers ensured that in the end, in March 1938, he was fired as *Solidaridad Obrera* director. Left for exile in Argentina.

TREINTISTAS: The *treintistas* described themselves as gradualist revolutionaries and pure syndicalists, opposed to the "hare-brained" insurrectionists of the *faístas*. They preferred long-term trade union endeavor to short-term, hasty, insurrectionist action that drew down repression and disorganization.

The *Manifesto of the Thirty* (Trenta) in August 1931 was signed by, among others, Progreso Alfarache, Roldán Cortada (who finished up in the UGT), Juan López (who became the Republic's Industry minister), **Joan Peiró** (a very prominent trade unionist and a figure of great prestige), Ángel Pestaña, and so on. The main upshots of the *Manifesto of the Thirty* was a split within the CNT and the emergence of the so-called Opposition Unions that, in January 1933, went on to launch the Libertarian Syndicalist Federation (FSL). In Catalonia, the FSL built up great strength in towns like Sabadell, Mataró, Badalona, Manresa, etc. It also became very strong in the Valencia region. It had around 65,000 members.

The split was not resolved until the Zaragoza Congress of the CNT in May 1936, a few short months prior to the outbreak of civil war. Joan Peiró rejoined the reunified CNT fold with his tremendous prestige undiminished.

Ángel Pestaña quit the FSL to launch a minuscule Syndicalist Party in April 1934; this alienated him from the bulk of the CNT membership and can be regarded as his great personal and political failure.

UGT: *See General Union of Workers.*

UNCONTROLLABLES: The CNT and FAI higher committees restored public order, which is to say republican law and order, to the streets of Barcelona, cracking down on crime and hunting down embedded fascists, but also curtailing the revolutionary violence of the barrio committees and trade unions. The veil disguising this tackling of revolutionary expropriators was their professed purpose of wiping out fascist sympathizers, the clergy, and an arbitrary and opportunistic criminality that did actually exist and that was incontrovertibly a serious issue. All the antifascist organizations—including the Generalidad government and the higher committees—conflated criminality with the **revolutionary violence** of the barrio committees and unions, which were collectivizing or taking over factories, fields, and workshops; executing fascists, *pistoleros*, right-wingers, military, and priests; and seizing mansions, cars, luxury accommodations, barracks, convents, hospitals, hospices, properties abandoned by fugitive rebels, etc.

In the eyes of many, the revolutionary process had gone too far. The first step toward bringing it to heel was to curb it so that it would go no further. The time to wrest back lost ground would come after that. Which is where the new notion of "revolutionary order" came from: it meant nothing less than stopping the revolution from embedding itself and looking upon "revolutionary gains" as a new and **finished order** in need of protection from uncontrollable/revolutionaries, from maverick criminality, from the expropriated bourgeoisie, and from fascism.

The success of the label "uncontrollable" was rooted in this very ambiguity, in the incorporation and confounding of two separate meanings: the criminal and the revolutionary. This was achieved in a rather discreet and disguised fashion so as to win acceptance from the barrio, local, or trade union committees themselves—at which it was targeted. And it was done plainly and precisely enough that it could be used by the higher committees, the bourgeois parties, the Stalinists, and the government as a weapon against revolutionaries, the latter having been transfigured by the slanderous tag "uncontrollable" into scapegoats, whipping boys, and the number one target to be taken down.

The requisite and inescapable crackdown on chaotic, opportunistic criminality provided an excellent pretext for curbing and controlling the property-seizing revolutionaries as well. It was the product of the authentic nature of the CAMC, which was something less than the Generalidad government, but was the first step in the direction of its reconstruction, that is, a class collaborationist agency, a partnership between all the worker and bourgeois trade unions and political organizations, as well as representatives of the government. The ultimate aim, whether consciously or otherwise, was to restore the full authority of the bourgeois state. At each step, an appropriate agency was formed to oversee and channel the "July revolution" and pave the way for the future reconstruction of the state. The same thing happened with the Control Patrols. With the "real" Public Order forces (which is to say, the Civil Guard and Assault Guard) confined to their barracks, a "revolutionary" police force was needed, to protect this new "revolutionary" order and it needed the capability to crack down on random criminality, but it also had to "contain" the barrio and trade-union committees, regardless of any and all contradictions created by the unstable circumstances of the higher committees. These higher committees were in charge of an organization that was anti-state in its ideology, but a stakeholder in the business of government and in the rebuilding of the capitalist state.

Throughout history, revolutionary movements have never been pure and unblemished; they have been heterogeneous and contradictory, naïve and avant-garde, irksome and blinkered, surprising and farsighted, all at the same time.

UNIFIED SOCIALIST PARTY OF CATALONIA (PSUC): The product of the amalgamation of four small socialist and communist partiers on 24 July 1936. Its general secretary was **Comorera**. Controlled by Moscow through the Hungarian Erno Gerö (aka "Pedro'), who, in 1956, used tanks to crush the workers' insurrection in Budapest. The PSUC was the only party in the Third International formed through the coming together of socialists and communists and it was also the only party acknowledged as representing a country without a state of its own.

USC: *See Socialist Union of Catalonia.*

VIDIELLA, Rafael (1890–1982): Born in Tortosa in 1890. A printing worker who was active in the CNT in his early youth. During the Primo de Rivera dictatorship, he served as publisher of *Solidaridad Obrera* in Valencia. From 1925 on, he was active in the UGT. From 1931 on, he led the PSOE's Catalan Federation. In September 1935, the POUM was launched as the result of negotiations between the BOC and the ICE. On 24 July, the PSUC was launched as an amalgamation of four small socialist and communist parties: the Communist Party of Catalonia (PCC); the Catalan Federation of the PSOE, led by Vidiella; the Comorera-led USC; and the Partit Català Proletari.

In May 1936, Vidiella stepped down from his post on the PSOE National Committee. Some months after that, Comorera and Vidiella became members of the central committee of the PCE.

On 21 July 1936, he took charge of the CAMC's Investigation Department. In the very short-lived government formed by Companys on 31 July 1936, but vetoed by García Oliver, the PSUC had three councillorships: Joan Comorera at Economy, Rafael Vidiella at Communications, and Estanislau Ruíz Ponsetí at Supplies. On 6 August 1936, a new government was formed, without any PSUC presence.

The Generalidad government wanted to avoid trying those who were accused of murders carried out during the revolutionary period that followed the defeat of the army revolt in Catalonia in July 1936. Vidiella drafted a press statement in which it was stated that the Generalidad Council had unanimously agreed to its proposal that the magistrates be instructed not to treat "revolutionary incidents" as criminal. Companys remarked that this ought not to be made public, but Vidiella pressed on and the report was carried in the newspapers. No public denial followed.

On 17 December 1936, a brand new "trade union" Generalidad government was formed. Three PSUC members—representing the UGT—joined the government: Vidiella (at Justice), Comorera (at Supplies) and Miquel Valdés (at Labor and Public Works). On 16 April 1937, there was a cabinet reshuffle and Vidiella became labor and public works councillor. A few days after that, on 25 April, one of the PSUC's leaders, Roldán Cortada, was assassinated. Vidiella put the blame for the murder on the anarchists, helping to exacerbate existing tensions.

During the bloodletting in May 1937, Vidiella, replacing Antonio Sesé who had been killed on 5 May while en route to the Generalidad to take up his post, was appointed councillor for justice, Labor, Supplies, and Public Works. In the government of 30 June 1937, he was awarded the portfolio for Labor and Public Works.

He spent his exile in several countries before eventually settling permanently in Budapest. During the falling-out between Comorera and the PCE, Vidiella stuck by the party. For many years he was one of the main leaders of the PCE. He was a regular contributor to the PSUC review *Nous Horitzons*. In 1976, he returned to Spain and settled in Barcelona where he died on 23 September 1982.

VINALESA: On 8 March 1937, violent armed clashes erupted in Vinalesa (Valencia) between anarchists opposed to militarization and the Assault Guards who wanted to compel them to return to the front. The upshot was that several lives were lost and there were wounded on both sides. Upwards of two hundred anarcho-syndicalists were arrested, ninety-two of them militia members from the Iron Column. In the end, on 21 March, the Iron Column agreed to be militarized, becoming the 843rd Brigade.

WORKERS' PARTY FOR MARXIST UNIFICATION (POUM): Founded in September 1935 through the amalgamation of the BOC and the ICE. By July 1936, it had some 5,000 members in Catalonia. Being a Leninist party, it forbade the formation of fractions, any sort of discussion or debate, on pain of instant expulsion, except during the time of a congress. It was critical of Stalinism in the Soviet Union. On 16 June 1937, the party was outlawed, its Central Committee jailed, and its members persecuted. Its political secretary, **Nin**, was abducted, tortured, and murdered by the Soviets. The Hotel Falcón, previously lodgings for foreigners sympathetic to the POUM, was turned into a Stalinist prison.

WORKERS' TRADE UNION UNITY FEDERATION: Organization under the sway of the POUM and primarily Catalonia-based. Initially, it had been set up by unions excluded from the CNT. Nin ordered it to amalgamate with the UGT in September 1936, in a vain attempt to woo the latter away from the PSUC. In July 1936, its membership stood at around 50,000.

Bibliography

The basic texts that make possible a documented and rigorous interpretation of the May Events of Barcelona are marked with an asterisk (*).

1. Main Archival Sources:

Actes de les sessions del Consell Executiu de la Generalitat [ANC, AMTM, and others]

Bolloten Correspondence [HI]

FACA Correspondence [BAEL]

Correspondence and interviews of Agustín Guillamón [Guillamón Archive]

Fons Andreu i Abelló [ANC]

Fons Bosch i Gimpera [ANC]

Fons Brangui [ANC]

Fons Joan Casanovas Codina [AHCB]

Fons Fets de Maig del 27 [Tarradellas Papers] [ANC]

Fons Ronald Fraser d'entrevistes orals [AHCB]

Fons Generalitat Republicana [ANC]

Fonsa d'Ordre Públic [AHTM]

Fons Sagarra i Plana, Josep María [ANC]

Fons Rafael Vidiella [ANC]

Leaflets and Posters [CA, AEP, and elsewhere]

Reuniones de comités superiores libertarios, en Barcelona [FAL, IISH, and SA]

Sumari per troballa de dotze cadàvers en la carretera de Bellaterra. Jutjat Especial, 1937 [TSJC]

2. Books, theses, articles, and pamphlets

ABAD DE SANTILLÁN, Diego. *Por qué perdimos la guerra.* Esplugues del Llobregat: Plaza y Janés, 1977.

L'ADUNATA DEI REFRATTARI. *Barricate e Decreti, Spagna 36–37: La rivoluzione infranta.* n.p.: Gratis, 2012.

* "Affaire Sancho-Casanovas-Lluhí-Gassol, desde la Embajada de París y el Consulado de Toulouse." Investigation by Manuel Escorza's Information Service in concert with Dionisio Eroles's agency. [AEP]

AGUILERA POVEDANO, Manuel. "Listado de víctimas de los Hechos de Mayo de 1937 en

Barcelona." Blog of Manuel Aguilera Povedano. 2013. https://manuelaguilerapovedano.word-press.com/2013/12/31/listado-de-victimas-de-los-hechos-de-mayo-de-1937-en-barcelona.

———. "Los hechos de mayo de 1937: Efectivos y bajas de cada bando." *Hispania* 245 (2013): 789–816.

AGUZZI, Aldo. "Un anarquista italiano en las Jornadas de Mayo." In *Barcelona, mayo 1937: Testimonios desde las barricadas*, edited by GARCÍA, PIOTROWSKI, and ROSÉS, 155–62. Barcelona: Alikornio Ediciones, 2006.

BALCELLS, Albert. *Justicia i presons, després de maig de 1937, a Catalunya*. Barcelona: Dalmau, 1989. [Ground-breaking book, essential reading]

BALLESTER, David. *Els anys de la guerra. La UGT de Catalunya (1936–1939)*. Barcelona: Columna, 1998.

BARROT, Jean. *"Bilan": Contre-révolution en Espagne (1936-1939)*. Paris: Union Générale d'Éditions, 1979. [Required reading]

———. *Quand meurent les révolutions*. Paris: Adel, n.d.

BERENGUER, Sara. *Entre el sol y la tormenta*. Calella: Seuba Ediciones, 1988.

———. Correspondence with Agustín Guillamón (2009).

BERNECKER, W. *Colectividades y revolución social*. Barcelona: Crítica, 1982.

———. "La revolución social." In *La Guerra civil. Una nueva visión del conflicto que dividió España*, edited by PAYNE and TUSELL, 485–583. Madrid: Temas de Hoy, 1996.

BERTRÁN y MUSITU, José. *Experiencias de los Servicios de Información del Nordeste de España (SIFNA) durante la guerra*. Madrid: Espasa-Calpe, 1940.

BOLLOTEN, Burnett. *La Guerra Civil española*. Madrid: Alianza, 1989. [A classic that has stood the test of time.]

BONOMINI, Ernesto. "Semana sangrienta." In *Barcelona, mayo 1937: Testimonios desde las barricadas*, edited by GARCÍA, PIOTROWSKI, and ROSÉS, 145–54. Barcelona: Alikornio Ediciones, 2006.

BRENAN, Gerald: *El laberinto español*. Paris: Ruedo Ibérico, 1962.

BROUÉ, Pierre. *Trotsky y la guerra civil española*. Buenos Aires: Jorge Álvarez, 1966.

———. *La révolution espasgnole (1931–1939)*. Paris: Flammarion, 1973.

———. *Staline et la révolution. Le cas espagnol*. Paris: Fayard, 1993.

BROUÉ, Pierre, and N. DOREY. "Critiques de gauche et opposition révolutionnaire au Front Populaire 1936-1938." *Le Mouvement Social*, January–March (1966): 91–133.

BROUÉ, Pierre, Ronald FRASER, and Pierre VILAR. *Metodología histórica de la guerra y revolución españolas*. Madrid: Fontamara, 1980.

BROUÉ, Pierre, and Emile TÉMIME. *La Révolution et la Guerre d'Espagne*. Paris: Les Éditions de Minuit, 1961. [Spanish edition by FCE, Mexico, 1967.]

BUCCI, Fausto, and Paolo CASCIOLA. *Massimalisti, trotskisti e bordighisti italiani nella guerra civile spagnola (1936–1939)*. Paper written for the symposium, sponsored by the review *Spagna Contemporanea* on the topic of "Exiles and Fighters: 1930s Spain in the collective memory in Italy." Alessandria-Novi Ligure, 30 November–1 December 2007. Unpublished.

CABALLÉ, T. *Barcelona Roja, Dietario de la revolución*. Barcelona: Librería Argentina, 1939.

* CAMPOS, Severino. "Las ideas y los hombres. Objeciones al prologo de un libero III." *Le Combat syndicaliste* (23 December 1978): 6. [He confirms the existence of a secret revolutionary committee in May 1937. And he affords an insight into the part played by each individual: Merino as the insurrection's leader; Ruano, the man of action skilled in street-fighting; and Manzana, as the strategist behind the defense of the Casa CNT-FAI. He thereby adds nuance to the testimony of Suñer, by clearly differentiating the tasks they performed within that committee.]

————. *Una vida por un ideal*. 2006. Unpublished.

CASANOVAS, Joan. "La guerra civil a Barcelona: les patrulles de control de Sants vistes per un dels seus membres." *Historia y Fuente Oral* 11 (1994): 53–66.

CASANOVAS CODINA, Joan. *Joan Remi*. Fons oral, AHCB 3-332/5D.102.

CASCIOLO, Paolo and Agustín GUILLAMÓN, eds. *Biografías del 36*. Barcelona: Descontrol, 2016.

CHAZÉ, H. [pseudonym of Gaston Davoust]. *Chronique de la Révolution Espagnole. Union Communiste (1933–1939)*. Paris: Spartacus, 1979.

Comité Central de Milícies Antifeixistes, Junta de Seguretat Interior, Conselleria de Seguretat Interior. *Ordre públic I violencia a Catalunya* (Barcelona: Dau, 2011)

Correspondence of Agustín Guillamón and **Albert Masó March** (1996–1997)

Correspondence of Agustín Guillamón and **José Quesada Suárez** (1996)

Correspondence, interview, and questionnaire, Agustín Guillamón and **Josep Rebull Cabré** (1985)

CRUELLS, Manuel. *Mayo sangriento: Barcelona 1937*. Barcelona: Juventud, 1970. [A book that needs to be read with a very critical eye as it is fraught with errors and weird interpretations.]

EALHAM, Chris. *La lucha por Barcelona: Clase, cultura y conflicto 1898–1937*. Madrid: Alianza Editorial, 2005.

————. *Vivir la anarquía, vivir la utopia. José Peirats y la historia del anarcosindicalismo español*. Barcelona: Alianza Editorial, 2016.

EVANS, Daniel. *The Conscience of the Spanish Revolution: Anarchist opposition to state collaboration in 1937*. Doctoral thesis. University of Leeds. July 2016.

FRASER, Ronald. *Recuérdalo tú y recuérdalo a otros. Historia oral de la guerra civil española*, 2 volumes. Barcelona: Critica, 1979. [A beautiful, book, essential reading.]

FRASQUET, Eduard, and Jesus E. ALONSO. "Notes al voltant de la Guerra civil espanyola i el concepte de revolució." *Ullal* 10 (1986): 54–59.

FUKUYAMA, Francis. *The End of History and the Last Man*. New York: Free Press, 1992. [Non-historiographical account.]

Fundación de Estudios Libertarios "Salvador Seguí." *Sucesos de Mayo (1937)*. Madrid: Cuadernos de la Guerra Civil, Fundación Salvador Seguí, 1987. [Document no. 1 is a reprint of Agustín Souchy's *Los sucesos de Barcelona* (Ediciones Ebro, 1937).]

GALLEGO, Ferran. *Barcelona, mayo de 1937*. Barcelona: Debate, 2007. [Non-historiographical account.]

GARCÍA, Carlos, Harald PIOTROWSKI, and Sergi ROSÉS. *Barcelona mayo 1937. Testimonios desde las barricadas*. Barcelona: Alikornio Ediciones, 2006. [Essential reading.]

GARCÍA OLIVER, Juan. *El eco de los pasos*. Paris: Ruedo Ibérico 1978. [On Merino, see 420–21.]

GARCÍA VIVANCOS, Miguel. "La intervención de la CNT y la FAI en el proceso del POUM." *Cultura Proletaria* (February 1939).

GERVASINI, Virginia: "Gli insegnamenti della sconfitta della rivoluzione spagnola (1937–1939)." *Quaderni del Centro Studi Pietro Tresso* 30, Studie e richerche series (1993)

GODICHEAU, François: *Répression et Ordre Public en Catalogne pendant la guerre civile (1936-1939)*. Thesis, 3 volumes. Écoles des Hautes Études en Sciences Sociales. 2001. [Outstanding, pioneering work.]

———. "Los Hechos de Mayo d 1937 y los presos antifascisytas: identificación de un fenómeno represivo." *Historia Social* 44 (2002): 39–63.

———. *La Guerre d'Espagne, République et révolution en Catalogne*. Paris: Odile Jacob, 2004.

———. "La domestication de la révolution: du viol des principes doctrineaux à la patrimoinisation de l'identité anarchiste en passant pour l'intégration de la CNT à l'État républican (1936–1939)." *Regards* 9 (2006): 149–73.

GÓMEZ, Fredy. *Entrevista con Juan García Oliver, regisatrada el 29-6-1977 en París (Francia)*. Madrid: Fundación Salvador Seguí, 1990.

Govern de la Generalitat/Josep Tarradellas. *Crónica de la Guerra civil a Catalunya*. 2 volumes. Barcelona: DAU, 2008 and 2009. [Outstanding publication, the fruits of the erudition and rigorous standards set by Montserrat Catalán, director at the AMTM.]

GUILLAMÓN, Agustín. "I bordighisti nella guerra civile spagnola." *Quaderni del Centro Studi Pietro Tresso* 27, Studi e reicerche series (1993).

———. *Barricadas en Barcelona*. Barcelona: Espartaco Internacional, 2007. [Issued in French translation by Éditions Spartacus, 2009.]

———. *Los Comités de Defensa de la CNT en Barcelona (1933–1938)*. Barcelona: Aldarull, 2011. [Fourth corrected and expanded edition, 2013. Available in French, Italian, Catalan, Greek, and English translations. English edition: *Ready For Revolution: The CNT Defense Committees in Barcelona (1933–38)*. Oakland: AK Press and Kate Sharpley Library, 2014.

———. *La revolución de los comités. Hambre y violencia en la Barcelona revolucionaria. De julio a diciembre de 1936*. Barcelona: Aldarull/El grillo libertario, 2012. [Second corrected edition published by El grillo libertario, 2015.]

———. *El terror Stalinista en Barcelona (1938)*. Barcelona: Aldarull/Descontrol, 2013.

———. *Los Amigos de Durruti. Historia y antología de textos*. Barcelona: Aldarull/Descontrol, 2013.

*———. *Espagne 1937: Josep Rebull, la voie révolutionnaire*. Paris: Spartacus, 2014. [Issued in Spanish by Descontrol, 2017.]

————. *La guerra del pan. Hambre y violencia en la Barcelona revolucionaria. De diciembre de 1936 a mayo de 1937.* Barcelona: Descontrol, 2014.

————. *La represión contra la CNT y los revolucionarios. Hambre y violencia en la Barcelona revolucionaria. De mayo a septiembre de 1937.* Barcelona: Descontrol, 2015.

————. *Correspondencia entre Abel Paz y García Oliver. Tesis sobre la Guerra de España y la situación revolucionaria creada el 19 de julio en Cataluña.* Barcelona: Descontrol, 2016.

GUILLAMÓN, Agustín (Archives): Correspondence, interviews, and/or questionnaires traded between Agustín Guillamón and Sara Berenguer, Pierre Broué, Diego Camacho, Mary Low, César Martínez Lorenzo, Albert Masó, Munis, José Quesada, Josep Rebull, Wilebaldo Solano, and Pere Vigués.

GUILLAMÓN, Agustín, ed. *Documentación histórica del trosquismo español (1936-1948) De la guerra civil a la ruptura con la Cuarta Internacional.* Madrid: Ediciones La Torre, 1996. [Publication prepared by Agustín Guillamón, Paolo Casciola, Eulogio Izquierdo, Javier Chávez, and Marco Novarino.]

"HELD, Walter" [Heinz EPE]. "Thèses sur la guerre civile en Espagne." In *Les Cahiers du CER-MTRI* 41 (1986). [Essential reading.]

IZARD, Miquel, ed. *Entusiastas olvidados.* Barcelona: Descontrol, 2016.

KAMINSKI, H.E. *Los de Barcelona.* Foreword by José Peirats. Barcelona: Cotal, 1976.

KORSCH, Karl, Paul MATTICK, Anton PANNEKOEK, Otto RÜHLE, and Helmut WAGNER. *La contre-révolution bureaucratique.* Paris: Union Générale d'Éditions, 1973.

LEDESMA, José Luis et al., eds. *Culturas y políticas de la violencia. España siglo XX.* Madrid: Siete mares, 2005.

LIARTE, Ramón. *Entre la revolución y la guerra.* Barcelona: Picazo, 1986.

LÓPEZ SÁNCHEZ, Pere. *Rastros de rostros en un prado rojo (y negro).* Barcelona: Virus, 2013.

LORENZO, César M. [César Martínez Lorenzo]. *Los anarquistas españoles y el poder.* Paris: Ruedo Ibérico, 1969.

*————. *Le movement anarchiste en Espagne. Pouvoir et révolution sociale.* Saint-Georges-d'Oléron, France: Les Éditions Libertaires, 2006. [One of the best books on the history of Spanish anarchism. Not yet translated into Spanish. A quite different text from the one published by Ruedo Ibérico.] [**For Escorza alerting the defense committees and for Matías Suñer Vidal's evidence regarding a secret revolutionary committee made up of Julian Merino, Lucio Ruano and Sergeant Manzana, see page 347.**]

————. *Horacio Prieto. Mon père.* Saint-Georges-d'Oléron, France: Les Éditions Libertaires, 2012.

*————. *Les racines espagnoles du socialisme libetaire.* Unpublished. [Includes the biography of Matías Suñer Vidal, who testifies to the existence of the secret CNT revolutionary committee in May 1937.]

*————. Correspondence and conversations between Agustín Guillamón and César M. Lorenzo on the Events of May 1937 and the testimony of Matías Suñer Vidal.

MAGUID, Jacobo. *La revolución libertaria española (1936–1939).* Buenos Aires: Reconstruir,

1994.

MARÍN, Ángel. "Hombres y hechos de la Guerra civil española." In *Lo que Dante no pudo imaginar*, edited by Amedeo SINCA, 51–58. Barcelona: Producciones editoriales, 1980.

MÁRQUEZ, José Manuel, and Juan José GALLARDO. *Ortiz. General sin dios ni amo*. Barcelona: Hacer, 1999.

MARTÍN RAMOS, José Luís. *La rereguarda en guerra. Catalunya, 1936–1937*. Barcelona: L'Avenç, 2012. [From a pro-PSUC angle.]

———. *Territori capital. La guerra civil a Catalunya, 1937–1939*. Barcelona: L'Avenç, 2015. [Second part of the above title.]

*MASÓ, Albert. Correspondencia with Agustín Guillamón (1996–1997). Guillamón Archives.

MINTZ, Frank, and Miguel PECIA. *Los Amigos de Durruti, los trosquistas y los sucesos de mayo*. Madrid: Campo Abierto, 1978.

MONJO, Anna. *Militants*. Barcelona: Laertes, 2003.

MONJO, Anna, and Carme VEGA. *El treballadors i la guerra civil. Història d'una indústria catalana collectivitzada*. Barcelona: Editorial Empúries, 1986.

———. "La clase obrera durante la guerra civil española: una historia silenciada." *Historia y fuente oral* 3 (1990): 67–91.

MORROW, Felix. *Revolución y contrarrevolución en España*. Bogotá: Pluma, 1976.

MUNIS, G. *Jalones de derrota, promesa de victoria. Crítica y teoría de la revolución española 1930–1939)*. Brenes: Muñoz Moya, 2003.

NELLES, Dieter, Harald PIOTROWSKI, Ulric LINSE, and Carlos GARCÍA. *Antifascistas alemanes en Barcelona (1933–1939). El Grupo DAS: sus actividades contra la red nazi y en el frente de Aragón*. Barcelona: Sintra, 2010.

OEHLER, Hugo: "Barricadas en Barcelona: la primera revuelta del proletariado contra el Frente Popular capitalista: relato de un testigo. Barcelona, 15 de mayo de 1937." In *Barcelona, mayo 1937: Testimonios desde las barricadas*, edited by GARCÍA, PIOTROWSKI, and ROSÉS, 29–56. Barcelona: Alikornio Ediciones, 2006.

PAZ, Abel, et al., eds. *La Barcelona rebelde. Guía de una ciudad silenciada*. Barcelona: Octaedro, 2008.

PEIRATS, José. *La CNT en la revolución española*. 3 volumes. Paris: Ruedo Ibérico, 1971.

———. *Los anarquistas en la crisis política española*. Madrid-Gijón: Júcar, 1976.

———. *De mi paso por la vida. Memorias*. Barcelona: Flor del Viento, 2009.

PEIRÓ, Joan. *Perilla a la reraguarda*. Foreword by Julià Gual. Mataró: Edicions Llibertat, 1936.

———. *Problemas del sindicalismo y del anarquismo* (Toulouse: Ediciones Movimiento Libertario Español, 1945.

———. *Problemas y cintarazos*. Rennes: n.p., 1946.

PÉREZ-BARÓ, Albert. *Trenta mesos de collectivisme a Catalunya (1936–1939)*. Barcelona: Ariel, 1970.

———. *Historia de les cooperatives a Catalunya*. Barcelona: Critrica, 1989.

PIQUERAS ARENAS, José A. "Estado y Poder en tiempo de guerra." *Débats* 15 (March 1986): 14–18.

RADOSH, Ronald, Mary R. HABECK, and Grigory SEVASTIANOV. *España traicionada. Stalín y la guerra civil.* Barcelona: Planeta, 2002.

* "Reunión extraordinaria celebrada el día cuatro de mayo de 1937 por el Comité Regional y los demas Comités responsables de Cataluña." [IISH-CNT-85C1] **[Along with Campos's articles and Suñer's testimony as reported by César M Lorenzo, this meeting makes it plain that Julián Merino was acting as leader of the May 1937 insurrection.]**

ROCA, Francesc. *Política, economía y espacio. La política territorial en Cataluña (1936–1939).* Barcelona: Ediciones del Serbal, 1983.

ROIG, C. *El fenomen dels "incontrolats" a Catalunya Durant a guerra civil (1936–1939).* Dissertation. Universidad Autónoma de Barcelona: 2000. [Accessible via the Internet.]

SÁNCHEZ, Mario et al., eds. *Los sucesos de mayo de 1937. Una revolución en la República.* Barcelona: Pandora, 1988.

* "Segunda sesión del pleno local de Grupos Anarquistas de Barcelona ... convocada en la sala de actos de la Casa CNT-FAI, con asistencia de los grupos de Defensa confederal y Juventudes libertarias, Barcelona, 24 abril 1937." [SA-PS Barcelona 1307-07] **[First mention made of an insurrectionist committee having been formed. Plenum radicalized by the presence of Julián Merino, Pablo Ruiz, and Juan Santana Calero.]**

SIGNORINO, Mario. *Il massacro di Barcellona.* Milan: Fratelli Fabbri Editori, 1973.

SOLÉ, Josep, and Joan VILLARROYA. "Les victims dels Fets de Maig." *Recerques* 12 (1982): 197–207

SOUCHY, Agustín. *La verdad sobre los sucesos en la retaguardia leal. Los acontecimientos de Cataluña.* Buenos Aires: FACA, 1937.

TÉLLEZ, Antonio. *La red de evasión del grupo Ponzá: Anarquistas en la guerra secreta contra el franquismo y el nazismo (1936–1944).* Barcelona: Virus, 1996.

TORRALBA, Pedro. *De Ayerbe a la "Rjoa y Negra": 127 Brigada de la 28 División.* Barcelona: Self-published, 1980.

TROTSKY, Leon. *La revolución española (1930–1940).* 2 volumes. Barcelona: Fontanella 1977. [Texts selected and introduced by Pierre Broué.]

———. *España, la victoria era possible: escritos 1930–1940.* Buenos Aires: Ediciones IPS, 2014. [Volume 7 of Leon Trotsky's *Obras escogidas*]

VEGA, Carme, Anna MONJO, and Mercedes VILANOVA. "Socialización y Hechos de Mayo: una nueva aportación a partir del proceso a Mauricio Stevens (2 de junio de 1937)." *Historia y fuente oral* 3 (1990): 93–103.

VIDIELLA, Rafael. *Memòries.* Unpublished. Fons Vidiella at the ANC.

VIGUES, Pere. *Un món hostil. Narració autobiogràfica.* Ajuntament de Terrassa: Papers de Ciutat, 1994.

VIÑAS, Ángel. *El escudo de la República.* Barcelona: Crítica, 2007. [Liberal in outlook, favorably disposed toward the top levels of the central government.]

3. Press outlets, periodicals, reviews, bulletins

Acció Cooperatista. Organ of the Catalonian Federation of Cooperatives (1936–1938).

Acracia. Daily newspaper of the CNT and FAI in Lérida. Nos. 2–136 (28 July 1936 to 31 December 1936).

El Amigo del Pueblo. Mouthpiece of the Friends of Durruti. Nos. 1–12 (19 May 1937 to 1 February 1937).

Anarquía-FAI. Clandestine organ of the FAI. Barcelona. Nos. 1–5 (July 1937).

Anthropos. Cultural review with the occasional monograph devoted to leading Spanish anarchist figures.

Avant. POUM mouthpiece. Barcelona, 2nd series, nos. 1–12 (20 July 1936 to 1 August 1937).

Balance: Cuadernos de la historia del movimiento obrero (Barcelona 1993 to the present). Published by Agustín Guillamón.

La Batalla. Central mouthpiece of the POUM. Barcelona, 2nd series, nos. 1–253 (2 August 1936 to 27 May 1937); 3rd series (underground), nos. 1–34 (1937–1938).

Bilan (1933–1938). Monthly theoretical bulletin of the Left Fraction of the PCI. Nos. 1–22. Monthly theoretical bulletin of the Italian Fraction of the Communist Left. Paris, nos. 23–46.

Boletín de Información CNT-AIT-FAI. Reports and news supplied by the CNT and FAI. Barcelona, nos. 1–523 (22 July 1936 to 22 March 1938).

Boletín de Información del POUM. Published by the Executive Committee, no. 1 (23 February 1939); no. 2, London (15 March 1939); no. 5 (15 April 1939).

Boletín Interior: Órgano de discusión para el II Congreso del Comité Local de Barcelona del POUM. Barcelona, no. 1 (23 April 1937); no. 2 (29 May 1937).

Bollettino d'Informazione. Published by the Italian Bolshevik-Leninists affiliated to the Fourth International (Paris). No. 1 (25 June 1936); no. 2 (1 August 1936).

Bollettino d'Informazione del POUM. Italian edition (Barcelona). Several issues erratically numbered and some undated, September 1936–January 1937(?).

Les Cahiers du CERMTRI. Review of the history of revolutionary movements with some issues devoted to the Spanish Civil War.

Cahiers Léon Trotsky. Review published by the Institut Léon Trotsky. Director, Pierre Broué (St Martin d'Hères) nos. 1–61 (1979–2001).

La Commune. Organ of regroupment and revolutionary action. Nos. 1–14 (6 December 1935 to 6 March 1936). Central Organ of the Internationalist Communist Party (French Section of the Fourth International). Nos. 15–27 (13 March 1936 to 5 June 1936). Central Organ of the Internationalist Communist Party. Bolshevik-Leninist for the reconstruction of the Fourth International. Nos. 28–156 (October 1936 to December 1938).

Criticón. Satirical and humorous periodical. Barcelona (1937).

Cuadernos de Ruedo Ibérico. Paris, nos. 1–66 (1965–1979).

Diari Oficial de la Generalitat de Catalunya. (1936–1938).

Entre deux mondes: Antifascisme and Révolution en Espagne. No. 1 (December 1936).

Esfuerzo. Wall newspaper and organ of the Libertarian Youth of Catalonia. Barcelona, nos. 1–9 (1937)

L'Espagne nouvelle. Weekly organ published by the Secrétariat de documentation ouvrière. Montpellier. Nos. 1–17 (1937).

L'Espagne nouvelle. "*L'Espagne indomptee.*" Year 3, nos. 67–69 (July–September 1939).

L'expérience espagnole (La experiencia española): Faits et documents. Paris, no. 1 (1939). [Initiating the debate in the run-up to the POUM congress]; Paris, no. 2 (August 1939) [Articles by Gorkín, "O. Emem" [Eduardo Mauricio], Gironella, and Juan Vila on where the POUM made mistakes in the civil war.]

Gaseta Municipal de Barcelona (1937).

Guerra di Classe. Unione Sindacale Italiana (AIT). Barcelona, nos. 1–27; Paris, nos. 28–30 (1936–1937).

Juillet. POUM's International Review. Barcelona/Paris, no. 1 (June 1937).

Libertad. Clandestine organ of the CRTC. Nos. 1–3 and 6–11 (1937). Nos. 4–5 and 12 unavailable.

La Lutte Ouvrière. Organ of the Internationalist Workers' Party (Bolshevik-Leninist). French Section of the Fourth International. Paris, nos. 5–111 (24 July 1936 to 3 March 1939).

Mi Revista. Illustrated News. Barcelona, nos. 1–54 (15 October 1936 to 1 December 1938). Cinema and entertainment review carrying opinion articles and interviews. See no. 4 for interview with Dionisio Eroles.

La Noche. Barcelona, nos. 3348–3701 (22 July 1936 to 23 January 1939).

La Nueva Era. Monthly doctrinal and news review. Barcelona, nos. 1–7 (January 1936 to March/April 1937).

Nuevo Curso. Spanish News Bulletin of the Bolshevik-Leninists for Reconstruction of the Fourth International. Paris, nos. 1–3 (12 May 1939 to 23 January 1939).

Octobre. Monthly organ of the Bureau of Left Communist Fractions. Nos. 1–5 (February 1938 to August 1939).

Prometeo. Bi-monthly, Italian-language publication of the "Bordigist" Fraction. Brussels, nos. 1–153 (1928–1938).

Quaderni Centro Studi Pietro Tresso. History review specializing in Trotskyism and revolutionary movements, under the direction of Paolo Casciola (1987–1997).

Quaderni Pietro Tresso. History review specializing in Trotskyism and revolutionary movements, under the direction of Paolo Casciola (1997–present).

Révision. Revolutionary studies review published by "a group of young revolutionaries." Paris, nos. 1–6 (February 1938 to August 1939).

La Révolution Espagnole. Weekly French-language publication of Spain's Workers' Party for Marxist Unification. Barcelona, nos. 1–10 (3 September 1936 to 18 November 1936). See "The role of the Central Antifascist Militias Committee" in no. 2. And bi-monthly publication of the Workers' Party for Marxist Unification. Nos. 11–16 (18 December 1936 to 1 May 1937).

La Révolution Prolétarienne. Syndicalist-communist review. Paris, nos. 1–300 (January 1925 to October 1939).

Revolutionary History. (1992–1999).

La Rivoluzione Spagnolo. Italian-language fortnightly publication of the POUM. Barcelona, nos. 1–4 (1 March 1937 to 1 May 1937).

Ruta. Organ of the Libertarian Youth of Catalonia. Barcelona (1936–1937 issues consulted).

El Sembrador. Comarcal organ of the Libertarian Youth of Ter y Freser. Nos. 8 and 11–44 (1936–1937).

Solidaridad Obrera. Organ of the Regional Confederation of Labor in Catalonia. Mouthpiece of the CNT. Barcelona, nos. 1329–2105 (18 July 1936 to 25 January 1939). On Monday 20 July 1936, it published a supplement, distributed in the form of a flyer that was unnumbered and indeed was mistakenly dated 21 July: no. 1330 was on Sunday, 19 July, no. 1331 on Wednesday, 22 July. no. 1577 was published on Sunday, 2 May 1937; on Monday, 3 May, nothing was published; on Tuesday, 4 May, no. 1578 appeared; on Wednesday, 5 May, no. 1579; on Thursday, 6 May, no. 1580; on Friday, 7 May, two editions appeared, numbered 1581 and 1582; on Sunday, 9 May, no. 1584 appeared; on Monday, 10 May, *Solidaridad Obrera* did not appear, but on Tuesday, 12 May, it was back with no. 1585.

Solidaridad Obrera/Le Combat syndicaliste. Paris (issues from 1970 to 1982 consulted).

Le Soviet. Organ of the Bolshevik-Leninists of Spain for the Fourth International. Nos. 1–5 (January 1937 to January 1938). Published in Barcelona in French, and hand-colored by Virginia Gervasini.

The Spanish Revolution: Weekly English Bulletin of the Workers' Party of Marxist Unification of Spain (POUM). Barcelona, vol. 1, nos. 1–9 (21 October 1936 to 23 December 1936); vol. 2, nos. 1–8 (6 January 1937 to 19 May 1937). There is a reprint edition of the entire collection, complete with introduction by Russell Blackwell, published as *The Spanish Revolution, Volumes 1–2: 1936–1937.* New York: Greenwood Reprint Corporation, 1968.

Suplementos de Anthropos. Cultural review publishing monographs.

Treball. Barcelona (1936–1938).

La Vanguardia. Barcelona (1936–1938).

La Voz Leninista. Organ of the SBLE. Barcelona, nos. 1–3 (April 1937 to February 1938).

Index

What is the Kate Sharpley Library?

The Kate Sharpley Library is a library, archive, publishing outfit and affinity group. We preserve and promote anarchist history.

What we've got

Our collection includes anarchist books, pamphlets, newspapers and leaflets from the nineteenth century to the present in over twenty languages. The collection includes manuscripts, badges, audio and video recordings, and photographs, as well as the work of historians and other writers who have documented the anarchist movement.

What we do

We promote the history of anarchism by reprinting original documents from our collection, and translating or publishing new works on anarchism and its history. These appear in our quarterly bulletin or regularly published pamphlets. We have also provided manuscripts to other anarchist publishers. People come and research in the library, or we can send out a limited amount of photocopies.

Why we do it

We don't say one strand of class-struggle anarchism has all the answers. We don't think anarchism can be understood by looking at 'thinkers' in isolation. We do think that what previous generations thought and did, what they wanted and how they tried to get it, is relevant today. We encourage the anarchist movement to think about its own history—not to live on past glories but to get an extra perspective on current and future dangers and opportunities.

How we do it

Everything at the Kate Sharpley Library—acquisitions, cataloguing, preservation work, publishing, answering inquiries is done by volunteers. All our running costs are met by donations (from members of the collective or our subscribers and supporters) or by the small income we make through publishing.

How you can help

Please subscribe to our bulletin to keep up with what we're doing. There are four issues of the Bulletin a year. Or become a Friend, a KSL Friend subscription gets you the *Bulletin* and all our publications as they come out.

You can send us anarchist material that you don't need any more (from books to badges)—we can pay postage for large loads, but it doesn't have to be large. A couple of pamphlets will be as gratefully received as anything. Even if you send us duplicates we can trade with other archives for material we do not have. If you publish anarchist material, please add us to your mailing list!

You can send us money too. Details are on our website at: http://www.kate sharpleylibrary.net/doc/donations

Keep in touch!

www.katesharpleylibrary.net | www.facebook.com/katesharpleylibrary

Kate Sharpley Library
BM Hurricane
London, WC1N 3XX

AK PRESS is small, in terms of staff and resources, but we also manage to be one of the world's most productive anarchist publishing houses. We publish close to twenty books every year, and distribute thousands of other titles published by like-minded independent presses and projects from around the globe. We're entirely worker-run and democratically managed. We operate without a corporate structure—no boss, no managers, no bullshit.

The **FRIENDS OF AK PRESS** program is a way you can directly contribute to the continued existence of AK Press, and ensure that we're able to keep publishing books like this one! Friends pay $25 a month directly into our publishing account ($30 for Canada, $35 for international), and receive a copy of every book AK PRESS publishes for the duration of their membership! Friends also receive a discount on anything they order from our website or buy at a table: 50% on AK titles, and 30% on everything else. We have a Friends of AK ebook program as well: $15 a month gets you an electronic copy of every book we publish for the duration of your membership. *You can even sponsor a very discounted membership for someone in prison.*

Email **friendsofak@akpress.org** for more info, or visit the website: **https://www.akpress.org/friends.html**.

There are always great book projects in the works—so sign up now to become a Friend of AK Press, and let the presses roll!

Agustín Guillamón is an independent historian; editor of *Balance*, a magazine dedicated to new research on the Spanish Revolution; and the author of *The Friends of Durruti Group, 1937–1939* and *Ready for Revolution*, among numerous other books.

Paul Sharkey is an accomplished translator who has made a vast body of anarchist texts available to English-language readers. His numerous translations include the works of Nestor Makhno, Osvaldo Bayer, Errico Malatesta, Daniel Guérin, José Peirats, and Antonio Téllez.